PRAISE FOR *PROVOCATIONS*

"Ever-mindful of historical and cultural context, the authors present essays that cross borders of time and space to reveal women's emerging consciousness of self, sexuality, and intellect through the centuries. The result is a collection of proto-feminist and feminist thought stunning in its breadth and depth."

VICTORIA BYNUM, DISTINGUISHED PROFESSOR EMERITUS OF
HISTORY, TEXAS STATE UNIVERSITY, SAN MARCOS

"A wide-ranging collection of essays by recognized critics in the field, which begins with antiquity and closes with the twenty-first century—a reader that proves yet again, if proof were still needed, that feminism is a transnational (transhistorical and transcultural) movement."

DOMNA C. STANTON, DISTINGUISHED PROFESSOR OF FRENCH,
GRADUATE CENTER CUNY

"Coupling contextualizing analytical essays with the voices of women from all regions of the world, from antiquity to the present, *Provocations* affords new insights into women's self-understandings, aspirations, and resistance, as well as the expansive precursors, origins, and scope of feminist activism."

MARY HAWKESWORTH, AUTHOR OF *POLITICAL WORLDS OF WOMEN:
ACTIVISM, ADVOCACY AND GOVERNANCE IN THE 21ST CENTURY*

PROVOCATIONS

PROVOCATIONS

A Transnational Reader in the History of Feminist Thought

EDITED BY

Susan Bordo

M. Cristina Alcalde

Ellen Rosenman

UNIVERSITY OF CALIFORNIA PRESS

University of California Press, one of the most distinguished university presses in the United States, enriches lives around the world by advancing scholarship in the humanities, social sciences, and natural sciences. Its activities are supported by the UC Press Foundation and by philanthropic contributions from individuals and institutions. For more information, visit www.ucpress.edu.

University of California Press
Oakland, California

Library of Congress Cataloging-in-Publication Data

Provocations : a transnational reader in the history of feminist thought / edited by Susan Bordo, Cristina Alcalde, Ellen Rosenman.
    pages cm
  Includes bibliographical references and index.
  ISBN 978-0-520-26420-5 (cloth : alk. paper)
  ISBN 978-0-520-26422-9 (pbk. : alk. paper)
  1. Feminism—History.   I. Bordo, Susan, 1947– editor. II. Alcalde, María Cristina, editor. III. Rosenman, Ellen Bayuk, editor.
  HQ1121.P76   2015
  305.42—dc23   2014037768

Manufactured in the United States of America
24 23 22 21 20 19 18 17 16 15
10 9 8 7 6 5 4 3 2 1

CONTENTS

Acknowledgments · xiii

Foreword: The Challenges of Constructing a Transnational History
Susan Bordo, M. Cristina Alcalde, and Ellen Rosenman · xvii

PART 1. CHALLENGING MALE DOMINANCE: ANTIQUITY TO 1800

1. Amy Richlin: Feminist Thought before the Renaissance · 3
   Sappho, Fragment 16 · 10
   Nossis, Poem II · 11
   Sulpicia the Elegist, Poem I · 11
   Sulpicia the Satirist, Fragment · 11
   Hrotsvit, Preface to Her Plays · 12
   Hrotsvit, Letter to Certain Wise Men, Supporters of This Book · 13
   Euripides, Medea, *lines 230–51* · 14
   Plautus, Mercator, *lines 817–29* · 15
   Musonius Rufus, from That Women Too Should Study Philosophy · 15
   Musonius Rufus, from Should Daughters Receive the Same
   Education as Sons? · 17

2. Susan Bordo: Christine de Pizan and the *Querelle des
   femmes* · 19
   Christine de Pizan, from The Book of the City of Ladies · 23

3. Mónica Díaz: Sor Juana Inés de la Cruz: Early Feminism in the Americas or the Right of Every Woman to Study · 28

    Sor Juana Inés de la Cruz, from The Poet's Answer to the Most Illustrious Sor Filotea de la Cruz · 36

    Sor Juana Inés de la Cruz, First Dream · 44

4. Ruth Perry: Radical Doubt and the Liberation of Women · 62

    René Descartes, from Meditations on First Philosophy · 68

    Mary Astell, from A Serious Proposal to the Ladies, *Part I* · 69

    Mary Astell, from A Serious Proposal to the Ladies, *Part II* · 71

PART 2. ACTIVISM ON THREE CONTINENTS: NINETEENTH TO EARLY TWENTIETH CENTURIES

5. Ellen Rosenman: Sexual Politics in England and India: The Case of Prostitution · 77

    Josephine Butler, from Personal Reminiscences of a Great Crusade · 83

    Muvalur Ramamirthammal, from Web of Deceit · 88

6. Ellen Rosenman, Jill Abney, and Kathi Kern: Women's Suffrage: Transnational Connections · 98

    Lady Constance Lytton, A Speech Delivered at the Queen's Hall, January 31, 1910 · 109

    Millicent Garrett Fawcett, Home and Politics · 114

    Aruna Asaf Ali, from Woman's Suffrage in India · 119

    Carrie Chapman Catt, from an Untitled Manuscript on the Position of Women in the "Orient" · 124

    Clara Colby, An Attack on the Tagore "Craze" · 125

    Clara Colby, from Notes on the Writings of Rabindranath Tagore · 127

PART 3. TALKING BACK TO SEXISM BEFORE "WOMEN'S LIBERATION": NINETEENTH TO MID-TWENTIETH CENTURIES

7. Jacqueline Couti: The Mythology of the *Doudou*: Sexualizing Black Female Bodies, Constructing Culture in the French Caribbean · 131

    Lafcadio Hearn, from La fille de couleur · 139

    Lafcadio Hearn, from Youma: The Story of a West-Indian Slave · 142

8. Pramila Venkateswaran: Locating the Feminist Spirit in the Nineteenth and Early Twentieth Centuries in India: Tarabai Shinde and Lalithambika Antherjanam · 144

    Tarabai Shinde, from A Comparison of Men and Women · 150

    Lalithambika Antherjanam, The Goddess of Revenge · 160

9. Liang Luo: Problems of Translation and Transnational Feminisms:
On Gu Ruopu and Li Ruzhen · 169
Gu Ruopu, Rebuttal of Ridicule · 175
Li Ruzhen, from Flowers in the Mirror · 176

10. Ellen Rosenman: *A Room of One's Own* in Transracial
Perspective · 183
Virginia Woolf, from A Room of One's Own, *Chapter 1* · 187

11. Susan Bordo: Simone de Beauvoir: The Feminist Philosopher as
Other · 193
Simone de Beauvoir, from The Second Sex · 199
Simone de Beauvoir, Interview with Alice Schwarzer · 208

**PART 4. DISCOVERING GENDER AND REMAPPING FEMINISM:
1955–1975**

12. Karen W. Tice: The "Personal Politics" of Class · 213
Rita Mae Brown, The Last Straw · 221
Ginny Berson, Class Revisited: One Step forward, Two Steps Back · 226

13. Susan Bordo: Feminists Reimagine the Body · 231
Germaine Greer, Sex, *from* The Female Eunuch · 236
Anne Koedt, The Myth of the Vaginal Orgasm · 242
Luce Irigaray, This Sex Which Is Not One · 248
Audre Lorde, Uses of the Erotic: The Erotic as Power · 254

14. Cheryl R. Hopson: The U.S. Women's Liberation Movement and
Black Feminist "Sisterhood" · 260
Mary Ann Weathers, An Argument for Black Women's Liberation as a
Revolutionary Force · 270
Pauli Murray, The Liberation of Black Women · 273
Michele Wallace, Anger in Isolation: A Black Feminist's Search for
Sisterhood · 275
Audre Lorde, Eye to Eye: Black Women, Hatred, and Anger · 278

15. Maylei Blackwell: *Triple Jeopardy: The Third World Women's
Alliance and the Transnational Roots of Women-of-Color
Feminisms* · 280
Images from Triple Jeopardy, 1971–1975 · 289

16. Ann M. Ciasullo: Strained Sisterhood: Lesbianism, Feminism, and
the U.S. Women's Liberation Movement · 292
Radicalesbians, The Woman-Identified Woman · 301

Amber Hollibaugh and Cherríe Moraga, What We're Rollin' around in Bed With: Sexual Silences in Feminism · 305

17. Norma Mogrovejo: The Latin American Lesbian Movement: Its Shaping and Its Search for Autonomy · 312
Declaration of Lesbians from Mexico · 319

18. Paula Gunn Allen: Who Is Your Mother? Red Roots of White Feminism · 321
Cherokee Women and Nanye' hi / Nancy Ward, Speeches and Letters · 331

19. Tamara Beauboeuf-Lafontant: Suffering Like an African Girl: Trauma Embodied in Tsitsi Dangarembga's *Nervous Conditions* · 335
Tsitsi Dangarembga, Nervous Conditions, *Chapter 10* · 340

20. Fatima Mernissi: The Meaning of Spatial Boundaries · 350
Fatima Mernissi, from Dreams of Trespass · 363

PART 5. BEYOND "THE DECADE OF THE WOMAN": 1975 TO THE PRESENT

21. M. Cristina Alcalde: Mothers, Guerrillas, and Revolutionaries: Women's Mobilization and Activism in Latin America · 379
Carmen Robles de Zurita, from Matilde Mellibovsky, Circle of Love over Death: Testimonies of the Mothers of the Plaza de Mayo · 385
María Elena Moyano, from The Autobiography of María Elena Moyano: The Life and Death of a Peruvian Activist · 389

22. M. Cristina Alcalde, Srimati Basu, and Emily Burrill: Feminist Organizing around Violence against Women in Mali, Peru, and India · 402
from African (Banjul) Charter on Human and Peoples' Rights · 413
Inter-American Convention on the Prevention, Punishment, and Eradication of Violence against Women *(Convention of Belém do Pará, 1994)* · 415
Malini Bhattacharya, To Give a Daughter Away, *Scene 3* · 421

23. Bernadette Barton: Freedom from Sexism versus Sexual Freedom: A Short History of the Feminist Sex Wars · 430
Andrea Dworkin, Pornography and Grief · 436

Dorothy Allison, Public Silence, Private Terror · 440

24. Diane E. King: Two Generations of Feminist Activism: Snapshots
from the Middle East and North Africa since 1970 · 451
Gohar Kordi, from An Iranian Odyssey · 461
Iman Humaydan Younes, from B as in Beirut · 468

25. Michael Kimmel: Men and Women's Studies: Promise, Pitfalls,
and Possibility · 471
John Stoltenberg, How Men Have (a) Sex: An Address to College Students · 479
R. W. Connell, Masculinities and Globalization · 488

26. Ashley Bourgeois: Identity, Activism, and Third Wave
Feminism in the United States · 501
Kathleen Hanna, Riot Grrrl Manifesto · 508
Gwendolyn D. Pough, Do the Ladies Run This . . . ? Some Thoughts on
Hip-Hop Feminism · 510
Alana Suskin, Hearing the Daughter Voice: The *Bat Kol* as
Rrrabbi Grrrl · 515
Jennifer Baumgardner and Amy Richards, Third Wave Manifesta:
A Thirteen-Point Agenda · 520

27. Obioma Nnaemeka: Captured in Translation: Africa and
Feminisms in the Age of Globalization · 522

28. Nadje Al-Ali: Gendering the Arab Spring · 530

Contributors · 537
Credits · 543
Author and Title Index · 549
Subject Index · 552

ACKNOWLEDGMENTS

From the very first proposals we wrote to last-minute requests for help we have received nothing but the warmest and strongest support from both the University of Kentucky (UK) and the University of California (UC) Press. Several generous College Research Activity Awards (CRAA) from the College of Arts and Sciences at the University of Kentucky made the project possible. The first, in combination with an advance from the University of California Press, enabled us to hold an interdisciplinary faculty seminar in spring 2009, a vibrant collaborative project that generated an initial set of readings, concepts, and issues. Two other CRAAs covered the costs of transcribing sessions from that seminar and helped, along with funds from the University of California Press, to defray the significant costs involved in obtaining permissions. We were also supported by a University of Kentucky grant for research collaborations that promote diversity. We thank past and present administrators at UK and our editor at UC Press, Naomi Schneider, who worked so hard to make sure we received the funds we needed to bring the collection to fruition. Thanks too to English Department chair Jeff Clymer and Jennifer (Walton) White for their assistance in that process.

We gratefully acknowledge the contribution of the faculty who participated in that 2009 interdisciplinary seminar, facilitated by Susan Bordo, a seminar which in many ways was the intellectual laboratory for this collection: Rynetta Davis, Janice Oaks, Srimati Basu, Kathi Kern, Patricia Cooper, Lucinda Ramberg, Karen Tice, Emily Burrill, Liang Liu, Cheryl Hopson, and Cristina Alcalde, the last of whom went on to become a coeditor of this collection. All the participants contributed their energy and expertise to the project; we are especially grateful to those who went on to write essays for this collection.

The seminar, however, did not spring out of nowhere. It was the result of many years of collective brainstorming, discussion, and problem solving by the Women's Studies Steering Committee, which, long before Gender and Women's Studies became a department at the University of Kentucky, worked tirelessly and creatively developing curriculum, programming, and long-term plans under the directorship of Ellen Rosenman, Deborah Crooks, Pat Cooper, Susan Bordo, and, most significantly, Joan Callahan. The composition of the steering committee varied from year to year, so it is not possible to name every member. You know who you are; please accept our gratitude!

We are very grateful to the contributors to this anthology, both those who participated in the 2009 seminar and the many others who joined the project at different points of its development. Creating this collection was a long, arduous process that would not have been possible without their patience, diligence, and commitment. Communicating with and reading the insightful work of colleagues from multiple disciplines, universities, and countries have been an enriching experience for us.

A project of this magnitude involves numerous tasks that require different kinds of expertise and support. Sam Stoloff provided wise guidance from the beginning of the project, and Naomi Schneider was our good shepherd at UC Press all along the way. Others at UC Press who contributed their invaluable energy, expertise, and time to this project were Christopher Lura, Caroline Knapp, and Rachel Berchten. Several anonymous reviewers for UC Press provided constructive comments and suggestions. Particularly significant roles closer to home were played by Natalie Sweet, who compiled references and helped with other editorial tasks, Betty Pasley, who provided administrative advice and troubleshooting of various sorts, and most especially Michelle Del Toro, who performed the monumental, backbreaking, and often mind-bending job of requesting and compiling permissions—as well as providing general administrative assistance—with patience, precision, and good humor.

Last but not least, we wish to express our deep gratitude to our families. For Cristina, participation in the 2009 seminar coincided with the last weeks of pregnancy with her youngest son. In the five years since Emilio's birth, the love and support of her spouse, Joe O'Neil, and their sons, Santiago and Emilio, as well as of parents, Pilar and Xavier, parents-in-law, Paula and Dan, and siblings Gabriela and Gonzalo have helped make possible this and other projects that involved spending time away and a sometimes ridiculous amount of multitasking. As always, Ellen wishes to thank her mother, Jill Rosenman, a woman ahead of her time, and her husband, David Youngblood, who as always contributed support, wise counsel, and good humor. She also thanks daughter Liz Youngblood and semi-daughter Ardilla Deneys, young women shaping their lives in the twenty-first century. While, as this book suggests, we are far from a postfeminist (read postpatriarchal) era, their creativity and determination make her hopeful about our future. Susan, whose work on this project coincided with her daughter Cassie's growing-up years from ages seven to fifteen, has been reminded time and again, both by Cassie's courage and individuality as well as by the challenges that still face girls in this culture, of our indebtedness to feminist thought and activism—and of the fragility of our collective memory of that debt. Having an adolescent daughter did not make working on this book easier, but it did answer any doubts Susan had about the continuing importance of the ideas expressed within it. When that recognition gave way to despair at the sluggishness of change or the constancy of backlash, her husband, Edward, was there to crack a wry joke or simply share her anger. Susan is also grateful to the deep, unbreakable bonds she has with her sisters Mickey Silverman and Binnie Klein and her longtime friend LeeAnn Whites.

Finally, we thank one another for a collaboration that has been more mutually enriching, good-humored, and just plain fun than we ever could have imagined. The work was long, taxing, and sometimes frustrating, and doing it together is what made it possible.

FOREWORD: THE CHALLENGES OF CONSTRUCTING A TRANSNATIONAL HISTORY

Susan Bordo, M. Cristina Alcalde, and Ellen Rosenman

This book began with what seemed, at times, an impossible dream: to create a course in the history of feminist thought that would be both transnational in coverage *and* historically organized. From the first discussion, among the Gender and Women's Studies faculty at the University of Kentucky, the idea provoked surprisingly heated debate. Some among us considered the emphasis on history to be a Western imposition, carrying with it a whole raft of distortions about how to mark "periods" and plot appropriate narratives of crisis and change. Others felt that a lack of the sense of context and movement through time was our students' most serious barrier to understanding the motivations, controversies, and upheavals of feminist thought. The "pro-history" faction was outraged that many of our students had no idea that anything of value had been written before 1985, because earlier works had been so thoroughly dismissed as racist, heterosexist, essentialist, et cetera, et cetera in their feminist theory courses. Others among us bristled at the very word "history," and suggested that historical organization of a course would degenerate into ethnocentrism and essentialism; "Whose history?" they challenged. These discussions were among the most contentious we had as a faculty; not even the most delicious snacks (usually the crisis-averters in our department) could prevent us from leaving these sessions feeling misunderstood and angry.

Like many heated debates, this one was resolved only when we abandoned abstraction and decided to start *doing*. Our action took the form of what we affectionately (and sometimes ironically) called "Feminist Summer Camp": two weeks of daylong sessions in which each of us—a group now expanded to include invited participants from other institutions—had the opportunity to pick readings and lead discussion on the move-ments and ideas that each considered essential to include in the course. With partici-pants from a broad range of disciplines and areas of specialization, none of us could claim expertise over the whole; with actual texts in front of us, we were forced to recog-nize complexities and subtleties in works that we might have dismissed, and were delighted to be introduced to writers and traditions of which we had been ignorant. Lib-erated from abstract debate about "positions," we felt like students again. And from the very first day, the seminar exploded with the excitement of discovered connections, influ-ences, and convergences. We began to see the concrete historical reality of what we subscribed to in theory: that the world is not a collection of discrete and disconnected items, each existing in its own self-contained universe of values, but an infinite set of relations, interactions, exchanges, and conflicts, many of them anchored in inequalities and culture-bound perceptions. We never relinquished our individual passions and pri-orities, but we began to realize that in making them converse with each other, we were collectively creating new ways of telling familiar narratives, new ways of reading familiar texts, new understandings of feminist insight and activism.

What is new about the collection that ultimately emerged from this seminar? Perhaps first and foremost is its unique format, which pairs primary texts with original introduc-tory essays. Written by scholars of various nationalities, with disciplinary training in anthropology, educational policy, French, history, classics, English, sociology, philosophy, and women's studies, these essays provide navigation tools for reading and teaching the primary texts. Every text comes from somewhere, historically and geographically, with all the possibilities and limitations that its specific location entails. By emphasizing the spe-cifics of the "somewhere"—the particular histories of colonialism, nation-building, rac-ism, class, religion, and gender—rather than the sheer spectacle of "diversity," we hope to develop a sense of the dynamic emergence of feminist thought in response to specific contexts, encouraging readers to understand why particular lines of inquiry and argument appeared where, when, and in what form they did. Our primary sources are drawn from Asia, Africa, Europe, and the Americas. We hope that the accompanying essays will make what is new and unfamiliar accessible and meaningful to students, as well as provide teachers with convenient jumping-off points for discussion. To facilitate this goal, each original essay ends with a set of questions for classroom use—or private reflection.

One cannot do justice to such complexities—as we discovered in our seminar—so long as the goal is the representation of "diversity." It's an impossible goal to satisfy, of course, and in many ways not a very helpful one. We firmly believe in the value of culti-vating what philosopher María Lugones has called "world-travelling" habits of thought, which expand the horizons of the familiar and create a broader cultural map for students to explore (María Lugones, "Playfulness, World-Travelling, and Loving Perception," *Hypatia* 2, no. 2 [1987]: 11, 12). But in the absence of orienting contexts, the question remains as to what scholars and students are to *do* with all this diversity, beyond celebrat-ing it, tasting all the dishes on the smorgasbord table. It becomes too easy to put works into artificial dialogue with each other, culling out shared themes (e.g., "sexualities," "gender violence," "motherhood," etc.) that flatten cultural and historical difference. This approach invites a "compare-and-contrast" orientation that provides little sense of the realities of events, power, and conversations that drive ideas, and thus, ironically, may encourage the ethnocentrism of readers who have only their own culture as a frame of reference within which to evaluate the documents. The less familiar contributions remain what Simone de Beauvoir described as "the Other," marked by their divergence from the norms with which students are familiar.

Our approach, in contrast, is to encourage appreciation of each contribution or set of contributions in its own geographical and cultural context, while prodding history to reveal what is shared—and not shared—across those borders. When common themes seem to emerge across differences, the essays accompanying the primary texts and their discussion questions will encourage readers to think about the "why," "when," and "how," so that readers can go deeper than surface similarities. Thus, for example, chapter 22 in our collection highlights violence against women as a common issue for women's activism in Mali, India, and Peru. But the coauthored essay that accompanies these primary texts examines the national, historical, and legislative particularities that caution us against making generalizations about violence and women's activism. Similarly, arguments for the education of women are prominent among the writers included in part I—on ancient, medieval, and Renaissance views—but the historical periods and cultural/national differences that separate Musonius Rufus, Sor Juana Inés de la Cruz, and Mary Astell invite a "text in context" exploration that would not be possible without the accompanying essays.

These points of convergence/divergence can be found throughout the collection, as our selections were chosen to make them visible. Ann M. Ciasullo's and Norma Mogrovejo's pieces on the development of lesbian feminism in the United States and Latin America, for example, reveal fascinating differences—and some similarities—in the political contexts within which each of these movements emerged and in the issues that became central to each movement. The similarities are instructive, but even more so are the differences, which demonstrate that the path followed by feminists in the United States was not the model for the rest of the world. Similarly, in Obioma Nnaemeka's essay on African feminism, "womanism" appears as a significant concept—which may come as a surprise to those American feminists who believe it was coined by Alice Walker. These essays make clear, instead, that "womanism" was independently developed in the contexts of Africa and the United States; at the same time, African "womanism" clearly engages in dialogue with Western feminism and shares some characteristics with Walker's concept. This volume encourages readers to notice when ideas are talking to each other, influencing each other, and criticizing each other across borders, allowing us to trace and analyze what we call "cross talk" among writers and thinkers.

This cross talk represents one of the key structures of transnational feminism as it unfolds throughout history and throughout the collection, interrelating works without submerging their particularities. In some cases, this cross-talk is intentional and concrete, as in the fertile if highly charged interchanges among English, American, and Indian writers in the late nineteenth and early twentieth centuries, around the issues of sexuality and suffrage. More often, it has become visible in hindsight: Christine de Pizan and Sor Juana Inés de la Cruz both addressed the *"querelle des femmes,"* the woman question, from within their own cultural contexts (France and Mexico, respectively), in the process contributing to a transnational feminist conversation whose global scope they may not have been aware of, but that we can see as historically significant. Yet another example is the move away from biology and towards a "social constructionism" of the body, which began to preoccupy feminists in the 1970s. This shift in paradigm is often credited to male poststructuralist writers such as Michel Foucault, but history shows that feminists were the first to argue constructionist positions, although not always in the same theoretical form as their peers. Rather, the highly distinctive approaches of these feminist writers together coalesced around a change that was later consolidated in more unified theory. These approaches beg to be considered not just as the works of individual writers, but as racially and nationally inflected as well. Juxtaposing and critically analyzing texts by Germaine Greer, Anne Koedt, Luce Irigaray, and Audre Lorde reveals that, although these authors were not in explicit conversation with each other, their texts do "talk" to each other across cultural lines, at a moment when feminists were dramatically changing the intellectual landscape.

Our biggest challenge, in a project of such broad scope, was choosing what to include. Faced with an abundance of fascinating texts, we have highlighted key documents—from Christine de Pizan, Sor Juana Inés de la Cruz, Virginia Woolf, Simone de Beauvoir, Tsitsi Dangarembga, Paula Gunn Allen, Fatima Mernissi, and others—that were particularly influential or that raise issues that continue to occupy feminisms today. However, we also include lesser known texts, and define "feminist thought" broadly, including texts that were created before the terms and conversations with which we are familiar came into being. Our selections thus range from manifestos to imaginative writing to cartoons to philosophical essays. We want readers to appreciate that astute and creative feminist thinking reaches far back into history. Women were passionately imagining, theorizing, and arguing long before the first women's studies course was offered, long before the study of gender became splintered into disciplines, and long before Simone de Beauvoir and Virginia Woolf authored their groundbreaking studies. Highlighting this legacy was one of our prime motivations as we imagined putting together a collection that displayed the history of feminist thought. Women's studies courses can tacitly construct a narrative of progress, in which the limited thinking of earlier writers is improved upon by the superior insights of the present, in spite of the respect they pay to canonical women writers of the past, such as Sappho, Christine de Pizan, Virginia Woolf, and Simone de Beauvoir. The idea that theory is an invention of the late twentieth century has sometimes devalued the contributions of earlier writers, especially some Western women writers of what is sometimes called the Second Wave, particularly since a good deal of poststructuralist theory is built up out of criticism—and too often, rather harsh dismissal—of earlier works. Why, we wondered, are so many male writers permitted to retain a respected place in the social thought curriculum despite their blind spots, while so many feminist writers have been discarded because of theirs?

Although we wanted to restore historical consciousness, none of us was interested in telling "The Story of Feminism." Our pairings of primary texts and critical essays are organized chronologically not to create an overarching historical narrative but to give a sense of the movements, relations, and conversations that can justifiably be described as crossing or overlapping borders, as well as the differences between them. So, within four broad historical clusters—antiquity to 1800, nineteenth- to mid-twentieth centuries, 1955 to 1975, 1975 to the present—readers will find multiple essays focusing on particular countries and regions, and will be able to track moments of transnational significance for feminism, as well as themes that preoccupy feminists across national borders. These periods and themes are not signals of "sameness" but potential points for starting dialogues about the histories and meanings of feminisms.

So, for example, the first section of this collection, Challenging Male Dominance: Antiquity to 1800, highlights the emergence, in distinct places and times, of some of the earliest writings that can meaningfully be described as feminist. What "feminist" means in these contexts is ultimately something for readers to discover and debate. As editors, we group these texts together because they demonstrate that there always have been creative women protesting prevailing theories of female inferiority and various "natural" justifications for excluding women from full participation in education, culture, and politics. Simply by writing, these women challenge the assumption that they are intellectually inferior to men and naturally prefer modesty and silence. And they also argue, sometimes quite explicitly, with the dominant discourses of their time, as poets from classical antiquity revel in descriptions of women's desire, and writers like Sor Juana Inés de la Cruz and Christine de Pizan engage forcefully in debates about women's nature that were dominated by men.

The next section, Activism on Three Continents: Nineteenth to Early Twentieth Centuries, charts the dense interconnections among British, Indian, and American feminists as they become conscious of themselves *as* agents of change. In this period, from the mid-nineteenth to the mid-twentieth century, women come to see themselves as actors on the public stage, a vision that, in our selections, begins with the construction of "sexual politics" in prostitution reform and culminates in the fight for suffrage. Because of the historical links among these three countries, we can trace concrete interactions across national borders. For perhaps the first time in history, feminism becomes actively transnational: thanks to international travel, the circulations of books, newspapers, and letters, and the establishment of international women's organizations, feminist conversations unfold in "real time." These conversations allow us to understand the ways in which women found common agendas as well as the ways in which distinctive national contexts shaped different strategies aimed at the shared goals. They also reveal the currents of power that complicated the ideal of international sisterhood—though, contrary to what we might expect, power does not run in only one direction, nor do Western feminists have the final say in what constitutes "progressive" political change. This multisided case study raises many provocative issues, both strategic and ethical, that continue to preoccupy feminist politics.

The next section, Talking Back to Sexism before "Women's Liberation": Nineteenth to Mid-Twentieth Centuries, focuses on writing as a form of activism as images, concepts, and representations begin to be deconstructed and satirized, their sexism exposed. The selections range historically from the late nineteenth century through 1949, when *The Second Sex* was first published in France. The postwar movements for "Women's Liberation" had yet to bring the concept of "sexism" or notions such as "consciousness-raising" and "personal politics" to cultural prominence, yet it's clear from the works we have chosen that these ideas were under construction. This was a fertile period for women writers; making selections was difficult, and in the end we chose to go with a mix of well-known works and works that are probably less familiar to many readers. Essays on the French Caribbean and India focus on the racialized representation of women as erotic objects and on early feminist protests against the intertwining of sexism and colonialism. From China, a fantasy-narrative imagines "reform" within the patriarchal structure of Confucian thought, both extending and curtailing women's roles. From England and France, influential new concepts are developed and "catch hold" internationally, as Woolf and de Beauvoir challenge the particulars of male-dominated discourse and theorize the conceptual, political, and cultural scaffolding that supports it.

Discovering Gender and Remapping Feminism: 1955–1975 explores what are arguably the two most concentrated, influential decades of contemporary feminist thought. One way of thinking of this period is in terms of a progressive splintering of the myth of the unified "subject," as gender, class, race, nationality, and sexuality assert their claims against any notion of the "essential" or unmarked "human." First directed against assumptions of a male norm, groundbreaking work on class, sexuality, race, and the body, explorations of the collisions between "East" and "West," and considerations of the impact of colonialism dismantle the essentialist category of "woman" as well and thus the possibility of a single brand of feminism. While U.S. feminism, for example, was both shaped and redefined by racial, sexual, and class perspectives—and often, conflicts—among women, modern feminisms of Rhodesia/Zimbabwe and Morocco emerged from confrontations with imperialist and religious authorities, on the one hand, and indigenous patriarchal customs on the other.

Choosing readings for this section was particularly challenging, as we were constantly aware of everything that we were leaving out. We wanted to give readers a sense of the complexity of "Women's Liberation" in the United States—a movement too often caricatured as "white and middle-class"—but at the same time to emphasize that "Women's Liberation" had feminist counterparts in other places around the world. These movements should not be assumed to have taken their cue from white, middle-class feminist developments in the United States; for example, while many white, middle-class U.S. feminists were asserting the value of what we now call "identity politics," laying claim to a defining identity in order to gain solidarity, women of color in the United States, Latin America, and Africa were forming coalitions that depended on recognition of what we now call the "intersectionality" of identity—the ways in which women's identities and experiences of oppression are founded on multiple intersecting markers of difference, such as gender, race, sexuality, and class. At the same time, the increasingly global nature of commerce and culture inevitably affects every feminist struggle—as the selection from Tsitsi Dangerembga's *Nervous Conditions* demonstrates.

We titled our concluding section, Beyond "The Decade of the Woman": 1975 to Present, with several developments in mind. When the UN declared 1976–1985 the "Decade of the Woman," it placed gender politics at the center of the international stage, publicly recognizing the fact that the situation of women is not simply a matter of private or personal experience—just as feminist thinkers have argued for centuries. At the same time, the singular "woman" of that designation belies the global reach of gender politics, and evokes a notion of feminism that is no longer credible. Writers and activists in this section underscore their increasing awareness of the distinctive nature of their identities, values, and struggles, reminding readers that, as Obioma Nnaemeka writes, "feminism, as ideology and struggle, has taken location-specific and culturally defined forms across time and space." Those specifics, in this section, include not only the political innovations and critical challenges posed to mainstream feminism by postcolonial societies, but the emergence of men's studies and Third Wave reframings of feminisms' relationships to consumerism and pop culture.

Our shared goals as we began our work on this collection were to make the study of feminist thought fresh, accessible, and provocative—and to encourage transnational and interdisciplinary analysis rather than simply to represent "difference." But as editors and scholars positioned in different disciplines, generations, and cultural traditions, we came to the project with different ideas about how to achieve those goals. Working from and through those ideas has been intellectually exciting and personally rewarding. We came to understand each other better, and in many ways our own cross talk became the collection's true editor, as what each of us initially brought to the project—assumptions about each other, intellectual and political passions, sensitivities and hot-button issues—were transformed by our discussions. This is our hope, too, for teachers and students who use this collection: that they bring themselves to their discussion of feminist thought—and then find themselves transformed by it.

PART 1

CHALLENGING MALE DOMINANCE

Antiquity to 1800

1

FEMINIST THOUGHT BEFORE
THE RENAISSANCE

Amy Richlin

Did feminism exist before the Renaissance? Not as an organized political movement; furthermore, the category "women" is much complicated by slavery—we should always beware of saying "women" when we mean "free women," as too often happens. In ancient law, slaves' bodies were by definition available for sexual use, so that sex acts themselves were generally felt to be related to ownership. At times free women did band together to protest laws that affected them negatively (for example, the Oppian Law at Rome in 195 BCE); there were women writers who did resist male norms, although their cultures preserved very few of their works; male writers did create female characters who made speeches about women's rights (a sort of ventriloquism); and some thinkers did argue for equal treatment for women. A voice that argued for women always coexisted with a much louder misogynistic voice.

Ideas about women varied enormously over the enormous temporal and geographic span in which the cultures of the modern West were formed, from the ancient Near East through the Middle Ages. As always, in history, it depends whom you ask. The one huge break in the history of this period is the beginning of Christendom—the mapping of a single religion onto the territory of the Roman empire—from the 300s CE onward. Christianity was good for free women in that women (at first) were able to preach, travel, and attain some importance (e.g., as donors, saints, and martyrs); these women's writings and sayings are preserved, an outstanding example being the prison diary of Perpetua, written around 200 CE. But Christianity was disastrous in that Roman law had allowed easy divorce and full property rights for women, and in late antiquity

THE DIVERSITY OF THE ANCIENT WORLD

Hundreds of cultures flourished in the Near East, the Mediterranean basin (which includes North Africa), and Europe in the almost two thousand years that separate Sappho from Hrotsvit. All were slave cultures. The Greek language predominated in the eastern Mediterranean from around 500 BCE through the Middle Ages; throughout that time, Semitic languages were spoken in Syria, in Israel, and across North Africa, mixing with Greek in the east and, later, with Latin in the west. In 500 BCE, Latin was the language of just a small area in central Italy; by 100 CE Rome governed an empire stretching from Britain to Arabia. People throughout the empire continued to speak their local languages. Europe and North Africa fell to Germanic invaders in the 400s CE, but the empire continued in the east, ruled from the city of Constantinople (Byzantium), and the Byzantines called themselves Romans until the city fell to the Turks in 1453 CE. The Germanic-speaking cultures formed kingdoms until the rise of a second "Roman" empire in the 800s CE; in Spain and North Africa, Islamic cultures held sway from the 700s onward. Cultures overlapped, with Jews, for example, living and writing from Baghdad to Spain for most of this time, while the slave trade constantly moved people from the margins to the center. The best-known texts in Greek come from Athens in the 400s BCE, and the best-known texts in Latin from the city of Rome from the 80s BCE to the early 100s CE; the books of the Bible date from the 1100s BCE to the 100s CE; the Quran dates to the late 600s CE; but no one text or period sums up this complex whole.

this began to change, matching contemporary Christian attitudes; it might be argued that both Christian and legal attitudes were part of a wide-ranging shift towards cultural conservatism, or from urban to rural values—one that lasted a very long time. Slaves, however, who under Roman law were themselves property and under Christianity continued to be property, had nothing to lose. Women wore the veil in the ancient Mediterranean long before either Christianity or Islam: some women, in some places, sometimes.

WOMEN WRITING

Sappho is by far the best known of women writers in Greek, but she was not alone. We would not expect to find extant writings by a woman from the extremely androcentric culture of Athens in the 400s BCE, and indeed Sappho (who spelled her name Psappho) came from a very different culture, on the island of Lesbos in the 500s BCE: an aristocratic culture in which women seem to have been educated to write the same kind of poetry also produced by men on the island, known as "lyric" poetry because it was sung to the lyre. All but one of her extant poems are fragmentary—missing words, lines, or sections—and most of her work was destroyed by Christian extremists in the 100s CE. Sappho LP 16 is written in the stanza structure named after her (sapphics) and copied by many writers in both Greek and Latin—until the Christian takeover, she was revered as one of the greatest poets—and, as the critic Page duBois has demonstrated, in this poem Sappho stakes out a position opposing the dominant male tradition, the epic. Her poem is short, where an epic is book length; she chooses Helen, the much-blamed cause of the Trojan War (the prime subject of Greek epics), to be her role model here. Above all, she sets up the first stanza in a form called a "priamel"—"some say X, others say Y, I say Z"—but her priamel first rejects war heroes in favor of love, and, more fundamentally, rejects any one of a list of specific, competing candidates for "most beautiful," in favor of the indefinite, relative "whatever someone loves."

That Sappho finally nominates Anactoria's walk as surpassing the beauty of an army on the march—that is, that "what she loved" was a woman—was evidently not a problem on Lesbos, but Greek male writers had began to make fun of Sappho already in the 400s BCE, and mockery of Sappho as a *tribas* (lesbian) continued on into Latin. However, Sappho was an admired role model not only to Roman writers like Catullus and Horace but to Greek women writers, particularly Nossis, who lived in Locri in southern Italy in the 200s BCE; one of her poems is a message to Sappho. Arguably, one of the very few extant women poets writing in Latin also imitates Sappho in the first poem of her brief extant cycle; this was Sulpicia, an upper-class Roman woman, friend of Ovid, who lived in Rome in the 20s BCE. In that poem she boasts of how she prayed to Venus and got the man she wanted; compare Sappho LP 1, Sappho's only extant complete poem, which is a conversation with Aphrodite.

What makes Sulpicia's poem so interesting is the brassy way in which she upends contemporary Roman moral expectations for decent female behavior. She says it would be wrong for her to worry about her *fama*—her reputation, looking good in the eyes of the public—and, by writing this poem, she makes it so. Roman writers generally published their poems by reciting them to an invited audience; if Sulpicia did this, it would have been a bold act, although we know of at least one other woman poet in Ovid's circle. Sulpicia's boldness is echoed in a series of jokes attributed to Julia, daughter of Augustus (the first emperor, who exiled Ovid), in which Julia overturns all the moral strictures her father would impose on her. These jokes were probably collected in her lifetime by a writer in her circle, but are known now because they were re-collected, approvingly, by Macrobius in the early 400s BCE—a hint at his own contemporary, the empress Galla Placidia, and other imperial women then entangled in Christian court politics. We have only a tantalizing taste of the poetry of another Roman woman, oddly also named Sulpicia, who wrote just before 100 CE; in this one tiny fragment, just like her forerunner, she exposes herself to the public gaze, this time while having sex with her husband. Texts about women's desire for men are none too common before the rise of the novel; when we generalize about Roman misogyny we have to bear in mind that both Sulpicias, along with Julia, were admired by male writers for their wit. It conforms with ancient ideas of women's tendency toward lust that all these women writers take a stance that would now be identified within feminism as "sex positive"; this probably accounts for the survival of these scraps, and should also be taken as an index of how much nerve it took to write like this—as Michelle Cliff once put it, "claiming an identity they taught me to despise."

It is still not a good sign that almost everything women wrote before Christianity is lost, and we can be sure there was much more and that it would have surprised us. Laurie O'Higgins has argued that there was a whole tradition of women's joking and invective, even in otherwise oppressive Greek cultures; there were some women philosophers, there were poets who wrote about topics other than love (some of this survives), there were religious leaders, there were women who wrote memoirs and letters (we have hundreds of everyday women's letters preserved on Egyptian papyri, but not the letters written by Cicero's acquaintance Caerellia, who liked philosophy). From slave women we have only silence, except for the substantial amounts of information we can glean from their tombstones.

VENTRILOQUISM

Male writers of antiquity do try to speak for women, including slaves. One of the most exciting areas of literature in Latin is Roman comedy from around 200 BCE, especially the plays of Plautus. These plays were written by decidedly lower-class men—ex-slaves, workers, army veterans—and were performed by men of a similar background and by slaves, probably all male. The actors probably wore masks, and the costumes and settings were Greek although the plays were in a boisterous Latin, full of Greek words, invented words, puns, and alliteration. Free speech in Rome was plentiful but risky, so, even in these earliest extant literary texts, the riotous cultural critique is hedged about with plausible deniability: the masks, the "Greek" setting. In these plays, slaves are main characters, and constantly speak truth to power.

Unsurprisingly considering who wrote and acted in the plays, their perspective is that of male slaves, but there are plenty of female slave characters, and some are extremely outspoken: an unnamed female pimp, a freed slave, talks about married citizen women as a model of friendship among themselves, but haughty toward her own class out of envy of the whores who become their husbands' girlfriends (*Cistellaria* [The One about the Chest], lines 22–41); the whore's slave-woman Astaphium rants on behalf of whores and their bad reputation for greed, saying the customers steal too (*Truculentus* [Angry Man], lines 95–110, 209–47); in the same play, when an owner beats two female slaves because (he says) they allowed his daughter to be raped, they defy him, pointing out that it is men who commit rape—and then pointing to the rapist (lines 810–13). One of these slaves is named "Syra," a common slave name; it means "woman from Syria," and evokes a then-current belief that Syrians were natural slaves and that Syrian women were ugly and suited for household drudgery.

So when another "Syra" makes a big speech in the play *Mercator* (The Trader), it comes as a surprise. This character has already been established as an old woman, hence doubly abject; she belongs to a married woman who is incensed that her husband (she thinks) has moved his slave/whore/girlfriend into their house. It is in this play that a free character explains what a married woman's slave-woman should be like: ugly, a Syrian or an Egyptian (this probably means an Ethiopian), who can "grind grain, cook, spin wool, and be crushed by the whip" (lines 413–16). Plautus's plays were performed at big public festivals, on temporary stages set up in the street, competing for attention with all sorts of sideshows; we know that all kinds of people, slave and free, sat on the benches to watch them. In Rome around 200 BCE, in the midst of wars that devastated Italy, the crowd would have been multilingual, a cultural mix produced by war—some comic writers had been captured and sold into slavery, and Plautus's native language was not Latin. What would it have meant to the men and women in the audience when a man in a slave-woman's mask delivered Syra's monologue protesting the double sexual standard for married men and women? What kind of a joke was this? And why put this speech in Syra's mouth? Did slaves care about fairness to married women? Slaves were not allowed to marry.

The same kind of question besets our understanding of the female characters in Athenian comedy and tragedy from the 400s BCE: considering that proper Athenian women were not supposed to go out in public except to a religious festival or a funeral, and that all the writers and actors were male, what are all those "women" doing onstage? And what did it mean for a masked male actor to deliver their lines? Athenian actors were citizens, the dramatic festivals there were held in a specially dedicated ritual space, an outdoor theater; the audience in the seating area was probably made up of male citizens (the presence of women in the audience is debated, and it is now argued that all kinds of people, including women, stood at the back and sides). All the playwrights wrote starring roles for female characters, but Euripides (according to the send-up of him in Aristophanes' comedy *Women at the Thesmophoria*) was famous for it—as a misogynist. Yet feminists have claimed him as a proto-feminist because of plays like *Medea*, in which the title character triumphs (in a horrible way) over her despicable husband, Jason: he leaves her and their two sons to marry the king's daughter; she thwarts him by killing the princess, the king, and the children as well. The speech she makes about what it means to be a woman is memorably eloquent, but the name "Medea," from the 400s BCE onward, suggested "witch, evil woman." *Medea* continues to be performed today. Reception theorists believe that meaning is made at the point of reception; are we justified in reading Medea as a hero?

PHILOSOPHY

Feminism is both an attitude that can be held by anybody (hence the literary texts surveyed so far) and a kind of theory, developed by specialists in theoretical thinking. Political philosophy in the West goes back at least to the Greeks and is usually associated with them; *philosophia* is a Greek word meaning "love of wisdom." Most people today have only heard of Plato and Aristotle, while "stoic" has become an adjective, but in fact there were many kinds of philosophy, just as, once Christianity got going, there were many kinds of Christian theology. Unfortunately, the most misogynistic strands in both philosophy and Christianity were those that prevailed; still, as Kathy Gaca has demonstrated, there was a gender-egalitarian "road not taken."

Aristotle (late 300s BCE), the worst misogynist, has had the most far-reaching influence, having been adopted with enthusiasm by Saint Thomas Aquinas in the 1200s CE and thus feeding into modern Catholicism. In the *Politics*, Aristotle draws a set of analogies (1259a37, 1260a9): husband is to wife as father is to children as owner is to slave as human is to animal as ruler is to ruled. Elsewhere he says simply, "the male is by nature superior, and the female inferior; and the one rules, and the other is ruled" (1254b2). Plato (early 300s BCE) is often cited for the gender-egalitarian statements he makes in the *Republic* and *Laws*, but these texts manifest a good deal of ambivalence about women's capacities. Women were not among the followers of either Plato or Aristotle; we might expect better of some of the other philosophical schools that included women—the Epicureans, the Cynics, the Pythagoreans, and the early Stoics. However, very few of their works survive in other than fragmentary form, although we do have a few short essays attributed to female Pythagoreans.

The most strongly feminist statement from ancient philosophy comes, surprisingly, from a Roman Stoic, Musonius Rufus, a wealthy upper-class citizen who lived in Rome (except for periods spent in exile) from about 20 CE to the 80s or 90s CE. The titles of his extant essays, originally written up in Greek from notes by a student, include "That Women Too Should Study Philosophy," "Should Daughters Receive the Same Education as Sons?" and "Is Marriage a Handicap for the Pursuit of Philosophy?" Musonius comes out firmly in favor of women's education and of marriage, which is entirely consistent with the general trend of Roman culture: both boys and girls received an elementary education, and a few young women went on to further study (though usually not rhetoric, like their brothers); this was true not only for free children, as selected slave children received the same education. Further, despite misogynistic moralizing, wives held a respected position throughout Roman Italy, and women engaged in business, were involved in public life, and corresponded with writers like Cicero, Pliny, and Fronto. The degree of literacy in antiquity has been hotly debated, but (misspelled) graffiti by both men and women suggest that it was pretty pervasive.

As has often been pointed out, it is thought-provoking that Musonius Rufus was a contemporary of Saint Paul, whose ideas on the proper relations between the sexes still dominate Christendom. Yet the ideas of Saint Paul, and of other misogynistic theologians like Tertullian and Tatian, need not have won out; early gnostic Christianity held Mary Magdalene to have been the first among Christ's Apostles, in some North African sects women continued as leaders, and Epiphanes, in the 100s CE, advocated sexual communalism as opposed to the "procreationist monogamy" that won out (see Gaca, 272–91)—that is, he saw monogamy as a system in which husbands held wives like a kind of property, and argued that this was un-Christian and wrong. Moreover, the place established for women within the monastic movement (from the late 200s CE onward) meant that there continued to be women-only centers where, because of the need to read holy books, at least some women were educated. As education within Christendom came to be identical with religious education, this meant that women in convents might get something like an equivalent education to what was on offer in monasteries, although with fewer books in the library. This brings us to one last woman writer.

HROTSVIT

Hrotsvit (her name is also spelled "Roswitha" or "Hrotswitha") was an aristocratic woman who became a canoness (like a nun, but not as restricted) in the abbey of Gandersheim, in what is now Germany, in the 900s CE. She wrote in Latin in a range of poetic forms, including epic, and did a series of saints' lives in verse; she also had the wildly original idea of writing plays about (mostly female) saints and martyrs and casting them in the style of the Roman comic playwright Terence, who dramatized love stories about young men and whores. These are believed to be the first plays written anywhere in Europe after late antiquity. In the double preface to her plays she portrays herself as a little ignorant female (*nesciola*), a worthless little woman (*vilis mulierculae*) who has only a tiny talent (*ingenioli*), with many other professions of unworthiness. These apologies are embedded in a dazzling display of erudition and super-talented rhetorical flair, set in rhyming prose marked by internal divisions (it sounds like rap, and was certainly meant to be entertaining, but more in a high-culture than a pop-culture way; I've represented the internal breaks with extended spaces within the prose), decorated with literary as well as biblical allusions. Moreover, in the second part of the preface she uses the language of philosophy, showing a knowledge of Aristotle that would have been extremely rare in her day. In her biblical references, too, she subtly sets herself on a level with towering figures like John the Baptist and Saint Paul. Yet she makes some surprising plays on words: her previous ("worthless") talent has been *heroico ligatam strophio*, literally "tied up by the heroic brassiere/chest-binding," while she is now making it *dramatica vinctam serie*, "bound with dramatic lines." That is, she is turning from epic, which is written in hexameter (punning on *strophium*, "brassiere," *strophe*, "verse," and *stropha*, "trick"), to drama, originally written in a set of meters not found in epic; and she is putting on these styles like a brassiere—the "lines" of poetry turn into straps. Outrageous, especially for someone who throughout this double essay sets herself up in contrast to "truly" wise men. The statement that her work will give more credit to God "insofar as women's wits are believed to be slower" is definitely sarcastic. We note that she translates her name here, "Hrotsvit," as meaning "Strong Shout." The plays themselves depict women's triumphs in no uncertain terms, while male characters are often made to look stupid. Still, although the tactic of pretending to be ignorant was a well-worn rhetorical move (used by Socrates, for example, in Plato's *Apology*), the smokescreen of worthlessness Hrotsvit uses in these prefaces perhaps outlines the real-life barriers to women's speech.

Today we still live in Christendom. We used to write dates "B.C." ("Before Christ") and A.D. (*Anno Domini*, "In the Year of Our Lord"), and now we write "BCE" ("Before the

Common Era") and "CE" (in the "Common Era"), but to whom is that era common? Our dates still revolve around the (inaccurate) date of the birth of an illegitimate baby to a teenaged mother who spoke a Semitic language in an obscure corner of the Roman empire. As Daniel Boyarin once said, we are living in the very late Roman empire. Is that coming to an end any time soon?

DISCUSSION QUESTIONS

1. Imagine different classes of ancient women hearing these texts read aloud or performed. How would slavery affect the meaning of each text to the audience?

2. How was Christianity empowering for Hrotsvit?

3. What is the difference between texts produced by women (like Sappho, Nossis, the two Sulpicias, and Hrotsvit), texts written by men for women characters (like Medea and Syra) to speak, and texts written by men (like Musonius Rufus) about women?

SAPPHO, FRAGMENT 16

Some say a host of horsemen, others of foot-soldiers,
others of ships, upon the black earth
is the fairest thing, but I say it is
    whatever someone loves;
And it's entirely easy to make this intelligible
to everyone: Helen, who far excelled in beauty
among all people, left her husband,
    a most noble man,
and went sailing off to Troy,
remembering not at all her child
or her dear parents, but [Aphrodite?]
    led her aside
[2 fragmentary lines]
. . . which now makes me remember Anactoria,
    here no more;
her lovely step would I prefer to see
and the bright sparkle of her face,

SOURCES: Translations of Sappho, Sulpicia the elegist, Sulpicia the satirist, Hrotsvit, and Plautus are by Amy Richlin and were commissioned for this volume.

than the Lydian chariots and the foot-soldiers
in their full armor.

Translated by Amy Richlin

NOSSIS, POEM 11

This poem pretends to be the epitaph on the poet's gravestone.

Stranger, if you sail to the land of lovely dances, Mytilene,
to catch fire from the blossom of Sappho's graces,
say that a friend to her and the Muses, the Lokrian land
bore me. And knowing my name is Nossis, go on!

Translated by Diane Rayor

SOURCE: Nossis, "Poem 11," in *Sappho's Lyre: Archaic Lyric and Women Poets of Ancient Greece,* trans. Diane Rayor (Berkeley, University of California Press, 1991), 133.

SULPICIA THE ELEGIST, POEM 1 (TIBULLUS BOOK 3, POEM 13)

At last love has come, of a sort that to hide it would shame me
more than my bad reputation if I laid it bare.
Begged by my Muses, and Italy's, the goddess of Cythera
brought him to me and put him in my lap.
Venus kept her promise: let anyone tell my joys—
if they want it said they had none of their own.
Not I to trust a thing to sealed-up papers,
so no one could read me before my own man does,
but it feels good to sin—to put on a face to look good
bores me: with a man who's my match, let them say I'm a match for him.

Translated by Amy Richlin

SULPICIA THE SATIRIST, FRAGMENT

If my featherbed frame got fixed,
and [someone? something?] showed me lying naked with Calenus

Translated by Amy Richlin

Many Catholics are found,   and we can't fully cleanse ourselves of this state of mind,   who, for the eloquence   of its polished performance,   prefer the emptiness of pagan literature   to the usefulness of holy scripture.   There are even some who stick   to the pages of the holy book,   who even if they shun other pagan stuff,   still like to read Terence's more than enough,   and, while the sweetness of his style makes them happy,   reading about nasty things gets them dirty.   So I, the Strong Shout of Gandersheim, haven't said no to copying him in my speaking,   since other people go for him in their reading,   so that with the same style of speech,   in which the gross lewdnesses of sexy women were recited,   the praiseworthy virtuousnesses of holy virgins (up to the ability of my little talent) can be celebrated.   Still this pretty often makes me embarrassed   and by serious blushing to be harassed,   that, since this kind   of speaking forces my hand,   the despicable dementia of lovers outside the law   and their too-sweet to-and-fro,   which is not allowed into our hearing—   that's what I've been handling in my mind by speaking   and by my busy pen I've been signifying.   But if I left this out because of blushing,   I wouldn't complete my undertaking,   nor the praise of innocents (as best I can) would I be displaying—because, the more ready the seductions of madmen are to ensnare us,   so much both the glory of the helper above is higher over us,   and the victory of those who triumph is proven more glorious,   especially when female fragility is victorious   and manly brawn in confusion lies helpless.   Indeed there's no doubt in me   that some people are going to protest to me,   because the worthlessness of this speaking is much inferior,   much narrower,   and totally dissimilar   to what the man's whom I proposed to imitate were.   I agree;   but to them I decree,   that I cannot be judged by that rule,   as if I presumed to compare myself to those writers,   who have far surpassed my lack of skill in a knowledge much higher.   Nor indeed am I so   filled up with braggadocio,   that even with the most outsider   foster children of writers I'd presume to compare myself.

But this alone I strive for, that, even if I'm not strong enough to do it with perfection,   still by my mind's prayerful devotion   I can bend   my given talent back to the Giver, in the end.   So I am not so much a lover of myself, that to avoid a scolding   the virtue of Christ, who works in his saints, with whatever ability he will give me himself, I should cease from unfolding.   For if anyone likes my devotion,   I second that emotion;   but if either because of my lowliness   or because of my faulty style's boorishness   nobody likes it,   still it feels good to me myself, that I did it,   because, while the worthlessness of my personal diligence,   in the other little works of my ignorance   was tied up with heroic (bra)strap-lines,   and this time I wear it bound up in dramatic lines,   the vicious   pagans' pleasures   by ditching   I'm enriching.

Translated by Amy Richlin

Greetings to you, knowledge-full,   civil, gentle,   nor another's project begrudging,   but, as befits truly wise men, well-wishing;   from Hrotsvit, little ignorant girl,   and worthy of no approval;   who personally asks you to be well   and always asks you to rejoice.   So the magnitude of your laudable humbleness   I cannot admire enough,   the fullness of your magnificent kindness and esteem toward my worthlessness   with recompense of worthy thankfulness   I cannot pay back enough.   Since, when you have been brought up on philosophical studies especially,   and you've been perfected in knowledge far more excellently,   the little work of a worthless little woman (me)   you have judged worthy of your admiration   and you have praised the Bestower of the grace working in me,   with brotherly affection bestowing congratulation,   thinking there is in me a bit of the knowledge of the arts,   of which the subtleties far pass by my womanish heart.   Then the boorishness of my little speaking   until now I was hardly daring to show to a few, and only my friends;   and from this the work of speaking almost came to an end   beyond something of this kind,   because, just as there were few, who might get a good look at it with my permission,   so there weren't many to dig out what in it needed correction,   or, for me to dare something like it, to provide provocation.   But now, since we know that when three witnesses agree, truth is established [Deut. 19:15],   made strong by your opinion of me, I presume with more confidence both to embark on publication, if God gives the nod that I can,   and to undergo examination by any wise men.   Amongst all this, by conflicting emotions, namely by joy and fear, I am pulled apart: for indeed, because God, by whose grace alone I am what I am, is praised through me [I Cor. 15:10], I rejoice with all my heart;   but I am afraid to seem greater than I am,   since I don't doubt it is equally sinful, when God gives a free gift,   not to take it, as, when a gift is not given, to fake it.   So I don't deny that, by the Creator's grace, I have a knowledge of the arts in potentiality,   since I am an animal (as Aristotle says) with a trainable mentality,   but I confess that I am entirely ignorant in actuality.   I recognize, too, that a keen intellect has been allotted to me by God;   but, once the diligence of my teachers lapses, it's left unpolished,   and, due to the sluggishness of my personal laziness, it lies neglected.   So, lest the gift of God should be nullified in me because of my own negligence,   whatever chance thread or even fluff I have been able to pluck from the rags torn from Philosophy's raiment,   I have taken care to weave into this little composition I mentioned,   so that the worthlessness of my own ignorance should be brightened by the intermingling of a material that's nobler,   and so that the Bestower of intellect   might be justly praised through me the more,   insofar as women's wits are believed to be slower.

This is my intention in speaking,   this is the sole cause of my sweat;   nor do I boast by pretending   that I know unknown things,   but, as for me, I only know that I do not know.   For since I have been swayed, like the reed shaken by the wind [Matt. 11:7], by the touch of your favor and mention,   this little book, which I set out with such an intention,   but up until now because of its worthlessness I preferred to conceal   rather than to bring out and reveal,   to your scrutiny I yield,   and it is right that you should check it by correcting it with the diligence of no lesser care than you have accorded to my previous work.   And so, at last, reshaped to the standard of correctness, send it back to me,   so that, with your instruction to demonstrate it to me, I may recognize at what points I have most greatly gone astray.

Translated by Amy Richlin

EURIPIDES, *MEDEA*, LINES 230–51

Medea:

> Of all those beings capable of life and thought,
> we women are most miserable of living things.
> First we must buy ourselves a husband, at great cost,
> and thus acquire a master over our own bodies—
> a second evil still more grievous than the first.
> The greatest ordeal here is whether we will get
> a worthwhile or a bad one; for departure harms
> a woman's reputation, and she can't refuse
> a husband. Then she comes to new customs and ways,
> and must divine prophetically—not having learned
> at home—what kind of bed-mate she'll be dealing with.
> If we succeed in working all this out, and if
> our husband bears in peace the yoke of living with us,
> our life is enviable; if not, we must die.
> But when a man is burdened by the company
> within, he goes outside to ease his heart's distress
> [by turning to a friend or someone his own age];
> we, by necessity, must look to one alone.
> They say there is no danger in the life we lead,
> staying at home while they do battle with the spear.
> How wrongheaded they are! I'd rather stand three times
> behind a shield in war than give birth to one child!

Translated by Ruby Blondell

SOURCE: Euripides, "Medea," in *Women on the Edge: Four Plays by Euripides,* trans. Ruby Blondell (New York: Routledge, 1999), 177.

PLAUTUS, *MERCATOR*, LINES 817–29

Syra:

My goodness, women live by a hard law,
and, poor things, a much less fair way than men.
For if a husband hires a whore and hides it from his wife,
if the wife finds out, no problem for the husband;
but if a wife goes out of the house and hides it from her husband,
the husband has grounds to kick her out of the marriage.
I wish the law was the same for husbands as for wives;
for a wife is satisfied, if she's good, with just one husband:
why shouldn't a husband be satisfied with one wife?
My goodness, I'd fix it, if husbands were hit the same way—
whoever hired a whore and hid it from his wife—
the same way women are kicked out who've been guilty,
there'd be more husbands on their own than there are wives now.

Translated by Amy Richlin

MUSONIUS RUFUS, FROM *THAT WOMEN TOO SHOULD STUDY PHILOSOPHY*

When someone asked him if women too should study philosophy, he began to discourse on the theme that they should, in somewhat the following manner. Women as well as men, he said, have received from the gods the gift of reason, which we use in our dealings with one another and by which we judge whether a thing is good or bad, right or wrong. Likewise the female has the same senses as the male; namely sight, hearing, smell, and the others. Also both have the same parts of the body, and one has nothing more than the other. Moreover, not men alone, but women too, have a natural inclination toward virtue and the capacity for acquiring it, and it is the nature of women no less than men to be pleased by good and just acts and to reject the opposite of these. If this is true, by what reasoning would it ever be appropriate for men to search out and consider how they may lead good lives, which is exactly the study of philosophy, but inappropriate for women? Could it be that it is fitting for men to be good, but not for women? Let us examine in detail the qualities which are suitable for a woman who would lead a good life, for it will appear that each one of them would accrue to her most readily from the study of philosophy. In the first place, a woman must be a good housekeeper; that is, a careful accountant of all that pertains to the welfare of her house and capable of directing the household slaves. It is my contention that these are the very qualities which would be present particularly in

SOURCE: "The Roman Socrates," trans. Cora E. Lutz (Hartford: Yale University Press, 1947), 41, 43, 45, 47.

the woman who studies philosophy, since obviously each of them is a part of life and philosophy is nothing other than knowledge about life, and the philosopher, as Socrates said, quoting Homer, is constantly engaged in investigating precisely this: "Whatsoever of good and of evil is wrought in thy halls." But above all a woman must be chaste and self-controlled; she must, I mean, be pure in respect of unlawful love, exercise restraint in other pleasures, not be a slave to desire, not be contentious, not lavish in expense, nor extravagant in dress. Such are the works of a virtuous woman, and to them I would add yet these: to control her temper, not to be overcome by grief, and to be superior to uncontrolled emotion of every kind. Now these are the things which the teachings of philosophy transmit, and the person who has learned them and practices them would seem to me to have become a well-ordered and seemly character, whether man or woman. Well then, so much for self-control. As for justice, would not the woman who studies philosophy be just, would she not be a blameless life-partner, would she not be a sympathetic help-mate, would she not be an untiring defender of husband and children, and would she not be entirely free of greed and arrogance? And who better than the woman trained in philosophy—and she certainly of necessity if she has really acquired philosophy—would be disposed to look upon doing a wrong as worse than suffering one (as much worse as it is the baser), and to regard being worsted as better than gaining an unjust advantage? Moreover, who better than she would love her children more than life itself? What woman would be more just than such a one? Now as for courage, certainly it is to be expected that the educated woman will be more courageous than the uneducated, and one who has studied philosophy more than one who has not; and she will not therefore submit to anything shameful because of fear of death or unwillingness to face hardship, and she will not be intimidated by anyone because he is of noble birth, or powerful, or wealthy, no, not even if he be the tyrant of her city. For in fact she has schooled herself to be high-minded and to think of death not as an evil and life not as a good, and likewise not to shun hardship and never for a moment to seek ease and indolence. So it is that such a woman is likely to be energetic, strong to endure pain, prepared to nourish her children at her own breast, and to serve her husband with her own hands, and willing to do things which some would consider no better than slaves' work. Would not such a woman be a great help to the man who married her, an ornament to her relatives, and a good example for all who know her? Yes, but I assure you, some will say that women who associate with philosophers are bound to be arrogant for the most part and presumptuous, in that abandoning their own households and turning to the company of men they practice speeches, talk like sophists, and analyze syllogisms, when they ought to be sitting at home spinning. I should not expect the women who study philosophy to shirk their appointed tasks for mere talk any more than men, but I maintain that their discussions should be conducted for the sake of their practical application. For as there is no merit in the science of medicine unless it conduces to the healing of man's body, so if a philosopher has or teaches reason, it is of no use if it does not contribute to the virtue of man's soul. Above all, we ought to examine the doctrine which we think women who study philosophy ought to follow; we ought to see if the study which presents modesty as the greatest good can make them presumptuous, if the study which is a guide to the greatest self-restraint accustoms them to live heedlessly, if what sets forth intemperance as the greatest evil does not teach self-control, if what represents the management of a household as a virtue does not impel them to manage well their homes. Finally, the teachings of philosophy exhort the woman to be content with her lot and to work with her own hands.

Translated by Cora E. Lutz

MUSONIUS RUFUS, FROM *SHOULD DAUGHTERS RECEIVE THE SAME EDUCATION AS SONS?*

Once when the question arose as to whether or not sons and daughters ought to be given the same education, he remarked that trainers of horses and dogs make no distinction in the training of the male and the female; for female dogs are taught to hunt just as the males are, and one can see no difference in the training of mares, if they are expected to do a horse's work, and the training of stallions. In the case of man, however, it would seem to be felt necessary to employ some special and exceptional training and education for males over females, as if it were not essential that the same virtues should be present in both alike, in man and woman, or as if it were possible to arrive at the same virtues, not through the same, but through different instruction. And yet that there is not one set of virtues for a man and another for a woman is easy to perceive. In the first place, a man must have understanding and so must a woman, or what pray would be the use of a foolish man or woman? Then it is essential for one no less than the other to live justly, since the man who is not just would not be a good citizen, and the woman would not manage her household well if she did not do it justly; but if she is unjust she will wrong her husband like Eriphyle in the story. Again, it is recognized as right for a woman in wedlock to be chaste, and so is it likewise for a man; the law, at all events, decrees the same punishment for committing adultery as for being taken in adultery. Gluttony, drunkenness, and other related vices, which are vices of excess and bring disgrace upon those guilty of them, show that self-control is most necessary for every human being, male and female alike; for the only way of escape from wantonness is through self-control; there is no other. Perhaps someone may say that courage is a virtue appropriate to men only. That is not so. For a woman too of the right sort must have courage and be wholly free of cowardice, so that she will be swayed neither by hardships nor by fear; otherwise, how will she be said to have self-control, if by threat or force she can be constrained to yield to shame? Nay more, it is necessary for women to be able to repel attack, unless indeed they are willing to appear more cowardly than hens and other female birds which fight with creatures much larger than themselves to defend their young. How then should women not need courage? That women have some prowess in arms the race of the Amazons demonstrated when they defeated many tribes in war. If, therefore, something of this courage is lacking in other women, it is due to lack of use and practice rather than because they were not endowed with it. If then men and women are born with the same virtues, the same type of training and education must, of necessity, befit both men and women. [. . .] "Come now," I suppose someone will say, "do you expect that men should learn spinning the same as women, and that women should take part in gymnastic exercises the same as men?" No, that I should not demand. But I do say that, since in the human race man's constitution is stronger and woman's weaker, tasks should be assigned which are suited to the nature of each; that is the heavier tasks should be given to the stronger and lighter ones to the weaker. Thus spinning and indoor work would be more fitting for women than for men, while gymnastics and outdoor work would be more suitable for men. Occasionally, however, some men might more fittingly handle certain of the lighter tasks and what is generally considered women's work, and again, women might do heavier tasks which seem more appropriate for men whenever conditions of strength, need, or circumstance warranted. For all human tasks, I am inclined to believe, are a common obligation and are common for men and women, and none is necessarily appointed for either one exclusively, but some pursuits are more suited to the nature of one, some to the other, and for this reason some are called men's work and some women's. But whatever things have reference to virtue, these one would properly say are equally appropriate to the nature of both, inasmuch as we agree that virtues are in no respect more fitting for the one than the other. Hence I hold it reasonable that the things which have reference to virtue ought to be taught to male and female alike; and furthermore that straight from infancy they ought to be taught that this is right and that is wrong, and that it is the same for both alike; that this is helpful, that is harmful, that one must do this, one must not do that. From this training understanding is developed in those who learn, boys and girls alike, with no difference. [. . .] I do not mean that women should possess technical skill and acuteness in argument. It would be quite superfluous, since they will use philosophy for the ends of their life as women. Even in men I do not prize this accomplishment too highly. I only urge that they should acquire from philosophy goodness in conduct and nobility of character. Now in very truth philosophy is training in nobility of character and nothing else.

Translated by Cora E. Lutz

2

CHRISTINE DE PIZAN AND
THE *QUERELLE DES FEMMES*

Susan Bordo

From the very earliest Greek philosophers, women have created trouble for theories of human nature. The Greeks and the medieval Christian philosophers inspired by them were obsessed with establishing and defining a privileged place for "Man" in the hierarchy of living things—and often found an answer in the elevation of "mind" over "body." Man, alone among creatures, could transcend the desires and limitations of bodily existence to achieve rational thought and control of his animal instincts. It would be a struggle, involving will, dedication to a virtuous life, and the right kind of philosophical/ religious practice, but it could be done.

In this scheme, women represented a conundrum. They were humans, not animals. But they were disturbingly different from men, too. They bled every month, and gave birth to children; their service seemed to be to and of the body rather than the mind. And from the perspective of many male theologians, they embodied everything that pulled them away from their own spiritual quests, everything that aroused and comforted and tempted them, everything that reminded them of the facts of their own bloody, earthly origins, and the hard-to-conquer needs of their bodies.

Clearly, a separate "theory" of Woman's "difference" had to be formulated. Could a woman be virtuous? If so, what kind of virtue was distinctively hers? Was her intelligence less than man's? Was she capable of being educated? What about her physiology and psychology ruled her nature? The misogynist answers to these questions and their dominance in Western philosophy and theology are well known. But, as Amy Richlin's essay in chapter 1 points out, there has always been a "recessive" strain poking holes in (and sometimes, fun at) the official misogyny. And early in the fifteenth century, something remarkable happens: the voice of protest becomes strong enough to initiate a widespread cultural debate, lasting for at least four centuries (and arguably, still going today). The participants were both male and female; Catholic, Protestant, and Jew; French, German, Spanish, Italian, and English. They wrote pamphlets, poems, treatises, letters. They volleyed back and forth, some egalitarian, some misogynist, some arguing for woman's special "difference." The whole genre came to be known as the *Querelle des femmes,* or the "woman question."

It's impossible to specify the exact origins of the *Querelles,* but most scholars agree that Christine de Pizan's *Book of the City of Ladies* (1405), excerpted here, played a key role. *The City of Ladies* is not de Pizan's only work—she was a prolific writer who had many patrons among the French and English aristocracy—but it is probably her most famous, and most certainly the one that earned her Joan Kelly's assessment as the first "feminist theorist," for its thoroughgoing resistance to "the cultural and social colonization of women by men" (28). Some would call the label "feminist" an anachronism, of course; but the description—although de Pizan would puzzle at the word "colonization"—is apt.

The Book of the City of Ladies, like many tipping-point works, was the product of broad social change and particular circumstances. The broad social change was European "humanism," a loose label for the widespread intellectual questioning of medieval ideas and institutions, including the Catholic Church, which fueled the scientific revolution, Protestant Reformation, and philosophical "Enlightenment." Humanism, which began in Italy in the fourteenth century and quickly spread among the intellectual avant-garde throughout Europe, made sharp criticism of convention into something of an art form. Most tracts were dead serious in intent, but often delivered their arguments through irony and sarcasm. The Dutch scholar Erasmus, for example, whose *The Praise of Folly,* published in 1511, was a runaway best seller throughout Europe, lampooned all manner of human hypocrisy and foolishness, while sinking sharp barbs into the clergy, who "crucify" Christ "afresh by their scandalous life" (292).

The new humanism was provocative, it was "radical," it was antiestablishment. And although its most famous lights were males who had no interests in debunking ancient theories of female inferiority, it opened the door, both intellectually and practically, for women writers to walk through, armed with wit and erudition against their own chosen targets. They entered, not through the universities (where women were not allowed to study), but through private tutoring by humanist fathers (Thomas More most famously, but both de Pizan and Sor Juana, discussed in chapter 3, benefitted from their educated male relations) and the court salons, where the great intellects and artists of the day gathered and entertained each other with argument, playacting, and banter.[1] Young women of the nobility could acquire an informal education while serving as ladies-in-waiting, and older, more independent women with talent and wit could develop patrons among aristocrats and royalty. This was how Christine de Pizan, who "was perhaps the closest thing to a career woman in the fifteenth century" (she had turned to writing after she was widowed at the age of twenty-five, with three children and a mother to support), established her reputation (Gottlieb 282).

The Book of the City of Ladies seems to have been inspired, most immediately, by two works—Jean de Meun's version of *The Romance of the Rose* and Mathéolus's *Lamentations*—both of which contain passages that complain of woman's greedy, manipulative, lustful nature. Although the sequence of events is fuzzy, the *Querelles* over these works apparently began when a distinguished scholar circulated his praise for *The Romance*. Christine protested his views in letters to two royal secretaries, which set off a rally of counterattack, defense, and counterattack. At some point Christine must have decided it was time to make her voice heard more forcefully and present her arguments more systematically. *The Book of the City of Ladies* was the result. In it, de Pizan gathers heroines from history and her own time through which to protest the "many evil and reproachful things about women and their behavior" written in male treatises.

Although the controversy over *The Romance of the Rose* may have ignited the debate that led to *The Book of the City of Ladies,* Christine, in the introductory section reprinted here, refers instead to Malotheus's less influential *Lamentations,* possibly because she is not so much interested in refuting specific arguments, as in setting up a foil to stand for "male think" in general. "It seems that they all speak from one and the same mouth," she observes, and goes on to consider whether indeed this uniformity of opinion suggests that they may in fact be right about woman's wicked nature. This possibility leads her to great despair, until Lady Reason and Lady Rectitude step in to educate her—as all women, Christine argues, should be educated. Like other writers of her time, Christine may well be playing with the reader when she declares, having examined a "gushing fountain" of male authorities, that indeed "God formed a vile creature when He made woman," but when Lady Reason speaks, it is through serious, solid argument, pointing out the contradictions and self-deceptions in the men's indictment of woman's nature.

The Book of the City of Ladies was arguably the first, but not the last, shot fired in the transnational "gender wars" of the fifteenth and sixteenth centuries. Not surprisingly, it was still largely men who presented the public face of the debate. The "pro-woman" male faction included Juan Rodriguez del Padron (*The Triumph of Women,* 1438) and Martin Le Franc (*The Champion of Women,* 1440) The "anti-woman" male faction included Leon Battista Alberti (*On the Family,* 1434–37) and later but more influentially, Juan Luis Vives's *The Education of a Christian Woman* (1523). *The Education,* written expressly for Henry VIII's daughter Mary, insisted, against de Pizan's arguments, on the necessarily subordinate role of women. In it, young girls, reminded that they are "the devil's instrument," are given strict instructions for how to protect themselves and their virtue, while the married woman is advised leave the home as little as possible, speak "only when it would be harmful to keep silent," and "administer everything according to the will and command of her husband" (255).

The debate among the men continued in 1540 and 1542 with Sir Thomas Elyot's refutation of Vives's *Defence of Good Women,* which argued for women's full participation in public life (and skill at arms!), and Heinrich Cornelius Agrippa von Nettesheim's *Of the Nobilitie and Excellencye of Womankynde*. Anticipating later Enlightenment thinkers, Agrippa argues that the differences between men and women are only bodily and that "the woman hathe that same mynd that a man hath, the same reason and speche, she gothe to the same ende of blysfulnes [spirituality], where shall be no exception of kynde." Why then are they everywhere subordinate to men? Because they are not permitted to make the laws or write history, and therefore they, as historian Constance Jordan paraphrases Agrippa, "cannot contribute to or criticize the intellectual bases on which they are categorized as inferior" (85).

It wasn't long, however, before "the old tune was sung again," as Margaret King puts it. When Mary Tudor became queen of England in 1553, her Catholicism added fuel to the fire that was already burning in Protestant reformer John Knox, who argued, in his famously titled *The First Blast of the Trumpet against the Monstrous Regiment of Women*, "that any woman who presumed 'to sit in the seat of God, that is, to teach, to judge, or to reign above a man'" was "a monster in nature" (Jansen 1). For "Nature . . . doth paint them forth to be weak, frail, impatient, feeble, and foolish, and experience hath declared them to be unconstant, variable, cruel, and lacking the spirit of counsel and regiment" (Jansen 15). (No wonder Elizabeth I felt it important that people see her as having "the heart and stomach of a King"!)

The *Querelle* was far from concluded, however. But, as the selections from Sor Juana and Mary Astell in chapters 3 and 4 illustrate, as more women entered the debate in the early modern period, the very notion on which the earlier *Querelle* revolved—the moral and intellectual status of that "different" human, woman—began to be displaced by radical questioning of the idea that the mind or soul is "gendered" at all. Christine de Pizan does not go so far as this; her aim is to refute theories of female inferiority (and often, to shift the onus of vice onto men), not establish that men and women are "the same" in important respects. Still, one can see the seeds of this idea in the argument, presented forcefully by Lady Reason, that if women "usually know less than men" it is not because they are any less intellectually equipped than men, but because, consigned to the home, they have less opportunity to exercise the range of their capacities. De Pizan herself was living proof of this, and despite her playful pretense, she surely knew it.

NOTES

1. Francis I's sister Marguerite de Navarre, for example, turned the Valois court into a center of intellectual and artistic brilliance. Francis's counselor and confidante since he took the throne in 1515, Marguerite filled the court with poets, philosophers, and the most provocative reformist intellectuals of the time. In Marguerite's court, all the hot humanist topics of the day were debated, from the "Bible question" (did people need priests to interpret scripture for them or should vernacular versions be widely available?) to the "woman question."

WORKS CITED

Erasmus, Desiderius. "The Praise of Folly." In *Readings in Western Religious Thought II: The Middle Ages,* edited by Patrick V. Reid. New York: Paulist Press, 1995.

Jansen, Sharon. *The Monstrous Regiment of Women: Female Rulers in Early Modern Europe.* New York: Palgrave Macmillan, 2002.

Jordan, Constance. *Renaissance Feminism: Literary Texts and Political Models.* Ithaca: Cornell University Press, 1990.

Kelly, Joan. "Early Feminist Theory and the *Querelle des Femmes,* 1400–1789." *Signs* 8, no. 1 (1982): 4–28.

Pizan, Christine de. *The Book of the City of Ladies.* Translated by Earl Jeffrey Richards. New York: Persea Books, 1982.

Vives, Juan Luis. *The Education of a Christian Woman: A Sixteenth-Century Manual.* Translated by Charles Fantazzi. Chicago: Chicago University Press, 2000.

DISCUSSION QUESTIONS

1. In the selection, Christine de Pizan speaks in several different voices: that of the "I" telling the story and that of the ladies who instruct her. How would you describe the different personalities they embody, and how do they work together to form the argument of the piece? Where is de Pizan herself in all this?

2. Does a "woman question" still exist today? If so, what are the ideas being debated? Who are the participants?

3. Would you describe de Pizan as a feminist? Why or why not?

CHRISTINE DE PIZAN, FROM *THE BOOK OF THE CITY OF LADIES*

One day as I was sitting alone in my study surrounded by books on all kinds of subjects, devoting myself to literary studies, my usual habit, my mind dwelt at length on the weighty opinions of various authors whom I had studied for a long time. I looked up from my book, having decided to leave such subtle questions in peace and to relax by reading some light poetry. With this in mind, I searched for some small book. By chance a strange volume came into my hands, not one of my own, but one which had been given to me along with some others. When I held it open and saw from its title page that it was by Mathéolus, I smiled, for though I had never seen it before, I had often heard that like other books it discussed respect for women. I thought I would browse through it to amuse myself. I had not been reading for very long when my good mother called me to refresh myself with some supper, for it was evening. Intending to look at it the next day, I put it down. The next morning, again

SOURCE: Christine de Pizan, *The Book of the City of Ladies,* trans. Earl Jeffrey Richard (New York: Persea, 1982), 3–5, 62–64, 142, 164–65, 256–57.

seated in my study as was my habit, I remembered wanting to examine this book by Mathéo-lus. I started to read it and went on for a little while. Because the subject seemed to me not very pleasant for people who do not enjoy lies, and of no use in developing virtue or manners, given its lack of integrity in diction and theme, and after browsing here and there and read-ing the end, I put it down in order to turn my attention to more elevated and useful study. But just the sight of this book, even though it was of no authority, made me wonder how it happened that so many different men—and learned men among them—have been and are so inclined to express both in speaking and in their treatises and writings so many wicked insults about women and their behavior. Not only one or two and not even just this Mathéo-lus (for this book had a bad name anyway and was intended as a satire) but, more generally, judging from the treatises of all philosophers and poets and from all the orators—it would take too long to mention their names—it seems that they all speak from one and the same mouth. They all concur in one conclusion: that the behavior of women is inclined to and full of every vice. Thinking deeply about these matters, I began to examine my character and conduct as a natural woman and, similarly, I considered other women whose company I frequently kept, princesses, great ladies, women of the middle and lower classes, who had graciously told me of their most private and intimate thoughts, hoping that I could judge impartially and in good conscience whether the testimony of so many notable men could be true. To the best of my knowledge, no matter how long I confronted or dissected the problem, I could not see or realize how their claims could be true when compared to the natural behavior and character of women. Yet I still argued vehemently against women, saying that it would be impossible that so many famous men—such solemn scholars, possessed of such deep and great understanding, so clear-sighted in all things, as it seemed—could have spo-ken falsely on so many occasions that I could hardly find a book on morals where, even before I had read it in its entirety, I did not find several chapters or certain sections attacking women, no matter who the author was. This reason alone, in short, made me conclude that, although my intellect did not perceive my own great faults and, likewise, those of other women, because of its simpleness and ignorance, it was however truly fitting that such was the case. And so I relied more on the judgment of others than on what I myself felt and knew. I was so transfixed in this line of thinking for such a long time that it seemed as if I were in a stupor. Like a gushing fountain, a series of authorities, whom I recalled one after another, came to mind, along with their opinions on this topic. And I finally decided that God formed a vile creature when He made woman, and I wondered how such a worthy artisan could have deigned to make such an abominable work which, from what they say, is the vessel as well as the refuge and abode of every evil and vice. As I was thinking this, a great unhappiness and sadness welled up in my heart, for I detested myself and the entire feminine sex, as though we were monstrosities in nature. And in my lament I spoke these words:

"Oh, God, how can this be? For unless I stray from my faith, I must never doubt that Your infinite wisdom and most perfect goodness ever created anything which was not good. Did You Yourself not create woman in a very special way and since that time did You not give her all those inclinations which it pleased You for her to have? And how could it be that You could go wrong in anything? Yet look at all these accusations which have been judged, decided, and concluded against women. I do not know how to understand this repugnance. If it is so, fair Lord God, that in fact so many abominations abound in the female sex, for You Yourself say that the testimony of two or three witnesses lends credence, why shall I not doubt that this is true? Alas, God, why did You not let me be born in the world as a man, so that all my inclinations would be to serve You better, and so that I would not stray in anything and would be as perfect as a man is said to be? But since Your kindness has not been extended to me, then forgive my negligence in Your service, most fair Lord God, and may it not displease You, for the servant who receives fewer gifts from his lord is less obliged in his service." I spoke these words to God in my lament and a great deal more for a very long time in sad reflection, and in my folly I considered myself most unfortunate because God had made me inhabit a female body in this world. [. . .]

After hearing these things, I replied to the lady [Reason] who spoke infallibly: "My lady, truly has God revealed great wonders in the strength of these women whom you describe. But please enlighten me again, whether it has ever pleased this God, who has bestowed so many favors on women, to honor the feminine sex with the privilege of the virtue of high understanding and great learning, and whether women ever have a clever enough mind for this. I wish very much to know this because men maintain that the mind of women can learn only a little."

She answered, "My daughter, since I told you before, you know quite well that the opposite of their opinion is true, and to show you this even more clearly, I will give you proof through examples. I tell you again—and don't fear a contradiction—if it were customary to send daughters to school like sons, and if they were then taught the natural sciences, they would learn as thoroughly and understand the subtleties of all the arts and sciences as well as sons. And by chance there happen to be such women, for, as I touched on before, just as women have more delicate bodies than men, weaker and less able to perform many tasks, so do they have minds that are freer and sharper whenever they apply themselves."

"My lady, what are you saying? With all due respect, could you dwell longer on this point, please. Certainly men would never admit this answer is true, unless it is explained more plainly, for they believe that one normally sees that men know more than women do."

She answered, "Do you know why women know less?"

"Not unless you tell me, my lady."

"Without the slightest doubt, it is because they are not involved in many different things, but stay at home, where it is enough for them to run the household, and there is nothing which so instructs a reasonable creature as the exercise and experience of many different things."

"My lady, since they have minds skilled in conceptualizing and learning, just like men, why don't women learn more?"

She replied, "Because, my daughter, the public does not require them to get involved in the affairs which men are commissioned to execute, just as I told you before. It is enough for women to perform the usual duties to which they are ordained. As for judging from experience, since one sees that women usually know less than men, that therefore their capacity for understanding is less, look at men who farm the flatlands or who live in the mountains. You will find that in many countries they seem completely savage because they are so simple-minded. All the same, there is no doubt that Nature provided them with the qualities of body and mind found in the wisest and most learned men. All of this stems from a failure to learn, though, just as I told you, among men and women, some possess better minds than others. Let me tell you about women who have possessed great learning and profound understanding and treat the question of the similarity of women's minds to men's." [. . .]

"My lady, I see the endless benefits which have accrued to the world through women and nevertheless these men claim that there is no evil which has not come into the world because of them."

"Fair friend," she answered, "you can see from what I have already said to you that the contrary of what they say is true. For there is no man who could sum up the enormous benefits which have come about through women and which come about every day, and I proved this for you with the examples of the noble ladies who gave the sciences and arts to the world. But, if what I have said about the earthly benefits accruing thanks to women is not enough for you, I will tell you about the spiritual ones. Oh, how could any man be so heartless to forget that the door of Paradise was opened to him by a woman? As I told you before, it was opened by the Virgin Mary, and is there anything greater one could ask for than that God was made man? And who can forget the great benefits which mothers bring to their sons and which wives bring to their husbands? I implore them at the very least not to forget the advantages which touch upon spiritual good. Let us consider the Law of the Jews. If you recall the story of Moses, to whom God gave the written Law of the Jews, you will find that this holy prophet, through whom so much good has come about, was saved from death by a woman, just as I will tell you. [. . .]

"My lady [Rectitude], you have given me a remarkable account of the marvelous constancy, strength, endurance, and virtue of women. What more could one say about the strongest men who have lived? Men, especially writing in books, vociferously and unanimously claim that women in particular are fickle and inconstant, changeable and flighty, weak-hearted, compliant like children, and lacking all stamina. Are the men who accuse women of so much changeableness and inconstancy themselves so unwavering that change for them lies outside the realm of custom or common occurrence? Of course, if they themselves are not that firm, then it is truly despicable for them to accuse others of their own vice or to demand a virtue which they do not themselves know how to practice."

She replied, "Fair sweet friend, have you not heard the saying that the fool can clearly see the mote in his neighbor's eye but pays no attention to the beam hanging out of his own eye? Let me point out to you the contradiction in what these men say concerning the variability and inconstancy of women: since they all generally accuse women of being delicate and frail by nature, you would assume that they think that they are constant, or, at the very least, that women are less constant than they are. Yet they demand more constancy from women than they themselves can muster, for these men who claim to be so strong and of such noble condition are unable to prevent themselves from falling into many, even graver faults and sins, not all of them out of ignorance, but rather out of pure malice, knowing well that they are in the wrong. All the same, they excuse themselves for this by claiming it is human nature to sin. When a few women lapse (and when these men themselves, through their own strivings and their own power, are the cause), then as far as these men are concerned, it is completely a matter of fragility and inconstancy. It seems to me right, nevertheless, to conclude—since they claim women are so fragile—that these men should be somewhat more tolerant of women's weaknesses and not hold something to be a crime for women which they consider only a peccadillo for themselves. For the law does not maintain, nor can any such written opinion be found that permits them and not women to sin, that their vice is more excusable. In fact these men allow themselves liberties which they are unwilling to tolerate in women and thus they—and they are many—perpetrate many insults and outrages in word and deed. Nor do they deign to repute women strong and constant for having endured such men's harsh outrages. In this way men try in every question to have the right on their side—they want to have it both ways! You yourself have quite adequately discussed this problem in your *Epistre au Dieu d'Amour.*" [. . .]

In brief, all women—whether noble, bourgeois, or lower-class—be well-informed in all things and cautious in defending your honor and chastity against your enemies! My ladies, see how these men accuse you of so many vices in everything. Make liars of them all by showing forth your virtue, and prove their attacks false by acting well, so that you can say with the Psalmist, "the vices of the evil will fall on their heads." Repel the deceptive flatterers who, using different charms, seek with various tricks to steal that which you must consummately guard, that is, your honor and the beauty of your praise. Oh my ladies, flee, flee the foolish love they urge on you! Flee it, for God's sake, flee! For no good can come to you from it. Rather, rest assured that however deceptive their lures, their end is always to your detriment. And do not believe the contrary, for it cannot be otherwise. Remember, dear ladies, how these men call you frail, unserious, and easily influenced but yet try hard, using all kinds of strange and deceptive tricks, to catch you, just as one lays traps for wild animals. Flee, flee, my ladies, and avoid their company—under these smiles are hidden deadly and painful poisons. And so may it please you, my most respected ladies, to cultivate virtue, to flee vice, to increase and multiply our City, and to rejoice and act well. And may I, your servant, commend myself to you, praying to God who by His grace has granted me to live in this world and to persevere in His holy service. May He in the end have mercy on my great sins and grant to me the joy which lasts forever, which I may, by His grace, afford to you. Amen.

Translated by Earl Jeffrey Richard

3

SOR JUANA INÉS DE LA CRUZ
*Early Feminism in the Americas or the Right of
Every Woman to Study*

Mónica Díaz

The last three decades have witnessed an increased interest in the study of women writers of the early modern period (roughly 1500–1750). Influenced by a feminist agenda and theoretical trends that have shaped literary and historical studies, the project of recovering and studying the writings of women from Europe and its colonies has proved to be an important restorative endeavor in intellectual history. The Mexican nun Sor Juana Inés de la Cruz (1648/51–95) was one of the leading writers within a wide range of women intellectuals, and her work, which addresses the realities of patriarchalism and the strict religious politics of her time, illuminates contemporary women's issues. A woman of genius, Sor Juana wrote in all genres available to her, and accomplished the rare feat of having some of her works published during her own lifetime.

Juana Ramírez y Asbaje was born in Nepantla, in the valley of Mexico; she was the illegitimate daughter of Isabel Ramírez and Pedro Manuel de Asbaje. Mexico City was the capital of the viceroyalty of New Spain; its main square and administrative buildings had been built on top of Tenochtitlán, the pre-Hispanic center of power in Mesoamerica, ruled by the Mexicas until 1521. One of the most important institutions for the colonization was the Catholic Church. The Church's first purpose was to convert the indigenous populations, yet as colonial power consolidated and urban centers developed, new needs began to unfold. By the seventeenth century a growing population of Creoles *(criollos)*, people of Spanish descent born in America, inhabited the territory; they developed a consciousness of belonging to the land and began differentiating themselves from newly arrived Europeans. The religious environment in New Spain responded to developments in Counter-Reformation Spain, where the founding of convents became a symbol of prestige, and the nuns who lived in them acquired a special place in society. The first convent in New Spain, founded in 1540, was intended for the daughters of the conquistadors, but later convents catered mostly to the elite Creole population, to which Sor Juana belonged. The Catholic religion in the colonies filtered through many spheres of life, and helped to define and reinforce gender roles.

Although women were not able to acquire a formal education during this period, Juana was an avid reader of her grandfather's large library, which led her to achieve exceptional erudition. Sor Juana wrote in her famous autobiographical letter *La Respuesta* (Answer to Sister Filotea de la Cruz) that she wished to dress as a man in order to study at the university in Mexico City. When Juana was older, her mother sent her to live with relatives in the city, and she was introduced into the court of New Spain as a lady-in-waiting, where she quickly won the viceregal couple's favor. She continued cultivating her knowledge and writing poetry while in court.

After five years as a lady-in-waiting, she was persuaded by Antonio Núñez de Miranda, the viceroy and vicereine's confessor, to enter the convent. Her decision adhered to the custom in Counter-Reformation settings whereby "virtuous" women were compelled to enter the convent or be married. As she would explain in the *Respuesta* years later, she desired nothing more than to pursue her inclination to study; therefore she chose the convent rather than marriage in order to have the freedom to continue her intellectual career. Sor Juana first entered the strict convent of the Discalced Carmelites, but after a few months she was forced to leave the cloister due to illness. In 1669 she entered the hieronymite Convent of Saint Paula in Mexico City, where she took final vows.[1] Her illegitimate birth did not prevent her from entering the prestigious Convent of Saint Paula, and she received support from a wealthy relative, who paid the dowry needed to enter the cloister. Sor Juana Inés de la Cruz and her conventual sisters lived a comfortable life, received visitors, and did not follow strictly the vow of poverty or total enclosure.

Sor Juana continued to have close ties to the court, and was commissioned to write poetry for different religious and secular festivities. She composed love poems to the vicereines (the marquise of Mancera and later the countess of Paredes), philosophical sonnets, satiric verses on relationships between men and women, religious pieces dedicated to the Virgin Mary and other saints, *villancicos* (carols), plays, and a nine-hundred-line *silva* (a verse form of lines either eleven or seven syllables long) entitled *Primero sueño* (First Dream), the only piece that Sor Juana claims she composed of her own volition.

Sor Juana was a poet from an early age; she mastered the stylistic conventions of the Spanish baroque, surpassing the complexities of the form and subverting traditional themes for her own purposes. Sor Juana inverted the rhetoric of Petrarchan courtship in her poetry in order to criticize the objectification of female beauty.[2] She also put forth the idea that all human souls are equal and sexless.

Sor Juana's poem *Primero sueño* relates how at nightfall the body goes to sleep, while the soul engages in an intellectual journey towards knowledge. It fails at its several attempts until daylight comes and the body awakens. Keeping with Sor Juana's notion of the genderless soul, there are no boundaries for the curiosity of the soul in *Primero sueño*, which does not follow a mystical journey in search of union with God, as was usually attempted by women religious writers. Sor Juana's poem reflects the interest of a woman in universal epistemological matters. *Primero sueño* can be situated in a traditionally male genre of empirical and scientific reflection in which the soul travels to grasp knowledge, but the subject matter of the poem and the soul's quest to understand "the whole of reality in rational terms" is presented by Sor Juana as a genderless issue (Sabat-Rivers 128).[3]

In his polemical and monumental *Sor Juana Inés de la Cruz or The Traps of Faith*, Nobel Prize–winner Octavio Paz (1988) identifies how Sor Juana's poem differs from similar texts authored by men. First, it was composed in verse instead of prose; second, it does not identify the protagonist of the poem until the very end when the female *"despierta"* (I awake) is introduced; and finally, it does not include a guide to instruct the dreamer. Georgina Sabat de Rivers argues for her part that there is a preponderance of feminine characters and feminine nouns throughout the poem. The poem opens with "the goddess's orb," making direct reference to the triple mythological representation of the moon as "Hecate in the sky; as Diana on Earth; and as Proserpina in the underworld" (146). Later in the poem, more mythological female figures appear, all with key significance in Sor Juana's struggle to attain knowledge. Although the relationship and presence of all these female characters are not always harmonious, the universe that Sor Juana constructs in her poem is nevertheless ruled by women.

Tamara Harvey pursues a different feminist reading of *Primero sueño*, and proposes that the reason why the soul in the poem does not have a guide to take her into her intellectual journey is because the body is not entirely separate from the soul. According to Harvey, this interpretation offers a challenge to the symbolic separation of body and soul that underlies many misogynist ideas of the period.[4] One such classic understanding of the soul comes from Aristotle, who characterizes the souls of men and women as different: in his view, women have souls that are less developed than those of men. Although he does not fully separate the soul from the body (as Plato and Neoplatonists propose), Aristotle gives the soul a privileged place over the body. In Aristotle's schema, the male is rational, and the female is related to passion and to the body, so that women had a less powerful "rational soul" than did men.[5] Sor Juana defies this view by placing the intellect of the soul in a female body, and recognizing that the two are not fully separated.

Tamara Harvey elaborates by explaining that the dreamer of the *Primero sueño* is fundamentally both body and soul, and that the body is not valued as the basis for the symbolic significance of the soul (79). An important section of the poem is dedicated to a description of the vital relationship between soul and body; although the body is described as "a corpse with soul / is dead to living, living to the dead," it is also the one that "keeps life going." Sor Juana utilizes the symbolic separation of body and soul to ponder scientific matters related to the physiological functions of human bodies. Although Sor Juana's protagonist, the soul, is presented as female, the poem argues for a gender-neutral intellect by referring to the soul as "her immaterial being," one that does not have to conform to either gender.

From the time Sor Juana entered the convent until 1688, when the viceroys departed from New Spain, she wrote with extensive liberty and enjoyed the support of the vicereine Countess of Paredes. While Sor Juana was protected by the court, the Church was lenient with her transgressions in her literary pursuits, and she was quite prolific during this time. Yet her confessor, Núñez de Miranda, had expressed on different occasions the Church's disapproval of Sor Juana's literary career, demanding from her a more traditional and devotional religious life. Finally in 1682 Sor Juana wrote a letter in which she dismissed him from his charge as her confessor.[6] In her letter, Sor Juana questions Núñez de Miranda's right to command her to stop writing verses since doing so, according to her, is using the gifts God had given her. Moreover, she argues that she writes out of obedience, since much of her poetry is the result of commissions from the court or other high officials. After the viceroys departed, Sor Juana was left without protection, and having broken up with her confessor, she was an easy target for an intolerant Church. Archbishop Francisco de Aguiar y Seijas, another Jesuit and Sor Juana's superior within the Church's hierarchy, was a known misogynist, who disapproved of Sor Juana's irreverent literary interests.

In 1691 Sor Juana penned her famous reply (*La Respuesta* or *The Answer*) to bishop Manuel Fernández de Santa Cruz after he published, without her consent, a theological critique Sor Juana had written of a Jesuit's sermon. Fernández de Santa Cruz was her friend and had asked her to write her thoughts on Antonio de Vieyra's sermon. Sor Juana agreed while clarifying that she wished for her reflections to be for his eyes only. In an unexpected move, the motives for which are still unclear to scholars, Bishop Fernández de Santa Cruz published Sor Juana's brilliant refutation of Vieyra's sermon, entitling it "A Letter Worthy of Athena" (the Greek goddess of wisdom), preceded by an open letter authored by Fernández de Santa Cruz but signed by Sister Filotea de la Cruz. In his preface, Fernández de Santa Cruz disguised as Sister Filotea censures Sor Juana, a gesture that Sor Juana felt was an attack from which she needed to defend herself.

Sor Juana Inés de la Cruz has been characterized as "the first feminist in the New World" because of this *Respuesta*, in which she defends women's rights to develop intellectually. In their critical edition and translation of the *Respuesta*, Electa Arenal and Amanda Powell discuss the usage of the term "feminism" when referring to Sor Juana. They argue that although the term's current meaning is derived from twentieth-century women's movements for equal opportunity, there was also a debate during the medieval and early modern periods on the "woman question." Arenal and Powell state that since Sor Juana consciously participated in the debate through her many writings, "aware of her gender status and because she intended her arguments to be applied on behalf of other women *as women*," she clearly foreshadows what we call feminism (ix).

The debate Sor Juana joined along with other women from the early modern world, is known as the *querelle des femmes*. A key early text of the *querelle* is Christine de Pizan's

Book of the City of Ladies (1403–4; see chapter 2 in this collection), a critical reaction to the misogynist attacks of the *Roman de la Rose* and other texts. As Stephanie Merrim shows, participants in the *querelle* argued by example, using the catalogue of learned women to support their defense of the right of women to be educated. Sor Juana aligns herself with this kind of debate in the *Respuesta*, invoking a catalogue of comparable women from antiquity to the seventeenth century. Sor Juana's mentions of Hypatia and Paula, among many others, are not gratuitous; both were learned women who wrote and were regarded as wise.

The *Respuesta* is not just a reply to Bishop Fernández de Santa Cruz or a well-crafted personal defense in order to continue writing. Sor Juana utilized many different genres and rhetorical devices in the *Respuesta* that allow her to skillfully present her case, defend her God-given talents, and occupy a prominent place in the history of feminist thought.

Sor Juana was familiar with early women's Christian writings, particularly with those by women like Carmelite reformer Saint Teresa of Avila, who had been able to get around Inquisitorial and religious censors and have her writings published. Sor Juana's letter clearly resonates with the traditional genre of the spiritual life or *vida* written by nuns, which resembles the genre of the autobiography but with an inherent confessional voice. In the opening section of the *Respuesta* Sor Juana displays the rhetoric of humility, ignorance, and obedience while addressing "Sor Filotea" to thank her for having published her *borrones* (scratches). Sor Juana employs the conventions of the nun's *vida*, beginning with the narration of her childhood, but alters the traditional nun's narrative to present her call for an intellectual life, instead of a call to follow a mystical path. She narrates her interest in learning from an early age and references her strategies to force herself to be disciplined towards her goals by not eating cheese or cutting her hair when she did not master her subject. Sor Juana purposely skips the five years she remained in the viceregal court of New Spain; instead she underscores her stalled journey towards a full discernment of theology. In this way she directly engages with Fernández de Santa Cruz's criticism and advice in his preface to the "Letter Worthy of Athena."

Sor Juana also has recourse to elements of the hagiographic genre (the lives of saints) that followed the tradition of the *imitatio Christi* (imitation of Christ). Following this rhetoric, nuns would usually narrate a series of obstacles found in their secular (before entering the convent) or religious lives that prevent them from reaching the ultimate goal of perfection. In most cases these instances function as rhetorical devices that place them closer to the ideal the Church had for them, in which human physical and emotional suffering resembled that of Jesus. Sor Juana describes her sufferings by imitating the normative narration, but instead she narrates the persecution and criticism she had to endure for having written poetry and devoted hours to study. She proceeds to describe Jesus' capture and mockery by the Pharisees and draws a parallel with her own experiences of harassment because of her inclination to learn in the name of God.

As Sor Juana tells it in the *Respuesta*, when she was asked to stop studying by the prelate in the convent, she continued her quest for knowledge in everyday practices and empirical observations, instead of in her beloved books. She narrates that even while cooking, she had been able to acquire knowledge and ironically adds that "had Aristotle cooked, he would have written a great deal more" (75). Sor Juana proves that her inherent and God-given talent for study cannot be stopped in any way.

Sor Juana masterfully employs legal and rhetorical discourse in her defense. As Rosa Perelmuter Pérez shows in her analysis of the *Respuesta*, Sor Juana crafts her letter following Renaissance rhetoric conventions, by clearly dividing her narration into the classical sections of Ciceronian forensic style.[7] When she concludes the narration section, the longest section of the *Respuesta*, she offers proof for what she has argued, for her right to pursue knowledge. This section moves the *Respuesta* from an individualized defense against the affront made by Bishop Fernández de Santa Cruz, toward a general defense of the right of every woman to study.

Women aligned with the *querelle des femmes* would also reference male writers who were considered authoritative and who had defended women, in order to support their own argument in favor of women's rights. Sor Juana reinterprets Saint Jerome and Saint Paul's teachings about women, particularly Paul's statement in I Corinthians, "Let women keep silent in the churches." She inverts its meaning and supports it with an authoritative male source, that of Mexican theologian Juan Arce, who advocated women's study. Sor Juana contextualizes the quote to lessen its damaging effects, and adds her own interpretation, explaining that women used to teach one another in the temples and that the instruction "let them keep silent" is because their voices confused the apostle. Sor Juana brings out not only this best-known misogynist sentence by Paul but also another, less-celebrated passage that claims that aged women teach well.

Sor Juana references both the numerous learned women in her catalogue and authoritative male texts that seem to contradict each other, resolving any confusion by explaining at length that it is wrong for women to teach in public but that to study, write, and teach in private is not only acceptable but beneficial. She raises her tone at the end of the segment where the catalogue of learned women is provided, switching to a more personal defense and asking how she could be in error for writing, given that other women like María de Agreda and María de la Antigua were not canonized and yet the Church had allowed their writings to circulate. Sor Juana finishes by reiterating her point about the benefits that study can bring women, especially the study of sacred scripture for religious women.

Sor Juana used traditional discursive and literary genres to enter the historical debate about women's roles. As Josefina Ludmer states: "It is always possible to claim a space from which one can practice what is forbidden in others; it is always possible to annex other fields and establish other territorialities" (93). In her *Respuesta,* Sor Juana defended herself from censorship by turning the problem into a broader struggle for women's right to study. She followed the conventions expected in writings from religious women, yet she explored legal arguments that have allowed her voice to be heard up to this day.

Although Sor Juana's second collection of works was published in Seville in 1692 by her friend the former vicereine of New Spain, the hieronymite continued to face the wrath of the Church and was instructed to remain silent and stop writing. In a puzzling move, Sor Juana sold her library and scientific instruments, and limited her writing to the composition of carols to Saint Catherine. Although Sor Juana's last years continue to be a mystery, we can assert that even after she signed a general confession in 1693, Sor Juana continued writing. She composed the *Enigmas ofrecidos a la Casa del Placer (Enigmas Offered to the House of Pleasure)*, a collection of poems, specifically of rhymed puzzles, intended for a group of aristocratic nuns in a Lisbon convent. Finally in 1694 she signed a declaration of faith and one year later she died of an epidemic in the convent.

Sor Juana's work and person have been of interest to scholars in U.S. academia, from Dorothy Schons in the second decade of the twentieth century to scholars who brought new insights into her writings, like Georgina Sabat de Rivers, Electa Arenal, Stephanie Merrim, Marie-Cecile Bénassy-Berling, and Rosa Perelmuter Pérez, among many others. Sor Juana's feminism, according to Stephanie Merrim, instead of seeking to highlight difference between genders, intended to negate their difference (*Toward a Feminist Reading* 23). In both the *Respuesta* and *Primero sueño*, Sor Juana argues for equality in access to knowledge by emphasizing the historical existence of female figures of wisdom. She places herself within the context of other religious women writers of the early modern world by using the same stratagems and rhetorical devices they also had at hand, yet she surpasses this "female" tradition, making arguments on theological and scientific subjects. Although only two texts by Sor Juana Inés de la Cruz were highlighted here, *Primero sueño* and the *Respuesta*, all of Sor Juana's oeuvre was composed with a clear feminist agenda in mind. As she argued in the *Respuesta*, there is no difference between male and female in matters of knowledge; the only difference that exists is between the learned and the foolish.

NOTES

1. The "hieronymite" order was named after St. Jerome, since the constitutions that they followed were based on extracts from his writings.

2. The Petrarchan sonnet is a poetic style developed by Francesco Petrarca (1304–74) in Italy, in which the poet's voice objectifies the beloved, presenting her as a model of inspiration.

3. Examples of this genre include Johannes Kepler's *Somnium* (The Dream).

4. Many of these ideas come from Aristotle's formulations. Constance Jordan explains that Aristotle's politics were an extrapolation of his understanding of biology, one which "reflects the same preferential distinction for the soul over the body, the intellect over the passions. Because the male, exemplifying the rational element, is superior to the female, exemplifying the passionate element, it is natural, Aristotle writes in the *Politics*, that he rule, and she be ruled" (Jordan 32).

5. Plato writes in the *Republic* that "men and women alike possess the qualities which make a guardian [i.e., a person capable of command]; they differ only in their comparative strength or weakness" (qtd. in Jordan 33).

6. Nuns had the right to choose a confessor and to dismiss one as well.

7. This model follows the form Cicero established in *De Partitione Oratoria,* in which letters were the vehicle for proving a case. The traditional structure of these kinds of letters is the *exordium* or introduction, the narration or statement of facts, the proof, and finally the peroration or conclusion (Perelmuter Pérez 187).

WORKS CITED

de la Cruz, Sor Juana Inés. *The Answer/La Repuesta.* Edited and translated by Electa Arenal and Amanda Powell. New York: Feminist Press, 1994.

Harvey, Tamara. *Figuring Modesty in Feminist Discourse across the Americas, 1633–1700.* Burlington: Ashgate, 2008.

Jordan, Constance. *Renaissance Feminism: Literary Texts and Political Models.* Ithaca: Cornell University Press, 1990.

Ludmer, Josefina. "Tricks of the Weak." In *Feminist Perspectives on Sor Juana Inés de la Cruz,* pp. 86–93. Edited by Stephanie Merrim. Detroit: Wayne State University Press, 1990.

Merrim, Stephanie. *Early Modern Women's Writing and Sor Juana Inés de la Cruz.* Nashville: Vanderbilt University Press, 1999.

———. "Toward a Feminist Reading of Sor Juana Inés de la Cruz: Past, Present, and Future Directions in Sor Juana Criticism." In *Feminist Perspectives on Sor Juana Inés de la Cruz,* pp. 11–37. Edited by Stephanie Merrim. Detroit: Wayne State University Press, 1990.

Paz, Octavio. *Sor Juana, or, The Traps of Faith.* Translated by Margaret Sayers Peden. Cambridge: Belknap–Harvard University Press, 1988.

Perelmuter Pérez, Rosa. "The Answer to Sor Filotea: A Rhetorical Approach." In *Approaches to Teaching the Works of Sor Juana Inés de la Cruz,* pp. 186–92. Edited by Emilie Bergmann and Stacey Sclau. New York: MLA, 2007.

Sabat-Rivers, Georgina. "A Feminist Rereading of Sor Juana's Dream." In *Feminist Perspectives on Sor Juana Inés de la Cruz,* pp. 142–61. Edited by Stephanie Merrim. Detroit: Wayne State University Press, 1990.

Trueblood, Alan S., trans. *A Sor Juana Anthology.* Cambridge: Harvard University Press, 1988.

DISCUSSION QUESTIONS

1. Sor Juana's views on the relationship of mind and body, so central to philosophy and religion from the ancients on, have been interpreted in vastly different—and at times, diametrically opposed—ways by modern feminist commentators. What are these interpretations and how do they relate to the issue of Sor Juana's "feminism"?

2. Both Christine de Pizan and Sor Juana were arguably highly successful at developing ways to critique masculinist and sexist discourses of their times while remaining within acceptable norms of female comportment. How did they achieve this in their writings?

3. Where does Sor Juana stand with relation to woman's "difference" from man? Do you see any interesting departures from de Pizan?

SOR JUANA INÉS DE LA CRUZ, FROM *THE POET'S ANSWER TO THE MOST ILLUSTRIOUS SOR FILOTEA DE LA CRUZ*

Most illustrious Lady, my Lady:

It has not been my will, but my scant health and a rightful fear that have delayed my reply for so many days. Is it to be wondered that, at the very first step, I should meet with two obstacles that sent my dull pen stumbling? The first (and to me the most insuperable) is the question of how to respond to your immensely learned, prudent, devout, and loving letter. For when I consider how the Angelic Doctor, St. Thomas Aquinas, on being asked of his silence before his teacher Albertus Magnus, responded that he kept quiet because he could say nothing worthy of Albertus, then how much more fitting it is that I should keep quiet— not like the Saint from modesty, but rather because, in truth, I am unable to say anything worthy of you. The second obstacle is the question of how to render my thanks for the favor, as excessive as it was unexpected, of giving my drafts and scratches to the press: a favor so far beyond all measure as to surpass the most ambitious hopes or the most fantastic desires; so that as a rational being I simply could not house it in my thoughts. In short, this was a favor of such magnitude that it cannot be bounded by the confines of speech and indeed exceeds all powers of gratitude, as much because it was so large as because it was so unexpected. In the words of Quintilian: *"They produce less glory through hopes, more glory through benefits conferred."* And so much so, that the recipient is struck dumb.

When the mother of [John] the Baptist—felicitously barren, so as to become miraculously fertile—saw under her roof so exceedingly great a guest as the Mother of the Word, her powers of mind were dulled and her speech was halted; and thus, instead of thanks, she burst out with doubts and questions: *"And whence is this to me:. . ?"* The same occurred with Saul when he was chosen and anointed King of Israel: *"Am not I a son of Jemini of the least tribe of Israel, and my kindred the last among all the families of the tribe of Benjamin? Why then hast thou spoken this word to me?"* Just so, I too must say: Whence, O venerable Lady; whence comes such a favor to me? By chance, am I something more than a poor nun, the slightest creature on earth and the least worthy of drawing your attention? Well, *why then hast thou spoken this word to me? And whence is this to me?*

I can answer nothing more to the first obstacle than that I am entirely unworthy of your gaze. To the second, I can offer nothing more than amazement, instead of thanks, declaring that I am unable to thank you for the slightest part of what I owe you. It is not false humility, my Lady, but the candid truth of my very soul, to say that when the printed

SOURCE: Sor Juana Inés de la Cruz, "The Poet's Answer to the Most Illustrious Sor Filotea de la Cruz," in *The Answer/La Respuesta*, ed. and trans. Electa Arenal and Amanda Powell (New York: Feminist Press, 1994), 39, 41, 47, 49, 51, 53, 73, 75, 77, 79, 81, 85, 87.

letter reached my hands—that letter you were pleased to dub "Worthy of Athena"—I burst into tears (a thing that does not come easily to me), tears of confusion. For it seemed to me that your great favor was nothing other than God's reproof aimed at my failure to return His favors, and while He corrects others with punishments, He wished to chide me through benefits. A special favor, this, for which I acknowledge myself His debtor, as I am indebted for infinitely many favors given by His immense goodness; but this is also a special way of shaming and confounding me. For it is the choicest form of punishment to cause me to serve, knowingly, as the judge who condemns and sentences my own ingratitude. And so when I consider this fully, here in solitude, it is my custom to say: Blessed are you, my Lord God, for not only did you forbear to give another creature the power to judge me, nor have you placed that power in my hands. Rather, you have kept that power for yourself and have freed me of myself and of the sentence I would pass on myself, which, forced by my own conscience, could be no less than condemnation. Instead you have reserved that sentence for your great mercy to declare, because you love me more than I can love myself. [. . .]

My writing has never proceeded from any dictate of my own, but a force beyond me; I can in truth say, *"You have compelled me."* One thing, however, is true, so that I shall not deny it (first because it is already well known to all, and second because God has shown me His favor in giving me the greatest possible love of truth, even when it might count against me). For ever since the light of reason first dawned in me, my inclination to letters was marked by such passion and vehemence that neither the reprimands of others (for I have received many) nor reflections of my own (there have been more than a few) have sufficed to make me abandon my pursuit of this native impulse that God Himself bestowed on me. His Majesty knows why and to what end He did so, and He knows that I have prayed that He snuff out the light of my intellect, leaving only enough to keep His Law. For more than that is too much, some would say, in a woman; and there are even those who say that it is harmful. His Majesty knows too that, not achieving this, I have attempted to entomb my intellect together with my name and to sacrifice it to the One who gave it to me; and that no other motive brought me to the life of Religion, despite the fact that the exercises and companionship of a community were quite opposed to the tranquility and freedom from disturbance required by my studious bent. And once in the community, the Lord knows—and in this world only he who needs must know it, does—what I did to try to conceal my name and renown from the public; he did not, however, allow me to do this, telling me it was temptation, and so it would have been. If I could repay any part of my debt to you, my Lady, I believe I might do so merely by informing you of this, for these words have never left my mouth save to that [. . .] one to whom they must be said. But having thrown wide the doors of my heart and revealed to you what is there under seal of secrecy, I want you to know that this confidence does not gainsay the respect I owe to your venerable person and excessive favors.

To go on with the narration of this inclination of mine, of which I wish to give you a full account: I declare I was not yet three years old when my mother sent off one of my sisters, older than I, to learn to read in one of those girls' schools that they call *Amigas*. Affection and mischief carried me after her: and when I saw that they were giving her lessons, I so caught fire with the desire to learn that, deceiving the teacher (or so I thought), I told her that my mother wanted her to teach me also. She did not believe this, for it was not to be believed; but to humor my whim she gave me lessons. I continued to go and she continued to teach me, though no longer in make-believe, for the experience undeceived her. I learned to read in such a short time that I already knew how by the time my mother heard of it. My teacher had kept it from my mother to give delight with a thing all done and to receive a prize for a thing done well. And I had kept still, thinking I would be whipped for having done this without permission. The woman who taught me (may God keep her) is still living, and she can vouch for what I say.

I remember that in those days, though I was as greedy for treats as children usually are at that age, I would abstain from eating cheese, because I heard tell that it made people stupid, and the desire to learn was stronger for me than the desire to eat—powerful as this is in children. Later, when I was six or seven years old and already knew how to read and write, along with all the other skills like embroidery and sewing that women learn, I heard that in Mexico City there were a University and Schools where they studied the sciences. As soon as I heard this I began to slay my poor mother with insistent and annoying pleas, begging her to dress me in men's clothes and send me to the capital, to the home of some relatives she had there, so that I could enter the University and study. She refused, and was right in doing so; but I quenched my desire by reading a great variety of books that belonged to my grandfather, and neither punishments nor scoldings could prevent me. And so when I did go to Mexico City, people marveled not so much at my intelligence as at my memory and the facts I knew at an age when it seemed I had scarcely had time to learn to speak.

I began to study Latin, in which I believe I took fewer than twenty lessons. And my interest was so intense, that although in women (and especially in the very bloom of youth) the natural adornment of the hair is so esteemed, I would cut off four to six fingerlengths of my hair, measuring how long it had been before. And I made myself a rule that if by the time it had grown back to the same length [,] I did not know such and such a thing that I intended to study, then I would cut my hair off again to punish my dullwittedness. And so my hair grew, but I did not yet know what I had resolved to learn, for it grew quickly and I learned slowly. Then I cut my hair right off to punish my dull-wittedness, for I did not think it reasonable that hair should cover a head that was so bare of facts—the more desirable adornment. I took the veil because, although I knew I would find in religious life many things that would be quite opposed to my character (I speak of accessory rather than essential matters), it would, given my absolute unwillingness to enter into marriage, be the least unfitting and the most decent state I could choose, with regard to the assurance I desired of my salvation. For before this first concern (which is, at the last, the most important), all the impertinent little follies of my character gave way and bowed to the yoke. These were wanting to live alone and not wanting to have either obligations that would disturb my freedom to study or the noise of a community that would interrupt the tranquil silence of my books. These things made me waver somewhat in my decision until, being enlightened by learned people as to my temptation, I vanquished it with divine favor and took the state I so unworthily hold. I thought I was fleeing myself, but—woe is me!—I brought myself with me, and brought my greatest enemy in my inclination to study, which I know not whether to take as a Heaven-sent favor or as a punishment. For when snuffed out or hindered with every [spiritual] exercise known to Religion, it exploded like gunpowder; and in my case the saying *"privation gives rise to appetite"* was proven true.

I went back (no, I spoke incorrectly, for I never stopped)—I went on, I mean, with my studious task (which to me was peace and rest in every moment left over when my duties were done) of reading and still more reading, study and still more study, with no teacher besides my books themselves. What a hardship it is to learn from those lifeless letters, deprived of the sound of a teacher's voice and explanations; yet I suffered all these trials most gladly for the love of learning. Oh, if only this had been done for the love of God, as was rightful, think what I should have merited! Nevertheless I did my best to elevate these studies and direct them to His service, for the goal to which I aspired was the study of Theology. Being a Catholic, I thought it an abject failing not to know everything that can in this life be achieved, through earthly methods, concerning the divine mysteries. And being a nun and not a laywoman, I thought I should, because I was in religious life, profess the study of letters—the more so as the daughter of such as St. Jerome and St. Paula: for it would be a degeneracy for an idiot daughter to proceed from such learned parents. I argued in this way to myself, and I thought my own argument quite reasonable. However, the fact may have been (and this seems most likely) that I was merely flattering and encouraging my own inclination, by arguing that its own pleasure was an obligation.

[. . . .] I confess that I am far indeed from the terms of Knowledge and that I have wished to follow it, though *"afar off."* But all this has merely led me closer to the flames of persecution, the crucible of affliction; and to such extremes that some have even sought to prohibit me from study.

They achieved this once, with a very saintly and simple mother superior who believed that study was an affair for the Inquisition and ordered that I should not read. I obeyed her (for the three months or so that her authority over us lasted) in that I did not pick up a book. But with regard to avoiding study absolutely, as such a thing does not lie within my power, I could not do it. For although I did not study in books, I studied all the things that God created, taking them for my letters, and for my book all the intricate structures of this world. Nothing could I see without reflecting upon it, nothing could I hear without pondering it, even to the most minute, material things. For there is no creature, however lowly, in which one cannot recognize the great *"God made me"*; there is not one that does not stagger the mind if it receives due consideration. And so, I repeat, I looked and marveled at all things, so that from the very persons with whom I spoke and from what they said to me, a thousand speculations leapt to my mind: Whence could spring this diversity of character and intelligence among individuals all composing one single species? What temperaments, what hidden qualities could give rise to each? When I noticed a shape, I would set about combining the proportions of its lines and measuring it in my mind and converting it to other proportions. I sometimes walked back and forth along the fore-wall of one of our dormitories (which is a very large room), and I began to observe that although the lines of its two sides were parallel and the ceiling was flat, yet the eye falsely perceived these lines as though they approached each other and the ceiling as though it were lower in the distance than close by; from this I inferred that visual lines run straight, but not parallel, and that they form a pyramidal figure. And I conjectured whether this might be the reason the ancients were obliged to question whether the world is spherical or not. Because even though it seems so, this could be a delusion of the eye, displaying concavities where there were none.

This kind of observation has been continual in me and is so to this day, without my having control over it; rather, I tend to find it annoying, because it tires my head. Yet I believed this happened to everyone, as with thinking in verse, until experience taught me otherwise. This trait, whether a matter of nature or custom, is such that nothing do I see without a second thought. Two little girls were playing with a top in front of me, and no sooner had I seen the motion and shape than I began, with this madness of mine, to observe the easy movement of the spherical form and how the momentum lasted, now fixed and set free of its cause; for even far from its first cause, which was the hand of the girl, the little top went on dancing. Yet not content with this, I ordered flour to be brought and sifted on the floor, so that as the top danced over it, we could know whether its movement described perfect circles or no. I found they were not circular, but rather spiral lines that lost their circularity as the top lost its momentum. Other girls were playing at spillikins (the most frivolous of all childhood games). I drew near to observe the shapes they made, and when I saw three of the straws by chance fall in a triangle, I fell to intertwining one with another, recalling that this was said to be the very shape of Solomon's mysterious ring, where distantly there shone bright traces and representations of the Most Blessed Trinity, by virtue of which it worked great prodigies and marvels. And they say David's harp had the same shape, and thus was Saul cured by its sound; to this day, harps have almost the same form.

Well, and what then shall I tell you, my Lady, of the secrets of nature that I have learned while cooking? I observe that an egg becomes solid and cooks in butter or oil, and on the contrary that it dissolves in sugar syrup. Or again, to ensure that sugar will flow freely one need only add the slightest bit of water that has held quince or some other sour fruit. The yolk and white of the very same egg are of such a contrary nature that when eggs are used with sugar, each part separately may be used perfectly well, yet they cannot be mixed together. I shall not weary you with such inanities, which I relate simply to give you a full account of my nature, and I believe this will make you laugh. But in truth, my Lady, what can we women know, save philosophies of the kitchen? It was well put by Lupercio Leonardo [sic] that one can philosophize quite well while preparing supper. I often say, when I make these little observations, "Had Aristotle cooked, he would have written a great deal more." And so to go on with the mode of my cogitations: I declare that all this is so continual in me that I have no need of books. On one occasion, because of a severe stomach ailment, the doctors forbade me to study. I spent several days in that state, and then quickly proposed to them that it would be less harmful to allow me my books, for my cogitations were so strenuous and vehement that they consumed more vitality in a quarter of an hour than the reading of books could in four days. And so the doctors were compelled to let me read. What is more, my Lady, not even my sleep has been free of this ceaseless movement of my imagination. Rather, my mind operates in sleep still more freely and unobstructedly, ordering with greater clarity and ease the events it has preserved from the day, presenting arguments and composing verses. I could give you a very long catalogue of these, as I could of certain reasonings and subtle turns I have reached far better in my sleep than while awake; but I leave them out in order not to weary you. I have said enough for your judgment and your surpassing eminence to comprehend my nature with clarity and full understanding, together with the beginnings, the methods, and the present state of my studies.

If studies, my Lady, be merits (for indeed I see them extolled as such in men), in me they are no such thing: I study because I must. If they be a failing, I believe for the same reason that the fault is none of mine. Yet withal, I live always so wary of myself that neither in this nor in anything else do I trust my own judgment. And so I entrust the decision to your supreme skill and straightway submit to whatever sentence you may pass, posing no objection or reluctance, for this has been no more than a simple account of my inclination to letters.

I confess also that, while in truth this inclination has been such that, as I said before, I had no need of exemplars, nevertheless the many books that I have read have not failed to help me, both in sacred as well as secular letters. For there I see a Deborah issuing laws, military as well as political, and governing the people among whom there were so many learned men. I see the exceedingly knowledgeable Queen of Sheba, so learned she dares to test the wisdom of the wisest of all wise men with riddles, without being rebuked for it; indeed, on this very account she is to become judge of the unbelievers. I see so many and such significant women: some adorned with the gift of prophecy, like an Abigail; others, of persuasion, like Esther; others, of piety, like Rahab; others, of perseverance, like Anna [Hannah] the mother of Samuel; and others, infinitely more, with other kinds of qualities and virtues.

If I consider the Gentiles, the first I meet are the Sibyls, chosen by God to prophesy the essential mysteries of our Faith in such learned and elegant verses that they stupefy the imagination. I see a woman such as Minerva, daughter of great Jupiter and mistress of all the wisdom of Athens, adored as goddess of the sciences. I see one Polla Argentaria, who helped Lucan, her husband, to write the *Battle of Pharsalia*. I see the daughter of the divine Tiresias, more learned still than her father. I see, too, such a woman as Zenobia, queen of the Palmyrians, as wise as she was courageous. Again, I see an Arete, daughter of Aristippus, most learned. A Nicostrata, inventor of Latin letters and most erudite in the Greek. An Aspasia Miletia, who taught philosophy and rhetoric and was the teacher of the philosopher Pericles. An Hypatia, who taught astrology and lectured for many years in Alexandria. A Leontium, who won over the philosopher Theophrastus and proved him wrong. A Julia, a Corinna, a Cornelia; and, in sum, the vast throng of women who merited titles and earned renown: now as Greeks, again as Muses, and yet again as Pythonesses. For what were they all but learned women, who were considered, celebrated, and indeed venerated as such in Antiquity? Without mentioning still others, of whom the books are full; for I see the Egyptian Catherine, lecturing and refuting all the learning of the most learned men of Egypt. I see a Gertrude read, write, and teach. And seeking no more examples far from home, I see my own most holy mother Paula, learned in the Hebrew, Greek, and Latin tongues and most expert in the interpretation of the Scriptures. What wonder then can it be that, though her chronicler was no less than the unequaled Jerome, the Saint found himself scarcely worthy of the task, for with that lively gravity and energetic effectiveness with which only he can express himself, he says: "If all the parts of my body were tongues, they would not suffice to proclaim the learning and virtues of Paula." Blessilla, a widow, earned the same praises, as did the luminous virgin Eustochium, both of them daughters of the Saint herself [Paula]; and indeed Eustochium was such that for her knowledge she was hailed as a World Prodigy. Fabiola, also a Roman, was another most learned in Holy Scripture. Proba Falconia, a Roman woman, wrote an elegant book of centos, joining together verses from Virgil, on the mysteries of our holy Faith. Our Queen Isabella, wife of Alfonso X, is known to have written on astrology—without mentioning others, whom I omit so as not merely to copy what others have said (which is a vice I have always detested): Well then, in our own day there thrive the great Christina Alexandra, Queen of Sweden, as learned as she is brave and generous; and too those most excellent ladies, the Duchess of Aveyro and the Countess of Villaumbrosa.

The venerable Dr. Arce (worthy professor of Scripture, known for his virtue and learning), in his *For the Scholar of the Bible*, raises this question: *"Is it permissible for women to apply themselves to the study, and indeed the interpretation, of the Holy Bible?"* And in opposition he presents the verdicts passed by many saints, particularly the words of [Paul] the Apostle: *"Let women keep silence in the churches: for it is not permitted them to speak,"* etc. Arce then presents differing verdicts, including this passage addressed to Titus, again spoken by the Apostle: *"The aged women, in like manner, in holy attire [. . .] teaching well"*; and he gives other interpretations from the Fathers of the Church. Arce at last resolves, in his prudent way, that women are not allowed to lecture publicly in the universities or to preach from the pulpits, but that studying, writing, and teaching privately [are] not only permitted but most beneficial and useful to them. Clearly, of course, he does not mean by this that all women should do so, but only those whom God may have seen fit to endow with special virtue and prudence, and who are very mature and erudite and possess the necessary talents and requirements for such a sacred occupation. And so just is this distinction that not only women, who are held to be so incompetent, but also men, who simply because they are men think themselves wise, are to be prohibited from the interpretation of the Sacred Word, save when they are most learned, virtuous, of amenable intellect, and inclined to the good. For when the reverse is true, I believe, numerous sectarians are produced, and this has given rise to numerous heresies. For there are many who study only to become ignorant, especially those of arrogant, restless, and prideful spirits, fond of innovations in the Law (the very thing that rejects all innovation). And so they are not content until, for the sake of saying what no one before them has said, they speak heresy. Of such men as these the Holy Spirit says: *"For wisdom will not enter into a malicious soul."* For them, more harm is worked by knowledge than by ignorance. A wit once observed that he who knows no Latin is not an utter fool, but he who does know it has met the prerequisites. And I might add that he is made a perfect fool (if foolishness can attain perfection) by having studied his bit of philosophy and theology and by knowing something of languages. For with that he can be foolish in several sciences and tongues; a great fool cannot be contained in his mother tongue alone. [. . .]

Oh, how many abuses would be avoided in our land if the older women were as well instructed as Leta and knew how to teach as is commanded by St. Paul and my father St. Jerome! Instead, for lack of such learning and through the extreme feebleness in which they are determined to maintain our poor women, if any parents then wish to give their daughters more extensive Christian instruction than is usual, necessity and the lack of learned older women oblige them to employ men as instructors to teach reading and writing, numbers and music, and other skills. This leads to considerable harm, which occurs every day in doleful instances of these unsuitable associations. For the immediacy of such contact and the passage of time all too frequently allow what seemed impossible to be accomplished quite easily. For this reason, many parents prefer to let their daughters remain uncivilized and untutored, rather than risk exposing them to such notorious peril as this familiarity with men. Yet all this could be avoided if there were old women of sound education, as St. Paul desires, so that instruction could be passed from the old to the young just as is done with sewing and all the customary skills.

For what impropriety can there be if an older woman, learned in letters and holy conversation and customs, should have in her charge the education of young maids? Better so than to let these young girls go to perdition, either for lack of any Christian teaching or because one tries to impart it through such dangerous means as male teachers. For if there were no greater risk than the simple indecency of seating a completely unknown man at the side of a bashful woman (who blushes if her own father should look her straight in the face), allowing him to address her with household familiarity and to speak to her with intimate authority, even so the modesty demanded in interchange with men and in conversation with them gives sufficient cause to forbid this. Indeed, I do not see how the custom of men as teachers of women can be without its dangers, save only in the strict tribunal of the confessional, or the distant teachings of the pulpit, or the remote wisdom of books; but never in the repeated handling that occurs in such immediate and tarnishing contact. And everyone knows this to be true. Nevertheless, it is permitted for no better reason than the lack of learned older women; therefore, it does great harm not to have them. This point should be taken into account by those who, tied to the *"Let women keep silence in the churches,"* curse the idea that women should acquire knowledge and teach, as if it were not the Apostle himself who described them *"teaching well."* Furthermore, that prohibition applied to the case related by Eusebius: to wit, that in the early Church, women were set to teaching each other Christian doctrine in the temples. The murmur of their voices caused confusion when the apostles were preaching, and that is why they were told to be silent. Just so, we see today that when the preacher is preaching, no one prays aloud.

Translated by Electa Arenal and Amanda Powell

SOR JUANA INÉS DE LA CRUZ, *FIRST DREAM*

So entitled and so composed by Mother Juana Inés de la Cruz, in imitation of Góngora

Pyramidal, lugubrious,
a shadow born of earth
pushed heavenward its towering tips
like vacuous obelisks bent on scaling stars,
although those splendid lights
forever free, aglow forever,
spurned the shadowy war
which the dreadful moving shade
was waging in gaseous blackness, so far below
that even its frowning gloom stopped short
before it reached the convex side
of that fair goddess's orb[1]—
she, I mean, who shows herself
in threefold beauty,
the beauty of her three faces.
There was left it as sole domain
the air it kept defiling
with each dense breath exhaled,
within which soundless purview

SOURCE: Sor Juana Inés de la Cruz, "First Dream," in *A Sor Juana Anthology*, trans. Alan S. Trueblood (Cambridge, MA: Harvard University Press, 1988), 171–73, 179–81, 194–95.

1. The sphere of the moon is the innermost of the ten that revolve around Earth in the Ptolemaic system. The moon's three faces (waxing, waning, dark) correspond to the three forms in which the moon goddess is worshiped.—Ed.

of its silent realm,
it brooked none but the muted voices
of the birds of darkness,
sounds so deep and dim
as not to break the silence.

       With sluggish flight and song,
jarring on ear and even more on spirit,
shamefaced Nyctimene[2] keeps watch
by chinks in sacred portals
or at those gaping openings
of lofty, rounded windows
best suited to her purpose:
to desecrate the brightly shining
holy lamps perpetually lit,
extinguishing, even defiling them,
while drinking in clear liquid form
rich substance that Minerva's tree,
constrained by press, has sweated forth
out of her fruit, a tribute forced.

       And those women[3] who saw their house
become an out-of-doors; their weft, the grass;
defiant of Bacchus' godhead—
no longer telling various tales
but changed now ignominiously—
create an added fog,
fearing even in darkness to be seen,
featherless wingèd birds—
those three sisters I mean,
daringly laborious,
whose frightful punishment
gave them such ill-shaped wings
of drab and naked membranes
as to bring them jeers from other baleful birds.

       They, with Pluto's telltale

2. For tricking her father into incest with her, Nyctimene of Lesbos was changed into an owl, a bird believed to drink the oil of holy lamps in order to extinguish them. The olive tree was a gift of Athena (Minerva) to the Greeks.—Ed.

3. The daughters of Minyas of Thebes refused Bacchus's summons to join his cult, clinging instead to their looms in defense of Athena and telling stories to while away the time. As punishment, they were changed into bats, their weft into greenery (Ovid, *Metamorphoses*, 4.1–30, 389–415).—Ed.

one-time henchman,[4] now an omen

to superstitious persons,

alone made up

the fearsome jangling choir,

droning long and longer lengthened notes,

and pausing more than singing,

to hang on the torpid, lazy measure,

more dragged out still at times, kept by the wind

to a phlegmatic beat,

so slow in tempo, so sustained,

that sometimes the wind would doze between two notes.

This dismal intermittent dirge

of the fearful shadowy band

insisted on attention less

than it coaxed a listener asleep.

Indeed, with all deliberation

its dull and drawn-out harmony

invited all to rest,

urging repose on weary limbs,

while Night, an index finger

sealing her two dark lips—

silent Harpocrates[5]—enjoined

silence on all things living,

a summons, however peremptory,

complied with easily

and promptly obeyed by all.

The dog asleep, the wind at rest—

one prone, the other quiet—

stir not a single atom,

fearing lest sough or sigh should make

a sacrilegious noise, however slight,

to violate the reign of silence.

The sea, no longer roiled,

did not so much as rock the azure

unsteady cradle where the sun lay sleeping.

4. Ascalaphus, son of a nymph of the underworld and the river Acheron, revealed that Persephone had eaten seven pomegranate seeds while below; for this indiscretion he was changed into a screech owl, a bird of ill omen (Ovid, *Metamorphoses*, 5.533–50).—Ed.

5. Harpocrates is the Greek version of the name of the Egyptian sun god Horus, represented in Egypt as a boy with a finger on his mouth. This pose, misunderstood by the Greeks, led to their worshiping him as god of silence.—Ed.

The fish, mute always, now asleep
in the oozy beds
of their cavernous dark coves
were doubly silent,
and Halcyon[6] in their midst,
enchantress and deceiver,
by her own transformation brought revenge
to guileless lovers once transformed by her.
        In remote mountain hideaways,
misshapen hollow crags
whose ruggedness is less defense
than their darkness is protection,
abodes of utter blackness
where night is safe from daylight's glare,
to which sure foot of practiced hunter
has never yet ascended,
the legions of wild animals lay resting—
some shedding all ferocity,
others, their timorousness—
each to Nature's power
paying the tribute
imposed by her on all alike.
The king of beasts, though open-eyed
pretending to keep watch, lay fast asleep.
That once-illustrious monarch[7]
cornered by his own dogs,
now a timid hart,
pricks up an ear
to catch the slightest motion
of the peaceful surrounding night,
the merest shift of atom,
and twitching each ear in turn,
perceives the faint and muffled sound
uneasily through his sleep.
In the quietude of the nest

6. Halcyon, a daughter of Aeolus, god of the winds, threw herself from the shore onto the body of her drowned husband, Ceyx, king of Thrace, and along with him was changed into a kingfisher (halcyon). Thus, her earlier rejected suitors, metaphorically caught like fish in the nets of her allurements, were avenged (Ovid, *Metamorphoses,* 9.710–48).—Ed.

7. Actaeon, not himself a monarch but grandson of the king of Thebes, having inadvertently surprised Diana at her bath, was changed by her into a stag and torn to pieces by his own hounds (Ovid, *Metamorphoses,* 3.155–252).—Ed.

built out of twigs and mud—
hammock hung where foliage is thickest—
the light-pinioned tribe
slumbers away and gives the wind
a respite from the slashes of its wings.
       Jupiter's majestic bird,[8]
the dutiful king of fowl, rejects
complete repose, holding it a vice,
too far indulged, and taking care
not to fall unwittingly asleep.
Entrusting all his weight to a single leg,
he keeps a pebble in the other foot—
an alarm for his light sleep—
so that, when slumber impends,
it may not be prolonged,
will rather be interrupted
by kingly pastoral concern.
Uneasy lies the head that wears a crown!
Not for one instant may he lay it down.
Mysterious explanation this may be
why crowns are circular,
the golden round betokening
the unending obligation of the king.
       All was now bound in sleep,
all by silence occupied.
Even the thief was slumbering,
even the lover had closed his eyes.
       The hour of silence is drawing to a close,
the dark time is half over
when, worn out by daily tasks—
oppressed not only
by the heavy burden
of bodily exertion, but fatigued
by pleasure as well (for any object
continually before the senses,
even if pleasurable, will cloy them:
hence Nature is always shifting weight

---

8. Sor Juana attributes to the eagle, "Jupiter's majestic bird," a practice ascribed since Pliny (*Natural History* 10.23) to the crane, a traditional symbol of vigilance. The sound of the pebble falling once the bird's grasp is relaxed in sleep supposedly would awaken it.—Ed.

from one side of the balance to the other,
setting the unsettled needle to its task
of logging all activity—now leisurely,
now toilsome—as she directs
the universe's complicated clockwork);
the limbs, then, all were occupied
by deep and welcome sleep,
leaving the senses for a time
if not deprived, relieved
of their customary labor—
labor indeed but labor greatly loved,
if labor can be loved—
the senses, I say, had yielded
to the likeness of life's opponent,
who, slow to arm and cowardly in attack,
with sleepy weapons is a lazy victor
over lowly shepherd's crook and lofty scepter
and all that stands between,
purple and sackcloth being all one for him.
His level is all-powerful:
it never makes exceptions
for any man alive,
be he one who wears the sovereign tiara
made up of triple crowns,[9] or one
who dwells in hut of straw,
a man whom the Danube gilds in mirrored glory
or a denizen of humble rushes:
with one unvarying measuring-rod
(Morpheus being, after all,
a powerful image of death)
he graduates brocade and sackcloth.
        The soul now being released
from outward governance, activity
which keeps her materially employed
for better or for worse the whole day through,
at some remove although not quite cut off,
pays out their wages
of vegetal heat only

9. The papal tiara is made up of three superimposed crowns.—Ed.

to listless limbs and resting bones
oppressed by temporary death.
The body in unbroken calm,
a corpse with soul,
is dead to living, living to the dead,
the human clock attesting
by faintest signs of life
its vital wound-up state,
wound not by hand but by arterial concert:
by throbbings which give tiny measured signs
of its well-regulated movement.
   This sovereign member, very core of vital spirits,
with its allied breathing bellows—
the lung, a magnet drawing in the wind—
which, with movement always even,
now compressing, now expanding
the sinewy, soft aqueduct,
effects the inhalation
of the cool surrounding atmosphere,
warming it up;
but the latter, angered at being expelled,
continually carries off small traces
of native warmth one day to be lamented,
never to be recovered, although now
not even noticed by their possessor—
still no theft is small if it keeps recurring;
these two witnesses, then,
reliable, unimpeachable in fact,
as I was saying, kept life going
while the silent senses, vocal silently,
impugned their testimony,
citing their very silence,
and the torpid tongue by silence of its own
disputed them as well.
   And that most marvelous and scientific
manufacturer of heat,
provident supplier of the limbs,
always at work and never stinting,
which neither favors the closest member
nor overlooks the farthest
but keeps exact account

on her natural dial
of the share she apportions to each one
in the chyle, which unceasing heat distills
from the food—well-meaning intercessor,
innocent interposer of its substance
between heat and humid radical,[10]
who has to pay in full for good intentions
or foolish arrogance that leaves that food
exposed to its enemy's voracity,
punishment well deserved although unneeded
for one who intervenes when others quarrel—
so this, if not forge of Vulcan,
moderate bonfire of human warmth,
was sending to the brain
vapors from the four well-tempered humors,
humid but so clear
it not only failed to cloud with them
the images which the estimative sense[11]
furnished to the imaginative
and the latter, for safer keeping,
passed on in purer form
to diligent memory
to incise retentively and store with care,
but also offered the fantasy
a chance to put together
further images. In just the way
that on the polished surface—
a glassy marvel and unique protection
of Pharos Island—could be seen
far, far away, despite the distance,
in the quicksilver moon,
almost the entire realm of Neptune
with the ships that plowed it so far off,
their number, size, and fortune
and the risk they ran

10. In ancient physiology the "humid radical" was a "lymphatic humor, sweet, thin, and balmlike, which gave flexibility and elasticity to the body's tendons" (*Espasa Dict.* [Span.]). It was constantly contending with the body's "natural heat," which was unable to overcome it because the interposition of food kept restoring its destructiveness.—Ed.

11. Father Méndez Plancarte (*OC*, I. 590) believes Sor Juana means, by "estimative sense," the inner sense common to the five outer senses, which receives their percepts and passes them on to the other senses located in the brain: the image-making faculty, the memory, and fantasy.—Ed.

in the transparent
unsteady country of the deep
as their light sails cleaved the wind,
their heavy hulls the waters:
so the fantasy was calmly copying
the images of everything,
and the invisible brush was shaping
in the mind's colors, without light
yet beautiful still, the likenesses
not just of all created things
here in this sublunary world, but those as well
that are the intellect's bright stars,
and as far as in her power lay
the conception of things invisible,
was picturing them ingeniously in herself
and displaying them to the soul.

      Meanwhile the latter, all intent
on her immaterial being,
was contemplating that most lovely spark,
that portion of highest being
in whose likeness in herself she took delight.
She thought herself almost loosed
from that bodily chain,
that always blocks her path,
obstructing crudely and grossly interfering
with the flight of intellect through which she plumbs
the vast immensity of the firmament
or ponders the well-regulated orbits
in which the celestial bodies
variously run their courses—
a heavy sin with punishment inherent,
the relentless shattering of inner peace,
when it lapses into vain astrology—
placed, so she thought, on the towering crest
of a mountain next to which that very Atlas,
which like a giant dominates all others,
becomes a mere obedient dwarf,
and Olympus, whose tranquil brow
has never admitted violation
by buffeting winds,
is unworthy of foothill status.

For the clouds that form an opaque crown
for the topmost mass
of the loftiest volcano that from earth,
a rearing giant,[12] goads high heaven to war,
scarcely form a heavy sash
around its soaring height
or a girdle round its huge waist,
a turbulent one, rough and poorly fashioned,
which winds undo
or the nearness of the sun evaporates.
    The first level of its elevation
(the bottommost, I mean, if you divide
its limitless awesome body into three)
no rapid surging flight could ever reach
of eagle soaring to the very heavens,
drinking in sunbeams[13] and aspiring
to build her nest amidst the sun's own lights,
however hard she presses upward
with great flappings of her feathered sails
or combings of the air
with open talons, as she strives,
fashioning ladders out of atoms,
to pierce the inviolate precincts of the peak . . .
the goal of all his works, the circle
clasping heaven and earth in one,
utmost perfection of creation,
utmost delight of its Eternal Author,
with whom well pleased, well satisfied,
His immense magnificence took His rest;
creature of portentous fashioning
who may stretch proud arms to heaven
yet suffers sealing of his mouth with dust;
whose mysterious image might be found
in the sacred vision seen in Patmos
by the evangelic eagle,[14] that strange vision

12. After their unsuccessful assault on Olympus, the Giants or Titans were condemned by the gods to imprisonment under mountains.—Ed.
13. The eagle was considered the only living creature capable of gazing directly into the sun (Pliny, *Nat. Hist.*, 29. 123–60).—Ed.
14. The eagle is the iconographic emblem of Saint John the Evangelist. Though the congruence is not perfect, the "strange vision" appears to be that of Apocalypse 10:1–2: "And I saw another mighty angel come down from heaven . . . and he set his right foot upon the sea and his left foot upon the earth."—Ed.

which trod the stars and soil with equal step;
or else in that looming statue[15]
with sumptuous lofty brow
made of the most prized metal,
who took his stance on flimsy feet
made of the material least regarded,
and subject to collapse at the slightest shudder.

      In short, I speak of man, the greatest wonder
the human mind can ponder,
complete compendium
resembling angel, plant, and beast alike;
whose haughty lowliness
partook of every nature. Why?
Perhaps that, being more fortunate
than any, he might be lifted high
by a grace of loving union.
Oh, grace repeated often,
yet never recognized sufficiently,
overlooked, so one might think,
so unappreciated is it,
so unacknowledged it remains.

      These then were the stages over which
I sometimes wished to range; yet other times
I changed my mind, considering much too daring
for one to try to take in everything,
who failed to understand the very smallest,
the easiest part
of those effects of nature
that lie so close at hand;
who, seeing the laughing brook, could never grasp
the hidden means whereby
she steers her crystal course,
pausing at times for roundabout meanders,
conducting her bright search
through Pluto's grim recesses[16]
and through the frightful caverns
of the deep and terrifying chasm,

---

15. The "great statue" of Nebuchadnezzar's dream in Daniel 2:32–35.—Ed.

16. There is an implicit reference to Arethusa, a nymph of Artemis, who, pursued by the river Alpheus, was changed into a stream that went underground and under the sea to the island of Ortygia in the harbor of Syracuse, where she surfaced as a spring (Ovid, *Metamorphoses*, 5.504–8, 572–641).—Ed.

through lovely countryside,
the pleasant Elysian Fields,
once bridal chamber[17] for his triform wife
(useful inquisitiveness, however trivial,
that brought the goddess of the flaxen hair[18]
sure word of her fair missing daughter
when, searching high and low through woods and hills,
investigating every field and grove,
she sought her very life and all the while
was losing her life from grief);
who, seeing a tiny flower, could not tell
why with an ivory pattern
its fragile beauty is girt about;
why a mixture of colors—
scarlet blending into white of dawn—
tints its fragrant costume,
why its scent is of amber,
why it unravels in the breeze
a wrapping so delicately beautiful
(renewed in its every newborn child)
and makes a bright show of flounces
fluted with golden streaks,
which, once the bud's white seal is broken,
boastfully display the tincture
born of the Cyprian goddess' sweet wound,[19]
unless, indeed, the whiteness of the daybreak
or the redness of the dawn
has overwhelmed it, fusing
red snowflake with snow-whitened rose,
such opalescence soon eliciting
acclaim sought from the meadow;
perhaps a tutor in the vanity—
unless indeed an impious demonstration
of the feminine duplicity which makes
the deadliest poison twice as deadly

17. The reference is to Pluto's abduction of Persephone to be his consort in the underworld. Her three forms: first as maiden, the daughter of Demeter and Zeus; then, for half of the year, queen of the underworld; and for the other half, goddess of agriculture.—Ed.

18. Demeter (Ceres), goddess of grains and harvests, was associated with "flaxen hair."—Ed.

19. The red rose was said to have arisen from the blood of Venus when a thorn pricked her foot as she rushed to the aid of Adonis, who had been wounded by a wild boar.—Ed.

in the conspicuous overlay
of the woman who feigns a glowing countenance.
          Now if, from a single object—
my timid thought kept saying—
true knowledge shies away,
and reason ingloriously turns aside;
if on a species set apart
as independent of all others—
thought of as unrelated—
understanding turns her back;
if reason, overwhelmed, recoils
before so difficult a challenge,
refusing to take action resolutely,
doubting in her cowardice
that she can grasp even this single object,
how can she hope to function in the face
of so astounding and immense a system?
Its burden, terrible, unendurable—
were it not upheld[20] at its very center—
would make the shoulders even of Atlas[21] sag,
outdo the strength of Hercules,[22]
and they, who proved sufficient counterweight
to the sphere of heaven,
would judge its fabric far less burdensome,
its framework less oppressive,
than the task of investigating Nature.
          Bolder at other times,
my mind denounced as height of cowardice
yielding the laurels without one attempt
to meet the challenge of the lists.
Then it would seize upon the brave example
set by that famous youth, high-minded
charioteer of the chariot of flame;
then courage would be fired
by his grand and bold, if hapless, impulse,
in which the spirit finds
not, like timidity, a chastening lesson

20. The omniscience and omnipotence of God sustain the universe.—Ed.
21. Atlas was a Titan, king of Mauretania; he was turned by Perseus into the mountain that upholds the sky.—Ed.
22. Hercules for a time relieved Atlas of the burden of the heavens.—Ed.

but a pathway summoning it to dare;
once treading this, no punishment can deter
the spirit bent upon a fresh attempt
(I mean a thrust of new ambition).
Neither the nether pantheon—
cerulean tomb of his unhappy ashes—
nor the vengeful lightning bolt,
for all their warnings, ever will convince
the soaring spirit once resolved,
in lofty disregard of living,
to pluck from ruin an everlasting fame.
Rather, that youth is the very type, the model:
a most pernicious instance
(causing wings to sprout for further flights)
of that ambitious mettle,
which, finding in terror itself a spur
to prick up courage,
pieces together the name of glory
from letters spelling endless havoc.
Either the punishment should not be known
so that the crime would never become contagious,
a politic silence covering up instead,
with a statesman's circumspection,
all record of the proceedings;
or let a show of ignorance prevail,
or the insolent excess
meet its just deserts by secret sentence
without the noxious example
ever reaching public notice,
for broadcasting makes the wickedness
of the greatest crime all the greater
till it threatens a widespread epidemic,
while, left in unknown isolation,
repetition is far less likely
than if broadcast to all as a would-be lesson.
        But as judgment foundered in confusion
amid the reefs and skirted whirlpools
of no return, no matter which direction
it sought to follow, heat, no longer finding
the sustenance it needed,
since its tempered flame (however temperate,

a flame still, which, actively engaging
in its function, uses up materials
or else inflames them),
unable to act otherwise
had gradually
transformed its nutriment,
converting foreign matter into own.
The noisy boiling that resulted
from uniting the burning humor with the moist
in that most wonderful
and natural of vessels now had ceased,
with nothing left to feed on. In consequence
the humid and sleep-inducing vapors[23]
arising from it,
were affecting the seat of reason
(from which they carried to the limbs
a pleasant drowsiness);
and consumed by the gentle warming
resulting from the heat,
were loosening the chains of sleep.
The overtired limbs,
worn out by rest,
reacting to the lack of sustenance,
and neither wide-awake nor fast asleep,
were showing signs of wishing
to be stirring once again
by the languid, drawn-out stretching
the torpid sinews were engaging in.
Even without their owner's full assent,
the limbs were turning tired bones
from side to side;
the senses were beginning to resume
their functioning, despite mild interference
caused by the natural toxin,[24]
half-opening the eyes;
and from the brain, now cleared,
phantasms had taken leave

23. Sleep, according to Saint Thomas, following Aristotle, occurs when vapors from digestion rise to the brain ("the seat of reason") and numb the senses. With the ending of the digestive process, one awakens.—Ed.
24. The last lingering vapors arising from the digestive process.—Ed.

and, being formed of lightest vapor,
converted easily to smoke or wind,
now let their shapes be dissipated.
Just so, the magic lantern[25]
casts on white of wall
simulations of different painted figures,
made possible by shadow no less than light.
Maintaining amid shimmering reflections
the distances required
by the science of perspective
and confirmed in its true measurements
by a number of experiments,
the fleeting shadow
that fades into the brilliance of the light
simulates a body's form,
one possessing all dimensions, though it merits
no consideration even as surface.

      Meanwhile the father of flaming light
saw that the appointed hour was arriving
when he must climb the East.
He took his leave of our antipodes
with light departing down the West,
for through the flickers of his fading light
the same point serves to mark his going down
as ushers in the brightening of our East.
But not till Venus as the morning star,
beautiful and serene,
had pierced the first faint dawnlight,
and the fair wife of old Tithonus—[26]
amazon arrayed in countless lights
(her armor against the night),
beautiful though bold,
valiant although tearful—
had let her lovely brow be seen
crowned with the lights of morning.
a tender prelude though a spirited one,

---

25. The magic lantern was a recent invention whose functioning had been explained and illustrated in the *Ars Magna Lucis et Umbrae* (The Great Art of Light and Shade) of Athanasius Kircher (Amsterdam, 1667), a work that Sor Juana frequently cited.—Ed.

26. Eos or Aurora, the Dawn, has her youth renewed every day, while her husband, Tithonus, originally a mortal, grows older and older.—Ed.

to the fiery planet,
who was busy marshaling his troops
of glimmering novices—
reserving glowing veterans, more robust,
to fill the rearguard—
against the tyrannical usurper
of the empire of daylight,
who wore a laurel girdle with countless shadows
and with her dreadful nighttime scepter
ruled over shadows
of whom she stood in awe herself.
But scarcely had the lovely harbinger
and standard-bearer of the Sun unfurled
her luminous pennant in the East,
as all the bugles of the birds,
soft yet bellicose, sounded the call to arms
(resonant trumpeters and skilled,
though uninstructed)
when—cowardly as tyrants always are,
and beset by timorous misgivings—
although trying to put up a valiant front
with her forces, although flaunting
her funereal cloak as shield,
that took short wounds
from the stabbing brightness
(even though her uneasy bravery
was merely a crude cover for her fear
since she knew how weak was her resistance)—
as if relying more on flight
than belligerence for her salvation,
Night was blowing her raucous horn
to gather her swarthy squadrons in
and make an orderly retreat—
when a burst of bouncing light
assaulted her from closer by
as it bathed the topmost tip
of the loftiest of turrets in the world.
The Sun appeared, the circle now complete
which he carves in gold against the sapphire blue.
From his luminous circumference there sprang
a thousand times a thousand golden specks,

a thousand streams of gold—
lines, I mean, of brilliant light
ruled on heaven's cerulean page,
drawn up for orderly attack
upon the dismal despot of his realm
who, in hasty headlong flight,
stumbling over her native terrors,
was treading on her very shadow
as she sought to reach the West
with the routed, broken ranks
of her shadow army, harassed by light
in close pursuit upon her heels.
At last her fleeing footsteps reached the point
where the West came into view
and, though rushing, regaining her composure,
plucking courage up from her very ruin,
she resolved, rebelling once again,
to see herself made sovereign
in that half of the globe
left unprotected by the Sun
when the beauty of his golden locks
brought luster to our hemisphere.
Dealing judiciously with his light,
by orderly distribution he dispensed
to all things visible their colors,
restoring to every outer sense
full functioning,
flooding with light whatever had been opaque
throughout the world, and summoning me awake.

Translated by Alan S. Trueblood

4

RADICAL DOUBT AND THE LIBERATION OF WOMEN

Ruth Perry

[. . .] The seventeenth century was a time of loosening constraints on women. Particularly in England where the old order was giving way under the armed attacks of republican forces, women were accorded a new place in this "world turned upside down." New political and religious experiments made room for an occasional woman in public spaces—the meeting house, the printing shop, or the political planning session. The evolving system of capitalism, with its combination of a cash economy and the growth of large urban centers, made it possible for the "odd" woman to survive as an atomized individual, cut adrift from family and community, subsisting independently outside family obligations and protection—like Moll Flanders—living on wages or income from investments, in the anonymity of a big city. Not until later in the eighteenth century was the new configuration of restraint woven to keep women in their places, the gentle tyranny that Lawrence Stone has called the "companionate marriage," which assumed women's responsibility for the happiness of her family, a somewhat masochistic spiritual superiority, and a claustrophobic notion of gentility and middle-class respectability.

One important aspect of this general liberation of women can be found in the intellectual history of the seventeenth century, in the powerful and revolutionary philosophical method introduced by Descartes. Cartesian assumptions and Cartesian method, ironic as it may seem, liberated women intellectually and thus psychically, by making it possible for numbers of them to participate in serious mainstream philosophical discourse.

The "new philosophy," whether the rationalism of Descartes or the empiricism of Bacon, did women the incalculable service of taking formal thought out of the schools, from which women, even the most aristocratic, had always been excluded. The new philosophical practice did not require formal education or even familiarity with classical texts; anyone who could meditate and think logically about that meditation, might contribute to knowledge. Descartes himself had made it clear that an old-fashioned classical education was irrelevant to the most profound questions of philosophy—questions about the nature of knowledge itself.[1]

Poullain de la Barre, a feminist disciple of Descartes, held that since men and women had the same physiological equipment for receiving and registering sensations—the same bundles of nerve fibers—they therefore had the same potential for finding their way to Truth. Once put on an experiential basis, philosophy became the common intellectual ground on which men and women might meet to discuss the nature of thought and of physical matter.

They usually did not meet face to face, however, but wrote letters to one another about philosophical matters. Private correspondence, considered as much a woman's form as a man's, became the medium for the exchange of philosophical and theological ideas. Letters were the appropriate mode of communication between respectable women and men outside their circle of acquaintance. The very means of communication created and cemented these intellectualized relationships between strangers; the medium was suited to metaphysical speculation, and in itself constituted a kind of proof that disembodied friendships between members of the opposite sex could subsist on ideas alone.

Learned correspondence between intellectual men and women became quite the rage in the course of the seventeenth century, not the least of which was the celebrated exchange between Descartes and his friend Elizabeth, princess of Bohemia, herself a friend and correspondent of the feminist and intellectual Anna Van Schurman. Anna Van Schurman, linguist, painter, theologian, philosopher, was the most learned woman in Europe. "To have been in Utrecht without having seen Mademoiselle de Schurman," wrote a contemporary, "was like having been to Paris without having seen the king." Educated by an admiring father, and later by the Dutch reformed theologian Gisbert Voet (who arranged for her to attend his university lectures hidden behind a curtain), she corresponded with the leading intellectuals of her day: Constantijn Huygens, Pierre Gassendi, Queen Christine of Sweden, Bathsua Makin in England, Marin Mersenne, René Descartes, and Cardinal Richelieu.

Elizabeth of Bohemia initiated the correspondence with Descartes, as was usually the case in cross-sex intellectual friendships. She wrote to ask him to clarify his view of the nature and the locus of interaction between the immaterial mind and the material body. Her shrewd questions are still considered among the most trenchant critiques of Cartesian dualism, and their letters constitute an important part of the Cartesian *oeuvre*.[2]

Princess Elizabeth's relation to Descartes was special, of course, because she was also his patron. But many private women wrote as she did, out of the blue, to philosophers or clergymen to question them more closely about their published views. In time, a remarkable number of these philosophically minded women came to pen serious essays or treatises for the public themselves. Reassured no doubt by Descartes's claim that rationality was distributed throughout the population ("I never supposed my mind was above the ordinary," he remarked in *Discourse on Method*), they tested their wings—their quills—privately at first, practicing philosophical exposition on a smaller scale before taking the leap into public space. These experiences had a radicalizing effect on these women and emboldened them later to write feminist treatises—to publicly disown the cultural conceptions of women as shallow, frivolous, and ineducable, and to agitate for reconsideration of the power relations between the sexes.

Let us go back to the beginning again, to Descartes. As everyone knows, Descartes wanted nothing less than to establish a foundation for knowledge of the world—for science—on a mathematically verifiable basis. His universal, abstract notion of truth was one that required "a mind entirely free of all prejudice" and one that could readily "free itself from its attachment to the senses." As the inventor of analytic geometry, mathematical demonstration appealed to him, he said, because a proof did not depend on the fallible senses, or evidence of the external world. The proof was the same whether one was awake or dreaming. Needless to say, this notion of truth excluded history, custom, and indeed all other human beings.

Descartes invented a method appropriate to his purpose, a method which took prior learning as inessential, and which required no books or equipment of any sort—nothing but the quiet necessary for meditation. Indeed, he began by bracketing the entire material world in order to concentrate on the essential basis of all knowledge: immaterial thought itself. This was a method equally available to women living in rural isolation on country estates or in villages, and to those living in the city, although peace and quiet were harder to come by there. As Elizabeth of Bohemia lamented: "The life I am constrained to lead does not permit me enough time at my disposal to acquire a habit of meditation according to your rules. From time to time the interests of my House, which I must not neglect, or the conversations and amusements that I cannot evade, beset my feeble mind so strongly with annoyances and boredom that it becomes, for a long time thereafter, useless for anything else."[3]

Descartes was a peculiar man, and as he tells his story, lived in extreme isolation much of his life. "From my childhood I lived in a world of books," he tells us. And during the first stage of his quest for knowledge, he reports spending nine years wandering here and there throughout the world, trying to be a "spectator rather than actor in all the comedies that go on." At the end of that time, seeing that disputes existed everywhere among the learned, he concluded that it was necessary to build knowledge in a new manner. He retired to Holland where, in his own words, "in the midst of a great and busy people, more interested in their own affairs than curious about those of others, I was able to enjoy all the comforts of life to be found in the most populous cities while living in as solitary and retired a fashion as though in the most remote of deserts."[4]

It is one of the ironies of history that no woman, however wealthy and however highborn, would have been at liberty to live as alone as Descartes lived. To go further: no woman could have originated Descartes's epistemology because no woman could have grown up so primally disconnected from society as Descartes. Yet once invented, this meditative introspection which required leisure, isolation, and the willful doubting of all previous knowledge, was a mode of intellectual activity available to almost all literate middle-class and aristocratic women, trapped as they were in an economic system which increasingly relieved them of real tasks contributing to the subsistence of their house-holds, and in an old-fashioned moralism which condemned most pastimes (shopping, visiting, gossiping, gambling) other than reading and contemplation. Women with time on their hands, without a scholastic education yet able to read, might participate in the "new way of ideas" heartened by the fact that the introspective data of all thinking beings were equally important. As Elizabeth Berkeley (later Burnet) wrote to Locke in 1697: "You love to convers with children and see the naturall productions of the mind, unassisted by art, and unposest by other notions"—to which she added "mine is too much so."[5]

I suspect that women were also attracted to the new philosophy by virtue of their powerlessness in the material world, and that a discipline predicated on retreat from that world seemed a safe enough enterprise. In his *Discourse on Method,* Descartes wrote that he had early decided that it was better to try to "conquer" himself rather than fortune, "to change my desires rather than the established order," because "nothing except our thoughts is wholly under our control."[6] This approach appealed especially to women, who could control little else. His emphasis on abstract reasoning, and on the greater stability (and therefore reality) of ideas compared to slippery and contingent material "fact," found an immediately sympathetic audience, for instance, among those bookish women in France who came to be called *les précieuses.*[7] Molière's satiric play, *Les Femmes savantes,* shows these women reading Descartes and discoursing in an absurdly airy and pretentious manner. Modern feminists have suggested that despite the ridicule which *les précieuses* called down upon themselves because of their preoccupation with the abstract, their insistence on living in a world of pure ideas freed them at least from the tyranny of their reproductive systems. To refuse to live on a material plane was to escape the con-tinuous pregnancies, miscarriages, and lyings-in which were the lot of all fertile married women in the days before contraception.[8]

[. . . .]

. . . [T]here seems to be some connection between engaging in philosophical corre-spondence and later publishing, although the appropriate metaphor for describing it is uncertain—whether priming the pump, testing the waters, or trying one's strength. But the pattern is clear: the new philosophy indirectly aided women by giving them a subject and a method, and an opportunity to participate in public speech.

In the case of Mary Astell in particular, I think it is possible to go further, and to show that Cartesian rationalism was the very cornerstone of her feminism. Her belief in an imma-terial intellect which had no gender and which was the essential feature of all human nature, was the base upon which she built the rest. Because she believed in a firm and immutable Truth, which all minds were capable of reaching given time and training, women were equal to men in the only respect that mattered. The miracle of reason itself seemed to bless her logic, for surely that marvelous faculty was a sign of something "too Divine, to have it once imagin'd that it was made for nothing else but to move a portion of Matter 70 or 80 Years."[9] Everything in the divinely ordered universe had an end or purpose for which it was fitted and predestined, and human beings with their extraordinary faculties were obviously meant to engage in philosophic pursuits, to discover and disseminate Truth.

Mary Astell's insistence on the primacy of the intellect was the key to her confidence that women were meant for better things than frivolous pleasures or domestic labors. The mighty thing about human nature, she wrote, was an unwillingness to accept ignorance. Just as "a rational mind will be employed," women turned to plays and romances for lack of anything better, Astell explained sensibly. "She who has nothing else to value herself upon, will be proud of her Beauty, or Money and what that can purchase, and think her self mightily oblig'd to him, who tells her she has those Perfections which she naturally longs for." She understood the competitions of fashionable life as perversions of the instinct for excellence with which their Maker had endowed all human beings, and she doubted the protestations of those of her sex who claimed to be satisfied with their allotted roles as ignorant women.

> A being content with Ignorance is really but a Pretence, for the frame of our nature is such that it is impossible we should be so; even those very Pretenders value themselves for some Knowledge or other, tho' it be a trifling or mistaken one. She who makes the most Grimace at a Woman of Sense, who employs all her little skill in endeavoring to render Learning and Ingenuity ridiculous, is yet very desirous to be thought Knowing in Dress, in the Management of an Intreague, in Coquetry or good Housewifry. If then either the Nobleness or Necessity of our Nature unavoidably excites us to a desire of Advancing, shall it be thought a fault to do it by pursuing the best things?[10]

Astell did everything in her power to help other women pursue what she called "the best things," to be intellectually ambitious and to live fully the life of the mind. All her life she wrote, she taught, she urged women to live up to their potential capacity. Her first published book (she wrote six that we know of, and two long pamphlets in the years following her correspondence with John Norris) argued for institutions of higher learning for women. This book, titled *A Serious Proposal to the Ladies* (1694), proposed that women pool their resources to set up educational residences like Protestant convents, celibate women's colleges that could provide women with a much-needed education, and with an even more needed alternative to marriage. As Astell well knew, many women had no place to go if they left their parental homes, and no way to support themselves.

A few years later, seeing that no one had taken up her suggestion for women's colleges, and feeling that women were still in great need of intellectual discipline, she wrote a second part to *A Serious Proposal to the Ladies* (1697), in which she distilled the rules of thought set forth by the seventeenth-century French thinkers who had trained a generation of philosophers: Antoine Arnaud and René Descartes. Her third book, published in 1700, was more radical. There she attacked the power relations between men and women in marriage, and advised women not to marry at all, unless they could find men into whose keeping they could entrust their moral and intellectual progress.

Thus, in Mary Astell's case, her romance with seventeenth-century philosophy was related in both form and content to the growth of her own feminism. Descartes taught her to start with her own vantage point as a thinking woman to analyze the world. Norris's reception of her arguments about the nature of love and one's relation to God reinforced her sense of what she had to say. It was a great pleasure to her to think and read and write; and she determined to convince others of her sex to join her in these pursuits. She wrote from experience, replying to her culture's clichés about women as honestly as she could. And she addressed herself earnestly and directly to an audience of women as if she were writing a letter to a group of friends, engaging them and exhorting them, and arguing from undeniable premises.

NOTES

This chapter's introduction is an excerpt from Ruth Perry, "Radical Doubt and the Liberation of Women," *Eighteenth-Century Studies* 18, no. 4 (Autumn 1985): 472–93. The notes that follow are from that published text.

1. René Descartes, *Discourse on Method,* trans. Lawrence Lafleur (Indianapolis: Bobbs-Merrill Educational Publishing, 1960). All subsequent quotations are taken from this edition.

2. Selections from their correspondence are included in the volume edited and introduced by Margaret D. Wilson, *The Essential Descartes* (New York: New American Library, 1969), 373–80.

3. Wilson, *The Essential Descartes* , 376.

4. René Descartes, *Discourse on Method,* trans. L. Lafleur, 5, 22, 23.

5. *The Correspondence of John Locke,* ed. E. S. DeBeer, 8 vols. (Oxford: Clarendon Press, 1976–82), 6:197–204. Letter dated September 22, 1697.

6. René Descartes, *Discourse on Method,* trans. L. Lafleur, 20.

7. A. Foucher de Careil, *Descartes et la princesse palatine ou De L'influence Cartesianism sur les femme au XVII siecle* (Paris: August Durand, 1862), passim.

8. Dorothy Anne Liot Backer, *Precious Women* (New York: Basic Books, 1974), 180–82.

9. Mary Astell, *A Serious Proposal to the Ladies, Part II,* 233.

10. Astell, *A Serious Proposal* , 287.

DISCUSSION QUESTIONS

1. Feminists have sometimes argued that mind/body dualism, in elevating the mind (almost always coded as male) and disparaging the body (often associated with things female), has not been a particularly woman-friendly position. Yet Perry argues that dualism can also function to support gender equality,

especially arguments, like Astell's, for the education of women. What is Perry's argument? Looking at both the Descartes and Astell excerpts, can you find evidence for the influence of Descartes's dualism on Astell?

2. Compare and contrast Astell's arguments for the education of women with those of Sor Juana and Rufus Musonius. What are the similarities and differences? How, in your opinion, do the different time periods and national contexts figure into these differences?

3. What do you make of the fact that Astell directly addresses women ("the ladies") in her proposal? Is it just a tactic to make the work more palatable and less threatening to men—something that any woman writing in the period had to consider—or do you see something deeper at work?

DESCARTES, FROM *MEDITATIONS ON FIRST PHILOSOPHY*
First Meditation: Of the Things of Which We May Doubt

SEVERAL years have now elapsed since I first became aware that I had accepted, even from my youth, many false opinions for true, and that consequently what I afterward based on such principles was highly doubtful; and from that time I was convinced of the necessity of undertaking once in my life to rid myself of all the opinions I had adopted, and of commencing anew the work of building from the foundation, if I desired to establish a firm and abiding superstructure in the sciences. But as this enterprise appeared to me to be one of great magnitude, I waited until I had attained an age so mature as to leave me no hope that at any stage of life more advanced I should be better able to execute my design. On this account, I have delayed so long that I should henceforth consider I was doing wrong were I still to consume in deliberation any of the time that now remains for action. To-day, then, since I have opportunely freed my mind from all cares [and am happily disturbed by no passions],[1] and since I am in the secure possession of leisure in a peaceable retirement, I will at length apply myself earnestly and freely to the general overthrow of all my former opinions. [. . .]

Third Meditation: Of God: That He Exists

I WILL now close my eyes, I will stop my ears, I will turn away my senses from their objects, I will even efface from my consciousness all the images of corporeal things; or at least, because this can hardly be accomplished, I will consider them as empty and false; and thus, holding converse only with myself, and closely examining my nature, I will

SOURCE: René Descartes, *Meditations on First Philosophy*, eds. David B. Manley and Charles S. Taylor, trans. John Veitch, www.wright.edu/~charles.taylor/descartes/.

1. Bracketed text in original.

endeavor to obtain by degrees a more intimate and familiar knowledge of myself. I am a thinking (conscious) thing, that is, a being who doubts, affirms, denies, knows a few objects, and is ignorant of many,—[who loves, hates], wills, refuses, who imagines like-wise, and perceives; for, as I before remarked, although the things which I perceive or imagine are perhaps nothing at all apart from me [and in themselves], I am nevertheless assured that those modes of consciousness which I call perceptions and imaginations, in as far only as they are modes of consciousness, exist in me. [. . .]

Sixth Meditation: Of the Existence of Material Things, and of the Real Distinction between the Mind and Body of Man

[. . . .] To commence this examination accordingly, I here remark, in the first place, that there is a vast difference between mind and body, in respect that body, from its nature, is always divisible, and that mind is entirely indivisible. For in truth, when I consider the mind, that is, when I consider myself in so far only as I am a thinking thing, I can dis-tinguish in myself no parts, but I very clearly discern that I am somewhat absolutely one and entire; and although the whole mind seems to be united to the whole body, yet, when a foot, an arm, or any other part is cut off, I am conscious that nothing has been taken from my mind; nor can the faculties of willing, perceiving, conceiving, etc., properly be called its parts, for it is the same mind that is exercised [all entire] in willing, in perceiv-ing, and in conceiving, etc. But quite the opposite holds in corporeal or extended things; for I cannot imagine any one of them [how small soever it may be], which I cannot easily sunder in thought, and which, therefore, I do not know to be divisible. This would be sufficient to teach me that the mind or soul of man is entirely different from the body, if I had not already been apprised of it on other grounds. [. . .]

Translated by John Veitch

MARY ASTELL, FROM *A SERIOUS PROPOSAL TO THE LADIES*, PART I

[. . .] Now as to the Proposal it is to erect a *Monastery*, or if you will (to avoid giving offence to the scrupulous and injudicious, by names which tho' innocent in themselves, have been abus'd by superstitious Practices), we will call it a *Religious Retirement*, and such as shall have a double aspect, being not only a Retreat from the World for those who desire that advantage, but likewise, an institution and previous discipline, to fit us to do the greatest good in it; such an institution as this (if I do not mightily deceive my self)

SOURCE: Mary Astell, "A Serious Proposal to the Ladies," in *The Essential Feminist Reader*, ed. Estelle Freedman (New York: Modern Library, 2007), 20–23.

would be the most probable method to amend the present and improve the future Age. [. . .]

You are therefore Ladies, invited into a place, where you shall suffer no other confinement, but to be kept out of the road of Sin: You shall not be depriv'd of your Grandeur, but only exchange the vain Pomps and Pageantry of the world, empty Titles and Forms of State, for the true and solid Greatness of being able to despise *them*. You will only quit the Chat of insignificant people for an ingenious Conversation; the froth of flashy Wit for real Wisdom; idle tales for instructive discourses. The deceitful Flatteries of those who under pretence of loving and admiring you, really served their *own* base ends, for the seasonable Reproofs and wholsom Counsels of your hearty well-wishers and affectionate Friends, which will procure you those perfections your feigned lovers pretended you had, and kept you from obtaining. [. . .]

[Y]our Retreat shall be so manag'd as not to exclude the good Works of an *Active*, from the pleasure and serenity of a *contemplative* Life, but by a due mixture of both retain all the advantages and avoid the inconveniences that attend either. It shall not so cut you off from the world as to hinder you from bettering and improving it, but rather qualify you to do it the greatest Good, and be a Seminary to stock the Kingdom with pious and prudent Ladies; whose good Example it is to be hop'd, will so influence the rest of their Sex, that Women may no longer pass for those little useless and impertinent Animals, which the ill conduct of too many has caus'd them to be mistaken for.

We have hitherto consider'd our Retirement only in relation to Religion, which is indeed its *main*, I may say its *only* design; nor can this be thought too contracting a word, since Religion is the adequate business of our lives, and largely consider'd, takes in all we have to do. [. . .] But because, as we have all along observ'd, Religion never appears in its true Beauty, but when it is accompanied with Wisdom and Discretion; and that without a good Understanding, we can scarce be *truly*, but never *eminently* Good; being liable to a thousand seductions and mistakes; for even the men themselves, if they have not a competent degree of Knowledge, they are carried about with every wind of Doctrine. Therefore, one great end of this institution, shall be to expel that cloud of Ignorance, which Custom has involv'd us in, to furnish our minds with a stock of solid and useful Knowledge, that the Souls of Women may no longer be the only unadorn'd and neglected things. [. . .]

For since GOD has given Women as well as Men intelligent Souls, why should they be forbidden to improve them? Since he has not denied us the faculty of Thinking, why shou'd we not (at least in gratitude to him) employ our Thoughts on himself their noblest Object, and not unworthily bestow them on Trifles and Gaities and secular Affairs? Being the Soul was created for the contemplation of Truth as well as for the fruition of Good, is it not as cruel and unjust to preclude Women from the knowledge of the one, as well as from the enjoyment of the other? [. . .]

We pretend not that Women shou'd teach in the Church, or usurp Authority where it is not allow'd them; permit us only to understand our *own* duty, and not be forc'd to take it upon trust from others; to be at least so far learned, as to be able to form in our minds a true Idea of Christianity. [. . .]

But since such Seminaries are thought proper for the Men, since they enjoy the fruits of those Noble Ladies' Bounty who were the foundresses of several of their Colleges, why shou'd we not think that such ways of Education wou'd be as advantageous to the Ladies? or why shou'd we despair of finding some among them who will be as kind to their own Sex as their Ancestors have been to the other? [. . .]

The Men therefore may still enjoy their Prerogatives for us, we mean not to intrench on any of their Lawful Privileges, our only Contention shall be that they may not out-do us in promoting his Glory who is Lord both of them and us; And by all that appears the generality will not oppose us in this matter, we shall not provoke them by striving to be better Christians. They may busy their Heads with Affairs of State, and spend their Time and Strength in recommending themselves to an uncertain Master, or a more giddy Multitude, our only endeavour shall be to be absolute Monarchs in our own Bosoms. They shall still if they please dispute about Religion, let 'em only give us leave to Understand and Practise it. [. . .]

MARY ASTELL, FROM *A SERIOUS PROPOSAL TO THE LADIES*, PART II

[. . .] Contemplation requires a governable body, a sedate and steady mind, and the body and the mind do so reciprocally influence each other, that we can scarce keep the one in tune if the other be out of it. We can neither observe the errors of our intellect, nor the irregularity of our morals whilst we are darkened by fumes, agitated with unruly passions, or carried away with eager desires after sensible things and vanities. We must therefore withdraw our minds from the world, from adhering to the senses, from the love of material beings, of pomps and gaieties; for 'tis these that usually steal away the heart, that seduce the mind to such unaccountable wanderings, and so fill up its capacity that they leave no room for truth, so distract its attention that it cannot enquire after her. For though the body does partly occasion this fault, yet the will no doubt may in good measure remedy it by using its authority to fix the understanding on such objects as it would have contemplated; it has a rein which will certainly curb this wandering, if it can but be persuaded to make use of it. Indeed attention and deep meditation is not so agreeable to our animal nature, does not flatter our pride so well as this agreeable reverie, which gives us a pretense to knowledge without taking much pains to acquire it, and does not choke us with the humbling thoughts of our own ignorance, with which we must make such ado e're it can be enlightened. Yet without attention and strict examination we are liable to false judgments on every occasion, to vanity and arrogance, to impertinent prating of things we don't understand, are kept from making a progress, because we fancy ourselves to be at the top already, and can never attain to true wisdom. If then we would hereafter think to purpose, we must suffer ourselves to be convinced how oft we have already thought to none, suspect our quickness, and not give our desultory imagination leave to ramble.

And in order to the restraining it we may consider, what a loss of time and study such irregular and useless thoughts occasion, what a reproach they are to our reason, how they cheat us with a *show* of knowledge, which so long as we are under the power of this giddy temper will inevitably escape us. And if to this we add a serious perusal of such books as are not loosely writ, but require an attent and awakened mind to apprehend, and to take in the whole force of them, obliging ourselves to understand them thoroughly, so as to be able to give a just account of them to ourselves, or rather to some other person intelligent enough to take it and to correct our mistakes, it is to be hoped we shall obtain a due poise of mind, and be able to direct our thoughts to the through discussion of such subjects as we would examine. Such books I mean as are fuller of matter than words, which diffuse a light through every part of their subject, do not skim, but penetrate it to the bottom, yet so as to leave somewhat to be wrought out by the reader's own meditation; such as are writ with order and connection, the strength of whose arguments can't be sufficiently felt unless we remember and compare the whole system. 'Tis impossible to prescribe absolutely, and every one may easily find what authors are most apt to stay their attention, and should apply to them. But whenever they meditate, be it on what object it may, let them fix their minds steadily on it, not removing till it be thoroughly examined, at least not until they have seen all that's necessary to their present purpose.

Doing so we shall prevent rashness and precipitation in our judgments, which is occasioned by that volatileness we have been speaking of, together with an over-weaning opinion of ourselves. All the irregularities of our will proceed from those false judgments we make, through want of consideration, or a partial examination when we do consider. For did we consider with any manner of attention, we could not be so absurd as to call evil, good, and choose it as such, or prefer a less good before a greater, a poor momentary trifle before the purity and perfection of our mind; before an eternal and immutable crown of glory! But we seek no farther than the first appearances of truth and good, here we stop; allowing neither time nor thought to search to the bottom, and to pull off those disguises which impose on us. This precipitation is that which gives birth to all our errors, which are nothing else but a hasty and injudicious sentence, a mistaking one thing for another, supposing an agreement or disparity amongst ideas and their relations where in reality there is none, occasioned by an imperfect and cursory view of them. And though there are other things which may be said to lead us into error, yet they do it only as they seduce us into rash and precipitate judgments. We love grandeur and every thing that feeds our good opinion of ourselves, and therefore would judge off hand, supposing it a disparagement to our understandings to be long in examining, so that we greedily embrace whatever seems to carry evidence enough for a speedy determination, how slight and superficial soever it be. Whereas did we calmly and deliberately examine our evidence, and how far those motives we are acted by ought to influence, we should not be liable to this seduction. For hereby the impetuosity of a warm imagination would be cooled, and the extravagancies of a disorderly one regulated; we should not be deceived by the report of our senses; the prejudices of education; our own private interest, and readiness to receive the opinions whether true or false of those we love, and would appear to love because we think they will serve us in that interest; our inordinate thirst after a great reputation, or the power and riches, the grandeurs and pleasures of this world, these would no longer dissipate our thoughts and distract our attention, for then we should be sensible how little concern is due to them. We should neither mistake in the end and object by not employing our understandings at all about such things as they were chiefly made for, or not enough, or by busying them with such as are out of their reach, or beneath their application; nor should we be out in the method of our meditation, by going a wrong or a round about way. For the God of truth is ready to lead us into all truth, if we honestly and attentively apply ourselves to him.

In sum, whatever false principle we embrace, whatever wrong conclusion we draw from true ones, is a disparagement to our thinking power, a weakness of judgment proceeding from a confused and imperfect view of things, as that does from want of attention, and a hasty and partial examination. It were endless to reckon up all the false maxims and reasonings we fall into, nor is it possible to give a list of them, for there are innumerable errors opposite to one single truth. The general causes have been already mentioned, the particulars are as many as those several compositions which arise from the various mixtures of the passions, interests, education, conversation and reading, etc. of particular persons. And the best way that I can think of to improve the understanding, and to guard it against all errors proceed they from what cause they may, is to regulate the will, whose office it is to determine the understanding to such and such ideas, and to stay it in the consideration of them so long as is necessary to the discovery of truth; for if the will be right the understanding can't be guilty of any culpable error. Not to judge of anything which we don't apprehend, to suspend our assent till we see just cause to give it, and to determine nothing till the strength and clearness of the evidence oblige us to it. To withdraw ourselves as much as may be from corporeal things, that pure reason may be heard the better; to make that use of our senses for which they are designed and fitted, the preservation of the body, but not to depend on their testimony in our enquiries after truth. Particularly to divest ourselves of mistaken self-love, little ends and mean designs, and to keep our inclinations and passions under government. Not to engage ourselves so far in any party or opinion as to make it in a manner necessary that that should be right, lest from wishing it were, we come at last to persuade ourselves it is so. But to be passionately in love with truth, as being thoroughly sensible of her excellency and beauty. To embrace her how opposite soever she may sometimes be to our humors and designs, to bring these over to her, and never attempt to make her truckle to them. To be so far from disliking a truth because it touches us home, and lances our tenderest and dearest corruption, as on the contrary to prize it the more, by how much the more plainly it shows us our errors and miscarriages. For indeed it concerns us most to know such truths as these [;] it is not material to us what other people's opinions are, any farther than as the knowledge of their sentiments may correct our mistakes. And the higher our station is in the world, so much the greater need have we to be curious in this particular. [. . .]

PART 2

ACTIVISM ON THREE CONTINENTS

Nineteenth to Early Twentieth Centuries

5

SEXUAL POLITICS IN ENGLAND AND INDIA
The Case of Prostitution

Ellen Rosenman

BACKGROUND: ELITE WOMEN IN VICTORIAN ENGLAND

The nineteenth century was a time of enormous change for women. At the beginning of the century, women could not attend college or enter the professions. For the most part, wives could not own property, enter into contracts, or control their own wages; nor could they keep jewelry, money, or land they had inherited. Under the legal doctrine of coverture, the husband was assumed to "cover" or protect the wife and so took charge of all economic resources (though some wealthy families drew up what we would now call prenuptial agreements to protect their wealth). Though seldom granted to anyone, divorce law explicitly privileged husbands over wives and automatically granted child custody to the father. As writers and politicians debated "the woman question"—actually a group of interrelated issues involving education, employment, marriage, and economic power— the traditional gender hierarchy increasingly seemed oppressive and unfair. Persuaded by journalists, activists, and politicians, Parliament passed legislation to close the gap between men and women, husbands and wives, throughout the century.

Beginning with Mary Wollstonecraft's famous *A Vindication of the Rights of Women* (1792), which argued forcefully for female equality, the century was one of the most dense periods of feminist thinking: Caroline Norton called for greater maternal rights over children, which eventually resulted in the first Infant's Custody Act (1839); Florence Nightingale demonstrated middle-class women's capacity for challenging work as she trained nurses and organized medical care during the Crimean War (1853–56); journalist

Frances Power Cobbe brought the issue of spousal abuse to light; and, along with his wife Harriet Taylor, intellectual and politician John Stuart Mill insisted that culture, not an innate nature, inhibited female achievement. By the end of the century, women could petition for custody of children under the age of sixteen, they could attend one of two women's colleges at Cambridge University (although they did not receive full membership equal to men's until the mid–twentieth century), they could sue for divorce on the same grounds as men, and they could attend medical school. A breed of "new women," as they were called, sprang up, deliberately repudiating traditional women's roles in areas ranging from clothing and employment to sexuality and marriage.

THE CONTAGIOUS DISEASES ACTS IN ENGLAND

One surprising, apparently local cause that became a crucible for women's activism was the treatment of prostitutes. In an effort to curb the spread of venereal disease among sailors and soldiers, the British government passed a series of laws called the Contagious Diseases Acts in 1864, 1866, and 1869 for a few specific garrison towns. These acts empowered police to arrest anyone they thought might be a "common prostitute"—a term that was never defined by law—and required surgeons to inspect them forcibly, treat them for venereal disease, and imprison them in hospitals until they were no longer infectious. Sailors, of course, were not arrested, forcibly treated, or detained. Inadvertently, these acts shone a bright light on many unsavory assumptions about gender. Casually accepting male sexual adventuring, they enshrined the double standard, and they treated prostitutes' bodies with an equally casual brutality.[1] Sparking public outrage, they shocked many elite women into activism.

The repeal campaign attacked traditional beliefs about gender and sexuality head-on. It asserted that women's sexuality was a political issue, not only because it was subject to legislation but also because it was an arena in which unequal power relations between men and women played themselves out. Arguing that sexual norms were as much a part of women's oppression as political exclusion, the repeal campaign crystallized the idea that we now call "sexual politics." Tenuously and inconsistently, it also used "woman" as an inclusive category, proposing a solidarity based on gender that transcended the powerful class distinctions of Victorian England. Though other reform efforts directed at prostitutes existed before and alongside the campaign against the Contagious Disease Acts, they tended to treat prostitutes as helpless victims in dire need of rescue and moral guidance.[2] While the repeal campaign shared some of the condescension of this rescue work, it also advanced some radical claims about the rights of prostitutes. Thus, despite its narrow agenda, it forms an important chapter in the history of feminist thought.

The Ladies National Association (LNA) was the main agent of change, led by its charismatic leader, Josephine Butler. A social purity association, the LNA insisted that men, and women should adhere to the same high sexual standards. In a dramatic stroke, it used the rhetoric of chastity to attack not only the clients whose patronage kept prostitutes in business but also the officials who enforced the Contagious Diseases Acts. Branding the forcible penetration of working-class bodies in medical examinations "instrumental rape," reformers turned the acts on their head, accusing the medical, judicial, and legal establishments of committing sexual crimes against prostitutes. Butler recognized that police and surgeons, two occupational groups that were struggling to gain prestige, were using the bodies of poor women to advance their claims to expertise and social importance. These professions, she argued, were not neutral, rational bureaucracies but rather masculinist structures that institutionalized sexism.

Butler also took the bold step of declaring that all women had what amounts to a civil right to control their own bodies: "the inalienable rights of every woman, chaste or unchaste, over her own person" (12). This claim challenged prevailing views, which considered prostitutes as either degraded creatures who had forfeited all respect or pathetic wretches in need of pity and charity. In claiming these rights for "every woman," Butler swept away distinctions based on class and replaced them with a unified category defined by gender. A devout Christian dismayed by the immorality of her society, she also framed prostitution as a *political* issue, insisting on the equality of all women under the law. While feeding the public's moral outrage with tragic tales of virtue gone wrong, Butler also repeatedly compared her repeal efforts to American and British abolitionist movements, taking reform out of the realm of private charity or moral persuasion—the celebrated female "influence" that was supposed to be more effective than any direct exercise of power—and into the political arena.

In doing so, she also redefined the role of the middle-class women who protested the Contagious Diseases Acts. Rather than present their activities as mere extensions of their private roles as mothers, wives, and moral exemplars, Butler insisted that reformers define their efforts *as* public work: they must become "political women" (158) and fight the battle "*on the lines of law and government,—on political lines*" (184, italics in original).

Butler traveled throughout Europe to muster international support for the reform of prostitution laws, especially in France. Unlike Britain, France did criminalize prostitution, creating a Morals Police led by the infamous M. Lecour, who incarcerated prostitutes in St. Lazare, a notorious prison/hospital (see Butler's opinion of these measures below). The first Congress on Public Morality, held in Geneva in 1877, resulted in part from her efforts, bringing together over five hundred representatives from the United States and Europe, and producing a manifesto that asserted many of her arguments against the double standard and government oppression of prostitutes. After decades of protest, the acts were finally repealed in 1886. The legacy of this activism was profound: these women went on to fight for the vote, and women's sexuality was affirmed as a political issue

PROSTITUTION REFORM IN INDIA

The parallel reform movement in India was both like and unlike its British counterpart, in part because of India's status as a colony and in part because of its own traditions. This example of transnational "cross-talk"—direct interaction among women of different nations addressing a common problem—reveals both the power and the limitations of transnational women's alliances. Inevitably, British models were an imperfect fit with Indian culture; while they provided inspiration and support, they were reshaped within distinctive Indian narratives about womanhood and national progress. Reform saved many prostitutes from difficult lives, but the heavy weight of British imperialism, India's colonial status, and incompletely understood cultural differences ensured that its effects would not be wholly positive.

As part of its imperial mission, Great Britain also established versions of the Contagious Diseases Acts throughout its colonies, most notably in India, which was drawn directly under British rule after a wave of resistance in 1857. Butler and the LNA were equally active in opposing government and medical treatment of prostitutes abroad. They saw Indian women as doubly oppressed, first as women and second as colonial subjects. Again, Butler insisted that she was protesting "a political and illegal tyranny" (qtd. in Burton 150). As she did with her comments about "chaste and unchaste" women, Butler also continued to challenge distinctions within the category of "women" by claiming sisterhood with Indian prostitutes. But the imperial framework made her reform efforts problematic. Although unlike many other imperialists Butler did not consider Indian women racially inferior, she did view India as a corrupt civilization and Hinduism as a heathen religion. She shared the attitude noted in chapter 8 in this anthology that the "innocent subject, the Indian Woman," required British protection. Though Christianity's superiority made the immorality of the Contagious Diseases Acts that much more shameful in Butler's eyes, it also vested moral power in the West. In fact, reform work, which was concentrated in India (though Butler and most LNA workers never visited the country), benefited the reformers as much as prostitutes. Even as they critiqued empire, they were able to represent themselves as its supporters, seeking only to strengthen and stabilize it by placing it on firmer moral ground (Burton 17). Intervening in this colonial setting, women displayed their commitment to British interests, a point that suffragists were quick to make when they demanded the vote.

These reform activities also influenced Indian activism. Even from afar, Butler's charismatic aura and prolific publications attracted the attention of Indian women. The future legislator and suffragist Muthulakshmi Reddy joined forces with British social reform efforts, expressing her "love and gratitude for those of my Western sisters who have made our cause their own, have devoted themselves whole-heartedly to the regeneration of the Indian people" (232). A proponent of social purity like Butler, Reddy insisted that men and women should be held to equally high sexual standards and blamed male self-indulgence rather than female promiscuity for prostitution (see chapter 8 for further discussion of the attack on the sexual double standard by Indian women). Despite their shared commitment to social purity, though, Butler and Reddy operated in different national contexts. In India this movement embarked on a large-scale rethinking of marriage that made prostitution an even more dangerous practice, one that threatened not only individual men but also the institution of marriage itself. Traditionally, arranged marriages united high-caste men and women for the economic benefit of the families, sometimes when wives were mere children. In these marriages, women had little power, while men not only ruled over domestic life but were free to seek out sexual pleasure elsewhere. Critiquing these unions as degrading to wives, reformers promoted companionate marriages—that is, marriages motivated by the desire for a life-companion, based on affection and respect. Such marriages also appealed to nationalists fighting for an independent India, who saw them as part of the road to modernity, bringing Indian customs in line with those of the West while giving Indian womanhood the respect it deserved. Spreading far beyond the Contagious Diseases Acts, the fight against prostitution became part of a much larger agenda of gender reform. Reddy's crusade embraced not only the eradication of prostitution but also the end of child marriage and arranged marriages, as well as better medical care and education, initiatives that undoubtedly improved the lives of many women, including prostitutes. As in England, this activism trained many of the women who joined the suffrage movement.

In the case of the Hindu temple dancers called *devadasis*, however, the complicated contexts of imperial rule, Indian tradition, and Indian reform movements proved destructive, even fatal.[3] In accordance with ancient Hindu tradition, *devadasis* were pledged to the gods, dedicated to temples where they danced, sang, and recited poetry. Because of their religious role, they could not marry, but they frequently entered into liaisons with elite men. Consorting with a *devadasi* was a mark of status, even for a married man; insulting or molesting one was a ritual offense. Supported by their temple, these women were exempted from the property laws that disempowered Indian wives (as such laws did in England) and so enjoyed an unusual degree of economic autonomy. Thus, they joined spirituality, art, sexuality, economic privilege, and social status in a way that was unfathomable to the British. The colonial authorities quickly rewrote them as common prostitutes, making them targets of anti-prostitution legislation. At the same time, Indian activists argued that the custom of *devadasi* devalued Hindu womanhood. Indian reform movements, especially Reddy's social purity campaign, singled out the "*devadasi* problem" as a moral scourge and a roadblock to national progress (Reddy 56). Thus, in the name of morality and modernity, British and Indian reformers converged on the *devadasis*, stigmatizing the role and stripping women of their status, autonomy, and economic privilege. In fact, scholars have argued that it was "the apparent independence and success of these women," as much as their sexual freedom, that concerned reformers, who "attempted to 'normalize' them" by disempowering them (Forbes 182). Though *devadasis* attempted to organize in order to maintain their rights, they did not succeed; by 1947, temple affiliations were declared illegal and *devadasis* were officially classified as prostitutes.

As a transnational movement, prostitution reform created close ties between British and Indian women, nurturing a generation of activists in both countries who refused to leave the public stage. No longer could women be told that their delicate natures required seclusion in the private sphere—or at least, when they were told, they had ample evidence to the contrary. The very fact that they concerned themselves with prostitution—walking city streets, visiting brothels, debating the consequences of illicit sexual acts—exploded that stereotype. One can imagine the shared excitement of these women who, despite their different nationalities and positions, broke through the barrier of modesty and silence to take up such a scandalous cause. But their desire to end exploitation, undermine the double standard, and improve the lot of poor women was also refracted through the different contexts in which they worked. In particular, India's status as a colonial possession made gender activism a high-stakes game, one in which Western standards defined "reform." While gains made in women's education and social status represented genuine progress, the fate of the *devadasi* remains a stubborn reminder that "reform" is not necessarily a common good but serves particular interests and that "feminist thought" unfolds within particular contexts and constraints.

The two selections here represent different approaches to prostitution reform. The first is a section of Josephine Butler's *Personal Reminiscences of a Great Crusade*, which spells out her political argument against the Contagious Diseases Acts. The second is several chapters from Muvalur Ramamirthammal's *Web of Deceit (Dasigal Mosavalei)*. Forced to become a *devadasi* by her family for economic reasons, Ramamirthammal developed a forceful analysis of the tradition as degrading to women and became a public advocate for its abolition. *Web of Deceit* is a rare novel-length text by a woman at this time. Though it clearly opposes the role of *devadasi*, it is also noteworthy for giving *devadasi* characters a voice.

NOTES

1. It is interesting to note that, although prostitutes were harassed under vagrancy laws, prostitution was not criminalized in England because it was thought to be a necessary if unfortunate outlet for male sexual needs.

2. In reality, historian Judith Walkowitz argues, prostitution was a reasonable economic choice for urban working-class women, resembling "a trade largely organized by women" that gave rise to a "strong female subculture" (25).

3. Thanks to Lucinda Ramberg for her assistance on this section of the essay.

WORKS CITED

Burton, Antoinette. *Burdens of History: British Feminists, Indian Women, and Imperial Culture, 1865–1915*. Chapel Hill: University of North Carolina Press, 1994.

Butler, Josephine E. *Personal Reminiscences of a Great Crusade*. London: Horace Marshall & Son, 1911; rpt. Westport, CT: Hyperion Press, 1976.

Forbes, Geraldine. *Women in Modern India*. Cambridge: Cambridge University Press, 1996.

Ramamirthammal, Muvalur. *Web of Deceit: Devadasi Reform in Colonial India*. Edited by Kalpana Kannabiran and Vasanth Kannabiran. New Delhi: Kali for Women, 2003.

Reddy, Muthulakshmi. *My Experience as a Legislator*. Madras: Current Thought Press, 1930.

Walkowitz, Judith. *Prostitution and Victorian Society: Women, Class, and the State*. Cambridge: Cambridge University Press, 1980.

DISCUSSION QUESTIONS

1. Compare the treatments of women's sexuality by Butler and Ramamirthammal. What is gained by considering women's sexuality under the framework of political equality, as Butler does, as opposed to the more moral, interpersonal, character-based ideas such as chastity employed by Ramamirthammal? What is gained by Ramamirthammal's approach?

2. How do Butler and Ramamirthammal portray men and male sexuality? What kinds of power do men have? Are there ways in which, in spite of men's obvious authority, women have power over them?

3. Does the idea of "social purity"—that men and women should be sexually active only in marriage—seem relevant today? Is it still an idea that can be used in the service of a feminist agenda?

4. Do these two vignettes by Ramamirthammal add up to a stable point of view about the *devadasis* and women's sexuality, or do you see important differences between them? Can you tell where the author stands from the interactions and conversations among characters?

JOSEPHINE BUTLER, FROM *PERSONAL REMINISCENCES OF A GREAT CRUSADE*

Many persons, honestly judging the matter from the outside, have mistakenly imagined that the persecution which had to be endured, the ridicule by which we were constantly assailed in the Press, the social ostracism, the coldness of many who had before been friends and companions, the obloquy, false accusations, abuse and violence, continued for years, must have been the greatest of the trials incident to the part we were called to take in so dreadful an enterprise. So far as my own experience bears witness, those who judge so are mistaken. These things were for me light and easy to bear in comparison with the deep and silent sorrow, the bitterness of soul of the years which preceded. I recall those years of painful thinking, and of questionings which seemed to receive no answer and to be susceptible of no solution; those years in which I saw this great social iniquity (based on the shameful inequality of judgment concerning sexual sin in man and woman)

SOURCE: Josephine E. Butler, *Personal Reminiscences of a Great Crusade* (London: Horace Marshall and Son, 1911; rpt. Westport, CT: Hyperion Press, 1976), 4–12, 78–80.

devastating the world, contentedly acquiesced in, no great revolt proclaimed against it, a dead silence reigning concerning it, a voice feebly raised perhaps now and again, but quickly rebuked and silenced. The call to action, the field of battle entered, with all its perils and trials clearly set out before us, were a joyful relief, a place of free breathing, compared with the oppression and the heart-woe which went before.

Those alone who have trod the silent and secret "way of Calvary" will fully understand me. Those who have not may well think the discipline of being traduced, slandered, threatened, and "spitefully entreated" a very hard discipline. But one who has endured the deeper and keener spiritual discipline, when there seemed no escape, no ray of hope, must regard the outward persecution and violence only as a welcome sign that the battle is set in array, and that the enemy is roused to bitterest hatred because his claims are disputed and his sovereignty is about to be overthrown. The inward sorrow I believe to have been necessary for the vitalising of righteous action, and the insuring of depth, reality and constancy.

On the 1st January, 1870, was published the famous Women's Protest, as follows:

We, the undersigned, enter our solemn protest against these Acts.

1st.—Because, involving as they do such a momentous change in the legal safeguards hitherto enjoyed by women in common with men, they have been passed, not only without the knowledge of the country, but unknown, in a great measure, to Parliament itself; and we hold that neither the Representatives of the People, nor the Press, fulfil the duties which are expected of them, when they allow such legislation to take place without the fullest discussion.

2nd.—Because, so far as women are concerned, they remove every guarantee of personal security which the law has established and held sacred, and put their reputation, their freedom, and their persons absolutely in the power of the police.

3rd.—Because the law is bound, in any country professing to give civil liberty to its subjects, to define clearly an offence which it punishes.

4th.—Because it is unjust to punish the sex who are the victims of a vice, and leave unpunished the sex who are the main cause, both of the vice and its dreaded consequences; and we consider that liability to arrest, forced medical treatment, and (where this is resisted) imprisonment with hard labour, to which these Acts subject women, are punishments of the most degrading kind.

5th.—Because, by such a system, the path of evil is made more easy to our sons, and to the whole of the youth of England; inasmuch as a moral restraint is withdrawn the moment the State recognises, and provides convenience for, the practice of a vice which it thereby declares to be necessary and venial.

6th.—Because these measures are cruel to the women who come under their action—violating the feelings of those whose sense of shame is not wholly lost, and further brutalising even the most abandoned.

7th.—Because the disease which these Acts seek to remove has never been removed by any such legislation. The advocates of the system have utterly failed to show, by statistics or otherwise, that these regulations have in any case, after several years' trial, and when applied to one sex only, diminished disease, reclaimed the fallen, or improved the general morality of the country. We have, on the contrary, the strongest evidence to show that in Paris and other Continental cities where women have long been outraged by this system, the public health and morals are worse than at home.

8th.—Because the conditions of this disease, in the first instance, are moral, not physical. The moral evil through which the disease makes its way separates the case entirely from that of the plague, or other scourges, which have been placed under police control or sanitary care. We hold that we are bound, before rushing into experiments of legalising a revolting vice, to try to deal with the *causes* of the evil, and we dare to believe that with wiser teaching and more capable legislation, those causes would not be beyond control.

This Protest was published in the *Daily News,* and the fact of its appearance was flashed by telegram to the remotest parts of the Kingdom. The local press largely reproduced it. Among the two thousand signatures which it obtained in a short time there were those of Florence Nightingale, Harriet Martineau, Mary Carpenter, the sisters and other relatives of the late Mr. John Bright, all the leading ladies of the Society of Friends, and many well-known in the literary and philanthropic world.

A pause ensued, a silence on the part of our opponents and undecided or critical lookers on, induced by the first shock of this unexpected and powerful manifesto. A member of Parliament, fully sympathetic with us, said to me: "Your manifesto has shaken us very badly in the House of Commons; a leading man in the House remarked to me, 'We know how to manage any other opposition in the House or in the country, but this is very awkward for us—this revolt of the women. It is quite a new thing; what are we to do with such an opposition as this?'"

But this temporary pause was succeeded by signs of much agitation and business among our opponents in preparation for an organised stand against our attitude and claims; and simultaneously was inaugurated the great "Conspiracy of Silence" in the press, which continued unbroken until the autumn of 1874, when a well-known Ex–Cabinet Minister spoke powerfully at a public meeting on our behalf. After this one occasion, however, the press, as if by common consent, fell back into its old attitude of silence. This silence could not be in most cases attributed to a regard for the feelings of readers, for statements in favour of the Acts were continually admitted. We had, however, great encouragement from many and often unexpected parts of the world.

Many persons on the Continent, working for social reforms, were even then rejoicing in the trumpet-blast which had been sounded from England, in open opposition to this vicious system. We had inaugurated a line of action to the continuance of which we were pledged by sacred duty in regard to the hopes which it had awakened throughout Europe.

Amongst the reforms which, it was hoped, would be aided by the present agitation was one connected with the army, in the substitution of some better system of national defence than that of a military army of celibates, kept as a distinct class, and demoralized by unnatural provisions, supposed to be needful for their exceptional existence.

The purification of the medical profession was also hoped for, and the exposure and defeat of those deadly materialist doctrines respecting the necessity of unchastity, which had been secretly and widely promulgated, and which, together with the dogmatism and despotism of certain doctors, had begun to exercise so fatal an influence over our legislative counsels. The condition of the womanhood of our country for some time past we often compared with that of the afflicted woman of whom we read in the Gospels, of whom it was said, "She had endured many things of many physicians," and that she grew no better, but rather worse. The afflicted woman alluded to, approaching the person of the great Spiritual Physician, was healed by the touch of faith. A similar faith was coming to the succour of the womanhood of the present day. Their hearts were lifted up to God, with whom are the issues of life and death, and they were taught to scorn the perversions of physicians who, in the supposed interests of the body, trampled under foot the claims of decency and the inalienable rights of every woman, chaste or unchaste, over her own person. God would henceforth, we trusted, place His gifts of healing in holy hands, and say to the poor afflicted womanhood of this day, "Daughter, be of good cheer."

The purification we hoped for was already indicated by the fact that, among the men who gradually rallied around us in this cause, from all ranks and all professions, pure-hearted physicians were among the foremost, both in action and in indignant denunciation of the theories and practices which we abhorred. [. . .]

There was a whole world of misery contained within the walls of the St. Lazare. As I reached the stone portico leading out of the street to the large gates of the prison, a huge prison-van rolled in under the arch, drawn by stout horses with clattering hoofs, and followed by *gens-d'armes,* also on stout horses, and armed. The van was on high wheels, and had apparently no window at all; strongly secured, and dismal to look at, like an immense hearse. People fell back as if awed, and the great iron gates rolled open; the *cortège* rattled in, and the gates rolled back again. I tried to make my way through the gates in the wake of the prison-van, but there was no time, they closed so quickly and looked so inexorable when shut. What powerful ruffians, what dangerous, strong-sinewed criminals were they conveying with all this show of armed force into the prison? The van contained only a few poor, weak, helpless *girls,* guilty of the crime of not ministering to impurity in accordance with official rules. I could not help exclaiming to myself in my bitterness of soul: O, manly, courageous Frenchmen! ever athirst for "glory," how well it looks to see you exercising your brave military spirit against the womanhood of your own country! You cannot govern your own passions, but you can at least govern by physical force the poor women of your streets, and swagger to your hearts' content in your hour of triumph, as you proudly enter the prison gates with your trembling caged linnets. But no! miserable men, you cannot even do this; you are beaten by your own women. They cannot meet you on stout horses, with helmets and military swagger and police tyranny, but they beat you with other and more deadly weapons.

We speak much of women, under the vicious system we oppose, being the slaves of men, and we realise all the tyranny and oppression which has reduced women to so abject a state; but when I went to Paris I began to see the picture reversed in a strange and awful way, and to understand how the men who had rivetted the slavery of women for such degrading ends had become, in a generation or two, themselves the greater slaves; not only the slaves of their own enfeebled and corrupted natures, but of the women whom they have maddened, hardened, and stamped under foot. Bowing down before the unrestrained dictates of their own lusts, they now bow down also before the tortured and fiendish womanhood which *they have created*. Till now I had never fully realised Nemesis in this form. The degenerates of to-day plot and plan and scheme in vain for their own physical safety. Possessed at times with a sort of stampede of terror, they rush to International Congresses, and forge together more chains for the dreaded wild beast they have so carefully trained, and in their pitiful panic build up fresh barricades between themselves and that womanhood, the *femme vengeresse*, which they proclaim to be a "permanent source of sanitary danger." M. Lecour, in his last book which he gave me, appeared to regard every woman who is not under the immediate rule of some man as he would a volcano ready to burst forth under his feet; his terror had driven him to contrive a scheme by which all the single women of Paris, the virtuous as well as vicious, shall be netted by the police and held fast!

When a man abuses the good gifts of nature to brutalise himself by excess in wine, that passive agent, in itself unconscious and incapable of motive for good or evil, becomes to him a fiery scourge, his tyrant, and he its slave; "in the end it biteth like a serpent." Much more, and in a far more awful sense, does abused womanhood become the fiery scourge, the torment, and the tyrant of the men who systematically outrage, in her, God's best gift. Just so far as the soul of a woman is above all inanimate things which are susceptible of abuse, so far is the punishment of the man who outrages it increased. It is true he does not become the slave of the woman, but merely of the *female*. Yet, inasmuch as she is not a mere inanimate thing, like intoxicating drink, nor a mere animal, but is endowed with intellect, affections, will, responsibility, an immortal spirit, and inasmuch as men have turned *all this to poison*, so is the vengeance suffered by those men in exact proportion. The men who are guilty of the deliberate and calculating crime of organising and regulating the ruin of women prepare for themselves an enslavement, an overmastering terror and tyranny, compared with which the miseries and enslavements brought about by other vices, terrible as these are, are but as the foreshadowing of a reality. Already they cringe, the abject slaves of the tyrant they have created; they are ruled, cajoled, outwitted, mocked and scourged by her. They rave at and curse her, as a wretched dipsomaniac curses his intoxicating drink, madly grasping it all the time, and in the end she slays them.

MUVALUR RAMAMIRTHAMMAL, FROM *WEB OF DECEIT*

The Minor's Infatuation

Kamalapuram Kantha and Ganavathi, the daughters of Boga Chinthamani, were famous singers whose concerts were in great demand. They had learnt music from the Mysore Vidwan for a fee of Rs 5000. Noblemen flocked to their doors in carriages and cars filling the dasis[1] next door with great envy. One day they received a telegram and Boga Chinthamani sent her son, Karunakaran, off to Vakil Sundaram's house asking him to come and read the telegram out to them. Flattered by her request the lawyer asked a client to provide Karunakaran with coffee and some snacks. Translating the telegram into Tamil, he wrote it down on a sheet of glazed paper, placed it in an envelope bearing his name and gave it to Karunakaran promising to follow later. Karunakaran, flattered by the client's hospitality, was proud of being a dasi's brother and treated with such respect and courtesy.

The telegram invited Kantha and Ganavathi to perform at a concert in the Chennai Gana Sabha[2] on the 8th for a fee of seventy five rupees. Kantha, on reading this, tossed her head and said carelessly, "Mother what is this? It costs fifty rupees just to travel to Chennai. Tell them we can't go."

Boga Chinthamani retorted, "Oh you silly girl, did you learn music to earn money to build a palace? Or to deck yourself with ornaments? Even if the Gana Sabha pays a hundred rupees we won't save ten. Why do dasis learn music? It is to become famous. When you travel to other cities and perform, countless rich men and zamindars[3] will come to hear you. At least one or two will fall for your charms and fall into our net. It is their gifts that will add to our riches, not what you earn through music. Many zamindars, noblemen, professionals and businessmen come to a music concert in the Chennai Gana Sabha. If our luck holds we may have a wave of good fortune. It is good luck that has brought this telegram from the Gana Sabha. We must accept. Don't refuse." She promptly replied that they would be there on the 7th.

Boga Chinthamani's neighbour, a dasi called Chinnammal, had a daughter Kanakavalli. Chinnammal, an envious woman hearing the talk about the telegram, turned upon her daughter and said,

"Look at the telegrams coming and going in that house. Those girls earn both through conceits and through men. They grow richer each day. And you, ill-fated unlucky wretch

SOURCE: Muvalur Ramamirthammal, *Web of Deceit: Devadasi Reform in Colonial India*, eds. Kalpana Kannabiran and Vasanth Kannabiran (New Delhi: Kali for Women, 2003), 48–59, 82–84.

1. A *dasi* was a female servant or slave.
2. The Chennai Gana Sabha was a music society.
3. *Zamindars* are landlords.

cannot earn even a rupee a day. Here I am spending money on your disease and ill health. You cursed donkey! Look at the rich men queuing up at their door! No one even asks about you. Why didn't the god who gave you beauty also give you some luck? You are so dull. Who will turn to look at a dasi girl who has no charms? Foul faced crone why do you stand in front of me?"

Kanakavalli's eyes filled with tears. She turned silently to her bed and lay down thinking, 'Although I earn so much in spite of my ill health how I suffer. What life is this! What an existence! It is better to be born in a poverty-stricken home than as a girl in a dasi family. In a poor home even if there is suffering there is still some time to speak together as man and wife. God! Why was I born in a wretched shameless caste such as this? Is there really a god? If there was a god would he not punish wretches like this? What caste is this where there is not even a mustard seed of kindness, patience, love, or consideration for a daughter? While I suffer, her eyes turn towards the neighbour and she curses me. How low is her character? However ugly a rich dasi may be, rich men will flock to her daughter. However beautiful a poor dasi may be, rich men do not visit her. And in spite of knowing this truth she made me a dasi and now complains. It is better to commit suicide than to continue life like this. They say that suicide will send you to hell. But can hell be worse than this hellish torture of a dasi's life? If I run away then the caste elders will accuse me of eloping with a lover. I can invite any number of men into my home, but I cannot leave my house with one man. And this caste is praised so highly in the Puranas.[4] If there is a god then I pray that the author of these Puranas should be born in a dasi family in his next life. Oh, why was I born in this caste? If at least I had no beauty then I could have married one man and lived in comfort! Oh god! If you have any mercy then create the women in this caste without any beauty or intelligence. Make women with beauty and brains in other castes. Or else girls like me will say that there is no god. If anyone thinks this is sinful then he is an ignorant man and lacks intelligence. How can I believe in a god who does not punish such cruel sinners?' She lay there, her eyes brimming with tears.

Boga Chinthamani's house was bustling with activity. She asked Karunakaran to prepare for the journey to Chennai and to pack bedding, baggage and thamburas. She organized everything. She yelled at Karunakaran,

"Go fetch a cart to go to the station. Why do you stand there like a tree? Do you have to be told each and every thing? Don't you know what has to be done for a trip out of town?"

Karunakaran brought a cart, hastily loaded all the luggage into it and left for the station. Later Boga Chinthamani, Kantha and Ganavathi reached the railway station. She gave Karunakaran some money and told him to buy two first class and two third class tickets to Chennai. Kantha said, "Why Mother, we can all travel together in the third class." Her mother impatient at her lack of common sense said, "Kantha, you don't know

4. The Puranas are ancient Hindu texts in Sanskrit.

the secrets of the profession. Do you think I asked for first class tickets out of luxury? Zamindars, Minors[5] and noblemen travel first class. If you travel first class then they will notice you and start visiting us. If anyone asks you for your addresses, ask them whether they want to arrange a concert for a family wedding. That will convince them that you have no desire for men but live only by your music. Why do I say this? The times are bad. They say that dasis are deceitful. If you say that you are musicians not dasis, then they will not think ill of you. If they ask if you have a man then say that your voice will be spoilt for the practice of your music. Say you are waiting to find a man who is worthy and whose love is true. Say this smoothly and diplomatically." As she was advising Kantha, Karunakaran arrived with the tickets. He asked his mother whether he could call a porter as there was a lot of luggage. "You lout! Where is the anna to pay the porter? When you are there why this needless expense? There is still time. Take it to the train in two trips." Karunakaran couldn't say anything and obeyed her.

The train steamed in and Kantha and Ganavathi entered the first class compartment elegantly. In the first class compartment was seated a handsome well built youth, clad in rich clothes and ornaments, wearing a watch worth three hundred rupees and a cigarette dangling from his lips. He sat up, bolt upright on beholding the girls. His mind began to race madly without even a moment's calm. His eyes began to roll. All kinds of thoughts flooded his mind: 'They must be dasis. No I am wrong. [B]rahmin girls these days are playing all kinds of instruments and they even perform at concerts. So they must be brahmins. No! No! if they are then where are their men? The men would be in this compartment, so they must be dasis.' Being a Minor, his mind worked in strange ways and seeing the two girls he wanted to embrace both Kantha and Ganavathi at the same time! 'Tcha! that is not proper. They might think I am a lunatic. If I manage to speak a few words to them then I can take it from there.' Noticing his plight Ganavathi, glancing at the Minor, said to her sister, "I wonder when this train reaches the City." Seizing the opportunity he said, "This train reaches Ezhumbur at 6.00 a.m. Where do you ladies come from? I feel I have seen you before. Please do not mistake me."

The sisters realising quickly that he was a wealthy Minor and that to enter into a conversation would be profitable said, "We are from Thanjavur. We are going to Chennai to sing at a concert. You must have seen us in many places. How can Minors remember people whom they have seen just once? How can you remember us? We wondered why although you knew us you did not speak to us. And so we were also quiet." This was Kantha. The Minor was thrilled.

"Oh so you are from Thanjavur. You must have seen me often. I visit lower street Kanakambujam's house often. Even an hour before leaving for the station, I sent her a sari worth two hundred rupees with her brother Govindaswami and other things worth a hundred rupees. I am also going to the January festival in Chennai." And he began to brag

5. *Minors* in this context are young unmarried men.

about his feats by the dozen. Listening to him Kantha and Ganavathi realized he was a dullard. Kantha gave him a teasing look, "Aren't you the person who performed the santhi muhurtham[6] for Thanjavur Bagyathammal's daughter Tripura Sundari?" she asked.

On hearing the word santhi the Minor felt wildly possessed and his head began to spin at great speed. He was delighted that he had made their acquaintance. If they already knew so much about him they must have great love and desire for him. He felt that he must bring them into his clutches somehow. "What! You know Tripura Sundari? How is it you know so much about me? I performed Tripura Sundari's santhi. I spent five thousand on her santhi, I gave her a diamond set worth ten thousand rupees. The other expenses came to about five thousand. All this in the space of two months." On hearing these boastful claims the two girls realized that he was a simpleton who would dance to their tune.

The train stopped at Villipuram. The Minor ordered the Spencer butler to get three glasses of iced, coloured drinks. He then asked a vendor the cost of oranges and apples. The vendor seeing a good chance said, "Sir! you asking the price? Is this the first time you are buying things from me? As if you don't know the cost!" The butler brought three glasses of coloured drinks. He gave Kantha a glass. She said, "We are not in the habit of taking these things. I drink this only to please you." He gave Ganavathi another glass, drank the other and gave back the glasses and money to the butler. The fruit vendor asked him how many dozens he wanted. He sorted out the good fruit and chose the seconds for the Minor who then asked the vendor to fetch some flowers. He then placed the flowers and fruit before them. "Why did you get all this? Why didn't you ask me? Anyway let me pay." And she pulled out a ten rupee note from her purse like one who spends freely and held it out to the vendor without stretching her elbow. "I won't take it from you. My master will be angry if I take it from you[,]" said the clever lad. So the Minor said, "How much?" "How vexatious! Why are you so formal? Is there a difference between your money and mine?" Kantha said glancing at the Minor. The Minor was happy and paid the vendor and asked him to go. Watching this performance the girls were mighty pleased to have found a real fool. The Minor wanted to make witty conversation. But what could he talk about? There had to be a subject. So he decided to say the first thing that came to mind. Looking at the tambur lying there he said, "What is that long thing there?" Kantha deciding he was crazy said, "That is a tambur." "Which district is that Uru?"[7] asked the Minor. Kantha said, "Oh, what a bother. This is not a village, it is an instrument to sing with." The Minor replied with a smile, "I was joking. I also have some knowledge of music. Can I have your address?" Ganavathi looked at her sister and pretending to be angry said, "This is a bad habit with all passengers. When the English travel they mind their own business and do not indulge in gossip. Why do you gossip needlessly, sister? You have to sing tomorrow in the concert and your voice will grow hoarse! The rail journey, sleeplessness, this needless gossip will all

6. *Santhi muhurtham*, literally, a time of bliss, signaled the consummation of a marriage.
7. *Uru* means village; the Minor is asking where Tambur is located.

exhaust you. Do not talk. Many vidwans and lords will come to listen to the concert tomorrow. Our performance must be good. What about our reputation? Can you make an excuse that you were gossiping on the train? What does he care? He is a big lord."

The Minor was amazed. He thought, 'Look at this little chit of a girl. She is talking so intelligently. The girls of this caste are truly intelligent. Only our girls are dull, unlucky wretches.' He said happily, "Why do you think I am not worth even a paisa[8] Ganavathi? Know the truth before you speak. If you knew how I came to be known as the famous Minor then you would not speak as if I was not worth a paisa. I spent one lakh of rupees[9] in the space of three months. Ask any of the *Dafar Mamas* and they will tell you of my greatness. Why do you think so cheaply of me without knowing these facts?"

Kantha indicated to her sister that this was a first class dullard and signalled that she should take his watch.

Ganavathi: "I spoke without knowing. I thought you are a woman and spoke too quickly. Please don't be offended."

"What! I, a woman? Don't you know the difference between a man and woman. And you were advising your sister. What intelligence! And you who do not even know the difference between a man and woman, I thought you very intelligent."

"Don't be offended. It is the way your hair is parted and your ladies watch which made me assume that you were a Malayali woman. If you are a man, that's okay. A wealthy man like you should wear a gold pocket watch and chain. I would not have made fun of you. It was because of your ladies wristwatch that I joked." The Minor was ashamed. He regretted his stupidity in talking to the witty Ganavathi. Then he asked her, "Why Ganavathi, if this is a lady's watch why are you not wearing one?"

Ganavathi said, "I am just an unmarried maid. How can I wear a watch unless someone like you gives me one? Do I have a husband?"

The Minor was very excited and thought, 'This girl is the size of a cluster bean and yet she is so bright. Every word is so graceful, melodious, packed with meaning. When our girls talk it is like pouring hot melted iron ore into the ear.' And he said, "Ganavathi you seem to like this watch. Take it."

Ganavathi: "This is awful. You and I are fellow travellers on a train. When we alight we will go our different ways. Why these jokes? Haven't you heard of rail relationships? I don't want this. I will wear only my own watch. What pleasure can I get out of wearing a borrowed watch? Passengers speak of all sorts of things to while away the time. I do not want this."

The Minor was in a fix. What could he do? After boasting that he had spent a lakh of rupees in three months, if he hesitated to give her the three hundred rupee watch she would think him cheap. So he decided to gift her the watch. And he said, "Ganavathi I am giving you this watch as a reward for your intelligence. It is your own now. Stretch out your hand and let me fasten it for you."

8. A *paisa* would be roughly equal to a penny.
9. A *lakh* is a unit meaning one hundred thousand.

Ganavathi said, "What words are these? Can you touch the hand of an unmarried maid? If my mother hears do you know what my fate will be?"

The Minor said, "I did not intend anything wrong. I am used to western ways. Don't be annoyed."

Ganavathi said, "Does your western culture ask you to part with a three hundred rupee watch so foolishly? Do westerners behave like this?"

The Minor: "What, you have called me a fool! Is it foolish to reward someone for intelligence?"

Ganavathi: "I am only a young girl. I thought only foolish people are given the title of Minor. Don't be angry. I will not cut any more jokes."

Minor: "Even if you call me a fool twice over I do not mind. What does it matter what one hears from the lips of one who is intelligent? You speak with such affection for me it matters little what words you choose. I must have performed good deeds to deserve those loving words from your lips. . . . Would you open your mouth in front of a miser even if he owned crores?[10] After all you are speaking to me because I spend in lakhs. Am I a foolish fellow? Don't think I am like others. If ten people run around me every day I might feed them but I will not part with a single paisa. I do not object to your jokes."

Ganavathi, sarcastically: "Feeding ten flatterers is not foolishness, it is great cleverness. How clever you must be to spend a lakh in three months! How can I describe your intelligence and greatness? It is really something."

Minor: "Oh you are already using the familiar thou. You are very bold. You are an amusing girl. I have spoken with many dasis in fun but never have I come across anyone as humorous as you. I am happy with your words. The more you talk the more I enjoy it."

Ganavathi: "What is this sir, you are imagining all kinds of things when I speak of ordinary things. Don't address me and I will not speak to you any more." She then looked at her sister and said, "This is like that story of the foolish king." And proceeded to tell the story.

Dasis usually make fun of the gentlemen who visit their houses. But the gentlemen seldom feel insulted and are so excited that as the ridicule grows they sit there smiling. Even the most intelligent, wealthy, well born gentlemen perform tasks for dasis which ordinary people would find distasteful. These same rich men get angry if their wives talk to them about family matters. They even demonstrate their bravery by using abuse and a stick.

"You wretched slave! Don't I know! You presume to advise me. Do you know how I am respected? Don't you know that I was invited to the Governor's tea party? Do you know how much respect I received? Did they think I was a fool? I should have married a donkey instead of you. I feel disgraced if I look upon your face. Go to your mother's house and I will send you money every month for your maintenance." And so on. The

10. *Crores* are tens of millions (here, of rupees).

same men will put up with anything from dasis. So it is no matter for surprise that Gana-vathi spoke so contemptuously to the Minor or that he listened so quietly.

Soon they neared Chennai.

The Minor realized he had not got their address and he said, "What is this Ganavathi, you have not given me your address and particulars."

Ganavathi then said, "Sir, along with the address when you say particulars what does that mean?"

The Minor said, "Are you making fun of me? I need your address but I also need to know if both of you have any men and then I can be at peace."

Ganavathi: "So you want to know. All right. Who will believe a dasi who speaks the truth? Even if she spends her life with a single man people will think she is a dasi and has many men. Who will believe my words? Forget it."

Minor: "Are there no good women among dasis?"

Ganavathi: "There is a Vellalar from Mayavaram district who visits my sister. He is a very quiet person. He treats my sister with dignity. She will not even look at another man. As for me I am not married yet."

The Minor then thought, 'I had wanted to fix up both Kantha and Ganavathi. Now she says Kantha will not consider another man. Let us see to that later. She is so careless of me when I spend in lakhs. If only I had spent that money on these good women they would have taken care of me till my very end. Now what am I to do? I was deceived. Let me not cry over spilt milk. If I marry Ganavathi then I will become the head of their household. Then I can get rid of the Vellalar who visits Kantha and enjoy both of them myself.'

With these thoughts the Minor said, "Ganavathi, these slaves who are prostitutes have no gratitude however much you spend on them. I understand that you are good women. I have seen many dasis but never have I seen a woman with such faith. I implore you to have faith in me and do not forget me. I will sell my remaining property, send my wife to her maternal home and come and live in your house. You can protect me or punish me."

Ganavathi pretended to be shocked and said, "Don't use such terrible words. Mother might hear. So many gentlemen are willing to marry me and have offered me ten and twenty thousand. We have not replied because it would harm my music. Please don't talk like this. Even this light conversation till we alight will have to stop." The Minor was surprised. 'Can dasis even be like this? They offered to pay for the fruit and soda in Vil-lipuram. I promised to give them a three hundred rupee watch and there is no mention of it. They have no desire for material things.'

And he said, "Ganavathi, take this watch."

"No, no, if you will take the money from me then I will accept it. We are not like other dasis who grab what they can get and deceive. We live by our music. Do not think we are like other dasis," said Ganavathi.

This caste can act like great saints when they are certain that the goods will not slip out of their hands. If they see them slipping then they start talking humorously and seize hold of the goods. These dasis can size up a man's character and his aim at first sight. The men who go to dasis prefer them to stroke their thighs and snatch the gift from them rather than to give it to them outright. Then they come out and boast to their friends,

"What is this, whatever it is they accept it with such pleasure. When we carry sweetmeats home to our wives, they turn their faces and march off. Who will feel like buying anything for such crones? Once Dasi Sornam took my watch, earrings, ring and shoes and wore them and came out. Those girls don't feel any awkwardness. I was so delighted that I asked her to keep them and wear them for me whenever I visited her. Till today she does this. So tell me, is the woman who heeds your words the one who loves you passionately or is it the one who ignores you? Will the women in our households do all this for us?"

This is the kind of stuff they blabber. They little realize that these women dance to their tune to acquire their wealth. Love is blind and the Minor was blind to Ganavathi's character.

He said[,] "Ay! Ganavathi! Don't mistake me. If you want my favour take this."

The mother in the servant compartment was listening attentively. The Minor is a lord only for three months. This watch has not yet been grabbed by either of the girls. It is destined to come to us. If the girls take the watch then this fellow will follow us and strut around. And the rich men at the concert will think we have brought a man with us thus ruining our professional chances.

So Boga Chinthamani spoke very meaningfully, "What is this little sister? I have been silent all this while. Brother seems a very good man. Why do you make fun of him? He probably has only this watch left. He is sure to have expenses in Chennai. What will he do? Don't take the watch."

Ganavathi understood her mother's message and turned to the Minor and said, "Did you hear my mother scold me? I told you in the very beginning that we do not deceive to live. Will another dasi refuse a three hundred rupee watch? Although we were born into that evil caste we can never have the heart to cheat anyone." The Minor's faith grew greater. "Ganavathi, I implore you don't be so careless of my request. If you want my favour take this watch without your mother's knowledge." He forced her to take it.

Ganavathi said, "All right, I don't want to refuse you. I will give you a favour sometime. Give it to me without my mother's knowledge." And she took it. The Minor was happy that after so much uncertainty he had at last achieved his desire. Then he began to write the address with his fountain pen.

Ganavathi then said, "I will give you the Chennai address, come there and we can discuss everything." She then gave him the wrong address and said it was on Thangasalai street. The Minor touched the paper with the address to his eyes reverently and put it away carefully. It was six in the morning and the train steamed into Ezhumbur station. They hired a car and four of them set off. The Minor asked if he could join them in the car. But Ganavathi said there was no room and the car left.

The Minor felt humiliated and thought, 'What a mistake to ask if I can go with them! After all I have the address and I could go there in a separate car. What a mistake.'

The Minor who had spent the whole night conversing with both the girls found it unbearable to be alone. 'What beauty! What sweet words! I didn't even know it was dawn. Her beauty is still fresh in my mind.' The Minor was in a daze. A porter thinking he was mad went up to him and asked if he wanted a coolie. The Minor asked him to get lost. Finally he had to carry his own baggage and kept looking around in case Ganavathi came back looking for him. He hastily completed his ablutions, refreshed himself, hired a car and set off to the address Ganavathi had given him.

The Craze for Jewels and the Cure

Unable to bear the disgrace of having beaten up the innocent Somasekaran the man called his wife and said, "I beat up a good man because of you. When 'other' women desire modern clothes and ornaments they are bound to get a bad reputation. Do you realize the effects of neglecting natural beauty and turning instead to artificial beauty aids? Because you decked yourself so grandly and stood at the door, I beat up a stranger. If this news spreads is it not bad for our reputation? If your dressing up was decent then these problems would not arise. If I say anything you get angry immediately."

The wife replied, "I agree I should not be angry at your words. My only sin was in marrying you, who cannot bear to see me dressed beautifully. Women like me are dressed in saris worth three hundred and four hundred rupees and although I wear only saris worth ten rupees you speak to me like this. If I were like other women then I would be impossible to control. There are many women who deck themselves with jewels and rich clothes and travel from place to place visiting temple fairs and festivals without the permission of their husbands. And their husbands are happy listening to the stories they tell of their travels and the sights they have seen. That is their good fortune. This is mine. It is my fate that I suffer like this. If some fellow asks whether this is a dasi's house you behave as if the roof has fallen. Men never speak like this to women who are wearing expensive lotus necklaces and earrings. I don't know why even these few jewels irritate your eyes. My father brought me up affectionately and gave me to you because he did not want me to marry into a house where there was a mother-in-law or sister-in-law. And you treat me as if I am a cheap nobody. It is better for me to go far away out of sight than bear these troubles." Saying this she wept bitterly.

And her husband thought, 'It was my foolishness to believe that those who advocated education for women lacked understanding. It is her lack of education that prevents her from understanding the difference between what is good and bad!'

"Listen to me. Why is it that instead of taking to heart the conduct of good women you only look at women who are ignorant? After all, the whole world believes that a dasi practices prostitution and is bad in character. Is it not important to gain a good name? Rid your mind of those women who are dressed in silver laced silks and heavy jewellery who visit all festivals. Look at the countless women who are sensible. Do they go around wearing jewellery like beasts of burden? Like bullocks whose noses are pierced to rope them? Women pierce their noses and ears and parts of their face mutilating and ruining their faces. Then thieves cut these parts to steal the jewels. This is unbearable cruelty. Why don't you understand that these women are being treated worse than animals? Do you think that English women do not have property? Do they disfigure themselves with ornaments like the women of this country? Have you not seen families suffer intensely because they have borrowed money at high interest to buy jewellery and deck themselves? It is only when women give up this meaningless ornamentation that the poverty and backwardness of this country will go. Women will stop competing with each other to buy more and more useless ornaments. Quarrels in the family will vanish like smoke and life will become more meaningful. You cannot even carry a pot of water. You need a servant for every task. How you are able to carry such heavy jewellery is beyond me! Think deeply, observe and then decide for yourself. I have bought you jewels but let us come to a decision today. At least now let us mend our ways and live in a thrifty and careful manner. I need your help. You can keep the money from your jewellery yourself. But stop this meaningless *Vedanta*."[11]

Wife: "I can see some sense in what you say. I answered you back out of sheer habit. I realize that artificial beauty can't be compared to natural beauty. Forgive me. Because I decked myself in the manner of a dasi, a man who mistook me for one was beaten up. I am responsible for this. If matters are explained rationally then women accept the truth. A good bullock needs one branding and a good woman needs one word, they say. Here are my jewels. Sell them and invest the money for interest. But I have one question."

Man: "Ask me your question."

Woman: "You ask me not to wear any jewels but all the goddesses in temples are decked with plenty of jewels and have ceremonies and rituals." Since the man was one who had deep faith in god he could not answer this question and started thinking. He felt that if he did not answer the question she might take back the jewels she had given him. So he hastily said that all those practices must go and was very happy that his wife had given him the jewels. It is because women are beaten brutally and no one explains matters to them that they are unable to grasp the truth. Because he explained things so calmly and logically she understood his ideas and his only fault which was his blind faith in god was also removed by her. Now the couple live happily together.

---

11. *Vedanta* in this context means something like "philosophizing."

6

WOMEN'S SUFFRAGE
Transnational Connections

Ellen Rosenman, Jill Abney, and Kathi Kern

"From its inception women's struggle for the vote was explicitly global," according to scholars Louise Edwards and Mina Roces (1). It was nurtured by interconnections among women around the world who read each other's essays and manifestos, avidly followed each other's progress, borrowed each other's tactics, traveled to other nations to meet with their counterparts, and gathered in international meetings devoted to women's rights. The fight for suffrage is one of the first and most visible examples of deliberate transnational collaboration, in which women recognized the power of gender solidarity on a grand scale. It was crucial in establishing "woman" as a political category, a part of the structure of public life that could not be ignored.

At the same time, the phrase "women's suffrage" masks divisions within this overarching category and suggests a too-simple view of progressive social change and global sisterhood. Predictably, Western imperial nations were only too happy to advise women whose cultures they considered backward and uncivilized; imperialist thinking and racial prejudice often infected transnational collaboration. But the influence flowed in both directions, as some American feminists turned to India as a spiritually superior society whose example could renovate Western politics. Within nations, existing hierarchies were equally persistent. For example, social class played a critical role in the British suffrage movement, as race did in that of the United States. As we will see in many other parts of this anthology, just as the category "women" can productively draw together the shared interests and experience of many diverse people, it can also hide and thus perpetuate inequalities of power and privilege. And, despite their shared goals, suffrage movements depended on different justifications and different constructions of woman-hood. The transnational nature of women's suffrage should not imply a single banner under which women around the world marched hand in hand. Rather, global intercon-nections were complex and varied as these movements unfolded within specific national contexts.

WOMEN'S SUFFRAGE IN ENGLAND

The women's suffrage movement in England fought many long battles against the British government and conservative public opinion, and it fought many internal battles as well. From the early organized suffrage work of the 1860s to the final achievement of univer-sal adult suffrage in 1928, the movement gathered activists of many different stripes, split into different organizations, extended itself into a host of local committees, voiced an array of different justifications, and employed a variety of tactics. British suffragists par-ticipated in the International Women's Suffrage Alliance, initially headquartered in London, and eagerly volunteered their expertise to other countries, but they also found themselves at odds with their putative sisters from other nations. The story of women's suffrage in Great Britain includes both bold nonconformity and strategic compromise, radical demands and incremental change. It reveals as much about competing versions of feminism—even within a single nation—as it does about conflicts between men and women.

A brief overview of the movement is probably helpful. While not enfranchised, British women found ways to infiltrate the political sphere even before the twentieth century, participating actively in the campaign to abolish British slave trade in the early 1800s and leading the charge against the Contagious Diseases Acts of the 1860s. But while women of property could vote in municipal elections, they could not vote for members of Parlia-ment (MPs) or serve in Parliament. Unsuccessfully, radical politicians such as John Stu-art Mill introduced legislation in the 1860s, but the suffrage movement gathered momentum only when groups of elite women founded their own organizations: the moderate National Union of Women's Suffrage Societies (NUWSS), organized by Milli-cent Garrett Fawcett, and the militant Women's Suffrage Political Union (WPSU), led by Emmeline Pankhurst and her daughters Christabel and Sylvia.

Both groups had to contend with the existing qualifications for voting—not only gen-der but property ownership. In many ways, British society was strongly divided according to social class. In contrast to the American ideology of political equality for all—contra-dicted by the exclusion of white women and African Americans from the franchise but still advanced as a defining feature of the nation—Britain considered the ownership of property a sign of education and independence, prerequisites for informed voting. Thus

This section is by Ellen Rosenman and Jill Abney.

both women and non-property-owning men, who fought for inclusion in the nineteenth century, were frequently pitted against each other. Extending the male franchise was considered a more important priority by the British establishment, which feared an uprising by disgruntled working-class men but—naively, as we shall see—had no fear of violence from women.

Suffragists faced indifference, condescension, resistance, and sometimes outright brutality from men. For the most part, in the first half of the nineteenth century, women were commonly understood to be less intellectual, more emotional, and more moral than men—this last quality the happy result of their exclusion from the competitive, heartless public world. Opponents feared that political participation would compromise this purity and damage women's delicate constitutions. Moreover, under the doctrine of coverture, wives had no legal existence apart from their husbands. How, then, could they be granted a separate political voice? Though legislation throughout the century extended the rights of both single women and wives, suffrage represented perhaps the most dramatic frontier of equality. The prospect called forth an avalanche of satirical cartoons representing suffrage workers as either mannish and aggressive or absurdly unfit for serious responsibilities. The NUWSS worked diligently "within the system," using constitutional means to argue for and demonstrate women's capacity for rational public action.

However, repeated rejections by the government and a lack of public support drove more radical women to found the WSPU, which engaged in more militant tactics. Holding public demonstrations, smashing windows, throwing bricks at the prime minister's car, these women also demolished the image of womanhood as delicate and demure. But their radical actions also gave ammunition to their opponents—especially the tactic of self-harm. When Emily Davison threw herself in front of King George V's horse at the 1913 Epsom Derby, critics were horrified. If an educated woman could act like this, they asked, then what would a mass of uneducated women voters do? The suffragists' subversion of gender ideology called forth a shocking reprisal. On November 18, 1910—"Black Friday"—police assaulted women protesters, tearing at their clothes, grabbing them in sexually suggestive ways, striking them, and knocking them down. Imprisoned, several protesters went on hunger strikes and were violently force-fed, an act that suffragists likened to rape because of its physical restraint and bodily penetration.

While historians debate the impact of these events on the ultimate achievement of suffrage, generally granting the steady pressure of the more moderate NUWSS more credit for the movement's ultimate success, militancy achieved a critical end by unveiling the gender hierarchy as a site of violence as well as interdependence and protection. Male hostility was itself an argument for empowering women.

But suffrage also contended with internal tensions. Dispersed geographically and through different organizations, and adapting over time, it did not speak with a single voice. The arguments for suffrage represent two classic positions in feminist thought. One is the argument for human rights: women are entitled to the same rights as men;

since both are human, both should enjoy equal access to public forms of privilege and power. The second position claims that women deserve inclusion because of their distinctive natures: they are more moral, more sympathetic, more attuned to human suffering. This second position was already part of the history of Victorian women's activism, since it had been used to justify participation in campaigns against slavery and prostitution. This division did not map neatly onto different groups and, in fact, individuals might use both arguments at different times, depending on context and audience. Suffragists adapted the second argument into a more pragmatic assertion that is still in play in today's politics: because women are more familiar with and passionate about issues involving families and children, they can make uniquely informed contributions to public policy in these areas.

Questions of strategy and emphasis were more divisive. The conflict between the constitutional tactics of the NUWSS and the militancy of the WSPU split the movement into warring camps. Constitutional feminists deplored the militants for alienating the public, while the militants were exasperated by the conservatism of their counterparts. This conflict represents a question that faces any group advocating for significant change: is it better to work within existing structures or attack them? In Cristina Alcalde's essay in this anthology "Mothers, Guerrillas, and Revolutionaries," we see Latin American activists confronting the same choices: is violence an acceptable way of working toward a more fair and peaceful world? Can a group use violence without weakening the ethical foundation of its opposition? Does women's willingness to commit acts of aggression level the playing field, so to speak, or constitute a refusal to be victimized by the violence of others? While the brutal oppression in Peru, detailed in Alcalde's essay, makes these questions especially pressing in that context, they also preoccupied British activists, who struggled with their ethical and strategic implications.

The issue of sexuality also divided the movement. Many of its earliest members had been active in prostitution reform, which laid an important foundation for future activism: it identified politics as an appropriate arena for women's action; it insisted on women's bodily "self-ownership," which could extend logically to the concept of citizenship; and it designated sexuality as a political issue (see Rosenman, "Sexual Politics in England and India," in this anthology). But, concerned about their image and the ease with which the press could discredit them, not all suffragists wanted sexuality on the agenda—including Fawcett, who had been a supporter of Josephine Butler's reform efforts, albeit a quiet one. Again, women confronted the question of whether to move ahead by direct confrontation or by relatively unthreatening persuasion—though it would be a mistake to underestimate the challenge to the status quo posed by this more moderate wing.

The movement was further divided over thorny ethical issues. One was the question of what exactly it should demand. Should it insist on adult suffrage—that is, the vote for everyone—or equal suffrage—that is, suffrage for women who met the same property qualifications as voting men? Many women, including Fawcett and the NUWSS, supported the more modest demand for equal suffrage, and not only because it was more likely to be accepted. Class prejudice played a part in their position: elite women felt themselves more qualified to vote than working-class men, many of whom had been enfranchised by the Reform Acts of 1867 and 1884. Why should they not have the same rights as "'a rabble of illiterates," asked Frances Power Cobbe, a journalist and one of the more conservative members of the movement (qtd. in Levine 61). This line of argument sought to regroup elite women with elite men by virtue of their shared cultural capital and economic privilege, creating an affiliation based on class rather than a division based on gender.

As World War I erupted, the issue of war also split suffragists. A strong internationalist, socialist component supported an ambitious agenda that, today, seems both conservative and radical: arguing that male aggression and territoriality were destroying society, they promoted pacifism and international cooperation, seeing female suffrage as a step toward creating a more just, peaceful world. Their assumptions about gender were stereotypical, but they sought transformative change. But others were staunch nationalists who identified pacifism with treason—including the influential Fawcett, who broke with the International Women's Suffrage Alliance because it supported negotiation with Germany, Britain's enemy. These suffragists were Britons first, withdrawing from a fragile international community of pacifist women. This stance was probably crucial in securing the government's support for suffrage, granted for women over the age of thirty in 1918, when the war ended, and for all women in 1928. But the "nation first" attitude reminds us that political "progress" is actually a complex series of choices and changes. Like the issue of equal suffrage, the war required feminists to decide between different identifications. While the ideal of global sisterhood was powerful, it competed with the agenda of the national movement.

WOMEN'S SUFFRAGE IN INDIA

The women's suffrage movement in India was extremely complex—shaped, enabled, and constrained by the imperialism of Great Britain, the influence of British feminists, and the demand for Indian independence as well as the powerful voices of Indian women. India was a diverse country with regional centers of power, divided by multiple religions, especially Hinduism and Buddhism, and further divided into castes. As a British colony, officially annexed in 1857 after many decades of unofficial imperialism, India was also partially reshaped in the image of Western culture: many traditional customs were branded as barbaric, especially those involving women, sexuality, and marriage, while the practices of British society and government were promoted to "modernize" the country— though always with the ethnocentric belief that no mere colony could ever approach the

This section is by Ellen Rosenman.

high standards of Western civilization. At the same time, the western Enlightenment concept of human rights provided one powerful justification for women's suffrage, and American and especially British activists helped mobilize Indian women. This fragmented context posed considerable challenges for Indian women suffragists. As both women and colonial subjects, they were caught in an uncomfortable position of double jeopardy. They struck a delicate balance—or rather, had to strike several delicate balances at the same time—in order to capitalize on the momentum of the global women's suffrage movement and the movement for Indian independence.

The first national organization devoted to suffrage along with other women's issues was the Women's Indian Association, founded in 1917. The name itself suggests the complicated allegiances that defined the movement. "Women's" was deliberately placed before "Indian" to claim membership in an international community first and foremost. And, in fact, the organization embraced both Indian and British women. It was co-founded by Margaret Cousins, a veteran of the Pankhursts' radical suffragette movement who had come to India in search of a more spiritual, less materialistic way of life, along with other women from England and America (see the Kern essay on American women and Indian spirituality). Muthulakshmi Reddy, its vice president and the first woman to serve in an Indian legislature, and Sarajini Naidu, a prominent nationalist, were among its earliest and most active members. The group promised to achieve a powerful alliance among women of different nations, defying national boundaries and the imperial/colonial power structure of empire.

To some extent, it achieved this promise. With more extensive political experience and greater access to the British imperial government in India, British women undoubtedly contributed to Indian women's suffrage. Aruna Asaf Ali, author of the reading below, calls English suffragists "a beacon of light for women the world over" (349). But the presence of Western women was a mixed blessing. They could be condescending: Cousins felt that a backwards India would probably take one hundred years to grant women suffrage. British women identified with Indian women, but they also identified with England, however much they critiqued its patriarchal culture. Not all British women shared this belief. Annie Besant, a veteran of British suffrage and other women's rights issues who also sought a spiritual life in India, served as president of both the Women's India Association and the Indian National Conference in 1917. A radical, forthright activist who denounced "the mad dog, Imperialism," Besant had no patience for the tyrannies of the British government (qtd. in Anderson). However, many British women were suffragists but also, at least in part, imperialists, representatives of the conquering nation that imposed its values and customs on its colony in the name of progress.

For many Indian women who chafed under this assumption, nationalism was an alternative foundation for women's rights. They were patriotically invested in the future of their nation once freed from colonial rule. Furthermore, an independent India promised greater freedom for women: when the British colonial government rejected a proposal to enfranchise women, the nationalist Indian National Congress took up the cause.

For many, women's suffrage was part of the vision of a unified India and a national citizenship that transcended more specific identities of region and caste that had dominated India in the past. While the colonial government had offered limited forms of political participation to women of property, following the model of the British system, many Indian suffragists opposed anything short of complete enfranchisement. In particular, the issue of reservations—holding some legislative positions for Muslins or for women of a particular region—became a rallying point. While colonial government commissions and many British women endorsed such a plan, most Indian women's organizations rejected it as divisive and incomplete. In India, nationalist fervor trumped the strategic advantage that British suffragists embraced when they agreed to a partial franchise.

In the 1940s, the women's suffrage movement submerged itself into the nationalist movement, folding its agenda into the universal adult suffrage achieved as part of Indian independence in 1947. Indian suffragists prided themselves on having avoided the messy demonstrations of their British counterparts, attributing their peaceful achievement of the vote to their respect for the rule of law and the more egalitarian attitude of their own Indian government.

But nationalism was also a conflicted allegiance. As Pramila Venkateswaran notes in her essay in this anthology, Indian women were adopted as a symbol of Indian tradition, embodying an essence of purity, morality, and domestic devotion that did not fit well with the exercise of public activism. Indian women were victims of double jeopardy, caught in the patriarchal formulas of Indian nationalism as well as the racist assumptions of British imperialism. As Anupuma Roy explains, it was difficult for activists to "voice women afresh" (166). Often they felt compelled to work within the outlines of a stereotypical femininity. Naidu, for example, expressed her commitment to Indian politics by citing the home as "the unit of central government in India" (Pearson 212). Much like some British feminists, Naidu posited a continuity between domestic and public life, both in need of women's purifying influence. Thus Indian women were represented— and represented themselves—as incarnations of traditional Indian gender roles and as citizens of the modern nation, equal to men if not identical to them.

The selections below represent some of the different positions on women's suffrage discussed in this essay. "A Speech by Lady Constance Lytton" describes her imprisonment and force-feeding. Lytton was a member of the British aristocracy, the daughter of the viceroy of India who proclaimed Queen Victoria "Empress of India." Though this pedigree made her perhaps an unlikely member of the militant WSPU, she was able to see firsthand that, in spite of her wealth and education, she was not a citizen in the eyes of her country. "Home and Politics" is authored by Millicent Garrett Fawcett, head of the moderate NUWSS, which disapproved of dramatic tactics such as civil disobedience and hunger strikes. The third is an essay by Aruna Asaf Ali, "Women's Suffrage in India," which was published in 1938, in the midst of the Indian suffrage movement, when women were gaining the vote in regional elections. Ali (1909–96) is best known as a nationalist, a cause for which she was imprisoned several times. Tracing the history of the suffrage movement, Ali explains the logic of women's insistence on universal suffrage.

U.S. SUFFRAGE, CLARA COLBY, AND INDIA

Embedded in transnational networks of women's organizations, women's suffrage in the United States began with a distinctively American flavor. The famous 1848 Seneca Falls Convention crafted a "Declaration of Sentiments" based on the Declaration of Independence. Announcing "We hold these truths to be self-evident, that all men and women are created equal," this document insisted that the values upon which the nation was founded could not be fully realized until women gained the vote. But this apparently self-evident truth did not immediately become law. It took from 1848, the year of the conference, until 1920 for the Nineteenth Amendment to be passed. (While the Nineteenth Amendment officially removed "sex" as a barrier to voter participation, many African American women were not able to exercise their right to vote until the passage of the Voting Rights Act of 1965.) In this period, the suffrage movement was both energized and divided by many of the forces with which British suffragists also grappled. And, when American values did not seem to offer a powerful enough logic for women's citizenship, some members of the movement took a fascinating journey to India. This transnational link reverses the currents of authority we saw in the British suffrage movement, in which Western women styled themselves as experts who could civilize the heathen East. While some American suffragists such as Elizabeth Cady Stanton and Carrie Chapman Catt maintained this condescending attitude, Clara Colby turned to India as a superior civilization, one that could provide the spiritual guidance necessary for political progress.

The Seneca Falls Convention reflected the ideal of equality its participants hoped to achieve on the national scene. Some of its most prominent attendees were members of the abolitionist movement, so the convention included African Americans as well as whites; among others, it was attended by Frederick Douglass, who arranged for the printing of the Declaration of Sentiments. But the cross-racial unity did not last. In 1870, the passage of the 15th Amendment, granting the vote to black men, offended prominent feminists such as Elizabeth Cady Stanton and Susan B. Anthony, just as the Reform Acts that enfranchised working-class men angered British suffragists. Many refused to support the amendment. Some even allied themselves with white supremacists, arguing that their votes would counterbalance the insurrectionary desires of newly freed slaves. The movement became painfully split over race, with some groups turning to a state-by-state strategy to avoid the racial conflict while others continued to push for a constitutional amendment.

As in England, suffragists were also split on the issue of whether women should vote because they were men's equals or because they possessed a unique moral nature that

This section is by Kathi Kern and Ellen Rosenman.

would improve the quality of public life, a claim that complicated the decisive statement of the Declaration of Sentiments with a different construction of womanhood. Again, as in England and India, many women entered the cause of suffrage from other reform work with a social purity agenda. During the Gilded Age and the Progressive Era in the 1890s, reformers insisted on the need to arrest the degeneration of society, to value morality and spirituality above material gain and sensual pleasure. Many suffragists took up these values as part of their platform, arguing that women were in a special position to renew a corrupt, masculinist nation. In the end, American values provided the leverage for universal national suffrage, thanks in part to the rhetoric of democracy used to justify American intervention in World War I. How could the Untied States claim it was fighting for democracy in Europe, suffragists asked, if it was not willing to embrace democracy fully at home? As more and more states passed suffrage legislation, the national government was persuaded to do so as well.

THE EXAMPLE OF INDIA: CLARA COLBY AND RABINDRANATH TAGORE

This philosophical and tactical contest between human equality and female essentialism, and the question of the relationship between spirituality and politics in women's movements, is incomplete without knowledge of the place of the "East"—especially India—in the thinking of progressive US feminists such as Clara Colby. Longtime editor of the suffrage paper *The Woman's Tribune*, Colby sought to counteract the reigning assumption that the subjection of women was of divine design. Like other progressives engaged in metaphysical "border-crossings," Colby drew upon a discourse of affirmative or romantic "Orientalism" whereby the insights of the "East" might counteract the spiritual poverty of the "West" (the term "Orientalism" was coined by scholar Edward Said, who argued that European and American thinkers constructed a binary opposition between their cultures and the allegedly more primitive cultures of other countries). In her effort to reform Western democracy, Colby drew on a powerful, persistent idea of "Indian spirituality" and its potential to transform the West. Not all suffragists shared Colby's enthusiasm for Indian culture. For example, Carrie Chapman Catt, the successor to Susan B. Anthony, carefully documented the "barbaric" practices of "Eastern" cultures in her 1912 world suffrage tour. Catt was typical of Anglo-American women suffragists, much like women reformers in Western Europe, who manipulated the language of "civilization" to bolster their own cause.

But others, like Clara Colby, found support and vision for feminism in foreign cultures, arguing that American women and their campaign for emancipation could be

This section is adapted from Kathi Kern, "Spiritual Border-Crossings in the U.S. Women's Rights Movement," in *American Religious Liberalism*, 162–81, eds. Leigh E. Schmidt and Sally M. Promey (Bloomington and Indianapolis: Indiana University Press, 2012).

positively influenced by the spiritual ideas of other nations. Though, unlike Catt and other feminists, Colby never traveled to India, she mined in both its ancient texts and its modern, nationalist writers, whose work resonated deeply with her own spiritual and political aspirations. Like social purity advocates in England, Colby envisioned a future in which woman's moral power would triumph over men's carnal natures (see Rosenman, "Sexual Politics in England and India," in chapter 5).

Colby gained inspiration and theoretical support for her critique of male sexual desire from a seemingly unlikely source: the romantic poetry and plays of the Bengali poet Rabindranath Tagore. Tagore's published work, for which he was awarded the Nobel Prize in Literature in 1913, coupled with his pilgrimages to England and the United States, touched off a "Tagore craze." Women were especially drawn to Tagore. They found his work compelling because of his ability to infuse daily life with sacred meaning, his interpretation of human passion as an expression of divine love, his creation of complex, rebellious female characters.

Colby harmonized her reading of Tagore with her critique of male desire. In her notes on Tagore, she articulated her grasp of Tagore's analysis of gender relations. Women, because of their traditional roles of serving, loving, and comforting, had throughout time "developed harmony and beauty." Man, on the other hand, was stymied by "diverse, untamed passions [that] stood in the way of his development" (Colby, "Tagore the Feminist"). Especially in the West, Tagore argued, this essential difference in orientation wreaked havoc. Men's passions drive imperialism, Tagore suggested, so that men of the West seek "shelter in distant nooks & corners on the earth" in a "crushing struggle for existence which is partly due to wants artificially created" (qtd. in Colby, "Tagore the Feminist"). This imbalance, this "social discord," is what necessitated the campaign for women's rights in the West. In Tagore's analysis, to be "Western" was to be materialistic, imperialistic, and sexually undisciplined; men's (not women's) behavior and status should be the object of scrutiny. A feminist reader like Colby was able to absorb Tagore's critique of "Western" men and use it to shift the terms of the debate about women's rights toward the degradation of the Western man.

Clearly, even radical suffragists like Colby succeeded only in manipulating the binaries of Orientalist logic: the imaginary construction of "the East" as an exotic Other remains the opposite of the modern, rational "West." Adherents of Eastern religions were either morally retrograde and in need of Western intervention, as Catt would have it, or they were spiritually endowed and capable of benefiting the "West" with their mystical gifts. The dualism may be inverted, but the East remains mysterious and irrational.

Still, suffragists' respect for the insights of ambassadors from abroad ran counter to the views that dominated Anglo-American life, according to which the East was perpetually to be the recipient of uplift and knowledge from the West. (It is worth noting, too, that Indians themselves adhered to this romanticized view of their culture, especially when it was strategically useful. Nineteenth-century Indian nationalists, for example, capitalized on the idea that India was inherently "more spiritual" and redirected that idea toward anti-colonial aims.) While trafficking in Orientalist tropes, feminists such as Colby offered a rare and largely unwelcomed critique of their nation's untroubled sense of power. While her spiritual proclivities rendered Colby a liability to a national political movement bent on gaining respectability, Colby and seekers like her may have been particularly well situated to transcend their own privilege and find solidarity with people who were different from them.

WORKS CITED

Anderson, Nancy Fix. "Bridging Cross-Cultural Feminisms: Annie Besant and Women's Rights in England and India, 1874–1933." *Women's History Review* 3, no.4 (1994): 563–80.

Catt, Carrie Chapman. *Diary,* February 1–April 1, 1912, p. 36, 41. Carrie Chapman Catt Papers, Library of Congress, Washington, D.C.

———. Excerpt, untitled manuscript on the position of women in the "Orient," 1913. Box 7, Folder 1, Carrie Chapman Catt Papers, New York Public Library.

Colby, Clara. "An Attack on the Tagore 'Craze.'" *The Literary Digest,* August 21, 1915, p. 352. Clipping, box 5, folder 11, Clara Bewick Colby Papers, State Historical Society of Wisconsin.

———. Excerpt, Clara Colby's notes on the writings of Rabindranath Tagore. Box 5, folder 11, Clara Bewick Colby Papers, State Historical Society of Wisconsin.

———. "Tagore the Feminist," handwritten manuscript. Box 5, folder 11, Clara Bewick Colby Papers, State Historical Society of Wisconsin.

Edwards, Louise, and Mina Roces, eds. *Women's Suffrage in Asia: Gender, Nationalism and Democracy.* London: Routledge Curzon, 2004.

Levine, Philippa. *Victorian Feminism, 1850–1900.* Tallahassee: The Florida State University Press, 1987.

Roy, Anupama. *Gendered Citizenship: Historical and Conceptual Explorations.* Hyderabad: Orient Longman, 2005.

Said, Edward. *Orientalism.* New York: Vintage, 1978.

DISCUSSION QUESTIONS

1. What different views of womanhood do you see in these documents? Do they imply different versions of citizenship as well?

2. Lytton's speech is a graphic account of her imprisonment and force-feeding. Do you think it qualifies as "feminist thought"? What feminist ideas and values do you see in it?

3. Do you agree with Ali that the vote in itself is not very meaningful unless it "opens up to women new opportunities of services and of self and national development"? Would these other writers agree with Ali? What opportunities might follow from the vote? What are the limitations of voting? Why do you think suffrage became such a prominent international issue and such a rallying point for women worldwide?

4. Based on the excerpts from Clara Colby's clipping files and notes on the Nobel Prize–winning author Rabindranath Tagore, what explains Tagore's popularity among American women? Why did some authors find Tagore's popularity controversial?

LADY CONSTANCE LYTTON, *A SPEECH DELIVERED AT THE QUEEN'S HALL, JANUARY 31, 1910*

I am grateful for your kindness, and I appreciate it as fully and as deeply as any human being can, but let me remind the strangers here that though what I have done is something rather different perhaps to what other women have done, because the circumstances concerning me were different, and because there was something to lay hold rather freshly of the imagination of outsiders; yet they must remember this fact, that thirty-five other women have been treated as I have been treated, and of these women I have suffered almost the least. Before I tell you my story I want to impress that fact on the strangers and the outsiders. I am one of thirty-five to whom this has been done, and of this number there are two women in the prison from which I come, who are now being treated like that; two women who, as I did, are watching the waning of the light, and knowing that when the light fades it is only a question of minutes before this torture—one can call it by no other name—is inflicted on their helpless bodies at the bottom of a prison cell, where there will be no witnesses and no appeal.

Since I have been released I have had many letters not only from strangers, but from personal friends, who try to show sympathy, but who say in a curious, blind, and ignorant fashion: "But, after all, what is it all about? Why do it? It is all unnecessary." Therefore I want to give as briefly as I can a little sketch of my experiences during the last year. When first I joined this movement my life was literally transformed by contact with the four great leaders, who in these brief years have framed and created a movement which, I think, even in the history of the whole world will ever be considered as remarkable.

When I first came across those great forces I stood as an absolute outsider, an impartial critic. Let me tell a little incident which occurred in the country town where I was. One day I came on a great crowd forming a ring round a sheep being taken to the slaughter house. It looked old and misshapen. I suddenly saw a vision of what it should have been, on its native mountain side, when all its forces were rightly developed, and there was a hideous contrast between that vision and the creature in the crowd. It seemed to be an ungainly thing. Presently it was caught again, and one man gave it a great cuff on the head. At that I felt exasperated. I said, "If you have got this creature in your power, don't you know your own business? If you were holding it properly it would be still. You think that insult is the

SOURCE: Lady Constance Lytton, "A Speech by Constance Lytton," in *Speeches and Trials of the Militant Suffragettes: The Women's Social and Political Union, 1903–1918*, ed. Cheryl R. Jorgensen-Earp (Madison, NJ: Farleigh Dickinson Press, 1999), 107–13.

proper thing at this moment?" Over and over again I have thought of that incident, of how women have been thought unwomanly, unnatural, held in contempt, a thing outside the pale, and laughed at and then insulted, because of conditions which they had not produced, but which were the result of mistakes and injustice of civilisation. When one joins this cause one must expect derisive misunderstanding, and misinterpretation of all one's motives. A friend told me recently that her brother, who had an important post in South Africa, condemned the movement when first he heard of her joining it. Presently, he came back from South Africa, and said he was a complete convert to Woman Suffrage. His reason was that as he moved among the aboriginal tribes he found that the status of the tribe was exactly gauged by the status of the women in that tribe. Where they were honoured and respected it was the same with the tribe, and where it was otherwise the tribe was dishonoured. I think that is a very good instance of what happens in all countries, civilised as well as uncivilised. Only the very day before I went into Liverpool prison as Jane Warton, I met at one of my meetings a factory inspector. She seemed what you could describe as a "red tape" official, an unimaginative, official woman. Yet she said this: "If only one of these well-to-do, happy women could sit in the police-court, as I have to do, there would be no need to argue with them about the position of women in this country at the present moment." She told me she was in a police-court the other day when three prisoners were brought before the magistrate, a man and two women. The man and a woman were arrested for being together in the public street at night, the other woman for mounting guard. The facts were clear—the man had bribed the woman and had paid her money—and yet this was the verdict: The two women were sent to prison and the man was allowed to go free. People talk of sex war. Is not that sex war? It is sex peace we want.

Women's Weapons

People say, what does this hunger-strike mean? Surely it is all folly. If it is not hysteria, at least it is unreasonable. They will not realise that we are like an army, that we are deputed to fight for a cause, and for other people, and in any struggle or any fight, weapons must be used. The weapons for which we ask are simple, a fair hearing, but that is refused us in Parliament, refused us by the Government, refused us in the magistrates' courts, refused us in the law courts. Then we must have other weapons. What do other people choose when they are driven to the last extremity? What do men choose? They have recourse to violence. But what the women of this movement have specially stood out for is that they will not kill, they will not harm while they have other weapons left them. These women have chosen the weapon of self-hurt to make their protest, and this hunger-strike brings great pressure upon the Government. It involves grave hurt and tremendous sacrifice, but this is on the part of the women only, and does not physically injure their enemies. Can that be called violence and hooliganism? But it is no good taking a weapon and being ready to drop it at the very first provocation, so when the Government retaliated with their unfair methods, with their abominable torture and tyranny of feeding by force, did you expect the women to drop their weapons? No, of course not. I had been in this movement many months, and although I absolutely approved of the method of getting in our messages by means of stones which did nothing but convey our meaning to the Ministers and to the world, still I felt I could not throw a stone myself. However, as I have told you here before when I saw the first of these women released—a mere girl—from Birmingham Gaol, I took another view. I went to Newcastle for a protest, meaning to share what these women endured. I went in my own name, and, as you know, I was released after a very short hunger-strike, a heart specialist being called in, who examined me for something like a quarter of an hour. I made a tremendous protest. I said that in that same prison where I was, there was a woman, a first offender, who had done much less violence than I had, and she was fed by force without having her heart tested at all. "Whatever you think of the subject," I said "whatever you think of the militant movement, surely you can see that justice is done between one human being and another!" I tried all I could, when I came out, and I got others whom I know to fight that question with truth and exposure, and what did they give us back?

Lies, and Nothing but Lies!

Well, I thought, you choose your weapons, I will fight with the same weapon, and you shall take my life, and do with it what you will! So I disguised myself; I changed my personality, and I went and made my protest outside that very gaol where these hideous, abominable things were being done. It was easier than I thought. I merely cut my hair. I bought clothes of a different type to my own, I removed the initials from my underclothes, I put on glasses, and that was more than sufficient. I had one rather unhappy moment. They had taken my belongings, brooches, handkerchief, etc. I saw in the first bundle a reel of cotton with "Lytton" on it, and a handkerchief from which I had omitted to remove the initials. I thought the game was up, but they were so little suspicious that I simply placed my hand upon these two things and put them into the fire. The prison world is so used to Suffragettes doing strange things that they were not at all surprised.

I was always on the alert for being discovered, but the first day of the hunger-strike went by, the second day went by, and the third day went by, and it was quite obvious from the way they treated me they did not suspect my identity. It was the first time I had been to prison without my name, and I can assure you it made a great deal of difference. Perhaps it is only human. I do not complain of position influencing people like wardresses or policemen, but when it comes to law and the Home Office, surely one can expect something more like justice? On the fourth day of my hunger-strike the doctor came to my cell and said he must feed me at once. I was so desirous of gaining my object—I knew that if I was only fed once it would be a test—that I did not look upon it with horror—I welcomed it. To my surprise and to my great relief they did not examine my heart, which I had managed for two days, but which by the fourth day of starvation was becoming difficult.

At last they came. It is like describing a hospital scene—and much worse. The doctor and four wardresses came into my cell. I decided to save all my resistance for the actual feeding, and when they pointed to my bed on the floor I lay down, and the doctor did not even feel my pulse. Two wardresses held my hands, one my head. Much as I had heard about this thing, it was infinitely more horrible and more painful than I had expected. The doctor put the steel gag in somewhere on my gums and forced open my mouth till it was yawning wide. As he proceeded to force into my mouth and down the throat a large rubber tube, I felt as though I were being killed; absolute suffocation is the feeling. You feel as though it would never stop. You cannot breathe, and yet you choke. It irritates the throat, it irritates the mucous membrane as it goes down, every second seems an hour, and you think they will never finish pushing it down. After a while the sensation is relieved, then the food is poured down, and then again you choke, and your whole body resists and writhes under the treatment; you are held down, and the process goes on, and, finally, when the vomiting becomes excessive the tube is removed. I forgot what I was in there for, I forgot women, I forgot everything except my own sufferings, and I was completely overcome by them.

What was even worse to me than the thing itself was the positive terror with which I anticipated its renewal. Very soon I thought to try and appeal to that man as a doctor to perform the operation in a better way, but whatever one said or suggested was treated with most absolute contempt.

There was one even worse thing, and that was the moral poisoning, if one may call it that, of one's whole mind. I always closed my eyes. I tried not to see the beings who came to do this thing. I felt it was all too hideous, and I did not wish it imprinted on my eyes. Nevertheless I got to hate those men and women, I got to hate infinitely more the powers that stood behind them, I got to hate the blindness, the prejudice, in those who turn away and won't look or listen to what is being done under their very eyes. I tried to think of the splendid heroes and heroines since the world began, of all the martyrs, all the magnificent women in this movement, and I felt a tremendous gratitude to them, an admiration which overpowered me. But it was no use to me—it did not help me and it did not strengthen me.

I must go back a little, and tell you that when the chaplain visited me he seemed to have said to himself, "This is a Suffragette; one must mend her ideas of women." So he began speaking in this style: "I can tell you one thing, any woman you see in this prison, you may take it from me, is as bad as bad can be. Everything has been done to help her, but she is absolutely hopeless." These remarks came back to me later, and I thought, "Here is this man, the only man in this prison who could strike a different note, who could help the wretched souls, and that is his summing up of all the unhappy people under him—'as bad as bad can be.'"

Two Pictures

Then one evening, as I lay on the bed on the floor of my cell, I looked up. There were three panes of clear glass, and on them as the light fell there came shadows of the moulding that looked like three crosses. It brought to my mind the familiar scene of Calvary with its three crosses, and I thought: What did they stand for? One for the Lord Christ who died for sinners, and one for the sinner who was kind, and one for the sinner who had not yet learnt to be kind, and behind those crosses I saw those hateful faces, the self-righteous, all those hateful institutions of superior goodness and moral blindness of officialdom, of all the injustice done, not only in prison, but in the world outside, and I thought surely it was for these that Christ died and is dying still and will have to die until they begin to see. When I thought that my blind hatred should be standing between these people and their better selves, I felt the hatred and the hell-like surroundings go from me. I was grateful to those panes, and the next day I put the table and the chair together and roused myself to wash the three windows cleaner, and as I looked through the glass, I saw, in the waning evening light, suffused by a pink glow, a scene which was to me more beautiful than the most beautiful picture I had ever seen. Outside was a little exercise yard, into which I had never been. Wandering round and round in the evening light, quite alone, was a slight figure of a woman, and as she turned the corner I saw that in her arms, under her shawl, she had another little prisoner, a baby, and she was happy and talking and singing to it; she seemed the very symbol of what we are fighting for, fighting to restore what has been lost—and I looked at that woman, who seemed so helpless, and I thought of the parson's words, "Bad as bad can be." And I felt as strong as Samson! A strength which no stories of heroic people had been able to give to me came to me.

After each time the hideous process of forcible feeding was repeated it meant a ghastly kind of washing up. Two or three times I was so completely unmanned that I was not able to do it myself, and an ordinary prisoner came in to do it. She was a new hand, and the wardresses said contemptuously in her presence, "Just look at that; look at the way she is doing it." But the woman's face never changed, there was no resentment and no anger. I ventured to say, "At any rate, she is doing the work I ought to do myself, and I am very grateful to her," and from that woman there came to me an immense strength, and I felt I could fight on and live on to the end. As I was taken out to be weighed I passed a little girl, she was not more than a child. She may for aught I know have been taken straight off the streets, but she had at that moment the face of an angel, and she looked down on me with a smile which you can never see out of prison. She gave me that angel's smile, and it positively touched my very soul. When I went out of the prison, I felt my resentment and anger were gone. In a way my physical courage was no better than before, but at least I could go on. I knew that I should last out.

Then you come out of prison, and you hear people say: "You have gone in as a practical joke to do the Home Secretary," or "You went in for a piece of hooliganism," and so on. What are these people made of? Is that what we want? No. We want that from those helpless officials who are only blindly doing what they are told to do, there should be removed these hideous orders from high quarters, that it should become impossible for orders of that kind to be carried out on women who can in no sense be compared with ordinary criminals. It must not be left to the magistrates and the law, but in public opinion it must be made impossible.

Even now there are many people to-day who kindly extend their personal sympathy to me. What are those people? Everyone counts immensely. Do not, at any point where you touch this movement, think you are of no account. Do your part and leave the rest. We want your sympathy, and are glad of it. We want your money, and I will tell you a story about that. One woman, a poor working woman, wrote to the Union, and enclosed a postal order for half-a-crown, and she said: "Will you take this and use it in any way Constance Lytton would like best." Another said: "I should have liked to send you flowers, but I thought you would like the money better." With this I mean to start a fund simply for educating this blind world, for trying to take the scales from the eyes of those who do not yet understand. We want your help for that, and we want your money for that, but we want, even more than that, that you should stand by us. Let me tell you one more personal anecdote. When the doctor first came into my cell I said: "Will you shake me by the hand?" And what I had been going to say to him if he had granted me my request was, "I want to shake hands with you for you have taken service on the wrong side. Those who back the Government in this matter are on the wrong side, and when they discover it they will have a very black moment, so let us shake hands over it now." Well the doctor, being a prison official, could probably do nothing else; he did not shake hands. But do not let it come to you—that black moment when you will find you have taken service on the wrong side. This is the most glorious fight that has ever been. Become a member of our Union. It is so easy to do that. Before you leave this hall, say: "I will stand by you whatever the world says, whatever public opinion says, I am for you now, before another minute goes by."

MILLICENT GARRETT FAWCETT, *HOME AND POLITICS*

It is now more than twenty years ago since I delivered the first lecture I had ever given in public, on a Brighton platform, in support of women's suffrage. Twenty years is a long time in the life of an individual; it is a very short time in the life of a great movement, and I think, as we look back over these twenty years, those who have devoted themselves to the cause of the enfranchisement of women have good reason to congratulate themselves on the substantial progress which has been made.

We have a direct increase of our strength in Parliament, and we have further cause for congratulation on side issues bearing upon the general position of women; their admission to the Municipal and School Board Suffrages; their activity in many invaluable efforts of social and moral regeneration; their work as Poor Law guardians; and their success in the higher fields of education. There is also the increased activity of women

SOURCE: Millicent Garrett Fawcett, "Home and Politics," in *Before the Vote Was Won: Arguments for and against Women's Suffrage*, ed. Jane Lewis (New York: Routledge and Kegan Paul, 1987), 418–24.

in political life. Each party now seems to vie with the other in its eagerness in calling upon the women within its ranks to come forward and work for what they believe to be the right side in politics. But, perhaps, more encouraging than any of these direct evidences of the progress the women's movement is making, is the general feeling that is beginning to prevail that women's suffrage is a thing that is bound to come. The tendency of public opinion is felt to be set in that direction, and even those who oppose us seem to know that they are fighting a lost battle. Mr Lowell used to say, "There is a sort of glacial drift in English public opinion; you cannot see it move, but when you look again you see that it has moved." I think there is no doubt that the glacial drift of English public opinion has moved and is moving in the direction of the active participation of women in politics. We have evidence of this in all parties.

With regard to the differences between men and women, those who advocate the enfranchisement of women have no wish to disregard them or make little of them. On the contrary, we base our claim to representation to a large extent on them. If men and women were exactly alike, the representation of men would represent us; but not being alike, that wherein we differ is unrepresented under the present system.

The motherhood of women, either actual or potential, is one of those great facts of everyday life which we must never lose sight of. To women as mothers, is given the charge of the home and the care of children. Women are, therefore, by nature as well as by occupation and training, more accustomed than men to concentrate their minds on the home and domestic side of things. But this difference between men and women, instead of being a reason against their enfranchisement, seems to me the strongest possible reason in favour of it; we want the home and the domestic side of things to count for more in politics and in the administration of public affairs than they do at present. We want to know how various kinds of legislative enactments bear on the home and on domestic life. And we want to force our legislators to consider the domestic as well as the political results of any legislation which many of them are advocating. We want to say to those of our fellow-countrywomen who, we hope, are about to be enfranchised, "do not give up one jot or tittle of your womanliness, your love for children, your care for the sick, your gentleness, your self-control, your obedience to conscience and duty, for all these things are terribly wanted in politics. We want women, with their knowledge of child life, especially to devote themselves to the law as it affects children, to children's training in our pauper schools, to the question of boarding out, to the employment of children of tender years, and the bearing of this employment on their after life: to the social life of children and young persons of both sexes in the lower stratum of our towns and villages, to the example set by the higher classes to the lower, to the housing of the poor, to the provision of open spaces and recreation grounds, to the temperance question, to laws relating to health and morals, and the bearing of all these things and many others upon the home, and upon the virtue and the purity of the domestic life of our nation."

Depend upon it, the most important institution in the country is the home. Anything which threatens the purity and stability of the home threatens the very life-blood of the country; if the homes of the nation are pure, if the standard of duty, of self-restraint and of justice is maintained in them, such a nation has nothing to fear; but if the contrary of all these things can be said, the nation is rotten at the core, and its down fall is only a question of time. Up to the present, my belief is that the home side and the political side of things have been kept too far apart, as if they had nothing to do with one another. We have before us the picture of the whole of Europe armed to the teeth, and the great neighbouring nations ready to spring like wild beasts at each other's throats, all for the sake of fancied political advantage, while the true domestic interests of the nation concerned would be almost as much injured by victory as by defeat. I confess that I think women are all too apt to forget their womanliness, even in such cases as this, and allow their aspirations to be guided by those of the masculine part of the society in which they find themselves. But by strengthening the independence of women, I think we shall strengthen their true native womanliness;[1] they will not so often be led away by the gunpowder and glory will-o'-the-wisp, which is really alien to the womanly nature, but will much more certainly than now cast their influence on whatever side seems to them to make for peace, purity, and love.

A large amount of opposition to Women's Suffrage is based on the fact that to women has been given, by nature, the charge of the domestic and home side of things, and there is also the fear that contact with political life would blunt the gentler qualities of women. Let us look at these two objections separately. To women, it is said quite truly, has been given the charge of the home and the domestic side of things. That is to say, most women's lives are wholly or almost wholly devoted to work for their husband and children within their home. I will apply myself to meet the argument against Women's Suffrage based on the fact that the daily business of most women's lives lies in the routine of domestic affairs. For the proper discharge of these duties many very high and noble qualities are needed, and no insignificant amount of practical knowledge. Women who are immersed in domestic affairs should be good economists, knowing how to save and how to spend judiciously; they should know a good deal about the health and training of children, about education, about what influences character and conduct; no quality is more important in the management of servants and children than a strong sense of justice. In proportion as women are good and efficient in what concerns their domestic duties, they will, if they become voters, bring these excellent qualities to bear upon public affairs. Most men are as much taken up by some trade, business, or profession in their everyday life as women are by their domestic duties; but we do not say that this man is so industrious and experienced in his business that it is a great pity that he should be admitted to the franchise; we rather feel that all that makes him a useful member of society in his private life will also make him a good citizen in his public duties. I am well

1. Mr R. L. Stevenson in one of his stories makes his hero refer to this, when a woman to flatter him repeats, parrot-like, what she conceives to be the man's formula on love and honour. "My honour?" he repeated, "For a woman you surprise me. . . . You speak, Madame von Rosen, like too many women, with a man's tongue."—*Prince Otto*, p. 205.

aware that there are some women who are not good for much in the home; in one class they think more of balls and fine clothes, than of home duties; cases have been known, I grieve to say, in all classes, where they have broken up their homes through drunkenness and idleness; though for one home broken up and destroyed by a drunken woman there are probably three or four broken up and destroyed by a drunken man. These women who are not good for much domestically will most likely not be good for much politically; but exactly the same thing can be said of the existing male voters. Taking women in the mass, I believe it can be claimed for them that they are faithful and conscientious in the fulfilment of the duties already confided to them, and if this be so, it is the best assurance we can have that they will be faithful and conscientious in the new ones that may be entrusted to them.

I think we may surely claim for women in general a high standard of goodness and virtue. Most of us are probably fortunate enough to know many women who live up to the ideal described by the late Poet Laureate.

> Because right is right
> To follow right, were wisdom in the scorn
> Of consequence.[2]

In so far as conduct is a test of virtue, we have a rough test in the number of men and women respectively who are committed for trial, for serious offences against the law, and we find that the women thus committed are less than a fifth the number of the men, although women are more numerous than men by about four per cent. I do not stop now to enquire what the causes of this may be, but I think the bare fact is a strong evidence that the admission of women to the suffrage would raise rather than lower the average quality, as regards conduct, of the existing constituencies.

Duty is what upholds all the structure of national greatness; why then exclude from the responsibilities of citizenship a large number of women among whom the standard of duty as measured by their conduct is conspicuously high and pure?

Let us now consider the fear that has been expressed that contact with political life will blunt the gentler qualities of women. We know that a very similar fear has been expressed with regard to the extension of higher education to women. It was thought that if a woman knew Greek she would not love her children, and that if she learned mathematics she would forsake her infant for a quadratic equation. Experience has set these fears at rest. It was imagined that if women were admitted to the studies pursued by young men at Oxford and Cambridge, they would imitate the swagger and slang of the idlest type of undergraduates. Experience has proved that these fears were baseless; may we not also hope that the fears expressed by some of the effects of political life on

---

2. The quoted lines are from Alfred, Lord Tennyson, "The Death of Oenone."—Ed.

womanly graces may prove to be equally unfounded? It seems to me very inconsistent and illogical to say with one breath Nature has made women so and so, and so and so, mentioning all kinds of graceful and delightful qualities, and then to add that all these qualities will disappear if a certain alteration takes place in the political constitution of the country. Nature is not so weak and ephemeral as this. All the Acts of Parliament that ever have been or ever can be passed cannot shake the rock upon which the institutions of Nature are founded. To think that we can upset the solemn edicts of Nature by the little laws of human invention is the most grotesque infidelity to Nature that has ever been dreamed of.

If you descend from these general considerations to look at the experience we have thus far had of the result of political activity upon the gentler qualities of women[,] I think we cannot do better than cite the example which has now for more than fifty years been given us by Queen Victoria. She has been from her early girlhood immersed in a constant succession of political duties and responsibilities, and yet no woman, as wife, mother, or friend, has ever shown herself more entirely womanly in her sympathy, faithfulness, and tenderness. I like very much the story told of the Queen in the early years of her reign, when one of her ministers apologised for the trouble he was giving her in regard to public business. "Never mention that word to me again," she replied, "only tell me how the thing is to be done, and done rightly, and I will do it if I can." That is womanly in the best sense, and the very quality we want more of, not in politics only, but everywhere and in every department of life.

When we speak of womanliness and the gentler qualities of the feminine nature, we must be careful not to mistake true for false, and false for true. Is there anything truly feminine in fainting fits, or in screaming at a mouse or at a black beetle? Fifty years ago a female of truly delicate susceptibilities was supposed to faint on the slightest provocation; but there was, I venture to think, nothing truly and essentially womanly in this accomplishment: it was merely a fashion which has now happily passed away. Women don't faint now unless their heart or their digestion is out of order. Merely foolish foibles ought not to be dignified by the name of womanliness; their only advantage lies in their providing a cheap and easy means to persons of the other sex of establishing their own superiority. Those men who are not very sure, in the bottom of their hearts, of their own superiority, naturally like to be assured of it by finding a plentiful supply of women who go into hysterics if a mouse is in the room, know nothing of business except that consols are things which go up and down in the city, or of history except that Alexander the Great was not the son-in-law of Louis XIV. The world would wag on if this kind of womanliness disappeared altogether; what we cannot afford to lose is the true womanliness, mercy, pity, peace, purity and love; and these I think we are justified in believing will grow and strengthen with all that strengthens the individuality and spontaneity of womanhood.

In conclusion, I will only add that I advocate the extension of the franchise to women because I wish to strengthen true womanliness in woman, and because I want to see the womanly and domestic side of things weigh more and count for more in all public concerns. It is told in Nehemiah that when the walls of Jerusalem were rebuilt after the captivity, women as well as men shared in the work. Our country now wants the hearts and brains of its daughters as well as the hearts and brains of its sons, for the solution of many perplexing and difficult problems. Let no one imagine for a moment that we want women to cease to be womanly; we want rather to raise the ideal type of womanhood and to multiply the number of those women of whom it may be said:—

> Happy he
> With such a mother; faith in womankind
> Beats with his blood, and trust in all things high
> Comes easy to him, and though he trip and fall
> He shall not blind his soul with clay.[3]

3. The quoted lines are from Alfred, Lord Tennyson, "The Princess."—Ed.

ARUNA ASAF ALI, FROM *WOMAN'S SUFFRAGE IN INDIA*

The rise and rapid growth of political agitation for self-Government in the country from the early years of this century made the women of India also conscious of their exclusion by British Law from any share in the Government of their land. The famous Home Rule movement sponsored by that great leader Mrs. Annie Besant and her subsequent imprisonment helped to stimulate political activity in general but it was also instrumental in creating a general political consciousness among the educated women of India. A direct proof of this general awakening was given when in 1917 the Secretary of State for India, Mr. E. S. Montagu, came out to investigate and study Indian conditions prior to the framing of a new constitution for India. Leading Indian women gave for the first time public expression to their feelings. Their first claim for suffrage was made by the All India Women's Deputation (including representatives from all parts of India) which waited on Mr. Montagu on the 1st of December, 1917, in Madras. Apart from claiming their share in the Government of the country, it brought to the notice of those who had come to devise a new constitution for India, the various reforms which women were specially desirous of recommending to Government to carry out. The paragraph setting forth the claims of Indian women will bear quotation here.

> Our interest, as one-half of the people, is directly affected by the demand in the united (Hindu-Muslim Reform) scheme (1.3) that the members of the council should be elected directly by the people on as broad a franchise as possible and in the memorandum 3 that the franchise should be broadened and extended directly to the people. We pray that when such a franchise is being drawn up, women may be recognised as people, and that it may be worded in such terms as will not disqualify our sex, but allow our women the same

SOURCE: Aruna Asaf Ali, "Women's Suffrage in India," in *Our Cause: A Symposium by Indian Women*, ed. Shyam Tumari Neiru (Allahabad, Kitabistan: n.p., n.d.), 364–71.

opportunities of representation as our men. In agreeing with the demand of the above-mentioned memorandum that a 'full measure of the Local Self-Government should be immediately granted,' we request that it shall include the representation of our women, a policy that has been admittedly successful for the past twenty years in Local Self-Government elsewhere in the British Empire. The precedent for including women in modern India [sic?] political life has been a marked feature of the Indian National Congress, in which since its inception women have voted and been delegates and speakers, and which this year finds its climax in the election of a woman as its president. Thus the voice of India approves of its women being considered responsible and acknowledged citizens; and we urgently claim that, in drawing up of all provisions regarding representation, our sex shall not be made a disqualification for the exercise of the franchise or for service in public life.

[. . . .] The Statutory Commission which came out to India in 1928 to draw up a scheme of Reforms laid special stress on the need for enfranchising a much larger proportion of women for the future Legislatures and said that "the beginning of a movement among certain Indian women, however comparatively few in number they may yet be, to grapple with problems which specially affect home and health and children, is one of the most encouraging signs of Indian progress, and we believe that the movement would be strengthened by increasing the influence of women at elections." This desire to increase the number of women electors so that "Indian women should have a direct opportunity of influencing the course of politics in the land to which they belong" was subsequently made clear by the Franchise Sub-Committee of the Round Table Conference. The Report of this Committee says: "No system of franchise can be considered satisfactory or as likely to lead to good Government where such a great disparity exists between the voting strength, of the two sexes. We feel, therefore, that special qualifications should be prescribed for women." The disproportionate strength of women as against men voters will show why such stress was being laid on special qualification for women. The following table shows the then existing proportion of men and women voters in various provinces, as noted by the Lothian Committee.

With a view to redressing this absurd position the Lothian Committee was led to recommend special qualifications for women. Of these, the first is what is commonly known as the literacy qualification, i.e., every woman who can read or write in any language will be entitled to vote, the second is what is called the "wifehood" qualification, i.e., the wives and widows of voters who possess property qualification will be entitled to vote. These qualifications have been the subject of a great deal of controversy. Apart from the fact that the wifehood qualification was and still is considered objectionable on the grounds that it places a premium on marriage and perpetuates the idea of women's dependence on man, and does not recognise their independent right of suffrage, the controversy also raged round what was regarded a heavy handicap, namely the condition that women voters who claimed special qualification would be enrolled only on making

	Women	Men
Madras	1	10
Bombay	1	10
Bengal	1	16
The Punjab	1	29
Bihar and Orissa	1	62
Central Provinces	1	25
Assam	1	114

an application to the authorities concerned. It was felt that this condition would defeat the very object for which special qualifications were devised and reduce the number of specially qualified women, as few would be in a position to fulfil the latter condition.

In spite of repeated protests from all major women's organisations, the application condition has not been removed, the plea being the impracticability of registering literate women. [. . .]

The arguments advanced by the Lothian Committee against the other objection, namely the "wifehood" qualification[,] makes interesting reading. They say: "It is a reasonable view that marriage gives a community of interest and that in it a woman enters into a partnership with her husband which may well confer civic rights as well as domestic duties" and add, "nor does there seem any valid reason why a woman should be more under the influence of her husband because her name is in the electoral roll for one reason rather than another."

As a result, however, of these additional qualifications, however inadequate they may be, it is roughly estimated that about six million women will be enfranchised throughout India out of a total electorate of thirty-five million and the ratio of men voters to women will be approximately five to one. Even these figures, higher though they are than ever before[,] show the inadequate voting strength of women as compared to men. [. . .]

The principle of reserving seats for women was one which has never been acceptable to any of the representative women's organisations and in spite of the view held by the Simon Commission ("We do not think it is in the real interest of Indian women or of the progress of representative institutions in India, to secure the inclusion of women members by such a method") a system of reserved seats on communal lines has been introduced in the future framework of the Indian Constitution. [. . .] The arguments advanced in favour of these special constituencies are numerous and some would hardly stand the test of logic but they are in the main as follows:—

"We wish to provide a representative electorate, and to ensure that the constituencies in which the women's seats are filled are small and select, and so framed as to minimise the difficulties of canvassing (particularly marked as a result of social conditions still prevalent in many parts of India), the hardships of communication in rural areas in that country, and the obstacles likely to be met by a member in maintaining contact with her constituents." [. . .]

The creation of these special constituencies again stresses the tendency to segregate women into a separate compartment and it is indeed unfortunate that the Committee could not accept the other alternative of reserving seats for women in the fuller territorial multimember constituencies. [. . .] This pampering attitude towards women will in no way help to create self-confidence in them and it is feared that notwithstanding the proposed aim of the Committee to secure "quality rather than quantity" these special constituencies will help to bring about the reverse state of affairs. One can only hope that women who command the confidence of the people will seek election not only from the special but also from the territorial constituencies which they are not debarred from contesting. [. . .]

A study of the latest figures available giving the percentage of women voters who went to the polls shows that they have not yet taken full advantage of their electoral right.

These figures make melancholy reading. In view of the leniency and generosity with which the vote had been conceded, to women this apathy has been much commented upon. This lack of response, however, is due to the fact that representative forms of administration are new to India and [it] will be some time before even the entire adult male population can grasp the full significance of the vote. Women will naturally take time to understand the implications of their electoral rights, unless active steps are taken to educate and train them. Besides they have not had the same opportunities of political education as men, who first learnt to handle electoral machinery as early as the later half of the nineteenth century.

It has been said that Local Self-Government in India is a representative organisation, responsible to a body of electors enjoying wide powers of administration and taxation and functioning both as a school for training in responsibility and a vital link in the chain of organisms that make up the Government of the country. Municipalities and District Boards form the basic units on which rests the superstructure of the large administration of the country, and if women are to participate in the discharge of civic duties and to realise their civic and political responsibilities, they must acquaint themselves increasingly with the working of these local bodies and exercise their right of franchise as well as that of entering them. It is through these bodies that people's primary needs like Health, Sanitation, Education, etc., are provided. Since woman's domestic duties have familiarised her with such needs and their fulfilment, she should have an advantage over men in tackling problems which[,] though affecting larger areas than her domestic circle, are of a similar nature. While . . . she cannot and should not be apathetic towards the wider problems of administration, it is essential that women should be thoroughly conversant with the work of Municipal Committees in the urban areas and District Boards in the rural areas. Apart from serving as training grounds for wider responsibilities, the work in these departments of administration is of vital importance to the day to day existence of a nation. [. . .]

Women Voters

	Number enrolled	Number enrolled in contested constituencies	Number who voted	Percentage of enrolled women voters who voted in contested constituencies
Provincial Legislative Council Elections				
Madras	127,969	98,680	17,836	18.1
Bombay	47,256	35,877	2,331	6.5
Bengal	*	*	*	*
United Provinces	56,224	31,360	1,208	3.9
Punjab	25,199	14,907	840	5.6
Central Provinces and Berar	7,679	3,926	347	8.8
Bihar and Orissa	6,924	4,229	229	5.4
Assam	2,324	1,314	85	6.5
Burma	124,404	100,275	13,774	14.0
Legislative Assembly Elections				
Madras	19,491	10,338	1,194	11.5
Bombay	5,644	2,617	34	3.2
Bengal	16,360	198	*	*
United Provinces	7,424	3,175	106	3.3
Punjab	3,413	2,193	165	7.5
Central Provinces and Berar	931	40	*	*
Bihar and Orissa	1,676	810	25	3.0
Assam	*	*	*	*
Burma	5,960	*	*	*
Ajmere-Merwara	0	–	–	–
Delhi	*	*	*	*

* Figures not recorded.

In conclusion one can only add that the enfranchisement of women merely for the sake of recognising a right loses all save an ornamental significance, if this does not also call into being a keen realization of corresponding responsibilities. The gaining of the vote will prove meaningless if it does not open up to women new opportunities of services and of self and national development. Women should realise that the vote is not an objective in itself, although it is that consent, which is said to be the basis of that final legal repository of the social will, the State. It should help to make women conscious citizens with an active sense of responsibility participating not only in the administration of the country but fulfilling their roles in all "the numerous forms of associative and institutional life of the Community." Otherwise the right to vote will degenerate into a useless, or even a dangerous, potentiality. France is an illustration of just the reverse situation, where women enjoy the fullest liberty in the various functional organisations of the country but they are deprived of the political vote. This hampers them to some extent but it has not prevented them from enjoying that liberty which is essential if human beings are to rise to their fullest stature. This note of warning here has been struck to remind ourselves that in countries where the parliamentary system has been tested for some time it is now openly acknowledged that "a democratically elected parliament can be, at best only *one* vital expression of the consciousness of the community," and therefore while fully utilising the primary right of franchise, and participating in the active administration of the country, the other social institutions and associations which form as vital a part of the total life of the community must not be neglected.

CARRIE CHAPMAN CATT, FROM AN UNTITLED MANUSCRIPT ON THE POSITION OF WOMEN IN THE "ORIENT"

No one can visit the Orient without realizing that religion occupies a far more influential place in the life and thought of the people than with us. Perhaps this is not strange since all the great religions of the world had their origin in Asia, and probably it is quite natural that these indigenous religions should have become immovably entrenched in the land of their birth. I had a notion quite common among our people, that Europe and America were civilizing and westernizing Asia. It was a bit startling to discover that the democratic movements in Egypt, Turkey, Persia, India and Dutch India, of which we had all heard were not so much political as religious manifestations. Every conversation with the leaders of these movements disclosed the fact that religious motives were the spur of every thought and act. These people are far more anxious to free themselves from their European over-lords because they are Christians than because they desire self- government. Yet the feeling is not so much religious intolerance as it is a desire to foster and prove their own faith before the world. It is even more bewildering to discover that the Eastern woman has no more desire to follow the lead of the Western women into the state of liberty they enjoy, than has her brother to follow the Western man. Thanks to the jar which an influx of stirring Westerners have given the people of the East, they are awake and thinking and out of their thoughts has come a genuine normal desire among men for a better social order and among women for more independence, but these aspirations are progressing though their own religions. They refuse to become British or Dutch, or American, or to

SOURCE: Carrie Chapman Catt, Untitled manuscript on the position of women in the "Orient," 1913. Box 7, Folder 1, Carrie Chapman Catt Papers, New York Public Library.

follow the line of development of Christian nations. That would be conceding too much. They propose to work out their own destiny in their own way. They are certain to keep as a foundation those institutions and faiths which for centuries they have held dear and they will erect upon it only such edifice as will be in perfect harmony with it.

I am convinced that Asia will never be Christianized nor Westernized, but I am equally sure that it will stand still no longer. Its new evolution is well under way and it is coming though and by means of oriental religions.

The healthiest sign of a better time for women lies in the fact that two of the three great religions of Asia, Brahmanism and Buddhism are apologizing for the seclusion of women. Both declare it is no part of their religion, and assert that the Mohammedans are responsible for it. They waged wars everywhere until no woman's life, or virtue, was secure and they were driven to seek safety behind the walls of their homes. What had been a necessity in time became established custom, and no one asked its origin. Now they disclaim all responsibility for it, and in consequence women are coming forth from their hiding places in astonishing numbers. The Maharanee of Baroda, a progressive Indian State, has written a book in which she appeals to the women of India to come forth and seek a more useful life, to encourage education, to take up employment for the common welfare, but she adjures them to do this in strict accord with Indian thought. The picture of the unveiled Maharanee herself in a preface to the book is a bolder example to her country women than those unfamiliar with Hindu custom can realize. Hindu women have started and are maintaining many schools for girls. They have organized the Seva Sedan Sisterhood, composed of Hindu, Parsee and Mohammedan women the object being to break down the barriers of religions.

CLARA COLBY, *AN ATTACK ON THE TAGORE "CRAZE"*

The smashing of literary idols is a pursuit rarely cultivated nowadays. We read that it flourished in earlier, ruder times. But now, when the nations of Europe are occupied with wholesale murder as the best part of the day's work, too often we hear the complaint that all criticism can do is to purr pleasantly or shriek discoveries of geniuses twice a week. Consequently there is an air of novelty about a caustic notice in *America* (New York) of the Tagore "craze." The Hindu poet and dramatist has appeared before in the pages of *The Literary Digest* as the subject of high and authoritative praise. At present he passes under a different kind of review, while his American and English devotees are sharply reminded that they are Christians, not Hindus. The article is written by Mr. Joyce Kilmer, known as a poet and a critic, who on this occasion performs in the latter capacity with "a big stick." Mr. Kilmer is far from denying the actual gifts of Tagore, but when William Butler Yeats, the Irish poet, ranks the Hindu with St. Francis, Thomas à Kempis, and

SOURCE: Clara Colby, "An Attack on the Tagore 'Craze,'" *The Literary Digest*, August 21, 1915, p. 352. Clipping, box 5, folder 11, Clara Bewick Colby Papers, State Historical Society of Wisconsin.

William Blake, it seems about time to protest against such "a weird combination," and against the whole "mystic" bag of tricks with which the Tagore legend is conjured. The quaint exoticism of the man is what makes women's clubs delight in him, we read, whereas "if Tagore had been born in Brooklyn, he would never be a fashionable poet."

We read then:

No one will deny that Tagore is an able literary craftsman. He is not, as he has been called, the greatest living poet, but he is the most versatile writer living; he is almost as versatile as the late Andrew Lang. He writes in English as skillfully as in his native Bengali; his love-songs are graceful; his poems about children are whimsical and dainty; his one-act plays, although not strikingly original, are imaginative and dexterously put together; and his philosophical essays are thoughtful.

But Blake and St. Francis and Thomas a Kempis! What have they to do with this talented Hindu? An enthusiastic young woman, reviewing Tagore's work in a New York newspaper, desired to go Mr. Yeats one better, and actually compared the subject of her critique to Joan of Arc, of all people!

Considering the books that have been written about Tagore, the practice some clergymen have of reading his verse in the pulpit, and the critical enthusiasm he has awakened, this critic asks the "why" of it all, and explains the marvel as follows:

It is not because Tagore received the Nobel Prize. It is not because he is nearly as clever a lyricist as Mr. Clinton Scollard and nearly as clever a playwright as Mr. Henry Arthur Jones. It is because, in the first place, he is an East-Indian: like that dear, dear Swami who tells you all about your "aura" at those wonderful afternoon teas at Mrs. Van Dusenbury's! If Tagore had been born in Brooklyn, he would never be a fashionable poet. There is a quaint exotic aroma about his poems, like sandalwood or stale cigarets [sic] or the back room of a Chinese laundry. He writes about temple-bells and water-jars and the desert: it is all so nice and Oriental! And then he teaches such a comfortable philosophy: just have a good time and love everybody and your soul will migrate and migrate and migrate until finally it pops off into the Infinite! The pearl slips into the lotos; Om mani padme hum—and that sort of thing.

Well that is all right in its way unless you happen to be a Christian. "Go to the dogs and be drunken," says Tagore, "Be drunken and go to the dogs." M. Baudelaire gave the same advice in a poem which this well-read poet may possibly have seen. But M. Baudelaire was merely praised with faint damns for writing it. Tagore is almost worshipped; he is hailed as a genius, a philosopher, a benefactor of the world, a religious leader, and—of course—a mystic.

It is all very well for Tagore's compatriots and coreligionists to raise him aloft as far as they care to, the writer goes on to say, but it is puzzling and offensive to find "American and Englishmen who are humbly kneeling before the clever Oriental journalist who bids them 'leave this chanting and singing and telling of beads,' who would substitute fatalism for hope, Nirvana for heaven, and . . . Krishna for Jesus Christ."

CLARA COLBY, FROM *NOTES ON THE WRITINGS OF RABINDRANATH TAGORE*

It has been usual with Hindus that after a deep religious experience they become ascetics. But R's clung to the world more closely & to his family. He had married at 23. It is only those who do not get the philosophy of unity who wish to renounce. This is brought out in a poem which he has translated.

At midnight the would-be ascetic announced: This is the time to give up my home, and seek for God. Ah, who has held me so long in delusion here? God whispered "I" but the ears of the man were stopped.

With a baby asleep at her breast lay his wife, peacefully sleeping on one side of the bed. The man said "Who are ye that have fooled me so long?" The voice said again "They are God," but he heard it not. The baby cried out in its dream, nestling close to its mother.

God commanded "Stop fool leave not thy home!" But still he heard not. God sighed & complained "Why does my servant want to seek me, forsaking me?"

Tagore held that the "greater" cannot be great without the small, the infinite is only the fullest expression of the finite and that there is no liberation without love[;] wherever love is there dwells the Infinite within the finite[.] (Compare Whitman's "A kelson of the creation is love" after his illumination[.])

Tagore was about thirty at the time of the vision and from this time his poems are filled with love of God. In all his poems there is one single theme. His religious songs became more universal, and they have that effect on devout Hindus that a single passage often produces a religious ecstasy. Here is one of them.

I have made you the polar star of my existence. Never again can I lose my way in the voyage of life.

(Wherever I go you are always there to shower your beneficence all around me. Your face is ever present before my mind's eyes. I almost lose my mind, if I lose sight of you even for a moment.

Whenever my heart is about to go astray; just a glance of you makes it feel ashamed of itself.)

One of these religious songs was sung by R. in the presence of his father who was so moved by it that he presented his son with a check for 500 rupees.

SOURCE: Clara Colby, "Notes on the Writings of Rabindranath Tagore." Box 5, folder 11, Clara Bewick Colby Papers, State Historical Society of Wisconsin.

PART 3

TALKING BACK TO SEXISM BEFORE "WOMEN'S LIBERATION"

Nineteenth to Mid-Twentieth Centuries

7

THE MYTHOLOGY OF
THE *DOUDOU*

Sexualizing Black Female Bodies, Constructing Culture in the
French Caribbean

Jacqueline Couti

Since the eighteenth century, Caribbean white Creoles and travelers to Martinique and Guadeloupe have extolled the beauty of the mulatto woman, transfiguring her into a Venus-like symbol.[1] So much so that this figure has come to be known nowadays in French studies and mainstream culture as the *doudou*. In the 1890s, for an American audience and then in the 1920s for a French readership, the works of international traveler and journalist Lafcadio Hearn showcase this exotic and racialized discourse around French Caribbean women. Yet, it is only in the interwar period that writers from these islands living in Paris—namely, Suzanne Lacascade, and Paulette and Jane Nardal—noticeably denounce such a colonial as well as masculine eroticization and exoticization of the black female body. Consequently, this introduction contrasts Hearn's writing to that of Lacascade and the Nardal sisters, to suggest that for these French Caribbean writers during the interwar period, awareness of the gendered self went hand-in-hand with awareness of the racial self . At that time in Paris, negrophilia and primitivism were thriving: the often demeaning craze for anything black or African was inescapable. Thus, these writers had to confront European representations of their blackness, Creoleness, and femininity, that is to say of their Caribbean culture. These exoticizing works illustrate—as Brent Hayes Edwards argues, reclaiming Etienne Balibar—that "racism always 'presupposes' sexism" (132). To understand what these women were up against, this essay first examines the polysemy inherent in the term *doudou,* then discusses Hearn's racialized and exotic discourse, before exploring the responses of Lacascade and the Nardal sisters.

Today in French Caribbean studies, as in mainstream culture, the Creole term *doudou* designates the mesmerizing mulatto woman as the ideal or potential lover who offers her favors to the white man. The *da*, the asexual dark-skinned maternal figure who takes care of white Creole children frequently stands as the stark counterpart to the enchantress of color. In French Caribbean–based Creole, *doudou* means "darling." This term originated from the French word *doux* (soft or sweet) repeated twice (Hearn, *Two Years* 349). Anyone can be called *doudou*. This Creole word entered standard French dictionaries such as *Le petit Robert* in 1929, before the 1931 colonial exhibition in Paris. The gallicized *doudou* has come to signify a beautiful, loved French Caribbean woman, most likely light skinned or mixed race. Studying these representations of the black female body in the French Caribbean as a metaphor for both colonized islands and islanders reveals the manifestation of the male gaze in a French colonial context. That is, the white male defines the black female.

This masculine vision exemplifies what Robert Young terms "colonial desire"—a peculiarly sexual expression of patriarchy and colonialism (152). Thus, the paradigmatic stereotypes of the courtesan or *doudou,* and the dark-skinned maternal figure of the mammy or *da* feed a sexual and colonial mythology. These images extolling either sexual or maternal traits embody the same racialized and masculine ideology that promotes white culture. Biased and dangerous ideologies lurk behind these stereotypes; the pervasive aspects of exotic imagery have long-lasting implications for contemporary Martinican culture.

The French meaning of *doudou*—in contrast to the more expansive meaning in Creole—does more than encourage a perception of the female body in Caribbean literature as a mere object of desire or metonymic promotion of the beauty of the island. This female body often symbolizes the French Caribbean as a so-called place of leisure and pleasure that also hides dire social problems. We all think we know what femininity entails, but do we understand the political and cultural undertones specific to this particular construct of femininity? Examining the polysemy—that is, the multiple implications—of the term *doudou* demonstrates the extent to which a community creates myths and imagery of femininity or accepts external representation of its women as its own.

Nowadays the *doudou* has become a cultural icon that symbolizes the beauty of her island or region; her graces frequently promote her homeland in a touristic way, as shown in numerous postcards (see opposite page). In his article *"La doudou et la da"* ("The Lover and the Mammy"), R. D. Burton attempts to trace the history of this female figure. For that purpose, he draws on the work of the researcher Régis Antoine to explain that this exotic model of femininity originates from the eighteenth century and took shape in the song *"Adieu foulard, adieu madras"* in 1769–70 (Burton 133–34). Yet, in his study of the song, Antoine does not use the term *doudou* but rather talks about "a certain

Postcard image of the *doudou*.

image of the French West Indian woman separated from her friend, a French sailor" (Antoine 209).[2]

In fact, Antoine is discussing the free mulatto woman, the *belle affranchie* of the Ancien Régime—the aristocratic, social, and political system established in France from the fifteenth century to the eighteenth century. Caribbean white Creoles and travelers to the island extolled the bounty of this Venus-like figure, whose beauty and sensuality were irresistible. In the late nineteenth century, international traveler and journalist Lafcadio Hearn became a mouthpiece of this exotic and racialized discourse in his work on Martinique.[3] In his texts, light-skinned women of African heritage, reduced to sexual objects, embody an exotic model of femininity that mainstream French culture would define in the 1920s as the *doudou*. In Hearn's vision, little distinguishes the figures of the *da* and the *doudou*, as their sexual and maternal traits are closely intertwined. Eventually, the black female body appears to be a mirror reflecting Hearn's own biases while flattering the white masculine ego.

COLONIAL DESIRE AT PLAY IN THE FRENCH CARIBBEAN

In 1887, *Harper's Weekly* sent Hearn to the Caribbean as a correspondent for two years, most of which he spent in Martinique. In 1890 he then published two books based on the experience: a "Martinican" novel, *Youma: The Story of a West-Indian Slave,* and an account of his trip, *Two Years in the French West Indies,* filled with illustrations, many of them depicting Martinican women. In *Youma,* Hearn narrates a supposedly true incident that took place in Martinique before the abolition of slavery in 1848: a female domestic slave chose to perish with her masters during a slave riot. Studying Hearn's construction of French Caribbean femininity first brings to the fore his attempts to contrast light-skinned women's sex appeal with dark-skinned women's maternal traits. Yet he cannot help underscoring their attractiveness due to miscegenation and therefore their mixed "racial" heritage as well as their dedication to the white man.

In *Two Years in the French West Indies*, Hearn devotes an illustrated chapter, *"La fille de couleur,"* to the exotic beauty of Martinican women of color, which fascinates him. In the first edition of his book, a postcard of a mixed-raced woman titled "A Martinique Métisse" serves as the frontispiece, thus framing the ideology of the whole text. In this short chapter there are seven images of women, derived from a thriving trade in postcards and photographs in Martinique and Guadeloupe. In *"La fille de couleur,"* Hearn praises the graces of mulatto women and quotes white Creole writers from Martinique and white travelers without questioning his informants' accuracy or motives, as the endnotes of *Two Years in the French West Indies* attest. His descriptions may at first appear positive, as he seems to celebrate the wonders of *métissage*—miscegenation or racial mixing. Yet Hearn's writings illustrate white masculine discourse and racial biases. For instance, discussing the mystical charms of the *belle affranchie*, Hearn explains that these "women, whose tints of skin rivaled the color of ripe fruits, and whose gracefulness—peculiar, exotic and irresistible—made them formidable rivals to the daughters of the dominant race, were no doubt physically superior to the modern *filles de couleur*" (324). More than once Hearn associates mulatto women with fruits, particularly when he talks about their skin color. These women become a mere object of consumption and desire that needs to be taken. Moreover, he sees the "modern *fille de couleur*" as a sexual object, "as the half-breed girl destined from her birth to a career like that of the *belle affranchie* of the old regime" (328). This light-skinned woman appears not only as a beautiful fruit ready for consumption but as the epitome of the courtesan-prostitute. Sex is her trade. Yet Hearn also considers the courtesan's dedication to the white man as learned behavior inherited from slavery (330). Thus, he acknowledges that her desire to please her lover, the master, the white Creole or European traveler, derives from the social structure of the plantation system. His vision of gender relationship within the plantocracy remains problematic.

In the introduction to *Youma*, Hearn argues that the *"da* was, in general, a Creole Negress—, more often, at all events, of the darker than of the lighter hue,—more commonly a *capresse* [of chocolate or bronze complexion] rather than a *mestive* [honey or gold]" (1). As a matter of fact, like the archetype of the mammy within U.S. slavery, the *da*, also a maternal, domestic slave, was characterized by her dark skin. Hearn adds that: "In her particular case, the prejudice of color *did not exist*. The *da* was a slave; but *no freedwoman*, however beautiful and cultivated, could enjoy social privileges equal to those of certain *das*" (my emphasis). The *da* was respected and loved as a mother: "She was at once a foster-mother and a nurse" (1). According to Hearn this maternal figure, enslaved and devoid of any sexuality or individual identity, often fared best in a plantation system. Of course, he also praises her moral values: "She represented the highest development of natural goodness possible in a race mentally undeveloped, kept half savage by subservience . . . her special type was a product of slavery: the one creation of slavery perhaps not unworthy of regret" (5). His nostalgic discourse implies that this mode of enslavement could have positive aspects for slaves and betrays that Hearn has embraced the cultural ideal of white Creoles and Americans. His comments in the introduction to the novel frame his fictional discourse and display potential racial biases feeding his American readership.

In addition, comparing Hearn's depiction of the *da* in the introduction to *Youma* with the depiction in *"La fille de couleur"* in *Two Years in the French West Indies* sheds a particular light on his ambivalent representation of femininity. He cannot help associating the *da* with the enticing *belle affranchie* or the courtesan (314). In *"La fille de couleur,"* his conflicting representations of the maternal figure as a sexualized "Byzantine Virgin" demonstrate how Hearn's sexual and exotic biases contaminate his construction of this maternal figure (314). In *Youma*, the narration first underscores the *da*'s dark color and as such her ethnoclass, to construct her as an archetypal maternal figure. Yet the narrator comments in detail upon Youma's physical attributes and concentrates on her phenotype or racial traits and her beauty before extolling her virtue. The narrator notices that "her tint was of a clear deep red—; there was in her features a soft vague beauty,—a something that suggested the indefinable face of the Sphinx" (14). This depiction of an untouchable Oriental virginal figure recalls the sexualized "Byzantine Virgin" in *"La fille de couleur."* Despite the maternal role to which Hearn relegates the *da* in his introduction, the novel's narration alternates between an emphasis on Youma's sexual attributes and her altruistic motherly role. Eventually, the story concentrates on this *da*'s selflessness toward her mistress's family.

Youma has a heightened sense of duty and risks her life more than once to protect the small Mayotte, the white Creole child under her care. She also refuses to run away to marry Gabriel; she loves him against her mistress's will so she cannot elope with him. The narrator underscores her strong moral sense, her sense of duty and her Catholic beliefs. Her implicit refusal to embrace her sexuality with a black man promotes the ideal of life of the white community. The end of the novel offers a striking example of Youma's solicitude toward whiteness. On the eve of the abolition of slavery in Martinique in 1848, a mob of angry slaves and freedmen, including her suitor, sets on fire the house where Youma's "adoptive family" or masters take refuge. She declines the assistance of rioters trying to help her escape the burning building because they refuse to save the little Mayotte. Being a *da* for Youma is a calling. So she dies with her white Creole family. She chooses to stay with the little Mayotte instead of loving a black man and starting her own family. Her sacrificial stance emphasizes the maternal characteristics of the *da* and transforms her into the mouthpiece of a political ideology glorifying the white Creole way of life, including the subservience of people of color on which it depends. The novel *Youma* constructs a racialized family romance narrative that ultimately excludes blackness. Black women can nurture white Creole families but women of color held up as examples cannot have families of their own.

HEARN'S AUDIENCES AND THE LASTING LEGACY
OF COLONIAL DESIRE

When Hearn published his two texts in the 1890s, his audience was the American bourgeoisie, which acquired wealth after the Civil War and the abolition of slavery. After
quenching the American thirst for tropical exoticism in the 1890s, Hearn's vision remained
mostly unchallenged and fed France's yearning for all things black in the 1920s. Indeed,
Marc Logé translated *Youma* and the chapter "Martinique Sketches" from *Two Years* into
French in 1923 and 1924, respectively. Logé did so during the zenith of primitivism and
negrophilia surrounding colonial exhibitions in France. In the 1930s, Hearn's texts and
his vision of femininity influenced anticolonial Martinican writers, such as Aimé Césaire
(Arnold 71). Later in the 1980s, the *créolistes* Raphael Confiant and Patrick Chamoiseau
among others would also appreciate his work. All those thinkers praise Hearn for preserving Martinican folklore to the point that his vision often feeds their own promotion of
Creole culture and blackness. Rather than rejecting his exoticizing vision, they embraced
his representations as authentic images. These male Martinican writers, who discovered
a version of their culture through the eyes of an outsider writing above all for an American
audience and feeding its racial biases, did not challenge his vision. On the contrary, they
started to use black female bodies to mirror their own ideologies and vision of the world.
Yet since the 1920s , female voices from Martinique and Guadeloupe had warned against
the perpetuation of this exotic and erotic imagery, in vain, it seems. For these French
Caribbean female writers, reducing female islanders to the *doudou*, an object of desire
symbolizing the Caribbean and its inhabitants, feminized Caribbean men as well.

TRANSATLANTIC WOMEN'S VOICES: THE *DOUDOU* WRITES BACK

In Paris from 1919 to 1935, the explosion of modernist ideas, which fed negrophilia and
primitivism, impacted the development of black consciousness and French proto-feminism of color. Suzanne Lacascade, Suzanne Roussi-Césaire, and Paulette and Jane Nardal
denounced the detrimental exoticization of the French Caribbean islands and their inhabitants, as well as of the black world as a whole. These women fought the type of sexual
exoticism that Lafcadio Hearn among others embraced and are often viewed as precursors
of negritude (Sharpley-Whiting 14). Critics often question their feminism and political
activism, as these French Caribbean writers' claims were not as radical or politicized as
those of their European counterparts. In her work to undermine the motif of the *doudou*,
Suzanne Lacascade, of Guadeloupe, challenges the notion of political assimilation and
the place of the French Caribbean colonies in the French empire, not the role of women
as such. The sisters Paulette and Jane Nardal in turn, carefully spell out why black Creoles
should avoid perpetuating French exotic and erotic imagery. So doing, these female thinkers do not present a feminist agenda per se but rather a cultural and political one based
on denouncing racial biases. Yet their work illustrates the claim that "racism always
'presupposes' sexism" (132). Through their ambivalent critique of exoticism à la française,

also called *doudouisme,* these women living in Paris expose the threat to black culture in general and to French Caribbean culture in particular. They also make a transatlantic commentary on the condition of black women in a French colonial space.

Suzanne Lacascade's *Claire-Solange: Âme-africaine* (1924) represents the first attempt at female literary promotion of black consciousness through racial essentialism (Sharpley-Whiting 16). Lacascade deconstructs the objectifying *topos* of the enchanting and docile mixed-race woman. The resentful and biting character Claire-Solange promotes the worth of the colonies that an ungrateful France does not recognize. This young mulatto woman stands as a complex protagonist, one who claims her black African and Creole ancestry over her French and white one. Her portrait initially brings forth her feisty spirit, her cultural and political agenda, and her rejection of all things French, not her sensuality. To some extent, Claire-Solange speaks back to exoticism and French imperialism. Yet, she remains the product of a wealthy mulatto middle class that wants to be recognized by France as useful citizens and as equals. At the end of the novel, she marries a white man, her cousin.

Jane and Paulette Nardal denounced the representation in colonial discourse of the colonies and their inhabitants as exotic in their salon in Clamart and in journals such as *La Dépêche africaine* (1928–30) and the bilingual *Revue du monde noir* (1931–32). For these Martinican women, this imagery threatened their identity and integrity while preventing black people from being valued. In their thinking, Caribbean men are complicit in the colonial discourse and their own emasculation. Yet, they did not challenge "the implicit superiority of French culture and civilization" (Sweeney 119). In her article *"Pantins exotiques"* (*La Dépéchêche africaine,* 1928), Jane, the younger of the two sisters, explores how Europe sees Caribbean people as a source of entertainment and the black woman as a beautiful animal, as symbolized by the dancer Josephine Baker. She explains: "Should it come to be known or perceived that you are 'exotic,' you will arouse a lively interest, preposterous questions, the dream and regrets of those who have never traveled: 'Oh! The golden Islands! the marvelous lands! With their happy people, naive people, carefree natives!' In vain, you strive to destroy so many legends, they hardly believe you" (qtd. in Sharpley-Whiting 108). In addition, Jane critiques the dark imagery sold by the best-selling author Paul Moran (a representative of exoticism in colonial French literature) and exposes the dangers of exotic and erotic reification of black female bodies by the colonial discourse or *doudouisme.* This Martinican woman explores the social and emotional consequences upon black women living in a Paris that fetishizes them in its thirst for the exotic.

Paulette Nardal also decries the exoticism that was all the rage in interwar Paris. In 1932, in *"L'éveil de la conscience noire"* ("Awakening of Race Consciousness") she explains: "The coloured women living alone in the metropolis, until the Colonial Exhibition, have certainly been less favored than coloured men who are content with a certain easy success. Long before the latter, they have felt the need of a racial solidarity" (Nardal 29). She understood "the emergence of race consciousness as a specifically feminine ordeal" (Boittin 153). She also perceived the European interest in the other as a manifestation of colonialism, and often sexual in content. At the time, Jane and Paulette Nardal would not have been able to label this expression of colonialism as "colonial desire." Yet this is exactly what they fight against in their articles, through attacking white and black men's objectification of black women.

Lacascade offers a challenging rewriting of the mulatto woman that emphasizes not only her political and cultural values but also the validity of Caribbean culture and eventually of French civilization. The Nardal sisters on the other hand emphasize the danger of auto-eroticism and the sexualization of black women by both white and black men. Ultimately, the Nardal sisters noticed the danger in the representation of an exotic, feminized, and sexualized Caribbean. Their work demonstrates that the immeasurable love that the *doudou* is assumed to feel for Frenchmen/white men and ultimately for France, flattering and reassuring as it may be for American and French audiences, conveys an idea of the French nation that erases local Creole realities. This image of women of color that scholars nowadays in French studies often call the *doudou* hides a complex transatlantic discourse deforming the French Caribbean and its culture. In fact, this construction of femininity reflects political, cultural, and national ideologies that frequently vilify the blackness or darkness that these women are supposed to represent. And yet, this is the same vision of womanhood that contemporary Martinican male thinkers such as the Creolists Raphael Confiant and Patrick Chamoiseau often seem to praise. This shows the obstacles that feminism has had to overcome in the French Caribbean particularly when dealing with feminine images inherited from a colonial discourse that both black women and men have integrated as theirs.

NOTES

1. The expression *mulatto woman* (*mulâtresse* in French) when used in the French Caribbean is a complex concept, recalling a hierarchy of color and class inherited from the plantation system: often, the whiter, the better. The terms *mulâtre/mulâtresse* are widely used in Martinique to describe in a positive fashion members of the elite or middle class and light-skinned individuals or in a derogatory way "sellouts" and mercenaries betraying their blackness.

2. Unless otherwise noted, translations from French to English are mine.

3. Lafcadio Hearn (27 June 1850—26 September 1904) was known also by the Japanese name Koizumi Yakumo. He is famous for his writings about Japan, less so for his work on New Orleans and Martinique.

WORKS CITED

Antoine, Régis. *Les écrivains français et les Antilles: Des premiers Pères Blancs aux surréalistes noirs.* Paris: Maisonneuve & Larose, 1978.

Boittin, Jennifer Anne. "In Black and White: Women, *La Dépêche Africaine*, and the Print Culture of the Diaspora." In *Colonial Metropolis: The Urban Grounds of Anti-Imperialism and Feminism in Interwar Paris*, 133–69. Lincoln: University Press of Nebraska, 2010.

Burton, Richard D. E. *La famille coloniale: La Martinique et la mère patrie 1789–1992.* Paris: L'Harmattan, 1994.

Edwards, Brent Hayes. *The Practice of Diaspora: Literature, Translation, and the Rise of Black Internationalism.* Cambridge: Harvard University Press, 2003.

Hearn, Lafcadio. *"La fille de couleur."* In *Two Years in the French West Indies,* 311–37. New York: Harper & Brothers, 1890.

———. *Youma: The Story of a West-Indian Slave.* New York: Harper & Brothers, 1890.

Nardal, Jane. *"Pantins exotiques."* La Dépêche africaine (May 30, 1929): 3.

Nardal, Suzanne. *"L'éveil de la conscience de race chez les étudiants noirs."* La Revue du monde noire 6 (April 1932): 25–31.

Sharpley-Whiting, T. Denean. *Negritude Women.* Minneapolis: University Press of Minnesota, 2002.

Young, Robert, J. C. *Colonial Desire: Hybridity in Theory, Culture and Race.* London: Routledge, 1995.

DISCUSSION QUESTIONS

1. Why would Lafcadio Hearn's description of eighteenth- and nineteenth-century women of color be positive to twentieth-century cultural and political figures from Martinique?

2. From a feminist point of view, why is Hearn's construction problematic? Does one need to be a feminist to understand its shortcomings?

3. After reading Hearn's description of Martinican women, how do you perceive them? What are the cultural and political implications of this author's depiction of black Caribbean femininity?

4. Why it is important to know Hearn's audience? Why is it important that he first wrote for an American audience at the end of the 1880s?

5. Do the postcards present a single version of Martinican women or do they have multiple implications? What features of each postcard lead you to a specific interpretation of Martinican women?

LAFCADIO HEARN, FROM *LA FILLE DE COULEUR*

[. . . .] The *da* (nurse) or "porteuse-de-baptême" who bears the baby to church holds it at the baptismal font, and afterwards carries it from house to house in order that all the friends of the family may kiss it, is thus attired; but nowadays, unless she be a professional (for there are professional *das*, hired only for such occasions), she usually borrows the jewellery. If tall, young, graceful, with a rich gold tone of skin, the effect of her costume is dazzling as that of a Byzantine Virgin. I saw one young da who, thus garbed, scarcely seemed of the earth and earthly;—there was an Oriental something in her appearance

SOURCE: Lafcadio Hearn, *"La fille de couleur,"* in *Two Years in the French West Indies* (New York: Harper and Brothers, 1890), 311–37.

La fille de couleur **THE MARTINIQUE TURBAN, OR "MADRAS CALENDÉ."**

difficult to describe,—something that made you think of the Queen of Sheba going to visit Solomon. She had brought a merchant's baby, just christened, to receive the caresses of the family at whose house I was visiting; and when it came to my turn to kiss it, I confess I could not notice the child: I saw only the beautiful dark face, coiffed with orange and purple, bending over it, in an illumination of antique gold.... What a da!... She represented really the type of that *belle affranchie* of other days, against whose fascination special sumptuary laws were made: romantically she imaged for me the supernatural godmothers and Cinderellas of the creole fairy-tales. For these become transformed in the West Indian folklore,—adapted to the environment, and to local idealism: Cinderella, for example, is changed to a beautiful métisse, wearing a quadruple *collier-choux, zépingues tremblants*, and all the ornaments of a da.[1] [...]

I. ... "*Vouèla Cendrillon evec yon bel ròbe velou grande lakhè.... Ça té ka bail ou mal ziè. Li té tini bel zanneau dans zòreill li, quate-tou-chou, bouoche, bracelet, tremblant,—toutt sòte bel baggaïe conm ça.*"...—[*Conte Cendrillon,— d'après Turiault*]

"There was Cendrillon with a beautiful long trailing robe of velvet on her!... It was enough to hurt one's eyes to look at her. She had beautiful rings in her ears, and a collier-choux of four rows, brooches, *tremblants*, bracelets,—everything fine of that sort"—[Story of Cinderella in Turiault's *Creole Grammar*]

[. . .] What successes she achieved in this regard may be imagined from the serious statement of creole historians that if human nature had been left untrammelled to follow its better impulses, slavery would have ceased to exist a century before the actual period of emancipation! By 1738, when the white population had reached its maximum (15,000), and colonial luxury had arrived at its greatest height, the question of voluntary enfranchisement was becoming very grave.[2] So omnipotent the charm of half-breed beauty that masters were becoming the slaves of their slaves. It was not only the creole *negress* who had appeared to play a part in this strange drama which was the triumph of nature over interest and judgment: her daughters, far more beautiful, had grown up to aid her, and to form a special class. These women, whose tints of skin rivalled the colors of ripe fruit, and whose gracefulness—peculiar, exotic, and irresistible—made them formidable rivals to the daughters of the dominant race, were no doubt physically superior to the modern *filles-de-couleur*. They were results of a natural selection which could have taken place in no community otherwise constituted;—the offspring of the union between the finer types of both races. But that which only slavery could have rendered possible began to endanger the integrity of slavery itself: the institutions upon which the whole social structure rested were being steadily sapped by the influence of half-breed girls. Some new, severe, extreme policy was evidently necessary to avert the already visible peril. Special laws were passed by the Home-Government to check enfranchisement, to limit its reasons or motives; and the power of the slave woman was so well comprehended by the Métropole [. . . .]

Physically, the typical *fille-de-couleur* may certainly be classed, as white creole writers have not hesitated to class her, with the "most beautiful women of the human race."[3] She has inherited not only the finer bodily characteristics of either parent race, but a something else belonging originally to neither, and created by special climatic and physical conditions,—a grace, a suppleness of form, a delicacy of extremities (so that all the lines described by the bending of limbs or fingers are parts of clean curves), a satiny smoothness and fruit-tint of skin,—solely West Indian. . . . Morally, of course, it is much more difficult to describe her; and whatever may safely be said refers rather to the *fille-de-couleur* of the past than of the present half-century. The race is now in a period of transition: public education and political changes are modifying the type, and it is impossible to guess the ultimate consequence, because it is impossible to safely predict what new influences may yet be brought to affect its social development. Before the present era of colonial decadence, the character of the *fille-de-couleur* was not what it is now. Even when totally uneducated, she had a peculiar charm,—that charm of childishness which has power to win sympathy from the rudest natures. One could not but feel attracted towards this *naïf* being, docile as an infant, and as easily pleased or as easily pained,—

2. I am assured it has now fallen to a figure not exceeding 5,000.

3. *La race de sang-mêlé, issue des blancs et des noirs, est éminement civilizable. Comme types physiques, elle fournit dans beaucoup d'individus, dans ses femmes en général, les plus beaux specimens de la race humaine.—* Le Préjugé de Race aux Antilles Françaises, par G. Souquet-Basiège. (St. Pierre, Martinique: 1883). pp. 661–62.

artless in her goodnesses as in her faults, to all outward appearance;—willing to give her youth, her beauty, her caresses to some one in exchange for the promise to love her,— perhaps also to care for a mother, or a younger brother. Her astonishing capacity for being delighted with trifles, her pretty vanities and pretty follies, her sudden veerings of mood from laughter to tears,—like the sudden rainbursts and sunbursts of her own passionate climate: these touched, drew, won, and tyrannized. Yet such easily created joys and pains did not really indicate any deep reserve of feeling: rather a superficial sensitiveness only,—like the *zhèbe-m'amisé*, or *zhébe-manmzelle*, whose leaves close at the touch of a hair. Such human manifestations, nevertheless, are apt to attract more in proportion as they are more visible,—in proportion as the soul-current, being less profound, flows more audibly. But no hasty observation could have revealed the whole character of the *fille-de-couleur* to the stranger, equally charmed and surprised.

LAFCADIO HEARN, FROM *YOUMA: THE STORY OF A WEST-INDIAN SLAVE*

The *da*, during old colonial days, often held high rank in rich Martinique households. The *da* was usually a Creole negress,—more often, at all events, of the darker than of the lighter hue,—more commonly a *capresse* than a *mestive;* but in her particular case the prejudice of color did not exist. The *da* was a slave; but no freedwoman, however beautiful or cultivated, could enjoy social privileges equal to those of certain *da*s. The *da* was respected and loved as a mother: she was at once a foster-mother and nurse. For the Creole child had two mothers [. . . .]

[S]he had sacrificed so much of her own maternal pleasures for the sake of others' children. She was unselfish and devoted to a degree which compelled gratitude even from natures of iron;—she represented the highest development of natural goodness possible in a race mentally undeveloped, kept half savage by subservience, but physically refined in a remarkable manner by climate, environment, and all those mysterious influences which form the characteristics of Creole peoples.

[. . . .] Youma's tint was a clear deep red;—there was in her features a soft vague beauty,—a something that suggested the indefinable face of the Sphinx, especially in profile;—her hair, though curly as a black fleece, was long and not uncomely; she was graceful furthermore, and very tall. At fifteen she had seemed a woman; at eighteen she was taller by head and shoulders than her young mistress; and Mademoiselle Aimée, though not below the average stature, had to lift up her eyes, when they walked out together, to look into Youma's face. The young *bonne* was universally admired: she was one of those figures that a Martiniquais would point out with pride to a stranger as a type of the beauty of the mixed race. Even in slave days, the Creole did not refuse himself the

SOURCE: Lafcadio Hearn, *Youma: The Story of a West-Indian Slave* (New York: Harper and Brothers, 1890), 1, 5, 14–15.

pleasure of admiring in human skin those tones none fear to praise in bronze or gold: he frankly confessed them exquisite;—aesthetically, his " color prejudice" had no existence. There were few young whites, nevertheless, who would have presumed to tell their admiration to Youma: there was something in the eyes and the serious manner of the young slave that protected her quite as much as the moral power of the family in which she had been brought up.

Madame Peyronnette was proud of her servant, and took pleasure in seeing her attired as handsomely as possible in the brilliant and graceful costume then worn by the women of color. In regard to dress, Youma had no reason to envy any of the freed class: she had all that a capresse could wish to wear, according to local ideas of color contrast [. . . .]

8

LOCATING THE FEMINIST SPIRIT IN THE NINETEENTH AND EARLY TWENTIETH CENTURIES IN INDIA

Tarabai Shinde and Lalithambika Antherjanam

Pramila Venkateswaran

The nineteenth and early twentieth centuries in India generated multiple narratives about women's issues. These narratives converged and diverged, marking tensions between British and nationalist ideas of womanhood, between traditional Hindu and nationalist ideas, and between women's ideas of gender and nationalist and colonial ideas about Indian women. Each of these groups used the Hindu mythoreligious context to their own purposes to underscore their positions. In all of these narratives about Indian and Hindu womanhood, it is useful to ask, where does the feminist spirit lie in the colonial period and what gave rise to it? In order to answer these questions, let us look at two writers of this period in Indian history, Tarabai Shinde and Lalithambika Antherjanam. Shinde's and Antherjanam's positions were to locate the sacredness of women's bodies as separate from the patriarchal and nationalist notion of possessing the female and equating her— the chaste Hindu woman—with the idea of a pure and independent nation.

The colonial perspective on Indian women was to look at the woman as a unitary subject and project onto her all the qualities that were the opposite of British women, thus creating a binary, in which British women were superior and Indian women were inferior. The colonial attitude toward the subject race was further intensified in its description of Indian women, where imperial and patriarchal attitudes converged in the colonial desire to protect that innocent subject, the Indian woman. In reaction, the nationalist attitude was to raise the image of the Indian woman to an iconic status, give her all the qualities of a goddess, and expect her to live up to that rarefied image. Thus the images of nation and woman got conflated; the nation had to wrest itself from colonial domination and retain its purity and independence, which was exemplified in its woman, the mother of the nation. Within this nationalist depiction of woman were tensions between the reformists and the old school: while the reformists were on the path to uplift women from the ravages of tradition (widow remarriage, education, and the banning of *sati* and child marriage), the traditionalists maintained that the "reforming" of women was a Western and therefore impure influence that was detrimental to the nation and its efforts toward independence.

Both Tarabai Shinde and Lalithambika Antherjanam, who spanned the middle nineteenth through early twentieth centuries, questioned the nationalist insistence on the Indian female as impure outside her status of marriage. Shinde's prose is a riposte against patriarchal arguments about female inferiority, while Antherjanam's stories are forceful indictments against patriarchal control of female sexuality. Both writers question the very idea of purity as well as the growing conflation of national purity with women's purity. It is useful to understand that within Hindu culture, as reflected in some of its sacred texts, the female body is not seen as inferior but as the site of spiritual realization. While Hinduism has several philosophies, some of which propose transcending the body to attain spiritual realization, many of the goddess-based philosophical texts propound the goddesses as embodying the marriage of spirit and body. Goddesses are not transcendent, but immanent. Ordinary women are considered goddesses in the sense that their bodies are the sites of spiritual realization. The virgin goddess and the unmarried goddess are considered powerful because they are complete in themselves. Unfortunately, the nationalist interpretation of this philosophy was to make woman signify goddess-like qualities, elevating the image of the sexually pure, self-sacrificing, and uncomplaining wife. In reality, the sacred texts describe active, creative, fierce goddesses who balance out male energy, violent or passive. As Samita Sen points out, "nationalism inherited [the] language of colonialism. Thus nationalists, like earlier reformists (and indeed the colonial state to some extent) subjected the domestic to redefinition according to invented categories of 'tradition'" (467).

It is useful to remember that the equation between woman and nation that surfaced in the mid- to late nineteenth century in India, in parallel with a newly minted Hinduism with its prescriptions for women, is not peculiar to the colony. This equation of gender and nation is also seen in the British view of womanhood and femininity. As the colonizing power, Britain extended its patriarchal control not only to its colonial subjects but also to its female white subjects. British male and female commentary about the gender subjugation of the subject races, when seen against this mind-set, becomes ironic and hypocritical.

Shinde and Antherjanam are attacking a sexism that had sharpened in India under colonial rule. Conflating woman and nation forced women to follow some impossible standards created by nationalist leaders and forced men to maintain these standards in the family and in society.

Shinde, in *"Stri Purush Tulana"* ("A Comparison of Men and Women"), says, "One comes across several charges against women both in the written literature and in everyday discourse." She dispenses with any formal introduction in her piece and launches into her attack, addressing men and "Gods" mockingly in the same breath. She questions the omnipresence of gods just as she questions men's entitlement, whether it be in casting aspersions on female character or in defining and restricting female sexuality. Since the gods are not able to help her out, she summarily dismisses them and launches into her argument with the male sex, taking up each of their indictments against women and answering back. Whether it be male aspersions about women's suspicious nature, weakness of intellect, impudence, or adultery, in comparing women and men, Shinde uses examples from everyday life to point out that men in fact are the villains, who are projecting these negative qualities onto women.

Shinde's footnotes are as astringent and informative as the body of her essay. In one footnote she supports her argument that men are treacherous by showing that they take bribes from both rich and poor. She says, "Slimy beggars! That's what you are! All the paper in the world wouldn't be enough to write a panegyric on these most noble, excellent, and commendable merits of yours!" Her mockery of men's deeds cripples the argument thrown at her that "women are as stupid as buffaloes in the cow pen!" If indeed women are to be blamed for their illiteracy, men's literacy seems to have borne no fruit, she argues.

Shinde's retort about adultery is the crowning moment of the piece. Her first argument asks why women should be blamed for it if men indeed have also a share in the blame. Second, if the gods themselves do not consider it a crime, why should men? Quoting from the religious texts, she throws testimony in the face of society that dares blame women for remarriage by calling such an act adulterous. Shinde's answer comes at a time when there was a wave of reformers calling for remarriage as a way out of poverty and pariah status for young widows, some of whom were children.

Even literature seems to mimic the view men have about women. Shinde, one of the first female literary critics in India, critiques the stories *Manjugosha*, *Muktamala*, and *Manorama* and points out that such stories can only come from a male imagination that thinks the worst about women while ignoring that the vices they list actually are pervasive among men.

In "Comparison," Shinde does not simply show these sexual politics but also sets the record straight, doing an exposé of men and how their acts in fact hurt women and cast them further into a second-class status that Shinde finds both annoying and worrisome. Can't a woman be more than "whore" or "goddess incarnate"? Can't women (plural) be infinitely ordinary and diverse and be granted their rights that are their due?

This idea is echoed a few decades later in Antherjanam's story *"Praticaradevatha"* or "The Goddess of Revenge," in which the protagonist, Tatri, who is cast aside by husband and family despite her innocence, is provoked into action to bring about justice for herself and all women who are thus maligned by a cruel and entitled patriarchy. Antherjanam, in novel after novel, story after story, is in search of a just world for women; what unfolds in the pages of "The Goddess of Revenge" is a masterpiece that drives its fist right into the face of a rule-hardened male establishment of the Namboodri Brahmins, the upper-caste males of this particular sect in Kerala.

Where, indeed, does Antherjanam's, and her female protagonist, Tatri's, feminist spirit arise from? It would be both simplistic and a misconception to think that Antherjanam superimposed British views of female independence onto the development of her female characters. Rather, the Hindu mythic culture, which is goddess-centered, provides the language and the psychological and material knowledge to both men and women to carve out their self-determination and self-preservation. Secondly, it is also a misconception that British views of women were uniform, since it is out of the sexism of British society that the suffragist movement arose in England in the early part of the twentieth century, when Antherjanam began writing. Therefore, her writing should be viewed within the context that produced it as well as within the tradition of feminist writing and thinking in Indian literature. Reading Antherjanam, Shinde, and other women's writing in this manner takes readers, especially Western readers, away from the terrible misreading of Indian women as passive, or simply aping British women.

The most interesting part of the story, besides Tatri's use of prostituting herself to wreak revenge on her husband and men of high station, is the question Tatri asks the writer: Are you judging me as a woman of crass values and do you shun me? The writer answers for her readers and for herself and women like her that she does not judge her, that in fact, she is eager to hear her story so she can tell the truth and redeem Tatri from the inglorious hell she has been banished to. Antherjanam's retelling is itself a kind of justice for the woman who is used sexually by patriarchy and is blamed for seeking justice especially since, in Tatri's case, she uses sex to get even.

Out of Tatri's wounded body, which is marked by patriarchy, arises her feminist spirit that dares to "seek pleasure," the ultimate pleasure of revenge. Tatri's pleasure-pain marked body is the source of Antherjanam's feminism, which squarely places the blame at the feet of the Namboodri male Brahmin. In taking up her pen every night when the children are asleep and the house is quiet, she invokes her muse-goddess, who may be Tatri to any other wronged woman, to mark the body of her paper with their stories. Hence the muse or the goddess is not some divine, out-of-reach figure but a flesh-and-blood person who is having her polemics with the world.

As for Tatri's feminist spirit, it lies in her argument:

Fear ceases to exist when life and death seem no different from each other. . . . My capacity to err or cause to err must become more powerful: if I was to be cast out of society, if I was to be ostracized and excommunicated, I wanted to be sure I was not innocent. . . . If I was going to be pushed aside, others who were mean and cruel were going to fall with me. . . . If justice and fair play really existed, would it not be necessary to excommunicate more Namboodri men than women?

In this quotation, we clearly see that Tatri does not follow convention. Had she been conventional, she would have continued to live in misery with her family. But she makes a choice that if she is to be banished, she will not go down as an innocent woman, since that is what society is trained to accept. She is not willing to be a martyr; instead, she will seek her justice through revenge against the men who exploit women like her and use double standards to judge women as lacking virtue or self-respect. In exposing the men, Antherjanam and Tatri expose the society that makes Namboodri wives accept in silence the husbands who have extramarital affairs and bring in new wives or mistresses; they expose the hypocrisy of a society that holds a high standard of morality for women and yet enables a system in which women are expendable.

Shinde counters this very hypocrisy in her piece when she shows how sages, who are considered the acme of perfection and prescribe rules of behavior to society, commit the worst offences: "You sit on the *ghats* after bathing in the river, smearing yourselves with sackfuls of ash, pretending to be lost in meditation. But at the first sound of tinkling anklets, don't your eyes race up all fifty steps of the ghat?"

The reform in girls' education, the tenor of the nationalist movement, the concomitant rise of workers' struggles, which became full-fledged later with Gandhi's satyagraha movement, the active disagreements and dialogue among various political groups, and the burgeoning of newspapers in the vernacular languages and in English, all formed the background for Shinde's and Antherjanam's works. But beneath it all, as women, they carried a tradition of feminist rhetoric—from Gargi to Draupadi to Rani of Jhansi—that took full force when seen against the tumultuous sociopolitical context of Indian history in the late nineteenth and early twentieth centuries.

Both Shinde and Antherjanam, in comparing men and women, find men terribly wanting. One can hear the frustration in their voices at having to deal with this particular species of human. Both go against the grain not only in using the pen as their weapon, but also in choosing the style of their writing. Shinde's forceful rhetoric uses straightforward language that is accessible to the general public and dispenses with anything remotely flowery. One can hear the defiance in her voice and picture her expressing herself with her hands on her hips. In short, she is unrelentingly critical, a total opposite of the "angel in the house" that Virginia Woolf critiques, who is a simpering idiot afraid to be critical of men's writing lest she offend them. Like Shinde, Antherjanam achieves a sharp critical and satirical tone by invoking Tatri, the figure that her community had tried to banish from memory so as to erase her damning testimony from their collective psyche. In placing herself as a writer who is writing in the middle of the night and is visited by this infamous woman, Tatri, Antherjanam suggests that she and Tatri have fused; she has taken on Tatri's challenge to society and is willing to go out into the changing world of a nation struggling for independence and fight for her and all women. Unlike Tatri who used her body to seek justice for women, Antherjanam uses the body of her writing to challenge men into acknowledging women's rights.

Irreverence, sarcasm, banter, satire, and wit characterized much of women's writing in the mid- to late nineteenth and early twentieth centuries. Shinde's and Antherjanam's feminism is marked by this same irreverence and sarcasm, both in attitude and language. Shinde uses the everyday, nonliterary discourse, and Antherjanam uses the domestic, everyday language of women and men to highlight domestic dramas that have national repercussions. Both writers make their mark as literary critics as well as severe critics of patriarchy. Shinde seems to anticipate Antherjanam's story in many ways, but especially when she says, "I'm sure there are very few men who are ruined by women. But it would be difficult even to guess at the number of women ruined by men." This statement is the opposite of the havoc that Tatri unleashes. Antherjanam believes that if women's efforts to bring men to consciousness about justice are to be effective, not individual effort but collective action is necessary.

The patriarchy of the nineteenth and twentieth centuries in India, the colonial rulers, the nationalists, the traditionalists, anyone who had power and hegemony in society were asking the wrong questions about female sexuality. With Shinde and Antherjanam, the reader realizes that questions about female sexuality are feminist questions, beginning with women's rights as human beings, who feel that the liberty and sacredness of their bodies in everyday life should be held with utmost respect. The narrator's response to Tatri in Antherjanam's story is instructive: "Fired as you were with the intoxication of revenge, why did you not try to inspire all the other weak and slavish Namboodri women? Why did you shoulder the burden of revenge all alone?" Antherjanam, like other women of her time and Shinde's, is calling for women to organize around issues of injustice. The late nineteenth and twentieth centuries can be seen as an era of organizing around national independence; women's rights in the areas of education, marriage, and health; *harijan* struggle for human rights; and the beginning of a Marxist tenor to the struggles of agricultural workers and workers in the coir industry and others for fair wages.

One leaves Shinde's riposte and Antherjanam's story highly charged. Their works were timely and called men and women to right a wrong, to do whatever was in ordinary people's power to bring about justice—write, organize, march, anything but accept the status quo.

WORKS CITED

Antherjanam, Lalithambika. "Praticaradevatha (The Goddess of Revenge)." In *Women Writing in India 600 B.C. to the Present.* Edited by Susie Tharu and K. Lalita. Vol. 1. New York: Feminist Press, 1991.

Sen, Samita. "Toward a Feminist Politics? The Indian Woman's Movement in Historical Perspective." In *The Violence of Development: The Politics of Identity, Gender and Social Inequalities in India.* Edited by Karin Kapadia. New Delhi: Kali for Women, 2002.

Shinde, Tarabai. "Stri Purush Tulana (A Comparison of Men and Women)." In *Women Writing in India 600 B.C. to the Present.* Edited by Susie Tharu and K. Lalita. Vol. 1. New York: Feminist Press, 1991.

1. Although Tarabai Shinde and Lalithambika Antherjanam are addressing the average Indian reader, discuss how their works counter some of the assumptions that British rulers—and their Indian subjects—had about Indian women.

2. From your reading of British women writers of the nineteenth and twentieth centuries, examine the similarities in some key ideas between writers like Shinde and Antherjanam with writers like Mary Wollstonecraft and Virginia Woolf.

3. Very often writers from the past sound eerily contemporary. Write a letter either to Shinde or Antherjanam about how you find parallels between their writing and your own life or what you see as the relationship between men and women in your part of the world.

TARABAI SHINDE, FROM *A COMPARISON OF MEN AND WOMEN*

Let me ask you something, Gods! You are supposed to be omnipotent and freely accessible to all. You are said to be completely impartial. What does that mean? That you have never been known to be partial. But wasn't it you who created both men and women? Then why did you grant happiness only to men and brand women with nothing but agony? Your will was done! But the poor women have had to suffer for it down the ages.

One comes across several charges against women both in the written literature and in everyday discourse. But do men not suffer from the same flaws that women are supposed to have? Do men not cheat as women do? Theft, incest, murder, robbery, deception, fraud, swindling of government funds, taking bribes, changing truth to falsehood and falsehood to truth—do men not do any of these? . . .

First, if, as you claim, a woman has more power than a device for witchcraft or black magic, let me ask you, you who are endowed with an intellect far more powerful than hers, what have you not achieved with your intellect? You who have made possible what was believed to be impossible, of what worth can a woman's power be before your valiant deeds? Of none.

Second, it may be true that women are a whirlpool of suspicion. But that is because they are uneducated and all kinds of doubts inhabit their minds. But even then, it must be borne in mind that their suspicions are usually and necessarily about their own relationships. But if one casts just a fleeting glance at the webs of doubt in your minds, one's

SOURCE: Tarabai Shinde, "Stri Purush Tulana" (A Comparison of Men and Women), in *Women Writing in India 600 BC to the Present*, vol. 1, eds. Susie Tharu and K. Lalita, trans. Maya Pandit (New York: Feminist Press, 1991), 223–35.

eyes will surely be dazed. Your minds are full of all kinds of treacherous plans. "Let's bluff this moneylender and pocket a thousand rupees from him." Or, "Let's tell that *jagirdar* such and such a thing and swindle him out of some five hundred rupees." Or, "Let's lie to that officer about that particular case and change his judgment in X's favor." Or, "Let's register those false documents instead of the true ones." Or, "That woman Y, what a coquette she really is! What airs she gives herself! Must corner her one of these days, and see whether some affair with her can be managed. My current affair has begun to bore me. This is the chance to end it once and for all and begin a new one." Such disgusting thoughts never enter a woman's mind. This is, of course, not to say that all the women in the world are as luminous as the sun and as pure as the waters of the Holy Ganges. But even if one takes into account the entire female community in the world, it would be difficult to come across more than 10 percent of them who, like you, are caught in the whirlwind of such insidious perfidies, though not a single one of you is free of them.

Third, women are called the acme of impudence. But does your own species lack this quality in any measure? A judicious comparison would reveal the balance weighted far heavier on your side in this respect. Fourth, women are considered a megapolis of inadvertent acts. But what about you, the dastardly, perfidious, treacherous people that you are? You, who would not hesitate even for a moment in cutting somebody's throat immediately after winning his confidence. Do you never commit such insidious acts? You speak as if you are Holy Temples of Reason! Bravo! Bravo, indeed! You consider yourselves erudite and judicious, don't you? Yet can you find a match, anywhere, at any time, for the perfidious acts that you commit every day? On top of all this, you have the audacity to call yourselves judicious! What can anyone say?

Granted, women are as stupid as buffaloes in the cow pen! They are ignorant and do not know how to read or to write. But does that mean God did not grant them even an iota of intelligence? Thoughtless and rash they may sometimes be, but even then they are far preferable to you. Yes! To you who are the bastions of erudition and wisdom! Why, one has only to visit a prison to get a proof of this! The prisons are packed to capacity with such people. One can't even find a place to stand there, they are so packed! As for the "wisdom," the "knowledge" that they have, it's a little too much, if you really ask me! Everyone there has a "wise" head on his shoulders, and a "wise" deed to his credit! Some come there because they have printed false notes, some have taken bribes,[1] some for

1. Look, the government employs you for various jobs. It pays you salaries ranging from ten rupees to a couple of thousand, according to your qualifications, puts its complete trust in you, and agrees to whatever terms and conditions you make! Why? For merely putting your signatures across some papers here and there! Now, is it any of the government's fault that you pocket the pay and insist upon taking bribes as well? You never hesitate in accepting anything—just anything—as bribe. From hard cash to horses, cows, cloth, gold, and even pots and pans! And in the absence of any of these, even shoes! No one can escape from your clutches. You have no scruples whatsoever in extracting bribes from both the rich and the poor. Now doesn't this prove beyond any doubt that you are treacherous? That you commit treason? Further, if you fail to get any of these things, you are willing to accept as bribes any other thing, like provisions for a day, guavas, a couple of sticks of sugarcane, or even wood, jaggery, or even the husk of grain! But you will make people cough up something and grab it. Do you

having eloped with someone else's wife, some for having been in a rebellion, some for poisoning people, some for treason, some for perjury, some for impersonating kings and deceiving the public, some for murders. . . . Or would it be more correct to say that the government has most reverently offered you an honorable place in this prison, I mean, this palace, of merriment for committing such great, why, such superbly valiant deeds? Now tell me, what woman ever commits such atrocious deeds? Can you show me any prisons that claim to hold only women prisoners in their fold? I am sure the number of such women will not be more than a hundred at the most for every two thousand men.

Furthermore, we need to ask, what is the greatest crime that women commit? Adultery. That is the highest peak of their criminal ventures. They behave recklessly only because of such inclinations. But then, who takes the first step of sowing the seed of such designs in their minds? Who else but you? However shameless a woman may be, she will never throw herself into the arms of a strange man. That is an eternal truth. Do you know what a woman's idea of happiness is? First, a husband of her choice. One whom she can love. Once their hearts are united, she will not worry about poverty. She will endure any calamity for him. She will suffer hunger or thirst and put up with any kind of harassment for the sake of the man she loves. She will be happy even in the worst circumstances possible. But she will never, in her remotest dreams, think on her own of committing that crime. But let me tell you something. Can adultery really be considered an act of the most heinous nature? Our *shastras* certainly do not seem to think so![2] There is no need to think that such things did not happen in the past. In fact, those very shastras that you so very glibly quote are full of the most supreme confusion regarding this problem. For example, the shastras most freely sanctioned such practices in several circumstances. Suppose a king died, leaving behind him a queen who did not have a son, she could select any *rishi* of her choice and beget sons from him in order to augment the family.[3] And she could keep him till she had as many children as she wanted. What was this if not adultery? But wasn't it sanctioned by the shastras? Now, instead of sanctioning such things, had they sanctioned widow remarriages, that would have made even the kingdom of the deceased king stronger. As you know, many of our states, *jahagirs, inams,* and other hereditary revenue rights were dissolved by the government for want of legal heirs. Now that could easily have been avoided and even the country need not have become a slave.[4] The estates and properties of many were seized by the government and

ever let anybody escape without paying up? Never! By hook or crook, grab you will—anything that you can lay your hands on! Do you know what you are? Slimy beggars! Yes, that's what you are! All the paper in the world wouldn't be enough to write a panegyric on these most noble, excellent, and commendable merits of yours! Why, there won't be any place in the world large enough to stock all those papers! The entire world would overflow with them. And the oceans won't be sufficient to make ink to write that eulogy! And armies of carpenters will have to be employed to carve pens to write it with!

2. The term *shastra* here refers to ancient books of law, guidelines for moral, social, and political action; compilations belonging to the postvedic period.—Ed.

3. A *rishi* is a sage or seer.—Ed.

4. That is, had widows been allowed to remarry.—Ed.

added to the treasury, for lack of legal heirs. Besides, many times it so happened that when a king died, he left behind him a bunch of widows and there was no one to protect that crowd. What happened then? You men swooped down on them like a swarm of locusts and caused downright ruin. Those royal women, whose feet were never soiled with earth, were as beautiful as goddesses; but your insatiable lust reduced them to nothing but beggars in exile.

Another charge against women is that they are extremely mean minded and shallow. But they are never obsessed by such thoughts as "How will I get promoted to a higher office? How will I get more money? When will I rise to dizzy heights in public esteem? When will people address me as 'Sir' or 'Sahib' and speak humbly and meekly to me?" Women never waste their lives as you do, trying to achieve such impossible things. Then why do you pretend all these things are absolutely unknown to you and charge women with being the sole proprietors of "reckless vanity"?

The fifth charge against women is that they are the treasure houses of transgressions. But in fact, it is you who fit that description best. It's you who cause women to transgress. Let me substantiate this. Many fathers give away their beautiful and very young daughters, who are hardly ten or eleven years old, to men who are eighty or ninety in exchange for a purse of gold. They do it with an eye only on his wealth. Their reasoning is, "Even if the husband dies, there's no need to worry. She will be rolling in money. She will be able to get the best of things to eat, and be able to wear nice clothes—at least for a few days. She will have nothing to worry about. So what if she doesn't have a husband?" That is what they think. So without any scruples, they give their daughters away to such old men as lambs to a tiger. But once he who is her love, her real happiness, passes away, what meaning does life hold for her? The only man to delight in her new clothes, admire her, and consider her more precious than his life is her husband. Without him her life is like a desert. Then why would she hanker after those dry festivities? It might seem far better in the past when women used to burn themselves on their husbands' funeral pyres.[5] At least when one was reduced to a heap of ashes along with the husband, there was nothing left to worry about. In this world who is there who would love a woman as much as the husband does, apart from her mother, of course? That is a fact. But what about her who loses both? Who can she depend on when the red-hot fire of youth is

---

5. What a great service the Sarvajanik Sabha in Pune has rendered to women! In their journal, or whatever it is that they publish annually or biannually, they very pompously declared, "It would be better if the government allowed women to burn themselves on the funeral pyres of their husbands." But tell me, if you want women to do that, why don't you propose the same plan for yourselves? Why do you want to survive your wives? To knead cow dung and pat it into cakes for your own cremation? Why shouldn't you burn yourselves on the pyres of your wives? Better you than her. Because her passing away proves to be far more detrimental than yours. Do you want to know how? Well, she is always survived by her young children. Who would look after them for her?

There is a proverb, "Let a prosperous father die but even a pauper of a mother should never die." If the father dies, the mother will endure any amount of grief and sorrow but maintain her children. But what do you do in such circumstances? If your wife dies today, you rush to bring another the very next day and render your children homeless. Don't you? Admit it now! Already there is a great outcry about this! In fact it's you who should be thrown into that pyre before your wives.

burning in the pallav of her sari? This, then, is the fate of the women who are married off to old husbands. . . .

Many rich men get their favorite daughter married to a boy of rather humble origin and keep the couple in their house because they love their daughter. Everything goes well while the boy and the girl are both young and immature. But once she comes of age, this daughter of the rich man, clever, pampered, and used to wealth right from her birth, starts realizing the difference between herself and her husband. Now, that boy is a wretched creature of a lowly origin and is ignorant of the real comforts in life. As a result of the marriage, he is able to experience them for the first time. It is probably solely because of the good deeds he had done in a previous birth that he married into such a family. But his behavior is far from becoming to his newly acquired prosperity. The wretched creature is used only to the coarsest things in life! Even if a donkey is fed twice a day and decorated with silken threads, a saddle, a plume of feathers, and silver knobs, will it ever equal a noble horse though it be lean and on the brink of death? Naturally she doesn't like him, since he is a rough patch on a delicate shawl—and then the inevitable happens. I don't have to write about that extensively. All those ridiculous and despicable things that result from such a state of affairs are public knowledge. Now of what use is the father's pampering to the daughter? Had he found a suitable husband for her in the first place it would have been better. He would have the joy of seeing her happily settled in her married life.

You would not like a bad, ugly, cruel, uneducated wife, full of vices; why then should a wife like such a husband? Just as you desire a good wife, she also longs for a good husband. Let me remind you of something. When you are young and your parents are very poor, they are greatly worried about your marriage. At that time, they borrow heavily and somehow manage to marry you off. In such circumstances you can hardly expect to get a beautiful girl for a wife. At that time, even a wife who is as ugly as an owl seems like a Venus to you. But later on, when you are blessed by the goddess Saraswati, and have become "learned" and educated, when you get promoted in your job, you are ashamed of this first wife. Because you are wealthy now, you consider her to be worthless. She is nothing more to you than a servant or a cook whom you can hire to keep house for you for a few small coins. For you, she is just a slave you have bought for a thousand rupees. Perhaps you love even your dog or your horse more than your wife. A wife is nothing but a dark corner or a heap of rubbish in the house. Who cares for her? But why would a rich man care for his wife? For him wives come a dime a dozen. The rich are ready to be bridegrooms any day—indeed every day. It is only because Yama, the God of Death, doesn't have time to carry off their wives so fast. Otherwise they wouldn't mind tying the knot thrice a day. Such men find it very difficult to call an ugly wife their own. When they were poor, in the past, nobody took any notice of them. But now that they have acquired wealth and prestigious jobs, they have risen in public esteem. So they want a wife who will match that pomp with her beauty. Just watch all those silly pranks they get up to at the time of their second or third marriages. Now tell me, do women ever behave in this fashion? Whether in prosperity or in poverty, they always behave obediently, according to your commands. Have you ever heard of a woman running off with another man just because her husband is ugly or poor? Now who deserves to be blamed? Women or men?

The sixth argument against women is that a woman is enveloped in a hundred guises of fraud and deceit. My friends, as far as these particular merits are concerned, the honor of the first rank undoubtedly goes to you. How can I describe your deceit? One comes across it virtually at every step. Oh, what guises you don! Those yellow-black stripes that you draw on your body—like a tiger! You are a Gosavi, a fakir, a Haridas, a brahmachari, a sadhu, a dudhahari, a Giripuri, a bharati, a Nanak, a kanfate, a yogi[6] . . . what a fanfare you create. You smear your body with the so-called holy ash, grow your hair long into a mass of matted locks, proclaim that you have renounced the world, and roam all over cheating and deceiving people with your beguiling tricks. "Who's this?" "Ramgirkar-buwa." "Who's that?" "Shastribuwa." "And this?" "The great sage, Ganpatbuwa Phaltankar, a mahasadhu!" "That one there?" "A follower of Nanaka." Somebody just has to say "Look at his virtues! They defy any description! He's wonderful. Besides, he is free from all worldly desires. He has great magical powers," and so on. That is enough of an introduc-tion for a credulous public! Then the fake sadhu goes on prolonging his stay, putting on grander and grander pretensions. He gorges himself with rich, sweet food like a fat tomcat, and then begins his "worship." That is, reposing in a corner, he closely eyes all the women who come for an audience with him, and selects a few beautiful ones whose names he reiterates on his rosary. That's the end! All gods are forgotten promptly and forever. And these "goddesses," in the form of beautiful women, occupy that place. In his eyes, their lovely, smiling faces and in his heart a burning desire for money. Torn between these two cravings, the sadhu hovers between the worlds of sanity and madness. . . .

A tulsi necklace around the neck, God's name on your lips . . . with this paraphernalia you roam around in the guise of a Haridas, but what are you really? Nothing but beggars! Respectable-looking beggars! You go to Kashi, don't you? But just because you have shaved off your mustache and your beard, do you think you are absolved of all sin? . . .

Once you become sannyasis, you shouldn't hanker after any worldly ambitions. With your holy saffron clothes, your staffs and pails of holy water in your hands, you declare that all the creatures in this world are the manifestations of God. You sit on the *ghats* after bathing in the river, smearing yourselves with sackfuls of ash, pretending to be lost in meditation. But at the first sound of tinkling anklets, don't your eyes race up all the fifty steps of the ghat? The *buwa* is so utterly flustered that he drops the pail of holy water from his hand. . . . With what words can I describe your guile? You will assure somebody that he is like a brother to you, but at the same time wish for his ruin in your heart. You call another your father, but with your eye on his purse. And when you are friends with

---

6. Note from original editors Susie Tharu and K. Lalita: "These titles for holy men are Tarabai's satirical inventions."

someone, you eye everything, from his dog to his wife, with malicious desire. There are very few among the male sex who are pure. One should hear your gossip with your friends. "Why, that Mr. X shows off so much these days! What fun if he is ruined! How that Mr. Y has risen! What a marvel it is! There were times when that son of a donkey didn't have enough food to eat! But now the son of a bitch goes around in a two-horse carriage!" This is your favorite hobby, isn't it? The moral of the story is, with evil in your mind, like a crow, you roam around looking for the weaknesses of people to wreck them. Do women ever behave like that? Tell me. Did any woman ever disguise herself as a sadhu and carry any man off? Give me just one example. . . .

The next argument against women is this: A woman is temptation incarnate. All right. A woman is full of charm from top to toe. Everything about her—her limbs, her voice, her gait, her speech—fascinates and attracts men like a magnet, like a honeycomb attracts a honeybee. But is that any of her fault?

If a great brahmachari sadhu is asked to choose between a pot of gold coins and a beautiful woman, he will undoubtedly forsake the pot of gold for the golden complexion. . . .

In these days, because of the spread of education and because of the printing press, many works of fiction have been published. For example, *Manjughosha, Muktamala*, the play *Manorama*, and so on. Now it is true that no story becomes really interesting without a sprinkling of romance, humor, and pathos. But the composers of these stories should at least check whether such stories are plausible, or whether they have any historical validity, before starting the composition.

Let's take a look at *Manjughosha* first. Manjughosha is the favorite daughter of an emperor. Is it possible that she could deceive her old father and impudently run away with Vasantamadhava in his airplane? Wouldn't she have any sympathy for her old father, who treated her with so much love and affection? She was known as virtue incarnate; then how could she desert her jeweled palace and forsake its pleasures for a strange prince whose name and origin she did not know? Didn't the image of her old father rise before her eyes when she left? Didn't she feel guilty in any way? Dear readers, you can judge for yourselves the truth of such a story. It's thousands of years since the Dwaparyuga ended and the Kaliyuga began.[7] Even the English rule in this country is two hundred and fifty years old. The writer of this book, I'm sure, was born in this century itself. But I'm sure that all our ancestors put together couldn't ten generations ago visualize anything like Vasantamadhava's airplane.

The English people have invented many machines: trains, airplanes, and so on. But even they haven't got the trick of using an airplane for anything they want to. You can decide for yourselves how incredible it is to imagine that Vasantamadhava mastered its entire intricate mechanism for the sole purpose of carrying off Manjughosha.

---

7. Dwaparyuga is the third of the world's four ages; Kaliyuga is the present age.—Ed.

Another book in the same tradition is *Muktamala*. Muktamala was the daughter of a famous knight. Her husband had been thrown into prison as a result of the king's wrath. In her attempts to meet him, she got into the clutches of the despotic officer Bhadraksha. He tortured her and kept her prisoner in a thick forest. But she never surrendered her virtue, which is a woman's true religion. It is probably the intention of the writer to demonstrate this. Now what I want to debate is this. A woman is as frail as an ant compared to the towering strength of a man; why, all the strength in the whole of her body would be less than the strength contained in the arm of a man. If such a lustful tiger chased a poor helpless cow in a lonely and unprotected place, would he refrain from killing her as well?

Why, even your gods are treacherous. No wonder you are the same. Indra impersonated Gautama to seduce a virtuous wife like Ahalya. Didn't His Holiness, Lord Krishna, go and ruin the virtue of a great wife like Chandrawal, who loved her husband so much? No, if you start wrecking houses treacherously, what can a woman's *pativratadharma* do?[8] How can a woman protect her true religion, her loyalty to her husband?

Krishna at least is a God. He holds in even balance sins and moral achievements. He is omnipotent and knows the truth. A woman could save herself from your hands only if God himself takes pity on her and cuts you into tiny pieces at such times. Otherwise she can't even dream of being rescued. Such stories are true only in books. The preacher tells us from his pulpit that eating aubergines is forbidden in the Puranas and one shouldn't eat them. But the moment he is back from his preaching, all that he has said is promptly forgotten and he stuffs himself with a hearty meal of those very vegetables. Obviously what he preaches is only for other people to follow. What use is such knowledge? And who follows such dicta? Who cares about the sufferings of a woman? She can escape a tyrant only by smashing her head at his feet. Otherwise escape is impossible. So what is the intention behind writing such books? They are based on such obviously childish logic. One who knows the ways of the world can easily see how false the whole thing is.

Let us now turn to the play *Manorama*. The playwright has delineated four types of situations here. In the first, the couple Manorama and Ganapatrao are shown to have come to a good end because they are both cultured and educated. The couple Godubai and Ramrao Phadnis, on the other hand, are most ill matched. This is apparently to show how young wives ignore their old husbands and how contemptuously they treat them. Later on the writer presents elaborate descriptions of Godubai reveling in her native vileness after Ramrao's death, her becoming a laughingstock in the court of law, the police inspector's style of working, and the testimony of Saraswatibai and Tuka the barber. In the third situation, we have the couple Gangu and poor Vinayakrao. Gangu doesn't love her husband because of his poverty, and through the machinations of Saraswatibai, she becomes friendly with loafers and runs off to Karachi to openly become a whore. There,

---

8. Note from original editors Susie Tharu and K. Lalita: "*Pativratadharma* refers to a wife's religion. This is a concept somewhat like that of 'virtue' with many dimensions and many implications. A wife's religion is the worship of a husband, whom she must consider a god."

once again we find descriptions of the false affections of whores, their false words, their hollow promises, and so on.

The fourth section consists of the account of Rambhatji's daughter-in-law Thaku, who is a widow. Later she becomes pregnant and after going through every kind of suffering imaginable, she dies in extreme distress of some horrible disease in Bottlebhoy's hospital in Bombay.

All these different types of stories have been cooked up by the dramatist, but the question is, To what end? In fact, by writing such a play the writer has exposed himself in public and made himself a butt of ridicule. It's true that a clenched hand contains a million, every house has skeletons in its cupboards, and every house has some darkness and some light. Every house, however, also has a widow—either a sister, or mother, or daughter-in-law, or daughter. A stigma to one is a stigma to all. What a grand achievement it is that this author has managed to malign all widows by one stroke of his pen! Who can claim that all parents will learn their lesson from this play and get their daughters married only to good and virtuous husbands; and that Lady Luck will smile upon all women as she did on Manorama!

Similarly, old dogs like Ramrao will never learn a lesson from the play just because they see how Ramrao married a young adventuress only to have his prestige auctioned off in the crowded court of law. That will never stop them from marrying young girls in their old age. There shouldn't be any doubt that those who marry when they are so old will be disgraced and subjected to ridicule both in private and in public. But it is impossible to believe that all women will run away from husbands who are inferior to them.

Now it is hardly surprising that Thaku died in the hospital. After all, she was going to die anyway. Either at home or in the hospital. Dear authors, please don't imagine, even in your wildest dreams, that you will be able to strike terror into the hearts of people and persuade them never to do such things again simply by writing such stories.

In short, it is you who are vice incarnate. Why blame women? Women like Anadibai, the aunt of the Peshwas who was notorious for her murderous deeds, are far less in number than similar men. There will not be more than ten women like Vijayalakshmi in a hundred, either.[9]

And even if a woman is guilty of any monstrous deeds, she is, nonetheless, superior to man. Once you win her over with your various tricks, and become the king of her heart, she trusts you implicitly and loves you with every fiber of her being. Then you become the most precious thing for her, next to her virtue, of course. She offers you nothing less than her life. How can she see through your treacherous game? Because at such times you behave like a slave to her. You win her favors with such an obtrusive and officious manner that you are ready to even lick her shoes. Yes, your love knows no bounds, but for how long? Until your lust is satiated. Once your desire is fulfilled, and

9. From the context it seems likely that Vijayalakshmi would have been familiar to readers as an example of a "notorious" woman.—Ed.

she becomes pregnant, you leave all the worrying and suffering to her and hide your face like a scorpion, behind a stone. When that mortified woman, innocent as a deer, crushed to death by that burden on her soul, begs the wicked man, that beast in disguise, to help her, he answers her with such indifference as if it were none of his concern. "What can I do about it? You have sinned and now you must suffer for it." Ah, what an answer! What must she feel when she hears such words from the same mouth that had uttered words dripping with love, which she regarded with utmost love, for which she was prepared to throw away her life and soul? They are not words, they are poisoned arrows. Think of her condition when she hears such words. But what can the poor woman do? Utterly destitute, she had no courage left but to abandon the child, her own flesh and blood, to save the honor for which she has to undergo so severe a punishment.

Here under the British rule, not a leaf can be moved without a witness! But in such delicate affairs, witnesses are conspicuously absent. The government also deserves to be blamed for this. They have passed a law that the punishment given to him who offers a bribe will be double that given to him who accepts it. Similarly, I would suggest that they should pass a law in such cases as well by which the man should get twice as much punishment as woman gets. Why shouldn't it be so? Even in ancient civilizations like Rome and Greece such crimes used to be punished most severely. I have one suggestion to offer in this regard. The government should brand the stupid prattling mouths of these men with red-hot irons. This will strike terror in their hearts and such crimes will never be committed! Think of that miserable woman who later on spends her life in some godforsaken corner, or in the jail, mourning her fate, weeping her heart out, trying to wash the stains off her character. All her honor is torn to rags by such public disgrace. Many commit suicide, many abandon their relatives, give up their wealth, and go into exile. Even a cobra is preferable to you. At least it kills immediately. But the poison that you inject into her afflicts her with intolerable agony and causes her to die a slow, slow death. Thus, you are more treacherous than even a poisonous snake. You can judge who has a more generous mind. Will you ever suffer as much as she does for you?

Never, never will you be so kind! Never can you be so generous! No sooner have you ruined one than you are ready to go after another. Then you won't remember the first one even in a dream. But a woman's love is as deep as an ocean. She will value the man she loves even more than her own life. He may torture her, but she will always be on his side. Thus her heart is always full of tender love for him, but look how she's rewarded.

I'm sure there are very few men who are ruined by women. But it would be difficult even to guess at the number of women ruined by men. You are far too clever for women. You are, in fact, nothing but scoundrels of the first order! You are so cunning that you will pass through a sugarcane field without letting those sharp leaves touch you, let alone scratch you. You organize big meetings every day, deliver impressive speeches, offer unwanted advice to all and sundry, and do a hundred other such stupid things. You are nothing but learned asses! Yes, that's what you are really. It is said that it's always dark just under a lamp! You are no exception to that rule! If only you realized how much evil you contain, it would break your heart! . . .

Translated by Maya Pandit

LALITHAMBIKA ANTHERJANAM, *THE GODDESS OF REVENGE*

It was nearly midnight. I was sitting alone in the room where I usually did all my writing. The compassionate goddess of sleep stood by me, waiting to enfold in her caress the wounds that my spirit had accumulated in the course of all the hard work I had been doing. But I knew that if I threw down the pen and paper I had taken up to write my story, I would not be able to touch them again till this time tomorrow. And the same obstacles would present themselves tomorrow. I sat there, wrapped in thought. Silence lay deep around me, interrupted now and then by the sounds of two rats engaged in love talk in the attic above, or the snores of the children sleeping in the next room. The light from the lamp on the table crept out through the window and threw fearful shadows onto the thick darkness outside. The hooting of the many owl families that were my neighbors sounded like a warning in my ears. I must confess: I am a coward by nature. Especially at this deceptive hour of night.

I closed and bolted the window. And raised the wick of the lamp. I checked whether any of the children were awake or whimpering, then came back to my usual place. I had to finish writing today, come what may, but what was I going to write about? How was I to begin? Now that I had sat down to write, all the attendant problems rose up to confront me. Story writing is not a pleasant task. Especially for a woman like me, who nurtures her ideals on a sense of status and prestige, on an awareness of being nobly born. When fictional characters come to life and argue heatedly about contemporary issues, the author has to face opposition from many quarters. If an opponent were to use the weapon of obscene language against me, would I be able to defend myself with a like weapon? And then, the subject of caste distinctions was taboo, and religious restrictions were to be avoided at all costs. Indeed, we have arrived at a point at which writers have perforce to decide well in advance which particular literary theorist's recriminations they will have to face. It was all very distressing. I suddenly wanted to give it all up.

I threw my pen onto the table, filled with an obscure sense of anger, and closed my eyes. Innumerable characters passed through my mind as I sat there: people I had seen and not seen, people who were still alive and those who were dead. Women and men. Creatures tormented by pain. Those who had lost their voices, though their throbbing hearts thudded like thunderclouds, flashed like lightning. Were they demanding to be transcribed? I was afraid. But also inspired. Suddenly, I heard the sound of footsteps coming toward me, from the next room.

SOURCE: Lalithambika Antherjanam, "Praticaradevatha" (The Goddess of Revenge), in *Women Writing in India 600 B.C. to the Present*, vol. 1, eds. Susie Tharu and K. Lalita (New York: Feminist Press, 1991).

What could it mean? I sat up, startled. I had closed the door, bolted it securely, and locked it. And I had not even heard it being pushed open. It was midnight. Although I did not believe in ghosts, I trembled in fear. My head began to spin. My eyes closed tight. The footsteps grew firmer and firmer. They came and actually stood next to me, but I could not move.

The seconds ticked by. Did five minutes pass, or a whole hour? I can't say. Time stopped for a long while. Then I heard a woman's voice just in front of me, a firm, yet fine and delicately modulated voice:

"Are you asleep? Or afraid?" she said.

I remained very still. I did not have the strength to move, anyway. The voice went on, its sweetness tinged with a shade of mockery.

"When I heard that you wrote stories, I did not imagine that you would be such a coward. After all, a good writer usually witnesses so many scenes of agony and terror."

The eagerness to know the identity of this person, who had made such detailed enquiries about me, drove my fear away. I opened my eyes. In front of me, the figure of a woman took shape from the surrounding texture of dream. A woman . . . not a young girl. Not bold or proud. Not old either. All I can say is that she seemed a wonderful manifestation of meaning itself. Sorrow, a certain austerity, disgust, disappointment: all these mingled in her expression. The sparks of an intense fire of revenge burned fearfully in her eyes—I recognized the emotion as from the leaves of some forgotten book from the distant past. She went on, in a voice filled with power and tenderness.

"I've come with a purpose. I know you are looking for a story to write, that you are having trouble finding one. I have one in my keeping, a first-class one, which is going to waste for lack of someone to use it. If you agree . . . if you can listen to it without being terrified. . . . "

I had mustered my courage by now. "It's true that I panicked. But isn't that because of the time, the circumstances? But, please, for heaven's sake, tell me who you are. And how you got here at this time of night, through a locked door."

"Who am I?" She burst out laughing. "So you want to know who I am, do you? "Whether I'm a human being, or an evil spirit, a ghost or a witch. What superb courage."

She laughed out loud again, sounding like a forest stream that breaks its banks and overflows. Her laughter thudded against the walls of the room. But this time, I did not wince.

"I confess that I am a coward," I said. "But how can I have anything to do with you unless I know who you are? Human beings come to know the very stars in the sky by giving them names and positions of their own."

"Human beings? For heaven's sake, don't count me among them, Sister," she interrupted, looking displeased. "There was a time when I loved to be known as a human being, when I expended my greatest efforts on staying one. But I have learned—and taught others—that I never want to be called a human being again, and particularly not a woman. To be human, how deceitful it is, how cruel, what an experience of agony."

"Maybe you are right," I admitted. "But the pain and agony are gifts that are granted only to human beings. They are links in a divine golden chain."

She shook her head, prevented me from going on: "Stop this foolish raving: 'divine,' 'golden.' What melodious descriptions! A 'golden chain' indeed. Let me ask you, what advantage do golden chains have over iron ones, if they are meant to be fetters? Only this: that iron shows its true colors. And gold? What a glitter. A mere coating. God! What does it prove but the difference between a human being and a devil?"

Her face, which was full of hatred for her fellow beings, seemed transformed into something nonhuman. I could not be certain whether her expression signified sorrow, hatred, pride, or revenge, but I found it a singularly attractive mixture of all these emotions, and my eyes were riveted on her. What deep despair, what grief that life must have experienced in the past!

"So you're waiting to hear my story," she continued, after a short silence. "All right. I've come for that, anyway. It is an old story. It happened more than a hundred years ago and it is a true story, one that shook the world to its foundations when it happened. You had not been born then, neither had your social organizations, with their penchant for debate, nor their leaders. And yet, the turmoil that this story created over a great part of Kerala still continues. Some of the characters who figured in it may still be alive. Have you heard of Thu-Tatri?"

Oh, oh, so this was her. I drew back sharply in fear. This was the woman whose name our mothers had forbidden us even to utter, the very memory of whose name awakened horror. This was—oh, what could I say?

She smiled, with evident delight at my distress. "Yes, yes, you're thinking, which Namboodiri woman has not heard of that unfortunate creature, aren't you?[1] No one says so in so many words. But everyone knows. But, look, child! Do you know for whom, for what, that ill-fated 'thing' sacrificed her life? She too was a pure and untainted young girl once, like all of you. She wove chains of sacred grass. She recited her prayers with a holy thread in her hands. She performed all the ritual fasts. She was as meek as a doll; after the age of ten, she never looked at a man's face, or spoke to him. Grandmothers advised young girls who had started their periods to learn from Tatri's shining example. But you and I know that all this is part of an outward show. By the time we are seventeen or eighteen, we acquire an amazing capacity to keep our feelings under control. As we sit in the veranda by the light of the new moon, chanting our prayers, we hold the sighs that rise in our hearts to ourselves; no one ever hears them. Singing the 'Parvathi Swayamvaram' and other auspicious marriage songs, moving our feet in time to their rhythm, we learn to control the trembling in our throats. Yet, do we not listen for the sound of men's footsteps from the living room? Even while struggling with the prickly, exasperating *kuvalam*, our hearts are full of the fragrance of mango blossoms.[2] And we wait. Not just days and

---

1. Namboodri is the term for a subcaste within the privileged Brahmin caste.—Ed.
2. The *kuvalam* is a tropical fruit with a hard shell.—Ed.

months, but years. Till at last one day our mothers come to us with henna and a silver ring. Whether our hands are placed in those of an old man or a young one, a sick man or a libertine, is all a matter of destiny. We can do nothing but endure.

"People told me that I had been singled out for a very special destiny. I was his first wife. And he was not an old man either. He had enough to live on at home. So I started married life with a boundless sense of happiness. He was a passionate man. I nurtured my desires to suit his. I did my utmost to satisfy his preferences in our conjugal life, with the same attention with which I prepared food to please his palate. After all, a husband is considered to be a god in person. It was to give pleasure to this god that I learned a harlot's ways, those talents that were to become so notorious later. It was he who taught them to me. If it had been otherwise, my sister! If I too had become a meek wife, ignored by her husband, like countless women in our society, I wonder whether this cursed happening would have been blown so much out of proportion. I don't know. Maybe the intoxication of physical pleasure crept insidiously into my mind and lingered there as a fragrance. But he was the sole person enclosed within that fragrance, I swear it. That is why I was so upset when we started to drift apart gradually. He began to stay away from home for many nights in succession. Occasionally, it was because he had to perform a religious rite, or attend a temple festival. He would stay in rich, princely houses then. When we met, more and more rarely, I would weep before him, find fault with him. To whom could I unburden my sorrows, except to him?

"He would laugh, indifferent to the pleas of a broken heart. Man is free. He lives for pleasure. Just because he had tied a thali around the neck of a woman—and a woman who is only half Namboodiri at that—he could not waste his youth on her.

"Anger and fury sharpened within me. I wanted to batter myself, I wanted to die. I even cursed myself for having been born. Why had I been born a Namboodiri woman? Couldn't I have been born into some other caste in Kerala, some caste that would have given me the right to answer this arrogant man in his own coin?

"And yet, on every birthday, I bathed and prayed for a long and happy married life. I offered ghee lamps and garlands of *thumba* flowers in the temple. All I wanted now was to see him sometimes so that I could fill my eyes with his presence. Just as when I began to have my periods I had begun to pray for a husband, I longed now for my husband's love.

"Thanks to the generosity of our *karyasthan*, we did not starve.[3] But emotions and sensations have their own hunger, don't they? Greed. Thirst. Once brought to life, they cannot be quelled. They creep into the bloodstream, into the veins, they melt in them and simmer there. That was what happened to him too. But then. Ha! He was a man, I a woman, a woman born into a cursed society.

"Like all Namboodiri women, I too endured, kept my feelings in check, and went on. It happened without any warning: one evening, he came home with his new wife. They

---

3. The *karyasthan* is a steward who manages the affairs of the estate in important landowning families.—Ed.

slept in the very room where I had slept with him. I did not mind serving food to that harlot. But though I had read Shilavathi's story a hundred times, making their bed was—[4] Although I was a Namboodiri woman, I was a human being too. Maybe I accused her of being a prostitute. Maybe I cursed her for being a slut and a harlot. That was the first time I thought of men as devils. The first time my husband became a murderer in my eyes. I could have borne the torture for myself. But when he, my husband, used the same words: 'I brought her home deliberately, knowing she's a harlot. I like harlots. Why don't you become one yourself?'

"Ah, what a cruel blow that was. Even to think of it petrifies me. Imagine a husband telling his chaste, highborn wife, a woman who worships him, 'If you want me to love you, you must become a prostitute.' An irrational, uncontrollable desire for revenge took hold of my mind. But only for an instant. My faith stood in the way. 'No, I can't stay here, even for a single day.'

"After that, I never spoke to him again. I never spoke to anyone. The days went by somehow, empty of events, empty of anyone to love. If only something would move in this hell of darkness! I went back to the house where I was born, my heart full of a limitless grief, a burden of sorrow that it could hardly bear. I thought I would find comfort and relief at home, but I was wrong. In truth, are not all Namboodiri houses a kind of prison? There is little to choose between them. My father was dead, but all my five mothers were still alive. My elder brother was looking for a wife to replace the fourth one, who had just died. Two of my older sisters, both widowed, were staying at home. The third one had gone mad, because her Namboodiri husband had tortured her, and was roaming around somewhere. Two younger sisters had grown up and become a burden on the house, a continual source of worry to their mother. I joined them, going from the frying pan into the fire. Who would not long for whatever small comfort one could grasp amid such grief? At least within the limits that society permitted—I was still young. My body bloomed with good health. I knew I could afford the arrogance of being certain that I was more beautiful than the prostitutes who kept my husband company. And yet, when I combed my hair, placed the bright red *kumkum* between my eyebrows and peeped out through the barred door, all I felt was a desire to see the world, or, at most, an innocent longing that someone should notice how beautiful I was. There were men who met my eyes, returned my smile. After all, people tend to smile if you smile at them. It soon became a habit. Were not those highborn brahmins susceptible precisely because they knew I was a Namboodiri girl? They were aware of the consequences. But so long as nobody knew about them, they indulged in the basest actions.

"Scandalous reports began to spread. And meaningful looks. I heard murmurs. The women's quarters turned into a fifth column. Amma cursed whenever she caught sight of me. 'You sinner, born to ruin the family's honor! Why were you ever born in my womb?'

4. Shilavathi is the archetypal figure of a selfless woman whose entire life is given to pleasing her husband.—Ed.

"My brother's wife said one day, 'Tatri, don't come into the kitchen anymore. I'd rather you didn't touch anything there.'

"I did not understand the nature of the crime for which I was being punished. I had touched no man except my husband. I had not even dared to think of another man that way. If I peeped out of the window, if someone saw me and was attracted to me, how could that be my fault? But the world does not concern itself with such questions. My heart hardened as stones of mockery were hurled at me. My mind whirled with the fear of degradation. Then suddenly, I knew I could take anything that came to me. I had reached a point where I could bear anything. Darkness surrounded me on all sides. My enemies hissed at me from within a smoke-filled darkness like poisonous serpents. They stung me, bit me. To defend myself in this battle unto death, I had to become a poisonous serpent too. The desire for revenge and the hatred that had lain dormant within me blazed high. If I tell you about the decision they forced me to, it will make you draw back in fear. You will tremble, and drive me out of here. Oh, my sister, what I did was as much for your sake as mine. For the sake of all Namboodiri women who endure agonies. So that the world would realize that we too have our pride. I wanted to prove that we have strength and desire and life in us too. I delighted in the sorrow each man had to bear, for not a single tear shed by a Namboodiri woman has value. But, alas, all of you, for whom I did this, despised me. My very name was uttered with disgust, even in my lifetime. I was feared more than a devil. Even in the fashionable world of today, Tatri remains despicable; even you look upon me as a fallen and disgraced woman."

Her voice trembled at this point in her story. Her eyes filled. Weighed down by an unbearable sadness, she put her head down on the table. Silently, without moving, I sat watching that personification of hopelessness. The destiny of a woman like her, placed in such a situation, could take so many directions. If that broken life were to disintegrate completely, if its shattered remnants were to be scattered on the roadside like fragments of broken glass, surely it could not be her fault. Only the base tenets that had made her what she was could be blamed. For a Namboodiri woman who feels the heat of emotion, who feels proud to be alive, there is only one of two ways possible. Either she must go mad, or fall from grace. Both ways are hard.

Maybe she had no tears left to shed. She sat up. A flame that would have burned up even the fires of hell blazed in her eyes.

"No, child! I will not cry anymore. This is my last moment of weakness. I knew I would never be terrified again, not even if the seas swept over me or the skies fell down. Fear ceases to exist when life and death seem no different from each other. I had made my decision. If this was my ultimate destiny, I must transform it into an act of revenge. I must avenge my mothers, my sisters, countless women who had been weak and helpless. I laid my life, my soul, everything I possessed, at this sacrificial altar of revenge and sought the blessing of the gods. Let everyone see—and learn—that not only man, but woman also could bring herself down to the lowest level. My capacity to err or cause to err must become more powerful: if I was to be cast out of society, if I was to be ostracized and excommunicated, I wanted to be sure that I was not innocent. No one was going to punish me for a crime that I had not committed. If I was going to be pushed aside, others who were mean and cruel were going to fall with me. I wanted people to learn a lesson from the event, If justice and fair play really existed, would it not be necessary to excommunicate more Namboodiri men than women?

"From that night onward, a new face was seen at all the temple festivals, the face of a fascinating woman. She was passionate and beautiful. But more than her loveliness, it was a bewitching air of shyness, a gentleness of nature, that attracted men to her. Princes, titled chiefs, noblemen of all ranks crowded around her. I told them all that I was a married woman and not a prostitute. I told them I had a husband, I told them everything, openly, offering them a chance to break free. But the answer that they gave never varied: that bondage to a husband was not stipulated in this land of Parasurama.[5] All women, except those of one single caste, are free here. They could do as they liked. This was the pattern their comforting excuses followed. Oh, the minds of these men, who pretended to be self-respecting, pure and saintly, even ascetic. If only men who insisted that their wives remain chaste did not deliberately seduce other men's wives.

"Would not a woman who was aware that so many were attracted to her succumb finally, in spite of herself? Particularly one condemned to the women's quarters of a Namboodiri household, whom other women spit on and kicked? It was an age when the greed for flesh knew no bounds. The fame of this new harlot spread far and wide. Those who came to her went away gladdened. Nor did she forget to persuade them to express their satisfaction through gifts to her. And so the reputation of many who swaggered as honorable men of society came into the keeping of this prostitute.

"Only one man was left to come to me. The man I had waited for unceasingly. Surely, he would not fail to come when he heard of this beautiful, strong-willed woman, for he loved a passionate life. It was five years since we had met. Although I recognized him when we met at the trysting place in the temple courtyard, he did not make me out. How could he have recognized me? How could anyone have guessed that this proud and confident woman, this jewel among prostitutes, was that humble Namboodiri wife of long ago?

"That was an unforgettable night. It was the night I had lived for for so long, the night for which I had let myself be degraded. At least I was able to delight him that once. Ever since he had said to me, 'Go and learn to be a prostitute,' his command had lain simmering in my consciousness. If a woman who learns the ways of a prostitute in order to delight her husband can be considered chaste, I was another Shilavathi. I think it was a blissful night for him too. For, a little while before we parted, he said to me, 'I've never been with anyone as intelligent and beautiful as you. I wish I could always stay with you.'

"He had trapped himself. I asked, 'Are you certain that you've never met anyone like me?'

---

5. Parasurama is a mythological hero who killed his mother at the command of his father.—Ed.

"He lifted his sacred thread, held it high in his hand, and swore, 'By this wealth I possess as a brahmin, this symbol of my caste, I have never seen a woman as passionate and intelligent as you in all my life.'

"A triumphant smile was on my lips. I raised my voice a little and said, 'That's a lie. Remember your wife. Was she not as pleasing as I am?'

"Light was dawning on him. He looked suddenly at my face, screamed and got up. 'Oh God! Is it Tatri! Tatri! Tatri!' I do not know where he went, or when he stopped, when he ran out that day.

"The story is nearly over. You know what happened after that. The affair provoked an ethical debate that rocked Kerala to its very foundations. From great prince to highborn brahmin, men trembled, terrified because they did not know whose names this harlot was going to betray. Some men ran away and escaped. Others performed propitiatory rites, praying that she would forget their names at the time when she was being cross-examined.

"One man's ring, with his name engraved on it. Another's gold waist chain. Yet another's *kashavu angavastram*.[6] The incriminating pieces of evidence were used to prove the guilt of sixty-five men, including scholars well versed in the Vedas. I could have made it possible to excommunicate not just these sixty-five, but sixty thousand men. And not I alone. In those days, any lovely and intelligent woman who practiced this profession could have brought ruin upon entire families of landlords and wealthy aristocrats. And yet, I did not go that far, even though I knew the power of a Namboodiri woman's curse. That historically famous debate had to end there. A longstanding grievance was assuaged. Could it be considered simply an act of revenge performed by a prostitute? Or was it also the expression of the feeling of revenge experienced by all Namboodiri women who are caught in the meshes of evil customs, who are tortured and made to suffer agonies? Tell me, Sister! Tell me! Who is more culpable: the man who seduces a woman in order to satisfy his lust for flesh, or the woman who transgresses the dictates of society in an attempt to oppose him? Whom would you hate more? Whom would you reject? Give me an answer at least now, after so many years have gone by."

I sat amazed, unable to utter a single word while she recounted this extraordinary autobiography. I felt frozen, helpless.

Remarking on my silence, she continued, with an air of profound hopelessness, "So, perhaps I've made a mistake. Why did I come here today? Why did I try to talk to yet another of those Namboodiri women who are without shame or self-respect, another slave among slaves? They will never learn to improve their lot. Never." Her voice trembled with anger and grief.

But I felt no anger toward her. I said to her softly, "My poor sister! I am not trying to find fault with you. On the contrary, I have deep sympathy for you. In truth, you are not

6. A cloth with a border of gold thread.—Ed.

an individual anymore; you are society itself. You are timidity and weakness, weeping before strength, helpless womanhood screaming for justice, bloodstained humanity whose desires and talents have been ground into dust.

"How can the expression of that irremediable hopelessness and helplessness be identified with your own? Think of it, there is another side to all this. I have been thinking about it. Fired as you were with the intoxication of revenge, why did you not try to inspire all the other weak and slavish Namboodiri women? Why did you shoulder the burden of revenge all alone? In matters of this kind, Sister, individuals cannot triumph. On the other hand, they can bring disaster upon themselves. Consider, now, what good did it do to society, that hurricane you set in motion? Men began to torture Namboodiri women all the more, using that incident as a weapon. We are close now to bowing our heads once again under the same yoke. Not even the women in the families of the sixty-five who were excommunicated have been released from their agony."

I too was shaken by emotion. I continued, my voice trembling. "So, forgive me, Thu-Tatri sacrificed her very soul, but in the eyes of the world her sacrifice is remembered only as a legal affair involving a prostitute. An affair that certainly created a turmoil, but did not succeed in pointing the way to anything positive. The end cannot justify the means, Sister. Even while I recognize your courage and self-respect, I disagree with you. But Namboodiri society can never forget Tatri. From the heart of a great silence, you managed to throw out an explosive, brightly burning spark. It was a brave warning, a cry of victory. Falling into the minds of the generations to come, the torch it ignited still burns high and threatening. By the fire of its radiance, all the sins of that avenging angel are forgiven."

I held out my hands to that woman's form in affection and sympathy. Its face had paled. Its eyes grew lifeless. "Oh, I am a sinner. A fallen woman. An evil spirit. Even my shadow must never fall over society."

Continuing to talk, her form faded slowly, like the dissolving of a mist from the past. The crowing of a cock woke me from my dream, which of course was of no consequence.

Translated by Gita Krishnankutty

9

PROBLEMS OF TRANSLATION AND TRANSNATIONAL FEMINISMS
On Gu Ruopu and Li Ruzhen

Liang Luo

Literary translations, according to Walter Benjamin, are the "afterlife" of literary works (Benjamin 71–73). When Gu Ruopu's poetic rebuttal against criticism on women's education is translated from its seventeenth-century classical Chinese into English, and included in the current volume as part of a translational history of feminist thought, problems arise. There are many layers of translation at work. In order to make this specific literary sample of Gu's thoughts accessible to a contemporary English-speaking reader concerned with feminist thought, translingual, transhistorical, and transcultural interpretations are called for.

Gu Ruopu lived an extraordinarily long life, from 1592 to 1681, in the city of Hangzhou around the famous West Lake. She is variously described as "a seventeenth-century matriarch and poet," "the famous poet and a long-time chaste widow," or "the eminent woman writer and teacher." She has long been known as the teacher and "grandma" figure of a group of talented young female poets who formed the Banana Garden Poetry Club *(jiaoyuan shishe)* in Hangzhou in the seventeenth century. Gu's identity as wife, mother, grandmother, teacher, poet, and advocate of women's education in a Confucian society is constantly highlighted in her short poem included here.

Gu's poetry was collected, prefaced, and published by her sons on her sixtieth birthday in 1652. In presenting Gu's voice from seventeenth-century China, many forces functioned on many levels in this translating process. Two rather different English translations are available in two representative contemporary anthologies on Chinese women writers, Chang and Saussy (1999) and Idema and Grant (2004). By looking at two different renditions of the title to the poem, we emphasize the interpretation and mediation inevitably involved in translation:

> Translation 1: "When I Hired a Teacher to Instruct the Girls, Someone Ridiculed Me, So as a Joke I Have Written This Retort to Explain Matters" (Chang and Saussy 309–10)
>
> Translation 2: "Purposely Written as a 'Rebuttal of Ridicule' after Having Been Criticized for Hiring a Teacher to Instruct My Daughters" (Idema and Grant 418–19)

Translation 1 follows rather strictly the sentence structure of the original Chinese, which is composed of three sets of four-character phrases: *yanshi xunnü, huoyou fengzhe, guzuo jiechao*. Each of the three English clauses in translation 1 corresponds to each set of the four-character Chinese phrase. Translation 2 shifts the last phrase, *guzuo jiechao* (and the purposeful action of writing it conveys), to the beginning, and introduces the first two phrases last (as an explanation of that action).

On one hand, one could argue, as Benjamin would have it, that the first translation "incorporate[s] the original's mode of signification, thus making both the original and the translation recognizable as fragments of a greater language, just as fragments are part of a vessel" (Benjamin 78). On the other hand, although the second translation seems to deviate from the distinctively Chinese sentence structure of "leaving blank," and to "cater" to an English readership's reading habit, it at the same time liberates the meaning of the original Chinese from its form, "so that it gives voice to the intention of the original not as reproduction but as harmony, as a supplement to the language in which it expresses itself, as its own kind of intention" (Benjamin 79).

What I am referring to in the case of the second translation is the word *jiechao* in the third phrase, *guzuo jiechao*. The translator supplied a footnote to the term and translated it as "Rebuttal of Ridicule," pointing out that it was used here as an allusion, referring to the title of a text by the male scholar Yang Xiong (53 BCE—18 CE) in the style of a rhapsody, in which he defended himself against criticisms by others. By virtue of this allusion, the second translation gives voice to the original, not by imitating its formal structure, but by entering deep into the genealogy of a masculine genre convention in a Chinese literary historical context.

How to read Gu's "Rebuttal of Ridicule," be it a translation of a masculine canon staple or not, as a possible site for the cultivation of a feminist sensibility in seventeenth-century China? Gu's conservatism seems rather obvious at first sight. She begins, as everyone else would at the time, with a grand opening describing the separation of yin (the feminine sphere) and yang (the masculine sphere) and the cultivation of ethics in human relationships. Although in the translation included in this volume, the translator chose to render the Chinese original *fuzi* as "husband" instead of "Confucius" (both interpretations are possible), one does not need to go further than the first four phrases of the poem to encounter the Confucian term *nüzhen*, namely, "women should be chaste."

Gu was a living model of female chastity of her time. Her husband died when she was twenty-nine and she had to shoulder every responsibility regarding household management and the education of her children. As a model "chaste widow," a "matriarch," and a respected poet, she was well positioned to translate and interpret Confucian classics with her distinctly strong feminine voice.

In defending her choice to hire a teacher for her daughters, Gu safely positions her argument within the accepted realm of Confucian ethics. She uses exemplary women in history to support her argument. In particular, she upholds Ban Zhao's instruction for women as a standard. Women's education becomes part of the self-cultivation process necessary not only to reach personal fulfillment, but most importantly (at least rhetorically), to maintain family reputation. It is in no way threatening to man, as Gu repeatedly puts it in her rebuttal. She would not want her daughters to sit in the exam to pursue fame and fortune.

How is such thought, safely operated within Confucianism, feminist? It is indeed difficult to argue for the feminism of Gu's position if we only focus on her poetic rhetoric, which could only have been preserved and published with a male preface on the outside and a grand opening on Confucian ethics inside the text. If we look beyond rhetoric, however, Gu's impact on a group of female poets and her instrumental role as a model for the younger women in forming poetry societies and other female communities in seventeenth-century China can not be ignored.

The other short excerpt this essay addresses is taken from the one-hundred-chapter Chinese vernacular fiction, *Jing hua yuan* (Flowers in the Mirror) by Li Ruzhen (also known in English as Li Ju-chen). It is often regarded as one of the best satires on the subjugation of women in Chinese history. Including Li Ruzhen's fiction from China of the early nineteenth century in this transnational history of feminist thought is itself an affirmation of a certain kind of "feminist" quality in this text. The "rediscovery" of the text by early twentieth-century scholars during the "new cultural movement" rested precisely on such a conviction. Foreign-educated Chinese male scholars such as Hu Shi upheld the text as "A Chinese Declaration of the Rights of Women" in an English article in 1924 (100–109, 124), while the bilingual writer Lin Yutang, famous for introducing Chinese culture to the American public, included the text in his study of "Feminist Thought in Ancient China" in 1935 (127–50). Hu Shi was a student of John Dewey at Columbia University while Lin Yutang was educated at Harvard University and the University of Leipzig—both upheld the story as a feminist text advocating equal rights for women. The current excerpt, in particular, could be interpreted as supporting evidence for such a claim. The story of a man being subjugated to foot-binding in a "woman's kingdom" in order to be cultivated as a perfect imperial consort for the woman "king" of the kingdom, seemed to have pushed social satire to its extreme.

In the remaining short critical analysis, I attempt to provide both a contextual guide to situate the excerpt in the narrative structure of the full text in regards to its "feminist" quality, and a historiographical critique of the use and abuse of the text for contemporary feminist agendas. A few words on the anthology itself are in order. As we are calling this anthology a "transnational history of feminist thought," we may want to first ask ourselves: what do we mean by feminism? What feminism? Whose feminism? Moreover, the choice of "history" rather than "theory" suggests that we are sensitive to a variety of texts with "feminist" potentials, including, but not limited to, theoretical treaties, (auto) biographical accounts, and fictional narratives. The emphasis on the latter two rather than the former suggests our departure from a rigid sense of feminism as theory. Instead, we are highlighting life experience as well as the imaginative realm in the service of social change.

Li Ruzhen's novel has been described as "an inimitable blend of mythologies and adventure story, fantasy and allegory, satire and straight instruction" (Chang 405). Experience and imagination seem to have worked hand-in-hand in this text. The story is set during the time of China's one and only woman sovereign, Empress Wu Zetian. With the real-life empress and her talented lady attendant as characters in the story, Li instilled a sense of reality into the fictional and utopian (dystopian) world he constructed as an alternative to the Confucian world (but deeply rooted in it as well) for the Chinese women.

The narrative structure of the work centers on "the fate of mirrored flowers," a literal translation of the title, *Jing hua yuan*. Here Li followed a long-established convention in the Chinese literary tradition of using flowers to depict women. *The Dream of the Red Chamber* most possibly provided him inspiration, as Li's prologue to *Flowers in the Mirror* contained whole phrases lifted straight out of the prologue of the former. Li hopes, he says, to preserve a record of the lives of these outstanding women so that the memory of them may be kept; however, the obvious irony is that these hundred women were all "celestial" beings, namely, flower spirits who took female forms. This intentional crossing between the real and the fictive and the express purpose of preserving life experience in the form of fiction urge us to link the two realms in our considerations of the feminist potential of the text.

The story starts with Empress Wu ordering the flowers to bloom in the winter, hence disrupting the natural order of things. The flowers are banished into the stream of human life and scattered all over in the form of women. Through various vicissitudes, the flower girls are united and given an opportunity to demonstrate their talent in the examinations set up for women by Empress Wu. The girls then display their loyalty to the Tang (the dynasty overtaken by Wu) by participation in the military campaigns that would bring down the Empress. The representation of women is extremely contradictory throughout the narrative structure. In this story, Empress Wu is the initiator of great reforms such as setting up schools and examination systems to bring about opportunity for women's liberation; at the same time, she is the root of the problem. As a woman she takes control of the nation, hence disrupting the "natural order of things" under the Confucian universe. That aberration has to be tamed in the end, as the flower spirits-turned-talented girls must rid the land of her for the sake of continuing the legitimate rule of the patriarchal Tang Dynasty.

Situating the short excerpt included here in the narrative structure of the flower spirits' journey "back to normal," that is, their eventual return to the Confucian order governing women's subordinate place in the family and society, one can hardly argue for a feminist reading of the text in the sense of equal rights for women. Rights for women were indeed advocated, but they were not equal. They were advocated so that women could be educated and better serve men. In Li's text, schools and examinations had to be set up specifically for women, and this rigorous schooling did not lead to political or social engagement; rather, the educated girls were returned to households and palaces to better serve others.

Then what kind of "feminist" sensibility is the text conveying? And within what framework? To answer these questions, a close reading of Li's prologue to the story offers important clues. Li's model of ideal womanhood came from the Han Dynasty female scholar Ban Zhao, whose *Precepts for My Daughters (nü jie)* has long been considered a textbook for women's proper behaviors within the framework of Confucian ethical norms. Ban advocated women's education as a way to help women to best fulfill their potential within the limits set by Confucian society. Gu Ruopu, discussed earlier, followed a similar rhetoric. They were compelled to uphold the "proper order of things," namely, the Confucian (in Gu's case, Neo-Confucian) ethics regulating women's subordinate position in the family and society, serving her father, husband, son, and, by association, the emperor.

Since the second half of the twentieth century, scholars have paid increasing attention to this "conservative" side of Li's text, and revised the early twentieth-century craze for "rediscovering" feminism in the Chinese tradition. Hu Shi's and Lin Yutang's high praise for Li has been subjected to criticism. Recognizing that the text "promotes an emancipation for women," Frederick P. Brandauer nevertheless argues against reading the text as "promoting sexual equality and equal rights for women." For him, the emancipation potential of the text "is conceived within a traditional Chinese context very clearly defined by an early Confucian ideal of womanhood" (647–60).

I agree with Brandauer in his historically situated reading of the text and share his insistence on reading the text on its own terms. However, rereading the excerpted part from the novel does invite us to associate it with a profound critique of the patriarchic Confucian gender system. The wisdom and the humor of the text, and its excellent rendition into English, make it accessible to a reader living in the twenty-first century, faraway from China. In its excerpted form, this text takes on a life of its own and presents a hilarious social satire of the bodily and psychological sufferings of women under Confucianism. That alone justifies its inclusion here, as it takes shape as what Hannah Arendt regards as a forgotten pearl in the depth of the sea (51). Though fragmented and possibly not fitting "the standard," it nonetheless crystallized illuminating insights that should not be left in the dark.

WORKS CITED

Arendt, Hannah. "Introduction: Walter Benjamin, 1892–1940." In *Illuminations: Essays and Reflections*, edited by Hannah Arendt, translated by Harry Zohn. New York: Schocken Books, 1969.

Benjamin, Walter. "The Task of the Translator, An Introduction to the Translation of Baudelaire's *Tableaux Parisiens*." In *Illuminations: Essays and Reflections*, edited by Hannah Arendt, translated by Harry Zohn, 71–73. New York: Schocken Books, 1969.

Brandauer, Frederick P. "Women in the Ching-hua yüan *(Jing hua yuan)*: Emancipation toward a Confucian Ideal." *Journal of Asian Studies* 36, no. 4 (1977): 647–60.

Chang, H. C., trans. *Chinese Literature*. Edinburgh: Edinburgh University Press, 1973.

Chang, Kang-I Sun, and Haun Saussy. *Women Writers of Traditional China: An Anthology of Poetry and Criticism*. Stanford: Stanford University Press, 1999.

Gu Ruopu. "Rebuttal or Ridicule." In *The Red Brush: Writing Women of Imperial China*, edited and translated by Wilt Idema and Beata Grant, 418–19. Cambridge: Harvard University Asia Center, 2004.

Hu Shih. "A Chinese Declaration of the Rights of Women." *Chinese Social and Political Review* 8, no. 3 (Apr. 1924): 100–109.

Idema, Wilt, and Beata Grant, eds. *The Red Brush: Writing Women of Imperial China*. Cambridge: Harvard University Asia Center, 2004.

Li Ju-chen (Li Ruzhen). "Flowers in the Mirror." In *The Essential Feminist Reader*, edited by Estelle Freedman, translated by Lin Tai-yi, 37–46. New York: Modern Library, 2007.

Lin Yutang. "Feminist Thought in Ancient China." *Tien Hsia Monthly* 1, no. 2 (1935): 127–50.

DISCUSSION QUESTIONS

For Gu Ruopu, *Rebuttal of Ridicule*

1. How did Gu justify educating her daughters when she was scolded for doing so?

2. The Four Virtues are "respectful speech, chaste conduct, proper women's work, and modest demeanor"; the Three Obediences are to one's father, one's husband, and one's oldest son. How fully did Gu work within the limits set by these ideas?

3. Gu disdains women "who cultivate appearances—they are only pretty dresses." How would you compare this with Mary Wollstonecraft's attitude toward women who are only taught to please?

For Li Ruzhen, *Flowers in the Mirror*

1. How has the male body been mistreated and feminized in the story?

2. Discuss the relationships among beauty, gender, and freedom expressed in this story.

3. As a student of feminist thought living in the twenty-first century, what do you think are the strengths and limitations of the presentation of feminism made by this fictional piece written in China roughly two hundred years ago?

GU RUOPU, *REBUTTAL OF RIDICULE*

Purposely Written as a "Rebuttal of Ridicule" after Having Been Criticized for Hiring a Teacher to Instruct My Daughters[1]

As soon as yin and yang were separated,
Social norms were created and laid out:
The husband should establish righteousness,
And the wife and daughter should be chaste.
But without studying the *Odes* and *Documents*,
One cannot fulfill one's nature and one's life.
Now some old crone has lambasted me:[2]
"You've fallen short of the Wifely Way!
You have hired a teacher for your daughters,
As if she were going to sit for the exams.
She'll pay no attention to her needlework,
And will focus instead on reading books!"
When I heard these words, [I said:]
"You fail to understand my intention!
In life, men and women are segregated.
But wifely virtue is not so easily achieved!
How can we, just because we're women,
Refuse to take the ancients as our teachers?
The wives of both King Wen and King Wu
Are praised among the 'Ten Administrators';[3]

SOURCE: Gu Ruopu, "Rebuttal of Ridicule," in *The Red Brush: Writing Women of Imperial China,* ed. and tran. Wilt Idema and Beata Grant (Cambridge, MA: Harvard University Asia Center, 2004), 418–20.

1. *Rebuttal of Ridicule* is the title of a text by Yang Xiong (53 BCE–18 CE), written very much in the style of a rhapsody, in which he defends his contentment with his lowly position against the criticisms of those who argue that his scholarship should be able to secure him a much higher position.—Ed.

2. We do not know who "the old crone" mentioned in this text refers to, but we do know that it cannot have been Gu Ruopu's mother-in-law, as she died within a month of Gu Ruopu's marriage. Gu Ruopu speaks of her mother-in-law's death in a letter written in 1632 to her two married sons on the occasion of the division of the family property. In this letter, Gu Ruopu emerges as a forceful character, very much aware that the continued prosperity of the Huang family has in large part been the result of her own efforts.—Ed.

3. The "Ten Administrators" are the ten sage ministers who assisted King Wen and King Wu in the founding of the Zhou Dynasty.—Ed.

The Venerable Madam left us her instructions,
The 'Inner Quarters' Rules' must be understood.
I am ashamed of my own ignorance,
And find I cannot minimize my faults,
And yet, I feel pity for those of today
Who worry about their looks and pretty clothes.
If I did not instruct them in their youth,
The reputation of our family would suffer.
It is through study that children are molded,
Questions and discussions sharpen and refine.
The 'Four Virtues' and 'Three Obediences':
Those ways of the ancients remain the norm.
But by chiseling and by adorning,
One can make one's person pure and good.
How could I be thinking of luster and glory?
I wish only to admonish against error and wrong!
If you can't accept these simple words of mine,
Then you should put your question to the wise!"

Translated by Wilt Idema and Beata Grant

LI RUZHEN, FROM *FLOWERS IN THE MIRROR*

[. . . .] When Tang Ao heard that they had arrived at the Country of Women, he thought that the country was populated entirely by women, and was afraid to go ashore. But Old Tuo said, "Not at all! There are men as well as women, only they call men women, and women men. The men wear the skirts and take care of the home, while the women wear hats and trousers and manage affairs outside. If it were a country populated solely by women, I doubt that even Brother Lin here would dare to venture ashore, although he knows he always makes a good profit from sales here!"

"If the men dress like women, do they use cosmetics and bind their feet?" asked Tang Ao.

"Of course they do!" cried Lin, and took from his pocket a list of the merchandise he was going to sell, which consisted of huge quantities of rouge, face powder, combs and other women's notions. "Lucky I wasn't born in this country," he said. "Catch me mincing around on bound feet!"

When Tang Ao asked why he had not put down the price of the merchandise, Lin said, "The people here, no matter rich or poor, from the 'King' down to the simplest peasant,

SOURCE: Li Ju-Chen (Li Ruzhen), "Flowers in the Mirror" (Jing hua yuan), in *The Essential Feminist Reader*, ed. Estelle B. Freedman, trans. Lin Tai-yi (New York: Modern Library, 2007), 37–46.

are all mad about cosmetics. I'll charge them what I can. I shall have no difficulty selling the whole consignment to rich families in two or three days."

Beaming at the prospect of making a good profit, Lin went on shore with his list.

Tang Ao and Old Tuo decided to go and see the city. The people walking on the streets were small of stature, and rather slim, and although dressed in men's clothes, were beardless and spoke with women's voices, and walked with willowy steps.

"Look at them!" said Old Tuo. "They are perfectly normal-looking women. Isn't it a shame for them to dress like men?"

"Wait a minute," said Tang Ao. "Maybe when they see us, they think, 'Look at them, isn't it a shame that they dress like women?'"

"You're right. 'Whatever one is accustomed to always seems natural,' as the ancients say. But I wonder what the men are like?"

Old Tuo discreetly called Tang Ao's attention to a middle-aged woman, who was sitting in front of her doorstep, sewing on a shoe. Her hair was braided and coiled smoothly on top of her head, and decorated with pearls and jade. She was wearing long golden loops of earrings with precious stones in them, and wore a long mauve gown with an onion-green shirt underneath, from which peeped the toes of tiny feet shod in red silk shoes. With long, tapering fingers, the woman was doing embroidery. She had beautiful eyes and was carefully powdered and rouged, but when she lifted her head, they saw that her lip was covered by a thick moustache.

Tang Ao and Old Tuo could not help laughing out loud.

The "woman" looked up and said, "What are you laughing at, lassies?"

The voice sounded as deep and hoarse as a cracked gong. Tang Ao was so startled that he took to his heels and ran.

But the "woman" shouted after them, "You must be women, since you have whiskers on your faces. Why are you wearing men's clothes and pretending to be men? Aren't you ashamed of yourselves! I know, you dress like this because you want to mingle with the men, you cheap hussies! Take a look at yourselves in the mirror. Have you forgotten that you are women? It's lucky for you you only met up with me! If it had been somebody else who had caught you casting those sneaky glances, you would have been beaten almost to death!"

"This is the first time I have ever had such an experience," muttered Tang Ao. "But I suspect Brother Lin will receive better treatment at their hands."

"Why?" said Old Tuo.

"Well, he is very fair, and since he lost his beard at the Country of Flaming People, he may be mistaken by these people for a real woman. But come to think of it, isn't it worrying?"

As they walked further on, they saw some "women" on the streets as well as "men." Some were carrying babies in their arms, and others leading children by the hand. All the "women" walked on dainty bound feet, and in crowded places, acted shy, as if they were embarrassed to be seen. Some of the younger ones were beardless, and upon careful study, Tang Ao discovered that some of the ageing or middle-aged "women" shaved their lips and chins in order to appear younger.

The two returned to the junk before Merchant Lin. But when the latter did not come back at supper time, and it was past the second drum, Mistress Lu began to be worried. Tang Ao and Old Tuo went on shore with lanterns to look for him, but discovered that the city gates were shut for the night.

The next day, they went to look again, but found not a trace of Lin. On the third day, some sailors went with them, but still they could not find him.

When a few days had passed, it seemed as if Merchant Lin had vanished, like a rock sinking to the bottom of the sea. Mistress Lu and Pleasant wailed with grief. Tang Ao and Old Tuo went to make inquiries every day.

They could not know that Merchant Lin had been told by one of his customers that the "King's uncle" wanted to buy some of his goods. Following instructions, he went to the "Royal Uncle's" Residence in the Palace, and handed his list of merchandise to the gate-keeper. Soon, the gatekeeper came back and said that it was just what the "King" was looking for for his "concubines" and "maids," and asked Lin to be shown into the inner apartments.

The attendant led Merchant Lin through guarded doors and winding paths until he was at the door of the inner apartments, where a guard told him, "Please wait here, madam. I shall go in and inquire what the royal wishes are." She took Lin's list, and after a short time, returned and said, "But madam hasn't put any prices on her list. How much do you charge for a picul of rouge? How much is a picul of perfumed powder? And hair lotion? And hair ribbons?"

Lin told her the prices, and the guard went in and came out again and asked, "How much is a box of jade ornaments, madam? And your velvet flowers? How much is a box of your fragrant beads? And what about the combs?"

Merchant Lin told her and the guard again went to report, and came back and said, "The King has been choosing imperial concubines and wants to buy some of your goods for them. He invites you to go inside, since you come from the Kingdom on Earth and we are friendly allies. However, madam must behave with courtesy and respect when she is in the presence of His Majesty."

Merchant Lin followed the guard inside, and was soon in the presence of the "King." After making a deep bow, he saw that she was a woman of some thirty years old, with a beautiful face, fair skin and cherry-red lips. Around her there stood many palace "maids."

The "King" spoke to Lin in a light voice, holding the list of articles in her slender hands, and looking at him with interest as he answered her questions.

"I wonder what she is staring at me like this for," Merchant Lin thought to himself. "Hasn't she ever seen a man from the Kingdom on Earth before?"

After a while, he heard her say that she was keeping the list of goods, and ordered palace "maids" to prepare a feast and wine for the "woman" from the Kingdom on Earth.

In a little time, Merchant Lin was ushered to a room upstairs, where victuals of many kinds awaited him. As he ate, however, he heard a great deal of noise downstairs. Several palace "maids" ran upstairs soon, and calling him "Your Highness," kowtowed to him and congratulated him. Before he knew what was happening, Merchant Lin was being stripped completely bare by the maids and led to a perfumed bath. Against the powerful arms of these maids, he could scarcely struggle. Soon he found himself being anointed, perfumed, powdered and rouged, and dressed in a skirt. His big feet were bound up in strips of cloth and socks, and his hair was combed into an elaborate braid over his head and decorated with pins. These male "maids" thrust bracelets on his arms and rings on his fingers, and put a phoenix headdress on his head. They tied a jade green sash around his waist and put an embroidered cape around his shoulders.

Then they led him to a bed, and asked him to sit down.

Merchant Lin thought that he must be drunk, or dreaming, and began to tremble. He asked the maids what was happening, and was told that he had been chosen by the "King" to be the Imperial Consort, and that a propitious day would be chosen for him to enter the "King's" chambers.

Before he could utter a word, another group of maids, all tall and strong and wearing beards, came in. One was holding a threaded needle. "We are ordered to pierce your ears," he said, as the other four "maids" grabbed Lin by the arms and legs. The white-bearded one seized Lin's right ear, and after rubbing the lobe a little, drove the needle through it.

"Ooh!" Merchant Lin screamed.

The maid seized the other ear, and likewise drove the needle through it. As Lin screamed with pain, powdered lead was smeared on his earlobes and a pair of "eight-precious" earrings was hung from the holes.

Having finished what they came to do, the maids retreated, and a black-bearded fellow came in with a bolt of white silk. Kneeling down before him, the fellow said, "I am ordered to bind Your Highness's feet."

Two other maids seized Lin's feet as the black-bearded one sat down on a low stool, and began to rip the silk into ribbons. Seizing Lin's right foot, he set it upon his knee, and sprinkled white alum powder between the toes and the grooves of the foot. He squeezed the toes tightly together, bent them down so that the whole foot was shaped like an arch, and took a length of white silk and bound it tightly around it twice. One of the others sewed the ribbon together in small stitches. Again the silk went around the foot, and again, it was sewn up.

Merchant Lin felt as though his feet were burning, and wave after wave of pain rose to his heart. When he could stand it no longer, he let out his voice and began to cry. The "maids" had hastily made a pair of soft-soled red shoes, and these they put on both his feet.

"Please, kind brothers, go and tell Her Majesty that I'm a married man," Lin begged. "How can I become her Consort? As for my feet, please liberate them. They have enjoyed the kind of freedom which scholars who are not interested in official careers enjoy! How can you bind them? Please tell your 'King' to let me go. I shall be grateful, and my wife will be very grateful."

But the maids said, "The King said that you are to enter his chambers as soon as your feet are bound. It is no time for talk of this kind."

When it was dark, a table was laid for him with mountains of meat and oceans of wine. But Merchant Lin only nibbled, and told the "maids" they could have the rest.

Still sitting on the bed, and with his feet aching terribly, he decided to lie down in his clothes for a rest.

At once a middle-aged "maid" came up to him and said, "Please, will you wash before you retire?"

No sooner was this said than a succession of maids came in with candles, basins of water and spittoon, dressing table, boxes of ointment, face powder, towels, silk handkerchiefs, and surrounded him. Lin had to submit to the motions of washing in front of them all. But after he had washed his face, a maid wanted to put some cream on it again.

Merchant Lin stoutly refused.

"But night time is the best time to treat the skin," the white-bearded maid said. "This powder has a lot of musk in it. It will make your skin fragrant, although I dare say it is fair enough already. If you use it regularly your skin will not only seem like white jade, but will give off a natural fragrance of its own. And the more fragrant it is, the fairer it will become, and the more lovely to behold, and the more lovable you will be. You'll see how good it is after you have used it regularly."

But Lin refused firmly, and the maids said, "If you are so stubborn, we will have to report this, and let Matron deal with you tomorrow."

Then they left him alone. But Lin's feet hurt so much that he could not sleep a wink. He tore at the ribbons with all his might, and after a great struggle succeeded in tearing them off. He stretched out his ten toes again, and luxuriating in their exquisite freedom, finally fell asleep.

The next morning, however, when the black-bearded maid discovered that he had torn off his foot-bandages, he immediately reported it to the "King," who ordered that Lin should be punished by receiving twenty strokes of the bamboo from the "Matron." Accordingly, a white-bearded "Matron" came in with a stick of bamboo about eight feet long, and when the others had stripped him and held him down, raised the stick and began to strike Lin's bottom and legs.

Before five strokes had been delivered, Lin's tender skin was bleeding, and the Matron did not have the heart to go on. "Look at her skin! Have you ever seen such white and tender and lovable skin? Why, I think indeed her looks are comparable to Pan An and Sung Yu!" the Matron thought to himself. "But what am I doing, comparing her bottom and not her face to them? Is that a compliment?"

The foot-binding maid came and asked Lin if he would behave from now on.

"Yes, I'll behave," Lin replied, and they stopped beating him. They wiped the blood from his wounds, and special ointment was sent by the "King" and ginseng soup was given him to drink.

Merchant Lin drank the soup, and fell on the bed for a rest. But the "King" had given orders that his feet must be bound again, and that he should be taught to walk on them. So with one maid supporting him on each side, Merchant Lin was marched up and down the room all day on his bound feet. When he lay down to sleep that night, he could not close his eyes for the excruciating pain.

But from now on, he was never left alone again. Maids took turns to sit with him. Merchant Lin knew that he was no longer in command of his destiny.

Before two weeks were over, Lin's feet had begun to assume a permanently arched form, and his toes begun to rot. Daily medical ablutions were given to them, and the pain persisted.

"I should have thought that Brother-in-law and Old Tuo would have come to my rescue by now," he thought one day as he was being led up and down his room. "I have endured all I can! I'd be better off dead!"

He sat down on the edge of the bed, and began to tear off his embroidered shoes and silk bandages. "Go tell your 'King' to put me to death at once, or let my feet loose," he told the Matron.

But when he returned, the Matron said, "The King said that if you don't obey his orders, you are to be hung upside down from the beam of the house."

"Then do it quickly! The quicker the better!" said Lin, impatient to have an end put to his agony.

Accordingly, they tied a rope around his feet and hung him upside down from the beam. Merchant Lin saw stars before his eyes. Sweat poured out of his body, and his legs became numb. He closed his eyes and waited for death to come to the rescue. But it did not come. At last he could stand it no longer, and began to scream like a pig being led to slaughter.

The order was given to cut him down.

From now on, Lin was completely in the power of the maids. Wanting to complete the task their "King" had assigned them as soon as possible, they tied the bandages around his feet tighter than ever. Several times, Lin thought of committing suicide, but with people watching him constantly, he had not a chance.

In due course, his feet lost much of their original shape. Blood and flesh were squeezed into a pulp and then little remained of his feet but dry bones and skin, shrunk, indeed, to a dainty size. Responding to daily anointing, his hair became shiny and smooth, and his body, after repeated ablutions of perfumed water, began to look very attractive indeed. His eyebrows were plucked to resemble a new moon. With blood-red lipstick and powder adorning his face, and jade and pearl adorning his coiffure and ears, Merchant Lin assumed, at last, a not unappealing appearance.

The "King" sent someone to watch his progress every day. One day, the Matron announced that the task of foot-binding had been completed. When the "King" herself came upstairs to have a look, she saw a Lin whose face was like a peach blossom, whose eyes were like autumn lakes, whose eyebrows suggested the lines of distant hills, and who stood before her in a willowy stance.

She was delighted. "What a beauty!" she thought to herself. "If I hadn't seen her hidden possibilities beneath her ridiculous man's costume, her beauty might never have come to light!"

She took a pearl bracelet and put it on Merchant Lin's wrist, and the maids persuaded him to sink down on his knees and give thanks. The "King" pulled him up and made him sit down beside her, and began to fondle his hands and smell them and look appreciatively at his dainty feet.

Lin went red with shame.

Extremely pleased, the "King" decided that Lin should enter her chambers the very next day. When Merchant Lin heard this, he saw his last hopes vanish. He was not even able to walk without someone to help him, and spent the whole night thinking about his wife and shedding tears.

In the morning, the "maids" came especially early to shave off the fine hairs from his face, and to powder him and comb him in preparation for his wedding. Supported by a pair of red embroidered high-heeled shoes, his longer-than-ordinary "golden lotuses" became not obtrusively large. He wore a bridal crown and gown, and with jewels dangling and waves of perfume issuing from his person, was if not notably beautiful, at least a rather charming "bride."

After breakfast, "Imperial Concubines" came to congratulate him, and he was kept fully occupied until the afternoon, when maids came again to straighten his clothes and freshen up his appearance before escorting him to the Reception Hall.

Soon, palace attendants holding red lanterns came in and knelt before him and said, "The propitious hour has come. Would Madam please come to the Main Reception Hall to await His Majesty? The ceremonies will be conducted there."

Merchant Lin was stunned. His body and soul almost parted company.

The attendants seized him and escorted him downstairs. Countless officials and guests had come to witness the ceremony in the Main Reception Hall, which was brightly lighted with candles. As Lin walked toward "His Majesty," swaying on the arms of attendants, he was like a sprig of fresh flowers waving in the wind. When he was standing directly in front of the "King," he had no alternative but to tug at his sleeves and make a deep bow.

Congratulations were showered upon the "King" by the attendants.

As Lin was about to be ushered into the "King's" chambers, there came a great hubbub of noise from the outside. The "King" was startled.

It was Tang Ao, who had come to the rescue. If the reader wants to know what happened next, please turn to the next chapter.

Translated by Lin Tai-yi

10

A ROOM OF ONE'S OWN IN TRANSRACIAL PERSPECTIVE

Ellen Rosenman

Virginia Woolf made an inspired choice when she titled her feminist literary history *A Room of One's Own* (1929). The phrase is powerful because it evokes a constellation of meanings: autonomy and freedom from the demands of domestic life and other-directed responsibilities; the privacy necessary to listen to one's own voice and to create; the economic power that makes it possible to claim a space and escape financial dependence on men; ownership of one's mind, body, and place in the world. The fact that the title has been adapted to name everything from a scholarly work about women science fiction writers in Soviet-era Russia to a store selling high-end baby furniture suggests its enduring if unpredictable resonance (try entering "a room of" in the Worldcat bibliographic database or in Google to see how widely it has been used and revised). In *Room,* Woolf marks out a distinctive literary-historical space populated by women—many forgotten or neglected—who have written letters and diaries as well as poetry and fiction, and devises a *theory* of literary history, an analysis of the cultural and economic forces that created this space and shaped the careers of these women.

Woolf's book began as a series of lectures on women and fiction delivered in 1928 to students of Girton and Newnham, the women's colleges that were founded within Cambridge University in 1869 and 1871, respectively. The moment was auspicious: the vote has just been extended to all women over the age of twenty-one. But in spite of her efforts on behalf of women's suffrage, Woolf considered the money women could earn with their education "infinitely more important" (37), prescribing five hundred pounds a year (equivalent to about 37,000 dollars today) along with a room of one's own as the prerequisites for creative freedom. With economic self-sufficiency, women would no longer need to censor themselves or conform to a stereotype to avoid offending men. Against the prevailing view that artists are instinctive geniuses who cannot help but produce masterpieces even if they are starving in a garret (perhaps especially if they are starving in a garret), Woolf argued that the money is essential to creativity because it can purchase education, leisure, and privacy.

This materialist, cultural analysis of gender is one of *Room*'s most important legacies. It allows Woolf to take a fresh look at early twentieth-century assumptions about women writers—or rather, about the absence of revered women writers throughout history. Surveying the British literary canon, Woolf admits that women have not produced the same array of self-assured literary masterpieces as men. But their sad showing is due to economic and intellectual barriers, not an innate, sex-based lack of talent, as many critics then claimed. Within *Room*'s literary history—some real, some invented—from the Renaissance to the present, these barriers deform women's writing, sometimes silencing women entirely. In one of the most famous sections of the book, Woolf introduces the myth of Judith Shakespeare, William's equally talented sister, as an example of this silencing. Expelled from her home for the sin of literary ambition, Judith finds London equally inhospitable. Unable to find work because of her sex, she allows herself to be seduced, becomes pregnant, and commits suicide without leaving a word behind. Brother William, of course, is embraced by the theatrical establishment (and the rest, as they say, is literary history).

But *Room* also questions whether male standards of artistic greatness and public recognition are appropriate for women's writing. Looking at women's liabilities from another angle, it reframes them as productive conditions that can give rise to a different tradition. This argument can be traced through some of the work's most famous phrases. When the narrator asserts "Anon was a woman," she regrets the absence of individual writers famous enough to leave their signatures, but she also implies a hidden history of achievement beneath this apparent absence that could be recovered with some creative investigating—or imagining—like that of *Room*. Woolf posits a tradition stretching from modern graduates of Newnham and Girton through unassuming women who raised families—including intellectual daughters—and left a legacy of traits such as modesty, subtlety, and resourcefulness that, though stereotypically feminine, could be refashioned into a distinctive writing style. "If we are women, we think back through our mothers," Woolf writes, discovering a different line of descent from the official literary canon. We can trace the idea of "foremothers," central to Anglo-American feminism of the twentieth century, to *Room*. Sketching the dynamics of a female literary tradition, *Room* also imagines new directions for novels themselves. Because of their marginality, women have a special perspective on men's privilege and priorities, finding their investment in heroism, conquest, and heterosexual passion hard to understand. Instead, women might prefer to write a novel in which "Chloe liked Olivia," a plot that diverges from the familiar story of heterosexual love to explore same-sex relationships—erotic, friendly, familial. Departing from approved conventions, this novel might seem eccentric, but *Room* values it for its gender-specific originality.

Thus, *Room* established some of the key "talking points" of "Second Wave" feminism, such as the historical oppression of women and its role in producing women's supposedly "natural" inferiority, and the value of constructing alternative bodies of knowledge that focus on women's experience. We can also credit *Room* with developing the concept of "difference" itself. It rejects the belief in a single "human nature"—which is really a set of masculine norms masquerading as universal traits—as well as the traditional hierarchy of "masculine" and "feminine," because both formulations automatically judge women in relation to masculinity and find them lacking. Instead, *Room* insists that "masculine" and "feminine" are interrelated, socially constructed categories, each with its own distinctive characteristics. While many of these assertions are familiar today, we should remember that they were fairly radical in Woolf's time. In fact, they are familiar in part because of *Room*, which was rediscovered in the 1970s by feminist literary critics after languishing for decades—an ironic fate for a work concerned with the erasure of women writers.

Room has also remained relevant to subsequent iterations of feminism. Its playful, elusive style has engaged French feminists like Luce Irigaray who resist "masculine" rigor and argumentation. In its poetic approach to ideas, *Room* represents the new kind of theorizing they sought to develop, while its defense of femininity as distinctive rather than inferior accords with the French feminist agenda. On the other hand, *Room* has been subject to critique on several grounds. Its poetic style results in inconsistencies that some critics have considered politically incorrect: though it celebrates a distinctive female tradition, it also closes with a tribute to androgyny as an escape from the limitations of both sexes; though it emphasizes the materialist basis of gender, it also links feminine literary style to the body in a way that has been interpreted as essentialist. Certainly it recycles very familiar gender stereotypes, painting masculinity and femininity—and literary history, for that matter—in broad brushstrokes.

Furthermore, because it dwells on a level of economic and professional achievement unattainable for most women around the world, it has also been critiqued as elitist, and Woolf has been accused of confining her concerns to the problems of a narrow and comparatively lucky subset of the enormous category "women," and even "women writers." Born into an elite intellectual family, Woolf was privileged intellectually and economically. Though she never attended university, she received an impressive education at home. At the time when she delivered her lectures at Newnham and Girton, Woolf was considered one of the greatest living writers. She was also politically active, working for the Adult Suffragists and the Women's Co-operative Guild, which fought for the political and economic equality of women of all classes. There is no doubt that Woolf's personal life was often traumatic: she was molested by her half-brothers, entered a sexless but stable marriage (though she had sexual and romantic relationships with several women), and eventually committed suicide, probably from a combination of continuing effects of sexual abuse and manic depression. But as a writer Woolf enjoyed many advantages. Though she implicitly claims outsider status in *Room*, it might be more accurate to

ALICE WALKER: MAKING ROOM FOR AFRICAN AMERICAN WOMEN WRITERS

One of Woolf's most conscious descendants and powerful critics is the African American writer Alice Walker, who talks back to Woolf about the issues of race and class in her essay "In Search of Our Mothers' Gardens" (see Cheryl Hopson's essay in chapter 14 for a related discussion of Walker). While Woolf critiques the "blind spot" that keeps men from seeing women's accomplishments and their own prejudices, Walker critiques Woolf, who does not see that economic and racial privilege enter her text in subtle ways. Walker fills this blind spot with the story of Phillis Wheatley, a slave with an extraordinary talent for poetry. Quoting *Room* explicitly, Walker uses brackets to insert Wheatley's life into Woolf's literary history:

> any woman born with a great gift in the sixteenth century [insert eighteenth century, insert Black woman, insert born or made a slave] would certainly have gone crazed, shot herself, or ended her days in some lonely cottage . . . a highly gifted girl who had tried to use her gift for poetry would have been so thwarted and hindered by contrary instincts [add chains, guns, the lash, the ownership of one's body by someone else, submission to an alien religion] that she must have lost her health and sanity to a certainty. (235)

Walker also critiques another important tenet of *Room:* the importance of public recognition for creative work. Although Woolf acknowledges the ordinary foremothers who came before her, she is most interested in writing as a profession and, in her imaginary life of Judith Shakespeare, suggests that if potential artists do not find a formal outlet, they will go mad or kill themselves. In contrast, Walker celebrates the traditional work of women who lack the resources to become public artists but who bring imagination and beauty to everyday life. Far from being a failed novel, Walker's mother's garden is an artistic achievement in its own right, "so brilliant with colors, so original in its design, so magnificent with life and creativity, that to this day people drive by our house in Georgia . . . and ask to stand or walk among my mother's art" (241). "Our Mothers' Gardens" thus establishes an important strain of feminist theory: the need to revalue women's daily domestic labor such as quilting, cooking, and nurturing relationships. Though today's media-driven "Mommy Wars" pit women who work outside the home against so-called stay-at-home mothers and housewives, Walker suggests important continuities between women's work in these two arenas.

consider her an insider-outsider, marginal enough to shine a bright light on social injustices but privileged enough to find an outlet and an audience for those insights.

This selection is from the first chapter of *Room*, written after Woolf's visit to Girton and Newnham, which obviously provided some of the key tropes that Woolf developed when she expanded her lectures for publication. Immediately, Virginia Woolf—visibly present before the students at Girton and Newnham, and present by name on the title page of the published book—turns the narration over to a mysterious "I" ("call me Mary Beton, Mary Seton, Mary Carmichael, or by any other name you please—it is not a matter of any importance"). This narrator contrasts a visit to Oxbridge—a common expression uniting Oxford and Cambridge, the two great men's colleges in England—with one to Fernham, her fictitious name for Girton/Newnham. In this brief section, you can see many of the themes of the work as a whole as described above. You can also get a flavor of her distinctive technique, for Woolf was one of the great stylists of the twentieth century. She does not construct a clear, linear argument about women's literary history by making straightforward assertions grounded in evidence but rather weaves her ideas together using the techniques of fiction: a narrator, a story, metaphors, symbolic actions. Though Woolf is analyzing power and culture, she remains a creative writer seeking to engage readers' imagination as well as their reason.

WORKS CITED

Walker, Alice. *In Search of Our Mothers' Gardens: Womanist Prose*. New York: Harvest, 2004.

DISCUSSION QUESTIONS

1. What do you think Woolf gains from writing her women's literary history as a piece of fiction? Consider some of the techniques and symbolic actions she uses: the anonymous narrator, the narrator's trespass off the path, the description of the Oxbridge dons as insects. What does she lose?

2. What insight does the narrator's position of marginality grant her?

3. If we consider the narrator a woman writer, what does her mental journey tell us about her psychological and creative development as she moves through her experiences at Oxbridge and Fernham?

VIRGINIA WOOLF, FROM *A ROOM OF ONE'S OWN*, CHAPTER 1

But, you may say, we asked you to speak about women and fiction—what has that got to do with a room of one's own? I will try to explain. When you asked me to speak about women and fiction I sat down on the banks of a river and began to wonder what the words meant. They might mean simply a few remarks about Fanny Burney; a few more about Jane Austen; a tribute to the Brontës and a sketch of Haworth Parsonage under snow; some witticisms if possible about Miss Mitford; a respectful allusion to George Eliot; a reference to Mrs. Gaskell and one would have done. But at second sight the words seemed not so simple. The title women and fiction might mean, and you may have meant it to

SOURCE: Virginia Woolf, *A Room of One's Own* (New York: Houghton Mifflin Harcourt, 1929), 3–24.

mean, women and what they are like; or it might mean women and the fiction that they write; or it might mean women and the fiction that is written about them; or it might mean that somehow all three are inextricably mixed together and you want me to consider them in that light. But when I began to consider the subject in this last way, which seemed the most interesting, I soon saw that it had one fatal drawback. I should never be able to come to a conclusion. I should never be able to fulfil what is, I understand, the first duty of a lecturer—to hand you after an hour's discourse a nugget of pure truth to wrap up between the pages of your notebooks and keep on the mantel-piece for ever. All I could do was to offer you an opinion upon one minor point—a woman must have money and a room of her own if she is to write fiction; and that, as you will see, leaves the great problem of the true nature of woman and the true nature of fiction unsolved. I have shirked the duty of coming to a conclusion upon these two questions—women and fiction remain, so far as I am concerned, unsolved problems. But in order to make some amends I am going to do what I can to show you how I arrived at this opinion about the room and the money. I am going to develop in your presence as fully and freely as I can the train of thought which led me to think this. Perhaps if I lay bare the ideas, the prejudices, that lie behind this statement you will find that they have some bearing upon women and some upon fiction. At any rate, when a subject is highly controversial—and any question about sex is that—one cannot hope to tell the truth. One can only show how one came to hold whatever opinion one does hold. One can only give one's audience the chance of drawing their own conclusions as they observe the limitations, the prejudices, the idio-syncrasies of the speaker. Fiction here is likely to contain more truth than fact. Therefore I propose, making use of all the liberties and licences of a novelist, to tell you the story of the two days that preceded my coming here—how, bowed down by the weight of the subject which you have laid upon my shoulders, I pondered it, and made it work in and out of my daily life. I need not say that what I am about to describe has no existence; Oxbridge is an invention; so is Fernham; "I" is only a convenient term for somebody who has no real being. Lies will flow from my lips, but there may perhaps be some truth mixed up with them; it is for you to seek out this truth and to decide whether any part of it is worth keeping. If not, you will of course throw the whole of it into the wastepaper basket and forget all about it.

Here then was I (call me Mary Beton, Mary Seton, Mary Carmichael or by any name you please—it is not a matter of any importance) sitting on the banks of a river a week or two ago in fine October weather, lost in thought. That collar I have spoken of, women and fiction, the need of coming to some conclusion on a subject that raises all sorts of prejudices and passions, bowed my head to the ground. To the right and left bushes of some sort, golden and crimson, glowed with the colour, even it seemed burnt with the heat, of fire. On the further bank the willows wept in perpetual lamentation, their hair about their shoulders. The river reflected whatever it chose of sky and bridge and burn-ing tree, and when the undergraduate had oared his boat through the reflections they closed again, completely, as if he had never been. There one might have sat the clock round lost in thought. Thought—to call it by a prouder name than it deserved—had let its line down into the stream. It swayed, minute after minute, hither and thither among the reflections and the weeds, letting the water lift it and sink it, until—you know the little tug—the sudden conglomeration of an idea at the end of one's line: and then the cautious hauling of it in, and the careful laying of it out? Alas, laid on the grass how small, how insignificant this thought of mine looked; the sort of fish that a good fisher-man puts back into the water so that it may grow fatter and be one day worth cooking and eating. I will not trouble you with that thought now, though if you look carefully you may find it for yourselves in the course of what I am going to say.

But however small it was, it had, nevertheless, the mysterious property of its kind—put back into the mind, it became at once very exciting, and important; and as it darted and sank, and flashed hither and thither, set up such a wash and tumult of ideas that it was impossible to sit still. It was thus that I found myself walking with extreme rapidity across a grass plot. Instantly a man's figure rose to intercept me. Nor did I at first under-stand that the gesticulations of a curious-looking object, in a cut-away coat and evening shirt, were aimed at me. His face expressed horror and indignation. Instinct rather than reason came to my help; he was a Beadle; I was a woman. This was the turf; there was the path. Only the Fellows and Scholars are allowed here; the gravel is the place for me. Such thoughts were the work of a moment. As I regained the path the arms of the Beadle sank, his face assumed its usual repose, and though turf is better walking than gravel, no very great harm was done. The only charge I could bring against the Fellows and Scholars of whatever the college might happen to be was that in protection of their turf, which has been rolled for 300 years in succession, they had sent my little fish into hiding.

What idea it had been that had sent me so audaciously trespassing I could not now remember. [. . .]

[. . . .] Still an hour remained before luncheon, and what was one to do? Stroll on the meadows? sit by the river? Certainly it was a lovely autumn morning; the leaves were fluttering red to the ground; there was no great hardship in doing either. But the sound of music reached my ear. Some service or celebration was going forward. The organ complained magnificently as I passed the chapel door. Even the sorrow of Christianity sounded in that serene air more like the recollection of sorrow than sorrow itself; even the groanings of the ancient organ seemed lapped in peace. I had no wish to enter had I the right, and this time the verger might have stopped me, demanding perhaps my bap-tismal certificate, or a letter of introduction from the Dean. But the outside of these magnificent buildings is often as beautiful as the inside. Moreover, it was amusing enough to watch the congregation assembling, coming in and going out again, busying themselves at the door of the chapel like bees at the mouth of a hive. Many were in cap and gown; some had tufts of fur on their shoulders; others were wheeled in bath-chairs; others, though not past middle age, seemed creased and crushed into shapes so singular that one was reminded of those giant crabs and crayfish who heave with difficulty across the sand of an aquarium. As I leant against the wall the University indeed seemed a sanctuary in which are preserved rare types which would soon be obsolete if left to fight for existence on the pavement of the Strand. [. . .]

[. . . .][1] Here, however, I shall take the liberty to defy that convention and to tell you that the lunch on this occasion began with soles, sunk in a deep dish, over which the college cook had spread a counterpane of the whitest cream, save that it was branded here and there with brown spots like the spots on the flanks of a doe. After that came the partridges, but if this suggests a couple of bald, brown birds on a plate you are mistaken. The partridges, many and various, came with all their retinue of sauces and salads, the sharp and the sweet, each in its order; their potatoes, thin as coins but not so hard; their sprouts, foliated as rosebuds but more succulent. And no sooner had the roast and its retinue been done with than the silent serving-man, the Beadle himself perhaps in a milder manifestation, set before us, wreathed in napkins, a confection which rose all sugar from the waves. To call it pudding and so relate it to rice and tapioca would be an insult. Meanwhile the wineglasses had flushed yellow and flushed crimson; had been emptied; had been filled. And thus by degrees was lit, halfway down the spine, which is the seat of the soul, not that hard little electric light which we call brilliance, as it pops in and out upon our lips, but the more profound, subtle and subterranean glow, which is the rich yellow flame of rational intercourse. No need to hurry. No need to sparkle. No need to be anybody but oneself. We are all going to heaven and Vandyck is of the company—in other words, how good life seemed, how sweet its rewards, how trivial this grudge or that grievance, how admirable friendship and the society of one's kind, as, lighting a good cigarette, one sunk among the cushions in the window-seat. [. . .]

[. . . .][2] A wind blew, from what quarter I know not, but it lifted the half-grown leaves so that there was a flash of silver grey in the air. It was the time between the lights when colours undergo their intensification and purples and golds burn in window-panes like the beat of an excitable heart; when for some reason the beauty of the world revealed and yet soon to perish (here I pushed into the garden, for, unwisely, the door was left open and no beadles seemed about), the beauty of the world which is so soon to perish, has two edges, one of laughter, one of anguish, cutting the heart asunder. The gardens of Fernham lay before me in the spring twilight, wild and open, and in the long grass, sprinkled and carelessly flung, were daffodils and blue-bells, not orderly perhaps at the best of times, and now wind-blown and waving as they tugged at their roots. The windows of the building, curved like ships' windows among generous waves of red brick, changed from lemon to silver under the flight of the quick spring clouds. Somebody was in a hammock, somebody, but in this light they were phantoms only, half guessed, half seen, raced across the grass—would no one stop her?—and then on the terrace, as if popping out to breathe the air, to glance at the garden, came a bent figure, formidable yet humble, with her great forehead and her shabby dress—could it be the famous scholar,

---

1. The narrator continues her tour of Oxbridge.—Ed.
2. The narrator has left Oxbridge to visit Fernham.—Ed.

could it be J— H— herself? All was dim, yet intense too, as if the scarf which the dusk had flung over the garden were torn asunder by star or sword—the flash of some terrible reality leaping, as its way is, out of the heart of the spring. For youth—

Here was my soup. Dinner was being served in the great dining hall. Far from being spring it was in fact an evening in October. Everybody was assembled in the big dining-room. Dinner was ready. Here was the soup. It was a plain gravy soup. There was nothing to stir the fancy in that. One could have seen through the transparent liquid any pattern that there might have been on the plate itself. But there was no pattern. The plate was plain. Next came beef with its attendant greens and potatoes—a homely trinity, suggest-ing the rumps of cattle in a muddy market, and sprouts curled and yellowed at the edge, and bargaining and cheapening, and women with string bags on Monday morning. There was no reason to complain of human nature's daily food, seeing that the supply was sufficient and coal-miners doubtless were sitting down to less. Prunes and custard followed. And if any one complains that prunes, even when mitigated by custard, are an uncharitable vegetable (fruit they are not), stringy as a miser's heart and exuding a fluid such as might run in misers' veins who have denied themselves wine and warmth for eighty years and yet not given to the poor, he should reflect that there are people whose charity embraces even the prune. Biscuits and cheese came next, and here the water-jug was liberally passed round, for it is the nature of biscuits to be dry, and these were bis-cuits to the core. That was all. The meal was over. Everybody scraped their chairs back; the swing-doors swung violently to and fro; soon the hall was emptied of every sign of food and made ready no doubt for breakfast next morning. Down corridors and up stair-cases the youth of England went banging and singing. And was it for a guest, a stranger (for I had no more right here in Fernham than in Trinity or Somerville or Girton or Newnham or Christchurch), to say, "The dinner was not good," or to say (we were now, Mary Seton and I, in her sitting-room), "Could we not have dined up here alone?" for if I had said anything of the kind I should have been prying and searching into the secret economies of a house which to the stranger wears so fine a front of gaiety and courage. No, one could say nothing of the sort. Indeed, conversation for a moment flagged. The human frame being what it is, heart, body and brain all mixed together, and not con-tained in separate compartments as they will be no doubt in another million years, a good dinner is of great importance to good talk. One cannot think well, love well, sleep well, if one has not dined well. The lamp in the spine does not light on beef and prunes. We are all *probably* going to heaven, and Vandyck is, we *hope,* to meet us round the next corner—that is the dubious and qualifying state of mind that beef and prunes at the end of the day's work breed between them. [. . .]

So I went back to my inn, and as I walked through the dark streets I pondered this and that, as one does at the end of the day's work. I pondered why it was that Mrs. Seton had no money to leave us; and what effect poverty has on the mind; and what effect wealth has on the mind; and I thought of the queer old gentlemen I had seen that morn-ing with tufts of fur upon their shoulders; and I remembered how if one whistled one of them ran; and I thought of the organ booming in the chapel and of the shut doors of the library; and I thought how unpleasant it is to be locked out; and I thought how it is worse perhaps to be locked in; and, thinking of the safety and prosperity of the one sex and of the poverty and insecurity of the other and of the effect of tradition and of the lack of tradition upon the mind of a writer, I thought at last that it was time to roll up the crumpled skin of the day, with its arguments and its impressions and its anger and its laughter, and cast it into the hedge. A thousand stars were flashing across the blue wastes of the sky. One seemed alone with an inscrutable society. All human beings were laid asleep—prone, horizontal, dumb. Nobody seemed stirring in the streets of Oxbridge. Even the door of the hotel sprang open at the touch of an invisible hand—not a boots was sitting up to light me to bed, it was so late.

11

SIMONE DE BEAUVOIR
The Feminist Philosopher as Other

Susan Bordo

My older sister is eight-and-a-half years my senior, and once she turned sixteen was granted the privilege of her own tiny bedroom. As I was going through adolescence in the second half of the 1950s and early '60s, her room was an exotic, sexy space to me, largely because of the bookshelf, which held titles like *Lady Chatterley's Lover, Marjorie Morningstar, Peyton Place, Lolita, Bonjour Tristesse,* and—perhaps most enticing of all—*The Second Sex,* which I of course presumed was about sex. This wasn't just a hormonally fueled mistake. My sister had the hardback, but the Bantam paperback edition, issued in 1961, had a blurry but unmistakably naked woman on the front cover, blonde hair cascading over her shoulders, pert breast (and even nipple) very visible, while on the back cover Beauvoir was described as "a Frenchwoman who never loses sight of the needs and desires of both sexes." "WOMEN AND SEX" announced the frontispiece, and the book promised to deliver an "unorthodox treatment of sex and the feminine personality." I snuck into Mickey's room when she wasn't home, quickly passing over the dense introduction, full of terms that I didn't understand, and sought out any mention of body parts.

This was pretty much what the original publisher, Alfred Knopf, had wanted, hoping to capture the same readers who were devouring Havelock Ellis, not Jean-Paul Sartre. It was one of the reasons he had enlisted zoologist H. M. Parshley to do the translation. Knopf and his wife, Blanche, considered existentialism a "dead duck" (Bair 436), and had instructed Parshley to minimize the philosophical content of the book. A zoologist, they hoped, would transform it into a best-selling guide to the mating habits of the female of the species. Fortunately, Parshley wouldn't do their bidding—at least, not entirely. Although he edited the book to make it more readable to a general audience, he considered existentialism to have provided philosophy with "certain new insights of permanent value" that he wasn't willing to excise. He studied up, corresponded with Beauvoir about the concepts he wasn't sure of, and although Beauvoir initially fought the edits, she ultimately found the translation "excellent" and the book "superb" (Bair 436). She was hopeful that an English-speaking audience wouldn't become as inflamed as the French had when the book was published in France in 1949. "What a festival of obscenity!" Beauvoir later recalled about the epithets thrown at her: "Unsatisfied, cold, priapic, nymphomaniac, lesbian, a hundred times aborted, I was everything, even an unmarried mother. People offered to cure me of my frigidity or to satisfy my ghoulish appetites" (Force 197). Camus said she made the French male look ridiculous, while the Vatican placed the book on its Index of Forbidden Books.

English speaking critics *were* less offended by the candor and explicitness of the book's sexual descriptions, but many were no less appalled by Beauvoir's feminism (although she had yet to identify with feminism herself). William Barrett, in *Irrational Man,* a bible for budding existentialists, described Beauvoir as "that woman, his [Sartre's] friend, who wrote a book of feminine protest, *The Second Sex,* which is in reality the protest against being feminine" (232). Dwight MacDonald called the book a "deformed work" which "carries the feminist grievance too far" (Bair 438). Beauvoir was seen as both irritatingly masculine and suffering from too large a dose of feminine narcissism. At the same time, the book was described as if it were her biological offspring. *Time* headlined its review with a birth announcement: "Weight: 2 3/4 lbs," in one economical image associating the book with the bodily realm that Beauvoir describes as continually culturally projected onto women, and women's "natural" role of child bearer. And so Beauvoir, that most unnatural of creatures, a woman philosopher, was put in her rightful place. Even today, as Margaret Simons notes, "Few surveys of contemporary continental philosophy, even those focusing on issues in socio-political philosophy . . . include discussions of her work" (144).

The supreme irony of all this is that this "othering" of *The Second Sex* as female (if "unnaturally" so) is a jaw-dropping example of precisely the phenomenon that Beauvoir had exposed—and brilliantly theorized—in the book. In the introduction, excerpted here, Beauvoir argues that within the social world, there are those who occupy the unmarked position of the "essential," the universal, the human, and those who are defined and marked by their (sexual, racial, religious) difference from the norm.[1] The accomplishments of those who are marked by their difference are not always disparaged; often, they are appreciated, but always in their special, peripheral place. So, there's "history," and then there's *"women's* history," and women's history (unlike military history, for example)—is imagined to belong outside history proper. There are the male philosophers' critiques of reason, which are of "general" interest, and then there are the feminist critiques, of interest to those concerned with gender. Edward Said, for example, while noting a slew of male poststructuralists responsible for "new critical trends" and "great advancements made in . . . humanistic interpretation," credits the most famous feminists of the twentieth century, from Greer to Spivak, as having "made it impossible to ignore gender" (xiv–xv).

Beauvoir recognized—as will become clear in the selections provided here—that gender is only one cultural form of Otherness. I had a non-Jewish colleague who, having found out that I am Jewish, became unable to converse with me about anything that didn't revolve around the brilliance, historical suffering, or sense of humor of "the Jewish people." On one occasion the conversation turned to our mutual love of Broadway show tunes. For a moment I thought I would be spared, but then he piped: "And what did you think about *Fiddler on the Roof*? Didn't you just love that one?" Every time black authors and journalists are consulted only for their views on race—expertise about "general" topics being reserved for white males, who are imagined to be without race and gender—the Otherness of the black is perpetuated. It's rarely noted, in the persistent identification of *The Second Sex* as a book "about women" (which of course it is, but no more *only* about women than Foucault's *Discipline and Punish* is only about prisons), how frequently Beauvoir makes the comparison between women and blacks, which she discussed at length with Richard Wright and her longtime lover, Nelson Algren, while visiting the United States during the writing of the book. Otherness has many faces. In developing the concept, Beauvoir contributed what is arguably the single most broadly, deeply, and enduringly significant insight of the twentieth and twenty-first centuries, one that has shaped numerous scholarly conversations—about race, colonialism, heterosexism, and disability, to name a few. The (admittedly clunky) term has even become something of a media colloquialism; once confined to academic articles and books, "othering" became common shorthand among pro-democratic television commentators during the 2012 national election when referring to "birtherism" and other tactics used by Barack Obama's right-wing enemies to suggest that Obama was not "really" an American. The concept of Otherness alone qualifies Beauvoir to be included in a transnational anthology.

The concept did not, however, come glibly to Beauvoir, in part because, despite the repressiveness of laws prohibiting women's freedoms in France during this time, she first had to recognize that it applied to herself. For much of her life, which was economically and culturally privileged in many ways, "I had never had any feeling of inferiority, no one had ever said to me: 'You think that way because you are a woman.'" When the insight hit her, in 1946, the year she began *The Second Sex*, "I was so interested in this discovery that I abandoned my project for a personal confession in order to give all my attention to finding out about the condition of women in its broadest terms" (Force 103).

"Broadest terms" meant first of all, applying the essentials of the existentialist framework—which Beauvoir firmly adhered to at this point in her life—to the specific conditions of women's lives. But with this very first move, Beauvoir was already significantly altering that framework, perhaps more than she herself realized. For at virtually every step, her research revealed to her that women experienced their place in the world very differently than men, and that these differences were the result, not of an "existential condition" but of the concrete inequalities, ideology, mythology, and limitations placed on their lives. "One is not born a woman, one becomes one," she wrote, defying the notions that either biology or an eternal feminine essence were women's natural

SOME BASIC EXISTENTIALIST CONCEPTS

Subjects *(pour-soi)* have the capacity to make decisions about what to do, what kind of person to try to become, what values and behaviors to accept and reject. Objects *(en-soi)* cannot decide what to be; their definition and value is dependent on what subjects confer on them. They thus belong to the realm of **immanence**, that is, they are full of **being**. Subjects, in contrast, are capable of—indeed, "condemned to"—**transcendence**, that is, to moving beyond what they already are toward their **possibilities**. Subjects are thus always **becoming**, that is, moving from what they have been to what they will be.

I am sitting now at my computer, writing away. But I can decide (as I just did a few minutes ago) to get up and make an English muffin pizza (the pizza, in contrast, cannot choose to be made). Or, more significantly, I am a mother. But I can always choose to resist this "role"—for example, go shopping at the mall instead of helping my daughter with her homework. The unavoidable nature of **choice** is, for the existentialist, the source of a most profound and ubiquitous human **anxiety**—sometimes referred to as "anguish"— from which the human being constantly tries to escape, for example, by explaining choices as "necessitated" by one's "role," "job," or "duty": "It's the way I was brought up," "I'm a good Catholic," "He's my husband," et cetera and by otherwise avoiding responsibility for our decisions. This is called **bad faith**.

Simone de Beauvoir makes use of all these concepts in *The Second Sex*. But her analysis of "Woman as Other" significantly transforms them. Some would claim that she is not even truly an existentialist thinker. Others, however, have seen her as little more than a clever discipline of Jean-Paul Sartre. What do you think?

inheritance. Yet women's lives could not be theorized in the same way as men's, either. One needed "broad terms," yes, but they could not be gender indifferent. This insight, arguably, was implicitly a major critique, not only of Sartre and his cohort, but also of every theory of an undifferentiated "human" subject advanced up until then. That is to say, virtually all philosophy and religion. Beauvoir had made the first "cut" (so to speak) in the mythology of the unified, universal, unmarked "human."

Take, as just one specific example, the concept of "the gaze" (or "the look"), which has played such a large role in contemporary theory in many disciplines. Sartre is famous for having declared, in *No Exit*, that "Hell is other people." The idea is philosophically grounded in *Being and Nothingness*, his magnum opus, which makes a powerful argument for human relations as a battle between subjectivities trying to escape or conquer each other's defining gaze. If I were alone in the world, Sartre argues, nothing would stand between my freedom to create and re-create myself—even if at times only in my imagination. But I am not alone. Other subjects are constantly observing me, if only in passing, and what they see is not necessarily what I want them to see, or imagine that they see, but how I appear to them, through whatever meanings and values *they* hold. This ability of other people to *objectify* me is unsettling, because try as I might (and we do all the time) I ultimately cannot control how the other person sees me. Much human interaction, for Sartre, is thus motivated by the desire to captivate (e.g., in sexual desire or love) or obliterate (e.g., in hate) the power that the other person's gaze has over me.

What Beauvoir brought to this scheme is significant. For one, she presents objectification as not only an "existential" category, but also a social/historical one. Since whole classes of people have historically been seen/defined/treated in stereotypical, ideologically mediated ways (e.g., as marked by their gender, race, class, ethnicity, disability, etc.), there are profound differences in the way they are gazed at and experience the gaze of others. Race studies and disability studies, in particular, have produced powerful accounts of what it feels like to move through the social world marked by one's skin color, for example, or one's wheelchair. Beauvoir, focusing on gender, was the first to recognize that being looked at may have a profoundly different meaning for women and men. Although Sartre had theorized the defining look of the other as threatening, encroaching on the freedom of the subject, Beauvoir understands that it can also be not only affirming, but necessary to one's sense of worth. In her chapter on "the woman in love, " she describes Albertine in Proust's *Remembrance of Things Past* feeling abandoned when her lover Marcel is asleep, because she needs his admiring eyes to give her value (657). This is not something that Beauvoir celebrates; she'd like to see this dependency overcome. But it is a fact of gendered difference to which Sartre is oblivious. Strikingly, in *Being and Nothingness* he refers to the same novel, describing the *relief* Marcel feels when Albertine is asleep, because only then is the judging, expecting, desiring, gaze obliterated and his freedom to self-define restored

(Sartre 342).[2] "The look" clearly requires more than an abstract philosophical analysis, and has to be placed in a cultural, historical, political context—a project that has since absorbed many twentieth-century theorists of sexuality, race, film, and literature.

The Second Sex didn't receive much commentary by feminist scholars until the 1970s and '80s, and when it did begin to be discussed, produced almost as much outrage— although of a more scholarly sort—as it had among the antifeminist critics of the 1950s. French feminists of the *"écriture feminine"* variety, seizing on Beauvoir's admittedly phobic descriptions of the female body, criticized her for not celebrating women's 'difference'" (Moi 201), which they viewed as the source of a liberating, "non-phallic" perspective on sexuality. At the other extreme, among those for whom essentialism was the feminist bogeyman, Beauvoir was criticized for falsely universalizing the female experience. British social anthropologist Judith Oakely, for example, decried the "pan-cultural generalizations" of *The Second Sex* and described it as at best an ethnographic study of an "urban village": mid-twentieth-century Paris, white and middle class (Simons 39).

Scholarly criticism did not prevent *The Second Sex* from being translated into forty languages, passed from woman to woman around the world, and ultimately becoming the centerpiece of international conferences. As German journalist Alice Schwarzer puts it, the book was "like a secret code that we emerging women used to send messages to each other" (Bair 478). Beauvoir would be the first to acknowledge, as she writes in *The Second Sex*, that women's lives are "dispersed, contingent, and multiple," and I believe she would recognize today just how many of the specifics of *The Second Sex* are indeed ethnocentric. But clearly, the big ideas of the book have struck a nerve far beyond Beauvoir's "urban village." When she died, memorial events were held by feminist groups in numerous countries, among them the Feministes de Grece, the Campaneras du Instituto la Mujer of Madrid, women's studies programs and women's centers throughout the United States and the United Kingdom, and groups in Africa and Iran (Bair 617). And perhaps, someday, she will even be recognized, not only as a *feminist* philosopher, but as a writer whose ideas changed the very contours of thought in the second half of the twentieth century.

NOTES

1. *The Second Sex* was retranslated by Constance Borde and Shelia Malovany-Chevalier (New York: Knopf, 2010) and has been the occasion of a sometimes heated controversy over which translation—the Parshley or the new one—is the more readable and/or the more philosophically accurate. In this controversy, I side with Toril Moi (2010) over Francine du Plessix Gray; I prefer the Parshley, and so that is the translation I have excerpted here.

2. As far as I know, neither Sartre nor Beauvoir noticed this revealing coincidence.

WORKS CITED

Bair, Dierde. *Simone de Beauvoir.* New York: Simon and Schuster, 1990.
Barrett, William. *Irrational Man.* Garden City, NY: Doubleday, 1958.

Beauvoir, Simone de. *Force of Circumstances*. Translated by Richard Howard. Middlesex: Penguin Books, 1968.

———. *The Second Sex*. Translated by H. M. Parshley. New York: Alfred A. Knopf, 1957.

Moi, Toril. *Simone de Beauvoir: The Making of an Intellectual Woman*. Oxford: Oxford University Press, 2009.

Said, Edward. *Musical Elaborations*. New York: Columbia University Press, 1956.

Sartre, Jean-Paul. *Being and Nothingness*. Edited and translated by Hazel Barnes. New York: Citadel Press, 1956.

Simons, Margaret. *Feminist Interpretations of Simone de Beauvoir*. University Park: Pennsylvania State Press, 1995.

DISCUSSION QUESTIONS

1. *The Second Sex* is one of those "benchmark" works which can be used to assess how much has changed and how much has remained the same since it was written. Drawing on the excerpt printed here, what statements remain as true as when Beauvoir wrote them—and which no longer hold?

2. "Otherness," Beauvoir writes, "is a fundamental category of human thought." What does she mean by this? Do you agree?

3. Alongside the excerpts from *The Second Sex*, we include a 1976 interview with Alice Schwarzer that originally appeared in *Marie Claire* (later reprinted), in which Beauvoir talks about sexuality, femininity, and "essentialism" in some of the feminisms of that period. If you had the opportunity to interview Beauvoir today, what kinds of questions would you ask her? What do you think she would make of the ideas of the Third Wave (see the essays in last section of this collection for more on what defines the Third Wave)?

SIMONE DE BEAUVOIR, FROM *THE SECOND SEX*

[. . . .] What is a woman?

To state the question is, to me, to suggest, at once, a preliminary answer. The fact that I ask it is in itself significant. A man would never get the notion of writing a book on the peculiar situation of the human male.[1] But if I wish to define myself, I must first of all say: "I am a woman"; on this truth must be based all further discussion. A man never begins by presenting himself as an individual of a certain sex; it goes without saying that

SOURCE: Simone de Beauvoir, *The Second Sex*, trans. H. M. Parshley (New York: Alfred A. Knopf, 1957), xv–xxx.

1. The Kinsey Report [Alfred C. Kinsey and others: *Sexual Behavior in the Human Male* (Philadelphia: W. B. Saunders Co., 1948)] is no exception, for it is limited to describing the sexual characteristics of American men, which is quite a different matter.

he is a man. The terms *masculine* and *feminine* are used symmetrically only as a matter of form, as on legal papers. In actuality the relation of the two sexes is not quite like that of two electrical poles, for man represents both the positive and the neutral, as is indicated by the common use of *man* to designate human beings in general; whereas woman represents only the negative, defined by limiting criteria, without reciprocity. In the midst of an abstract discussion it is vexing to hear a man say: "You think thus and so because you are a woman"; but I know that my only defense is to reply: "I think thus and so because it is true," thereby removing my subjective self from the argument. It would be out of the question to reply: "And you think the contrary because you are a man," for it is understood that the fact of being a man is no peculiarity. A man is in the right in being a man; it is the woman who is in the wrong. It amounts to this: just as for the ancients there was an absolute vertical with reference to which the oblique was defined, so there is an absolute human type, the masculine. Woman has ovaries, a uterus; these peculiarities imprison her in her subjectivity, circumscribe her within the limits of her own nature. It is often said that she thinks with her glands. Man superbly ignores the fact that his anatomy also includes glands, such as the testicles, and that they secrete hormones. He thinks of his body as a direct and normal connection with the world, which he believes he apprehends objectively, whereas he regards the body of woman as a hindrance, a prison, weighed down by everything peculiar to it. "The female is a female by virtue of a certain *lack* of qualities," said Aristotle; "we should regard the female nature as afflicted with a natural defectiveness." And St. Thomas for his part pronounced woman to be an "imperfect man," an "incidental" being. This is symbolized in Genesis where Eve is depicted as made from what Bossuet called "a supernumerary bone" of Adam.

Thus humanity is male and man defines woman not in herself but as relative to him; she is not regarded as an autonomous being. Michelet writes: "Woman, the relative being." And Benda is most positive in his *Rapport d'Uriel:* "The body of man makes sense in itself quite apart from that of woman, whereas the latter seems wanting in significance by itself. . . . Man can think of himself without woman. She cannot think of herself without man." And she is simply what man decrees; thus she is called "the sex," by which is meant that she appears essentially to the male as a sexual being. For him she is sex—absolute sex, no less. She is defined and differentiated with reference to man and not he with reference to her; she is the incidental, the inessential as opposed to the essential. He is the Subject, he is the Absolute—she is the Other.

The category of the *Other* is as primordial as consciousness itself. In the most primitive societies, in the most ancient mythologies one finds the expression of a duality—that of the Self and the Other. This duality was not originally attached to the division of the sexes; it was not dependent upon any empirical facts. It is revealed in such works as that of Granet on Chinese thought and those of Dumézil on the East Indies and Rome. The feminine element was at first no more involved in such pairs as Varuna-Mitra, Uranus-Zeus, Sun-Moon, and Day-Night than it was in the contrasts between Good and Evil, lucky and unlucky auspices, right and left, God and Lucifer. Otherness is a fundamental category of human thought.

Thus it is that no group ever sets itself up as the One without at once setting up the Other over against itself. If three travelers chance to occupy the same compartment, that is enough to make vaguely hostile "others" out of all the rest of the passengers on the train. In small-town eyes all persons not belonging to the village are "strangers" and suspect; to the native of a country all who inhabit other countries are "foreigners"; Jews are "different" for the anti-Semite, Negroes are "inferior" for American racists, aborigines are "natives" for colonists, proletarians are the "lower class" for the privileged. [. . .]

[. . . .] Why is it that women do not dispute male sovereignty? No subject will readily volunteer to become the object, the inessential; it is not the Other who, in defining himself as the Other, establishes the One. The Other is posed as such by the One in defining himself as the One. But if the Other is not to regain the status of being the One, he must be submissive enough to accept this alien point of view. Whence comes this submission in the case of woman?

There are, to be sure, other cases in which a certain category has been able to dominate another completely for a time. Very often this privilege depends upon inequality of numbers—the majority imposes its rule upon the minority or persecutes it. But women are not a minority, like the American Negroes or the Jews; there are as many women as men on earth. Again, the two groups concerned have often been originally independent; they may have been formerly unaware of each other's existence, or perhaps they recognized each other's autonomy. But a historical event has resulted in the subjugation of the weaker by the stronger. The scattering of the Jews, the introduction of slavery into America, the conquests of imperialism are examples in point. In these cases the oppressed retained at least the memory of former days; they possessed in common a past, a tradition, sometimes a religion or a culture.

The parallel drawn by Bebel between women and the proletariat is valid in that neither ever formed a minority or a separate collective unit of mankind. And instead of a single historical event it is in both cases a historical development that explains their status as a class and accounts for the membership of *particular individuals* in that class. But proletarians have not always existed, whereas there have always been women. They are women in virtue of their anatomy and physiology. Throughout history they have always been subordinated to men, and hence their dependency is not the result of a historical event or a social change—it was not something that occurred. The reason why otherness in this case seems to be an absolute is in part that it lacks the contingent or incidental nature of historical facts. A condition brought about at a certain time can be abolished at some other time, as the Negroes of Haiti and others have proved; but it might seem that a natural condition is beyond the possibility of change. In truth, however, the nature of things is no more immutably given, once and for all, than is historical reality. If woman seems to be the inessential which never becomes the essential, it is because she herself fails to bring about this change. Proletarians say "We"; Negroes also.

Regarding themselves as subjects, they transform the bourgeois, the whites, into "others." But women do not say "We," except at some congress of feminists or similar formal demonstration; men say "women," and women use the same word in referring to themselves. They do not authentically assume a subjective attitude. The proletarians have accomplished the revolution in Russia, the Negroes in Haiti, the Indo-Chinese are battling for it in Indo-China; but the women's effort has never been anything more than a symbolic agitation. They have gained only what men have been willing to grant; they have taken nothing, they have only received.

The reason for this is that women lack concrete means for organizing themselves into a unit which can stand face to face with the correlative unit. They have no past, no history, no religion of their own; and they have no such solidarity of work and interest as that of the proletariat. They are not even promiscuously herded together in the way that creates community feeling among the American Negroes, the ghetto Jews, the workers of Saint-Denis, or the factory hands of Renault. They live dispersed among the males, attached through residence, housework, economic condition, and social standing to certain men—fathers or husbands—more firmly than they are to other women. If they belong to the bourgeoisie, they feel solidarity with men of that class, not with proletarian women; if they are white, their allegiance is to white men, not to Negro women. The proletariat can propose to massacre the ruling class, and a sufficiently fanatical Jew or Negro might dream of getting sole possession of the atomic bomb and making humanity wholly Jewish or black; but woman cannot even dream of exterminating the males. The bond that unites her to her oppressors is not comparable to any other. The division of the sexes is a biological fact, not an event in human history. Male and female stand opposed within a primordial *Mitsein*, and woman has not broken it.[2] The couple is a fundamental unity with its two halves riveted together, and the cleavage of society along the line of sex is impossible. [. . .]

[. . . .] Now, woman has always been man's dependent, if not his slave; the two sexes have never shared the world in equality. And even today woman is heavily handicapped, though her situation is beginning to change. Almost nowhere is her legal status the same as man's, and frequently it is much to her disadvantage. Even when her rights are legally recognized in the abstract, long-standing custom prevents their full expression in the mores. In the economic sphere men and women can almost be said to make up two castes; other things being equal, the former hold the better jobs, get higher wages, and have more opportunity for success than their new competitors. In industry and politics men have a great many more positions and they monopolize the most important posts. In addition to all this, they enjoy a traditional prestige that the education of children tends in every way to support, for the present enshrines the past—and in the past all

2. Here Beauvoir adopts Heidegger's concept of *Mitsein* to apply to what she sees as the unique interconnectedness of women and men, an interconnectedness that stands in the way of women recognizing their shared situation.—Ed.

history has been made by men. At the present time, when women are beginning to take part in the affairs of the world, it is still a world that belongs to men—they have no doubt of it at all and women have scarcely any. To decline to be the Other, to refuse to be a party to the deal—this would be for women to renounce all the advantages conferred upon them by their alliance with the superior caste. Man-the-sovereign will provide woman-the-liege with material protection and will undertake the moral justification of her existence; thus she can evade at once both economic risk and the metaphysical risk of a liberty in which ends and aims must be contrived without assistance. Indeed, along with the ethical urge of each individual to affirm his subjective existence, there is also the temptation to forgo liberty and become a thing. This is an inauspicious road, for he who takes it—passive, lost, ruined—becomes henceforth the creature of another's will, frustrated in his transcendence and deprived of every value. But it is an easy road; on it one avoids the strain involved in undertaking an authentic existence. When man makes of woman the *Other*, he may, then, expect her to manifest deep-seated tendencies toward complicity. Thus, woman may fail to lay claim to the status of subject because she lacks definite resources, because she feels the necessary bond that ties her to man regardless of reciprocity, and because she is often very well pleased with her role as the *Other*.

But it will be asked at once: how did all this begin? It is easy to see that the duality of the sexes, like any duality, gives rise to conflict. And doubtless the winner will assume the status of absolute. But why should man have won from the start? It seems possible that women could have won the victory; or that the outcome of the conflict might never have been decided. How is it that this world has always belonged to the men and that things have begun to change only recently? Is this change a good thing? Will it bring about an equal sharing of the world between men and women?

These questions are not new, and they have often been answered. But the very fact that woman *is the Other* tends to cast suspicion upon all the justifications that men have ever been able to provide for it. These have all too evidently been dictated by men's interest. A little-known feminist of the seventeenth century, Poulain de la Barre, put it this way: "All that has been written about women by men should be suspect, for the men are at once judge and party to the lawsuit." Everywhere, at all times, the males have displayed their satisfaction in feeling that they are the lords of creation. "Blessed be God . . . that He did not make me a woman," say the Jews in their morning prayers, while their wives pray on a note of resignation: "Blessed be the Lord, who created me according to His will." The first among the blessings for which Plato thanked the gods was that he had been created free, not enslaved; the second, a man, not a woman. But the males could not enjoy this privilege fully unless they believed it to be founded on the absolute and the eternal; they sought to make the fact of their supremacy into a right. "Being men, those who have made and compiled the laws have favored their own sex, and jurists have elevated these laws into principles," to quote Poulain de la Barre once more.

Legislators, priests, philosophers, writers, and scientists have striven to show that the subordinate position of woman is willed in heaven and advantageous on earth. The religions invented by men reflect this wish for domination. In the legends of Eve and Pandora men have taken up arms against women. They have made use of philosophy and theology, as the quotations from Aristotle and St. Thomas have shown. Since ancient times satirists and moralists have delighted in showing up the weaknesses of women. We are familiar with the savage indictments hurled against women throughout French literature. Montherlant, for example, follows the tradition of Jean de Meung, though with less gusto. This hostility may at times be well founded, often it is gratuitous; but in truth it more or less successfully conceals a desire for self-justification. As Montaigne says, "It is easier to accuse one sex than to excuse the other." Sometimes what is going on is clear enough. For instance, the Roman law limiting the rights of woman cited "the imbecility, the instability of the sex" just when the weakening of family ties seemed to threaten the interests of male heirs. And in the effort to keep the married woman under guardianship, appeal was made in the sixteenth century to the authority of St. Augustine, who declared that "woman is a creature neither decisive nor constant," at a time when the single woman was thought capable of managing her property. Montaigne understood clearly how arbitrary and unjust was woman's appointed lot: "Women are not in the wrong when they decline to accept the rules laid down for them, since the men make these rules without consulting them. No wonder intrigue and strife abound." But he did not go so far as to champion their cause.

It was only later, in the eighteenth century, that genuinely democratic men began to view the matter objectively. Diderot, among others, strove to show that woman is, like man, a human being. Later John Stuart Mill came fervently to her defense. But these philosophers displayed unusual impartiality. In the nineteenth century the feminist quarrel became again a quarrel of partisans. One of the consequences of the industrial revolution was the entrance of women into productive labor, and it was just here that the claims of the feminists emerged from the realm of theory and acquired an economic basis, while their opponents became the more aggressive. Although landed property lost power to some extent, the bourgeoisie clung to the old morality that found the guarantee of private property in the solidity of the family. Woman was ordered back into the home the more harshly as her emancipation became a real menace. Even within the working class the men endeavored to restrain woman's liberation, because they began to see the women as dangerous competitors—the more so because they were accustomed to work for lower wages.

In proving woman's inferiority, the antifeminists then began to draw not only upon religion, philosophy, and theology, as before, but also upon science—biology, experimental psychology, etc. At most they were willing to grant "equality in difference" to the *other* sex. That profitable formula is most significant; it is precisely like the "equal but separate" formula of the Jim Crow laws aimed at the North American Negroes. As is well known, this so-called equalitarian segregation has resulted only in the most extreme discrimination. The similarity just noted is in no way due to chance, for whether it is a race, a caste, a class, or a sex that is reduced to a position of inferiority, the methods of justification are the same. "The eternal feminine" corresponds to "the black soul" and to "the Jewish character." True, the Jewish problem is on the whole very different from the other two—to the anti-Semite the Jew is not so much an inferior as he is an enemy for whom there is to be granted no place on earth, for whom annihilation is the fate desired. But there are deep similarities between the situation of woman and that of the Negro. Both are being emancipated today from a like paternalism, and the former master class wishes to "keep them in their place"—that is, the place chosen for them. In both cases the former masters lavish more or less sincere eulogies, either on the virtues of "the good Negro" with his dormant, childish, merry soul—the submissive Negro—or on the merits of the woman who is "truly feminine"—that is, frivolous, infantile, irresponsible—the submissive woman. In both cases the dominant class bases its argument on a state of affairs that it has itself created. [. . .]

[. . . .] People have tirelessly sought to prove that woman is superior, inferior, or equal to man. Some say that, having been created after Adam, she is evidently a secondary being; others say on the contrary that Adam was only a rough draft and that God succeeded in producing the human being in perfection when He created Eve. Woman's brain is smaller; yes, but it is relatively larger. Christ was made a man; yes, but perhaps for his greater humility. Each argument at once suggests its opposite, and both are often fallacious. If we are to gain understanding, we must get out of these ruts; we must discard the vague notions of superiority, inferiority, equality which have hitherto corrupted every discussion of the subject and start afresh.

Very well, but just how shall we pose the question? And, to, begin with, who are we to propound it at all? Man is at once judge and party to the case; but so is woman. What we need is an angel—neither man nor woman—but where shall we find one? Still, the angel would be poorly qualified to speak, for an angel is ignorant of all the basic facts involved in the problem. With a hermaphrodite we should be no better off, for here the situation is most peculiar; the hermaphrodite is not really the combination of a whole man and a whole woman, but consists of parts of each and thus is neither. It looks to me as if there are, after all, certain women who are best qualified to elucidate the situation of woman. Let us not be misled by the sophism that because Epimenides was a Cretan he was necessarily a liar[;] it is not a mysterious essence that compels men and women to act in good or in bad faith, it is their situation that inclines them more or less toward the search for truth. Many of today's women, fortunate in the restoration of all the privileges pertaining to the estate of the human being, can afford the luxury of impartiality—we even recognize its necessity. We are no longer like our partisan elders; by and large we have won the game. In recent debates on the status of women the United Nations has persistently maintained that the equality of the sexes is now becoming a reality, and already some of us have never had to sense in our femininity an inconvenience or an obstacle. Many problems appear to us to be more pressing than those which concern us in particular, and this detachment even allows us to hope that our attitude will be objective. Still, we know the feminine world more intimately than do the men because we have our roots in it, we grasp more immediately than do men what it means to a human being to be feminine; and we are more concerned with such knowledge. I have said that there are more pressing problems, but this does not prevent us from seeing some importance in asking how the fact of being women will affect our lives. What opportunities precisely have been given us and what withheld? What fate awaits our younger sisters, and what directions should they take? It is significant that books by women on women are in general animated in our day less by a wish to demand our rights than by an effort toward clarity and understanding. As we emerge from an era of excessive controversy, this book is offered as one attempt among others to confirm that statement.

But it is doubtless impossible to approach any human problem with a mind free from bias. The way in which questions are put, the points of view assumed, presuppose a relativity of interest; all characteristics imply values, and every objective description, so called, implies an ethical background. Rather than attempt to conceal principles more or less definitely implied, it is better to state them openly at the beginning. This will make it unnecessary to specify on every page in just what sense one uses such words as *superior, inferior, better, worse, progress, reaction,* and the like. If we survey some of the works on woman, we note that one of the points of view most frequently adopted is that of the public good, the general interest; and one always means by this the benefit of society as one wishes it to be maintained or established. For our part, we hold that the only public good is that which assures the private good of the citizens; we shall pass judgment on institutions according to their effectiveness in giving concrete opportunities to individuals. But we do not confuse the idea of private interest with that of happiness, although that is another common point of view. Are not women of the harem more happy than women voters? Is not the housekeeper happier than the working-woman? It is not too clear just what the word *happy* really means and still less what true values it may mask. There is no possibility of measuring the happiness of others, and it is always easy to describe as happy the situation in which one wishes to place them.

In particular those who are condemned to stagnation are often pronounced happy on the pretext that happiness consists in being at rest. This notion we reject, for our perspective is that of existentialist ethics. Every subject plays his part as such specifically through exploits or projects that serve as a mode of transcendence; he achieves liberty only through a continual reaching out toward other liberties. There is no justification for present existence other than its expansion into an indefinitely open future. Every time transcendence falls back into immanence, stagnation, there is a degradation of existence into the *"en-soi"*—the brutish life of subjection to given conditions—and of liberty into constraint and contingence. This downfall represents a moral fault if the subject consents to it; if it is inflicted upon him, it spells frustration and oppression. In both cases it is an absolute evil. Every individual concerned to justify his existence feels that his existence involves an undefined need to transcend himself, to engage in freely chosen projects.

Now, what peculiarly signalizes the situation of woman is that she—a free and autonomous being like all human creatures—nevertheless finds herself living in a world where men compel her to assume the status of the Other. They propose to stabilize her as object and to doom her to immanence since her transcendence is to be overshadowed and forever transcended by another ego *(conscience)* which is essential and sovereign. The drama of woman lies in this conflict between the fundamental aspirations of every subject (ego)—who always regards the self as the essential—and the compulsions of a situation in which she is the inessential. How can a human being in woman's situation attain fulfillment? What roads are open to her? Which are blocked? How can independence be recovered in a state of dependency? What circumstances limit woman's liberty and how can they be overcome? These are the fundamental questions on which I would fain throw some light. This means that I am interested in the fortunes of the individual as defined not in terms of happiness but in terms of liberty.

Quite evidently this problem would be without significance if we were to believe that woman's destiny is inevitably determined by physiological, psychological, or economic forces. Hence I shall discuss first of all the light in which woman is viewed by biology, psycho-analysis, and historical materialism. Next I shall try to show exactly how the concept of the "truly feminine" has been fashioned—why woman has been defined as the Other—and what have been the consequences from man's point of view. Then from woman's point of view I shall describe the world in which women must live; and thus we shall be able to envisage the difficulties in their way as, endeavoring to make their escape from the sphere hitherto assigned them, they aspire to full membership in the human race.

Introduction to Book II

The women of today are in a fair way to dethrone the myth of femininity; they are beginning to affirm their independence in concrete ways; but they do not easily succeed in living completely the life of a human being. Reared by women within a feminine world, their normal destiny is marriage, which still means practically subordination to man; for masculine prestige is far from extinction, resting still upon solid economic and social foundations. We must therefore study the traditional destiny of woman with some care. In Book II I shall seek to describe how woman undergoes her apprenticeship, how she experiences her situation, in what kind of universe she is confined, what modes of escape are vouchsafed her. Then only—with so much understood—shall we be able to comprehend the problems of women, the heirs of a burdensome past, who are striving to build a new future. When I use the words *woman* or *feminine* I evidently refer to no archetype, no changeless essence whatever; the reader must understand the phrase "in the present state of education and custom" after most of my statements. It is not our concern here to proclaim eternal verities, but rather to describe the common basis that underlies every individual feminine existence.

Translated by H. M. Parshley

SIMONE DE BEAUVOIR, *INTERVIEW WITH ALICE SCHWARZER*

Schwarzer: Five years have passed since you came out publicly as a feminist. You, Simone, the writer who most strongly inspired the new feminism, you were anti-feminist until the birth of the women's liberation movement. You were opposed to any autonomous movement. You thought that the socialist revolution would be the automatic solution to woman's oppression.

Much has happened since then. In 1971 you were one of the women who admitted, in public, to having had an abortion. You participated in a certain number of feminist actions and demonstrations. What is your relationship to the young feminists today?

Beauvoir: They are personal relations with women, not with groups or tendencies. I work with them on precise subjects. For example, on the editorial staff of the *Temps modernes* we regularly write a page on "everyday sexism."

I also chair the Ligue du droit des femmes [League for women's rights], and I help with efforts to create shelters for women who have been beaten. I am therefore not a militant in the strict meaning of the word—I'm not thirty, I'm sixty-seven, and I am an intellectual whose weapons are words—but I do follow the activities of the MLF and I am at their service.[1]

I find this project for battered women particularly important because, like abortion, the problem of violence concerns almost all women—independently of their social class. It goes beyond the frontiers of class. Women are beaten by husbands who are judges or magistrates as well as workers. So we created an "SOS Battered Women" and we try to organize centers that would give shelter at least temporarily—for a night or a few weeks—to a woman and her children if she can't go home because she might be beaten by her husband, sometimes beaten to death. . . .

Schwarzer: In your opinion, what role does sexuality, as it is conceived of today, play in the oppression of women?

Beauvoir: I think that sexuality can be a dreadful trap. There are women who become frigid—but that's not the worst thing that can happen to them. The worst thing is for women to find so much happiness in sexuality that they become more or less slaves of men and that strengthens the chain that binds them to their oppressor.

Schwarzer: If I understand you, frigidity seems to you, in the present state of discomfort created by the power play between men and women, a more prudent and reasonable reaction because it reflects this discomfort and therefore makes women less dependent on men.

Beauvoir: Exactly.

SOURCE: Simone de Beauvoir, "Interview with Alice Schwarzer and Simone de Beauvoir," in *New French Feminisms: An Anthology*, ed. Elaine Marks and Isabelle de Courtivron, trans. Elaine Marks (Amherst: University of Massachusetts Press, 1980), 151–53.

1. Movement de libération de femmes (MLF) was one of the dominant women's liberation movements in France at the time.

Schwarzer: There are women in the MLF who, in this world dominated by men, refuse to continue to share their private lives with men, to have sexual and emotional relationships with them. These women make of homosexuality a political strategy. What is your opinion?

Beauvoir: I understand fully the political refusal to compromise. Exactly for the reason I gave. Love can be a trap that makes women accept many things.

But this is only true in the present circumstances. In itself, homosexuality is as limiting as heterosexuality. The ideal should be the capacity to love a woman as well as a man, one or the other, a human being, without feeling fear or constraint or obligation.

Schwarzer: Your most famous sentence is: "One is not born, but rather becomes a woman." Today we can prove scientifically this "fabrication of the sexes" whose result is that men and women are very different: they think differently, they have different emotions, they walk differently. They are not born this way, they become this way. It is the result of their education and their daily life.

Almost everyone is in agreement about acknowledging this difference. But it is not only a difference: it implies at the same time an inferiority. So it is all the more astonishing that with the new revolt of women there should appear a rebirth of the eternal feminine, in short a mystification of the feminine.

That's what Jean Ferrat sings about in his latest hit: "Woman is the future of man." And even in the women's movement, some groups are brandishing these slogans.

Beauvoir: I think that today certain masculine shortcomings are absent in women. For example, a masculine manner of being grotesque, of taking oneself seriously, of thinking oneself important. Note that women who have a masculine career can also adopt these shortcomings. But all the same, women always retain a little nook of humor, a little distance between themselves and the hierarchy.

And that way of squelching competitors: in general, women do not act that way. And patience which is, up to a certain point, a quality (later it becomes a shortcoming), is also a characteristic of women. And irony, a sense of the concrete, because women are more strongly rooted in everyday life.

These "feminine" qualities have their origin in our oppression, but they should be preserved after our liberation. And men, too, should acquire them. But we must not exaggerate in the other direction. To say that woman has special ties to the earth, the rhythm of the moon, the tides, etc., that she has more soul, that she is less destructive by nature, etc. No, if there is something true in all that, it is not in terms of our nature, but of the conditions of our life.

"Feminine" little girls are also made and not born that way. Numerous studies prove this. A priori, a woman has no special value because she is a woman. That would be the most retrograde "biologism," in total contradiction with everything I think.

Schwarzer: *Then what does this rebirth of the "eternal feminine" mean?*

Beauvoir: When men say to us: "Just keep being good little women. Leave all the tedious things to us: power, honors, careers—Be happy to be there, bound to the earth, busy with human tasks—" That's very dangerous! On one hand it's a good thing that a woman is no longer ashamed of her body, of her pregnancy, of her menstruation. I think it is excellent that she should get to know her own body.

But it would be an error to make of it a value and to think that the feminine body gives you a new vision of the world. It would be ridiculous and absurd, it would be like constructing a counter-penis. The women who share this belief fall again into the irrational, into mysticism, into a sense of the cosmic. They play into the hands of men who will be better able to oppress them, to remove them from knowledge and power.

The eternal feminine is a lie, because nature plays an infinitesimal role in the development of a human being. We are social beings. Because I do not think that woman is naturally inferior to man, I do not think either that she is naturally superior to him.

Translated by Elaine Marks

PART 4

DISCOVERING GENDER AND REMAPPING FEMINISM

1955–1975

12

THE "PERSONAL POLITICS" OF CLASS

Karen W. Tice

> What is important is not that one person is middle class and the other is lower
> class. The words themselves are only used to loosely define general back-
> grounds and resulting patterns of behavior. . . . The label is there to help you
> find yourself: to help you understand how your background determines the way
> you act, and, understanding it, helps you to change it.
>
> GINNY BERSON, "CLASS REVISITED"

In 1968, feminists protesting the racism, militarism, and tyranny of beauty standards for women at the Miss America pageant tossed girdles, padded bras, high heels, and *Playboy* magazines into a "Freedom Trash Can." Although it is uncertain whether or not they actually burned bras, this protest action has become legendary, a lightning rod of debate for both feminists and nonfeminists ever since. For this reason, the term "bra burners" has become a common and often pejorative epithet for feminists. In 1971, a group of trade union women also brandished a bra (a cheap Woolworth's bra that fell apart after washing) to protest the meager wages paid to working women. This bra, and the working-class feminist activism for a living wage that it symbolized, however, has been relegated to the back burners of popular and feminist attention.

Despite the relative obscurity of the Woolworth's bra action, feminist activist-scholars working in both community organizations and women's studies programs have long asserted the importance of recognizing multiple forms of privilege and oppression including class and poverty. Course syllabi routinely list the importance of considering a nexus of gender, race, ethnicity, class, and sexualities regardless of the topical focus of the course. Despite these ambitions, class injustices often remain submerged, banished to the back seat relative to gender, race, and other identity markers. It is rare to find sustained dialogues about the politics of class within recent feminist theories and women's studies, despite lip service given to its significance for people's lives and identities. And when they do appear, notions of class have also tended to overemphasize purely structural, absolute, and either/or categorizations of class or to reduce class to mere matters of money and education. Meanwhile, the micropolitical, dynamic, and chameleon-like nature of class identities, status, and relations remains relatively muted and unproblematized.

Class, however, was not always in the closet, as numerous women throughout the twentieth century fought to improve wages, working conditions, and family and welfare policies to change the lives of women for the better. For many women activists and scholars who participated in the profusion of feminist organizations established in the 1970s, class mattered. Not content merely to debate the abstract and structural aspects of class and capitalist economies, many socialist feminist activists argued that frank talk about the subjective, personal, psychic, and emotional aspects of class and its effects on one's identity, body, behavior, aspirations, attitudes, and relationships was crucial to advance women's collective liberation. In this essay, I will explore some of these conversations about class and feminism as well as their relevance for feminist practice today. I will also examine some of the reasons why class is too often relegated to the margins of contemporary feminist thought and practice.

Many 1970s feminist activists had worked previously in mixed-gender civil rights, antiwar, and Marxist/left groups of the 1960s, and they were profoundly disturbed by the sexism they encountered. At the same time, many of them were also troubled by the middle-class orientations and emphases on individual advancement and personal empowerment that predominated in many strands of women's liberation groups. They argued that feminist organizations often neglected to confront the landmines of class privilege, power, and hierarchies within their own organizations and in everyday behavior, hampering the revolutionary potential of women's liberation. Ginny Berson, for example, warned that "class has been a problem in the women's movement since its inception. Both its internal dynamic (the way meetings are run, decisions are made) and the external dynamic (the issues we have tried to organize around) have essentially excluded working class women from full participation" (8). She urged feminists to interrogate and recognize patterns of classist behavior or risk fostering the exclusion of working-class and poor women.

Barbara Ehrenreich, a key spokeswoman for socialist feminism in the 1970s (as well as the author of numerous recent books, including *Nickel and Dimed: On (Not) Getting by in America* (2001), argued that an understanding of gender, class, capitalism, and male domination was needed to correct "truncated" and ahistorical feminist explanations of the universality of patriarchy/male supremacy and women's oppression that omitted the possibility of reconciliation with men and ignored important differences among women. She argued, however, that taking a "mechanical" Marxist approach that emphasized only the role of the economy and conflicts between wage laborers, managers, and the owners of the "means of production" was insufficient. Instead, a feminist analysis of class dynamics needed to be broadened to include the recognition that "in its search for markets, capitalism is driven to penetrate *every nook and cranny* of social existence" (Ehrenreich, "What Is Socialist Feminism," emphasis added). Class struggle, according to Ehrenreich, was thus not only about political economy, wages, and workplace issues, but also the atomization and individualization of community and family life, consumption and desires, sexuality, and leisure, since class penetrates "every arena where the interests of classes conflict, and that includes education, health, art, music, etc." She added, "We aim to transform not only the ownership of the means of production, but the totality of social existence." Ehrenreich argued that "if one is a woman in a capitalist society and you get pissed off: about the job, about the bills, about your husband (or ex), about the kids' school, the housework, being pretty, being looked at, not being looked at, and either way not listened to, etc. If you think about all of these things and how they fit together and what has to be changed, and you look for some words to hold all of these thoughts together," then, Ehrenreich insisted, a socialist feminism analysis was essential.

Many activists thus identified themselves as "socialist feminists" to differentiate themselves from other women's liberation groups that did not forcefully consider the significant roles that class plays in constituting women's oppression. Socialist feminists feared that ignoring class differences among women would limit the Women's Movement and undermine efforts to build broad coalitions of women across class and racial divides. In 1973, Ginny Berson asserted that a "feminist movement without class consciousness is going to leave lots of women in bondage. If we are really concerned about the welfare of all women, we had better start dealing with class" (Berson 9). Charlotte Bunch and Coletta Reid noted that, initially, many feminist discussions of class rarely went beyond guilt and superficial understandings of class.

> We never went beyond wondering why welfare mothers were not beating down our doors. Hours were spent beating our breasts with guilt. The verdict: Women's Liberation was middle-class and that's bad, but we never understood why. We never examined how our behavior created and perpetuated that kind of movement . . . I finally recognized that class in our society is not only an economic system that determines everyone's place, but also patterns of behavior that reflect one's status. (Bunch and Reid 2)

In the 1970s, feminist organizations of all sizes, shapes, and slants were established to challenge sexism, racism, imperialism, poverty, and homophobia, with widespread differences in their agendas, political strategies, and constructions of the problems and solutions. Socialist feminists, in particular, were engaged in an array of consciousness-raising activities and action projects designed to ignite class awareness and fuse class, race, and gender analyses. They believed that the failure to confront both class privilege and male chauvinism would hamper the effectiveness of women engaged in liberation struggles, since social relations under capitalism warped bodies, psyches, and relationships. Perhaps less well-known than groups such as the National Organization for Women and other predominantly white, middle-class organizations that received more mainstream media attention (a mixed blessing), socialist feminist organizations such as the Boston-based Bread & Roses, the Combahee River Collective, the Third World Women's

Alliance, the Chicago Women's Liberation Union, and numerous local socialist feminist unions across the country flourished.

These were exhilarating times for socialist feminist organizations as they established day care centers; organized waitresses, clerical, and hospital workers; and worked on issues such as equal wages, maternity leave, sexual objectification in the media, welfare and prisoners' rights, and sexism/classism in schools and unions. They established consciousness-raising workshops, national conferences, retreats, community-based liberation schools, and study groups in which they read a variety of socialist feminist thinkers such as Charlotte Perkins Gilman, Emma Goldman, and Julie Mitchell. Additionally, they offered community-based courses on women and their bodies, racism and women's politics, women's fiction, Marxism, women's psychology, auto repair, self-defense, et cetera. They published numerous newspapers, such as *Triple Jeopardy*, from the Third World Women's Alliance (an organization that included members from the Black Women's Alliance and the Puerto Rican independence movement; see chapter 15 in this volume), which integrated race, class, gender, and anti-imperialism into its analysis and promoted transnational and cross-class solidarities among women.

The Furies, a lesbian feminist collective in which twelve white working-class and middle-class women lived and worked together in Washington, D.C., was an especially important incubator for analyzing the interplay of class, gender, and sexuality for women's liberation through their educational programs and publications. Collective members included Charlotte Bunch (a human rights activist who established the Center for Women's Global Leadership at Rutgers University and wrote many classic and contemporary books on feminism including *Passionate Politics: Feminist Theory in Action*, 1987), Rita Mae Brown (a novelist), and Ginny Berson (the founder of Olivia Records). Berson noted that when the collective was formed, its members had been unprepared to deal with class and its destructive effects on the internal dynamics of the collective. Through their nationally distributed monthly magazine, *The Furies: Lesbian/Feminist Monthly*, collective members probed the complexities of class by focusing on the "personal politics" of class difference and privilege and their effects on organizational dynamics and interpersonal relationships among women. For collective members, class was not an abstraction but an immediate, personal, and affective set of social relations that threatened women's unity. The Furies collective was noteworthy for its concrete ways of talking about the perilous misunderstandings and emotional wounds that unrecognized class patterns had on attempts to forge women's solidarities and alliances. Class for them was not just a matter of who had more money, education, and leisure time but also of the assumptions that we make about the world, our place in it, the burdens we carry, and our feelings of security, vulnerability, comfort, confidence, and shame.

Collective member Rita Mae Brown noted that tokenism and U.S. mythologies of personal transformation, self-advancement, and mobility help to sustain patterns of class inferiority and superiority among women. She noted that:

America is a country reluctant to recognize class differences. The America myth crystallized is: This is the land of equal opportunity; work hard, stay in line, you'll get ahead. (Getting ahead always means money) . . . To prove that this is the land of golden opportunity, elastic capitalism has been able to produce enough tokens on many levels to keep this myth alive. . . . Visually parading the tokens promises working-class people, Blacks, Chicanos, and women the chance to get ahead. Tokenism also creates a smug security for middle-class whites. It also allows them to be blind to class differences by showing them people who "made it." The middle-class person then assumes that with extra effort a "disadvantaged" person can get ahead, she just has to work harder. (Brown 56)

Ginny Berson noted that regardless of class origins, all women needed to engage in critical self-examinations of problematic conceptions about a classless meritocracy. She observed that her parents believed in classlessness:

They knew there were rich people and they knew there were poor people, but the reasons for a person's economic status were personal and moral, not economic or political. Everything around me said the same thing—America was a classless society. My high school in particular confirmed this. The tracking started in early, and by 7th grade I was in classes with people with whom I would stay all through high school. It was clearly a classist system, but the division was explained in terms of smart and dumb. The dumbs were pretty much the same—the girls had teased hair, wore tight skirts, lots of makeup, and were considered easy lays . . . They didn't have school spirit. The whole school was set up so our lives would never touch. I went all through school thinking they were trash because that was the way they wanted to be and thinking I was "poor" but noble because I had risen above my circumstances to be smart and clean and active. (Berson 12)

Class was seen by these thinkers as an ever-present specter producing "literally hundreds of slaps in the face" for women to negotiate on a daily basis (Brown 57). Consequently, it was imperative that feminists overcome their "privileged passivity" about class dynamics in their theories, organizations, and interpersonal relations.

THE "NOOKS AND CRANNIES" OF CLASS

Members of the Furies collective regularly dissected the personal nuances of class within their collective, since they believed that dialogue and consciousness-raising were essential for overcoming class barriers and breaking the silences about class differences. Less concerned with abstract theorizing about the relationships among labor, capitalism, and patriarchy, collective members instead focused on the raw, nitty-gritty effects of class privilege. They recognized that guilt, shame, silencing, and denial often characterized the relationships among women. Berson, for example, asserted that "class is the way you see the world and your place in it. Class is where and how you get educated. Class is how you act towards people" (Berson 13). Rita Mae Brown argued that it was vital for feminists to take responsibility for examining their own class-coded attitudes and biographies, a process essential for building strong feminist collectivities. She wrote:

> Class is much more than Marx's definition of the relationship to the means of production. Class involves your behavior, your basic assumptions about life . . . how you are taught to behave, what you expect from yourself and others, your concept of a future, how you understand problems and solve them, how you think, feel, act. It is these behavioral patterns cemented in childhood that cause class conflicts in various movements. . . . It is these behavioral patterns that must be recognized, understood, and changed. (Brown 57)

Collective members all agreed that the long tentacles of class produced misunderstandings among movement women. Coletta Reid and Charlotte Bunch, for example, jointly observed that classist behavior occurs daily. They noted that "class supremacy is acted out in thinking that working-class women are less together, personally and politically, because they do not act or talk the way we do. Their politics may not be expressed in the same manner, their vocabulary may not be as 'developed' . . . or they may be hostile and emotional so one can hardly trust their political judgment; after all we've learned to keep ourselves in check, to be reasonable, to keep things in perspective." (Bunch and Reid 2)

They also bemoaned the numerous ways some middle-class women rationalized classist behaviors by denying that they were really middle-class, challenging the class identities of working-class women, retreating into guilt, romanticizing the lives of working-class women, and/or expecting working-class women to take responsibility for explaining classist behaviors and attitudes instead of middle-class women having to do the onerous work of self-reflection.

Many of the collective members described the difficulties of navigating class throughout their educations as well as the pressures to class pass and to be upwardly mobile. Coletta Reid, who described her childhood as shaped by being a member of the "rural poor where everything about us was wrong—the way we looked, talked, dressed, and moved," went to college on a scholarship. She poignantly recounted the concealments, accommodations, and silences she enacted to survive in college as a poor student.

> There I began a long apprenticeship in the art of appearing middle-class. I improved my grammar, increased my vocabulary, learned about classical music. College initiated me into an alien culture that I knew I had to master to go anywhere. From the first week on I stood demurely chatting and sipping tea, took showers and acted like I felt right at home in long-winded academic discussions. I found out that there were hundreds of books everyone else could discuss that I hadn't even heard of. I went to college so I wouldn't always be a waitress or nurse's aid, getting the smallest salary for the heaviest work in the place. But I found that college doesn't just prepare you for an easier, better paying job; it ensures that you dress, talk, and think like a member of the professional class—that includes thinking you're better than working-class people and their culture. (Reid 8)

Reid also noted that she continually felt shame and inadequacy because of her class background. Once she became a member of the Furies, however, she realized that she had to stop continually trying to "prove herself worthy" and "accommodating." She began to question some of the middle-class attitudes she had internalized, to determine which ones were oppressive and which ones were beneficial. She also acknowledged that because she had "worked her way up," she had partially blamed other working-class women for not having done so. Reid concluded that, as a working-class woman, she too had to interrogate her own problematic assumptions of class worthiness and mobility.

Nancy Myron, another Furies member, acknowledged that although she too was a working-class woman, she nonetheless had to contend with race privileging. "As a white working-class woman, I still got one small compensation from this scale of value . . . racial superiority. I grew up in poverty but I had white skin privilege. Despite all my feelings of inferiority, I could still 'improve' my lot and even make it into the middle-class. Not that I wouldn't pay for it with *bits of my soul* [emphasis added]. My education was not as bad as a Black woman's. As poor as we were, we still weren't as poor as Blacks in Roxbury." (Myron 3)

Collective members, however, did not consider obtaining a college degree to be the panacea that would heal the long-standing lacerations of class and racial oppression experienced in childhood. Rita Mae Brown asserted that just because some working-class women had "fought our way out of inadequate schools into the universities and became educated in no way removes the entire experience of our childhood and youth . . . a degree does not erase all that went before it." She continued by noting that "a white middle-class woman wouldn't dream of telling a Black lesbian with a college degree that she is no longer Black, yet she feels perfectly justified in telling a working class woman with a degree that she is no longer working class!" (Brown 57). Despite the many obstacles that poor and working-class women faced getting an academic education, college— if not a panacea for oppression—was nonetheless heralded as an important political opportunity. Brown noted that for many working-class women such as herself, "school was the first opportunity we had to have time to think politically. When you work all day, every day, there is little time to politically organize" (Brown 58).

Given socialist feminist hopes that higher education would foster critical class consciousness, what accounts for the relative lack of concrete conversations and theorizing about class and feminism today, especially given the ever-widening gulf between the rich and the poor and the growing insecurities and displacement of poor, immigrant, working-class, and middle-class women and men?

There are multiple reasons that help to maintain a relative silence about class and help to explain why so many people self-identify as middle-class and rarely as working-class (or the more pejorative label, "low-class"), despite vast differences in material resources, well-being, life experiences, and status. Class can be more easily hidden from view since it is not as explicitly inscribed on physical bodies as race and gender (though numerous makeover shows such as *Extreme Makeover, The Biggest Loser,* and *Flavor of*

Love: Charm School promise to repair and polish working-class and ethnic bodies and dispositions, perpetuating a long cultural tradition of celebrating rags-to-riches transformations and assimilation). Feelings of shame, guilt, and privilege further hamper class dialogue and consciousness. In an era of a deregulated and unstable economy and cutbacks in national safety nets for education, work, and welfare, discourses of equal opportunity, personal empowerment, self-enterprise, individual responsibility, and consumption continue to permeate public life and perpetuate ideas of classlessness in the United States.

Popular culture also plays a role by offering a steady diet of self-improvement and lifestyle programming that further blunts the awareness of class realities by promising that self-enhancement, personal transformation, and pulling oneself up by one's bras and bootstraps will yield upward mobility, assimilation, and prosperity. We are continually reminded to be proactive and energetic—to get up and be somebody—by making good choices. TV shows bombard us with class-coded self-help advice for how to be witty, tasteful, cosmopolitan, socially savvy, and confident while showcasing and disparaging the working-class and the poor for their bad choices, culture, and lack of ambition and discipline (for example, *Judge Judy, Jamie Oliver's Food Revolution, Bad Girl's Club*). Class mobility is marketed today as merely a matter of learning to enhance and invest in one's image, taste, and lifestyle (cosmopolitan and elite class proficiencies that include wine, food, art and culture, travel, etiquette, grammar, style, etc.). The failure to achieve middle-class lifestyles and securities is portrayed as a personal problem of choice, not a political one. The paucity of cross-class friendship networks also reduces opportunities for cross-class dialogues and for the recognition of the resiliencies and strengths of poor and working-class people.

Class is a relative and slippery concept that refers to processes and positionalities. It creates both confusion and silences. Class encompasses labor, income, wealth, power, position, status, education, mentorship and networks, moral value and stigma, security, debt and vulnerability, family and community origins, access to education, housing, health care, transportation, safety, food, and leisure and has profound effects on one's sense of self. It helps to choreograph our life experiences, our sense of self, our comfort zones, our sense of control and confidence in daily life, our dreams and desires, our fears of exposure for not fitting in, shame and awkwardness, and the exhausting challenges of passing, upward mobility, and class hybridity. Class is not a permanent home address, a rigid typology of characteristics neatly delineating various classes and their dispositions and resources, but rather a kaleidoscopic array of material and subjective dynamics that is also gendered and racialized. Class identities and statuses do change, as some manage to secure middle-class positions, yet at the same time, many immigrants experience class dislocation when they come to the United States. In an economy of bankruptcies, evictions, credit cards, and Wal-Mart, the realities of class continue to impact "the nooks and crannies" of our lives and make feminist dialogues about how class, race, sexuality, and gender are braided together even more urgent.

WORKS CITED

All of these articles are available online at www.rainbowhistory.org, and most of them were reprinted in Charlotte Bunch and Nancy Myron, eds., *Class and Feminism* (Baltimore: Diana Press, 1974). Barbara Ehrenreich, "What Is Socialist Feminism," *Win Magazine* (1976) and other writings on socialist feminism are available at www.cwluherstory.org.

Berson, Ginny. "Class Revisited: One Step Forward, Two Steps Back." *The Furies: Lesbian/ Feminist Monthly* 2, no. 3 (1973): 8–9.

———. "Slumming in the Middle Class." *The Furies: Lesbian/Feminist Monthly* 1, no. 3 (1972): 12–13.

Brown, Rita Mae. "The Last Straw." *Motive* 32, no. 1 (1972).

Bunch, Charlotte, and Coletta Reid. "Revolution Begins at Home." *The Furies: Lesbian/Feminist Monthly* 1, no. 4 (1972): 2–3.

Myron, Nancy. "Class Beginnings." *The Furies: Lesbian/Feminist Monthly* 1, no. 3 (1972): 2–3.

Reid, Coletta. "Recycled Trash." *The Furies: Lesbian/Feminist Monthly* 1, no. 5 (1972).

DISCUSSION QUESTIONS

1. How do you define class? When and why did you become aware of class differences?

2. What are the effects of class on student life, friendship circles, campus organizations and rituals, living arrangements, leisure, and interactions in the classroom?

3. How can one enhance opportunities for cross-class relationships and dialogues on campus?

4. What kind of messages do we get about class from TV shows?

5. How do new digital technologies such as the Internet and social networking sites reduce, exacerbate, or otherwise alter class inequalities?

RITA MAE BROWN, *THE LAST STRAW*

Now that lesbians are building a separate movement, class is a critical issue among us. Working class lesbians are determined that class will be the first issue resolved within our movement; otherwise the working class lesbians will be unable to work with middle class lesbians. Since class is so misunderstood, since it evokes such wild emotional responses, I will try to explain class in a concrete way, in terms of ideas and behavior. It would be repetitious to explain class in terms of the economy—Marx has already done that for us.

SOURCE: Rita Mae Brown, "The Last Straw," *Motive* 32, no. 1 (1972): 2–5.

America is a country reluctant to recognize class differences. The American myth crystallized is: This is the land of equal opportunity; work hard, stay in line, you'll get ahead. (Getting ahead always means money.) All public school children are fed this myth. It gives poor people hope and it reinforces middle class people's belief in their own superiority. To prove that this is the land of golden opportunity, elastic capitalism has been able to create enough tokens on many levels to keep the myth alive, i.e., the late Whitney Young, Diana Ross, Margaret Mead, etc. Visually parading the tokens promises working class people, Blacks, Chicanos, and women the chance to get ahead and channels them into the establishment where they will cut each others' throats to be capitalism's newest token. Tokenism also creates a smug security for middle class whites. It allows them to be blind to class differences by showing them the people who have "made it." The middle class person then assumes that with extra effort a "disadvantaged" person can get ahead, she just has to work harder. Since middle class people don't socialize or have close job relationships with workers there are no clashing experiences to challenge their false assumptions.

Due to America's peculiar blurring of class distinctions, middle class people do not think in class terms except for those who have become Marxist intellectuals. Middle class people often don't recognize that they are middle class. Even in the various political movements, they may recognize class intellectually but they don't understand how their personal behavior, shot through with middle class assumptions and ideas, is destructive to those of us from the working class. Even those who buy capitalism's line and want to "make it" know they are "inferior" due to class background and they work twice as hard to "overcome" it.

Class is much more than Marx's definition of relationship to the means of production. Class involves [how] your behavior, your basic assumptions about life, your experiences (determined by your class) validate those assumptions, how you are taught to behave, what you expect from yourself and from others, your concept of a future, how you understand problems and solve them, how you think, feel, act. It is these behavioral patterns cemented in childhood that cause class conflicts in the various movements. It is these behavioral patterns that middle class women resist recognizing although they may be perfectly willing to accept class in Marxist terms, a neat trick that helps them avoid really dealing with class behavior and changing that behavior in themselves. It is these behavioral patterns which must be recognized, understood and changed.

As lesbians it is crucial that we make these changes immediately. We have few privileges in male society if we come out because we threaten male supremacy at its core. Does that mean that because we have few class/race privileges in male society that we have no class/race differences among ourselves? No. While lesbians have little power to enforce their privileges once they *come out* they still continue to behave in the ways of their class/race. It is that behavior which infuriates those of us who are not middle class and who are not white. Our anger confuses the white, middle class lesbian because she can't understand what she is doing wrong—her behavior seems natural to her.

As examples, I have singled out two ideas and their consequent behavior current in the Lesbian Movement which are harmful to working class lesbians. All too often these mistakes are deliberate stalls on the part of the middle class lesbians to keep from changing themselves. Rather than hear us, they resist us with accusations and theories to negate our demand that they change oppressive behavior.

I. The Idea That a Working Class Woman with a College Education Escapes Her Class Background   Middle class women theorize that if you are working class but have a college degree then you must have just as much class privilege as they do so you are no longer working class. This idea is sheer arrogant blindness. Just because many of us fought our way out of inadequate schools into the universities and became "educated" in no way removes the entire experience of our childhood and youth—working class life. A degree does not erase all that went before it. A degree simply means that you have submitted to white, male, heterosexual, middle class educational standards and passed. It doesn't mean you accept those standards. If you have a college degree you can get a better job than if you don't have one. (Unless you are a lesbian who has come out.) None of us working class women are trying to pretend we can't get better jobs with degrees than without degrees . . . but a job is a way to earn money in adulthood, our pasts remain the same and our ways can remain intact.

A white, middle class woman wouldn't dream of telling a Black lesbian with a college degree that she is no longer Black, yet she feels perfectly justified in telling a working class woman with a degree that she is no longer working class! There is a reason for this double think. Working class lesbians with degrees push middle class lesbians very hard. We aren't intimidated by their high tone raps and we can talk "their" language only with "our" ideas. This scares the shit out of them, many of them want to believe the class stereotype: working class people are inarticulate, shy, passive, uninterested in ideas, etc. Those of us who fight back destroy those illusions and we also destroy the middle class person's class power by doing so. The women who are the most hostile to "educated" working class women are very often, middle class women who want to cling to class behavior and the power it gives them over other women. The other middle class women usually aren't hostile, just conveniently confused, so confused that it takes them a good long time before they believe us and change their own behavior. And disbelief of a working class woman's analysis of her class oppression is one more way to undermine us—we don't "know enough" to analyze our own goddamn oppression, we need a middle class woman to do it for us in fancy sociological language. Christ.

College was culture shock to many of us from the working class. College is middle class and reinforces the white middle class woman in her class ways. College for the working class woman challenges her entire life experience. The snobbism rampant in humanities departments, the enforced practice of saying in three polysyllabic paragraphs what could be said in two short sentences are counter to working class ways. There are literally hundreds of slaps in the face that a working class woman endures. Middle class women endure the sexism of college but not the classism. Working class women get both, Third World women get it three ways. For us, college was a journey through a hostile environment, an environment where we were forced to deny our class background in order to get our degree.

College caused some working class women to reject their early lives, adopt middle class values, become upwardly mobile (or if they joined a political movement, downwardly mobile) and fight their own working class sisters to be accepted into the middle class world. Others of us endured college because we didn't want to repeat the lives of drudgery and misery our parents had, but we did not adopt middle class ways. For many of us college was the last straw that pushed us into open class resistance.

Perhaps the most outrageous aspect of the middle class women's views on education and the working class women is their unspoken assumption that we went to college because we were upwardly mobile—in other words, we wanted to be like them. Only a woman far removed from bread and butter reality could harbor such an assumption. We watched our parents slave for nothing. School seemed the answer to our economic plight if we could just get there. So we studied, got scholarships, took out loans that kept us in hock for years—to avoid that same futile labor of our parents, to survive economically rather than subsist. And in this pursuit working class women suffered more than working class men because of sex discrimination in admission and scholarships. (Plus you had to hide being a lesbian or you'd get thrown out.) In spite of all these difficulties, this generation of working class lesbians and women from 22–35 has many college graduates, a testament of grit if ever there was one. For many of us school was the first opportunity we had to have time to think politically. When you work all day, every day there is little time to think and no time to politically organize. Yes we have college degrees, no we don't work in factories like our parents did and we learned from the rape of our parents—we want to make a revolution because of it.

II. Downward Mobility as the Road to Removing Class Differences Youth/drug culture, the New Left, the Women's Movement and unfortunately, the Lesbian Movement are all choking on this idea. Downward mobility is a mockery of working class life. It is poverty made fashionable. Behavior remains the same: Those who don't comply with this "hip" lifestyle are looked down upon. It is in the establishment of hierarchies that the middle class betrays itself—they always have to look down on somebody, a habitual attitude of power.

I don't want to live with mattresses on the floor, ragged clothes, dirt and spaghetti for supper every night. How anyone can imitate poverty and give it the flavor of "inness" is so alien to me that it is disgusting. I don't want to be above anybody but I do want decent housing, nice clothes and good food.

Downward mobility is the greatest insult yet devised by middle class people against the working class. If that alone isn't enough, downward mobility is married to the mistrust of the mind and a worship of the emotional. First of all, I don't understand intellect/emotional divisions yet millions of people seemed chained to that separation. A woman who thinks and analyzes is accused of being a power-hungry "heavy" in the movement while a woman who cries at every meeting is embraced as a true sister. Many middle class women, fearing that intellect will be mistaken for middle class behavior and remembering *their* college experience, bury their brains in a morass of "vibes," "gut feelings," and outright hysteria. This is dogmatically declared "true woman" behavior since men don't express their feelings. Serious organizing to end our oppression is suspect, ideological struggle is heresy; feelings are the way, the light and the truth—even when they result in political stagnation. Such an idea spells death to real political change if people cling to it.

It isn't intellect that working class women mistrust in middle class women, it is how middle class women use their intellect to rationalize holding onto class behavior that hurts us. Or simply, we mistrust bullshit, not brains.

Difficult as it is for middle class women to realize how downward mobility strikes us, they must open themselves and see what they are doing to us. I know that for many middle class women, downward mobility was a first attempt at trying to change their ways. However, those women must realize that the irony of downward mobility, its fatal flaw, is that they could *afford* to become downwardly mobile. Their class privilege enabled them to reject materialism. For those of us who grew up without material advantages downward mobility is infuriating—here are women rejecting what we never had and can't get! Valid as that emotional reaction is on our part, we working class women are being taught a lesson by the middle class women. That lesson is: lots of capitalistic possessions and social status do not bring happiness—another American myth shattered.

One good idea behind downward mobility is non-consumerism. The problem is not the idea but how it has become part of a new middle class "hip" lifestyle, an inverse snobbism that hits working class people both ways: Before downward mobility we were invisible or when visible, we were trash; with downward mobility we are "counterrevolutionaries" because we don't comply with the "hip" lifestyle. It's the same old shit—middle class people develop their values and measure us by their standards and have the effrontery to be enraged if we measure them by *our* standards. Downward mobility is the other side of the capitalist coin, or to put it more bluntly, the East Village is second generation Scarsdale.

Political working class lesbians are obviously going to practice non-consumerism but we aren't creating a behavioral code out of it. We aren't trucking around in patched pants mumbling about "gettin in touch with our feelins." (Another downward mobility insult, middle class women parody our speech to prove how they are no longer middle class. This is as unforgiveable as a white person putting on a broad Black "accent.")

Downward mobility also has one other dangerous effect upon those of us from the working classes—it prevents us from benefiting from the material privileges of white, middle class women. If you have money, sister, don't deny it, *share* it. If you have advanced skills don't make pottery in your loft, teach us those skills. If you have good clothes don't walk around in rags, give us some of your clothes. Downward mobility is a way to deny your material privileges to prove how "right on" you are. We know that anytime you get tired of poverty you can go right back to them (unless of course, you have publicly come out).

Downward mobility assumes that material benefits are bad. That's a mistake. Material benefits aren't bad, what's bad is that everyone doesn't have them. Downward mobility insures that working class women still won't have material benefits—we have more trouble getting them than the middle class woman and she won't share her privileges with us, she's too busy living in a dump. *Share* your material benefits.

Downward mobility and ideas centering around education are just two examples of how class can shatter alliances, make people hate each other, weaken us politically. Those examples are critical of middle class women and they deserve criticism but I'm not saying that middle class women are inevitably horrible. All I'm saying is that they have to change those ways. I am also not saying that being working class is wonderful and makes you an instant lesbian revolutionary. The fact is that there are class/race differences between lesbians and those differences have to be wiped out because they keep us apart and keep us at each others' throats. Behavior born of privilege granted from white, upper class, male heterosexuals is destructive to women and must be ended. The more privileged you were in that old world, the more you must work to free yourself from that destructiveness so that you can build the new world. But we have all lived in Amerika and in some ways we all have to change.

In the past those of us from working class backgrounds tried to make this clear to straight sisters. We are now making it crystal clear to our middle class lesbian sisters. It is not our job to explain our oppression to you, you must work to find out how class hurts other women. Don't waste our time by trying to prove you are an exception because your father was working class and your mother was middle class. All that means is that you have a mixture of class ways; stop trying to wriggle out of those middle class ways that you *do* have. Change them. You are your own responsibility. It is your job to examine yourself and change just as it is my job to examine myself and change. Our collective responsibility as lesbians is to annihilate, smash, destroy male supremacy and build a New World.

The real question is not whether you are middle class and white but whether you are serious about destroying male supremacy, about changing the world. If you are serious you will begin by changing yourself.

GINNY BERSON, *CLASS REVISITED: ONE STEP FORWARD, TWO STEPS BACK*

The class issue in the women's movement, always somewhere in the background, has recently been made a major priority by some of the lesbian media. Unfortunately, the issue has been raised only so that it can finally and irrevocably be smashed into oblivion. Class is being discussed as a non-issue, a force which divides us unnecessarily, a series

SOURCE: Ginny Berson, "Class Revisited: One Step Forward, Two Steps Back," *The Furies: Lesbian/Feminist Monthly* 2, no. 3 (1973): 8–9.

of nit-picking gripes made by illiterate or otherwise inadequate women, a political ploy to give one group control over another, a fad. It is all very reminiscent of the "arguments" used by straight women to discredit lesbianism as a political issue and lesbian separatism as sometimes necessary.

Class consciousness is not a fad. Class has been a problem in the women's movement since its inception. Both its internal dynamic (the way meetings are run, the way decisions are made) and the external dynamic (the issues we have tried to organize around) have essentially excluded lower class women from full participation. There are good articles about the way class operates in the lesbian movement in *The Furies* (especially #4) and *Ain't I a Woman* (especially June 16, 1972). What all the articles share is a conviction that women can change—that middle class women can recognise in themselves patterns of behaviour that are oppressive to lower class women, oppressive because they arise out of material privilege; and also that lower class women can recognise in themselves patterns of behaviour that result from their oppression. For example, a middle class woman may see that her ability to bullshit keeps her from having to deal honestly with other women, so she changes. The lower class woman sees that she is intimidated by the bullshit and decides to stop being intimidated.

What is important in this example is not that one person is middle class and the other is lower class. The words themselves are only used to loosely define general backgrounds and resulting patterns of behaviour. Just being a good bullshitter doesn't make you middle class, and being easily intimidated doesn't make you lower class. The label is only there to help you find yourself; to help you understand how your background determines the way you act, and, understanding it, help you change it. That is the exact process that thousands of women have gone through in order to develop feminist and lesbian consciousness.

Class Is Political

We know that being born a woman has had certain effects on us, and that these effects are not isolated to individuals. None of us thinks that if a woman is afraid of men that it's her own personal hang-up. We understand that fear is political in nature, that it is the result of a power system which puts men on the top. Within that power system are other power systems which say white is better than black, straight is better than gay, rich is better than poor. Add to that the pervasive American ideology of rugged individualism— anyone can make it, and anyone who doesn't is a personal failure.

In a society which places a premium, for example, on abstract thinking, is it unusual for a woman who can't think abstractly (because she has never been taught how, because she didn't go to college, because she took a commercial course in high school, etc.) to feel less together than and intimidated by someone who can? Is this her own personal problem? Obviously not. It's a political problem which is the result of people in power establishing values which reflect their own interests.

For years we believed it was our own fault that we couldn't find fulfillment in marriage and motherhood. For years lower class woman believed it was their own personal inadequacy that they couldn't think abstractly. But the Women's Liberation Movement has taught us that the personal is political: you are who you are because of the political forces that molded you. The early movement stopped at sex as the only determinant. It stopped there because it was largely a white, middle class, straight movement, which reaped the benefits of race, class and heterosexual privilege. They didn't do it deliberately; they did it because they didn't know that there were other forms of oppression that affect women. They thought that having women's consciousness was enough to free any woman from problems of class or race or anything else. But that is obviously not the case.

But we know, it is not enough to say that we have rejected all the class values that were shoved down our throats and have created our own. We're all trying to do that, but rejecting them intellectually and actually acting in ways that are completely free of the old values are two different things. Nobody says they want to be classist, any more than they want to be passive and gossipy. But how many of us are not occasionally passive, or gossipy, or ashamed of our bodies, or lacking in confidence? And we have been conscious of woman oppression much longer than we have been dealing with class.

The point of finding your identity in your class (or your sex) is not so that you can wear a badge to prove you're better than everyone else or that you have stopped at defining yourself as of a certain class. There is no more point in glorifying lower class values than there is in being ashamed because you're middle class. It's not a question of deciding which is better, but of recognizing that they are different.

I lived in a house once with lower and middle class women. The lower class women wanted their own rooms, and we were shocked: how un-revolutionary of them! We didn't understand that they had shared everything all their lives because there was never enough for everyone to have "her own." They wanted to keep financial books to keep track of our money; we thought it was unnecessary—if we spent too much we could always make it up somehow. But growing up with no financial security doesn't give you much faith in "somehow."

The Material Base

Another key area of class differences is in money and earning power. A woman with a college degree is more likely to get a better job than a high school drop-out. That is why sharing material privilege is so important. Otherwise, the people who have to work 40 hours a week are going to have less time and energy to put into the movement than the people who only have to work 20 hours a week. The people who have to work 40 hours are more likely to be the people without high-paying skills, like waitresses, typists, etc. Where there is a common political base, and a common commitment, people should share their privilege. If we are living and working collectively, and if I can make $100 a week for 23 hours of work, why should my friend have to work 40 hours a week as a waitress in order to make the same money? Is there something more inherently valuable in my contribution to the movement than hers? Is my time worth more than hers?

When *The Furies* was operating as a collective, we pooled our money on a percentage system in which the people with the most privilege and the best jobs gave the most money. That left us all with about the same amount of time for our political work. We also encouraged people to get the best jobs they could—to use their privilege so they could help the people who didn't have it. That means don't live off welfare if you can get a $5 an hour job. Just earning enough to "get by" is fine if there aren't a lot of people around who have to break their asses in order to just "get by." And I'm not talking about charity. I'm talking about women who are doing the same thing you're doing, or would be if they didn't have to work 8 hours a day.

Upward Mobility

If downward mobility is oppressive to lower class women, so is upward mobility. This is not because articulateness, education, and self-reliance are undesirable; but because upwardly mobile women tend to acquire classist attitudes in the process of moving up. As Coletta Reid says in *The Furies* (#5), "The most oppressive attitude I accepted was that because I had become middle class, worked my way 'up,' I was better than other working-class women who were still down there. . . . It was partially their own fault that now middle-class women still treated them with disrespect."

Recognizing and Acting on the Differences

Obviously not all working class women are inarticulate any more than all middle class women are articulate. There are a number of other determinants of our behaviour besides class—race, age, old gay/new gay. It is not particularly important to find the exact label that fits you. A middle class lesbian who came out long before there was a movement to support her is a victim of a different kind of oppression than the lower class woman who came out last week. There is no point in keeping a scorecard of who's more oppressed. The name just points you in the direction, and leads you to the people you might have the most in common with. It helps you understand why you are the way you are; it helps you understand the system that made you that way and what has to be done to create a new society which is free of oppressive power relationships.

The point is that there are differences between us, that some of those differences are based on class, and that to ignore them by saying they shouldn't exist is to perpetuate their existence.

So what should we do about it? How can both lower class and middle class women deal with the attitudes that are destructive to the movement that we are all trying to build? In the past, lower class women simply stayed away. Then they started confronting middle class women with their oppressive behaviour whenever it was possible. Often this meant devoting more time and energy to solving internal problems within a group than to solving the problems which brought the group together in the first place (i.e., this sexist world). It meant convincing middle class women that the experiences of lower class women were real and valid. Middle class women changed some, lower class women changed some, but it hasn't happened very fast. And lower class women are impatient— they want to get on with the task and middle class women are holding them back. So some of them are going off by themselves to do it. And just as we got tired of struggling with men first, and then with straight women, so they are tired of struggling with middle class women. That is why we must do it ourselves, if we expect to build a movement and a future society that is truly classless.

I think women can change. I think when middle class women change those parts of themselves which are oppressive to lower class women, we will be able to work together again. I'm not advocating that we all sit around and examine our navels for the next 5 years trying to figure out how we're oppressive. But I think that class consciousness has to be a part of whatever middle class women do. That doesn't mean that we drop what we're doing and run out to start organizing welfare mothers; it means that as we build our own institutions we are conscious that they meet the needs of all women, not just middle class women. It means that wherever politically practical we share our money and skills with lower class women. It means that we do not set up standards of leadership which can only be met by middle class women. It means that within our own groups we are conscious of each other's classism, and that instead of letting things slip by because they are not personally offensive, we criticize each other. It means that we accept criticism from other middle class women instead of acting as though the only legitimate class criticism can come from lower class women. It means that we stop relating to lower class women out of guilt and fear; that is what we do when we react to their criticism as if it were Truth. That is what we do when we retreat into passivity in order not to offend anyone.

A feminist movement without class consciousness is going to leave a lot of women in bondage. If we are really concerned about the welfare of all women, we had better start dealing with class.

13

FEMINISTS REIMAGINE
THE BODY

Susan Bordo

As cultural critics, twentieth-century feminists have produced some of the most powerful challenges to the conceptions of human nature, scientific theories and discoveries, philosophical and moral reason, and historical narratives established by male-dominated thinkers from antiquity through the first half of the twentieth century. Yet how often do we see feminist theorists listed along with Foucault, Derrida, or Kuhn as critics and reshapers of intellectual culture? More often, we encounter a version of Edward Said's formulation: "We ... know more about the way culture operates thanks to Raymond Williams, Roland Barthes, Michel Foucault, and Stuart Hall; we know about how to examine a text in ways that Jacques Derrida, Hayden White, Frederic Jameson, and Stanley Fish have significantly expanded and altered; and thanks to feminists like Elaine Showalter, Germaine Greer, Helene Cixous, Sandra Gilbert, Susan Gubar, and Gayatri Spivak it is impossible to avoid or ignore the gender issues in the production and interpretation of art" (xiv–xv). So: because of Barthes, Derrida, et al. we "know more" about culture and texts; "thanks to feminists," we are unable to "avoid" or "ignore" gender. Or, to invoke Simone de Beauvoir here, feminist thought remains the gendered "Other" in our narratives of "general" cultural transformation.

We can challenge this construction in any number of areas. The one that infuriates me the most, however—perhaps because feminist work in this area played such an important role in my own personal and intellectual development—is the notion that male poststructuralists rather than feminists are responsible for the twentieth-century "turn" to the body, and more specifically, the revolution in thinking about the body as socially, culturally, and politically "constructed" rather than a transparent biological entity. Both Black Power activists and women's liberationists, in the 1960s and 1970s, were centrally responsible for an awakening social consciousness of the body as an instrument of power and social control, from foot binding, corseting, and skin-color testing to compulsory heterosexuality, forced sterilization, and pornography. Indeed, as I read the history of thought, at the very center of "personal politics" was the conception of the body as profoundly shaped, both materially and representationally, by cultural ideology and what Foucault would *later* label "disciplinary" practice. Consider, for example, Andrea Dworkin, writing in 1974:

> Standards of beauty describe in precise terms the relationship that an individual will have to her own body. They prescribe her motility, spontaneity, posture, gait, the uses to which she can put her body. *They define precisely the dimensions of her physical freedom* . . . . This alteration is an ongoing, repetitive process. It is vital to the economy [and] the major substance of male-female differentiation. . . . It is commonly and wrongly said that male transvestites through the use of makeup and costuming caricature the women they would become, but any real knowledge of the romantic ethos makes clear that these men have penetrated to the core experience of being a woman, a romanticized construct. (113–14, emphasis in original)

Some readers may be amazed to discover that Dworkin is not the rabid "essentialist" that many later feminists have caricatured her as. When I read Dworkin in the seventies, I thought she was one of the most brilliant writers I'd encountered, who in many ways anticipated what would later become known as the "performitivity" of gender, and who regarded the female body, quite explicitly, as a politically "colonized" territory. The terms belong to the current lexicon, but the ideas are there, in Dworkin's work and many others. Yet, it is Foucault who is credited as the father of the "politics of the body." His central illustrations, in *Discipline and Punish*, written four years after Dworkin, involve gendered bodies no less than hers. Yet, when Dworkin talks about the discipline of the body required by the "art" of femininity, her work is read as having implications for women and the peculiarities of their condition, while when Foucault talks about the training of the soldier, it is read as gender-neutral and broadly applicable.

Ever since I started teaching and writing, I've been on something of a campaign to correct the record here, by returning to writers that have been virtually forgotten, to show that neither Foucault, Judith Butler, Iris Young, nor myself were the first to write about what has come to be known, among academics, as "the constructed body." The feminist resources are so rich, particularly if one includes the theory embodied in activism, that I teach a semester-long course on the topic. Here, space limitations have imposed a narrower focus and choice of selections. The topic is the politics of orgasm, and we've chosen four authors to represent four distinctive—and arguably nationally/ethnically inflected—views.

Australian Germaine Greer, represented here by a selection from 1970's *The Female Eunuch*, declares early in the book—countering centuries of philosophical thought privileging mind over body and arguing for the possibility of transcendence of mind over body—that "whatever else we are or may pretend to be, we are certainly our bodies." She then proceeds, in chapter after chapter, to travel through all the components of body, from the most "material" (e.g., bones, curves, hair) to the most elusive (e.g., energy, obsession, disgust), performing a historical/literary deconstruction of the myths and images that make up its history. She was among the very first to view the body, as we might say today, "as a product of discourse."

Greer was the first feminist I read whose work allowed me to believe that it was possible to combine political passion with literary sensibilities, sexual audaciousness, and cheeky humor—and produce work that is deliciously readable as well. I loved her for defying the media-produced stereotypes of the feminist as grim, male-bashing bluestocking, and the philosophy student in me was delighted to find the theories of my favorite "new left" writer—Herbert Marcuse—turned to feminist uses. Marcuse had argued, against Freud, that the genital organization of sexuality was not required for "civilization" to function, but rather to serve the interests of advanced capitalism. Freud had accepted that we are all "polymorphously perverse" by nature—we experience pleasure through every organ, every sense, every surface of the body. But unlike Freud, Marcuse and Greer believed that we could recover that "sexual involvement of the whole person" (as Greer refers to it in the selection reprinted here) without returning to some anarchistic, chaotic state of nature. Of course, realizing this would involve transformation of the social and economic machinery of capitalism (a staple of most sixties' social theory), but for me, just reading Greer made me feel more polymorphous.

Looking ahead to the Koedt selection, we should note that for Greer, the feminist celebration of the clitoral orgasm, which many women's libbers embraced as part of throwing off male oppression, is no less a constriction of eroticism than the sexist theories it attempted to debunk, in that it locates sexual pleasure in "a tiny cluster of nerves" rather than diffused throughout the body. As is hinted at in her discussion of the metaphors we use to describe the vagina—and the alternatives that we might employ instead—Greer was strongly opposed to any kind of biological reductionism. For her, the vagina is composed of cultural imagination as much as blood, muscle, and skin. Anne Koedt, whose extremely influential "Myth of the Vaginal Orgasm" (1973) is reprinted here, represents, to my mind, the more empirical strain of U.S. feminism. It is also very much the product of the ideology and practice of "consciousness-raising," in which women met to share their experiences, and in doing so, became aware of the political dimensions of their personal lives. Much early feminist theory grew out of such sessions, which often began with one woman tentatively offering a painful or shameful experience, and just as often discovering that she was far from alone. The group would then collectively (sometimes the most vocal, "politically advanced" member would lead the charge) examine the gendered power relations that they had previously imagined to be purely "personal" problems.

Koedt's challenge to the notion that the only "real" orgasm is a vaginal orgasm had many women, declared "frigid" by their therapists and doctors because they weren't aroused to orgasm during intercourse, cheering. And her dissection of why men have maintained the myth is one of the first exposures of what would later be called "phallocentric" thinking. However, it's also arguably the case that Koedt, in privileging what she described as "the small equivalent of the penis"—the clitoris—was engaging in another version of such thinking. It's easy to imagine Koedt and Greer in heated argument with each other, despite their shared annoyance at Freud and other male "experts." Greer might say that Koedt, while rightly debunking male myths, is still dominated by a scientistic, mechanistic view of sexual pleasure. For Koedt, it may be the clitoris rather than the vagina that is the privileged site of response, but for her no less than Freud, anatomy (rather than imagination and ideology) is still destiny.

Luce Irigaray's famous "This Sex Which Is Not One" (1980) does not mention Koedt, but opens with a paragraph that can be seen as both agreement and critique of her position. Like Koedt, Irigaray protests the privileging of the vagina by male sexologists. But unlike Koedt, what Irigaray objects to is not that the clitoris is ignored in this scheme, but that the vagina is imagined as it exists for men, as passive and receiving, existing only to provide a "home" for the penis. Thinking of the clitoris as a "little penis" (as Koedt does) does not escape this phallocentrism, but rather reproduces it on the other side of the equation. What is erotically "active" in woman (the clitoris) is what is most like the male; what is distinctively female (the vagina) is merely a hole to be filled up. To theorize female sexuality outside the "parameters" of the masculine will require something more radical than inverting its dualities. For Irigaray, this means rejecting the dualistic framework of malethink and accessing (or perhaps creating) a distinctively female "imaginary," neither serving "one" (the penis) nor—and here Irigaray can make literal-minded readers dizzy—"two." Woman's sexuality escapes the countable.

After Greer and Koedt, whose prose is accessible and argument style straightforward, Irigaray's piece may prove difficult, its meaning elusive. Even those well versed in continental philosophy have puzzled over her writing, which like much French feminism, tends to be more poetic, metaphorical and enigmatic than the "Second Wave" writing that came out of the United States and the United Kingdom. When Irigaray writes, "woman has sex organs just about everywhere," is she saying that "woman," by nature, is polymorphously perverse? If so, is this not to essentialize female sexuality just as centuries of male writers have done, but in a more appreciative mode? And if woman is "this sex which is not one," does this imply that men *are* "one"? What could that mean? Irigaray's writing resists definitive answers, but the key to understanding her, I believe, is to recognize that she is not talking about an empirical body. When Koedt talks about the vagina, she has an anatomical body part in mind; for Irigaray, in contrast, the vagina is always, inescapably discursive, impossible to describe outside one imaginary or another. You can't get at some biological bedrock. What you can do is create, or "write" the body in an alternative mode.

Our last selection, by Caribbean American writer and activist Audre Lorde, predates Irigaray by two years. I end my discussion with it because in many ways it embodies—rather than merely "calling for"—the transformative imaginary that Irigaray theorizes, and the polymorphous, anti-establishment sexuality that Greer celebrates. Lorde is perhaps most famous for having declared, in another piece titled by the phrase, that "the master's tools will never dismantle the master's house"—and although in that piece she had in mind the continuing racism of white feminism and its service to patriarchy, the phrase seems applicable as well to Lorde's conception of the erotic, which dispenses entirely with talk of sexual organs and orgasms. A debate about vagina versus clitoris will never dismantle the master's house, no matter which "side" you take. For the erotic is not about sensation, it cannot be confined to the bedroom, it is not about organs and what one does with them.

What is it then? Readers may at first be startled to find words like "power," "knowledge," and "work" associated with the erotic. Those familiar with Nietzsche, however, may be less baffled by the term "power"; for Lorde, as for Nietzsche, power is not *over* something or someone outside oneself, it is what comes from realizing one's "life-force": the full exercise of one's talents, energies, emotions. It can come to us in any number of ways, for, as Lorde writes, "the erotic is not a question only of what we do; it is a question of how acutely and fully we can feel in the doing. Once we know the extent to which we are capable of feeling that sense of satisfaction and completion, we can then observe which of our various life endeavors bring us closest to that fullness." Rereading Lorde, I recall the moment when, in 1968, twenty-one years old and suffering from a nervous condition that left me unable to leave my apartment, walk down the street, shop in stores, I was asked by one of the many therapists I consulted if I had orgasms with my husband. The fact that I had dropped out of school, stopped writing, and in a daze, married a man who did not share my values, were irrelevant facts to her. "Are you orgasmic?" was what she asked. Audre Lorde would have understood why the question itself only increased my despair. I had orgasms. But I had no joy.

The knowledge of what gives us joy, for Lorde, is the knowledge that most empowers us, and that makes us most dangerous to the established (capitalist, patriarchal) order. Like Greer (and Marcuse) Lorde believes our work can be just as erotic as our play, but is robbed of that potential by being governed by the principles of productivity for profit rather than human need. When our work is permitted to express our deepest nature and needs (Marx would say: when it is no longer alienated labor), then it is as full of delight as "moving into sunlight against the body of a woman I love." And "in touch with the erotic, I become less willing to accept powerlessness . . . resignation, despair, self-effacement, depression, self-denial." For me, that necessitated leaving a joyless marriage, orgasm-producing though it was, and writing again. Thank you, Germaine Greer. Thank you, Audre Lorde. Thank you, all those feminist authors who not only retheorized the sexual body but brought eros into their own work and renewed hope to my own life.

WORKS CITED

Dworkin, Andrea. *Woman-Hating*. New York: Dutton, 1974.

Said, Edward. *Musical Elaborations*. New York: Columbia University Press, 1991.

DISCUSSION QUESTIONS

1. Imagine Greer, Koedt, Irigaray, and Lorde on a panel together. What questions would you like each of them to address, and how do you think they might answer them?

2. Besides presenting different positions and arguments in terms of content, these four selections are very different stylistically. Do you see any connections between the ideas and the respective styles of these writers?

3. If you were to "update" the vagina/clitoris debate to reflect contemporary scientific thought and/or contemporary theories of sexuality, what positions not reflected in these four essays might be added to the debate?

GERMAINE GREER, *SEX*, FROM *THE FEMALE EUNUCH*

Women's sexual organs are shrouded in mystery.

It is assumed that most of them are internal and hidden, but even the ones that are external are relatively shady. When little girls begin to ask questions their mothers provide them, if they are lucky, with crude diagrams of the sexual apparatus, in which the organs of pleasure feature much less prominently than the intricacies of tubes and ovaries. I myself did not realize that the tissues of my vagina were quite normal until I saw a meticulously engraved dissection in an eighteenth-century anatomy textbook.[1] The little girl is not encouraged to explore her own genitals or to identify the tissues of which they are composed, or to understand the mechanism of lubrication and erection. The very idea is distasteful. Because of this strange modesty, which a young woman will find extends even into the doctor's office, where the doctor is loath to examine her, and loath to expatiate on what he finds, female orgasm has become more and more of a mystery, at the same time as it has been exalted as a duty. Its actual nature has become a matter for metaphysical speculation. All kinds of false ideas are still in circulation about women, although they were disproved years ago; many men refuse to relinquish the notion of female ejaculation, which although it has a long and prestigious history is utterly fanciful.

SOURCE: Germaine Greer, "Sex," in *The Female Eunuch* (New York: Harper Collins, 1970), 44–52.

1. E.g., Samuel Collins, *Systema Anatomicum* (London, 1685), p. 566, and Palfijn's *Surgical Anatomy* (London, 1856), plates facing pages 226 and 227, also his *Description Anatomique des Parties de la Femme* (Paris, 1708, the plates are not numbered), and Spigelius, *De humani corporis Fabrica* (1827), Tab XVII, Lib. VIII, and *Les Portraits Anatomique* of Vesalius (1569), and *Tabulae Anatomicae* of Eustachius (1714).

Part of the modesty about the female genitalia stems from actual distaste. The worst name anyone can be called is *cunt*. The best thing a cunt can be is small and unobtrusive: the anxiety about the bigness of the penis is only equaled by anxiety about the smallness of the cunt. No woman wants to find out that she has a twat like a horse-collar: she hopes she is not sloppy or smelly, and obligingly obliterates all signs of her menstruation in the cause of public decency. Women were not always so reticent: in ballad literature we can find lovely examples of women vaunting their genitals, like the lusty wench who admonished a timid tailor in round terms because he did not dare measure her fringed purse with his yard:

You'l find the Purse so deep,
You'l hardly come to the treasure.[2]

Another praised her shameful part in these terms:

I have a gallant Pin-box,
the like you ne'er did see,
It is where never was the Pox
something above my knee . . .
O 'tis a gallant Pin-box
you never saw the peer;
Then Ile not leave my Pin-box
for fifty pound a year.[3]

Early gynecology was entirely in the hands of men, some of whom, like Samuel Collins, described the vagina so lovingly that any woman who read his words would have been greatly cheered. Of course such books were not meant to be seen by women at all. He speaks of the vagina as the Temple of Venus and of the *mons veneris* as Venus's cushion, but he abandons euphemism to describe the wonders of the female erection:

. . . the Nymphs . . . being extended do compress the Penis and speak a delight in the act of Coition. . . . The use of the blood-vessels is to impart Vital Liquor into the substance of the Clitoris, and of the Nerves to impregnate it with a choyce Juyce inspired with animal Spirits (full of Elastick Particles making it Vigorous and Tense). . . . The Glands of the Vagina . . . being heated in Coition, do throw off the rarified fermented serous Liquor, through many Meatus into the Cavity of the Vagina, and thereby rendereth its passage very moist and slippery, which is pleasant in Coition. . . . The Hypogastrick Arteries do sport themselves in numerous Ramulets about the sides and other parts of the Vagina, which are so many inlets of blood to make it warm and turgid in the Act of Coition.[4]

2. *A Pleasant new Ballade Being a merry Discourse between a Country Lass and a young Taylor,* c. 1670.
3. *The High-prized Pin-Box. Tune of, Let every Man with Cup in's Hand* etc., c. 1665.
4. Samuel Collins (op. cit.), pp. 564–65.

Collins's description is an active one: the vagina *speaks, throws,* is *tense* and *vigorous.* He and his contemporaries assumed that young women were even more eager for intercourse than young men. Some of the terms they used to describe the tissues of the female genitalia in action are very informative and exact, although unscientific. The vagina is said to be lined "with tunicles like the petals of a full-blown rose," with "Wrinckle on wrinckle" which "do give delight in Copulations." The vagina was classified as "sensitive enough" which is an exact description. They were aware of the special role of the clitoris, in causing the "sweetness of love" and the "fury of venery."

> The Vagina is made so artificial [affabre is his word] that it can accommodate itself to any penis, so that it will give way to a long one, meet a short one, widen to a thick one, constringe to a small one: so that every man might well enough lie with any Woman, and every Woman with any Man. (*The Anatomy of Human Bodies Epitomised,* 1682, p. 156)

The notion that healthy and well-adjusted women would have orgasms originating in the vagina was a metaphysical interpolation in the empirical observations of these pioneers. Collins took the clitoris for granted, as a dear part of a beloved organ; he did not underemphasize the role of the vagina in creating pleasure, as we have seen. Unhappily we have accepted, along with the reinstatement of the clitoris after its proscription by the Freudians, a notion of the utter passivity and even irrelevance of the vagina. Love-making has become another male skill, of which women are the judges. The skills that the Wife of Bath used to make her husbands swink, the athletic sphincters of the Tahitian girls who can keep their men inside them all night, are alike unknown to us. All the vulgar linguistic emphasis is placed upon the *poking* element; *fucking, screwing, rooting, shagging* are all acts performed upon the passive female: the names for the penis are all *tool* names. The only genuine intersexual words we have for sex are the obsolete *swive,* and the ambiguous *ball.* Propagandists like Theodore Faithfull (and me) are trying to alter the emphasis of the current imagery. To a man who had difficulty getting an erection Faithfull wrote:

> If you ignore any idea of erection and concentrate your attention on your girl-friend, ignore the clitoris and use your fingers to caress her internally and if you follow such activity by a close association of your sex organs you may soon find that she can draw your sex organ into her vagina without any need on your part for erection.[5]

This sounds like therapeutic lying, nevertheless serious attempts have been made to increase women's participation in copulation. A. H. Kegel, teaching women how to overcome the bladder weakness that often afflicts women, showed them how to exercise the pubococcygeal muscles and found inadvertently that this increased their sexual enjoy-

5. Theodore Faithfull answering correspondence in *International Times,* no. 48, January 17–30, 1969.

ment.[6] What their mates thought of it is not on record. The incontinence resulted from the same suppression of activity that inhibited sexual pleasure; we might find that if we restored women's competence in managing their own musculature many of their pelvic disturbances would cease, and their sexual enjoyment might correspondingly grow. Of course we cannot do this until we find out how the pelvis ought to operate: as long as women cannot operate it, we cannot observe its action, and so the circle perpetuates itself. If the right chain reaction could happen, women might find that the clitoris was more directly involved in intercourse, and could be brought to climax by a less pompous and deliberate way than digital massage. In any case, women will have to accept part of the responsibility for their own and their partners' enjoyment, and this involves a measure of control and conscious cooperation. Part of the battle will be won if they can change their attitude towards sex, and embrace and stimulate the penis instead of *taking* it. Enlightened women have long sung the praises of the female superior position, because they are not weighed down by the heavier male body, and can respond more spontaneously. It is after all a question of communication, and communication is not advanced by the *he talk, me listen* formula.

The banishment of the fantasy of the vaginal orgasm is ultimately a service, but the substitution of the clitoral spasm for genuine gratification may turn out to be a disaster for sexuality. Masters and Johnson's conclusions have produced some unlooked for side-effects, like the veritable clitoromania which infects Mette Eiljersen's book, *I Accuse!* While speaking of women's orgasms as resulting from the "right touches on the button," she condemns sexologists who "recommend . . . the stimulation of the clitoris as part of the prelude to intercourse, to that which most men consider to be the 'real thing.' What is in fact the 'real thing' for them is *completely devoid of sensation* for the woman. This is the heart of the matter! Concealed for hundreds of years by humble, shy and subservient women."[7]

Not all the women in history have been humble and subservient to such an extent. It is nonsense to say that a woman feels nothing when a man is moving his penis in her vagina: the orgasm is qualitatively different when the vagina can undulate around the penis instead of vacancy. The differentiation between the simple inevitable pleasure of men and the tricky responses of women is not altogether valid. If ejaculation meant release for all men, given the constant manufacture of sperm and the resultant pressure to have intercourse, men could copulate without transport or disappointment with anyone. The process described by the experts, in which man dutifully does the rounds of the erogenous zones, spends an equal amount of time on each nipple, turns his attention to the clitoris (usually too directly), leads through the stages of digital or lingual stimulation and then politely lets himself into the vagina, perhaps waiting until the retraction of the clitoris tells him that he is welcome, is laborious and inhumanly computerized. The

---

6. A.H. Kegel, "Letter to the Editor," *Journal of the American Medical Association*, Vol. 153, 1953, pp. 1303–4. His work is discussed by Daniel G. Brown in "Female Orgasm and Sexual Inadequacy," in *An Analysis of Human Sexual Response*, ed. Ruth and Edward Brecher (London, 1968), pp. 163–64.

7. Mette Eiljersen, *I Accuse!* (London, 1969), p. 45.

implication that there is a statistically ideal fuck which will always result in satisfaction if the right procedures are followed is depressing and misleading. There is no substitute for excitement: not all the massage in the world will insure satisfaction, for it is a matter of psychosexual release. Real satisfaction is not enshrined in a tiny cluster of nerves but in the sexual involvement of the whole person. Women's continued high enjoyment of sex, which continues after orgasm, observed by men with wonder, is not based on the clitoris, which does not respond particularly well to continued stimulus, but in a general sensual response. If we localize female response in the clitoris we impose upon women the same limitation of sex which has stunted the male's response. The male sexual idea of virility without languor or amorousness is profoundly desolating: when the release is expressed in mechanical terms it is sought mechanically. Sex becomes masturbation in the vagina.

Many women who greeted the conclusions of Masters and Johnson with cries of "I told you so!" and "I am normal!" will feel that this criticism is a betrayal. They have discovered sexual pleasure after being denied it but the fact that they have only ever experienced gratification from clitoral stimulation is evidence for my case, because it is the index of the desexualization of the whole body, the substitution of genitality for sexuality. The ideal marriage as measured by the electronic equipment in the Reproductive Biology Research Foundation laboratories is enfeebled—dull sex for dull people. The sexual personality is basically antiauthoritarian. If the system wishes to enforce complete suggestibility in its subjects, it will have to tame sex. Masters and Johnson supplied the blueprint for standard, low-agitation, cool-out monogamy. If women are to avoid this last reduction of their humanity, they must hold out not just for orgasm but for ecstasy.

The organization of sexuality reflects the basic features of the performance principle and its organization of society. Freud emphasizes the aspect of centralization. It is especially operative in the "unification" of the various objects of the partial instincts into one libidinous object of the opposite sex, and in the establishment of genital supremacy. In both cases, the unifying process is repressive—that is to say, the partial instincts do not develop freely into a "higher" stage of gratification which preserved their objectives, but are cut off and reduced to subservient functions. This process achieves the socially necessary desexualization of the body, leaving most of the rest free for use as the instrument of labor. The temporal reduction of the libido is thus supplemented by its spatial reduction.[8]

If women find that the clitoris has become the only site of their pleasure instead of acting as a kind of sexual overdrive in a more general response, they will find themselves dominated by the performance ethic, which would not itself be a regression if the performance principle in our society included enterprise and creativity. But enterprise and creativity are connected with libido which does not survive the civilizing process. Women must struggle to keep alternative possibilities open, at the same time as they struggle to attain the kind of strength that can avail itself of them.

8. Herbert Marcuse, *Eros and Civilization* (Boston: Beacon Press, 1956).

The permissive society has done much to neutralize sexual drives by containing them. Sex for many has become a sorry business, a mechanical release involving neither discovery nor triumph, stressing human isolation more dishearteningly than ever before. The orgies feared by the Puritans have not materialized on every street corner, although more girls permit more (joyless) liberties than they might have done before. Homosexuality in many forms, indeed any kind of sex which can escape the dead hand of the institution—group sex, criminal sex, child-violation, bondage and discipline—has flourished, while simple sexual energy seems to be steadily diffusing and dissipating. This is not because enlightenment is harmful, or because repression is a necessary goad to human impotence, but because sexual enlightenment happened under government subsidy, so that its discoveries were released in bad prose and clinical jargon upon the world. The permit to speak freely of sexuality has resulted only in the setting up of another shibboleth of sexual normality, gorged with dishonesty and kitsch. Women who understand their sexual experience in the way that Jackie Collins writes of it are irretrievably lost to themselves and their lovers:

> He took her to the bedroom and undressed her slowly, he made love to her beautifully. Nothing frantic, nothing rushed. He caressed her body as though there were nothing more important in the world. He took her to the edge of ecstasy and back again, keeping her hovering, sure of every move he made. Her breasts grew under his touch, swelling, becoming even larger and firmer. She floated on a suspended plane, a complete captive to his hands and body. He had amazing control, stopping at just the right moment. When it did happen it was only because he wanted it to, and they came in complete unison. She had never experienced *that* before, and she clung to him, words tumbling out of her mouth about how much she loved him. Afterwards they lay and smoked and talked. "You're wonderful," he said. "You're a clever woman making me wait until after we were married!"[9]

Miss Collins's heroine is prudish, passive, calculating, selfish and dull, despite her miraculous expanding tits. When her husband grows tired of playing on this sexual instrument she can have no recourse but must continue to loll on her deflated airbed, wondering what went wrong. There is no mention of genitals: everything happens in a swoon or a swamp of undifferentiated sensation. He labors for her pleasure like a eunuch in the harem. Sex is harnessed in the service of counterrevolution.

> Embraces are cominglings from the Head even to the Feet, And not a pompous High
>   Priest entering by a Secret Place. (Blake, *Jerusalem*, pl. 69, ll. 39–40)

What Jackie Collins is expressing is the commonest romantic ideal of the perfect fuck. It shows how deeply we believe in the concept of male mastery. Miss Collins's heroine

9. Jackie Collins, *The World Is Full of Married Men* (London: W. H. Allen, 1969), 152–53.

was manipulating her mate's colonizing sexual urge, making him wait, as long as his importunacy lasts, until she is ready. In manipulating his violent impulses she exercised an illusory superiority, for she is tender, sentimental and modest, loving not for her own gratification, but in expression of esteem, trust and true love, until she could civilize him into marriage and the virtuoso sexual performance. The complicated psychic aspect of his love is undervalued; she is still alone, egotistical, without libido to desire him or bring him to new pleasure in her. Jackie Collins and the sex-books show that we still make love to organs and not people: that so far from realizing that people are never more idiosyncratic, never more totally *there* than when they make love, we are never more incommunicative, never more alone.

ANNE KOEDT, *THE MYTH OF THE VAGINAL ORGASM*

Whenever female orgasm is discussed, a false distinction is made between the vaginal and the clitoral orgasm. Frigidity has generally been defined by men as the failure of women to have vaginal orgasms. Actually, the vagina is not a highly sensitive area and is not physiologically constructed to achieve orgasm. It is the clitoris which is the center of sexual sensitivity and which is the female equivalent of the penis.

I think this explains a great many things. First of all, the fact that the so-called frigidity rate among women is phenomenally high. Rather than tracing female frigidity to the false assumptions about female anatomy, our "experts" have declared frigidity a psychological problem of women. Those women who complained about it were recommended psychiatrists, so that they might discover their "problem"—diagnosed generally as a failure to adjust to their role as women.

The facts of female anatomy and sexual response tell a different story. Although there are many areas for sexual arousal, there is only one area for sexual climax; that area is the clitoris. All orgasms are extensions of sensations from this area. Since the clitoris is not necessarily stimulated sufficiently in the conventional sexual positions, we are left "frigid."

Aside from physical stimulation, which is the common cause of orgasm for most people, there is also stimulation through primarily mental processes. Some women, for example, may achieve orgasm through sexual fantasies, or through fetishes. However, while the stimulation may be psychological the orgasm manifests itself physically. Thus while the cause is psychological, the *effect* is still physical, and the orgasm necessarily takes place in the sexual organ equipped for sexual climax—the clitoris. The orgasm experience may also differ in degree of intensity—some more localized, and some more diffuse and sensitive. But they are all clitoral orgasms.

All this leads to some interesting questions about conventional sex and our role in it. Men have orgasms essentially by friction with the vagina, not the clitoral area, which is

SOURCE: Anne Koedt, "The Myth of the Vaginal Orgasm," in *Radical Feminism*, ed. Anne Koedt, Ellen Levine, and Anita Rapone (New York: Quadrangle Books, 1973), 158–62.

external and not able to cause friction the way penetration does. Women have thus been defined sexually in terms of what pleases men; our own biology has not been properly analyzed. Instead, we are fed the myth of the liberated woman and her vaginal orgasm—an orgasm which in fact does not exist.

What we must do is redefine our sexuality. We must discard the "normal" concepts of sex and create new guidelines which take into account mutual sexual enjoyment. While the idea of mutual enjoyment is acknowledged in marriage manuals, it is not followed to its logical conclusion. We must begin to demand that if certain sexual positions now defined as "standard" are not mutually conducive to orgasm, they no longer be defined as standard. New techniques must be used or devised which transform this particular aspect of our current sexual exploitation.

Freud contended that the clitoral orgasm was adolescent, and that upon puberty, when women began having intercourse with men, women should transfer the center of orgasm to the vagina. The vagina, it was assumed, was able to produce a parallel, but more mature orgasm than the clitoris. Much work was done to elaborate on this theory, but not much was done to challenge the basic assumptions.

To fully appreciate this incredible invention, perhaps Freud's general attitude about women must first be realized. Mary Ellman (*Thinking about Women*) said it this way:

> Everything in Freud's patronizing and fearful attitude toward women follows from their lack of a penis, but it is only in his essay *The Psychology of Women* that Freud makes explicit . . . the deprecations of women which are implicit in his work. He then describes women as intellectually less able and prescribes for them the abandonment of the life of the mind, which will interfere with their sexual function. When the psychoanalyzed patient is a male, the analyst sets himself the task of developing the man's capacities; but with women patients, the job is to resign them to the limits of their sexuality. As Mr. Rieff puts it: for Freud, "analysis cannot encourage in women new energies for success and achievement, but only teach them the lesson of rational resignation."

It was Freud's feelings about women's secondary and inferior relationship to men that formed the basis for his theories on female sexuality.

Once having laid down the law about our sexuality, Freud not so strangely discovered a tremendous problem of frigidity in women. His recommended cure for a woman who was frigid was psychiatric care. She was suffering from failure to mentally adjust to her "natural" role as a woman. Frank S. Caprio, a contemporary follower of these ideas, states:

> . . . whenever a woman is incapable of achieving an orgasm via coitus, provided the husband is an adequate partner, and prefers clitoral stimulation to any other form of sexual activity, she can be regarded as suffering from frigidity and requires psychiatric assistance. (*The Sexually Adequate Female*)

The explanation given was that women were envious of men—"renunciation of womanhood." Thus it was diagnosed as an anti-male phenomenon.

It is important to emphasize that Freud didn't base his theory upon a study of the woman's anatomy, but rather upon his assumptions of women as an inferior appendage to the man, and her consequent social and psychological role. In their attempts to deal with the ensuing problem of mass frigidity, Freudians created elaborate mental gymnastics. Marie Bonaparte, in *Female Sexuality*, goes so far as to suggest surgery to help women back on their rightful path. Having discovered a strange connection between the non-frigid woman and the location of the clitoris near the vagina,

> It then occurred to men that where, in certain women, this gap was excessive, and the clitoridal fixation obdurate, a clitoridal-vaginal reconciliation might be effected by surgical means, which would then benefit the normal erotic function. Professor Halban, of Vienna, as much biologist as surgeon, became interested in the problem and worked out a simple operative technique. In this, the suspensory ligament of the clitoris was severed and the clitoris secured to the underlying structures, thus fixing it in a lower position, with eventual reduction of the labia minora.

But the severest damage was not in the area of surgery, where Freudians absurdly ran around trying to change the anatomy to fit their basic assumptions. The worst damage was done to the mental health of women who either suffered silently with self-blame or flocked to the psychiatrists, looking desperately for the hidden and terrible repression that kept from them their vaginal destiny.

One may perhaps at first claim that these are unknown and unexplored areas, but upon closer examination this is certainly not true today, nor was it true even in the past. For example, men have known that women suffered from frigidity often during intercourse. So the problem was there. Also, there is much specific evidence. Men knew that the clitoris was and is the essential organ for masturbation, whether in children or adult women. So obviously women made it clear where *they* thought their sexuality was located. Men also seem suspiciously aware of the clitoral powers during "foreplay" when they want to arouse women and produce the necessary lubrication for penetration. Foreplay is a concept created for male purposes, but works to the disadvantage of women since as soon as she is aroused the male changes to vaginal stimulation and leaves her both aroused and unsatisfied.

It has also been known that women need no anesthesia inside the vagina during surgery, thus pointing to the fact that the vagina is in fact not a highly sensitive area.

Today, with extensive knowledge of anatomy, with Kelly, Kinsey, and Masters and Johnson, to mention just a few sources, there is no ignorance on the subject. There are, however, social reasons why this knowledge has not been popularized. We are living in a male society which has sought change in women's role.

Rather than starting with what women *ought* to feel, it would seem logical to start out with what the anatomical facts are regarding the clitoris and vagina.

The Clitoris is a small equivalent of the penis, except for the fact that the urethra does not go through it as in the man's penis. Its erection is similar to the male erection, and the head of the clitoris has the same type of structure and function as the head of the penis. G. Lombard Kelly, in *Sexual Feeling in Married Men and Women*, says:

> The head of the clitoris is also composed of erectile tissue, and it possesses a very sensitive epithelium or surface covering, supplied with special nerve endings called genital corpuscles, which are peculiarly adapted for sensory stimulation that under proper mental conditions terminates in the sexual orgasm. No other part of the female generative tract has such corpuscles.

The clitoris has no other function than that of sexual pleasure.

The Vagina—Its functions are related to the reproductive function. Principally,

1. menstruation,
2. receive penis,
3. hold semen, and
4. birth passage.

The interior of the vagina, which according to the defenders of the vaginally caused orgasm is the center and producer of the orgasm, is:

> like nearly all other internal body structures, poorly supplied with end organs of touch. The internal entodermal origin of the lining of the vagina makes it similar in this respect to the rectum and other parts of the digestive tract. (Kinsey, *Sexual Behavior in the Human Female*)

The degree of insensitivity inside the vagina is so high that "Among the women who were tested in our gynecologic sample, less than 14% were at all conscious that they had been touched." (Kinsey)

Even the importance of the vagina as an *erotic* center (as opposed to an orgasmic center) has been found to be minor.

Other Areas—Labia minora and the vestibule of the vagina. These two sensitive areas may trigger off a clitoral orgasm. Because they can be effectively stimulated during "normal" coitus, though infrequently, this kind of stimulation is incorrectly thought to be vaginal orgasm. However, it is important to distinguish between areas which can stimulate the clitoris, incapable of producing the orgasm themselves, and the clitoris:

> Regardless of what means of excitation is used to bring the individual to the state of sexual climax, the sensation is perceived by the genital corpuscles and is localized where they are situated: in the head of the clitoris or penis. (Kelly)

Psychologically Stimulated Orgasm—Aside from the above mentioned direct and indirect stimulation of the clitoris, there is a third way an orgasm may be triggered. This is through mental (cortical) stimulation, where the imagination stimulates the brain, which in turn stimulates the genital corpuscles of the glans to set off an orgasm.

Confusion—Because of the lack of knowledge of their own anatomy, some women accept the idea that an orgasm felt during "normal" intercourse was vaginally caused. This confusion is caused by a combination of 2 factors. One, failing to locate the center of the orgasm, and two, by a desire to fit her experience to the male defined idea of sexual normalcy. Considering that women know little about their anatomy, it is easy to be confused.

Deception—The vast majority of women who claim vaginal orgasm to their men are faking it to, as Ti-Grace Atkinson says, "get the job." In a new bestselling Danish book, *I Accuse!*, Mette Ejlersen specifically deals with this common problem, which she calls the "sex comedy." This comedy has many causes. First of all, the man brings a great deal of pressure to bear on the woman, because he considers his ability as a lover at stake. So as not to offend his ego, the woman will comply with the prescribed role and go through simulated ecstasy. In some of the other Danish women mentioned, women who were left frigid were turned off to sex, and pretended vaginal orgasm to hurry up the sex act. Others admitted that they had faked vaginal orgasm to catch a man. In one case, the woman pretended vaginal orgasm to get him to leave his first wife, who admitted being vaginally frigid. Later she was forced to continue the deception, since obviously she couldn't tell him to stimulate her clitorally.

Many more were simply afraid to establish their right to equal enjoyment, seeing the sexual act as being primarily for the man's benefit, and any pleasure that the woman got as an added extra.

Other women, with just enough ego to reject the man's idea that they needed psychiatric care, refused to admit their frigidity. They wouldn't accept self-blame, but they didn't know how to solve the problem, not knowing the psychological facts about themselves. So they were left in a peculiar limbo.

Again, perhaps one of the most infuriating and damaging results of this whole charade has been that women who were perfectly healthy sexually were taught that they were not. So aside from being sexually deprived, these women were told to blame themselves when they deserved no blame. Looking for a cure to a problem that has none, can lead women on an endless path of self-hatred and insecurity.

Why Men Maintain the Myth

1. Sexual Penetration Is Preferred   The best stimulant for the penis is the woman's vagina. It supplies the necessary friction and lubrication. From a strictly technical point of view this position offers the best physiological condition, even though the man may try other positions for variation.

2. The Invisible Woman   One of the elements of male chauvinism is the refusal or inability to see women as total, separate human beings. Rather than this approach, men have chosen to define women only in terms of how they benefited men's lives. Sexually, a woman was not seen as an individual wanting to share equally in the sexual act, any more than she was seen as a person with independent desires when she did anything else in society. Thus, it was easy to make up what was convenient about women; for on top of that, society has been a function of male interests, and women were not organized to form even a vocal opposition to the male experts.

3. The Penis as the Epitome of Masculinity   Men define their lives greatly in terms of masculinity. It is a universal ego builder. Masculinity is defined culturally by what is the most non-female.

The essence of chauvinism is not the practical, economic, comfortable services women supply. It is the psychological superiority. This negative kind of definition of self, rather than a positive definition based upon one's own achievements and development of one's potentials, has of course chained the victim and the oppressor both. But *by far* the most brutalized of the two is the victim.

An analogy is racism, where the white racist compensates for his feelings of unworthiness by creating an image of the black man (it is primarily a male struggle) as biologically inferior to him. Because of his position in a white male power structure, the white man can socially enforce this mythical division.

To the extent that men try to rationalize and justify male superiority through physical differentiation, masculinity may be symbolized by being the *most* muscular, the most hairy, having the deepest voice, and the biggest penis. Women, on the other hand, are approved of (i.e., called feminine) if they are weak, petite; shave their legs; have high soft voices.

Since the clitoris is almost identical to the penis, one finds a great deal of evidence of men in various societies trying to either ignore the clitoris and emphasize the vagina (as did Freud), or, as in many places in the Mideast, actually performing clitoridectomy, Freud saw this ancient and still practiced custom as a way of further "feminizing" the female by removing this cardinal vestige of her masculinity. It should be noted also that a big clitoris is considered ugly and "masculine." Some cultures pour chemicals on the clitoris to make it shrivel up into proper size.

It seems clear to me that men in fact fear the clitoris as a threat to masculinity.

4. Sexually Expendable Male   Men fear that they will become sexually expendable if the clitoral organ is substituted for the vaginal as the basic pleasure for women. Actually this has a great deal of validity if one considers *only* the anatomy. The position of the penis inside the vagina, while perfect for reproduction, does not usually stimulate an orgasm in women because the clitoris is located externally and higher up. Women must rely upon indirect stimulation in the "normal" position.

Lesbian sexuality could make an excellent case, based on anatomical data, for the irrelevancy of the male organ. Albert Ellis says something to the effect that a man without a penis can make a woman an excellent lover.

Considering that the vagina is very desirable from a man's point of view, purely on physical grounds, one begins to see the dilemma for men. And it forces us to discard many "physical" arguments explaining why women go to bed with men. What is left, it seems to me, are primarily psychological reasons why women select men at the exclusion of women as sexual partners.

5. Control of Women   One reason given to explain the Mideastern practice of clitoridectomy is that it will keep the women from straying. By removing the sexual organ capable of orgasm, it must be assumed that her sexual drive will diminish. Considering how much men look upon their women as property, particularly in very backward nations, we should begin to consider a great deal more why it is not in the men's interest to have women totally free sexually. The double standard, as practiced for example in Latin America, is set up to keep the woman as total property of the husband, while he is free to have affairs as he wishes.

6. Lesbianism and Bisexuality   Aside from the strictly anatomical reasons why women might seek women lovers, there is a fear on men's part that women will seek the company of other women on a full, human basis. The recognition of clitoral orgasm as fact would threaten the heterosexual *institution*. For it would indicate that sexual pleasure was obtainable from either men *or* women, thus making heterosexuality not an absolute, but an option. It would thus open up the whole question of *human* sexual relationships beyond the confines of the present male-female role system.

LUCE IRIGARAY, *THIS SEX WHICH IS NOT ONE*

Female sexuality has always been theorized within masculine parameters. Thus, the opposition "virile" clitoral activity / "feminine" vaginal passivity which Freud—and many others—claims are alternative behaviors or steps in the process of becoming a sexually normal woman, seems prescribed more by the practice of masculine sexuality than by anything else. For the clitoris is thought of as a little penis which is pleasurable to masturbate, as long as the anxiety of castration does not exist (for the little boy), while the vagina derives its value from the "home" it offers the male penis when the now forbidden hand must find a substitute to take its place in giving pleasure.

According to these theorists, woman's erogenous zones are no more than a clitoris-sex, which cannot stand up in comparison with the valued phallic organ; or a hole-

SOURCE: Luce Irigaray, "This Sex Which Is Not One," in *New French Feminisms: An Anthology*, ed. Elaine Marks and Isabelle de Courtivron, trans. Claudia Reeder (Amherst: University of Massachusetts Press, 1980), 99–106.

envelope, a sheath which surrounds and rubs the penis during coition; a nonsex organ or a masculine sex organ turned inside out in order to caress itself.

Woman and her pleasure are not mentioned in this conception of the sexual relationship. Her fate is one of "lack," "atrophy" (of her genitals), and "penis envy," since the penis is the only recognized sex organ of any worth. Therefore she tries to appropriate it for herself, by all the means at her disposal: by her somewhat servile love of the father-husband capable of giving it to her; by her desire of a penis-child, preferably male; by gaining access to those cultural values which are still "by right" reserved for males alone and are therefore always masculine, etc. Woman lives her desire only as an attempt to possess at long last the equivalent of the male sex organ.

All of that seems rather foreign to her pleasure however, unless she remains within the dominant phallic economy. Thus, for example, woman's autoeroticism is very different from man's. He needs an instrument in order to touch himself: his hand, woman's genitals, language—And this self-stimulation requires a minimum of activity. But a woman touches herself by and within herself directly, without mediation, and before any distinction between activity and passivity is possible. A woman "touches herself" constantly without anyone being able to forbid her to do so, for her sex is composed of two lips which embrace continually. Thus, within herself she is already two—but not divisible into ones—who stimulate each other.

This autoeroticism, which she needs in order not to risk the disappearance of her pleasure in the sex act, is interrupted by a violent intrusion: the brutal spreading of these two lips by a violating penis. If, in order to assure an articulation between autoeroticism and heteroeroticism in coition (the encounter with the absolute other which always signifies death), the vagina must also, but not only, substitute for the little boy's hand, how can woman's autoeroticism possibly be perpetuated in the classic representation of sexuality? Will she not indeed be left the impossible choice between defensive virginity, fiercely turned back upon itself, or a body open for penetration, which no longer recognizes in its "hole" of a sex organ the pleasure of retouching itself? The almost exclusive, and ever so anxious, attention accorded the erection in Occidental sexuality proves to what extent the imaginary that commands it is foreign to everything female. For the most part, one finds in Occidental sexuality nothing more than imperatives dictated by rivalry among males: the "strongest" being the one who "gets it up the most," who has the longest, thickest, hardest penis or indeed the one who "pisses the farthest" (cf. little boys' games). These imperatives can also be dictated by sadomasochist fantasies, which in turn are ordered by the relationship between man and mother: his desire to force open, to penetrate, to appropriate for himself the mystery of the stomach in which he was conceived, the secret of his conception, of his "origin." Desire-need, also, once again, to make blood flow in order to revive a very ancient—intrauterine, undoubtedly, but also prehistoric—relation to the maternal.

Woman, in this sexual imaginary, is only a more or less complacent facilitator for the working out of man's fantasies. It is possible, and even certain, that she experiences vicarious pleasure there, but this pleasure is above all a masochistic prostitution of her body to a desire that is not her own and that leaves her in her well-known state of dependency. Not knowing what she wants, ready for anything, even asking for more, if only he will "take" her as the "object" of *his* pleasure, she will not say what *she* wants. Moreover, she does not know, or no longer knows, what she wants. As Freud admits, the beginnings of the sexual life of the little girl are so "obscure," so "faded by the years," that one would have to dig very deep in order to find, behind the traces of this civilization, this history, the vestiges of a more archaic civilization which could give some indication as to what woman's sexuality is all about. This very ancient civilization undoubtedly would not have the same language, the same alphabet—Woman's desire most likely does not speak the same language as man's desire, and it probably has been covered over by the logic that has dominated the West since the Greeks.

In this logic, the prevalence of the gaze, discrimination of form, and individualization of form is particularly foreign to female eroticism. Woman finds pleasure more in touch than in sight and her entrance into a dominant scopic economy signifies, once again, her relegation to passivity: she will be the beautiful object. Although her body is in this way eroticized and solicited to a double movement between exhibition and chaste retreat in order to excite the instincts of the "subject," her sex organ represents the horror of having nothing to see. In this system of representation and desire, the vagina is a flaw, a hole in the representation's scoptophilic objective. It was admitted already in Greek statuary that this "nothing to be seen" must be excluded, rejected, from such a scene of representation. Woman's sexual organs are simply absent from this scene: they are masked and her "slit" is sewn up.

In addition, this sex organ which offers nothing to the view has no distinctive form of its own. Although woman finds pleasure precisely in this incompleteness of the form of her sex organ, which is why it retouches itself indefinitely, her pleasure is denied by a civilization that privileges phallomorphism. The value accorded to the only definable form excludes the form involved in female autoeroticism. The *one* of form, the individual sex, proper name, literal meaning—supersedes, by spreading apart and dividing, this touching of *at least two* (lips) which keeps woman in contact with herself, although it would be impossible to distinguish exactly what "parts" are touching each other.

Whence the mystery that she represents in a culture that claims to enumerate everything, cipher everything by units, inventory everything by individualities. *She is neither one nor two.* She cannot, strictly speaking, be determined either as one person or as two. She renders any definition inadequate. Moreover she has no "proper" name. And her sex organ, which is not *a* sex organ, is counted as *no* sex organ. It is the negative, the opposite, the reverse, the counterpart, of the only visible and morphologically designatable sex organ (even if it does pose a few problems in its passage from erection to detumescence): the penis.

But woman holds the secret of the "thickness" of this "form," its many-layered volume, its metamorphosis from smaller to larger and vice versa, and even the intervals at which this change takes place. Without even knowing it. When she is asked to maintain, to revive, man's desire, what this means in terms of the value of her own desire is neglected. Moreover, she is not aware of her desire, at least not explicitly. But the force and continuity of her desire are capable of nurturing all the "feminine" masquerades that are expected of her for a long time.

It is true that she still has the child, with whom her appetite for touching, for contact, is given free rein, unless this appetite is already lost, or alienated by the taboo placed upon touching in a largely obsessional civilization. In her relation to the child she finds compensatory pleasure for the frustrations she encounters all too often in sexual relations proper. Thus maternity supplants the deficiencies of repressed female sexuality. Is it possible that man and woman no longer even caress each other except indirectly through the mediation between them represented by the child? Preferably male. Man, identified with his son, rediscovers the pleasure of maternal coddling; woman retouches herself in fondling that part of her body: her baby-penis-clitoris.

What that entails for the amorous trio has been clearly spelled out. The Oedipal interdict seems, however, a rather artificial and imprecise law—even though it is the very means of perpetuating the authoritarian discourse of fathers—when it is decreed in a culture where sexual relations are impracticable, since the desire of man and the desire of woman are so foreign to each other. Each of them is forced to search for some common meeting ground by indirect means: either an archaic, sensory relation to the mother's body, or a current, active or passive prolongation of the law of the father. Their attempts are characterized by regressive emotional behavior and the exchange of words so far from the realm of the sexual that they are completely exiled from it. "Mother" and "father" dominate the couple's functioning, but only as social roles. The division of labor prevents them from making love. They produce or reproduce. Not knowing too well how to use their leisure. If indeed they have any, if moreover they want to have any leisure. For what can be done with leisure? What substitute for amorous invention can be created?

We could go on and on—but perhaps we should return to the repressed female imaginary? Thus woman does not have a sex. She has at least two of them, but they cannot be identified as ones. Indeed she has many more of them than that. Her sexuality, always at least double, is in fact *plural*. Plural as culture now wishes to be plural? Plural as the manner in which current texts are written, with very little knowledge of the censorship from which they arise? Indeed, woman's pleasure does not have to choose between clitoral activity and vaginal passivity, for example. The pleasure of the vaginal caress does not have to substitute itself for the pleasure of the clitoral caress. Both contribute irreplaceably to woman's pleasure but they are only two caresses among many to do so. Caressing the breasts, touching the vulva, opening the lips, gently stroking the posterior wall of the vagina, lightly massaging the cervix, etc., evoke a few of the most specifically female pleasures. They remain rather unfamiliar pleasures in sexual difference as it is currently imagined, or rather as it is currently ignored: the other sex being only the indispensable complement of the only sex.

But *woman has sex organs just about everywhere.* She experiences pleasure almost everywhere. Even without speaking of the hysterization of her entire body, one can say that the geography of her pleasure is much more diversified, more multiple in its differences, more complex, more subtle, than is imagined—in an imaginary centered a bit too much on one and the same.

"She" is indefinitely other in herself. That is undoubtedly the reason she is called temperamental, incomprehensible, perturbed, capricious—not to mention her language in which "she" goes off in all directions and in which "he" is unable to discern the coherence of any meaning. Contradictory words seem a little crazy to the logic of reason, and inaudible for him who listens with ready-made grids, a code prepared in advance. In her statements—at least when she dares to speak out—woman retouches herself constantly. She just barely separates from herself some chatter, an exclamation, a half-secret, a sentence left in suspense—When she returns to it, it is only to set out again from another point of pleasure or pain. One must listen to her differently in order to hear an *"other meaning" which is constantly in the process of weaving itself, at the same time ceaselessly embracing words and yet casting them off to avoid becoming fixed, immobilized.* For when "she" says something, it is already no longer identical to what she means. Moreover, her statements are never identical to anything. Their distinguishing feature is one of contiguity. They touch *(upon)*. And when they wander too far from this nearness, she stops and begins again from "zero": her body-sex organ.

It is therefore useless to trap women into giving an exact definition of what they mean, to make them repeat (themselves) so the meaning will be clear. They are already elsewhere than in this discursive machinery where you claim to take them by surprise. They have turned back within themselves, which does not mean the same thing as "within yourself." They do not experience the same interiority that you do and which perhaps you mistakenly presume they share. "Within themselves" means *in the privacy of this silent, multiple, diffuse tact.* If you ask them insistently what they are thinking about, they can only reply: nothing. Everything.

Thus they desire at the same time nothing and everything. It is always more and other than this *one*—of sex, for example—that you give them, that you attribute to them and which is often interpreted, and feared, as a sort of insatiable hunger, a voracity which will engulf you entirely. While in fact it is really a question of another economy which diverts the linearity of a project, undermines the target-object of a desire, explodes the polarization of desire on only one pleasure, and disconcerts fidelity to only one discourse—

Must the multiple nature of female desire and language be understood as the fragmentary, scattered remains of a raped or denied sexuality? This is not an easy question to answer. The rejection, the exclusion of a female imaginary undoubtedly places woman in a position where she can experience herself only fragmentarily as waste or as excess in the little structured margins of a dominant ideology, this mirror entrusted by the (masculine) "subject" with the task of reflecting and redoubling himself. The role of "femininity" is prescribed moreover by this masculine specula(riza)tion and corresponds only slightly to woman's desire, which is recuperated only secretly, in hiding, and in a disturbing and unpardonable manner.

But if the female imaginary happened to unfold, if it happened to come into play other than as pieces, scraps, deprived of their assemblage, would it present itself for all that as *a* universe? Would it indeed be volume rather than surface? No. Unless female imaginary is taken to mean, once again, the prerogative of the maternal over the female. This maternal would be phallic in nature however, closed in upon the jealous possession of its valuable product, and competing with man in his esteem for surplus. In this race for power, woman loses the uniqueness of her pleasure. By diminishing herself in volume, she renounces the pleasure derived from the nonsuture of her lips: she is a mother certainly, but she is a virgin mother. Mythology long ago assigned this role to her in which she is allowed a certain social power as long as she is reduced, with her own complicity, to sexual impotence.

Thus a woman's (re)discovery of herself can only signify the possibility of not sacrificing any of her pleasures to another, of not identifying with anyone in particular, of never being simply one. It is a sort of universe in expansion for which no limits could be fixed and which, for all that, would not be incoherency. Nor would it be the polymorphic perversion of the infant during which its erogenous zones await their consolidation under the primacy of the phallus.

Woman would always remain multiple, but she would be protected from dispersion because the other is a part of her, and is autoerotically familiar to her. That does not mean that she would appropriate the other for herself, that she would make it her property. Property and propriety are undoubtedly rather foreign to all that is female. At least sexually. *Nearness,* however, is not foreign to woman, a nearness so close that any identification of one or the other, and therefore any form of property, is impossible. Woman enjoys a closeness with the other that is *so near she cannot possess it, any more than she can possess herself.* She constantly trades herself for the other without any possible identification of either one of them. Woman's pleasure, which grows indefinitely from its passage in/through the other, poses a problem for any current economy in that all computations that attempt to account for woman's incalculable pleasure are irremediably destined to fail.

However, in order for woman to arrive at the point where she can enjoy her pleasure as a woman, a long detour by the analysis of the various systems of oppression which affect her is certainly necessary. By claiming to resort to pleasure alone as the solution to her problem, she runs the risk of missing the reconsideration of a social practice upon which *her* pleasure depends.

For woman is traditionally use-value for man, exchange-value among men. Merchandise, then. This makes her the guardian of matter whose price will be determined by "subjects": workers, tradesmen, consumers, according to the standard of their work and their need-desire. Women are marked phallically by their fathers, husbands, procurers. This stamp(ing) determines their value in sexual commerce. Woman is never anything more than the scene of more or less rival exchange between two men, even when they are competing for the possession of mother-earth.

How can this object of transaction assert a right to pleasure without extricating itself from the established commercial system? How can this merchandise relate to other goods on the market other than with aggressive jealousy? How can raw materials possess themselves without provoking in the consumer fear of the disappearance of his nourishing soil? How can this exchange in nothingness that can be defined in "proper" terms of woman's desire not seem to be pure enticement, folly, all too quickly covered over by a more sensible discourse and an apparently more tangible system of values?

A woman's evolution, however radical it might seek to be, would not suffice then to liberate woman's desire. Neither political theory nor political practice have yet resolved nor sufficiently taken into account this historical problem, although Marxism has announced its importance. But women are not, strictly speaking, a class and their dispersion in several classes makes their political struggle complex and their demands sometimes contradictory.

Their underdeveloped condition stemming from their submission by/to a culture which oppresses them, uses them, cashes in on them, still remains. Women reap no advantage from this situation except that of their quasi-monopoly of masochistic pleasure, housework, and reproduction. The power of slaves? It is considerable since the master is not necessarily well served in matters of pleasure. Therefore, the inversion of the relationship, especially in sexual economy, does not seem to be an enviable objective.

But if women are to preserve their auto-eroticism, their homo-sexuality, and let it flourish, would not the renunciation of heterosexual pleasure simply be another form of this amputation of power that is traditionally associated with women? Would this renunciation not be a new incarceration, a new cloister that women would willingly build? Let women tacitly go on strike, avoid men long enough to learn to defend their desire notably by their speech, let them discover the love of other women protected from that imperious choice of men which puts them in a position of rival goods, let them forge a social status which demands recognition, let them earn their living in order to leave behind their condition of prostitute—These are certainly indispensable steps in their effort to escape their proletarization on the trade market. But, if their goal is to reverse the existing order—even if that were possible—history would simply repeat itself and return to phallocratism, where neither women's sex, their imaginary, nor their language can exist.

Translated by Claudia Reeder

AUDRE LORDE, *USES OF THE EROTIC: THE EROTIC AS POWER*

There are many kinds of power, used and unused, acknowledged or otherwise. The erotic is a resource within each of us that lies in a deeply female and spiritual plane, firmly rooted in the power of our unexpressed or unrecognized feeling. In order to perpetuate itself, every oppression must corrupt or distort those various sources of power within the culture

SOURCE: Audre Lorde, "Uses of the Erotic: The Erotic as Power" (Tucson, AZ: Kore Press, 1978), pamphlet. Paper delivered at the Fourth Berkshire Conference on the History of Women, Mount Holyoke College, August 25, 1978; first published as a pamphlet by Out and Out Books.

of the oppressed that can provide energy for change. For women, this has meant a suppression of the erotic as a considered source of power and information within our lives.

We have been taught to suspect this resource, vilified, abused, and devalued within western society. On the one hand, the superficially erotic has been encouraged as a sign of female inferiority; on the other hand, women have been made to suffer and to feel both contemptible and suspect by virtue of its existence.

It is a short step from there to the false belief that only by the suppression of the erotic within our lives and consciousness can women be truly strong. But that strength is illusory, for it is fashioned within the context of male models of power.

As women, we have come to distrust that power which rises from our deepest and nonrational knowledge. We have been warned against it all our lives by the male world, which values this depth of feeling enough to keep women around in order to exercise it in the service of men, but which fears this same depth too much to examine the possibilities of it within themselves. So women are maintained at a distant/inferior position to be psychically milked, much the same way ants maintain colonies of aphids to provide a life-giving substance for their masters.

But the erotic offers a well of replenishing and provocative force to the woman who does not fear its revelation, nor succumb to the belief that sensation is enough.

The erotic has often been misnamed by men and used against women. It has been made into the confused, the trivial, the psychotic, the plasticized sensation. For this reason, we have often turned away from the exploration and consideration of the erotic as a source of power and information, confusing it with its opposite, the pornographic. But pornography is a direct denial of the power of the erotic, for it represents the suppression of true feeling. Pornography emphasizes sensation without feeling.

The erotic is a measure between the beginnings of our sense of self and the chaos of our strongest feelings. It is an internal sense of satisfaction to which, once we have experienced it, we know we can aspire. For having experienced the fullness of this depth of feeling and recognizing its power, in honor and self-respect we can require no less of ourselves.

It is never easy to demand the most from ourselves, from our lives, from our work. To encourage excellence is to go beyond the encouraged mediocrity of our society. . . . But giving in to the fear of feeling and working to capacity is a luxury only the unintentional can afford, and the unintentional are those who do not wish to guide their own destinies.

This internal requirement toward excellence which we learn from the erotic must not be misconstrued as demanding the impossible from ourselves nor from others. Such a demand incapacitates everyone in the process. For the erotic is not a question only of what we do; it is a question of how acutely and fully we can feel in the doing. Once we know the extent to which we are capable of feeling that sense of satisfaction and completion, we can then observe which of our various life endeavors bring us closest to that fullness.

The aim of each thing which we do is to make our lives and the lives of our children richer and more possible. Within the celebration of the erotic in all our endeavors, my work becomes a conscious decision—a longed-for bed which I enter gratefully and from which I rise up empowered.

Of course, women so empowered are dangerous. So we are taught to separate the erotic demand from most vital areas of our lives other than sex. And the lack of concern for the erotic root and satisfactions of our work is felt in our disaffection from so much of what we do. For instance, how often do we truly love our work even at its most difficult?

The principal horror of any system which defines the good in terms of profit rather than in terms of human need, or which defines human need to the exclusion of the psychic and emotional components of that need—the principal horror of such a system— is that it robs our work of its erotic value, its erotic power and life appeal and fulfillment. Such a system reduces work to a travesty of necessities, a duty by which we earn bread or oblivion for ourselves and those we love. But this is tantamount to blinding a painter and then telling her to improve her work, and to enjoy the act of painting. It is not only next to impossible, it is also profoundly cruel.

As women, we need to examine the ways in which our world can be truly different. I am speaking here of the necessity for reassessing the quality of all the aspects of our lives and of our work, and of how we move toward and through them.

The very word *erotic* comes from the Greek word *eros*, the personification of love in all its aspects—born of Chaos, and personifying creative power and harmony. When I speak of the erotic, then, I speak of it as an assertion of the lifeforce of women; of that creative energy empowered, the knowledge and use of which we are now reclaiming in our language, our history, our dancing, our loving, our work, our lives.

There are frequent attempts to equate pornography and eroticism, two diametrically opposed uses of the sexual. Because of these attempts, it has become fashionable to separate the spiritual (psychic and emotional) from the political, to see them as contradictory or antithetical. "What do you mean, a poetic revolutionary, a meditating gunrunner?" In the same way, we have attempted to separate the spiritual and the erotic, thereby reducing the spiritual to a world of flattened affect, a world of the ascetic who aspires to feel nothing. But nothing is farther from the truth. For the ascetic position is one of the highest fear, the gravest immobility. The severe abstinence of the ascetic becomes the ruling obsession. And it is one not of self-discipline but of self-abnegation.

The dichotomy between the spiritual and the political is also false, resulting from an incomplete attention to our erotic knowledge. For the bridge which connects them is formed by the erotic—the sensual—those physical, emotional, and psychic expressions of what is deepest and strongest and richest within each of us, being shared: the passions of love, in its deepest meanings.

Beyond the superficial, the considered phrase, "It feels right to me," acknowledges the strength of the erotic into a true knowledge, for what that means is the first and most powerful guiding light toward any understanding. And understanding is a handmaiden which can only wait upon, or clarify, that knowledge, deeply born. The erotic is the nurturer or nursemaid of all our deepest knowledge.

The erotic functions for me in several ways, and the first is in providing the power which comes from sharing deeply any pursuit with another person. The sharing of joy, whether physical, emotional, psychic, or intellectual, forms a bridge between the sharers which can be the basis for understanding much of what is not shared between them, and lessens the threat of their difference.

Another important way in which the erotic connection functions is the open and fearless underlining of my capacity for joy. In the way my body stretches to music and opens into response, hearkening to its deepest rhythms, so every level upon which I sense also opens to the erotically satisfying experience, whether it is dancing, building a bookcase, writing a poem, examining an idea.

That self-connection shared is a measure of the joy which I know myself to be capable of feeling, a reminder of my capacity for feeling. And that deep and irreplaceable knowledge of my capacity for joy comes to demand from all of my life that it be lived within the knowledge that such satisfaction is possible, and does not have to be called *marriage*, nor *god*, nor *an afterlife*.

This is one reason why the erotic is so feared, and so often relegated to the bedroom alone, when it is recognized at all. For once we begin to feel deeply all the aspects of our lives, we begin to demand from ourselves and from our life-pursuits that they feel in accordance with that joy which we know ourselves to be capable of. Our erotic knowledge empowers us, becomes a lens through which we scrutinize all aspects of our existence, forcing us to evaluate those aspects honestly in terms of their relative meaning within our lives. And this is a grave responsibility, projected from within each of us, not to settle for the convenient, the shoddy, the conventionally expected, nor the merely safe.

During World War II, we bought sealed plastic packets of white, uncolored margarine, with a tiny, intense pellet of yellow coloring perched like a topaz just inside the clear skin of the bag. We would leave the margarine out for a while to soften, and then we would pinch the little pellet, to break it inside the bag, releasing the rich yellowness into the soft pale mass of margarine. Then taking it carefully between our fingers, we would knead it gently back and forth, over and over, until the color had spread throughout the whole pound bag of margarine, thoroughly coloring it.

I find the erotic such a kernel within myself. When released from its intense and constrained pellet, it flows through and colors my life with a kind of energy that heightens and sensitizes and strengthens all my experience.

We have been raised to fear the *yes* within ourselves, our deepest cravings. But, once recognized, those which do not enhance our future lose their power and can be altered. The fear of our desires keeps them suspect and indiscriminately powerful, for to suppress any truth is to give it strength beyond endurance. The fear that we cannot grow beyond whatever distortions we may find within ourselves keeps us docile and loyal and obedient, externally defined, and leads us to accept many facets of our oppression as women.

When we live outside ourselves, and by that I mean on external directives only rather than from our internal knowledge and needs, when we live away from those erotic guides from within ourselves, then our lives are limited by external and alien forms, and we conform to the needs of a structure that is not based on human need, let alone an individual's. But when we begin to live from within outward, in touch with the power of the erotic within ourselves, and allowing that power to inform and illuminate our actions upon the world around us, then we begin to be responsible to ourselves in the deepest sense. For as we begin to recognize our deepest feelings, we begin to give up, of necessity, being satisfied with suffering and self-negation, and with the numbness which so often seems like their only alternative in our society. Our acts against oppression become integral with self, motivated and empowered from within.

In touch with the erotic, I become less willing to accept powerlessness, or those other supplied states of being which are not native to me, such as resignation, despair, self-effacement, depression, self-denial.

And yes, there is a hierarchy. There is a difference between painting a back fence and writing a poem, but only one of quantity. And there is, for me, no difference between writing a good poem and moving into sunlight against the body of a woman I love.

This brings me to the last consideration of the erotic. To share the power of each other's feelings is different from using another's feelings as we would use a kleenex. When we look the other way from our experience, erotic or otherwise, we use rather than share the feelings of those others who participate in the experience with us. And use without consent of the used is abuse.

In order to be utilized, our erotic feelings must be recognized. The need for sharing deep feeling is a human need. But within the european-american tradition, this need is satisfied by certain proscribed erotic comings-together. These occasions are almost always characterized by a simultaneous looking away, a pretense of calling them something else, whether a religion, a fit, mob violence, or even playing doctor. And this misnaming of the need and the deed [gives] rise to that distortion which results in pornography and obscenity—the abuse of feeling.

When we look away from the importance of the erotic in the development and sustenance of our power, or when we look away from ourselves as we satisfy our erotic needs in concert with others, we use each other as objects of satisfaction rather than share our joy in the satisfying, rather than make connection with our similarities and our differences. To refuse to be conscious of what we are feeling at any time, however comfortable that might seem, is to deny a large part of the experience, and to allow ourselves to be reduced to the pornographic, the abused, and the absurd.

The erotic cannot be felt secondhand. As a Black lesbian feminist, I have a particular feeling, knowledge, and understanding for those sisters with whom I have danced hard, played, or even fought. This deep participation has often been the forerunner for joint concerted actions not possible before.

But this erotic charge is not easily shared by women who continue to operate under an exclusively european-american male tradition. I know it was not available to me when I was trying to adapt my consciousness to this mode of living and sensation.

Only now, I find more and more women-identified women brave enough to risk sharing the erotic's electrical charge without having to look away, and without distorting the enormously powerful and creative nature of that exchange. Recognizing the power of the erotic within our lives can give us the energy to pursue genuine change within our world, rather than merely settling for a shift of characters in the same weary drama.

For not only do we touch our most profoundly creative source, but we do that which is female and self-affirming in the face of a racist, patriarchal, and anti-erotic society.

14

THE U.S. WOMEN'S LIBERATION MOVEMENT AND BLACK FEMINIST "SISTERHOOD"

Cheryl R. Hopson

I can pinpoint when I became a "Black feminist." The year was 1991, and I was a freshman at a historically white, private, liberal arts college in Virginia. The day came when my professor, a white female, posed a question to the class: "How many of you identify as feminist?" Of the twenty-five students in the class, I was the only person to raise my hand. Even as I did so, I amended in thought the declaration made by my raised hand: "I am a 'Black' feminist." I grew up in southwest Virginia during the 1970s and 1980s and in a lower-middle-class home. I matriculated at a private and predominantly white college, and am the third of my mother's four daughters. It is to my benefit that my mother was an enthusiastic reader of contemporary Black women's fiction. I was always, in an unconscious way, aware of and opposed to the lack of parity (emotional, psychological, physical, and economic) within the heterosexual Black male/female relationships to which I was accustomed. I know today that my awareness of intraracial gender exploitation and bias was enhanced by my reading the very novels by Black women my mother read and discussed with her sisters. When I raised my hand at eighteen I was identifying with a materiality and a political philosophy it would take me decades to fully understand and embrace: I was then and am now Black, female, feminist, and a writer. Mine has never been the lone raised hand. I stand and write in esteemed company.

There have been critiques about the "whiteness" of the U.S. Women's Liberation Movement of the late 1960s and 1970s since its inception. Black women who participated in the movement were labeled "race traitors," often derided as being lesbians (a fact of sexual identity for some), and regarded as dupes of white feminists, promoting a cause in which they were not even a consideration.[1] Nevertheless, Black women who identified as feminist participated in and helped shape Women's Liberation Movement politics on [the] national [level] as well [as on] local levels, and contributed greatly to what we today think of as Second Wave feminism.

Despite narratives to the contrary, the U.S. Women's Liberation Movement is and always has been a transracial social and political movement advocating for and working on behalf of the empowerment and equal rights for all women.

ON SISTERHOOD

A key organizing principle of Women's Liberation Movement politics was the idea of feminists as "sisters" joined together in a "sisterhood" of sometimes contesting though unified women, and against a patriarchal order. While some Second Wave feminists chafed at the idea of feminists as sisters, still others regarded feminist sisterhood as a powerful and uniting force, a natural alliance against the oppressions of men and against sexism.[2] Black feminists of the Second Wave regarded "sisterhood" or alliance between women and in particular between Black women, as sensible, considering Black women's shared sex/racial history; they also recognized that there were serious roadblocks to this symbolic sister relationship. As such, within contemporary Black feminist perspectives there was a general recognition of feminist sisterhood as a *process* by which women came together to work toward common goals. This process-oriented approach suggested an awareness of the ways intraracial difference—that is, class, educational, ideological, sexuality—works on and mediates (often in disruptive ways) interactions between Black women.

ON SISTERS

The very notion of Black women as *sisters*, that is as figurative family predicated on race and gender sameness, was influenced by a 1960s Black Movement standpoint, which itself was influenced by African American cultural practices that predated even the Civil Rights movement of the 1950s. Black Movement politicos' use of the designations "sister" and "brother" to refer to Black women and Black men who may or may not have shared biological sibling ties was a carryover from earlier African American cultural practices, especially in the realm of religion and the church. Geneva Smitherman and Gloria Thomas Randle write that "a significant aspect of the sense of community within African American culture is the shared spirituality of many of its members." As such, "the sense of collective historical experience and spiritual kinship account for the extension of the traditional Black church terms 'Brother' and 'Sister' . . . into the secular arena" (4). Black feminists joined together as "sisters" in a "sisterhood" was not much of an imaginative leap for many Black women. In practice, however, this social, political, and *affective*, interpersonal relationship often remained just beyond their reach.

When exploring the Second Wave feminist concept of "sisterhood" from a contemporary Black feminist perspective, what becomes most clear is the great hope and palpable desire women such as Mary Ann Weathers, Pauli Murray, Michele Wallace, Audre Lorde, and Alice Walker, to name but a few, had for this relationship. Also clear is the fact that for many Black feminists, the attainment of such a relationship remained unfulfilled.

U.S. Second Wave Black feminists articulated interrelated though distinct ideas about feminist sisterhood, especially as it pertained to Black women. They wrote about feminist sisterhood or what is variously referred to in their works as communion, coalition, and alliance between Black women, often at the same time as they detailed aspects of their coming to consciousness both as "Black" and as "feminist." Their ideas about Black feminist sisterhood are classed, gendered, raced (with the added nuance of variations in skin tone), historically and regionally situated, and informed by their sexual identifications. Second Wave Black feminists theorized and wrote as writers, artists, activists, mothers, daughters, sisters (actual and figurative), friends, and lovers. They wrote and write from firsthand knowledge of the challenges and benefits of unity between Black (feminist) women specifically, and feminists generally.

During the late 1960s and throughout the 1970s, Black feminists questioned and directly challenged what they experienced as a paternalist, sexist status quo within Black Movement politics and Black culture. Sociologist Maxine Leeds Craig writes that "Black movement communities were centers of intensive exploration in which activists questioned existing meanings of black identity, reevaluated conventional practices, and created new ways of living day-to-day life" (164). However, there was within these communities little challenge to the "existing gender norms" of the surrounding culture, which were instead incorporated and reinforced (165). Black feminists responded in writing, through proposed legislation, and by the example of their lives to any and all imperatives that Black women subordinate themselves to Black men while at the same time propagating and "elevating the race" by bearing children and supporting Black males, *regardless.* Black feminists wrote in opposition to perpetual and pervasive ideas of Black women as less oppressed than the Black man; as well as in opposition to the idea that by virtue of Black women's asserting their personhood, they not only jeopardized "the Black family" but also emasculated Black males.

At the same time that the works of Black feminists such as Mary Ann Weathers, Pauli Murray, Michele Wallace, Audre Lorde, and Alice Walker grapple with notions of (Black) feminist sisterhood, they also provide perspective on Women's Liberation and Black Movement politics. The writings included and referenced here date from 1969 to the early 1980s.

U.S. SECOND WAVE BLACK FEMINIST PERSPECTIVES ON "SISTERHOOD"

In her 1969 essay "An Argument for Black Women's Liberation as a Revolutionary Force," Mary Ann Weathers writes as a Black and feminist revolutionary willing to take up arms to effect a necessary and fundamental change in society. She argues for the comingling of Black Movement politics with Women's Liberation Movement politics, and links both movements to what she regards as a class-based and necessary larger world movement "consisting of women, men, and children" (158). Weathers's essay builds from a desire to increase Black women's participation in Women's Liberation, and to incorporate a gender-based, feminist political perspective into ongoing Black Movement efforts. She sees and suggests a direct link between race bias, gender bias, and economic poverty as they accrue to Black women, and in particular Black mothers. Weathers is critical of what she regards as Black Movement politicos' demand that Black women submit themselves to race-based gender oppression in the name of racial solidarity, and she is critical of what she sees as Black women's willingness to do so.

Similar to Mary Ann Weathers, Pauli Murray, in "The Liberation of Black Women" (1970), argues that there is a "natural" alliance between women that, were it not for a race- and class-stratified society, would be wholly valuable to effecting societal changes that benefit women generally. Pauli Murray writes in favor of a class- and gender-based feminist political relationship between middle-class "Negro" or Black women and middle-class white women, who, she argues, share core tastes and values as a result of economic and educational opportunities. In Murray's schema, the middle-class Black woman would serve as an interpreter between Black and white female communities, conveying the interests and experiences of poor and working-class Black females to a white feminist middle-class constituency. Murray concludes that it is only by claiming leadership roles within the bourgeoning feminist movement that middle-class Black women can align feminist movement objectives with the "objectives of black liberation"—i.e., civil rights initiatives, social equality, access to power, a governing voice—and at the same time work "to advance [. . .] the interests of all women" (197).

In "Anger in Isolation: A Black Feminist's Search for Sisterhood" (1975), Michele Wallace details her coming to consciousness first as "Black" in 1968 through her participation in Black Movement politics, and then subsequently as feminist. This consciousness shift is largely due to her dawning awareness that the "Black" in "Black Movement" and "Black Nationalism" was gendered as male. Wallace quickly learned through her experience with the National Black Theatre, a cultural arm of the Black Movement, that Black women in the movement were cast in the role of overbearing, yet supportive, submissive and self-negating doormats for Black men. After this dawning realization, Wallace came to identify as a feminist and in particular a self-identified *Black* feminist. She was following the lead of her mother, Faith Ringgold, already a well-known Black feminist artist.

Significantly, Wallace argues in "Anger in Isolation" that there is between middle-class, heterosexual, Black women anger and a distrust that halts action. This anger and distrust are often tied to Black women's desire to win the approval of Black males and a Black male mate, according to Wallace. Wallace connects this anger and distrust of one another as Black women to our limited understanding and recognition of our true value as Black women, however well-educated, well-traveled, and influential we are. With respect to the possibility of sisterhood between Black women and white women, Wallace writes in the essay of her shocking awareness that white feminists considered Black men to be "less oppressive [than white men] . . . [,] less of a threat to women," and "fellow victims" of a white male patriarchal society. Wallace argues that such interpretations of Black men by white feminists discounted Black women's knowledge and experiences.

In keeping with the Second Wave feminist recognition that "the personal is political," Audre Lorde also situates her ideas, in "Eye to Eye: Black Women, Hatred, and Anger" (1983), in her personal experiences as a Black lesbian feminist. Lorde writes from the perspective of a first-generation, African American female born in Harlem in a pre–Civil Rights / pre-Black and Women's Liberation Movement era, and to West Indian immigrant parents. "Eye to Eye" is divided into eight sections, each one detailing her coming to consciousness about herself as a Black girl and woman in a national and cultural landscape that devalued Blackness and femaleness. Lorde writes that she learned early through her interactions with family as well as with the outside world that her "life [as a Black female] was not a high priority" (149). In "Eye to Eye" Lorde speaks directly to Black women who regard her as "unnatural" because she is both Black and lesbian—a "sister outsider." She writes that "often we [Black women] give lip service to the idea of mutual support and connection between Black women because we have not yet crossed the barriers to the possibilities, nor fully explored the angers and fears that keep us from realizing the power of a real Black sisterhood" (153). It is possible to see in "Eye to Eye," perhaps more so than in the essays of Weathers, Murray, and to a degree, Wallace, a valorization of the *affective*, self-affirming aspects of "mutual support and connection" between Black women (153). Both Michele Wallace and Audre Lorde emphasize intraracial conflicts between Black women such as anger and distrust, and both recognize that such conflicts are serious inhibitors to the attainment of Black feminist sisterhood.

In introducing and defining her now iconic idea for "a Black feminist or feminist of color" (i.e., womanist) at the opening of her 1983 collection *In Search of Our Mothers' Gardens: Womanist Prose,* Alice Walker imagines for herself and for unnumbered others a relationship that is intergenerational, transhistoric, Southern, Black female centered, and dialogic. In Walker's womanist schema, mothers and daughters join together as figurative sisters and in defense against oppressive forces. Alice Walker knows, as she writes in her 1979 essay "*One* Child of One's Own: A Meaningful Digression within the Work(s)," that the number of white feminists who are racist far outnumber the number of nonracist white feminists. She also knows that too often Black feminists participate in their own oppression and the oppression of their sisters, in the name of race solidarity and allegiance to Black men. As such, Black women who are truly feminist, who are self-liberating and aware, are not necessarily the norm. As such, and as a creative writer, Alice Walker turns to her craft to construct a concept that connotes, embodies, and engenders activist and creative Black women such as Harriet Tubman, Sojourner Truth, Ida B. Wells Barnett, and Alice Walker herself.

AN ARGUMENT FOR BLACK WOMEN'S LIBERATION AS A REVOLUTIONARY FORCE

In her invocation of a necessary and expressed "love" for and between Black women, as well as in her delineation of "the petty jealousies" that separate Black women, Mary Ann Weathers advances a distinctly heterosexual model of Black womanhood and Black sisterhood, one that is steeped in romantic notions of the poor Black woman as "more realistic" about herself and society (160), due to her reduced socioeconomic status. In her understanding and expression of a need for solidarity between Black "sisters," Weathers anticipates the work of Pauli Murray, Michele Wallace, Audre Lorde, Alice Walker, and others. Weathers's essay is addressed to Black women who are mothers, economic laborers, activists, and who can also be trailblazing revolutionaries. Weathers argues that effective sisterhood or alliance is interclass and intergenerational by design, and connected to a larger world movement for social and economic change. Such a sisterhood is made possible when Black women who participate in and follow the lead of Black Movement politicos join up with the Women's Liberation Movement.

As Weathers sees it, what separates Black "sisters" from each other are extremes of poverty and financial security and limited or nonexistent intergenerational communication. What links us as "sisters" is a shared awareness of "the scourge of the male-superiority-oriented society" (159). Weathers writes of "sister" alliances between Black women as a process that requires action. She argues in favor of an interclass, intergenerational Black sisterhood; one that would provide Black women "a wealth of information and experience" and serve not only to close "the communication gap between generations," but also the great economic gap that exists between middle-class and poor Black women (160). What would result from such a relationship is Black women's awareness of one another's lives, an awareness that can be harnessed for political action. As Weathers sees it, "women's liberation offers . . . a channel for these energies," that is, for Black women's political action (159). Addressing both constituencies—poor and middle-class Black women—variously as the voice of the poor, and the voice of the middle-class Black woman, Weathers writes that "we women must unabashedly use the word 'love' for one another. We must stop the petty jealousies, the violence, that we black women have for so long perpetrated on one another about fighting over this man or the other" (160). Speaking directly to middle-class Black women, Weathers adds that "we must let the [poor Black] sisters know that we are capable, and some of us already do love them" (160). Weathers continues that while *all* women are oppressed under male supremacy, Black women generally "are clearly the most oppressed and degraded." As such, Black women must be willing to "turn to ourselves and one another for strength and solace," and to work together to "save ourselves" (159–60).

THE LIBERATION OF BLACK WOMEN

In "The Liberation of Black Women," Pauli Murray argues that a major deterrent to an otherwise natural alliance between women generally, an alliance predicated on gender sameness and the experience of being female in a patriarchal society, is an increasingly race-stratified and polarized society. Murray writes that as a result of our racially stratified and polarized society, "communication and cooperation" between Black and white women has been "hesitant, limited, and formal," and therefore ineffective (191).

Notably, Murray argues that "Black women . . . have often found sex bias is more formidable than racial bias" (186). She regards the middle-class Black woman, who "by virtue of her tradition of independence and her long experience in civil rights," as a tangible human link between Women's Liberation and Black Liberation. As Murray sees it, as a bridge between two seemingly opposing movements and two seemingly opposing demographics (i.e., black male politicos and middle-class white feminist politicos), the middle-class Black woman can serve as an interpreter of the emotions of "the black community" for "her white counterparts" (197). Middle-class white feminists and middle-class Black feminists are not engaged in the "power relationships" that present between white and Black men and as such there is the possibility of a more productive and equitable exchange of ideas, according to Murray's essay. This suggests a romantic consideration on Murray's part of women's relational dynamics; but Murray is writing from experience. As part of a legal defense team that included a small group of mostly white feminist lawyers, she helped to pass important legislation on behalf of women's rights.[3] Murray writes from firsthand knowledge of the transformative influence of interracial sisterhood between Black and white women.

ANGER IN ISOLATION: A BLACK FEMINIST'S SEARCH FOR SISTERHOOD

Michele Wallace writes in "Anger in Isolation" (1974) that while there are individual and known "sister" feminists such as Eleanor Holmes Norton, Florence Kennedy, Alice Walker, and her own mother, artist Faith Ringgold, as well as individual and unknown "sister" feminists such as herself, there is no Black feminist sisterhood she can comfortably claim for herself, nor is there a Black women's movement. Wallace considers herself to be a Black feminist sister without community. She writes that she and other known and unknown Black feminists "exist [then] as women who are black who are feminists, each stranded for the moment, working independently because there is not yet an environment in this society remotely congenial to our struggle" (Guy-Sheftall 227). Like Weathers and Murray, Wallace writes from a belief that heterosexual Black women's vying for the love and approval of Black men encourages a distrust of other Black women, and necessitates a shying away from feminism.

Wallace communicates a desire for a middle-class, Black feminist sisterhood that consists of a trusting community of women who share a common agenda, as Blacks and as feminists. These women would serve as comrades who provide one another a way out of isolation, and a way to diffuse anger and distrust between Black women. However, as Wallace sees it, there are several obstacles to the attainment of Black feminist sisterhood, obstacles that include differences of sexuality, a lack of trust between Black women, and a preoccupation with Black men as well as with white feminists. Wallace concludes that Black feminists "had no strength to give one another" at the time of her writing, and could not therefore provide the sisterhood—the trusting, supportive community—she so desired.

EYE TO EYE: BLACK WOMEN, HATRED, AND ANGER

Audre Lorde writes in "Eye to Eye" that sisterhood or interpersonal connection between Black women is essential as it satisfies the need for self-love and self-recognition, both of which are made possible by coming together as women with shared experiences. Lorde determines that there is a palpable anger that exists between Black women, and that this anger masks the pain of emotional, physical, and psychological separation one from another. She writes that though Black women's sex and race might suggest a compulsory bond, and though Black women are aware of "the possibilities of support and connection for which we all yearn, and . . . dream," Black women are also aware that such connections "are not automatic by virtue of our similarities" and that "the possibilities of genuine communication between us are not easily achieved" (153). Still, it is this very connection, according to Lorde, or the *process* of Black women bonding as "sisters" that empowers Black women. What sisterhood can mean is tenderness from and connection with those presumed to be most like the self (i.e., other Black females).

In "Eye to Eye" Lorde delves into her own personal experience of gender and race prejudice as a Black feminist lesbian, in an effort to unearth the roots of Black women's anger of and hatred toward one another. She argues that because Black women have been "steeped in hatred—for our color . . . sex . . . [and] our effrontery in daring to presume we had any right to live," Black women have developed a hatred of and anger towards the self that registers in our interactions with one another, that is with our actual and figurative "sisters." What has come to exist between Black women according to Lorde, is pretenses of connection, parodies of self-love, evasion "on the deepest level," and a "false respect." Lorde concludes that the attainment of a sisterhood in which there is compassion and vital connection between Black women is a process that is "lengthy and difficult" (174). It is the pursuit of such a sister-relationship that can and does lead to Black women's "empowerment—our strengthening in the service of ourselves and each other, in the service of our work and future" (Lorde 174).

WOMANIST SISTERHOOD

In imagining and defining "womanist," as she does at the opening of In Search of Our Mothers' Gardens: Womanist Prose (1983), Alice Walker invokes the voice of a figurative Black mother ("you acting womanish") whose presence and power of discernment is modeled for a figurative daughter. To be womanist (like the color purple) is to be bold, to seek out and to integrate awareness, and to demonstrate a sense of oneself as capable, loved, and loving. It is to refuse collusion in one's own oppression, and to contest traditions and ideologies that deny the fullness of one's experience. To be joined in a womanist sisterhood is to participate in a relationship, real and imagined, that is supportive, affirming, and that fosters Black women's autonomy, *in community*.

Alice Walker dedicates *In Search of Our Mothers' Gardens*, the collection in which her womanist concept is introduced, to her daughter Rebecca (née Leventhal) Walker, a woman who is today a recognized Third Wave feminist writer, activist, and mother. In a closing essay to the collection, "*One* Child of One's Own: A Meaningful Digression within the Work(s)," Alice Walker details her experience of and ideas about motherhood as a full-time writer, wife, and, ultimately as a newly single-artist/mother. Alice Walker also indicts, in "*One* Child of One's Own," Black women who "dissociate themselves from the women's movement" and who therefore as she sees it, "abandon their responsibilities to women throughout the world" (389). Alice Walker regards such dissociation as "a serious abdication and misuse of radical black herstorical tradition"; a tradition that includes Harriet Tubman, Sojourner Truth, Ida B. Wells, Fannie Lou Hamer, and Alice Walker herself. Alice Walker also calls to task white feminists and Black male politicos for their seeming inability or unwillingness to recognize her full humanity as a woman, as an artist, as Black, and as feminist—i.e., as a womanist:

> . . . it is not my child who tells me I have no femaleness white women must affirm. Not my child who says: I have no rights black men must respect. It is not my child who has purged my face from history and herstory and left mystory just that, a mystery; my child loves my face and would have it on every page, if she could, as I have loved my own parents' faces above all others, and have refused to let them be denied, or myself to let them go. . . . We are together, my child and I. Mother and child, yes, but *sisters* really, against whatever denies us all that we are. (392)[4]

Alice Walker has stated that *In Search of Our Mothers' Gardens* is her legacy to Rebecca Walker. In writing of herself and her daughter as "*sisters* really," Alice Walker constructs a mother-daughter relationship in which both she and her daughter can be in a mutually affirming relationship; one that allows for and anticipates the continuous development of both—a Black feminist sisterhood.

SISTERHOOD *IS* POWERFUL (AND A PROCESS)

Black feminist sisterhood in practice is impeded by Black women's development under patriarchy and in a racist, classist, ageist, and homophobic society. To achieve true Black feminist sisterhood is to acknowledge the diversity of experiences among Black and Black-identified women, while at the same time recognizing and embracing Black women's connectedness as women, as people of color, as human beings. To achieve true Black feminist sisterhood, we must get to know, question, and challenge the roots of our distrust of one another; we must also recognize, respect, and affirm our individual ideas and experiences as Black and Black-identified women.

"Sisterhood is powerful," as a rallying cry, masked the reality that the attainment of feminist sisterhood is a process, perhaps one that is never-ending. As each of the Black feminists discussed here reminds us, Black feminist sisterhood, whether actual or of the imagination, can foster change; it can allow for an interchange of ideas and shared knowledge that can enhance and transform lives, and it can mean a very necessary and encouraging community. Black feminist sisterhood is a force in the world. It has touched and transformed and elucidated my life, as well as the lives of countless others. And it has done so primarily through writing.

NOTES

1. For a point of reference, see Deborah McDowell's essay "Reading Family Matters" from her collection *The Changing Same* (1995). See also Toni Cade Bambara's *The Black Woman: An Anthology* (1970), and Barbara Smith's anthology *Home Girls: A Black Feminist Anthology* (1983).

2. See for example, feminist scholar Jane Gallop's *Anecdotal Theory* (2002), and bell hooks' *Ain't I A Woman: Black Women and Feminism* (1981). See also Audre Lorde's collection *Sister Outsider* (1984), in which Lorde, echoing the sentiment of many of her contemporaries writes, "there is a pretense to homogeneity of experience covered by the word *sisterhood* that does not in fact exist" (116).

3. Beverly Guy-Sheftall writes that Murray, an activist, lawyer, and Episcopalian minister, "was a member of President Kennedy's Commission on the Status of Women, where she joined a small but growing informal network of feminists. She was also involved in the struggle to pass Title VII of the landmark 1964 Civil Rights Act, which mandated equal employment opportunities for women" (*Fire* 185). Murray was also a founding member of the National Organization for Women.

4. We unfortunately could not reprint Alice Walker's essay "*One* Child of One's Own." Interested readers should refer to the collection *In Search of Our Mothers' Gardens: Womanist Prose* (1983).

WORKS CITED

Craig, Maxine Leeds. *Ain't I a Beauty Queen? Black Women, Beauty, and the Politics of Race.* New York: Oxford University Press, 2002.

Guy-Sheftall, Beverly, ed. *Words of Fire: An Anthology of African-American Feminist Thought.* New York: The New York Press, 1995.

Lorde, Audre. "Eye to Eye: Black Women, Hatred, and Anger." In *Sister Outsider: Essays and Speeches.* Berkeley: The Crossing Press, 1984.

McDowell, Deborah E. *The Changing Same: Black Women's Literature, Criticism, and Theory.* Bloomington: Indiana University Press, 1995.

Murray, Pauli. "The Liberation of Black Women." In *Words of Fire: An Anthology of African-American Feminist Thought,* 186–98. Edited by Beverly Guy-Sheftall. New York: The New Press, 1995.

Smitherman, Geneva, and Gloria Thomas Randle. "Forms of Address." In *The Oxford Companion to African American Literature*, 3–4. Edited by William L. Andrews, Frances Smith Foster, and Trudier Harris. New York: Oxford University Press, 1997.

Walker, Alice. "*One* Child of One's Own: A Meaningful Digression Within the Work(s)." In *In Search of Our Mothers' Gardens: Womanist Prose*. San Diego: Harcourt Brace Jovanovich, 1983.

———. "Womanist." In *In Search of Our Mothers' Gardens: Womanist Prose*. San Diego: Harcourt Brace Jovanovich, 1983.

Wallace, Michele. "Anger in Isolation: A Black Feminist's Search for Sisterhood." In *Words of Fire: An Anthology of African-American Feminist Thought*, 220–28. Edited by Beverly Guy-Sheftall. New York: The New Press, 1995.

Weathers, Mary Ann. "An Argument for Black Women's Liberation as a Revolutionary Force." In *Words of Fire: An Anthology of African-American Feminist Thought*, 158–62. Edited by Beverly Guy-Sheftall. New York: The New Press, 1995.

White, Evelyn C. *Alice Walker: A Life*. New York: W.W. Norton, 2005.

DISCUSSION QUESTIONS

1. If, as Pauli Murray argues, middle-class Black women can function as interpreters of "Black community" for white women and men, what might the middle-class Black woman's role as interpreter require of her? Of those for whom she is serving as interpreter?

2. In what ways is the biographical slant of Michele Wallace and Audre Lorde demonstrative of the Second Wave feminist adage "the personal is political"?

3. Audre Lorde self-identified as a Black lesbian feminist, mother, warrior, and poet. How might Lorde's lesbian sexuality as well as her identifications as a mother, activist, and a poet be seen to mediate her desire for and expectations of solidarity between Black women?

MARY ANN WEATHERS, *AN ARGUMENT FOR BLACK WOMEN'S LIBERATION AS A REVOLUTIONARY FORCE*

"Nobody can fight your battles for you; you have to do it yourself." This will be the premise used for the time being for stating the case for black women's liberation, although certainly it is the least significant. Black women, at least the black women I have come in contact with in the movement, have been expounding all their energies in "liberating" black men (if you yourself are not free, how can you "liberate" someone else?). Consequently, the movement has practically come to a standstill. Not entirely due however to

SOURCE: Mary Ann Weathers, "An Argument for Black Women's Liberation as a Revolutionary Force," in *Words of Fire: An Anthology of African-American Feminist Thought*, ed. Beverly Guy-Sheftall (New York: The New Press, 1995), 158–62.

wasted energies, but adhering to basic false concepts rather than revolutionary principles, and at this stage of the game we should understand that if it is not revolutionary it is false.

We have found that women's liberation is an extremely emotional issue, as well as an explosive one. Black men are still parroting the master's prattle about male superiority. This now brings us to a very pertinent question: How can we seriously discuss reclaiming our African heritage—cultural living modes which clearly refute not only patriarchy and matriarchy, but our entire family structure as we know it. African tribes live communally where households, let alone heads of households, are nonexistent.

It is really disgusting to hear black women talk about giving black men their manhood—or allowing them to get it. This is degrading to other black women and thoroughly insulting to black men (or at least it should be). How can someone "give" one something as personal as one's adulthood? That's precisely like asking the beast for your freedom. We also chew the fat about standing behind our men. This forces me to the question: Are we women or leaning posts and props? It sounds as if we are saying if we come out from behind him, he'll fall down. To me, these are clearly maternal statements and should be closely examined.

Women's liberation should be considered as a strategy for an eventual tie-up with the entire revolutionary movement consisting of women, men, and children. We are now speaking of real revolution (armed). If you cannot accept this fact purely and without problems, examine your reactions closely. We are playing to win and so are they. Viet Nam is simply a matter of time and geography.

Another matter to be discussed is the liberation of children from a sick slave culture. Although we don't like to see it, we are still operating within the confines of the slave culture. Black women use their children for their own selfish needs of worth and love. We try to live our lives, which are too oppressing to bear, through our children and thereby destroy them in the process. Obviously the much acclaimed plaudits of the love of the black mother has some discrepancies. If we allow ourselves to run from the truth, we run the risk of spending another 400 years in self-destruction. Assuming of course the beast would tolerate us that long, and we know he wouldn't.

Women have fought with men, and we have died with men, in every revolution, more timely in Cuba, Algeria, China, and now in Viet Nam. If you notice, it is a woman heading the "Peace Talks" in Paris for the NLF [National Liberation Front]. What is wrong with black women? We are clearly the most oppressed and degraded minority in the world, let alone the country. Why can't we rightfully claim our place in the world?

Realizing fully what is being said, you should be warned that the opposition for liberation will come from every place, particularly from other women and from black men. Don't allow yourselves to be intimidated any longer with this nonsense about the "Matriarchy" of black women. Black women are not matriarchs, but we have been forced to live in abandonment and been used and abused. The myth of the matriarchy must stop, and we must not allow ourselves to be sledgehammered by it any longer—not if we are serious about change and ridding ourselves of the wickedness of this alien culture. Let it be clearly understood that black women's liberation is not antimale; any such sentiment or interpretation as such cannot be tolerated. It must be taken clearly for what it is— pro-human for all peoples.

The potential for such a movement is boundless. Whereas in the past only certain type black people have been attracted to the movement—younger people, radicals, and militants. The very poor, the middle class, older people, and women have not become aware or have not been able to translate their awareness into action. Women's liberation offers such a channel for these energies.

Even though middle-class black women may not have suffered the brutal suppression of poor black people, they most certainly have felt the scourge of the male-superiority-oriented society as women, and would be more prone to help in alleviating some of the conditions of our more oppressed sisters by teaching, raising awareness and consciousness, verbalizing the ills of women and this society, helping to establish communes.

Older women have a wealth of information and experience to offer and would be instrumental in closing the communications gap between the generations. To be black and to tolerate this jive about discounting people over thirty is madness.

Poor women have knowledge to teach us all. Who else in this society see more and are more realistic about ourselves and this society and about the faults that lie within our own people than our poor women? Who else could profit and benefit from a communal setting that could be established than these sisters? We must let the sisters know that we are capable, and some of us already do love them. We women must begin to unabashedly learn to use the word "love" for one another. We must stop the petty jealousies, the violence, that we black women have for so long perpetrated on one another about fighting over this man or the other. (Black men should have better sense than to encourage this kind of destructive behavior.) We must turn to ourselves and one another for strength and solace. Just think for a moment what it would be like if we got together and internalized our own 24-hour-a-day communal centers knowing our children would be safe and loved constantly. Not to mention what it would do for everyone's egos, especially the children's. Women should not have to be enslaved by this society's concept of motherhood through their children; and then the kids suffer through a mother's resentment of them by beatings, punishment, and rigid discipline. All one has to do is look at the statistics of black women who are rapidly filling the beast's mental institutions to know that the time for innovation and change and creative thinking is here. We cannot sit on our behinds waiting for someone else to do it for us. We must save ourselves.

We do not have to look at ourselves as someone's personal sex objects, maids, baby sitters, domestics, and the like in exchange for a man's attention. Men hold this power, along with that of the breadwinner, over our heads for these services, and that's all it is—servitude. In return we torture him, and fill him with insecurities about his manhood, and literally force him to "cat" and "mess around" bringing in all sorts of conflicts.

This is not the way really human people live. This is whitey's thing. And we play the game with as much proficiency as he does.

If we are going to bring about a better world, where best to begin than with ourselves? We must rid ourselves of our own hang-ups, before we can begin to talk about the rest of the world and we mean the world and nothing short of just that. (Let's not kid ourselves.) We will be in a position soon of having to hook up with the rest of the oppressed peoples of the world who are involved in liberation just as we are, and we had better be ready to act.

All women suffer oppression, even white women, particularly poor white women, and especially Indian, Mexican, Puerto Rican, Oriental, and black American women whose oppression is tripled by any of the above mentioned. But we do have females' oppression in common. This means that we can begin to talk to other women with this common factor and start building links with them and thereby build and transform the revolutionary force we are now beginning to amass. This is what Dr. King was doing. We can no longer allow ourselves to be duped by the guise of racism. Any time the white man admits to something, you know he is trying to cover something else up. We are all being exploited, even the white middle class, by the few people in control of this entire world. And to keep the real issue clouded, he keeps us at one another's throats with this racism jive. Although whites are most certainly racist, we must understand that they have been programmed to think in these patterns to divert their attention. If they are busy fighting us, then they have no time to question the policies of the war being run by this government. With the way the elections went down, it is clear that they are as powerless as the rest of us. Make no question about it, folks, this fool knows what he is doing. This man is playing the death game for money and power, not because he doesn't like us. He couldn't care less one way or the other. But think for a moment if we all go together and just walk on out. Who would fight his wars, who would run his police state, who would work his factories, who would buy his products?

We women must start this thing rolling.

PAULI MURRAY, *THE LIBERATION OF BLACK WOMEN*

Black women, historically, have been doubly victimized by the twin immoralities of Jim Crow and Jane Crow. Jane Crow refers to the entire range of assumptions, attitudes, stereotypes, customs, and arrangements that have robbed women of a positive self-concept and prevented them from participating fully in society as equals with men. Traditionally, racism and sexism in the United States have shared some common origins, displayed similar manifestations, reinforced one another, and are so deeply intertwined in the country's institutions that the successful outcome of the struggle against racism

SOURCE: Pauli Murray, "The Liberation of Black Women," in *Words of Fire: An Anthology of African-American Feminist Thought*, ed. Beverly Guy-Sheftall (New York: The New Press, 1995), 186–98.

will depend in large part upon the simultaneous elimination of all discrimination based upon sex. Black women, faced with these dual barriers, have often found that sex bias is more formidable than racial bias. If anyone should ask a Negro woman in America what has been her greatest achievement, her honest answer would be, "I survived!"

Negro women have endured their double burden with remarkable strength and fortitude. With dignity they have shared with black men a partnership as members of an embattled group excluded from the normal protections of the society and engaged in a struggle for survival during nearly four centuries of a barbarous slave trade, two centuries of chattel slavery, and a century or more of illusive citizenship. Throughout this struggle, into which has been poured most of the resources and much of the genius of successive generations of American Negroes, these women have often carried a disproportionate share of responsibility for the black family as they strove to keep its integrity intact against a host of indignities to which it has been subjected. Black women have not only stood shoulder to shoulder with black men in every phase of the struggle, but they have often continued to stand firmly when their men were destroyed by it. Few blacks are unfamiliar with that heroic, if formidable, figure exhorting her children and grandchildren to overcome every obstacle and humiliation and to "Be somebody!"

Because black women have an equal stake in women's liberation and black liberation, they are key figures at the juncture of these two movements. White women feminists are their natural allies in both causes. Their own liberation is linked with the issues that are stirring women today: adequate income maintenance and the elimination of poverty, repeal or reform of abortion laws, a national system of child-care centers, extension of labor standards to workers now excluded, cash maternity benefits as part of a system of social insurance, and the removal of all sex barriers to educational and employment opportunities at all levels. Black women have a special stake in the revolt against the treatment of women primarily as sex objects, for their own history has left them with the scars of the most brutal and degrading aspects of sexual exploitation.

The middle-class Negro woman is strategically placed by virtue of her tradition of independence and her long experience in civil rights and can play a creative role in strengthening the alliance between the black revolution and women's liberation. Her advantages of training and her values make it possible for her to communicate with her white counterparts, interpret the deepest feelings within the black community, and cooperate with white women on the basis of mutual concerns as women. The possibility of productive interchange between black and white women is greatly facilitated by the absence of power relationships, which separate black and white males as antagonists. By asserting a leadership role in the growing feminist movement, the black woman can help to keep it allied to the objectives of black liberation while simultaneously advancing the interests of all women.

The lesson of history that all human rights are indivisible and that the failure to adhere to this principle jeopardizes the rights of all is particularly applicable here. A built-in hazard of an aggressive ethnocentric movement that disregards the interests of other disadvantaged groups is that it will become parochial and ultimately self-defeating in the face of hostile reactions, dwindling allies, and mounting frustrations. As Dr. Caroline F. Ware has pointed out, perhaps the most essential instrument for combating the divisive effect of a black-only movement is the voice of black women insisting upon the unity of civil rights of women and Negroes as well as other minorities and excluded groups. Only a broad movement for human rights can prevent the black revolution from becoming isolated and can insure its ultimate success.

Beyond all the present conflict lies the important task of reconciliation of the races in America on the basis of genuine equality and human dignity. A powerful force in bringing about this result can be generated through the process of black and white women working together to achieve their common humanity.

MICHELE WALLACE, *ANGER IN ISOLATION: A BLACK FEMINIST'S SEARCH FOR SISTERHOOD*

I discovered my voice, and when brothers talked to me, I talked back. This had its hazards. Almost got my eye blackened several times. My social life was like guerrilla warfare. Here was the logic behind our grandmothers' old saying, "A nigga man ain't shit." It was shorthand for "The black man has learned to hate himself and to hate you even more. Be careful. He will hurt you."

I am reminded of a conversation I had with a brother up at City College one mild spring day. We were standing on a corner in front of the South Campus gates; he was telling me what the role of the black woman was. When a pause came in his monologue, I asked him what the role of the black man was. He mumbled something about, "Simply to be a man." When I suggested that might not be enough, he went completely ape. He turned purple. He started screaming. "The black man doesn't have to do anything. He's a man he's a man he's a man!"

Whenever I raised the question of a black woman's humanity in conversation with a black man, I got a similar reaction. Black men, at least the ones I knew, seemed totally confounded when it came to treating black women like people. Trying to be what we were told to be by the brothers of the "nation"—sweet and smiling—a young black woman I knew had warmly greeted a brother in passing on Riverside Drive. He responded by raping her. When she asked the brothers what she should do, they told her not to go to the police and to have the baby though she was only seventeen.

Young black female friends of mine were dropping out of school because their boyfriends had convinced them that it was "not correct" and "counter-revolutionary" to strive to do anything but have babies and clean house. "Help the brother get his thing together," they were told. Other black women submitted to polygamous situations where sometimes they were called upon to sleep with the friends of their "husband." This later duty

SOURCE: Michele Wallace, "Anger in Isolation: A Black Feminist's Search for Sisterhood," in *Words of Fire: An Anthology of African-American Feminist Thought,* ed. Beverly Guy-Sheftall (New York: The New Press, 1995), 220–28.

was explained to me once by a "priest" of the New York Yoruban Temple. "If your brother has to go to the bathroom and there is no toilet in his house then wouldn't you let him use your toilet?" For toilet read black woman.

The sisters got along by keeping their mouths shut, by refusing to see what was daily growing more difficult to ignore—a lot of brothers were doing double time—uptown with the sisters and downtown with the white woman whom they always vigorously claimed to hate. Some of the bolder brothers were quite frank about it. "The white woman lets me be a man."

The most popular justification black women had for not becoming feminists was their hatred of white women. They often repeated this for approving black male ears. (Obviously the brother had an interest in keeping black and white women apart—"Women will chatter.") But what I figured out was that the same black man who trembled with hatred for white men found the white woman irresistible because she was not a human being but a possession in his eyes—the higher-priced spread of woman he saw on television. "I know that the white man made the white woman the symbol of freedom and the black woman the symbol of slavery" *(Soul on Ice,* Eldridge Cleaver).

When I first became a feminist, my black friends used to cast pitying eyes upon me and say, "That's whitey's thing." I used to laugh it off, thinking, yes there are some slight problems, a few things white women don't completely understand, but we can work them out. In *Ebony, Jet,* and *Encore,* and even in *The New York Times,* various black writers cautioned black women to be wary of smiling white feminists. The women's movement enlists the support of black women only to lend credibility to an essentially middle-class, irrelevant movement, they asserted. Time has shown that there was more truth to these claims than their shrillness indicated. Today when many white feminists think of black women, they too often think of faceless masses of welfare mothers and rape victims to flesh out their statistical studies of woman's plight.

One unusually awkward moment for me as a black feminist was when I found out that white feminists often don't view black men as men but as fellow victims. I've got no pressing quarrel with the notion that white men have been the worst offenders, but that isn't very helpful for a black woman from day to day. White women don't check out a white man's bank account or stockholdings before they accuse him of being sexist—they confront white men with and without jobs, with and without membership in a male consciousness-raising group. Yet when it comes to the black man, it's hands off.

A black friend of mine was fired by a black news service because she was pregnant. When she proposed doing an article on this for *Ms,* an editor there turned down the proposal with these words: "We've got a special policy for the black man." For a while I thought that was just the conservative feminist position until I overheard a certified radical feminist explaining why she dated only black men and other nonwhite men: "They're less of a threat to women; they're less oppressive."

Being a black woman means frequent spells of impotent, self-consuming rage. Such a spell came upon me when I recently attended a panel discussion at a women artists' conference. One of the panel members, a museum director and a white feminist, had come with a young black man in a sweatshirt, Pro-Keds, and rag tied around the kind of gigantic Afro you don't see much anymore. When asked about her commitment to black women artists, she responded with, "Well, what about Puerto Rican women artists, and Mexican women artists, and Indian women artists? . . . " But she doesn't exhibit Hispanic women any more than she does black women (do I have to say anything about Indian women?), which is seldom indeed, though her museum is located in an area that is pre-dominantly black and Puerto Rican. Yet she was confident in the position she took because the living proof of her liberalism and good intentions sat in the front row, black and unsmiling, six foot something and militant-*looking*.

In the spring of 1973, Doris Wright, a black feminist writer, called a meeting to discuss "Black Women and Their Relationship to the Women's Movement." The result was the National Black Feminist Organization [NBFO], and I was fully delighted until, true to Women's Movement form, we got bogged down in an array of ideological disputes, the primary one being lesbianism versus heterosexuality. Dominated by the myths and facts of what white feminists had done and not done before us, it was nearly impossible to come to any agreement about our position on anything; and action was unthinkable.

Many of the prime movers in the organization seemed to be representing other inter-est groups and whatever commitment they might have had to black women's issues appeared to take a back seat to that. Women who had initiative and spirit usually attended one meeting, were turned off by the hopelessness of ever getting anything accomplished, and never returned again. Each meeting brought almost all new faces. Overhearing an aspiring political candidate say only half-jokingly at NBFO's first conference, "I'm gonna get me some votes out of these niggas," convinced me that black feminists were not ready to form a movement in which I could, with clear conscience, participate.

I started a black women's consciousness-raising group around the same time. When I heard one of my friends, whom I considered the closest thing to a feminist in the room, saying at one of our sessions, "I feel sorry for any woman who tries to take my husband away from me because she's just going to have a man who has to pay alimony and child support," even though she was not married to the man in question, I felt a great sinking somewhere in the chest area. Here was a woman who had insisted (at least to me) upon her right to bear a child outside of marriage, trying to convince a few black women, who were mostly single and very worried about it, that she was really married—unlike them. In fact, one of the first women to leave the group was a recent graduate of Sarah Law-rence, her excuse being, "I want to place myself in situations where I will meet more men." The group eventually disintegrated. We had no strength to give to one another. Is that possible? At any rate, that's the way it seemed, and perhaps it was the same on a larger scale with NBFO.

Despite a sizable number of black feminists who have contributed much to the leader-ship of the women's movement, there is still no black women's movement, and it appears there won't be for some time to come. It is conceivable that the level of consciousness

feminism would demand in black women wouldn't lead to any sort of separatist movement, anyway—despite our distinctive problems. Perhaps a multicultural women's
movement is somewhere in the future.

But for now, black feminists, of necessity it seems, exist as individuals—some well
known, like Eleanor Holmes Norton, Florynce Kennedy, Faith Ringgold, Shirley
Chisholm, Alice Walker, and some unknown, like me. We exist as women who are black
who are feminists, each stranded for the moment, working independently because there
is not yet an environment in this society remotely congenial to our struggle—because,
being on the bottom, we would have to do what no one else has done: we would have to
fight the world.

AUDRE LORDE, *EYE TO EYE: BLACK WOMEN, HATRED, AND ANGER*

Theorizing about self-worth is ineffective. So is pretending. Women can die in agony who
have lived with blank and beautiful faces. I can afford to look at myself directly, risk the
pain of experiencing who I am not, and learn to savor the sweetness of who I am. I can
make friends with all the different pieces of me, liked and disliked. Admit that I am kinder
to my neighbor's silly husband most days than I am to myself. I can look into the mirror
and learn to love the stormy little Black girl who once longed to be white or anything other
than who she was, since all she was ever allowed to be was the sum of the color of her
skin and the textures of her hair, the shade of her knees and elbows, and those things
were clearly not acceptable as human.

Learning to love ourselves as Black women goes beyond a simplistic insistence that
"Black is beautiful." It goes beyond and deeper than a surface appreciation of Black
beauty, although that is certainly a good beginning. But if the quest to reclaim ourselves
and each other remains there, then we risk another superficial measurement of self, one
superimposed upon the old one and almost as damaging, since it pauses at the superficial. Certainly it is no more empowering. And it is empowerment—our strengthening in
the service of ourselves and each other, in the service of our work and future—that will
be the result of this pursuit.

I have to learn to love myself before I can love you or accept your loving. You have to
learn to love yourself before you can love me or accept my loving. Know we are worthy of
touch before we can reach out for each other. Not cover that sense of worthlessness with "I
don't want you" or "it doesn't matter" or "white folks feel, Black folks DO." And these are
enormously difficult to accomplish in an environment that consistently encourages non-
love and cover-up, an environment that warns us to be quiet about our need of each other,
by defining our dissatisfactions as unanswerable and our necessities as unobtainable.

SOURCE: Audre Lorde, "Eye to Eye: Black Women, Hatred, and Anger," in *Sister Outsider: Essays and Speeches*
(Berkeley: The Crossing Press, 1984), 174–75.

Until now, there has been little that taught us how to be kind to each other. To the rest of the world, yes, but not to ourselves. There have been few external examples of how to treat another Black woman with kindness, deference, tenderness or an appreciative smile in passing, just because she IS; an understanding of each other's shortcomings because we have been somewhere close to that, ourselves. When last did you compliment another sister, give recognition to her specialness? We have to consciously study how to be tender with each other until it becomes a habit because what was native has been stolen from us, the love of Black women for each other. But we can practice being gentle with ourselves by being gentle with each other. We can practice being gentle with each other by being gentle with that piece of ourselves that is hardest to hold, by giving more to the brave bruised girlchild within each of us, by expecting a little less from her gargantuan efforts to excel. We can love her in the light as well as in the darkness, quiet her frenzy toward perfection and encourage her attentions toward fulfillment. Maybe then we will come to appreciate more how much she has taught us, and how much she is doing to keep this world revolving toward some livable future.

It would be ridiculous to believe that this process is not lengthy and difficult. It is suicidal to believe it is not possible. As we arm ourselves with ourselves and each other, we can stand toe to toe inside that rigorous loving and begin to speak the impossible—or what has always seemed like the impossible—to one another. The first step toward genuine change. Eventually, if we speak the truth to each other, it will become unavoidable to ourselves.

15

TRIPLE JEOPARDY
The Third World Women's Alliance and the
Transnational Roots of Women-of-Color Feminisms

Maylei Blackwell

In 1971, the Third World Women's Alliance (TWWA) came out with a new bold publication called *Triple Jeopardy*. This newspaper, as a historical document, provides one of the keys not only to historicizing the emergence of women-of-color political identities in the United States but to understanding the transnational roots of this political formation. The masthead read: *Triple Jeopardy: Racism, Imperialism, Sexism*. On every issue until its final publication in 1976, the emblem of the upraised fist of the people power movement with a machine gun, signifying third-world national liberation movements, appeared within the women's sign—symbolically merging the multiple insurgencies of women-of-color activists of the TWWA.

These early political projects and forms of solidarity between third-world women helped create a political subjectivity and gendered racial formation specific to the United States—or what we have come to understand today as the problematized and porous category women of color. Rather than viewing women of color as given political and social subjects, this history interrogates *how* in the post-WWII era, women of color *became* a gendered racial formation that had not existed in any other time in U.S. history.[1] The possibility of a movement of third-world peoples was first ignited at the 1955 Banduung Conference where delegates from across the world met in Indonesia to discuss the end of colonial rule. A key turning point for third-world women (especially those in North America) was the 1971 Vancouver conference where women leaders of third-world liberation movements gathered and consolidated a women's emancipation agenda. The historical roots of a U.S. women-of-color political identity was conceived as part of this

community of resistance. They invented a political subjectivity capable not only of crossing national borders by linking their struggles to a growing third-world liberation movement, but also of giving them analytical tools and a notion of solidarity that crossed
racial, class, and community lines within the United States.

Triple Jeopardy is a window through which to understand the political subject U.S.
"third-world women" and the political sites where women from diverse social locations
began to build solidarity and a coalitional, and sometimes conflictual, political identity
in between and sometimes in opposition to the social movements they participated in.
The newspaper calls us to rethink our notion of transnationalism as something that
occurs only outside of U.S. borders and to challenge the ways in which women-of-color
politics and its radical roots have been seen as something quintessentially "domestic," or
some essentialist staging of identity politics. Indeed, this echoes the critiques made by
Chicana theorist Sandra Soto, who has asked: "Where in the Transnational World are
U.S. Women of Color?" (Soto 2003). Women of color's feminist political subjectivities
have gone often ignored because they occurred *between* and sometimes in contestation
to various social movements. Contesting the periodization and politics of telling that
have erased U.S. third-world women, I propose a new historiographic framework that
theorizes the multiple feminist insurgencies of women of color.[2] This is an historiographic model that names feminist subjects who were multiply insurgent, those who
struggled on numerous fronts to challenge multiple oppressions, and thereby provides
a corrective to social movement historical narratives that have had difficulty elucidating
women of color as multiply constituted political subjects. It moves us beyond a dichotomy that sees the emergence of women-of-color feminism as either stemming from a
gendered critique of ethnic nationalism, on the one hand, or as an antiracist critique of
the women's liberation movement, what Chela Sandoval has called "hegemonic feminism," on the other. Taking multiple insurgencies as a model helps us see the varied
other sites of emergence including how internationalism, third-world liberation, and
anti-imperialist analysis brought women of color into solidarity with each other in order
to initiate on-the-ground organizing that gave them the opportunity to take action
together.

FORMATION

The Third World Women's Alliance's roots reach back to December of 1968 when the
Black Women's Liberation Committee formed to address problems women were having
within SNCC [Student Nonviolent Coordinating Committee]. Their critiques emerged,
according to Frances Beal, a founding member and editor of Triple Jeopardy, from being
"confined to secretarial and/or supportive roles and no matter what a woman's capabili-
ties were, we never seemed to be able to rise above this situation" (Triple Jeopardy Vol. 1,
No. 1, 1971: 8). Black women formed the organization to counter the myth of the black
matriarchy, prominent at the time.[3] Their philosophy stated, "There was also the wide-

spread concept that by some miracle, the oppression of slavery for the black woman was not as degrading, not as horrifying, not as barbaric as it had been for the black man. However, we state that in any society where men are not yet free, women are less free because we are further enslaved by our sex" (*Triple Jeopardy* Vol. 1, No. 1, 1971: 8).

The Black Women's Alliance articulated a critique of patriarchal nationalism, which linked the rejection of white cultural norms and the assertion of black "tradition" with the construction of gender ideologies that tended to limit black women's roles to reproductive labor. One early issue of the newspaper reported: "They stated that our role was a supportive one, others stated that we must become breeders and provide an army; still others stated that we had Kotex or pussy power. We opposed these concepts[,] stating that a true revolutionary movement must enhance the status of women." Also a founding member of the Black Women's Alliance and the Third World Women's Alliance, Frances Beal described how they began to organize as a way to critique a developing black revolutionary machismo in SNCC, where "women should be ten steps behind or having babies for the revolution." When they sat down as a collective to analyze these ideologies, they were mystified by how on the one hand they were put down as being "white" when they brought up women's liberation and on the other hand, they felt the "guys had this white middle-class female model" of domesticity that they were trying to impose on black women. "And we said, in fact, it's a model that does not match us historically or today. And that's how we began to look back [and understand] black women as laborers, all the way since slavery times. The dual family, you know, when we had to work at home and Ms. Ann's kitchen."[4]

Within the Black Women's Alliance, their analysis of the conditions of oppression they confronted began to shift, leading to a larger coalition among U.S. third-world women based on shared material realities and legacies of imperialism. They describe this shift in the following manifesto published in 1971:

> The development of an anti-imperialist ideology led us to recognize the need for Third World solidarity. Although Asian, Black, Chicana, Native American and Puerto Rican sisters have certain differences, we began to see that we are all affected by the same general oppressions. Industries employing mainly third world women are among the most exploitive in the country. Domestic workers, hospital workers, factory workers and farm laborers are prime objects of this exploitation as are the garment workers. . . . We realized that we would be much more effective and unified by becoming a third world women's organization.

In their founding documents, they challenged the critique that they were dividing "the national liberation struggle" by illustrating the interrelated nature of oppressions that they confronted as "third-world wom[e]n consciously aware of the depth of [their] oppression and willing to fight against it[,who] will never give up until all forms of racist, sexist, and economic exploitation [are] eliminated." Their political platform, articulated in the standard ten-point plan of the era, asserts a model of communal family structures with shared housework and child care, the right to decide if and when to have children (that there is no such thing as an "illegitimate child"), *safe* family planning including abortion when necessary, and an end to sterilization, mandatory birth control, and other genocidal practices against third-world peoples and the poor. The "employment" platform calls for full and equal nonexploitative employment controlled collectively by workers, adequate income for all, an end to racism and sexism resulting in lower pay for third-world women, and free day-care centers. The "sex roles" platform states that oppositional sex roles are oppressive to both men and women, that true revolutionaries should relate to people as human beings and not sex objects, and that "whether homosexuality is societal or genetic in origin, it exists in the third-world community. The oppression and dehumanizing ostracism that homosexuals face must be rejected and their right to exist as dignified human beings must be defended" (*Triple Jeopardy* Vol. 1, No. 1, 1971: 9). While not often recognized, lesbians of color played a vanguard role in creating new feminist communities across racial lines. This was despite, or perhaps as a remedy to, their marginalization in the multiple social movements (ethnic nationalist, feminist, gay and lesbian) they helped to build.

CONTINGENT COALITIONS

Triple Jeopardy reveals that third-world women's political subjectivity was built as a deeply *coalitional* project. U.S. third-world women activists began to build coalitional identities and politics around shared conditions and analysis, as witnessed by the editorials and coverage in *Triple Jeopardy* surrounding the racial and sexual politics of violence, incarceration, and employment issues (including how-to guides to maternity leave, unemployment, affirmative action, and child care). Several pieces covered sterilization cases against Puerto Rican, American Indian, and Black women, as well as articles on abortion and reproductive justice, signaling new kinds of coalitions across racial lines. Key among these coalitions was a series of prison cases that highlighted the high rates of violence against women of color. Throughout the 1970s there were a series of mobilizations, demonstrations, civil disobedience, and arrests in support of women who had been imprisoned for defending themselves against rape and violence, such as Joanne Little, charged with killing a prison guard who had repeatedly raped her, or Inéz Garcia, incarcerated for second-degree murder for killing the man who held her down while another man raped her.[5] These cases of violence against women of color were part of the local, grassroots issues that U.S. third-world women activists had in common and used to collectively mobilize. Other campaigns focused on police repression and the issue of political prisoners, perhaps best epitomized by the solidarity movements built around the black radical activist Angela Davis and Lolita Lebron, a Puerto Rican independence figure.

Other shared political interests that led to coalitional politics included a call to end forced sterilization and the articulation of a broader reproductive health agenda for women of color than the one taken up by the larger Women's Movement. Several of these early coalitions contributed to a legacy of women of color creating enduring analyses and organizations such as women-of-color reproductive justice movements. Further, various organizations started third-world women's child-care centers and collectives to address the need for child care in a way that was attentive to linguistic and cultural differences. Other convergences also occurred around labor rights, the welfare rights movement, access to education, and affirmative action. Besides covering issues of welfare and women's history, general interest articles in *Triple Jeopardy* ranged from "Changing a Fuse" to "Meatless Recipes" to an article on platform shoes called "The Platform Peril," all thrown into the mix with self-help guides on "Vaginal Ecology" and "Guerrilla Theater." Local reports covered New York rent strikes, union actions, boycotts and anticorporate campaigns, reports on sexual politics in the movement, critiques of U.S. drug policy, and solidarity statements from the prison movement. Third-world women activists used a transnational imaginary of anti-imperialism and third-world resistance to unite multiple struggles that had been up to that time viewed as separate. In addition, it was members of *Triple Jeopardy* who created the multifaceted lens of race, class, and gender through which to understand the intersecting, simultaneous nature of those oppressions. This view challenged the ways in which struggles to end class oppression, attain racial equality, or liberate women had been defined: until then, not only had each movement seen itself as separate from the others but also each saw their oppression as the primary struggle, which often created a hierarchy of oppression in which women-of-color activists, in their attempt to name their multiple oppressions, were either told that their race/class/gender concerns were secondary to the "real" struggle, at best, or that they were divisive, sold-out, or counterrevolutionary, at worst.

GENDERING THIRD-WORLD SOLIDARITY

Triple Jeopardy covered issues ranging from African and Indochinese movements for decolonization; women deputies to China's National People's Congress; the role of women in revolutionary struggles in Yemen, Cuba, Vietnam, Guinea-Bissau, Latin America, and the Arab struggles against the Israeli occupation; and the CIA. A crucial feature of the newspaper was to print letters and statements from international third-world women leaders and reports from U.S. third-world women solidarity delegations to China; each edition had an "International News" section that gave updates on various anti-imperialist struggles. Importantly, because the Third World Women's Alliance had wide participation from Puerto Rican women and the newspaper served a larger Latina feminist community in New York, many issues were bilingual, and there were several special issues in Spanish and many articles on Latin American feminist and women's struggles, including the Puerto Rican independence movement and the Chilean and Cuban solidarity movements.[6] The Third World Women's Alliance dedicated a special issue of *Triple Jeopardy* to "International Women's Year" in 1975, making it an homage to third-world women revolutionaries, and included articles on the role of women in African liberation struggles, and on Latin American women's movements in Brazil, Paraguay, and Uruguay. This issue also contained excerpts of a speech that the cofounder of the South Vietnam Liberation Women's Union gave to the National Congress of Vietnamese Women in Hanoi in 1974. Locally and nationally, that issue reported on the sterilization of American Indian women, the mid-1970s recession, and an exposé revealing that the Los Angeles Police Department was training in the use of tear gas in the case of food riots.

This mix of news coverage in the 1975 International Women's Year issue is important because the TWWA covered international events while grounding its analysis of imperialism, racism, and sexism in the events affecting its own communities. This strategy is what lesbian feminist scholar Adrienne Rich would later call the politics of location, contrasting it with the refusal of location, which was a criticism of other 1970s feminist interpretations of "Sisterhood is global." The TWWA was aware of how it was situated within geopolitical struggles and it localized a transnational imaginary of third-world solidarity among women to forge coalitional politics among women of color locally. The TWWA deployed a transnational imaginary in its print community coverage in celebration of International Women's Year and celebrated new forms of third-world feminist transnational solidarity.[7] In 1975 while U.S. feminists expanded their forms of solidarity globally through their conceptualization of "global sisterhood," U.S. third-world women participated in constructing an alternative transnational imagined community of shared feminist visions predicated on anticolonial and antiracist struggles in a way that refused claims to universality by working from their own situated struggles, their political locations.

ICONOGRAPHY OF THIRD-WORLD WOMEN: REJECTING THE REVOLUTIONARY (M)OTHER

Finally, *Triple Jeopardy* provided an alternative to the ways in which the New Left and cultural nationalists alike built solidarity around often highly romanticized notions of revolutionary masculinity through the image of the male revolutionary guerrilla, perhaps best epitomized in the figure of Che Guevara. Benedict Anderson has theorized how national identities were built through the publication of newspapers that were read across disparate geographies, regions, and other social divides, thereby creating what he calls the "imagined community" of the nation. Social movements also created imagined communities of resistance, often through newspaper, art, poetry, and other cultural work. For example, it could be argued that the powerful images of women in armed insurrections, from national liberation movements across the world, in each issue of *Triple Jeopardy* created an image(d) community, reworking Benedict Anderson's original formulation of imagined communities.[8] Such image(d) communities constituted in the circulation of print media are crucial, as symbolic politics is a main strategy in building transnational solidarity: the production of new visual images is pivotal in creating or imaging new political subjectivities. The circulation of these new symbols articulated a political practice and collective conversation, reimagining historical subjectivity, and was a powerful constitutive element in forming counterpublics whereby members of this alternative discursive community changed the gendered mode of address inherent in the revolutionary iconography at the time.[9]

By imaging new forms of revolutionary female subjectivity, the editors of *Triple Jeopardy* shifted the symbolic and material context constructed through nationalist discourse. The gendered iconography of revolution often included cultural images of women revolutionaries where women were represented not just as mothers of the nation (the standard nationalist conflation of woman/nation) but mothers of a new nation, bearing arms of revolutionary struggle. The image of what I call the revolutionary (m)Other in the Cuban and Nicaraguan cases depicts a woman with a machine gun over one shoulder as she cradles and nurses a baby at her breast. Significantly *Triple Jeopardy* never included images of revolutionary (m)Otherhood, which not only shifted the centrality of this image but suggested that women have political roles beyond the reproduction of the nation. *Triple Jeopardy* consistently offered other images of women through artwork as well as photojournalistic images that showed women working as domestics, factory workers, or secretaries; women meeting at conferences or picketing them; and girls playing double-dutch alongside a montage of women in action at big marches and meetings.

CONCLUSION: REFUGEES OF A WORLD ON FIRE

Examining the legacy of the Third World Women's Alliance reveals different genealogies of feminist transnationalism, and tells a different story about the role of race and transnationalism in feminist formations in the United States. A shift away from the term "third-world woman" to the term "women of color" emerged in the 1980s and is associated with the publication of *This Bridge Called My Back: Writings by Radical Women of Color*. The 1980s marked the era of deindustrialization, the ravages of Reaganomics, the beginning of the war on drugs—all political processes which motivated many women-of-color feminist organizers to turn inwards toward the struggles of their own communities for survival. Yet, in the preface to the second edition of *Bridge* in 1983, Cherríe Moraga herself shifts back to the term third-world women. There she argues that if *Bridge* had been conceived in 1983 rather than 1979, it would have needed to be much more international in perspective, linking people of color to new immigrants as we "begin to see ourselves all as Refugees of a World on Fire." While there was a turn inward, the theories and practices of women-of-color feminisms were also reshaped by new forms of transnational solidarity, especially in the South African divestment and Central American solidarity movements of the 1980s. As amorphous political subjectivities that are more than the sum of [their] possible constituency groups, women-of-color political identities challenged fixed racial and sexual boundaries and have been transformed by new generations of mixed-race women and queer and transgender people. The interrelationship between geopolitics and women of color as a gendered racial formation and community of resistance in the United States is again being illustrated in a post–September 11 context, as more and more Arab American, Muslim, and Southeast Asian communities have come under attack and women within them have joined with other immigrant and women-of-color feminists to redefine political identities, strategies, and visions. A close analysis of these forms of gendered racial formations and political coalitions is even more important as we enter a new era. Women-of-color identities and political urgencies are being stretched by a new global war on terror which has produced an ever-increasing number of refugees of a world on fire.

NOTES

1. By this I mean the political subject and political project "women of color," which signified an alternative project of belonging and a community of resistance rather than terms that have been assigned to African American and other racially marginalized women such as "colored women."

2. For more on multiple insurgencies of women of color see Blackwell, ¡Chicana Power!.

3. Frances Beal, interview with author, Oakland, CA, September 21, 1999.

4. Ibid.

5. See, for example, "38 Arrested," Triple Jeopardy.

6. Almost every issue of Triple Jeopardy has articles in Spanish and special editions were published in Spanish entitled "Puerto Rico" and "La Mujer."

7. For discussion of women of color and the 1975 UN International Women's Year conference in Mexico City, see Chavez, "Pilgrimage to the Homeland."

8. This concept is further developed in my essay "Bearing Bandaleras" and in ¡Chicana Power!.

9. See chapter 4, in Blackwell, ¡Chicana Power! and Fregoso, Bronze Screen. For a different rendering of the ways in which alternative discursive formations cause a crisis the system of signification and mode of address of a national culture, see Bhabha, "DissemiNation," 297.

WORKS CITED

"38 Arrested in Demonstration to Support Inéz Garcia." Triple Jeopardy, Summer 1975.

Bhabha, Homi K. "DissemiNation: Time, Narrative, and the Margins of the Modern Nation." In Nation and Narration. New York: Routledge, 1990.

Blackwell, Maylei. "Bearing Bandaleras: Transfigurative Liberation and the Iconography of la Nueva Chicana." In Beyond the Frame: Women of Color and Visual Representations, 171–96. Edited by Angela Y. Davis and Neferti X. M. Tadiar. New York: Palgrave Macmillan, 2005.

———. ¡Chicana Power! Contested Histories of Feminism in the Chicano Movement. Austin: University of Texas Press, 2011.

Chavez, Marsiela. "Pilgrimage to the Homeland: California Chicanas and International Women's Year, Mexico City, 1975." In Memories and Migrations: Mapping Boricua and Chicana Histories, 170–95. Edited by Vicki L. Ruiz and John R. Chavez. Chicago: University of Illinois Press, 2008.

Fregoso, Rosa Linda. *The Bronze Screen: Chicana and Chicano Film Culture.* Minneapolis: University of Minnesota Press, 1993.

"La Mujer en la Lucha de Liberación." *Triple Jeopardy,* n.d.

"The Puerto Rican Struggle for Independence." *Triple Jeopardy,* 1974.

Soto, Sandra K. "Where in the transnational world are U.S. women of color?" In *Women's Studies for the Future: Foundations, Interrogations, Politics,* 111–124. Edited by E. L. Kennedy and A. Beins. New Brunswick, NJ: Rutgers University Press, 2005.

DISCUSSION QUESTIONS

1. Blackwell argues that transnational feminism also occurred within the borders of the United States. What evidence does she provide for this? Do you agree or disagree? Why?

2. What political interests do women of color share with one another? How do these compare to the political interests of white, middle-class women?

3. Discuss some of the topics covered in *Triple Jeopardy.* How do these compare to contemporary feminist concerns and issues?

TRIPLE JEOPARDY

25¢
30¢ outside N.Y

RACISM, IMPERIALISM, SEXISM

Sept.-Oct. 1972

THIRD WORLD WOMEN'S ALLIANCE
346 W. 20 ST., N.Y.
vol. I
no. 7

TRIPLE JEOPARDY

RACISM IMPERIALISM SEXISM

A WOMAN'S PAPER

25¢

30¢ OUTSIDE N.Y.

artículos en
espanol

ÉDICION ESPECIAL:
La Mujer En La Lucha de Liberación

16

STRAINED SISTERHOOD
Lesbianism, Feminism, and the U.S. Women's Liberation Movement

Ann M. Ciasullo

Feminism at heart is a massive complaint. Lesbianism is the solution.

JILL JOHNSTON, *LESBIAN NATION*

. . . of course when most feminists talk about sexuality, including lesbianism, they're not talkin about Desire.

AMBER HOLLIBAUGH AND CHERRÍE MORAGA, "WHAT WE'RE ROLLIN AROUND IN BED WITH"

The year is 1970. It's been two years since the inaugural event of the Second Wave of feminism—the "No More Miss America" protest of 1968—and in that short span of time, the Women's Liberation Movement (WLM) has moved from the realm of fringe political activism to a position at the forefront of American consciousness. It is, in effect, a force to be reckoned with, a powerful chorus of voices calling for change. But by 1970, the harmony of these voices is being challenged by women in the movement who do not find sisterhood to be all that powerful, women for whom feminism's desire to be "respectable" translates into oppression within the movement. These women are lesbians, or what Betty Friedan famously called the "Lavender Menace," and on May 1, 1970, they decided it was time not only to speak out against the heterosexism of the WLM but also to assert the centrality of lesbianism to the feminist cause. Wearing "Lavender Menace" T-shirts, they stormed the second Congress to Unite Women, disrupted the convention, and took over the proceedings, demanding to be heard.[1] Just as the No More Miss America protest marked the start of the Women's Liberation Movement, the Lavender Menace protest marked the start of the complicated, tenuous, and sometimes even hostile relationship between lesbianism and feminism in the Second Wave.

From our Third Wave, twenty-first-century viewpoint, it may seem strange that lesbian feminists and straight feminists were frequently at odds with one another in a movement that purported liberation for *all* women, but within its historical context, their contentious relationship makes sense. From its nascence, the Women's Liberation Movement was assumed by the mainstream U.S. media to be a militant political enterprise run by man-hating lesbians; in the eyes of the average American, there was no other way to explain why women would publicly critique men as they did. Hence Friedan's fears over the lesbian presence in the movement—particularly in the National Organization for Women (NOW), which she cofounded—and hence the sense among lesbian feminists that they were unwanted in the movement. The fact is, they were. Political movements have always struggled with the desire to present a "respectable" face to the public versus the desire to embrace the diversity inherent within any group, and the WLM was no different in this regard. But in order to grow as a movement, Second Wavers had to face the fact that there *was* a relationship between feminism and lesbianism, a relationship of profound significance vis-à-vis issues of gender, power, and personal and political identity. This acknowledgment did not come easily to feminists like Friedan, those who fought to protect the "reputation" of feminism, but it came nonetheless. Embracing their identities as Lavender Menaces, lesbian feminists refused to be silent, refused to deny who they were for the sake of reputability. They understood that, if taken seriously, the Women's Liberation Movement was revolutionary, and that in any revolution, all voices—even those that challenge the leadership of the movement—need to be heard.

Based on the above account alone, it is tempting to cast lesbian feminists as the "serious" politicos or "true" revolutionaries in a movement that was becoming too concerned with public image, but to do so would gloss over the ways in which lesbian feminism, while radicalizing the Second Wave in extraordinarily important ways, also presented a political program that was idealistic at its best and militant at its worst. That is, like any political intervention, lesbian feminism demanded change, and often times those demands were highly dogmatic (and therefore problematic)—most significantly, the directive that feminists truly committed to the cause should embrace lesbianism as a political act. As Charlotte Bunch proclaimed in her 1972 essay "Lesbians in Revolt":

> If women do not make a commitment to each other, which includes sexual love, we deny ourselves the love and value traditionally given to men. We accept our second class status. When women do give primary energies to other women, then it is possible to concentrate fully on building a movement for our liberation. Woman-identified Lesbianism is, then, more than a sexual preference, it is a political choice. It is political because relationships between men and women are essentially political, they involve power and dominance. Since the Lesbian actively rejects that relationship and chooses women, she defies the established political system.[2]

At the heart of the Second Wave—its theories, its politics, and its commitment to consciousness-raising—lay the notion that "the personal is political." In claiming that sexuality was not simply a matter of personal preference but rather a profound political choice, lesbian feminists issued a challenge to straight feminists—a challenge that raised important questions about the power dynamics of heterosexual relationships and the potentially harmful influence of male-centered and male-identified culture.

All of this is not to say, however, that lesbian feminists presented a unified, unassailable front in their decade-long confrontations with straight feminists. Indeed, over the course of the Second Wave, dissent among lesbian feminists become more prominent, particularly around questions regarding the political efficacy of lesbian separatism and the erasure of sexual desire from discussions of sexuality. By 1982, arguments about the latter issue came to a head at the now-famous Barnard Conference, in which feminists from two opposing camps—the antipornography activists and the "sex positive" contingent—engaged in a heated battle over the sexual behaviors, practices, and desires of gay and straight women alike. Illustrating a major shift from earlier articulations of lesbian feminism that posited lesbianism as an ideal sexual identity because it was free from power struggles, "sex positive" feminists—many of whom were lesbians—insisted both on the inextricable relationship between power and desire and on the right of any feminist to explore this relationship in myriad ways, even ways that might seem oppressive to her. Whereas twelve years earlier, the Lavender Menace had challenged their marginalization in the Women's Liberation Movement and demanded to be included by their straight sisters in the struggle for equality, by 1982 the gay/straight split was no longer the defining fissure in the movement. The issue was no longer sexual orientation but sexuality itself.

The essays chosen for discussion in this section of the anthology both mirror and embody the trajectory outlined above; in subject, tone, and purpose they are representative of the interventions of lesbian feminism during the Second Wave. The first essay, "The Woman-Identified Woman," by Radicalesbians—a manifesto distributed by the Lavender Menace at the aforementioned takeover of the second Congress to Unite Women in 1970—confronts the WLM with a fundamental question: why do feminists' allegiances lie more with men than with lesbian women?[3] In posing this question—and in providing a thoughtful yet challenging analysis by way of response—the Radicalesbians posed the first major internal challenge to the feminist movement, a challenge not just to theorize feminism but to *live* it in all its implications. The second selection, Adrienne Rich's 1980 essay "Compulsory Heterosexuality and Lesbian Existence," is perhaps the most well-known and certainly the most influential of the three.[4] Though Rich's work is considered a landmark text (and rightly so), in many ways it reiterates a crucial point from the Radicalebians' manifesto, which appeared ten years prior: the notion that heterosexuality should be understood and analyzed as an *institution,* not simply as a personal choice. Rich also articulates a politics of lesbian feminism that would become one of the most widely debated by feminists in the Second Wave and beyond: the concept of the lesbian continuum. According to Rich, the lesbian continuum refers to the range of women-identified experiences that allow women to "discover the erotic in female terms," whether in the form of mothering, friendship, or romantic partnership.[5] While Rich aimed at redefining the erotic for women as an experience that was neither patriarchal nor male-identified in nature, her conceptualization of it differed greatly from that presented in the third essay discussed here, the 1983 conversation between Amber Hollibaugh and Cherríe Moraga, "What We're Rollin around in Bed With: Sexual Silences in Feminism." If the Radicalesbians represent the emergence of lesbian feminism as a powerful, significant voice in the movement, Hollibaugh and Moraga exemplify the direction that lesbian feminism had taken by the early 1980s: away from an idealization of lesbianism as the highest form of feminism and toward a recognition of the importance of sexual pleasure and fantasy, even those pleasure and fantasy practices that seem counter-feminist.

One of the central tenets of the Second Wave was the belief that women have long accepted their status as second-class citizens because they live in a patriarchal culture: a culture that tells them to not only expect their status but to embrace it. Patriarchy rewards women who sacrifice their own desires, ambitions, and needs—as well as those of other women—to fulfill the desires of men, thereby affirming the primacy of men at the expense of women. Such widespread oppression is made possible by having all aspects of culture—art, literature, music, politics, business—privilege men and male experience. While feminism on the whole exposed the insidiousness of male culture (e.g., Kate Millett's influential book *Sexual Politics* offers a brilliant analysis of sexism in literature), lesbian feminists in particular examined both the practices and the consequences of male identification. And they insisted that in order to be politically efficacious, feminists had to shift from being male-identified women to being woman-identified women.

The Radicalesbians first articulated the notion of the "woman-identified-woman" in their eponymous essay, and for this reason alone the essay is among the most important in the history of lesbian feminism of the Second Wave. But it is also important because of the incisive analysis it offers regarding the rewards of male identification, even among feminists. Indeed, the Radicalesbians assert that the WLM's fear and rejection of lesbianism stems above all from a desire to be accepted by *men:*

> Women in the movement have in most cases gone to great lengths to avoid discussion and confrontation with the issue of lesbianism. . . . They would rather not talk about it. . . . But it is no side issue. It is absolutely essential to the success and fulfillment of the women's liberation movement that this issue be dealt with. As long as the label "dyke" can be used to frighten women into a less militant stand, keep her separate from her sisters, keep her from giving primacy to anything other than men and family—then to that extent she is controlled by the male culture.[6]

The denial of lesbianism within the movement, according to the Radicalesbians, amounts to a denial of feminism itself—and, concomitantly, of the primacy of women.

In order to break the pattern of inauthenticity and self-hate that comes with "identifying with the oppressor, living through him, gaining status and identity from his ego, his power, his accomplishments," women must create a "new sense of self" through *each other*:

> Our energies must flow toward our sisters, not backwards towards our oppressors. As long as women's liberation tries to free women without facing the basic heterosexual structure that binds us in one-to-one relationships with our oppressors, tremendous energies will continue to flow into trying to straighten up each particular relationship with a man . . . trying to make the "new man" out of him, in the delusion that this will allow us to be the "new woman." . . . It is the primacy of women relating to women, of women creating a new consciousness of and with each other which is at the heart of women's liberation, and the basis for the cultural revolution.[7]

The woman-identified woman is a feminist who recognizes the relationship between sexism and heterosexism, who understands the intersections between one's personal choices and the larger political consequences, and who chooses to value women over men—regardless of her own sexual orientation. While the Radicalesbians never offer a direct statement regarding the need for feminists to become lesbians, the implications in their argument are clear: within the structures of heterosexuality, liberation and revolution are not possible. Or, as they succinctly put it, "until women see in each other the possibility of a primal commitment which includes sexual love, they will be denying themselves the love and value they readily accord to men."[8]

Though the Radicalesbians' critique of feminism was also inherently a critique of feminists' attachment to heterosexuality, and though other lesbian feminists—most notably the outspoken, charismatic Jill Johnston, who was a visible face of lesbianism during the Second Wave—continued to raise the question of how feminism and heterosexuality could be reconciled, it was Adrienne Rich's "Compulsory Heterosexuality and Lesbian Existence," published ten years after "The Woman-Identified-Woman," that brought the discussion of heterosexuality as an institution to the forefront of feminist consciousness. Rich's essay opens with an analysis of several feminist books whose aim is to reveal how sexism permeates social structures but that, despite these intentions, unwittingly participate in heterosexist enterprises. Rich asks why, "in none of [these books] is the question ever raised, whether in a different context, or other things being equal, women would *choose* heterosexual coupling and marriage."[9] The Radicalesbians asserted that heterosexuality was a serious impediment to feminist revolution; Rich takes this argument one step further, contending that heterosexuality is *ideological*, systematically maintained by "a pervasive cluster of forces, ranging from physical brutality to control of consciousness."[10] Women often choose heterosexuality, Rich maintains, not because it is "natural" or "normal," but because in patriarchal societies it is compulsory— and its compulsory status is enforced in myriad ways.

Rich devotes a substantial portion of her essay—over ten pages—to examining how this enforcement occurs in ways both explicit and implicit. In a careful and often brilliant analysis, she underscores how patriarchy hinges upon "assuring male access to women."[11] Two sites of male power she addresses at length are the workplace and the pornography industry, both of which she identifies as "social institutions . . . where women have learned to accept male violation of our psychic and physical boundaries."[12] She also provides readers with an extensive list of the "forms of compulsion" that are common in male-dominated societies: "the chastity belt; child marriage; erasure of lesbian existence (except as exotic or perverse) in art, literature; film; [and the] idealization of heterosexual romance and marriage."[13] Like the Radicalesbians before her, Rich urges feminists to acknowledge the inextricable link between patriarchy and compulsory heterosexuality:

> when we look hard and clearly at the extent and elaboration of measures designed to keep women within a male sexual purlieu, it becomes an inescapable question whether the issue we have to address as feminists is, not simple "gender inequality," [or] the domination of culture by males, [or] mere "taboos against homosexuality," but the enforcement of heterosexuality for women as a means of assuring male right of physical, economical, and emotional access.[14]

In many ways, Rich's challenge to feminists to "examine heterosexuality as an institution" is at once an act of repetition and of revolution.[15] It is an act of repetition insofar as the need for such an examination was implicit in the Radicalesbians' manifesto, as well as in several other lesbian feminist works throughout the 1970s, including the earlier cited essay by Charlotte Bunch, "Lesbians in Revolt," as well as Jill Johnston's *Lesbian Nation: The Feminist Solution*. In other words, the notion of compulsory heterosexuality was not a new idea. But Rich's *articulation* of that idea—her naming of it as such, her thorough evidence and analysis of it as an ideology, and her demand that feminists confront it in all its ramifications—*was* new. It functioned as a wake-up call to feminists, pushing them to recognize their long-standing theoretical blinds spots and the consequences of this blindness.

Also groundbreaking—and controversial—was Rich's conceptualization of the lesbian continuum.[16] While it may seem simply like a reiteration of the idea of the woman-identified woman, the lesbian continuum is in fact a far more nuanced concept:

> [It] include[s] a range . . . of woman-identified experience; not simply the fact that a woman has had or consciously desired genital sexual experience with another woman. If we expand it to embrace many more forms of primary intensity between and among women, including the sharing of a rich inner life, the bonding against male tyranny, the giving and receiving of practical support . . . we begin to grasp breadths of female history and psychology which have lain out of reach as a consequence of limited, mostly clinical, definitions of "lesbianism."[17]

The notion of the continuum gave feminists something that no other theorist before Rich had given them: a framework for recognizing the existence of lesbianism across the centuries, an existence that she insists is at once separate from that of gay men (in equating male homosexuality and lesbianism, according to Rich, we "deny and erase female reality once again"), *and* characterized by "the breaking of a taboo and the rejection of a compulsory way of life."[18] And unlike some of her lesbian feminist predecessors, Rich did not demand that all feminists become lesbians (although she did claim that "there is a *nascent* feminist political content in the act of choosing a woman lover or life partner in the face of institutionalized heterosexuality");[19] rather, she suggested that feminists expand the definition of lesbianism to include all forms of female intimacy and thereby to recognize the radical nature of allegiances among women. Such a recognition would help women to free themselves of the shackles of male identification, leading them "to discover the erotic in female terms: as that which is unconfined to any single part of the body or solely to the body itself, as an energy not only diffuse but, as Audre Lorde has described it, omnipresent."[20]

Rich's mention of the erotic is significant because it foreshadows the soon-to-be predominant (if not final) concern of the Second Wave: the desire among feminists to discuss desire itself—how it has been defined under patriarchy, how it can be redefined, and what forms it might take. In the ten years between "The Woman-Identified Woman" and "Compulsory Heterosexuality and Lesbian Existence," issues of sex and desire vis-à-vis the WLM had become secondary to issues of economic and political equity and, in the late 1970s, the problem of pornography. As feminist activists became increasingly vocal in their condemnation of pornography, they also became increasingly aligned politically with conservative forces, thereby raising a red flag for those feminists who were not active in the antipornography contingent of the movement. The concern among the latter group was how—and whether—it was possible to talk about sex, pleasure, and desire as feminists. The lesbian feminist text that most effectively and candidly addresses the often-fraught relationship between feminism and sex is Amber Hollibaugh and Cherríe Moraga's "What We're Rollin around in Bed With: Sexual Silences in Feminism." While the authors recognize the important work of the lesbian feminists before them (like Rich), they also boldly assert that "by analyzing the institution of heterosexuality, feminists learned what's oppressive about it and why people cooperate with it or don't, but we didn't learn what is *sexual.*"[21] The authors aim at developing a "sexual theory" for feminism, one that acknowledges the inextricability of pleasure and power. The battle cry of the Second Wave had long been "the personal is political," and in their conversation about their own sexual fantasies and practices, Hollibaugh and Moraga take this charge seriously.

"What We're Rollin around in Bed With" is a landmark essay for many reasons, above all for its frank and fearless discussion of sexual desire in all its forms: role-playing, fantasy, sadomasochism. But it is also as frank and fearless in its critique of feminism. The authors take feminists—straight and lesbian alike—to task on several issues: for idealizing lesbian relationships as "transcendent" and free of power dynamics; for denying the erotic dimension of power; and for essentially condemning women who might take pleasure in power relationships.[22] According to Hollibaugh and Moraga, the Second Wave had long defined gender relationships in a limited and judgmental way: "in feminism, . . . there is a masculine oppressor and a female oppressee. So whether you might fantasize yourself in a role a man might perform or a woman in reaction to a man, this makes you sick, fucked up, and you had better go and change it."[23] By focusing discussions of sexuality on "how much pain women had suffered around sex in relation to men," feminists overlooked one of the most personal aspects of sex: pleasure.[24] The extent to which the WLM had silenced these discussions is exemplified in what may be the boldest statement in the entire essay: "It seems feminism is the last rock of conservatism."[25] In recognizing the very real alliance between feminism and conservatism on the issue of pornography, and the frustration many feminists felt over the denial of sexuality in all its forms, Hollibaugh and Moraga's essay signals at once the start of what would be the most contentious issue among feminists and the end of the Second Wave itself.

Toward the end of their conversation, Amber Hollibaugh declares, "I won't give my sexuality up and I won't *not* be a feminist. So I'll build a different movement, but I won't live without either one."[26] Her proclamation could very well represent the sentiments of so many lesbian feminists who participated in the Second Wave. Refusing to deny their sexuality and, at the same time, refusing to abandon feminism, they changed history. Taken together, these three essays—though appearing at different historical moments in the movement and as such, performing different kinds of interventions—represent the ways in which lesbian voices were crucial to the development of a feminism that was more nuanced and more demanding both in its theory and in its activism. While we know now that lesbianism is not the highest form of feminism, not the "practice" required of those dedicated to feminist theory, we also know that feminism would not be what it is today without lesbianism.

NOTES

Epigraphs: Jill Johnston, *Lesbian Nation* (New York: Touchstone Books, 1973), 166; Amber Hollibaugh and Cherríe Moraga, "What We're Rollin around in Bed With: Sexual Silences in Feminism," in *Powers of Desire: The Politics of Sexuality*, ed. Ann Snitow et al. (New York: Monthly Review Press, 1983), 401.

1. Alice Echols, *Daring to Be Bad: Radical Feminism in America, 1967–1975* (Minneapolis: University of Minnesota Press, 1989), 214–15.

2. Charlotte Bunch, "Lesbians in Revolt," in *Radical Feminism: A Documentary Reader*, ed. Barbara A. Crow (New York: NYU Press, 2000), 332–33.

3. Radicalesbians, "The Woman-Identified Woman," in *Radical Feminism: A Documentary Reader*, ed. Barbara A. Crow (New York: NYU Press, 2000), 233–37. Echols, *Daring to Be Bad*, 215.

4. Due to copyright issues, Rich's essay is not reprinted in this anthology.

5. Adrienne Rich, "Compulsory Heterosexuality and Lesbian Existence," *Signs* (Summer 1980), 650.

6. Radicalesbians, "The Woman-Identified Woman," 235.

7. Ibid., 236.

8. Ibid., 235.

9. Rich, "Compulsory Heterosexuality," 633.

10. Ibid., 640.

11. Ibid., 643.

12. Ibid., 642.

13. Ibid., 640.

14. Ibid., 647.

15. Ibid., 648.

16. In the years following the publication of Rich's essay, there has been much debate about the concept of the "lesbian continuum"; in particular, some feminists have expressed concern over how "the sense of range and gradation that [Rich's] description evokes [has] completely disappeared." The result is that often, even among activists with the best of intentions, "lesbianism and female friendship [become] exactly the same thing." This conflation of sexual identity and female intimacy is obviously a problem for many reasons, the least of which is that lesbians often suffer real social consequences for their lesbianism in a way that female friends—even those who see themselves on a lesbian continuum—do not. See Adrienne Rich, "Afterward [1986]," in *The Lesbian and Gay Studies Reader,* ed. Henry Abelove, Michèle Aina Barale, and David M. Halperin (New York and London: Routledge, 1993), 247.

17. Rich, "Compulsory Heterosexuality," 648–49.

18. Ibid., 649.

19. Ibid., 659.

20. Ibid., 650.

21. Hollibaugh and Moraga, "What We're Rollin around in Bed With," 395.

22. Ibid., 395.

23. Ibid., 397.

24. Ibid., 395.

25. Ibid., 403.

26. Ibid., 403.

DISCUSSION QUESTIONS

1. We are no longer in the midst of the Women's Liberation Movement, and the themes, concerns, and tone of Second Wave texts can sometimes be strange, disconcerting, or offensive to us as Third Wave readers. Above all, we may feel defensive of our personal choices, particularly those under specific attack in works of the Second Wave feminists. Take, for example, the proclamation by Radicalesbians in "The Woman-Identified Woman" that "when you strip off all the packaging, you must finally realize that the essence of being a 'woman' is to get fucked by men." At the same time, Third Wave feminism rarely offers

such bold proclamations about gender and sexuality. What is gained and what is lost by the political approaches of each of the two waves?

2. In the thirty years that have passed since its publication, Rich's notion of the "lesbian continuum," which Ciasullo describes, has been widely debated. How useful is it to us now? What, if anything, can be gained by understanding *all* intimate relationships between women as located somewhere on this continuum?

3. The questions raised by Hollibaugh and Moraga about sex, desire, and power, while more openly addressed and acknowledged in the Third Wave, still remain today. How do we reconcile political efficacy and sexual desire, particularly when they are at odds with one another? Is the personal *always* political?

RADICALESBIANS, *THE WOMAN-IDENTIFIED WOMAN*

What is a lesbian? A lesbian is the rage of all women condensed to the point of explosion. She is the woman who, often beginning at an extremely early age, acts in accordance with her inner compulsion to be a more complete and freer human being than her society—perhaps then, but certainly later—cares to allow her. These needs and actions, over a period of years, bring her into painful conflict with people, situations, the accepted ways of thinking, feeling and behaving, until she is in a state of continual war with everything around her, and usually with her self. She may not be fully conscious of the political implications of what for her began as personal necessity, but on some level she has not been able to accept the limitations and oppression laid on her by the most basic role of her society—the female role. The turmoil she experiences tends to induce guilt proportional to the degree to which she feels she is not meeting social expectations, and/or eventually drives her to question and analyze what the rest of her society more or less accepts. She is forced to evolve her own life pattern, often living much of her life alone, learning usually much earlier than her "straight" (heterosexual) sisters about the essential aloneness of life (which the myth of marriage obscures) and about the reality of illusions. To the extent that she cannot expel the heavy socialization that goes with being female, she can never truly find peace with herself. For she is caught somewhere between accepting society's view of her—in which case she cannot accept herself—and coming to understand what this sexist society has done to her and why it is functional and necessary for it to do so. Those of us who work that through find ourselves on the other side of a tortuous journey through a night that may have been decades long. The perspective gained from that journey, the liberation of self, the inner peace, the real love

SOURCE: Radicalesbians, "The Woman-Identified Woman," in *Out of the Closets: Voices of Gay Liberation*, ed. Karla Jay and Allen Young (New York: NYU Press, 1972, 1978, 1992).

of self and of all women, is something to be shared with all women—because we are all women.

It should first be understood that lesbianism, like male homosexuality, is a category of behavior possible only in a sexist society characterized by rigid sex roles and dominated by male supremacy. Those sex roles dehumanize women by defining us as a supportive/serving caste in relation to the master caste of men, and emotionally cripple men by demanding that they be alienated from their own bodies and emotions in order to perform their economic/political/military functions effectively. Homosexuality is a byproduct of a particular way of setting up roles (or approved patterns of behavior) on the basis of sex; as such it is an inauthentic (not consonant with "reality") category. In a society in which men do not oppress women, and sexual expression is allowed to follow feelings, the categories of homosexuality and heterosexuality would disappear.

But lesbianism is also different from male homosexuality, and serves a different function in the society. "Dyke" is a different kind of put-down from "faggot," although both imply you are not playing your socially assigned sex role ... are not therefore a "real woman" or a "real man." The grudging admiration felt for the tomboy, and the queasiness felt around a sissy boy point to the same thing: the contempt in which women—or those who play a female role—are held. And the investment in keeping women in that contemptuous role is very great. Lesbian is a word, the label, the condition that holds women in line. When a woman hears this word tossed her way, she knows she is stepping out of line. She knows that she has crossed the terrible boundary of her sex role. She recoils, she protests, she reshapes her actions to gain approval. Lesbian is a label invented by the Man to throw at any woman who dares to be his equal, who dares to challenge his prerogatives (including that of all women as part of the exchange medium among men), who dares to assert the primacy of her own needs. To have the label applied to people active in women's liberation is just the most recent instance of a long history; older women will recall that not so long ago, any woman who was successful, independent, not orienting her whole life about a man, would hear this word. For in this sexist society, for a woman to be independent means she can't be a woman—she must be a dyke. That in itself should tell us where women are at. It says as clearly as can be said: women and person are contradictory terms. For a lesbian is not considered a "real woman." And yet, in popular thinking, there is really only one essential difference between a lesbian and other women: that of sexual orientation—which is to say, when you strip off all the packaging, you must finally realize that the essence of being a "woman" is to get fucked by men.

"Lesbian" is one of the sexual categories by which men have divided up humanity. While all women are dehumanized as sex objects, as the objects of men they are given certain compensations: identification with his power, his ego, his status, his protection (from other males), feeling like a "real woman," finding social acceptance by adhering to her role, etc. Should a woman confront herself by confronting another woman, there are fewer rationalizations, fewer buffers by which to avoid the stark horror of her dehumanized condition. Herein we find the overriding fear of many women toward being used as a sexual object by a woman, which not only will bring her no male-connected compensations, but also will reveal the void which is woman's real situation. This dehumanization is expressed when a straight woman learns that a sister is a lesbian: she begins to relate to her lesbian sister as her potential sex object, laying a surrogate male role on the lesbian. This reveals her heterosexual conditioning to make herself into an object when sex is potentially involved in a relationship, and it denies the lesbian her full humanity. For women, especially those in the movement, to perceive their lesbian sisters through this male grid of role definitions is to accept this male cultural conditioning and to oppress their sisters much as they themselves have been oppressed by men. Are we going to continue the male classification system of defining all females in sexual relation to some other category of people? Affixing the label lesbian not only to a woman who aspires to be a person, but also to any situation of real love, real solidarity, real primacy among women, is a primary form of divisiveness among women: it is the condition which keeps women within the confines of the feminine role, and it is the debunking/scare term that keeps women from forming any primary attachments, groups, or associations among ourselves.

Women in the movement have in most cases gone to great lengths to avoid discussion and confrontation with the issue of lesbianism. It puts people up-tight. They are hostile, evasive, or try to incorporate it into some "broader issue." They would rather not talk about it. If they have to, they try to dismiss it as a "lavender herring." But it is no side issue. It is absolutely essential to the success and fulfillment of the women's liberation movement that this issue be dealt with. As long as the label "dyke" can be used to frighten women into a less militant stand, keep her separate from her sisters, keep her from giving primacy to anything other than men and family—then to that extent she is controlled by the male culture. Until women see in each other the possibility of a primal commitment which includes sexual love, they will be denying themselves the love and value they readily accord to men, thus affirming their second-class status. As long as male acceptability is primary—both to individual women and to the movement as a whole—the term lesbian will be used effectively against women. Insofar as women want only more privileges within the system, they do not want to antagonize male power. They instead seek acceptability for women's liberation, and the most crucial aspect of the acceptability is to deny lesbianism—i.e., to deny any fundamental challenge to the basis of the female. It should also be said that some younger, more radical women have honestly begun to discuss lesbianism, but so far it has been primarily as a sexual "alternative" to men. This, however, is still giving primacy to men, both because the idea of relating more completely to women occurs as a negative reaction to men, and because the lesbian relationship is being characterized simply by sex, which is divisive and sexist. On one level, which is both personal and political, women may withdraw emotional and sexual energies from men, and work out various alternatives for those energies in their own lives. On a different political/psychological level, it must be understood that what is crucial is that women begin disengaging from male-defined response patterns. In the privacy of our own psyches, we must cut those cords to the core. For irrespective of where our love and sexual energies flow, if we are male-identified in our heads, we cannot realize our autonomy as human beings.

But why is it that women have related to and through men? By virtue of having been brought up in a male society, we have internalized the male culture's definition of ourselves. That definition consigns us to sexual and family functions, and excludes us from defining and shaping the terms of our lives. In exchange for our psychic servicing and for performing society's non-profit-making functions, the man confers on us just one thing: the slave status which makes us legitimate in the eyes of the society in which we live. This is called "femininity" or "being a real woman" in our cultural lingo. We are authentic, legitimate, real to the extent that we are the property of some man whose name we bear. To be a woman who belongs to no man is to be invisible, pathetic, inauthentic, unreal. He confirms his image of us—of what we have to be in order to be acceptable by him—but not our real selves; he confirms our womanhood—as he defines it, in relation to him—but cannot confirm our personhood, our own selves as absolutes. As long as we are dependent on the male culture for this definition, for this approval, we cannot be free.

The consequence of internalizing this role is an enormous reservoir of self-hate. This is not to say the self-hate is recognized or accepted as such; indeed most women would deny it. It may be experienced as discomfort with her role, as feeling empty, as numbness, as restlessness, as a paralyzing anxiety at the center. Alternatively, it may be expressed in shrill defensiveness of the glory and destiny of her role. But it does exist, often beneath the edge of her consciousness, poisoning her existence, keeping her alienated from herself, her own needs, and rendering her a stranger to other women. They try to escape by identifying with the oppressor, living through him, gaining status and identity from his ego, his power, his accomplishments. And by not identifying with other "empty vessels" like themselves. Women resist relating on all levels to other women who will reflect their own oppression, their own secondary status, their own self-hate. For to confront another woman is finally to confront one's self—the self we have gone to such lengths to avoid. And in that mirror we know we cannot really respect and love that which we have been made to be.

As the source of self-hate and the lack of real self are rooted in our male-given identity, we must create a new sense of self. As long as we cling to the idea of "being a woman," we will sense some conflict with that incipient self, that sense of I, that sense of a whole person. It is very difficult to realize and accept that being "feminine" and being a whole person are irreconcilable. Only women can give to each other a new sense of self. That identity we have to develop with reference to ourselves, and not in relation to men. This consciousness is the revolutionary force from which all else will follow, for ours is an organic revolution. For this we must be available and supportive to one another, give our commitment and our love, give the emotional support necessary to sustain this movement. Our energies must flow toward our sisters, not backward toward our oppressors. As long as woman's liberation tries to free women without facing the basic heterosexual structure that binds us in one-to-one relationship with our oppressors, tremendous energies will continue to flow into trying to straighten up each particular relationship with a man, into finding how to get better sex, how to turn his head around—into trying to make the "new man" out of him, in the delusion that this will allow us to be the "new woman." This obviously splits our energies and commitments, leaving us unable to be committed to the construction of the new patterns which will liberate us.

It is the primacy of women relating to women, of women creating a new consciousness of and with each other, which is at the heart of women's liberation, and the basis for the cultural revolution. Together we must find, reinforce, and validate our authentic selves. As we do this, we confirm in each other that struggling, incipient sense of pride and strength, the divisive barriers begin to melt, we feel this growing solidarity with our sisters. We see ourselves as prime, find our centers inside of ourselves. We find receding the sense of alienation, of being cut off, of being behind a locked window, of being unable to get out what we know is inside. We feel a real-ness, feel at last we are coinciding with ourselves. With that real self, with that consciousness, we begin a revolution to end the imposition of all coercive identifications, and to achieve maximum autonomy in human expression.

AMBER HOLLIBAUGH AND CHERRÍE MORAGA, *WHAT WE'RE ROLLIN AROUND IN BED WITH: SEXUAL SILENCES IN FEMINISM*
The Critique

Ironically, the whole notion of "the personal is political," which surfaced in the early part of the women's liberation movement (and which many of us have used to an extreme), is suddenly dismissed when we begin to discuss sexuality. We have become a relatively sophisticated movement, so many women think they now have to have the theory before they expose the experience. It seems we simply did not take our feminism to heart enough. This most privatized aspect of ourselves, our sex lives, has dead-ended into silence within the feminist movement.

For a brief moment in its early stages, the feminist movement did address women's sexual pleasure, but this discussion was quickly swamped by recognition of how much pain women had suffered around sex in relation to men (e.g., marriage, the nuclear family, wife-battering, rape, etc.). In these early discussions, lesbianism was ignored and heterosexuality was not understood as both an actual sexual interaction *and* a system. No matter how we play ourselves out sexually, we are all affected by the system inasmuch as our sexual values are filtered through a society where heterosexuality is considered the

SOURCE: Amber Hollibaugh and Cherríe Moraga, "What We're Rollin around in Bed With: Sexual Silences in Feminism," in *Powers of Desire: The Politics of Sexuality*, ed. Ann Snitow, Christine Stansell, and Sharon Thompson (New York: Monthly Review Press, 1983), 395–98, 401–5.

norm. It is difficult to believe that there is anyone in the world who hasn't spent some time in great pain over the choices and limitations that characterize the system.

By analyzing the institution of heterosexuality, feminists learned what's oppressive about it and why people cooperate with it or don't, but we didn't learn what is *sexual*. We don't really know, for instance, why men and women are still attracted to each other, even through all that oppression. There is something genuine that happens between heterosexuals, but gets perverted in a thousand different ways. There *is* heterosexuality outside of heterosexism.

What grew out of this kind of "nonsexual" theory was a "transcendent" definition of sexuality where lesbianism (since it exists outside the institution of heterosexuality) came to be seen as the practice of feminism. It set up a "perfect" vision of egalitarian sexuality, where we could magically leap over our heterosexist conditioning into mutually orgasmic, struggle-free, trouble-free sex. We feel this vision has become both misleading and damaging to many feminists, and in particular to lesbians. Who created this sexual model as a goal in the first place? Who can really live up to such an ideal? There is little language, little literature that reflects the actual sexual struggles of most lesbians, feminist or not.

The failure of feminism to answer all the questions about women, in particular about women's sexuality, is the same failure the homosexual movement suffers from around gender. It's a confusing of those two things—that some of us are both female and homosexual—that may be the source of some of the tension between the two movements and of the inadequacies of each. When we walk down the street, we are both female and lesbian. We are working-class white and working-class Chicana. We are all these things rolled into one and there is no way to eliminate even one aspect of ourselves.

The Conversation

Cherríe Moraga: *In trying to develop sexual theory, I think we should start by talking about what we're rollin around in bed with. We both agree that the way feminism has dealt with sexuality has been entirely inadequate.*

Amber Hollibaugh: Right. Sexual theory has traditionally been used to say *people have been forced to be this thing; people could be that thing.* And you're left standing in the middle going, "Well, I am here; and I don't know how to get there." It hasn't been able to talk realistically about what people *are* sexually.

I think by focusing on roles in lesbian relationships, we can begin to unravel who we really are in bed. Hiding how profoundly roles shape your sexuality can be seen as an example of how other things about sex get hidden. There's a lot of different things that shape the way that people respond—some not so easy to see, some more forbidden, as I perceive sadomasochism to be. Like with sadomasochism—when I think of it I'm frightened. Why? Is it because I might be sexually fascinated with it and I don't know how to accept that? Who am I there? The point is that when you deny that roles, sadomasochism, fantasy, or any sexual differences exist in the first place, you can only come up with neutered sexuality, where everybody's got to be basically the same because anything different puts the element of power and deviation in there and threatens the whole picture.

CM: *Exactly. Remember how I told you that growing up what turned me on sexually, at a very early age, had to do with the fantasy of capture, taking a woman, and my identification was with the man, taking? Well, something like that would be so frightening to bring up in a feminist context—fearing people would put it in some sicko sexual box. And yet, the truth is, I do have some real gut-level misgivings about my sexual connection with capture. It might feel very sexy to imagine "taking" a woman, but it has sometimes occurred at the expense of my feeling, sexually, like I can surrender myself to a woman; that is, always needing to be the one in control, calling the shots. It's a very butch trip and I feel like this can keep me private and protected and can prevent me from fully being able to express myself.*

AH: But it's not wrong, in and of itself, to have a capture fantasy, the real question is: Does it *actually* limit you? For instance, does it allow you to eroticize someone else, but never see yourself as erotic? Does it keep you always in control? Does the fantasy force you into a dimension of sexuality that feels very narrow to you? If it causes you to look at your lover in only one light, then you may want to check it out. But if you can't even dream about wanting a woman in this way in the first place, then you can't figure out what is narrow and heterosexist in it and what's just play. After all, it's only *one* fantasy.

CM: *Well, what I think is very dangerous about keeping down such fantasies is that they are forced to stay unconscious. Then, next thing you know, in the actual sexual relationship, you become the capturer, that is, you try to have power over your lover, psychologically or whatever. If the desire for power is so hidden and unacknowledged, it will inevitably surface through manipulation or what-have-you. If you couldn't play capturer, you'd be it.*

AH: Part of the problem in talking about sexuality is *it's so enormous* in our culture that people don't have any genuine sense of dimension. So that when you say "capture," every fantasy you've ever heard of from Robin Hood to colonialism comes racing into your mind and all you really maybe wanted to do was have your girlfriend lay you down.

But in feminism, we can't even explore these questions because what they say is, in gender, there is a masculine oppressor and a female oppressee. So whether you might fantasize yourself in a role a man might perform or a woman in reaction to a man, this makes you sick, fucked-up, and you had better go and change it.

If you don't speak of fantasies, they become a kind of amorphous thing that envelops you and hangs over your relationship and you get terrified of the silence. If you have no way to describe what your desire is and what your fear is, you have no way to negotiate with your lover. And I guarantee you, six months or six years later, the relationship has paid. Things that are kept private and hidden become painful and deformed.

When you say that part of your sexuality has been hooked up with capture, I want to say that absolutely there's a heterosexist part of that, but what part of that is just plain dealing with power, sexually? I don't want to live outside of power in my sexuality, but I don't want to be trapped into a heterosexist concept of power either. But what I feel feminism asks of me is to throw the baby out with the bathwater.

For example, *I think the reason butch/femme stuff got hidden within lesbian-feminism is because people are profoundly afraid of questions of power in bed.* And though everybody doesn't play out power the way I do, the question of power affects who and how you eroticize your sexual need. And it is absolutely at the bottom of all sexual inquiry. Given the present state of the movement, it's impossible to say I'm a femme and I like it—no apologies—without facing the probability of a heavy fight.

CM: *But what is femme to you? I told you once that what I thought of as femme was passive, unassertive, and so forth, and you didn't fit that image. And you said to me, "Well, change your definition of femme."*

AH: My fantasy life is deeply involved in a butch/femme exchange. I never come together with a woman, sexually, outside of those roles. It's saying to my partner, "Love me enough to let me go where I need to go and take me there. Don't make me think it through. Give me a way to be so in my body that I don't have to think; that you can fantasize for the both of us. You map it out. You are in control."

It's hard to talk about things like giving up power without it sounding passive. I am willing to give myself over to a woman equal to her amount of wanting. I expose myself for her to see what's possible for her to love in me that's female. I want her to respond to it. I may not be doing something active with my body, but more eroticizing her need that I feel in her hands as she touches me.

In the same way, as a butch, you want and conceive of a woman in a certain way. You dress a certain way to attract her and you put your sexual need within these certain boundaries to communicate that desire. . . . And yet, there's a part of me that feels maybe all this is not even a question of roles. Maybe it's much richer territory than that.

CM: *Yes, I feel the way I want a woman can be a very profound experience. Remember I told you how when I looked up at my lover's face when I was making love to her (I was actually just kissing her breast at the moment), but when I looked up at her face, I could feel and see how deeply every part of her was present? That every pore in her body was entrusting me to handle her, to take care of her sexual desire. This look on her face is like nothing else. It fills me up. She entrusts me to determine where she'll go sexually. And I honestly feel a power inside me strong enough to heal the deepest wound.*

AH: Well, I can't actually see what I look like, but I can feel it in my lover's hands when I look the way you described. When I open myself up more and more to her sensation of wanting a woman, when I eroticize that in her, I feel a kind of ache in my body, but it's not an ache to *do* something. I can feel a hurt spot and a need and it's there and it's just the tip of it, the tip of that desire and that is what first gets played with, made erotic. It's light and playful. It doesn't commit you to exposing a deeper part of yourself sexually. Then I begin to pick up passion. And the passion isn't butch or femme. It's just passion. [. . .]

CM: *How I fantasize sex roles has been really different for me with different women. I do usually enter into an erotic encounter with a woman from the kind of butch place you described, but I have also felt very ripped off there, finding myself taking all the sexual responsibility. I am seriously attracted to butches sometimes. It's a different dynamic, where the sexuality may not seem as fluid or comprehensible, but I know there's a huge part of me that wants to be handled in the way I described I can handle another woman. I am very compelled toward that "lover" posture. I have never totally reckoned with being the "beloved" and, frankly, I don't know if it takes a butch or a femme or what to get me there. I know that it's a struggle within me and it scares the shit out of me to look at it so directly. I've done this kind of searching emotionally, but to combine sex with it seems like very dangerous stuff.*

AH: Well, I think everybody has aspects of roles in their relationships, but I feel pretty out there on the extreme end. . . . I think what feminism did, in its fear of heterosexual control of fantasy, was to say that there was almost no fantasy safe to have, where you weren't going to have to give up power or take it. There's no sexual fantasy I can think of that doesn't include some aspect of that. But I feel like I have been forced to give up some of my richest potential sexually in the way feminism has defined what is, and what's not, "politically correct" in the sexual sphere.

CM: *Oh, of course when most feminists talk about sexuality, including lesbianism, they're not talkin about Desire. It is significant to me that I came out only when I met a good feminist, although I knew I was queer since eight or nine. That's only when I'd risk it because I wouldn't have to say it's because I want her. I didn't have to say that when she travels by me, my whole body starts throbbing.*

AH: Yes, it's just *correct*.

CM: *It was okay to be with her because we all knew men were really fuckers and there were a lot of "okay" women acknowledging that. Read: white and educated. . . . But that's not why I "came out." How could I say that I wanted women so bad I was gonna die if I didn't get me one, soon! You know, I just felt the pull in the hips, right?*

AH: Yes, really—. . . well, the first discussion I ever heard of lesbianism among feminists was: "We've been sex objects to men and where did it get us? And here when we're just learning how to be friends with other women, you got to go and sexualize it." That's what they said! "Fuck you. Now I have to worry about you looking down my blouse." That's exactly what they meant. It horrified me. "No no no," I wanted to say, "that's not me. I promise I'll only look at the sky. *Please* let me come to a meeting. I'm really okay. I just go to the bars and fuck like a rabbit with women who want me. You know?"

Now from the onset, how come feminism was so invested in that? They would not examine sexual need with each other except as oppressor/oppressee. Whatever your experience was you were always the victim. So how do dykes fit into that? Dykes who wanted tits, you know?

Now a lot of women have been sexually terrorized and this makes sense, their needing not to have to deal with explicit sexuality, but they made men out of every sexual dyke. "Oh my god, *she* wants me, too!"

So it became this really repressive movement, where you didn't talk dirty and you didn't want dirty. It really became a bore. So after meetings, we *ran* to the bars. You couldn't talk about wanting a woman, except very loftily. You couldn't say it hurt at night wanting a woman to touch you. . . . I remember at one meeting breaking down after everybody was talking about being a lesbian very delicately. I began crying. I remember saying, "I can't help it. I just . . . want her. I want to feel her." And everybody forgiving me. It was this atmosphere of me exorcising this *crude* sexual need for women.

CM: [. . . .] *Most women are not immune from experiencing pain in relation to their sexuality, but certainly lesbians experience a particular pain and oppression. Let us not forget, although feminism would sometimes like us to, that lesbians are oppressed in this world. Possibly, there are some of us who came out through the movement who feel immune to "queer attack," but not the majority of us (no matter when we came out), particularly if you have no economic buffer in this society. If you have enough money and privilege, you can separate yourself from hetero-sexist oppression. You can be sapphic or somethin, but you don't have to be queer.*

The point I am trying to make is that I believe most of us harbor plenty of demons and old hurts inside ourselves around sexuality. I know, for me, that each time I choose to touch another woman, to make love with her, I feel I risk opening up that secret, harbored, vulnerable place . . . I think why feminism has been particularly attractive to many "queer" lesbians is that it kept us in a place where we wouldn't have to look at our pain around sexuality anymore. Our sisters would just sweep us up into a movement. . . .

AH: Yes, it's not just because of feminism we were silent. Our own participation in that silence has stemmed from our absolute terror of facing that profound sexual need. Period.

There is no doubt in my mind that the feminist movement has radically changed, in an important way, everybody's concept of lesbianism, straight or gay. There's not a dyke in the world today (in or out of the bars) who can have the same conversation that she could have had ten years ago. It seeps through the water system or somethin, you know? Still, while lesbianism is certainly accepted in feminism, it's more as a political or intellectual concept. It seems feminism is the last rock of conservatism. It will not be sexualized. It's *prudish* in that way. . . .

Well, I won't give my sexuality up and I won't *not* be a feminist. So I'll build a different movement, but I won't live without either one.

Sometimes, I don't know how to handle how angry I feel about feminism. We may disagree on this. We have been treated in some similar ways, but our relationship to feminism has been different. Mine is a lot longer. I really have taken a lot more shit than you have, specifically around being femme. I have a personal fury. The more I got in touch with how I felt about women, what made me desire and desirable, the more I felt outside the feminist community and that was just terrifying because, on the one hand, it had given me so much. I loved it. And then, I couldn't be who I was. I felt that about class, too. I could describe my feelings about being a woman, but if I described it from my own class, using that language, my experience wasn't valid. I don't know what to do with my anger, particularly around sexuality.

CM: *Well, you've gotta be angry. . . . I mean what you were gonna do is turn off the tape, so we'd have no record of your being mad. What comes out of anger . . . if you, one woman, can* *say* I have been a sister all these years and you have not helped me . . . *that speaks more to the failure of all that theory and rhetoric than more theory and rhetoric.*

AH: Yeah. . . . Remember that night you and me and M. was at the bar and we were talkin about roles? She told you later that the reason she had checked out of the conversation was because she knew how much it was hurting me to talk about it. You know, I can't tell you what it meant to me for her to know that. The desperation we all felt at that table talking about sexuality was so great, wanting people to understand why we are the way we are.

CM: *I know. . . . I remember how at that forum on sadomasochism that happened last spring, how that Samois* [a lesbian feminist S/M group in the San Francisco Bay Area] *woman came to the front of the room and spoke very plainly and clearly about feeling that through sadomasochism she was really coping with power struggles in a tangible way with her lover. That this time, for once, she wasn't leaving the relationship. I can't write her off. I believed her. I believed she was a woman in struggle. And as feminists, Amber, you and I are interested in struggle.*

The Challenge

We would like to suggest that, for dealing with sexual issues both personally and politically, women go back to consciousness-raising (CR) groups. We believe that women must create sexual theory in the same way we created feminist theory. We simply need to get together in places where people agree to suspend their sexual values, so that all of us can feel free to say what we do sexually or want to do or have done to us. We do have fear of using feelings as theory. We do not mean to imply that feelings are everything. But they are the place to start if we want to build a broad-based, cross-cultural movement that recognizes the political implications of sexual differences.

We believe our racial and class backgrounds have a huge effect in determining how we perceive ourselves sexually. Since we are not a movement that is working-class-dominated or a movement that is third world, we both hold serious reservations as to how this new CR will be conceived. In our involvement in a movement largely controlled by white middle-class women, we feel that the values of their cultures (which may be more closely tied to an American-assimilated puritanism) have been pushed down our throats. The questions arise then: *Whose* feelings and *whose* values will be considered normative in these CR groups? If there is no room for criticism in sexual discussion around race and class issues, we foresee ourselves being gut-checked from the beginning. [. . .]

Essentially, we are challenging other women and ourselves to look where we haven't, to arrive at a synthesis of sexual thought that originates and develops from our varied cultural backgrounds and experiences. We refuse to be debilitated one more time around sexuality, race, or class.

17

THE LATIN AMERICAN LESBIAN MOVEMENT

Its Shaping and Its Search for Autonomy

Norma Mogrovejo

The formation of the Latin American feminist lesbian movement has not been simple or straightforward. In a region in which the Catholic religion permeates the state and its institutions, shapes moral norms, and consequently validates women according to their loyalty to the family, heterosexuality, and reproduction, lesbians had to begin their struggle behind closed doors. They searched for spaces of legitimization first within civil society and then independently, in order to reconfigure themselves as political subjects capable of generating public discourse.

The beginning of the lesbian movement in Latin America is intimately linked to our continent's history. The installation of authoritarian regimes in the 1960s and 1970s provoked responses from diverse social sectors, including guerrilla groups that sought to violently overthrow authoritarianism and to establish more equitable and just living conditions. In their demand for democratization and respect for human rights, civil society organizations of workers, peasants, indigenous peoples, women, youth, popular sectors, and homosexuals, among others, also sought societal change (Mogrovejo, *Amor*). This effervescence made possible a new generation of youth that challenged authority and responded with countercultural attitudes, influenced by the achievements of the Cuban revolution, Che Guevara, and the student struggles in Europe and North America, where new concepts regarding sexual freedom were being aired, and which took roots in Mexico and Latin America in the early sixties (Lumsdem, *Homosexualidad*).

The Latin American lesbian movement emerged in this context, influenced by the region's political context as well as by the political demands of the 1969 Stonewall riots, also the year in which the first homosexual group, Nuestro Mundo, emerged in Argentina in the middle of military dictatorship. Its members, the majority of whom were union activists from the lower middle class, were led by a former communist militant who had been ostracized from the party because of his homosexuality; for two years they were devoted to blasting the editorial staffs of Buenos Aires media outlets with mimeographed bulletins preaching sexual liberation. In August 1971, the linkage of Nuestro Mundo with a group of gay intellectuals inspired by the U.S. gay power movement gave birth to Argentina's Frente de Liberación Homosexual (FLH). Under the same FLH name, and in the same year, the first organized group emerged in Mexico, having as its main public face theater director Nancy Cárdenas (Mogrovejo, *Amor*).

Although smaller in number, lesbians were part of these homosexual groups. It was under the influence of Latin American feminism (labeled as Second Wave) that they began to think of themselves in terms of their particularities as women. Indeed, they had initially called themselves "feminine homosexuals"; the "lesbians" term appeared in 1975 at the Conference for the International Women's Year, under the influence of feminism.

Since the earliest mixed groups, lesbians had identified the oppression they faced from male homosexuals. Feminism provided them with the theoretical and methodological tools to analyze the unequal relations between men and women, and they were greatly surprised to find that same sexual discrimination operating inside homosexual organizations (Mogrovejo, *Amor*).

This first experience began to shape a characteristic of Latin American lesbians, insubordination against power relations that could put their autonomy at risk. And it was from this point that lesbians chose separatism as a strategy of political organization and positioning that allowed them to elaborate theoretical spaces based on autonomy (Mogrovejo, *Algunos*).

Thus, in almost all mixed groups, lesbians began to organize in specific committees and to separate from organizations of gay men in order to form autonomous groups. In Mexico, the Lambda de Liberación homosexual group that began in 1978 had a Comité de Lucha Feminista that brought feminist discussions to full meetings and where many activists were shaped by feminist principles. In Brazil, in the same year, the group Somos was formed, and the Sub-grupo Lésbico Feminista began, which later separated to form the Grupo de Acción Lésbico Feminista (GALF) and years later gave place to the Um Outro Olhar group. GALF was characterized by the promotion of political-cultural events in feminist, homosexual, and political party spaces and in civil society. They began to build a lesbian library and starting in 1981 they published twelve editions of the *Chana com chana* bulletin, which was important as one of the first lesbian-feminist publications in the region (Mogrovejo, *Amor*).[1]

AUTONOMOUS LESBIAN ORGANIZATION

The autonomous organization experience of Latin American lesbians began in 1977 in México with the Lesbos group, formed by lesbians who had participated in feminist groups and who had also experienced exclusion by heterosexual feminists. Lesbos's foundational statements were articulated to express solidarity with the struggles of all marginalized groups against repressive socioeconomic systems and to support the construction of *a new social organization*. Despite their political statement, the first discussions that caused difference and ruptures in the group were between members who felt a need to enter the public space and become involved in the lesbian struggle in the political-public dimension, which began to be called "coming out of the closet," and others who defended maintaining their status as a closed, contained group and expressed a fear of possible reprisals in a lesbophobic society, mainly in the family, work, and educational environments. Therefore, although lesbian groups started to emerge in some Latin American countries in the 1970s and 1980s, the climate of violence determined that the majority operated in a semi-underground manner, especially in the early stages.

Lesbos gave place to the famous Ollin Iskan Katuntat Bebeth Thot (OIKABETH), which in Mayan means "Movement of warrior women who open paths and spread flowers." OIKABETH had a somewhat mystical characteristic, feeding the collective imagination about the training of Amazon-like women, warriors willing to carry out the lesbian revolution and transform social relations. They worked in a coordinated manner with the Lambda lesbians and with the Frente Homosexual de Acción Revolucionaria (FHAR) and built communication links with heterosexual feminists (Mogrovejo, *Amor*). At these meetings, heterosexual feminists had the opportunity to question their fears about being stigmatized as lesbians and their resistance to accepting lesbians as peers, and how their proposals for the feminist agenda resulted from those attitudes. Lesbians named this "heterocentric hermeticism." Feminist demands were conceived for women in heterosexual relations; but the right to abortion, the struggle against violence against women, and the fight for voluntary and free maternity were not given new meanings for lesbians until some years later. At these meetings, feminists were able to cast sexuality as a space that produces power, and as a political practice linked to pleasure and negotiation and, therefore, a subject-generating experience. This relationship also served, significantly, to call into question the reproductive model of sexuality, and in this sense allowed many heterosexuals to become liberated from an imposed sexuality thanks to experimentation and constructionist concepts (Mogrovejo, *Algunos*). These same reflections were experienced in varied countries where hetero-feminism had been characterized by lesbophobia and where the presence of lesbians helped to transform the dynamics of relationships, theoretical concepts, and agendas.

OIKABETH gave place to the Lesbianas Socialistas group, which in turn gave place to the Seminario Marxista Leninista de Lesbianas Feministas group, all of which were influenced by Yan Maria Castro, a tireless activist who linked class analysis to feminism. The early 1980s also saw the emergence of La Comuna de Morelos, an interesting experiment conducted in a state near the Distrito Federal, constituted mainly by peasant lesbians who practiced a form of community economy and collective work. It ceased to exist due to the fear experienced by its members regarding possible persecution by the state (Mogrovejo, *Amor*).

THE INFLUENCE OF THE ENCUENTROS FEMINISTAS

The Encuentros Feministas Latinoamericanos y del Caribe (Latin American and Caribbean Feminist Meetings) that began in the 1980s were an important influence that allowed the Latin American lesbian movement to become regionally articulated and to deploy its autonomous current with greater strength. At the first meeting, in Colombia in 1981, the lesbianism issue was not contemplated, yet lesbians organized a forum on lesbianism in the Sexuality and Daily Life commission (Mogrovejo, *Encuentros*). At the second Encuentro Feminista, in Peru in 1983, the workshop on patriarchy and lesbianism became the most attention-grabbing workshop of the entire event. After this Encuentro the following groups emerged: Peru's GALF, Brazil's GALF, Cuarto Creciente, Oasis and MULA in Mexico, Ayuquelén in Chile, and Mitilene in the Dominican Republic.[2] After the third Encuentro Feminista in Brazil in 1985, Grupo Autogestivo de Lesbianas (GAL) began in Argentina, driven by Ilse Fuskova, who formed the Convocatoria Lesbiana group after a massive lesbian response to a television interview.[3] Preparations for the fifth Encuentro Feminista, held in 1990, mobilized an important number of lesbians who participated in Frente Sáfico (FRESA). The Las Lunas y las Otras group was formed that same year, which marked a new lesbian-feminist generation, and later the Grupo de Reflexión de Lesbianas (GRL).

After attending a 1986 conference in Geneva organized by the International Lesbian Information Service (ILIS) and experiencing the lack of spaces for lesbians within feminism, a Costa Rican lesbian proposed the need to constitute a new lesbian organization that could fight against lesbian oppression, and so it was that Las Entendidas were born in Costa Rica in March 1987 (Mogrovejo, *Amor*).[4]

THE NEED FOR THEIR OWN *ENCUENTROS*

At the third Encuentro Feminista in Brazil in 1985, GALF-Brasil and GALF-Peru sent out a call for a workshop on the question "How should we as lesbians organize ourselves?" where they expressed the need for Latin American lesbian *encuentros* outside the framework of Encuentros Feministas, and the need to foster a network for support and information exchange among the continent's lesbians (Mogrovejo, *Encuentros*).

This inclination towards autonomy among Latin American lesbians should be understood as a result of their experiences in other sectors, and their resistance to both the heterocentric policies of feminism and the phallocentric and misogynistic practices of the homosexual movement and the left (Mogrovejo, *Amor*). Calling for their own *encuentro* implied the need to rethink lesbian identities and to work on proposals that emerged from experience and the body itself. It was not easy to maintain this practice.

The first ELFLAC (Encuentros Lésbicos Feministas de América Latina y el Caribe) was held in Mexico in 1987, prior to the fourth Encuentro Feminista. The presence of international cooperation actors made this Encuentro particularly conflicted and marked a dynamic of institutionalization and struggle for power, representation, and financing that had never previously existed for lesbian work. However, a few days later at the Encuentro Feminista, lesbians presented a solid discourse that questioned the heterocentrism of feminism's collective action and agenda.

The interests of international cooperation, Eurocentric gay organizations, the party dynamics of some localities, and the lesbophobia of the state, church, and some sectors of civil society, also directly or indirectly affected the following meetings. To date, seven ELFLACs have been held with many difficulties because of these influences and also because of the organizational weakness of some countries. Nevertheless, lesbian contributions to the feminist movement, the homosexual movement, and society at large have been important.

Although in the 1970s and 1980s lesbo-feminism re-created an autonomous tradition within feminism, the coming of neoliberalism and globalization in the 1990s completely transformed social dynamics both in the production of discourse and in analyses and approaches. Lesbo-feminism's questioning of class-based, racist, generational, androcentric, and heterocentric power relations lost its central place to global-scale demands for rights. With the weakening of the nation-state due to the transformations brought by globalization, the scales of social action moved from the local to the global level, and demands promoted by supranational organizations, such as human rights, sexual and reproductive rights, and sexual diversity, took center stage (Mogrovejo, *Feminismo*). According to this logic, "minorities" were grouped under the "sexual diversity" heading, which also includes heterosexuals, thus obscuring the critique of hegemonic and normative sexuality (Mogrovejo, *Diversidad*). Interest in financing motivated this sector to become grouped under the "LGTTTB" (Lesbian, Gay, Transgender, Transsexual, Bisexual) denomination, which gives priority to dimensions of identity and where lesbian presence lost its importance or was reformulated under a masculine logic (Curiel).

The nineties also brought new philosophical concepts. With the critique of naturalism and the assumption of constructionist principles of gender, postfeminism ceased to consider the feminine subject as the center of its politics. Also according to this logic, it no longer made sense to maintain differentiated spaces based on identities, since being a man or woman, lesbian or homosexual was not an unchangeable identity or an essential nature, and thus fixed conceptions of justice and truth lost favor (Mogrovejo, *Algunos*).

In this context, the search for autonomy followed winding paths and has carried significant costs at the level of organizational experience. The institutionalization processes of the feminist movement and other social movements also affected the lesbian movement, modifying the logics of social action. In most cases, financing prioritized agendas that integrated the values of heterosexuality and the neoliberal market, generating representative bureaucracies and false leaderships. Institutionalization put in place a hegemonic feminism and lesbo-feminism, a type of discourse and logic of thought that was more European and more North-centered than Latin American. Resistance and challenges came from sectors that were critical of new forms of colonialism and dependence, and which defended self-management and thematic policies that conceptualized lesbianism as an issue beyond the dimensions of sexuality and identity.

Within this experience, it is important to highlight, both in the organization of lesbians in self-managing groups and in ELFLAC, the production of a lesbian culture that served as a reference for many lesbians in the region, who lacked a history and genealogy in which they could recognize themselves, and the construction of a culture of their own that disputed the hegemonic values of womanhood established by obligatory heterosexuality. Motivated by the desire to recuperate a femininity that had been mutilated by patriarchy and a genealogy of knowledge that had been able to escape (insofar as possible) from masculine thought, lesbians forged lesbian activist groups, groups of friends, sports groups, communes, self-managing and self-sustaining experiences, and shared economies. They shared urban and rural, spiritual, and materialistic experiences, experiences of complicity and solidarity among women, to make private spaces for reflection and political practice, and to make public spaces where day-to-day and spiritual elements converged. Artists created lesbian art; groups of painters, poets, theater-makers, and musicians organized expositions, recitals, and film festivals; these groups published magazines, organized lesbian archives and lesbian marches, and, above all, founded political parties only for lesbians. All these actions were understood as a form of political practice. And it is possible that this process also contributed to feminism an approach to the differences contained within difference.

Even though the ELFLACs, one of the most important points of political confluence of Latin American lesbians, express an autonomous and separatist conviction at the level of social organization, their nexus with feminism has been important: feminist theory has nourished lesbian reflections. In turn, feminism became more transformational, analytical, propositional, and enriching when lesbians began to generate more radical thinking and political action in the process of explaining how heterosexuality was a normative and obligatory system that had nefarious effects for women in the economic, social, cultural, symbolic, and emotional planes, limiting their autonomy and freedom (Curiel, "Lesbianismo Feminista").

Lesbo-feminism, having affirmed itself as a political option for any woman, that is, as more than sexual preference (De Lauretis, "Sujetos excéntricos"), has positioned itself as a political current that challenges one of the most imposing political regimes, heterosexuality, which determines that relationships between men and women should be relationships of domination based on the division of labor according to sex, and on the imposition of reproductive sexuality. It is a transformational proposal that assumes no sexual, emotional, economic, or cultural dependence on men. Now more than ever, the autonomous tradition puts forward the challenge of reasserting its eminently political posture, which makes of the lesbian subject a positioning against patriarchy, obligatory heterosexuality, racism, classism, neocolonialism, and neoliberalism.

Translated by Gonzalo Alcalde

NOTES

1. *Chana com chana* translates literally as "vulva with vulva."

2. Peru's GALF published the *Al Margen* magazine and assumed the organization of the second ELFLAC in 1989 but, due to violence generated by terrorist groups like Sendero Luminoso (Shining Path) and Movimiento Revolucionario Tupac Amaru (MRTA) and by the state, they asked Costa Rica's Entendidas to organize the Encuentro of 1990. Cuarto Creciente, one of the most important cultural spaces in the Mexican lesbian movement, offered a place for workshops and meetings, a cafeteria, and a library in the heart of Mexico City's historical district. Cuarto Creciente proposed to bring political analysis to personal practice and considered activism to be an intervention in daily life. Oasis was a space for meetings and documentation in Tepoztlán in Morelos, a town that is said to be magic, and to which many "alternative" people have come to live, including hippies, artisans, communes of foreigners, and a significant lesbian population, who have named the town "Lesbostlán." Oasis has also been characterized as an exclusive space for lesbians, based on separatism, autonomy, and difference. MULA worked principally on sexuality, eroticism, and lesbophobia workshops in hetero-feminist spaces. Ayuquelén emerged in 1983, during a military dictatorship, due to segregation by heterosexual feminists and to the murder of a lesbian by a police officer on a city street. Despite an adverse political context that kept them in a semi-underground state, they carried out an Encuentro Nacional and various workshops that contributed to subsequent generations.

3. They first published *Codo a Codo* in 1986 and *Cuadernos de Existencia Lesbiana* in 1987.

4. Las Entendidas published eleven issues of *La Boletina*, which allowed them to infiltrate certain spaces of Costa Rican society, principally lesbian and homosexual. In order to approach the lesbian community, for years they organized "women only nights," cultural and literary activities, and workshops to strengthen self-esteem at the La Avispa bar. They organized the second ELFLAC in 1990, in the midst of strong lesbophobic repression by the state and church.

WORKS CITED

Curiel, Ochy. "El Lesbianismo feminista en América Latina y el Caribe: Una propuesta política transformadora." Presented at the first Encuentro de Diversidad Sexual de las Mujeres, 2006. Bogota: Colectivo Triangulo Negro, 2006.

Lauretis, De. "Sujetos excéntricos: La teoría feminista y la conciencia histórica." In *De mujer a género, teoría, interpretación y práctica feministas en las ciencias sociales*, 73–113. Buenos Aires: Centro Editor de América Latina, 1993.

Lumsden, Ian. *Homosexualidad, sociedad y Estado en México*. Mexico: Colectivo Sol, 1991.

Mogrovejo, Norma. "Algunos aportes del lesbofeminismo al feminismo latinoamericano." In *Nuevos retos del feminismo colloquium*. Buenos Aires: Universidad de Buenos Aires, 2009.

———. "Diversidad sexual un concepto problemático." *Trabajo Social* 18 (2008): 62–71.

———."El feminismo en la era del neoliberalismo hegemónico." In *Mujer y violencia: El Feminismo en la era de la globalizacion:* Cuadernos del seminario 2, Ciencias Politicas y Administracion Urbana. UACM, 2009.

———. "Los Encuentros lésbico feministas de América Latina y el Caribe." In *Teoría lésbica, participación política y literatura*. Mexico City: UACM, 2004.

———, ed. *Un amor que se atrevió a decir su nombre: La lucha de las lesbianas y su relación con los movimientos feminista y homosexual en América Latina*. Mexico City: Plaza y Valdés; UACM, 2000.

DISCUSSION QUESTIONS

1. What does Mogrovejo mean when she writes that the development of the lesbian movement was influenced by the region's political context?

2. Discuss the relationship between the heterosexual feminist movement and the lesbian feminist movement.

3. What are the main characteristics Mogrovejo ascribes to lesbo-feminism? In what ways are they similar to and different from characteristics popularly associated with feminism more broadly?

DECLARATION OF LESBIANS FROM MEXICO

Publicly read at the forum on lesbianism organized by the lesbians who participated in the World Conference of the International Year of the Woman, 1975.

We lesbians from Mexico struggle so that everyone who feels attracted to others of the same sex knows that their feelings are natural, normal, dignified, and just.

Unfortunately our efforts have not been sufficiently effective, because we have not achieved a solid organization.

It is difficult, we know, to awaken the consciousness of our oppressed sisters about their own conceptions of self-denigration, but that is the unavoidable first step.

This preliminary stage, as well the sensitization of the society in which we live, is tremendously limited by the legal provisions that a judge may implement if the judge chooses to do so: laws against indecency, advocacy of a vice, printing and distribution of materials that incite someone to commit the crimes previously stated would be the most obvious indictments and would result in up to six years in prison without the right to parole.

This and the constant political action, unconstitutional but welcome by a *machista*, repressive, and depressed society, renders open organizing almost impossible.

SOURCE: This text of *Declaration of Lesbians from Mexico* is by Norma Mogrovejo and was commissioned for this volume.

We trust, however, that the tactics of struggle of our homosexual sisters and brothers in other parts of the world help us find our own path.

The liberation of homosexuals is one more form of social liberation.

Mexico City, June 1975

Translation by M. Cristina Alcalde

18

WHO IS YOUR MOTHER?
Red Roots of White Feminism

Paula Gunn Allen

At Laguna Pueblo in New Mexico, "Who is your mother?" is an important question. At Laguna, one of several of the ancient Keres gynocratic societies of the region, your mother's identity is the key to your own identity. Among the Keres, every individual has a place within the universe—human and nonhuman—and that place is defined by clan membership. In turn, clan membership is dependent on matrilineal descent. Of course, your mother is not only that woman whose womb formed and released you—the term refers in every individual case to an entire generation of women whose psychic, and consequently physical, "shape" made the psychic existence of the following generation possible. But naming your own mother (or her equivalent) enables people to place you precisely within the universal web of your life, in each of its dimensions: cultural, spiritual, personal, and historical.

Among the Keres, "context" and "matrix" are equivalent terms, and both refer to approximately the same thing as knowing your derivation and place. Failure to know your mother, that is, your position and its attendant traditions, history, and place in the scheme of things, is failure to remember your significance, your reality, your right relationship to earth and society. It is the same as being lost—isolated, abandoned, self-estranged, and alienated from your own life. This importance of tradition in the life of

SOURCE: Paula Gunn Allen, "Who Is Your Mother? Red Roots of White Feminism," in *The Sacred Hoop* (Boston: Beacon Press, 1992), 209–21.

every member of the community is not confined to Keres Indians; all American Indian Nations place great value on traditionalism.

The Native American sense of the importance of continuity with one's cultural origins runs counter to contemporary American ideas: in many instances, the immigrants to America have been eager to cast off cultural ties, often seeing their antecedents as backward, restrictive, even shameful. Rejection of tradition constitutes one of the major features of American life, an attitude that reaches far back into American colonial history and that now is validated by virtually every cultural institution in the country. Feminist practice, at least in the cultural artifacts the community values most, follows this cultural trend as well.

The American idea that the best and the brightest should willingly reject and repudiate their origins leads to an allied idea—that history, like everything in the past, is of little value and should be forgotten as quickly as possible. This all too often causes us to reinvent the wheel continually. We find ourselves discovering our collective pasts over and over, having to retake ground already covered by women in the preceding decades and centuries. The Native American view, which highly values maintenance of traditional customs, values, and perspectives, might result in slower societal change and in quite a bit less social upheaval, but it has the advantage of providing a solid sense of identity and lowered levels of psychological and interpersonal conflict.

Contemporary Indian communities value individual members who are deeply connected to the traditional ways of their people, even after centuries of concerted and brutal effort on the part of the American government, the churches, and the corporate system to break the connections between individuals and their tribal world. In fact, in the view of the traditionals, rejection of one's culture—one's traditions, language, people—is the result of colonial oppression and is hardly to be applauded. They believe that the roots of oppression are to be found in the loss of tradition and memory because that loss is always accompanied by a loss of a positive sense of self. In short, Indians think it is important to remember, while Americans believe it is important to forget.

The traditional Indians' view can have a significant impact if it is expanded to mean that the sources of social, political, and philosophical thought in the Americas not only should be recognized and honored by Native Americans but should be embraced by American society. If American society judiciously modeled the traditions of the various Native Nations, the place of women in society would become central, the distribution of goods and power would be egalitarian, the elderly would be respected, honored, and protected as a primary social and cultural resource, the ideals of physical beauty would be considerably enlarged (to include "fat," strong-featured women, gray-haired and wrinkled individuals, and others who in contemporary American culture are viewed as "ugly"). Additionally, the destruction of the biota, the life sphere, and the natural resources of the planet would be curtailed, and the spiritual nature of human and nonhuman life would become a primary organizing principle of human society. And if the traditional tribal systems that are emulated included pacifist ones, war would cease to be a major method of human problem solving.

The belief that rejection of tradition and of history is a useful response to life is reflected in America's amazing loss of memory concerning its origins in the matrix and context of Native America. America does not seem to remember that it derived its wealth, its values, its food, much of its medicine, and a large part of its "dream" from Native America. It is ignorant of the genesis of its culture in this Native American land, and that ignorance helps to perpetuate the long-standing European and Middle Eastern monotheistic, hierarchical, patriarchal cultures' oppression of women, gays and lesbians, people of color, working-class people, unemployed people, and the elderly. Hardly anyone in America speculates that the constitutional system of government might be as much a product of American Indian ideas and practices as of colonial American and Anglo-European revolutionary fervor.

Even though Indians are officially and informally ignored as intellectual movers and shapers in the United States, Britain, and Europe, they are peoples with ancient tenure on this soil. During the ages when tribal societies existed in the Americas largely untouched by patriarchal oppression, they developed elaborate systems of thought that included science, philosophy, and government based on a belief in the central importance of female energies, autonomy of individuals, cooperation, human dignity, human freedom, and egalitarian distribution of status, goods, and services. Respect for others, reverence for life, and, as a by-product, pacifism as a way of life; importance of kinship ties in the customary ordering of social interaction; a sense of the sacredness and mystery of existence; balance and harmony in relationships both sacred and secular were all features of life among the tribal confederacies and nations. And in those that lived by the largest number of these principles, gynarchy was the norm rather than the exception. Those systems are as yet unmatched in any contemporary industrial, agrarian, or postindustrial society on earth.

[. . .] there are many female gods recognized and honored by the tribes and Nations. Femaleness was highly valued, both respected and feared, and all social institutions reflected this attitude. Even modern sayings, such as the Cheyenne statement that a people is not conquered until the hearts of the women are on the ground, express the Indians' understanding that without the power of woman the people will not live, but with it, they will endure and prosper.

Indians did not confine this belief in the central importance of female energy to matters of worship. Among many of the tribes (perhaps as many as 70 percent of them in North America alone), this belief was reflected in all of their social institutions. The Iroquois Constitution or White Roots of Peace, also called the Great Law of the Iroquois, codified the Matrons' decision-making and economic power:

> The lineal descent of the people of the Five Fires [the Iroquois Nations] shall run in the female line. Women shall be considered the progenitors of the Nation. They shall own the land and the soil. Men and women shall follow the status of their mothers. (Article 44)
>
> The women heirs of the chieftainship titles of the League shall be called Oiner or Otinner [Noble] for all time to come. (Article 45)

If a disobedient chief persists in his disobedience after three warnings [by his female relatives, by his male relatives, and by one of his fellow council members, in that order], the matter shall go to the council of War Chiefs. The Chiefs shall then take away the title of the erring chief *by order of the women in whom the title is vested*. When the chief is deposed, the women shall notify the chiefs of the League . . . and the chiefs of the League shall sanction the act. The women will then select another of their sons as a candidate and the chiefs shall elect him. (Article 19) (Emphasis mine)

The Matrons held so much policy-making power traditionally that once, when their position was threatened they demanded its return, and consequently the power of women was fundamental in shaping the Iroquois Confederation sometime in the sixteenth or early seventeenth century. It was women

who fought what may have been the first successful feminist rebellion in the New World. The year was 1600, or thereabouts, when these tribal feminists decided that they had had enough of unregulated warfare by their men. Lysistratas among the Indian women proclaimed a boycott on lovemaking and childbearing. Until the men conceded to them the power to decide upon war and peace, there would be no more warriors. Since the men believed that the women alone knew the secret of childbirth, the rebellion was instantly successful.

In the Constitution of Deganawidah, the founder of the Iroquois Confederation of Nations had said: "He caused the body of our mother, the woman, to be of great worth and honor. He purposed that she shall be endowed and entrusted with the birth and upbringing of men, and that she shall have the care of all that is planted by which life is sustained and supported and the power to breathe is fortified: *and moreover that the warriors shall be her assistants*." (Emphasis mine)

The footnote of history was curiously supplied when Susan B. Anthony began her "Votes for Women" movement two and a half centuries later. Unknowingly the feminists chose to hold their founding convention of latter-day suffragettes in the town of Seneca [Falls], New York. The site was just a stone's throw from the old council house where the Iroquois women had plotted their feminist rebellion.[1]

Beliefs, attitudes, and laws such as these became part of the vision of American feminists and of other human liberation movements around the world. Yet feminists too often believe that no one has ever experienced the kind of society that empowered women and made that empowerment the basis of its rules of civilization. The price the feminist community must pay because it is not aware of the recent presence of gynarchical societies on this continent is unnecessary confusion, division, and much lost time.

THE ROOT OF OPPRESSION IS LOSS OF MEMORY

An odd thing occurs in the minds of Americans when Indian civilization is mentioned: little or nothing. As I write this, I am aware of how far removed my version of the roots of American feminism must seem to those steeped in either mainstream or radical versions of feminism's history. I am keenly aware of the lack of images Americans have about our continent's recent past. I am intensely conscious of popular notions of Indian women as beasts of burden, squaws, traitors, or, at best, vanished denizens of a long-lost wilderness. How odd, then, must my contention seem that the gynocratic tribes of the American continent provided the basis for all the dreams of liberation that characterize the modern world.

We as feminists must be aware of our history on this continent. We need to recognize that the same forces that devastated the gynarchies of Britain and the Continent also devastated the ancient African civilizations, and we must know that those same materialistic, antispiritual forces are presently engaged in wiping out the same gynarchical values, along with the peoples who adhere to them, in Latin America. I am convinced that those wars were and continue to be about the imposition of patriarchal civilization over the holistic, pacifist, and spirit-based gynarchies they supplant. To that end the wars of imperial conquest have not been solely or even mostly waged over the land and its resources, but they have been fought within the bodies, minds, and hearts of the people of the earth for dominion over them. I think this is the reason traditionals say we must remember our origins, our cultures, our histories, our mothers and grandmothers, for without that memory, which implies continuance rather than nostalgia, we are doomed to engulfment by a paradigm that is fundamentally inimical to the vitality, autonomy, and self-empowerment essential for satisfying, high-quality life.

The vision that impels feminists to action was the vision of the Grandmothers' society, the society that was captured in the words of the sixteenth-century explorer Peter Martyr nearly five hundred years ago. It is the same vision repeated over and over by radical thinkers of Europe and America, from François Villon to John Locke, from William Shakespeare to Thomas Jefferson, from Karl Marx to Friedrich Engels, from Benito Juarez to Martin Luther King, from Elizabeth Cady Stanton to Judy Grahn, from Harriet Tubman to Audre Lorde, from Emma Goldman to Bella Abzug, from Malinalli to Cherríe Moraga, and from Iyatiku to me. That vision as Martyr told it is of a country where there are "no soldiers, no gendarmes or police, no nobles, kings, regents, prefects, or judges, no prisons, no lawsuits. . . . All are equal and free," or so Friedrich Engels recounts Martyr's words.

Columbus wrote:

Nor have I been able to learn whether they [the inhabitants of the islands he visited on his first journey to the New World] held personal property, for it seemed to me that whatever one had, they all took shares of. . . . They are so ingenuous and free with all they have, that no one would believe it who has not seen it; of anything that they possess, if it be asked of them, they never say no; on the contrary, they invite you to share it and show as much love as if their hearts went with it.

At least that's how the Native Caribbean people acted when the whites first came among them; American Indians are the despair of social workers, bosses, and missionaries even now because of their deeply ingrained tendency to spend all they have, mostly on others. In any case, as the historian William Brandon notes,

> the Indian *seemed* free, to European eyes, gloriously free, to the European soul shaped by centuries of toil and tyranny, and this impression operated profoundly on the process of history and the development of America. Something in the peculiar character of the Indian world gave an impression of classlessness, of propertylessness, and that in turn led to an impression, as H. H. Bancroft put it, of "humanity unrestrained . . . in the exercise of liberty absolute."

A FEMINIST HEROINE

Early in the women's suffrage movement, Eva Emery Dye, an Oregon suffragette, went looking for a heroine to embody her vision of feminism. She wanted a historical figure whose life would symbolize the strengthened power of women. She found Sacagawea (or Sacajawea) buried in the journals of Lewis and Clark. The Shoshoni teenager had traveled with the Lewis and Clark expedition, carrying her infant son, and on a small number of occasions acted as translator.

Dye declared that Sacagawea, whose name is thought to mean Bird Woman, had been the guide to the historic expedition, and through Dye's work Sacagawea became enshrined in American memory as a moving force and friend of the whites, leading them in the settlement of western North America.

But Native American roots of white feminism reach back beyond Sacagawea. The earliest white women on this continent were well acquainted with tribal women. They were neighbors to a number of tribes and often shared food, information, childcare, and health care. Of course little is made of these encounters in official histories of colonial America, the period from the Revolution to the Civil War, or on the ever-moving frontier. Nor, to my knowledge, has either the significance or incidence of intermarriage between Indian and white or between Indian and Black been explored. By and large, the study of Indian-white relations has been focused on government and treaty relations, warfare, missionization, and education. It has been almost entirely documented in terms of formal white Christian patriarchal impacts and assaults on Native Americans, though they are not often characterized as assaults but as "civilizing the savages." Particularly in organs of popular culture and miseducation, the focus has been on what whites imagine to be degradation of Indian women ("squaws"), their equally imagined love of white government and white conquest ("princesses"), and the horrifyingly misleading, fanciful tales of "bloodthirsty, backward primitives" assaulting white Christian settlers who were looking for life, liberty, and happiness in their chosen land.

But, regardless of official versions of relations between Indians and whites or other segments of the American population, the fact remains that great numbers of apparently "white" or "Black" Americans carry notable degrees of Indian blood. With that blood has come the culture of the Indian, informing the lifestyles, attitudes, and values of their descendants. Somewhere along the line—and often quite recently—an Indian woman was giving birth to and raising the children of a family both officially and informally designated as white or Black—not Indian. In view of this, it should be evident that one of the major enterprises of Indian women in America has been the transfer of Indian values and culture to as large and influential a segment of American immigrant populations as possible. Their success in this endeavor is amply demonstrated in the Indian values and social styles that increasingly characterize American life. Among these must be included "permissive" childrearing practices, for in Indian societies imprisoning, torturing, caning, strapping, starving, or verbally abusing children [were] considered outrageous behavior. Native Americans did not believe that physical or psychological abuse of children would result in their edification. They did not believe that children are born in sin, are congenitally predisposed to evil, or that a good parent who wishes the child to gain salvation, achieve success, or earn the respect of her or his fellows can be helped to those ends by physical or emotional torture.

The early Americans saw the strongly protective attitude of the Indian people as a mark of their "savagery"—as they saw the Indian's habit of bathing frequently, their sexual openness, their liking for scant clothing, their raucous laughter at most things, their suspicion and derision of authoritarian structures, their quick pride, their genuine courtesy, their willingness to share what they had with others less fortunate than they, their egalitarianism, their ability to act as if various lifestyles were a normal part of living, and their granting that women were of equal or, in individual cases, of greater value than men.

Yet the very qualities that marked Indian life in the sixteenth century have, over the centuries since contact between the two worlds occurred, come to mark much of contemporary American life. And those qualities, which I believe have passed into white culture from Indian culture, are the very ones that fundamentalists, immigrants from Europe, the Middle East, and Asia often find the most reprehensible. Third- and fourth-generation Americans indulge in growing nudity, informality in social relations, egalitarianism, and the rearing of women who value autonomy, strength, freedom, and personal dignity—and who are often derided by European, Asian, and Middle Eastern men for those qualities. Contemporary Americans value leisure almost as much as tribal people do. They find themselves increasingly unable to accept child abuse as a reasonable way to nurture. They bathe more than any other industrial people on earth—much to the scorn of their white cousins across the Atlantic, and they sometimes enjoy a good laugh even at their own expense (though they still have a less developed sense of the ridiculous than one might wish).

Contemporary Americans find themselves more and more likely to adopt a "live and let live" attitude in matters of personal sexual and social styles. Two-thirds of their diet and a large share of their medications and medical treatments mirror or are directly derived from Native American sources. Indianization is not a simple concept, to be sure, and it is one that Americans often find themselves resisting; but it is a process that has taken place, regardless of American resistance to recognizing the source of many if not most of Americans' vaunted freedoms in our personal, family, social, and political arenas.

This is not to say that Americans have become Indian in every attitude, value, or social institution. Unfortunately, Americans have a way to go in learning how to live in the world in ways that improve the quality of life for each individual while doing minimal damage to the biota, but they have adapted certain basic qualities of perception and certain attitudes that are moving them in that direction.

AN INDIAN-FOCUSED VERSION OF AMERICAN HISTORY

American colonial ideas of self-government came as much from the colonists' observations of tribal governments as from their Protestant or Greco-Roman heritage. Neither Greece nor Rome had pluralistic democracy as that concept has been understood in the United States since Andrew Jackson, but the tribes, particularly the gynarchical tribal confederacies, did. It is true that the *oligarchic* form of government that colonial Americans established was originally based on Greco-Roman systems in a number of important ways, such as its restriction of citizenship to propertied white males over twenty-one years of age, but it was never a form that Americans as a whole have been entirely comfortable with. Politics and government in the United States during the Federalist period also reflected the English common law system as it had evolved under patriarchal feudalism and monarchy—hence the United States' retention of slavery and restriction of citizenship to propertied white males.

The Federalists did make one notable change in the feudal system from which their political system derived on its Anglo side. They rejected blooded aristocracy and monarchy. This idea came from the Protestant Revolt to be sure, but it was at least reinforced by colonial America's proximity to American Indian nonfeudal confederacies and their concourse with those confederacies over the two hundred years of the colonial era. It was this proximity and concourse that enabled the revolutionary theorists to "dream up" a system in which all local polities would contribute to and be protected by a central governing body responsible for implementing policies that bore on the common interest of all. It should also be noted that the Reformation followed Columbus's contact with the Americas and that his and Martyr's reports concerning Native Americans' free and easy egalitarianism were in circulation by the time the Reformation took hold.

The Iroquois federal system, like that of several in the vicinity of the American colonies, is remarkably similar to the organization of the federal system of the United States. It was made up of local, "state," and federal bodies composed of executive, legislative, and judicial branches. The Council of Matrons was the executive: it instituted and determined general policy. The village, tribal (several villages), and Confederate councils determined and implemented policies when they did not conflict with the broader Council's decisions or with theological precepts that ultimately determined policy at all levels. The judicial was composed of the men's councils and the Matrons' council, who sat together to make decisions. Because the Matrons were the ceremonial center of the system, they were also the prime policy makers.

Obviously, there are major differences between the structure of the contemporary American government and that of the Iroquois. Two of those differences were and are crucial to the process of just government. The Iroquois system is spirit-based, while that of the United States is secular, and the Iroquois Clan Matrons formed the executive. The female executive function was directly tied to the ritual nature of the Iroquois politic, for the executive was lodged in the hands of the Matrons of particular clans across village, tribe, and national lines. The executive office was hereditary, and only sons of eligible clans could serve, at the behest of the Matrons of their clans, on the councils at the three levels. Certain daughters inherited the office of Clan Matron through their clan affiliations. No one could impeach or disempower a Matron, though her violation of certain laws could result in her ineligibility for the Matrons' council. For example, a woman who married *and took her husband's name* could not hold the title Matron.

American ideas of social justice came into sharp focus through the commentaries of Iroquois observers who traveled in France in the colonial period. These observers expressed horror at the great gap between the lifestyles of the wealthy and the poor, remarking to the French philosopher Montaigne, who would heavily influence the radical communities of Europe, England, and America, that "they had noticed that in Europe there seemed to be two moities, consisting of the rich 'full gorged' with wealth, and the poor, starving 'and bare with need and povertie.' The Indian tourists not only marveled at the division, but marveled that the poor endured 'such an injustice, and that they took not the others by the throte, or set fire on their house.'" It must be noted that the urban poor eventually did just that in the French Revolution. The writings of Montaigne and of those he influenced provided the theoretical framework and the vision that propelled the struggle for liberty, justice, and equality on the Continent and later throughout the British empire.

The feminist idea of power as it ideally accrues to women stems from tribal sources. The central importance of the Clan Matrons in the formulation and determination of domestic and foreign policy as well as in their primary role in the ritual and ceremonial life of their respective Nations was the single most important attribute of the Iroquois, as of the Cherokee and Muskogee, who traditionally inhabited the southern Atlantic region. The latter peoples were removed to what is now Oklahoma during the Jackson administration, but prior to the American Revolution they had regular and frequent communication with and impact on both the British colonizers and later the American people, including the African peoples brought here as slaves.

Ethnographer Lewis Henry Morgan wrote an account of Iroquoian matriarchal culture, published in 1877, that heavily influenced Marx and the development of communism, particularly lending it the idea of the liberation of women from patriarchal dominance. The early socialists in Europe, especially in Russia, saw women's liberation as a central aspect of the socialist revolution. Indeed, the basic ideas of socialism, the egalitarian distribution of goods and power, the peaceful ordering of society, and the right of every member of society to participate in the work and benefits of that society, are ideas that pervade American Indian political thought and action. And it is through various channels—the informal but deeply effective Indianization of Europeans, and christianizing Africans, the social and political theory of the confederacies feuding and then intertwining with European dreams of liberty and justice, and, more recently, the work of Morgan and the writings of Marx and Engels—that the age-old gynarchical systems of egalitarian government found their way into contemporary feminist theory.

When Eva Emery Dye discovered Sacagawea and honored her as the guiding spirit of American womanhood, she may have been wrong in bare historical fact, but she was quite accurate in terms of deeper truth. The statues that have been erected depicting Sacagawea as a Matron in her prime signify an understanding in the American mind, however unconscious, that the source of just government, of right ordering of social relationships, the dream of "liberty and justice for all" can be gained only by following the Indian Matrons' guidance. For, as Dr. Anna Howard Shaw said of Sacagawea at the National American Woman's Suffrage Association in 1905:

> Forerunner of civilization, great leader of men, patient and motherly woman, we bow our hearts to do you honor! . . . May we the daughters of an alien race . . . learn the lessons of calm endurance, of patient persistence and unfaltering courage exemplified in your life, in our efforts to lead men through the Pass of justice, which goes over the mountains of prejudice and conservatism to the broad land of the perfect freedom of a true republic; one in which men and women together shall in perfect equality solve the problems of a nation that knows no caste, no race, no sex in opportunity, in responsibility or in justice! May "the eternal womanly" ever lead us on!

NOTE

1. Stan Steiner, *The New Indians* (N.Y.: Dell, 1968), 219–20.

DISCUSSION QUESTIONS

1. One of the most provocative ideas in "Who Is Your Mother?" is that while "Indians think it is important to remember . . . Americans believe it is important to forget." Do you agree with Gunn Allen that Americans believe that "history, like everything else in the past, is of little value and should be forgotten as quickly as possible"? What's the evidence for this, both in her essay and in your own experience?

2. Discuss the importance of motherhood as a source of power in Native American culture, as described by Gunn Allen and illustrated by the Cherokee documents, noting any connections you see with motherhood as a source of power in Latin America, as described in chapter 21.

3. Which of the ideas that Gunn Allen describes as originating with Native American cultures are, in your opinion, the most valuable to emphasize, appropriate, or perhaps revive for feminist politics today?

CHEROKEE WOMEN AND NANYE'HI / NANCY WARD, *SPEECHES AND LETTERS*

As the large and powerful Cherokee nation faced the challenges of maintaining its sovereignty, culture, and vast territory against the continuing encroachments of white settlers in the eighteenth century, it relied upon the authority, courage, and intelligence of Cherokee women. In traditionally matriarchal Cherokee society, women anchored their families, oversaw the use of the land, and held political offices like *Ghighua,* or Beloved Woman. They participated fully in the political life of their nation.

Four documented speeches from the 1780s demonstrate how in addressing Euro-American colonists, Cherokee women diplomats consistently drew from a powerful rhetorical tradition that established motherhood as the grounds for political authority and judgment. The first document is a speech made by a group of Cherokee women to a diplomatic commission organized by General Nathanael Greene (1742–86), a major general of the Continental Army during the Revolutionary War.[1] In this speech, the Cherokee women assert their authority as women and "mothers" over the male Euro-American diplomats whom they characterize as "sons," and they remind their Euro-American auditors of the great rates of intermarriage between Cherokee and European-descended peoples in the South, underscoring their common stake in peace and reconciliation.

The second document is a speech by Nanye'hi / Nancy Ward.[2] Born around the year 1738 into a politically powerful family of the Wolf Clan, at Chota, a Cherokee city traditionally designated as a "mother town," "peace town," or place of refuge, the Cherokee warrior and diplomat Nanye'hi married a Cherokee man named Tsu-la, or Kingfisher, in 1751. Tsu-la and Nanye'hi fought side by side during a conflict between the Cherokee and Creek nations; when Tsu-la was shot, Nanye'hi picked up his rifle and helped lead the Cherokee to victory. For her valor, she was selected to hold the traditional office of *Ghighua,* or Beloved Woman. (Nanye'hi became known as Nancy

SOURCE: Nanye'hi/Nancy Ward (Cherokee, 1738?–1824), "Speeches to the U.S. Treaty Commissioners," and Cherokee Women, "Speech to General Greene's Commission" and "Letter to Governor Benjamin Franklin," in *Transatlantic Feminism in the Age of Revolutions,* ed. Lisa L. Moore, Joanne Brooks, and Catherine Wigginton (New York: Oxford University Press, 2011), 178–82.

1. The speech is from *Report of Proceedings of a Commission Appointed by General Nathanael Greene on 26 February 1781 to Conduct Talks with the Cherokees,* Nathanael Greene Papers, 1775–1785, folder 5, Library of Congress.

2. The speech is from *Report of Proceedings,* Nathanael Greene Papers, 1775–1785, folder 5, Library of Congress.

Ward after marrying Bryant Ward, an Irish trader, in the 1750s. Some historians have viewed their marriage as a conscious act of international diplomacy to foster peace and trade. Under the matrilineal Cherokee system, Bryant Ward married into Nanye'hi's clan and family, benefiting from her political status.)

As a Beloved Woman, Nanye'hi held a voting position on the Cherokee General Council, served as the leader of the Cherokee Women's Council, and acted as a diplomat and negotiator. During her tenure, the vast Cherokee Territory—encompassing parts of Tennessee, Kentucky, Virginia, North Carolina, South Carolina, Alabama, and Georgia—was under constant threat from white settlers. In July 1781, at a treaty negotiation on the Holston River in Tennessee, Ward called for peace and demanded that U.S. treaty commissioners "let [their] Women hear our Words." Her words echo those of her mother's brother Chief Attakullakulla, who once demanded of white negotiators, "Where are your women?" To Cherokee people accustomed to matrilineal social structures and women's political participation, the political voicelessness of women in the United States was symptomatic of the imbalance, disorder, and violence of white colonial society. In her speech to U.S. commissioners at the negotiation of the Treaty of Hopewell (1785), the third document in this selection, Nanye'hi used the rhetoric of motherhood to counter Anglo-American rhetorical conventions that positioned whites as "fathers" or "elder brothers" to Native people, to establish her moral and political authority as a mother figure to both Native peoples and whites, and to indicate that kinship is the proper framework for diplomatic relations.

A fourth document by Cherokee women diplomats marshals the same powerful rhetoric of political motherhood to address Benjamin Franklin, then governor of Pennsylvania. Some scholars believe that this document, which was endorsed by at least three Cherokee women, was authored by Nancy Ward. Others, including Cherokee scholars Daniel Heath Justice and Virginia Carney, suggest that "Katteuha" may have been the name of another Beloved Woman of Chota or a collective of lesser-known Beloved Women.[3]

Cherokee Women, **Speech to General Greene's Commission,** *July 26–August 2, 1781*

Beloved Men and Warriors

We the Women of the Cherokee Nation now speak to you. We are Mothers, and have many sons, some of them Warriors, an[d] beloved Men. We call you also our sons: We have a right to call you so, because you are the sons of Mothers, and all descended from the same Woman at first. We say you are our Sons, because by Women, you were brought forth into this World, nursed, suckled, and raised up to be men befo[re] you reached your present Greatness. You are our Son[s.] Why should there be any Difference amongst us,

3. Headnote adapted with permission from Lisa L. Moore, Joanna Brooks, and Caroline Wigginton, *Transatlantic Feminisms in the Age of Revolutions.*

we liv[e] on the same Land with you, and ou[r] Peo[ple] [ar]e mixed with white Blood: one third of our [people are] mixed with white Bl[oo]d: why will you ga[*text missing*] for us. Here is wha [*text missing*]indled. I placed our elder Brother Col. [Martin] here to take care of it for us. There has been a little [disturb]ance betwixt you and us, and so has it been, [betwixt] [you a]nd your Fathers over the great Water: but a[ll is w]ell again. Col. Martin our elder Brother will take care of it for us. We hope although there has been a sho[w?] [of] [d]isturbance between us that our elder Brothers will not [thin]k of taking away this beloved spot reserved to hold g[ran]d Talks on.

Nanye'hi / Nancy Ward, **Speech to the U.S. Treaty Commissioners, 1781**

we did never concern in the [for]mer Treaty, which has been broken, but we do in this, and on our account, who are your Mothers, let it never [be] broken. You know Women are always looked upon as nothing; but we are your Mothers; you are our sons. Our cry [is] all for Peace; let it continue because we are Your Mothers. This Peace must last forever. Let your Womens sons be Ours, and let our sons be yours. Let your Women hear our Words.

Nanye'hi / Nancy Ward, **Speech to the U.S. Treaty Commissioners, 1785**

I am fond of hearing that there is a peace, and I hope you have now taken us by the hand in real friendship. I have a pipe and a little tobacco to give the commissioners to smoke in friendship. I look on you and the red people as my children. Your having determined on peace is most pleasing to me, for I have seen much trouble during the late war. I am old, but I hope yet to bear children, who will grow up and people our nation, as we are now to be under the protection of Congress, and shall have no more disturbance.—[A string, little old pipe, and some tobacco.][4]

The talk I have given, is from the young warriors I have raised in my town as well as myself. They rejoice that we have peace, and we hope the chain of friendship will never more be broke.—[A string of beads.][5]

Cherokee Women, **Letter to Governor Benjamin Franklin, *September 8, 1787***

Brother,

I am in hopes my Brothers & the Beloved men near the water side will heare from me. This day I filled the pipes that they smoaked in piece, and I am in hopes the smoake has Reached up to the skies above. I here send you a piece of the same Tobacco, and am in

---

4. This list indicates wampum, a traditional implement of indigenous diplomacy, and other ceremonial items presented by Nanye'hi during her speech.—Ed.

5. Wampum.—Ed.

hopes you & your Beloved men will smoake it in Friendship—and I am glad in my heart that I am the mother of men that will smoak it in piece.

Brother,

I am in hopes if you Rightly consider it that woman is the mother of All—and that woman Does not pull Children out of Trees or Stumps nor out of old Logs, but out of their Bodies, so that they ought to mind what a woman says, and look upon her as a mother—and I have Taken the privelage to Speak to you as my own Children, & the same as if you had sucked my Breast—and I am in hopes you have a beloved woman amongst you who will help to put her Children Right if they do wrong, as I shall do the same—the great men have all promised to Keep the path clear & straight, as my Children shall Keep the path clear & white so that the Messengers shall go & come in safety Between us—the old people is never done Talking to their Children—which makes me say so much as I do. The Talk you sent to me was to talk to my Children, which I have done this day, and they all liked my Talk well, which I am in hopes you will heare from me Every now & then that I keep my Children in piece—tho' I am a woman giving you this Talk, I am in hopes that you and all the Beloved men in Congress will pay particular Attention to it, as I am Delivering it to you from the Bottom of my heart, that they will Lay this on the white stool in Congress, wishing them all well & success in all their undertakings—I hold fast the good Talk I Received from you my Brother, & thanks you kindly for your good Talks, & your presents, & the kind usage you gave to my son.

From KATTEUHA, The Beloved woman of Chota.[6]

[Indorsed by Kaattahee, Scolecutta, and Kaattahee, Cherokee women.]

6. Scholars believe that Katteuha was either a mistranscription of Nanye'hi's title *ghighua*, the name of the Cherokee women's council, or the name of another Cherokee woman who authored this document.—Ed.

19

SUFFERING LIKE AN AFRICAN GIRL

Trauma Embodied in Tsitsi Dangarembga's
Nervous Conditions

Tamara Beauboeuf-Lafontant

[I]f you don't think of yourself as neatly fitting into either the category of the
unified, universalizing subject, which white men usually claim, or the category
of the "Other," usually spoken for by white women or men of color, . . . if you
happen to think of yourself as occupying two categories simultaneously—if you
are black and a woman . . .—or if you simply wish to write about such issues
conjunctively, then you're in danger of not making much sense, because you are
attempting to "speak" from the still radically unspeakable position of the
"other" of the "other."

MICHELE WALLACE, "VARIATIONS ON NEGATION AND
THE HERESY OF BLACK FEMINIST CREATIVITY"

The history of colonization, imperialism is a record of betrayal, of lies, and
deceits. The demand for that which is real is a demand for reparation, for
transformation. In resistance, the exploited, the oppressed work to expose the
false reality—to claim and recover ourselves. We make the revolutionary history,
telling the past as we have learned it, mouth-to-mouth, telling the present as we
see, feel, and know it with our hearts and in our words.

BELL HOOKS, *TALKING BACK*

I encountered Tsitsi Dangarembga's first novel, *Nervous Conditions* (1989), in my early
twenties, as I was beginning a program in Africana studies. This audacious, first-person,
coming-of-age story of a rural African girl engaging with a British colonial education in
the Southern Rhodesia of the 1960s crystallized many of what became my long-standing
interests—the development of girls in the institution of adolescence, the embodiment of
racialized gender, and the emergence of psychological and physical distress traceable not
to biology but to the material and ideological constraints of womanhood. The

novel remains a visceral exploration of the realities made visible when the colonial subject and "native" is intentionally written as a girl or woman. Like Toni Morrison's *The Bluest Eye* (1970), Jamaica Kincaid's *Annie John* (1985), and Merle Hodge's *Crick Crack, Monkey* (1981), *Nervous Conditions* takes seriously the psyche of Black diasporic girls and women.

Articulating the experience and violence of white colonialism and Black patriarchy from within and underneath, Dangarembga constructs a novel that provides two African girls, the cousins Tambudzai and Nyasha Sigauke, with epistemic privilege and narrative authority. Hers is a novel of young women subjugated through both tradition and modernity, and thereby forced to exist in the social location of what Black feminist Michele Wallace usefully terms the other's other—a space of presumed "nothingness that results from the intense pressure of being the wrong race, the wrong class and the wrong sex" (219). Through the cousins' emotional intimacy, which the adult narrator Tambu describes as "my first love affair, the first time that I grew to be fond of someone of whom I did not wholeheartedly approve" (78), the novel explores a fundamental relatedness between the body, colonialism, and gender, bringing to light an epistemological space twice removed from white patriarchal centers of power and knowledge.

Nervous Conditions chronicles Tambu's girlhood and adolescence, between the ages of eight and fifteen, and her move (some would say "ascent") from second-born village girl to scholarship student at an exclusive Roman Catholic private school, Young Ladies College of the Sacred Heart. The excerpt conveys her sense of accomplishment and triumph over her peasant background as she enters an environment more English than anyone else in her extended family has experienced. But this very self-absorbed enthusiasm is belied by the presence and comments of Nyasha, who refuses to submit to any external authority in the name of goodness.

Tambu's Uncle Babamukuru and Aunt Maiguru, Nyasha's parents, serve as surrogate parents during her two years of attendance at the mission school that he directs. Throughout this period of living at the school and sharing a room, the lives and psyches of Tambu and Nyasha become increasingly interdependent. Although Tambu exhibited much pluck earlier in the novel, pushing for her own education despite Shona tradition, which held out only the prospects of marriage and motherhood for her, as an adolescent Tambu increasingly comports herself as a thankful poor relative and a good girl. Both are safe personas to adopt as she seeks alternatives to the situation to which her mother has become resigned—being crushed by "the poverty of blackness on one side and the weight of womanhood on the other" (16).

Despite her strategy of accommodation, Tambu is drawn to Nyasha's staunch refusal to behave like a dutiful young woman. Unlike most "good" Shona adolescent girls and women, Nyasha is "volatile and strong-willed" and "respond[s] to challenges . . . [with an] intensity and determination" (116). She is forthright in a way perhaps tolerated in girlhood, in that developmental period Tambu describes as "before [one's] breasts grew too large" (4), but her assertiveness is clearly at odds with a girl's physical and cultural entrance into womanhood. By maintaining what girls' studies scholar Annie Rogers terms "ordinary courage" well into her adolescence, Nyasha dramatically refuses to edit down her knowledge and feelings about life as the other's other. In the process, she is vilified by her father as a whore and characterized by her extended family as overtaken by a destructive Englishness.

Throughout the novel, Nyasha insists on the existential danger of subordination.

> But when you've seen different things you want to be sure you're adjusting to the right thing. You can't go on all the time being whatever's necessary. You've got to have some conviction, and I'm convinced I don't want to be anyone's underdog. It's not right for any-one to be that. But once you get used to it, well, it just seems natural and you just carry on. And that's the end of you. You're trapped. They control everything you do. (117)

This caution is relevant not just to her own situation as the willful daughter of a highly esteemed patriarch but to that of the other gender-disadvantaged girls and women of the novel. As she articulates during her full-bodied tirade in the excerpt, even African boys and men—such as her father and older brother Chido—can only move forward in the colonial situation by "groveling," that is, behaving like "a good munt. A bloody good kaf-fir" (200) in deference to white power. In Tambu's case, her servility takes the form of optimistically minimizing the fact that she is viewed and treated as one of "the Africans," rather than as a full-fledged member of this elite school community of white girls and women. In pre-liberation Zimbabwe, Nyasha and the text remind us, there is no one nervous condition, but many, and they articulate with the structures of domination that press both African women and men into particular racialized and gendered forms of servitude to white colonial authority.

The novel *Nervous Conditions* also speaks to embodiment and the form rebellion takes when one is relatively powerless as the other's other. The European psychiatrist's categori-cal and brutally unfeeling pronouncement and dismissal of Nyasha's anorexia on the grounds that "Africans did not suffer in the way we had described. She was making a scene" (201) is disturbingly familiar. It parallels a still audible presumption that diasporic Black girls and women operate wholly outside of discourses, material realities, and degradations known to impact white women. To suffer like a European would mean that Nyasha had the complexity, sensibilities, and vulnerabilities that have long exalted white women over oth-ers and kept in place a dual and hierarchical construction of womanhood along racial lines (Hurtado). To appreciate Nyasha as more than an impersonating hysteric, we have to revisit "the historical view of Black women as bodies without minds" (Thompson 15).

What Dangarembga so boldly insists on and reveals in the novel is that Black girls and women have a subjectivity in excess of their social roles or utility to social dominants. Both the novel and feminist clinical literature account for anorexia as the distress of individuals who are forced through physical or psychological trauma to live on two dis-connected levels, blocked in their ability to live with integrity in their social worlds. Like

Dangarembga, sociologist Becky Thompson, in her study *A Hunger So Wide and So Deep*, highlights the traumatic origins to problem eating among women. And like Dangarembga's postcolonial novel, Thompson's multiracial feminist focus challenges mainstream approaches in both psychology and feminism for their collusion in reifying an image of eating disorders as limited to the most socially advantaged girls and women. Anorexia and other eating problems are stereotypically but not experientially limited to white Western women: The images of the nineteenth-century hysteric and the twentieth-century anorectic as young, white, and materially comfortable reflect the narrow population of women among whom such disorders have been studied (Bordo, Thompson). Examining how and why lesbians, poor women, and women of color develop symbolic relationships to food, eating, and their bodies, Thompson argues that anorexia, bulimia, and compulsive overeating are "logical, creative responses to trauma" that begin as "survival strategies—as sensible acts of self-preservation—in response to myriad injustices including racism, sexism, homophobia, classism, the stress of acculturation, and emotional, physical, and sexual abuse" (1–2). For Nyasha, as well as the profile-atypical women with eating problems whom Thompson studied, the body is the site of their domination, as well as their last refuge from material, physical, and psychic violations.

Nyasha's body as well as her anorexia are multiply determined. Her initial slimming of her body is a way to fit into British society while her parents are studying, on scholarship, for their advanced degrees. She alters its size and adornment to become more fashionable and modern, and less "backwardly" African. Upon returning home to Southern Rhodesia as an uncomfortable cultural hybrid and under heavy pressure as a young thirteen-year-old to be compliant and good, Nyasha begins utilizing her body for self-protection. Although Western beauty norms are implicated in Nyasha's anorexia, it is fundamentally about protest, not appearance, using the limited means at her disposal—her voice and, failing that, her body.

Nyasha's anorexia is a form of vigilance, as she steels herself against the incorporation of harmful knowledge and expectations. It is a regime, a discipline of mind and body, that allows her to question an adolescence comprising a steady diet of Englishness in schools and male dominance in her family and community. Many forces estrange her—not only the Englishness that Tambu's mother singles out, but also the native patriarchy and the intense silencing of women it rests upon. Nyasha's body literally holds meaning that others would prefer to ignore—it sees and lives at the intersection of lies, ruses, and psychic wounding, all justified under the guise of social progress. Regarding such knowledge, these inconvenient truths about colonial reality, Nyasha has struggled to "keep it in but it's powerful" (201).

Nyasha's anorexia is an embodied protest. Her spectacular fit of yelling, swearing, destruction of items, and self-harm dramatizes a colonial condition in which people are divided, turned against each other, and pressed into stunting patterns of deference to white authority. As Dangarembga herself understood at the time of writing, "the sentiments I was expressing were dangerous: they were untempered, conceding nothing to the tastes of the society about which I was writing" (43). And with assertiveness and without apology, Dangarembga challenges the framing of Black women (on the continent, but also throughout the diaspora) through a one-dimensional ideal of fortitude, invulnerability, and psychological absence. To appreciate that Black women can and do develop symbolic relationships to their bodies and eating is to recognize that the cultural and societal imagery of Black women as monochromatically strong and invulnerable is itself based in a reductive view of them as other than, less than, human, and inherently devoid of the capacity to develop a layered understanding of self and society.

WORKS CITED

Bordo, Susan. "Not Just 'A White Girl's Thing': The Changing Face of Food and Body Image Problems." In *Critical Feminist Approaches to Eating Disorders,* 46–59. Edited by Helen Malson and Maree Burns. New York: Routledge, 2009.

Dangarembga, Tsitsi. *Nervous Conditions.* Seattle: Seal Press, 1989.

———. "This Year, Next Year . . . ." *The Women's Review of Books* 8, no. 10–11 (1991): 43–44.

George, Rosemary Marangoly, and Helen Scott. "An Interview with Tsitsi Dangarembga." *Novel: A Forum on Fiction* 26, no. 3, Special issue on African literature (1993): 309–19.

Hodge, Merle. *Crick Crack, Monkey.* London: Heinemann, 1981.

hooks, bell. *Talking Back: Thinking Feminist, Thinking Black.* Cambridge: South End Press, 1989.

Hurtado, Aida. "Relating to Privilege: Seduction and Rejection in the Subordination of White Women and Women of Color." *Signs* 14, no. 4 (1989): 833–55.

Kincaid, Jamaica. *Annie John.* New York: Farrar, Straus and Giroux, 1985.

Morrison, Toni. *The Bluest Eye.* New York: Holt, Rinehart and Winston, 1970.

Rogers, Annie G. "Voice, Play, and a Practice of Ordinary Courage in Girls' and Women's Lives." *Harvard Educational Review* 63, no. 3 (1993): 265–96.

Thompson, Becky. *A Hunger So Wide and So Deep: A Multiracial View of Women's Eating Problems.* Minneapolis: University of Minnesota, 1994.

Wallace, Michele. "Variations on Negation and the Heresy of Black Feminist Creativity." In *Invisibility Blues: From Pop to Theory,* 213–40. New York: Verso, 1990.

DISCUSSION QUESTIONS

1. Regarding the difficulty she encountered in trying to publish her novel in Zimbabwe and recognizing that she was the first Zimbabwean woman novelist to be published in English (initially by the British Women's Press), Dangarembga stated in an interview that "it seems to be very difficult for men to accept the things that women write and want to write about" (George and Scott 311). What is gained and lost by men's unwillingness to realize the gendered construction of colonial and postcolonial realities?

2. The callous first psychiatrist is not alone in racializing certain forms of mental distress as "white." Within white and Black communities, there is a continued reluctance to subscribe to a notion of Blacks in the diaspora as vulnerable to psychological harm. Why might each group be invested in such a view of Black populations?

3. Dangarembga admits that while the events of the novel transpired during Zimbabwe's protracted fight for independence (1965–79), this political reality is barely addressed in the story. How can we understand her decision to focus on the experiential and psychological realities of two adolescent girls during this consequential period in Zimbabwean history?

TSITSI DANGAREMBGA, *NERVOUS CONDITIONS*, CHAPTER 10

Excitement. Anticipation. Elation and exultation. It was all very much the same as it had been on that first day that I went to the mission, the day that I began my new life. Yes, it had begun so thoroughly that January afternoon two years ago when I went to the mission, and it was continuing. Everything was coming together. All the things that I wanted were tying themselves up into a neat package which presented itself to me with a flourish. There should have been trumpets, truly there should have been. For was I—I, Tambudzai, lately of the mission and before that the homestead—was I, Tambudzai, so recently a peasant, was I not entering, as I had promised myself I would, a world where burdens lightened with every step, soon to disappear altogether? I had an idea that this would happen as I passed through the school gates, those gates that would declare me a young lady, a member of the Young Ladies College of the Sacred Heart. I was impatient to get to those gates. The drive was too long. The car had to go faster to get me there in time.

We were all in the car, all four of us, Babamukuru, Maiguru, Nyasha and me. Babamukuru was not happy about the arrangement, thinking Nyasha ought not to miss her classes just to take me to mine, but she had free periods that afternoon and her form-master had given her permission to miss the prep that usually took up the time. Maiguru must have talked to Babamukuru as well because though he looked annoyed when Nyasha climbed into the car beside me, he did not tell her to get out.

Maiguru, who had not fussed for a long time, could not resist the temptation on this occasion. A marvellous chicken lunch had been prepared in my honour, with chocolate cake afterwards so deliciously rich and sticky with icing that even Nyasha had forgotten her figure long enough to put away two slices of it. Somehow the question of tuck had escaped Maiguru's maternal attention and although I insisted to her that I did not need chocolate biscuits and potato crisps and orange juice, she insisted that I did, and so we stopped in

SOURCE: Tsitsi Dangarembga, *Nervous Conditions* (Banbury, UK: Ayebia Clarke, 1988), 195–208.

town to buy these things, adding twenty endless minutes to the time I had calculated the journey would take. Maiguru bought enough tuck to feed a small colony for several months. Nyasha warned me that if I ate all of it, even over the course of a term, I would end up unable to see past my stomach to admire my dainty new uniform shoes. We had a rather wild laugh at this even though it wasn't very funny. But we needed to laugh to forget that this was the end of our closeness and to that extent our friendship. So we giggled foolishly as we piled the packets and bottles and tins into the car. There was jam, tomato sauce, all sorts of things besides the biscuits and squash and crisps. Then, just as Babamukuru started the engine, Maiguru remembered that I would need a tumbler to drink my orange juice out of and went back to buy it. Eventually we arrived at Sacred Heart.

None of us had been there before, except Babamukuru. He had been several times to discuss my admission with Sister Emmanuel, who was both Mother Superior and Principal, and to pay her the only expenditure, the cost of my uniform, which, he told me dourly, would have paid for my whole year's board and tuition at his mission. Because I had not seen the place before, I was infatuated when we turned into the school gates. The grounds were majestically spacious. I never did discover how many hectares of land those nuns owned, but to the eye it looked like hundreds. We drove, slowly because there were humps, up past the hockey pitches, four of them neatly laid out side by side, past the tennis courts and the netball, yes, netball courts, to a thicket of conifers that seemed to signify that within this rich kingdom we had left the province of the physical and entered the realm of mental activity, because beyond the trees was a roundabout at the top of which stood the school buildings. The dormitories, bright and shimmering white in the clear summer sun, stretched towards us on one side of the roundabout, the classrooms stretched down on the other. Between them was an archway, supported by ornate plaster pillars in, I was to be told, the Greek style, not the Roman, and above this long archway rose the dining-room and chapel. The roundabout itself was serenely green with a lavish, permanently moist lawn, the latter relieved in places carefully selected so that the green would not be too monotonous, by flowering shrubs. Delicate mimosa fluffed puffs of yellow and silvery white, robust poinsettia splashed patches of crimson and peach against the green. Two swans cruised elegantly across a pond in the middle of the lawn and later I found there shoals of goldfish, goldfish which were not a pale imitation but definitely gold. Their rich, ruddy glow flitted in and out of water weeds in the company of more exotic species that shot flashes of red and blue and silver through the gold. I was enchanted, so obviously so that Nyasha thought she ought to remind me that I had come to school and not on holiday. Reluctantly I remembered.

Ours was not the only car on the wide tarmac drive complete with road markings. Dozens of cars were winding their way up one arm of the roundabout, stopping at the top for whatever period of time it took to get daughter settled, and then winding away again down the other side. There were more cars in the parking area at the top of the roundabout than I had ever seen in one place in my life. I imagined that every girl, every single one of the three hundred pupils at Sacred Heart must have brought with her her very own car. And what cars they were, long, lean and gleaming. I sent up a little prayer of thanksgiving that Babamukuru had seen fit to drive the green Ford, but I noticed that he always arrived in the Rover after that. Nyasha accurately perceived that all this affluence was dazzling me. Delicately, she cleared her throat. "Excuse me," she murmured in cultured tones, "but are you sure this is the right place?"

"What do you mean?" growled my uncle. "Of course this is the place!" His foot pressed down, certainly unconsciously, on the accelerator, sending us swinging over a hump which left our stomachs behind and caused Maiguru and me to catch our breath sharply, while Nyasha let out a sharp yelp. Perhaps Babamukuru was worrying about the cost of my uniform. Maybe that was why his nerves were so sharply on edge that afternoon, making it a bad day for both the man and his daughter. "Nyasha," he snapped, "stop that. What's the matter with you? Why can't you keep quiet like Tambudzai there?"

We found a parking space, though this was not easy, and disembarking, walked, taking the general direction of the stream of parents and pupils ahead of us, over crazy-paving of geometrically cut stone, through a corridor of creamy-white roses to the door that appeared to be the main entrance. Anticipation. Disappointment. I looked and looked and searched carefully through the crowd, but I could not find a single black face which did not belong to our party, except of course for the porters. The porters were carrying trunks, but none of them offered to carry mine.

At the door a nun, smiling beatifically, made us welcome by shaking our hands and asking us "Which one is this?" before taking us up steps and down corridors to a room at the end of a long hallway.

"All the first-formers live on this corridor," she explained as she led the way. "And the Africans live in here," she announced, triumphantly flinging the door to my new life wide open. The room was empty. I was, it seemed, the first black first-former to have arrived. It was not a small room but then neither was it large. It certainly was not large enough for the six beds that stood in it, three along one wall and three along the other, all of necessity so closely arranged that there was barely space to walk between them.

"This is your room," the nun said, smiling first at Nyasha and then at me, and then confessing her confusion. "Mr See-ga-ookey," she smiled, "you have only one coming. Which one is it?" She had forgotten already although we had been introduced at the door. I wished I had been wearing uniform like the other girls I had seen. Then she would have known who I was. But I was getting my uniform second-hand. The nuns would give it to me later.

"I have been wondering, Sister," began Babamukuru politely. "I was under the impression that the girls sleep four to a room, but I see there are six beds here."

"Ah, yes," agreed the Sister, proud of the fact. "We have more Africans here than usual this year and so we had to put them all in here."

"There are only four wardrobes," objected my uncle.

"It is inconvenient, isn't it?" sympathised Sister. "The youngest will have to share. We've got a sixth-former in here and a fourth-former as well. They have to have their own."

Babamukuru turned to me. "Come Tambudzai, let us help you get settled."

Baba and Maiguru made my bed for me, Nyasha, wanting to help but not having anything to do, only tweaking a sheet once or twice. While they made the bed, I unpacked. With my uniform still to be provided I had brought with me, besides the bedding, only toiletries, underwear and the two casual dresses that the uniform list stipulated, so I was soon through. When we had finished, we said our goodbyes. These were stern and exhortatory on my uncle's part, briskly cheerful from Maiguru, determinedly gay from Nyasha. We walked down to the car. In the courtyard Nyasha hugged me. "Have a good time, you African," she grinned. We parted with laughter and requests and promises to write and reply and to visit.

Term began and progressed but Nyasha did not come to visit. I hardly noticed the omission. You will say again that I was callous but I was not, only overwhelmed. It was all so heady and affluent and new that I was sure I was on the path of progress. I did not want to be left behind, so I threw myself into everything: exotic languages, like Latin and French and Portuguese, with unfamiliar sentence structures that told of brave legionnaries the enemy laying waste and pupils who wrote with the pen of their aunts. I wondered a while at such strange constructions, and then remembered that I was no longer writing in English, finding on closer inspection that the structures were quite similar to our own. Still, I mused, those foreign people had strange things on their minds: it did not seem likely that you could hold normal conversations in those languages. There were new games to play too, basketball, tennis and hockey, with interesting rules and intricate scoring procedures to be learnt. There were nuns to be observed and classified according to whether they were human or not, lay-teachers whose idiosyncrasies had to be identified so that you did not fall prey to them. The white students needed careful study to decide whether they were different or similar to me, whether they were likeable or not and what their habits were. Most importantly, most wonderfully, there was the library, big, bright, walled in glass on one side and furnished with private little cubicles where you could do your homework, or simply lose yourself in any one of the hundreds of tantalising books whose glossy covers never seemed to get dirty or torn. The sheer number of books in that library made me deeply ashamed of my ignorance. I resolved to read every single one of those informative volumes from the first page to the last.

With all those new books, reading took up so much of my time that there was none left in which to miss Nyasha, or my uncle and aunt; and if I had ever really missed my home, I had long since stopped doing that during my stay with Babamukuru. Besides, although Nyasha did not visit, she wrote often. She wrote long, expansive, entertaining letters full of lucid, irreverent detail: my father's latest method of extorting money from Babamukuru; the most recent gossip gleaned from the girls' hostel (Josie and Maidei were no longer speaking); Maiguru's progress with respect to her emancipation and the way Babamukuru was coping with his more adamant wife; that Lucia had passed her Grade One so well that they were moving her into Grade Three; news about my mother—she was well. This was the bulk of her news. She did not write much about herself until one day I received a serious letter from her.

"I am missing you badly," she wrote, "as I knew I would and told you so, but I did not want to worry you with it because I know about your guilts, and I did not want guilt over your luck to stop you enjoying it. But the fact is I am missing you and missing you badly. In many ways you are very essential to me in bridging some of the gaps in my life, and now that you are away, I feel them again. I find it more and more difficult to speak with the girls at school. I try, Tambu, but there is not much to speak of between us. They resent the fact that I do not read their romance stories and, if I do not read them, then of course I cannot talk about them. If only they knew that when I was ten my mother used to scold me very severely indeed for sneaking them down from the bookshelf. But I was ten six years ago and that is a long time to have grown out of such habits. I should, I suppose, have acquired more useful habits instead. I should have learnt to be light-hearted and gay, but it's difficult, you know. Besides, I am convinced that they have other reasons for disapproving of me. They do not like my language, my English, because it is authentic and my Shona, because it is not! They think that I am a snob, that I think I am superior to them because I do not feel that I am inferior to men (if you can call the boys in my class men). And all because I beat the boys at maths! I know that I should not complain, but I very much would like to belong, Tambu, but I find I do not. I spend a lot of time reading and studying now that you are not here for us to distract each other, but I must admit I long for those distractions—it's not virtue that keeps me so busy! I think, though, that your uncle is pleased with the quieter environment and I have discovered that it is restful to have him pleased, and so these days I am doing my best not to antag-onise him. You can imagine how difficult that is. Impossible, it seems. I cannot help thinking that what antagonises is the fact that I am me—hardly, I admit, the ideal daugh-ter for a hallowed headmaster, a revered patriarch. I have asked him several times if we may come to see you (through my mother, of course—it's always best to be quiet in his presence), but he believes it will spoil you."

This letter did cause a pang of guilt. I believed I was being irresponsible. Folding the pages away in my desk where I would see it often and be reminded to write, I resolved to reply as soon as I had a spare moment. But the pang of guilt was no more than a pang which dissolved quickly in the stream of novelty and discovery I had plunged into. No spare moment came my way, nor did I find the time to make one, before I received my cousin's next letter. This letter was of the usual kind. Bubbly and bouncy, Nyasha updated me on the mission gossip and announced that she had embarked on a diet "to discipline my body and occupy my mind, When you come back you will find a svelte, sensuous me."

That was one of the last letters I received from her. During the second half of the term her letters became less regular and eventually stopped altogether. Again I must confess that I did not really notice. The thirteen weeks of term galloped by so quickly that while I was still wondering when she would write next, Babamukuru came to fetch me. Preoc-cupied and tense, he came alone, informing me that Nyasha was keeping to her books. There was no conversation during the ride home, no enquiries from my uncle about the lessons, the dormitories, my friends or the food, and when I asked about Maiguru and the mission, he grunted so distractedly that I gave up the attempt. I was disappointed because Nyasha's letters had led me to believe that his disposition had improved, but I did not dwell on disappointment. If not Babamukuru, there was Nyasha to turn an attentive ear to the torrent of news about the goings on at Sacred Heart that was positively bursting to be told.

Nyasha was indeed looking svelte when she dashed out to hug me, flinging her arms round me almost before I had stepped out of the car. In fact too svelte. By my standards she had grown definitely thin, but I knew that she preferred bones to bounce and so I said nothing.

I did not stay at the mission long that vacation. Babamukuru drove me home the very next day. Nor did I pass through the mission on my way back to Sacred Heart at the beginning of the second term; so I did not see my cousin again until the August holiday. Three months had passed. In those three months she had grown skeletal. She was pathetic to see, but when she hugged me hello I was surprised at the strength in her arms, so frail they looked as though they would snap if she so much as picked up a pen. She hugged me briefly, hoped that my second term had been as interesting as the first and disappeared into the house with a suitcase while I unloaded the rest of my luggage and followed her to our bedroom. There I found her absorbed in a history text. She did not speak when I entered—a brief smile informed me she was busy. She worked until suppertime. When Anna called she put away her books and came to the table. She sat down very quietly and that was the beginning of a horribly weird and sinister drama. Babamukuru dished out a large helping of food for his daughter and set it before her, watching her surreptitiously as he picked casually at his own meal to persuade us that he was calm. Nyasha regarded her plate malevolently, darting anguished glances at her father, drained two glasses of water, then picked up her fork and shovelled the food into her mouth, swallowing without chewing and without pause except to sip between mouthfuls from a third glass of water. Maiguru ate steadily and fussed over me, placing another chunk of meat, another spoonful of vegetables on my plate and making cheerful conversation about my lessons, my friends and the food at Sacred Heart. When Nyasha's plate was empty they both relaxed and the atmosphere returned almost to normal. Nyasha excused herself immediately. I thought she had gone to the bedroom to read but when I followed her there the room was empty. I could hear retching and gagging from the bathroom.

She returned silently to her books, a mathematics exercise this time, and was still working when I rolled over to sleep at eleven o'clock. In the early hours of the morning something prodded me awake. It was Nyasha.

"Can you help me?" she asked timidly. "I can't get the right answer. I ought to be able to, but I keep getting it wrong." It was not a difficult problem. She had made a careless mistake. "Silly me," she said when I found her mistake. "I'm not concentrating hard enough."

Babamukuru wanted to take me home the next day, the day after I arrived. He told Maiguru to tell me at breakfast to be sure to be ready by lunchtime. I did not want to go,

I felt I could not. I could not leave my cousin in that state. You know how it is when something that has been a cornerstone of your security begins to crumble. You start worrying about yourself. For that reason alone, even if others were less selfish, I knew I could not leave. So my uncle had to be told. I had to tell him that I would not go, but how was that to be done? I might have been becoming a young lady and being educated at the convent, but what use were educated young ladies on the homestead? Or at the mission? I was and would remain Tambudzai, the daughter. Babamukuru was still and would always be the closest thing a human being could get to God. So although I knew I had to talk to him, I had no idea how that could be done.

I thought I would telephone him at his office, went so far as to dial the number and wait for a reply, but he was not there. The phone rang and rang. I grew more relieved with every buzz: I would not have to talk to him after all. I thought I would write a letter instead, then thought again and decided that since he would return for lunch I would take my courage in both hands, close my ears to my daughterly conscience and confront him then. And while I made these plans I knew all the time that it couldn't be done.

So I wasn't surprised when I nearly backed down. Babamukuru was angry at lunchtime because Nyasha refused to leave her bedroom. He was all for going in there himself to drag her to the table, but Maiguru managed to dissuade him. His daughter was so fragile, she said, the shock might do her serious harm. "And starving herself," he cried, "you mean starving herself does her no harm?" Eventually he allowed himself to be pacified. "Perhaps you are right," he conceded to Maiguru. "She does eat her supper when I have time to supervise her properly. Yes, I think you are right, Mai. It is not so serious. What she needs is to rest."

Yet it was serious. Nyasha was losing weight steadily, constantly, rapidly. It dropped off her body almost hourly and what was left of her was grotesquely unhealthy from the vital juices she flushed down the toilet. Did he not know? Did he not see? I could not ask him these questions. The most I could do was ask in a small, timid voice to be allowed to stay, with Nyasha, I specified, for a few more days. Nobody was more surprised by my audacity than I was. Babamukuru did not answer, but I was not taken home. I did not take it as a victory though. I took it as proof that Babamukuru was good.

Nyasha grew weaker by the day. She weaved when she walked and every night was the same. Although we were on vacation she studied fourteen hours a day to make sure that she passed her "O" levels. She worked late into the night to wake me up regularly and punctually at three o'clock with a problem—a chemical equation to balance, the number of amperes in a circuit to be calculated or an irregular Latin verb to be conjugated, although I was only in Form One and could not often help her. "I have to get it right," she would whisper with an apologetic smile. It was truly alarming, but nobody commented, nobody acted; we were all very frightened. One evening, at supper, she passed out into her plate. It didn't last long, only a minute or two, but it was enough to overtax her father's precarious patience. Babamukuru, who thought she was making a scene, ordered her to her bedroom, where she lay open-eyed and quiet all night. At three o'clock she woke me up.

"Can I get into bed with you, Tambu?" she whispered, but when I rolled over to make room for her to climb in she shook her head and smiled. "It's all right," she said: "I just wanted to see if you would let me." Then she sat on her bed and looked at me out of her sunken eyes, her bony knees pressed together so that her nightdress fell through the space where her thighs had been, agitated and nervous and picking her skin. "I don't want to do it, Tambu, really I don't, but it's coming, I feel it coming." Her eyes dilated. "They've done it to me," she accused, whispering still. "Really, they have." And then she became stern. "It's not their fault. They did it to them too. You know they did," she whispered. "To both of them, but especially to him. They put him through it all. But it's not his fault, he's good." Her voice took on a Rhodesian accent. "He's a good boy, a good munt. A bloody good kaffir," she informed in sneering sarcastic tones. Then she was whispering again. "Why do they do it Tambu," she hissed bitterly, her face contorting with rage, "to me and to you and to him? Do you see what they've done? They've taken us away. Lucia. Takesure. All of us. They've deprived you of you, him of him, ourselves of each other. We're grovelling. Lucia for a job, Jeremiah for money. Daddy grovels to them. We grovel to him." She began to rock, her body quivering tensely. "I won't grovel. Oh no, I won't. I'm not a good girl. I'm evil. I'm not a good girl." I touched her to comfort her and that was the trigger. "I won't grovel, I won't die," she raged and crouched like a cat ready to spring.

The noise brought Babamukuru and Maiguru running. They could do nothing, could only watch. Nyasha was beside herself with fury. She rampaged, shredding her history book between her teeth ("Their history. Fucking liars. Their bloody lies."), breaking mirrors, her clay pots, anything she could lay her hands on and jabbing the fragments viciously into her flesh, stripping the bedclothes, tearing her clothes from the wardrobe and trampling them underfoot. "They've trapped us. They've trapped us. But I won't be trapped. I'm not a good girl. I won't be trapped." Then as suddenly as it came, the rage passed. "I don't hate you, Daddy," she said softly. "They want me to, but I won't." She lay down on her bed. "I'm very tired," she said in a voice that was recognisably hers. "But I can't sleep. Mummy will you hold me?" She curled up in Maiguru's lap looking no more than five years old. "Look what they've done to us," she said softly. "I'm not one of them but I'm not one of you." She fell asleep.

The next morning she was calm, but she assured me it was an illusion, the eye of a storm. "There's a whole lot more," she said. "I've tried to keep it in but it's powerful. It ought to be. There's nearly a century of it," she added, with a shadow of her wry grin. "But I'm afraid," she told me apologetically. "It upsets people. So I need to go somewhere where it's safe. You know what I mean? Somewhere where people won't mind."

Nyasha's kamikazi behaviour jolted my uncle and aunt into action. Even as she was speaking to me in the bedroom, Babamukuru was on the telephone to Maiguru's brother in Salisbury. By ten o'clock we were on our way to the city, arriving there before twelve because Babamukuru drove like an August wind. Maiguru and I talked to Nyasha constantly all the way, to keep her with us, to prevent her mind from wandering too far. In the city Maiguru's brother immediately made an appointment with a psychiatrist. We felt better—help was at hand. But the psychiatrist said that Nyasha could not be ill, that Africans did not suffer in the way we had described. She was making a scene. We should take her home and be firm with her. This was not a sensible thing to say in front of my uncle, who found these words vastly reassuring and considered going back to Umtali at once, turning a deaf ear to Nyasha when she begged to see an African psychiatrist. Nyasha's uncle though, with the authority of seven years of learning to recognise suffering when he saw it, was able to persuade my uncle to wait.

There were no black psychiatrists, but she was persuaded to see a white one. This man was human. She needed to rest, he said. So Nyasha was put into a clinic, where she stayed for several weeks. Slowly, with the aid of doses of Largactil and the practical attention of her aunts who lived in the city, my cousin's condition improved, but I did not stay to see her improvement. Babamukuru, having a school to keep in order, was anxious to be back in Umtali and in three weeks' time I would have to be back at school, so I had to go back with him. I was upset. I felt Nyasha needed me but it was true: I had to go to school.

We did not talk on the drive back to Umtali, Babamukuru and I, and this was as things should be. Babamukuru's age alone merited the respect of silence. His education made him almost an elder. You simply could not talk. It would not have mattered if this had been my first car-ride along that road, but sophistication is acquired quickly. The vast rippling fields of maize and tobacco between Rusapi and Marandellas no longer impressed me, nor did Gomore Mhanda, whose stony baldness had been so intriguing on the outward journey. There was nothing to distract me. Although we had left at nine o'clock in the morning I forced myself to sleep; there was nothing to keep me awake except thoughts of Nyasha and these were thoughts I preferred to ignore. If Nyasha who had everything could not make it where could I expect to go? I could not bear to think about it because at that time we were not sure whether she would survive. All I knew was that the doctor would not commit himself. Nyasha's progress was still in the balance, and so, as a result was mine.

With this knowledge disturbing my mind, I was not unhappy when Babamukuru took me straight to the homestead. I did not want to stay at the mission, where there was too much that reminded me of Nyasha, and where she was. It was difficult to accept that this thing had happened, particularly difficult because I had no explanation. If you had asked me before it all began, I would have said it was impossible. I would have said it was impossible for people who had everything to suffer so extremely.

I may have had no explanation, but my mother had. She was very definite.

"It's the Englishness," she said. "It'll kill them all if they aren't careful," and she snorted. "Look at them: That boy Chido can hardly speak a word of his own mother's tongue and, you'll see, his children will be worse. Running around with that white one, isn't he, the missionary's daughter? His children will disgrace us. You'll see. And himself, to look at him he may look all right but there's no telling what price he's paying." She wouldn't say much about Nyasha. "About that one we don't even speak. It's speaking for itself. Both of them, it's the Englishness. It's a wonder it hasn't affected the parents too."

She went on like this for quite a while, going on about how you couldn't expect the ancestors to stomach so much Englishness. She didn't mention Nhamo, but I was beginning to follow her trend of thought. I knew she was thinking about him and I could see she considered me a victim too: "The problem is the Englishness, so you just be careful!"

It was a warning, a threat that would have had disastrous effects if I had let it. When you're afraid of something it doesn't help to have people who know more than you do come out and tell you you're quite right. Mother knew a lot of things and I had regard for her knowledge. Be careful, she had said, and I thought about Nyasha and Chido and Nhamo, who had all succumbed, and of my own creeping feelings of doom. Was I being careful enough? I wondered. For I was beginning to have a suspicion, no more than the seed of a suspicion, that I had been too eager to leave the homestead and embrace the "Englishness" of the mission; and after that the more concentrated "Englishness" of Sacred Heart. The suspicion remained for a few days, during which time it transformed itself into guilt, and then I had nightmares about Nhamo and Chido and Nyasha two nights in a row. That should tell you how much my mother's words disturbed me: I had not had a nightmare since the first time I went to the mission. But term-time was fast approaching and the thought of returning to Sacred Heart filled me with pleasure. The books, the games, the films, the debates—all these things were things that I wanted. I told myself I was a much more sensible person than Nyasha, because I knew what could or couldn't be done. In this way, I banished the suspicion, buried it in the depths of my subconscious, and happily went back to Sacred Heart.

I was young then and able to banish things, but seeds do grow. Although I was not aware of it then, no longer could I accept Sacred Heart and what it represented as a sunrise on my horizon. Quietly, unobtrusively and extremely fitfully, something in my mind began to assert itself, to question things and refuse to be brainwashed, bringing me to this time when I can set down this story. It was a long and painful process for me, that process of expansion. It was a process whose events stretched over many years and would fill another volume, but the story I have told here, is my own story, the story of four women whom I loved, and our men, this story is how it all began.

20

THE MEANING OF SPATIAL BOUNDARIES

Fatima Mernissi

Muslim sexuality is territorial. Its regulatory mechanisms consist primarily of a strict allocation of space to each sex and an elaborate ritual for resolving the contradictions arising from the inevitable intersections of spaces.[1] Apart from the ritualized trespasses of women into public spaces (which are, by definition, male spaces), there are no accepted patterns for interactions between unrelated men and women. Such interactions violate the spatial rules that are the pillars of the Muslim sexual order. Only that which is licit is formally regulated. Since the interaction of unrelated men and women is illicit, there are no rules governing it. Those people now experiencing sexual desegregation are therefore compelled to improvise. And, whereas imitation is possible, creation is far more difficult.

Boundaries are never established gratuitously. Society does not form divisions purely for the pleasure of breaking the social universe into compartments. The institutionalized boundaries dividing the parts of society express the recognition of power in one part at the expense of the other.[2] Any transgression of the boundaries is a danger to the social order because it is an attack on the acknowledged allocation of power. The link between boundaries and power is particularly salient in a society's sexual patterns.

Patterns or sexual dangers can be seen to express symmetry or hierarchy. It is impossible to interpret them as expressing something about the actual relation of the sexes. I suggest that many ideas about sexual dangers are better interpreted as symbols of the relation between parts of society, as mirroring designs of hierarchy or symmetry which apply in the larger social system.[3]

The symbolism of sexual patterns certainly seems to reflect society's hierarchy and power allocation in the Muslim order. Strict space boundaries divide Muslim society into two subuniverses: the universe of men (the *umma*, the world of religion and power) and the universe of women (the domestic world of sexuality and the family). The spatial division according to sex reflects the division between those who hold authority and those who do not, those who hold spiritual powers and those who do not.[4] The division is based on the physical separation of the *umma* (the public sphere) from the domestic universe. These two universes of social interaction are regulated by antithetical concepts of human relations, one based on community, the other on conflict.[5]

MEMBERSHIP OF THE TWO UNIVERSES

The Public Universe of the Umma: The believers. Women's position in the *umma* universe is ambiguous; Allah does not talk to them directly. We can therefore assume that the *umma* is primarily male believers.

The Domestic Universe of Sexuality: Individuals of both sexes as primarily sexual beings. But because men are not supposed to spend their time in the domestic unit, we may assume that the members are in fact women only.

Principles Regulating Relations between Members

The Umma	*The Family*
Equality	Inequality
Reciprocity	Lack of Reciprocity
Aggregation	Segregation
Unity, Communion	Separation, Division
Brotherhood, Love	Subordination, Authority
Trust	Mistrust

Communal Relationship   A social relationship will be so-called communal if and so far as the orientation of social action is based on the subjective feeling of the parties, whether affectual or traditional, that they belong together.[6]

The universe of the *umma* is communal; its citizens are persons who unite in a democratic collectivity based on a sophisticated concept of belief in a set of ideas, which is geared to produce integration and cohesion of all members who participate in the unifying task.

Conflict Relationship   A social relationship will be referred to as a "conflict" insofar as action within it is oriented intentionally to carrying out the actor's own will against the resistance of the other party or parties.[7]

The citizens of the domestic universe are primarily sexual beings; they are defined by their genitals and not by their faith. They are not united but are divided into two categories: men, who have power, and women, who obey. Women—who are citizens of this domestic universe and whose existence outside that sphere is considered an anomaly, a transgression—are subordinate to men, who (unlike their women) also possess a second nationality, one that grants them membership of the public sphere, the domain of religion and politics, the domain of power, of the management of the affairs of the *umma*. Having been identified as primarily citizens of the domestic universe, women are then deprived of power even within the world in which they are confined, since it is the man who wields authority within the family. The duty of Muslim women is to obey (as is very clear in the *Muduwana* and in Malik's *al-Muwatta*, from which it is inspired and on which it is based). The separation of the two groups, the hierarchy that subordinates the one to the other, is expressed in institutions that discourage, and even prohibit, any communication between the sexes. Men and women are supposed to collaborate in only one of the tasks required for the survival of society: procreation.

In fact, whenever cooperation between men and women is inevitable, as between the members of a couple, an entire array of mechanisms is set in motion to prevent too great an intimacy from arising between the partners. Sexual segregation thus fuels, and is fueled by, the conflicts that it is supposed to avoid between men and women. Or better, sexual segregation intensifies what it is supposed to eliminate: the sexualization of human relations.

The Seclusion of Women

In order to prevent sexual interaction between members of the *umma* and members of the domestic universe, seclusion and veiling (a symbolic form of seclusion) were developed. But paradoxically, sexual segregation heightens the sexual dimension of any interaction between men and women.

In a country like Morocco, in which heterosexual encounter is the focus of so many restrictions, and consequently of so much attention, seduction becomes a structural component of human relations in general, whether between individuals of the same sex or between men and women.

I have concentrated my discussion here on heterosexual relations, but our understanding of sexual identity cannot be complete without studies clarifying the interaction among individuals of the same sex. A society that opts for sexual segregation, and therefore for impoverishment of heterosexual relations, is a society that fosters "homosocial" relations on the one hand and seduction as a means of communication on the other.[8] Seduction is a conflict strategy, a way of seeming to give of yourself and of procuring great pleasure without actually giving anything. It is the art of abstaining from everything while playing on the promise of giving. It is a childish art in that the child has a vital need to protect itself, but for an adult it is the expression of an often uncontrollable emotional avarice. It is very rare that an individual who has invested years in learning seduction as a mode of interchange can suddenly open up and lavish all his (or her) "emotional treasures" on the person he has finally chosen to love.

In a society in which heterosexual relations are combated, emotional fulfilment is inhibited. As we are taught to fear and mistrust the other sex, and therefore to relate to its members through seduction, manipulation, and domination we become mere puppets who extend the games of seduction, acceptable during adolescence, into our relations as mature men and women.

The hedonistic enhancement of the beauty of the human body seems to have been a pronounced Mediterranean characteristic of Morocco which Islam failed to curb. Body adornment with both jewelry and cosmetics is an integral part of socialization. Even men, at least the generation now in their sixties, used to wear cosmetics to darken their eyelids *(khol)* and lips *(swak)* for religious rituals and festivals. Islam took an unequivocally negative attitude towards body ornamentation, especially for women.[9] It required pious women to be modest in their appearance and hide all ornamentation and eye-catching beauty behind veils.

> And tell the believing women to lower their gaze and be modest, and to display of their adornment only that which is apparent and to draw their veils over their bosoms, and not to reveal their adornment save to their own husbands or fathers or husband's fathers, or their sons or their husband's sons, or their women, or their slaves, or male attendants who lack vigour or children who know naught of women's nakedness. And let them not stamp their feet so as to reveal what they hide of their adornment. And turn unto Allah together, O believers, in order that ye may succeed.[10]

According to Ghazali, the eye is undoubtedly an erogenous zone in the Muslim structure of reality, just as able to give pleasure as the penis. A man can do as much damage to a woman's honor with his eyes as if he were to seize hold of her with his hands.

> To look at somebody else's wife is a sinful act. . . . The look is fornication of the eye, but if the sexual apparatus is not set in motion by it [if the man does not attempt to have sexual intercourse], it is a much more easily pardoned act.[11]

When the Prophet was asking God to protect him from the most virulent social dangers, he asked for help in controlling his penis and his eye from the dangers of fornication.[12]

The theory that seclusion in Islam is a device to protect the passive male who cannot control himself sexually in the presence of the lust-inducing female is further substantiated by verse 60 of sura 24, which explains that elderly women (supposed to be unattractive) can go unveiled. Belghiti's survey of rural women among whom seclusion is the prevailing mode, reveals that the restrictions on women's movements do not apply to elderly women, who consequently have a greater freedom.[13]

The seclusion of women, which to Western eyes is a source of oppression, is seen by many Muslim women as a source of pride.[14] The traditional women interviewed all perceived seclusion as prestigious. In rural Morocco seclusion is considered the privilege of women married to rich men.[15]

Harems, the ultimate form of seclusion, were considered even more prestigious, since they required huge economic assets. One of the women I interviewed, Salama, lived most of her life as a concubine in a harem. This is unusual even by Moroccan standards, and her experience contrasts sharply with that of most women. Because women are not allowed to leave a harem, sexual segregation is more successfully realized there than in the average, monogamous family. Successful seclusion of human beings requires considerable economic investment, because services must be provided at home for the secluded. Other women, who must go out to shop or go to the baths, are under many restrictions outside the home.

THE DESECLUSION OF WOMEN: ON THE STREET

Traditionally, women using public spaces, trespassing on the *umma* universe, are restricted to few occasions and bound by specific rituals, such as the wearing of the veil.[16] The veil is worn by Moroccan women only when they leave the house and walk through the street, which is a male space. The veil means that the woman is present in the men's world, but invisible; she has no right to be in the street.

If chaperoned, women are allowed to trespass into the men's universe on the traditional visits to the *hammam*, the public bath, and to the tomb of the local saint. According to my data, visits to the *hammam* used to be bi-monthly and to the saint's tomb not more than once or twice a year (usually the twenty-seventh day of Ramadan). Both required the husband's permission. The chaperoning was entrusted to an elderly asexual woman, usually the mother-in-law.

Traditionally, only necessity could justify a woman's presence outside the home, and no respect was ever attached to poverty and necessity. Respectable women were not seen on the street. In class-conscious Morocco, the maid, who has to go wherever she can to find a job, occupies the lowest rung of the social scale, and to be called a maid is one of the commonest insults. Only prostitutes and insane women wander freely in the streets. One expression for a prostitute is *rajlha zahqa*, "a woman whose foot is slipping." The Pascon-Bentahar survey revealed that when a rural youth visits a town he assumes that any woman walking down the street is sexually available.[17]

Women in male spaces are considered both provocative and offensive. Since schooling and jobs both require women to be able to move freely through the streets, modernization necessarily exposes many women to public harassment.[18]

In *The Hidden Dimension*, Edward Hall made two perceptive remarks about the use of space in Middle Eastern, Arab-Muslim societies. First, "there is no such thing as an intrusion in public. Public means public."[19] It is not possible for an individual to claim a private zone in a public space. This seems quite true for Morocco and has a particular bearing on women's presence in the street, as one might guess.

Second, space has a primarily social rather than physical quality. The notion of trespassing is related not so much to physical boundaries as to the identity of the person performing the act.[20] A friend, for example, never trespasses, while a foe always does.

A woman is always trespassing in a male space because she is, by definition, a foe. A woman has no right to use male spaces. If she enters them, she is upsetting the male's order and his peace of mind. She is actually committing an act of aggression against him merely by being present where she should not be. A woman in a traditionally male space upsets Allah's order by inciting men to commit *zina* [sexual transgression]. The man has everything to lose in this encounter: peace of mind, self-determination, allegiance to Allah, and social prestige.

If the woman is unveiled the situation is aggravated. The Moroccan term for a woman who is not veiled is *aryana*, "nude," and most women who frequent schools or hold jobs outside the home today are unveiled. The two elements together—trespassing and trespassing in the "nude"—constitute a open act of exhibitionism.

> Whether the indictable act consists of words spoken, gestures conveyed, or act performed, the communication structure of the event often consists of an individual initiating an engagement with a stranger of the opposite sex by means of the kind of message that would be proper only if they were on close and intimate terms. Apart from psychodynamic issues, exhibitionists often spectacularly subvert social control that keeps individuals interpersonally distant even though they are physically close to each other. The assault here is not so much directly on an individual as on the system of rights and symbols the individual employs in expressing relatedness and unrelatedness to those about him.[21]

The male's response to the woman's presence is, according to the prevailing ideology, a logical response to exhibitionist aggression. It consists in pursuing the woman for hours, pinching her, if the occasion is propitious, and possibly assaulting her verbally, all in the hope of convincing her to carry her exhibitionist propositioning to its implicit end.

During the Algerian revolution, the nationalist movement used women to carry arms and messages. One of the problems the revolutionary movement faced was the harassment of these women by Algerian "brothers" who mistook them for prostitutes and interfered with the performance of their nationalist task.[22] A similar incident was reported to have taken place near a refugee camp in Lebanon.

A female Palestinian militant was performing her task as a sentinel. She was posted in a deserted spot a few yards away from the camp, her machine-gun on her shoulder, when a Lebanese civilian who noticed her came by to make a proposition. When the woman rejected his advances with indignant words and gestures, the man got angry and said, "How do you want me to believe that a woman standing alone in the street the whole night has any honour?" The woman is said to have turned her gun towards her suitor and told him, "I am here in the street soiling my honour to defend yours because you are unable to do it yourself."[23] In spite of its revolutionary setting, the anecdote reveals that the female militant shares with the male civilian the belief that her being alone in the street is dishonourable. Her reflex was to justify her presence in the male space, not to claim her right to be there.

THE DESECLUSION OF WOMEN: IN THE OFFICE

The absence of modes of relatedness other than genital encounter helps to explain the form of heterosexual encounters in offices well as on the street.

The office is a recent development in Moroccan history, a legacy of the centralized bureaucracy set up by the French after 1912. After independence, public administration expanded both in terms of offices and posts and in terms of the portion of public resources it swallows. The state is now by far the most important employer in the country. A substantial number of literate working women are in government offices. These women, who often have not finished high school, are typists and secretaries and usually occupy positions subordinate to their male colleagues.[24]

The situation of the working woman in the office is reminiscent of her position in a traditional household and on the street. These conflicting images are likely to stimulate conflicting patterns of behavior in men. The boss's typist, like his wife and sister, is in a subordinate position, and he has the right to command her. Like them, she is dependent on him (more or less directly) for economic survival. He administers her salary, which is given to her because she provides him with specific services. Her advancement and promotion depend on him. It is therefore not surprising if he comes to confuse her with the woman he dominates because of his economic superiority and institutional authority (in other words, his wife), a step many men seem to take with ease. In any event, the drift that occurs in relations between the bureaucrat and his secretary, generated by his confusion of his privileges as a man and his rights and privileges as a bureaucrat, are not limited to sexual behavior. Max Weber identified this confusion as one of the problems of the bureaucratic system.

The confusion is inherent in any bureaucratic structure, but it assumes a particularly exaggerated character in third-world societies in which bureaucratization is relatively recent. Morocco, of course, already had its Makhzencentral, but that institution lacked the structures, resources, equipment, and personnel that it now commands. The harassment of the woman state employee occurs because she has transgressed the boundaries of the male space par excellence, the administration of affairs of state. The conflict and tension experienced by women who work in the state administration is proportional to the insolence of their intrusion into the sanctuaries of male power.

Women's increasing encroachment into traditionally male spaces greatly intensifies the sexual aspect of any encounter between men and women, especially in the urban centers. The process of integration of women into the modern circuits of the production system is now quite advanced, however unplanned or even undesired it may have been. A growing number of women, both educated and illiterate, are invading the labor market and the modern workshops. The aspiration for a *hadma mezyana* (well-paid job) is now shared by poor illiterate women and their more privileged sisters who have gained access to wealth and education.

When women go to work they are not only trespassing in the universe of the *umma* but are also competing with their former masters, men, for the scarce available jobs. The anxiety created by women seeking jobs in the modern sector, and thus demanding a role traditionally reserved for men, inevitably aggravates tension and conflict because of the scarcity of jobs and the high rate of unemployment among men.

[. . .]

THE FEAR OF FEMALE SEXUALITY

The perception of female aggression is directly influenced by the theory of women's sexuality. For Freud the female's aggression, in accordance with her sexual passivity, is turned inward. She is masochistic.

> The suppression of woman's aggressiveness which is prescribed for them constitutionally and imposed on them socially favours the development of powerful masochistic impulses, which succeed, as we know, in binding erotically the destructive trends which have been diverted inwards. Thus masochism, as people say, is truly feminine. But if, as happens so often, you meet with masochism in men, what is left for you but to say that these men exhibit very plainly feminine traits.[25]

The absence of active sexuality moulds the woman into a masochistic passive being. It is therefore no surprise that in the actively sexual Muslim female, aggressiveness is seen as turned outward. The nature of her aggression is precisely sexual. The Muslim woman is endowed with a fatal attraction which erodes the male's will to resist her and reduces him to a passive acquiescent role. He has no choice; he can only give in to her attraction, whence her identification with *fitna* (chaos) and with the antidivine and antisocial forces of the universe.

> The Prophet saw a woman. He hurried to his house and had intercourse with his wife Zaynab, then left the house and said, "When the woman comes towards you, it is Satan who is approaching you. When one of you sees a woman and he feels attracted to her, he should hurry to his wife. With her, it would be the same as with the other one."[26]

Commenting on this quotation, Imam Muslim, an established voice of Muslim tradition, reports that the Prophet was referring to the "fascination, to the irresistible attraction to women God instilled in man's soul, and he was referring to the pleasure man experiences when he looks at the woman, and the pleasure he experiences with anything related to her. She resembles Satan in his irresistible power over the individual."[27]

This attraction is a natural link between the sexes. Whenever a man is faced with a woman, *fitna* might occur: "When a man and a woman are isolated in the presence of each other, Satan is bound to be their third companion."[28]

The most potentially dangerous woman is one who has experienced sexual intercourse. It is the married woman who will have more difficulties in bearing sexual frustration. The married woman whose husband is absent is a particular threat to men: "Do not go to the women whose husbands are absent. Because Satan will get in your bodies as blood rushes through your flesh."[29]

In Moroccan folk culture this threat is epitomized by the belief in Aisha Kandisha, a repugnant female demon. She is repugnant precisely because she is libidinous. She has pendulous breasts and lips and her favourite pastime is to assault men in the streets and in dark places, to induce them to have sexual intercourse with her and ultimately to penetrate their bodies and stay with them forever.[30] They are then said to be inhabited. The fear of Aisha Kandisha is more than ever present in Morocco's daily life. Fear of the castrating female is a legacy of tradition and is seen in many forms in popular beliefs and practices and in both religious and mundane literature, particularly novels.

Moroccan folk culture is permeated with a negative attitude towards femininity. Loving a woman is popularly described as a form of mental illness, a self-destructive state of mind. A Moroccan proverb says:

Love is a complicated matter
If it does not drive you crazy, it kills you.[31]

The best example of this distrust of women is the sixteenth-century poet Sidi Abderahman al-Majdoub. His rhymes are so popular that they have become proverbs.

Women are fleeting wooden vessels
Whose passengers are doomed to destruction.

Or:

Don't trust them [women], so you would not be betrayed
Don't believe in their promises, so you would not be deceived
To be able to swim, fish need water
Women are the only creatures who can swim without it.

And finally:

Women's intrigues are mighty
To protect myself I run endlessly
Women are belted with serpents
And bejewelled with scorpions.[32]

The Muslim order faces two threats: the infidel without and the woman within.

The Prophet said, "After my disappearance there will be no greater source of chaos and disorder for my nation than women."[33]

The irony is that Muslim and European theories come to the same conclusion: women are destructive to the social order—for Imam Ghazali because they are active, for Freud because they are not.

Different social orders have integrated the tensions between religion and sexuality in different ways. In the Western Christian experience sexuality itself was attacked, degraded as animality and condemned as anticivilization. The individual was split into two anti-thetical selves: the spirit and the flesh, the ego and the id. The triumph of civilization implied the triumph of soul over flesh, of ego over id, of the controlled over the uncontrolled, of spirit over sex.

Islam took a substantially different path. What is attacked and debased is not sexuality but women, as the embodiment of destruction, the symbol of disorder. The woman is *fitna,* the epitome of the uncontrollable, a living representative of the dangers of sexuality and its rampant disruptive potential. [. . . .] Muslim theory considers raw instinct as energy which is likely to be used constructively for the benefit of Allah and His society if people live according to His laws. Sexuality per se is not a danger. On the contrary, it has three positive, vital functions. It allows the believers to perpetuate themselves on earth, an indispensable condition if the social order is to exist at all. It serves as a "foretaste of the delights secured for men in Paradise," thus encouraging men to strive for paradise and to obey Allah's rule on earth.[34] Finally, sexual satisfaction is necessary to intellectual effort.

The Muslim theory of sublimation is entirely different from the Western Christian tradition as represented by Freudian psychoanalytic theory. Freud viewed civilization as a war against sexuality.[35] Civilization is sexual energy "turned aside from its sexual goal and diverted towards other ends, no longer sexual and socially more valuable."[36] The Muslim theory views civilization as the outcome of satisfied sexual energy. Work is the result not of sexual frustration but of a contented and harmoniously lived sexuality.

The soul is usually reluctant to carry out its duty because duty [work] is against its nature. If one puts pressures on the soul in order to make it do what it loathes, the soul rebels. But if the soul is allowed to relax for some moments by the means of some pleasures, it fortifies itself and becomes after that alert and ready for work again. And in the woman's company, this relaxation drives out sadness and pacifies the heart. It is advisable for pious souls to divert themselves by means which are religiously lawful.[37]

According to Ghazali, the most precious gift God gave humans is reason. Its best use is the search for knowledge. To know the human environment, to know the earth and galaxies, is to know God. Knowledge (science) is the best form of prayer for a Muslim believer. But to be able to devote his energies to knowledge, man has to reduce the tensions within and without his body, avoid being distracted by external elements, and avoid indulging in earthly pleasures. Women are a dangerous distraction that must be used for the specific purpose of providing the Muslim nation with offspring and quenching the tensions of the sexual instinct. But in no way should women be an object of emotional investment or the focus of attention, which should be devoted to Allah alone in the form of knowledge-seeking, meditation, and prayer.

Ghazali's conception of the individual's task on earth is illuminating in that it reveals that the Muslim message, in spite of its beauty, considers humanity to be constituted by males only. Women are considered as not only outside of humanity but also a threat to it. Muslim wariness of heterosexual involvement is embodied in sexual segregation and its corollaries: arranged marriage, the important role of the mother in the son's life, and the fragility of the marital bond (as revealed by the institutions of repudiation and polygamy). The entire Muslim social structure can be seen as an attack on, and a defense against, the disruptive power of female sexuality.

NOTES

This introduction is excerpted from Fatima Mernissi, "The Meaning of Spatial Boundaries," in *Beyond the Veil: Male-Female Dynamics in Muslim Society* (London: Al Saqi Books, 1975), 137–47. The following notes are from that edition.

The version of the Koran used throughout this article is Mohammed Marmaduke Pickthall's *The Meaning of the Glorious Koran* (New York: New American Library, thirteenth printing). Abbreviations used in the notes are B for *bab* ("chapter"); H for *hadith* ("verbal tradition of Muhammad"); K for *kitab* ("book"); BESM for *Bulletin Economique et Social du Maroc*.

1. The term "territoriality," however, is really too primitive for the phenomenon, which is a sophisticated, manifold use of space. Hall's concept of "proxemics" is more suitable:

> Proxemics is the term I have coined for the interrelated observations and theories of man's use of space and a specialized elaboration of culture. (Edward Hall, *The Hidden Dimension*, New York, 1969, p. 1)

According to Hall, the dangers are great, given the sensuous dimension of any physical interaction, of involving the individuals in an atmosphere of ambiguous signs, unconsciously sent and received.

> Man's sense of space is closely related to his sense of self, which is in an intimate transaction with his environment. Man can be viewed as having visual, kinesthetic, tactile, and thermal aspects of

his self which may be either inhibited or encouraged to develop by his environment. (*The Hidden Dimension*, 63)

2. In *Purity and Danger* (Baltimore, 1970), Mary Douglas emphasized the links in social structure between the concept of boundaries, the concept of danger and the concept of power.

3. Douglas, *Purity and Danger*, 14.

4. In Moroccan folklore women are considered to be the repository of devilish forces: Edmund Doutte, *Magic et Religion dans l'Afrique du Nord* (Algiers, 1908), 33; also, E. Wester-mark, *The Belief in Spirits in Morocco*, 22. The Moroccan psychologist Abelwanad Radi in "Processus de socialisation de l'enfant marocain," *Etudes Philosophiques et Litteraires*, no. 4 (April 1969), attributes to women the responsibility for introducing children to the world of the irrational, of spirits.

5. The term "universe" is used here in the sense P. L. Berger and T. Luckman use it in *The Social Construction of Reality* (New York, 1967).

6. Max Weber, *The Theory of Social and Economic Organization* (New York, 1964), 136.

7. Weber, *Social and Economic Organization*, 132.

8. To foster "homosocial" relations does not necessarily mean to drive members of a society to practise what one Palestinian sociologist has called "homosociality": the inclination to spend most of one's time, most of one's life, with individuals of the same sex. Homosociality entails fear of the other sex and avoidance or limitation of controls with it. Obviously, homosociality is not peculiar to Arab society. Moreover, any institution or practice that tends to degrade the female body may be considered homosocial, and in this sense the advanced capitalist countries, with their pornography industry, would be prime examples.

9. More specifically, it condemned the practice of wearing wigs, which seems to have been quite common among Arab women in the seventh century (al-Bukhari, *al-Jami' al-Sahih*, 447, K: 67). Tattooing, also condemned by Islam, is still practised in Morocco, and some of the tattoos have unequivocal erotic meanings (J. Herber, "Tatouage du Pubis au Maroc," *Revue d'Ethnie*, vol. 3, 1922).

10. Koran, sura 24.

11. Abu-Hamid Al-Ghazali, *Revivification des sciences de la religion* (Paris: Editions Albouraq, 1999), 35.

12. Al-Ghazali, *Revivification*, 28.

13. Malika Belghiti, "Les Relations Féminines et le Statut de la Femme dans la Famille Rurale," *Collection du Bulletin Economique et Social du Maroc* (Rabat, 1970), 57.

14. The French anthropologist Germaine Tillion (*The Republic of Cousins* [London: Al Saqï Books, 1983]) noted that peasant women newly arrived to towns usually adopt the practice of veiling. She found it strange that women who were not veiled before adopted the veil willingly. I think that this phenomenon could be very easily interpreted if one remembers that, for the rural woman who has recently emigrated to the town, the veil is a sign of upward mobility—the expression of her newly acquired status as urbanite.

15. M. Belghiti, "Les Relations Féminines," 58.

16. Women are especially restricted when in a space they should have a right to: the mosque. In Morocco they may use only a specified area, usually a narrow, marginal, dark corner behind the male space. Although the Prophet allowed women to go to mosques, their

right to be there was, during Islam's fourteen centuries of existence, frequently in doubt and is often still subject to the husband's authorization. (Al-Bukhari, *al-Jami' al-Sahih*, p. 453, K: 67, B: 115.)

17. P. Pascon and M. Bentahar, "269 Jeunes Ruraux," 63.

18. My own experience has been that women are more or less harassed depending on the socioeconomic features of the place they are walking. Harassment is more systematic in small and medium-sized than in large cities. It is more intense in the poor neighborhoods and slums of Rabat and Casablanca than in the middle-class areas of these same cities. It also varies according to the legitimacy of the reason you are on the street: harassment is less intense at a post-office queue than it would be if you succumb to the desire to have an ice cream or some chips in a cafe in a poor neighborhood. Of course, there are some situations that concern only minorities. In those cases the mechanisms are more difficult to grasp, such as, for instance, the harassment of women who drive cars, which seems to be governed by a completely different system of references. Your chances of being harassed seem to be greater if you drive an old small car than if you are in a big gleaming machine.

19. E. Hall, *The Hidden Dimension*, 156.

20. Hall, *The Hidden Dimension*, 163.

21. Erving Goffman, *Behaviour in Public Places* (New York, 1966), 143.

22. Frantz Fanon, *A Dying Colonialism* (New York, 1967), 53. It is interesting to note that Fanon thought the incidents were "funny." For a man with Fanon's sensitivity to segregation and preoccupation with revolutionary assertion of human rights, his remark is puzzling to say the least.

23. Personal communication to the author.

24. Chérifa Alaoui el-Mdaghri, "Le Travail féminin: Cas de la Fonction publique au Maroc en 1980," Ecole Nationale d'Administration Publique, Rabat, cycle supérieur, no. 11, promotion 1980–81.

25. Sigmund Freud, *New Introductory Lectures on Psychoanalysis,* college edition (New York, 1965), 116.

26. Abu Issa al-Tarmidi, *Sunam al-Tarmidi*, vol. 2 (Medina, n.d.), p. 413, B: 9, H: 1167.

27. Abu-al-Hasan Muslim, *al-Jami' al-Sahih*, vol. 3 (Beirut, n.d.), Book of Marriage, 130.

28. Al-Tarmidi, *Sunam al-Tarmidi*, p. 149, B: 16, H: 1181. See also, al-Bukhari, *Kitab al-Jami' al-Sahih*, vol. 3 (Leiden, Holland, 1868), K: 67, B: 11.

29. Al-Tarmidi, *Sunam al-Tarmidi*, p. 149, B: 17, H: 1172.

30. Edward Westermark, *The Belief in Spirits in Morocco* (Abo, Finland, 1920).

31. Edward Westermark, *Wit and Wisdom in Morocco: A Study of Native Proverbs* (London, 1926), 330.

32. Sidi Abderahman al-Majdoub, *Les Quatrains du Mejdoub le Sarcastique, Poèt Maghrébin du XVIième Siècle*, ed. and trans. J. Scelles-Millie and B. Khelifa (Paris, 1966), 160–61.

33. Abu Abdallah Muhammad Ibn Ismal al-Bukhari, *Kitah al-Jami' al-Sahih* (Leiden, Holland, 1868), p. 419, K: 67, B: 18.

34. Al-Ghazali, *The Revivification of Religious Sciences*, vol. 2, p. 28.

35. Sigmund Freud, *Civilization and Its Discontents* (New York, 1962).

36. Sigmund Freud, *A General Introduction to Psychoanalysis* (New York, 1952).

37. Al-Ghazali, *Revivification*, 32.

DISCUSSION QUESTIONS

1. The family harem has strict rules about who can use certain spaces, and in what ways. How do these rules enforce a gender hierarchy? Are there spaces in your own life that are similarly gendered—at home, at school, at the gym, in public?

2. Mernissi writes that "trespassing leads only to sorrow and unhappiness. But women dreamed of trespassing all the time." How are women able to succeed in trespassing in spite of the harem's apparently rigid boundaries?

3. What are the pleasures and satisfactions of the beauty rituals practiced by these Moroccan women? How are they like or unlike your own experience with beauty treatments and cosmetics?

4. Morocco is part of the MENA region described in Diane King's essay "Two Generations of Feminist Activism" in chapter 24. Do you see forms of oppression and "trespass" that are common in all three selections? Do you see shared psychological and emotional experiences? Do you see important differences?

FATIMA MERNISSI, FROM *DREAMS OF TRESPASS*

1. My Harem Frontiers   I was born in a harem in 1940 in Fez, a ninth-century Moroccan city some five thousand kilometers west of Mecca, and one thousand kilometers south of Madrid, one of the dangerous capitals of the Christians. The problems with the Christians start, said Father, as with women, when the *hudud,* or sacred frontier, is not respected. I was born in the midst of chaos, since neither Christians nor women accepted the frontiers. Right on our threshold, you could see women of the harem contesting and fighting with Ahmed the doorkeeper as the foreign armies from the North kept arriving all over the city. In fact, foreigners were standing right at the end of our street, which lay just between the old city and the Ville Nouvelle, a new city that they were building for themselves. When Allah created the earth, said Father, he separated men from women, and put a sea between Muslims and Christians for a reason. Harmony exists when each group respects the prescribed limits of the other; trespassing leads only to sorrow and unhappiness. But women dreamed of trespassing all the time. The world beyond the gate was their obsession. They fantasized all day long about parading in unfamiliar streets, while the Christians kept crossing the sea, bringing death and chaos.

Trouble and cold winds come from the North, and we turn to the East to pray. Mecca is far. Your prayers might reach it if you know how to concentrate, I was to be taught how

SOURCE: Fatima Mernissi, *Dreams of Trespass: Tales of a Harem Girlhood* (Jackson, TN: Perseus, 1994), 1–10, 231–42.

to concentrate when the time was appropriate. Madrid's soldiers had camped north of Fez, and even Uncle 'Ali and Father, who were so powerful in the city and ordered around everyone in the house, had to ask permission from Madrid to attend Moulay Abdesslam's religious festival near Tangier, three hundred kilometers away. But the soldiers who stood outside our door were French, and of another tribe. They were Christians like the Spaniards, but they spoke another language and lived farther north. Paris was their capital. Cousin Samir said that Paris was probably two thousand kilometers away, twice as far away from us as Madrid, and twice as ferocious. Christians, just like Muslims, fight each other all the time, and the Spanish and the French almost killed one another when they crossed our frontier. Then, when neither was able to exterminate the other, they decided to cut Morocco in half. They put soldiers near 'Arbaoua and said from now on, to go north, you needed a pass because you were crossing into Spanish Morocco. To go south, you needed another pass, because you were crossing into French Morocco. If you did not go along with what they said, you got stuck at 'Arbaoua, an arbitrary spot where they had built a huge gate and said that it was a frontier. But Morocco, said Father, had existed undivided for centuries, even before Islam came along fourteen hundred years ago. No one ever had heard of a frontier splitting the land in two before. The frontier was an invisible line in the mind of warriors.

Cousin Samir, who sometimes accompanied Uncle and Father on their trips, said that to create a frontier, all you need is soldiers to force others to believe in it. In the landscape itself, nothing changes. The frontier is in the mind of the powerful. I could not go and see this for myself because Uncle and Father said that a girl does not travel. Travel is dangerous and women can't defend themselves. Aunt Habiba, who had been cast off and sent away suddenly for no reason by a husband she loved dearly, said that Allah had sent the Northern armies to Morocco to punish the men for violating the *hudud* protecting women. When you hurt a woman, you are violating Allah's sacred frontier. It is unlawful to hurt the weak. She cried for years.

Education is to know the *hudud*, the sacred frontiers, said Lalla Tam, the headmistress at the Koranic school where I was sent at age three to join my ten cousins. My teacher had a long, menacing whip, and I totally agreed with her about everything: the frontier, the Christians, education. To be a Muslim was to respect the *hudud*. And for a child, to respect the *hudud* was to obey. I wanted badly to please Lalla Tam, but once out of her earshot, I asked Cousin Malika, who was two years older than I, if she could show me where the *hudud* actually was located. She answered that all she knew for sure was that everything would work out fine if I obeyed the teacher. The *hudud* was whatever the teacher forbade. My cousin's words helped me relax and start enjoying school.

But since then, looking for the frontier has become my life's occupation. Anxiety eats at me whenever I cannot situate the geometric line organizing my powerlessness.

My childhood was happy because the frontiers were crystal clear. The first frontier was the threshold separating our family's salon from the main courtyard. I was not allowed to step out into that courtyard in the morning until Mother woke up, which meant that

I had to amuse myself from 6 A.M. to 8 A.M. without making any noise. I could sit on the cold white marble threshold if I wanted to, but I had to refrain from joining in with my older cousins already at play. "You don't know how to defend yourself yet," Mother would say. "Even playing is a kind of war." I'm afraid of war, so I would put my little cushion down on our threshold, and play *l-msaria b-lglass* (literally, "the seated promenade"), a game I invented then and still find quite useful today. You need only three things to play. The first is to be stuck somewhere, the second is to have a place to sit, and the third is to be in a humble state of mind, so you can accept that your time is worth nothing. The game consists in contemplating familiar grounds as if they were alien to you.

I would sit on our threshold and look at our house as if I had never seen it before. First, there was the square and rigid courtyard, where symmetry ruled everything. Even the white marble fountain, forever bubbling in the courtyard center, seemed controlled and tamed. The fountain had a thin blue-and-white faience frieze all around its circumference, which reproduced the design inlaid between the square marble tiles of the floor. The courtyard was surrounded by an arched colonnade, supported by four columns on each side. The columns had marble at the top and the bottom, and blue-and-white tilework in the middle, mirroring the pattern of the fountain and floor. Then, facing one another in pairs, across the courtyard, were four huge salons. Each salon had a gigantic gate in the middle, flanked by enormous windows, opening onto the courtyard. In the early morning, and in the winter, the salon gates would be shut tight with cedarwood doors carved with flowers. In the summer, the doors would be opened and drapes of heavy brocade, velvet, and lace let down, so breezes could flow in while light and noise were kept away. The salon windows had carved wooden shutters on the inside, similar to the doors, but from the outside all you could see were silver-plated, wrought-iron grilles, topped with wonderfully colored glass arches. I loved those colored glass arches, because of the way the rising morning sun kept changing their reds and blues to different hues, and softening the yellows. Like the heavy wooden doors, the windows were left wide open in the summer and the drapes were let down only at night or during afternoon naptimes, to protect sleep.

When you lifted your eyes toward the sky, you could see an elegant two-story structure with the top floors repeating the square arched colonnade of the courtyard, completed with a parapet of silver-plated ironwork. And finally, you had the sky—hanging up above but still strictly square-shaped, like all the rest, and solidly framed in a wooden frieze of fading gold-and-ocher geometric design.

Looking at the sky from the courtyard was an overwhelming experience. At first, it looked tame because of the man-made square frame. But then the movement of the early morning stars, fading slowly in the deep blue and white, became so intense that it could make you dizzy. In fact, on some days, especially during winter, when the purple and shocking-pink rays of the sun violently chased the last, stubborn twinkling stars from the sky, you could easily have become hypnotized. With your head tilted back, facing the squared sky, you would feel like going to sleep, but just then people would start invading the courtyard, coming up from everywhere, the doors and the stairs—oh, I almost forgot the stairs. Lodged in the four corners of the courtyard, they were important because even grownups could play a sort of gigantic hide-and-go-seek on them, running up and down their glazed green steps.

Facing me across the courtyard was the salon of Uncle and his wife and their seven children, which was an exact reproduction of our own. Mother would not allow any publicly visible distinctions to be made between our salon and Uncle's, although Uncle was the firstborn son, and therefore traditionally entitled to larger and more elaborate living quarters. Not only was Uncle older and richer than Father, but he also had a larger immediate family. With my sister and brother and my parents, we only numbered five. Uncle's family totalled nine (or ten, counting his wife's sister who visited often from Rabat, and sometimes stayed as long as six months at a time, after her husband married a second wife). But Mother, who hated communal harem life and dreamt of an eternal tête-à-tête with Father, only accepted what she called the 'azma (crisis) arrangement on the condition that no distinction be made between the wives. She would enjoy the exact same privileges as Uncle's wife, despite their disparities in rank. Uncle scrupulously respected this arrangement because in a well-managed harem, the more power you have, the more generous you ought to be. He and his children ultimately did have more space, but it was on the top floors only, well away from the highly public courtyard. Power need not manifest itself blatantly.

Our paternal grandmother, Lalla Mani, occupied the salon to my left. We only went there twice a day, once in the morning to kiss her hand, and a second time in the evening to do the same. Like all the other salons, hers was furnished with silk brocade–covered sofas and cushions running along all four walls; a huge central mirror reflecting the inside of the gate door and its carefully studied draperies; and a pale, flowered carpet which completely covered the floor. We were never, never supposed to step on her carpet wearing our slippers—or even worse, with wet feet, which was almost impossible to avoid doing in the summer, when the courtyard floor was cooled twice a day with water from the fountain. The young women of the family, such as my cousin Chama and her sisters, liked to clean the courtyard floor by playing *la piscine* (swimming pool), that is, by throwing buckets of water onto the floor and "accidently" splashing the person next to them. This, of course, encouraged the younger children—specifically, my cousin Samir and I—to run to the kitchen and come back armed with the waterhose. Then we would do a really good splashing job, and everyone would be screaming and trying to stop us. Our shouts would inevitably disturb Lalla Mani, who would angrily raise her drapes and warn us that she was going to complain to Uncle and Father that very night. "I will tell them that no one respects authority in this house anymore," she would say. Lalla Mani hated water splashing and she hated wet feet. In fact, if we ran to talk to her after we had been standing near the fountain, she would always order us to stop where we were. "Don't talk to me with wet feet," she would say. "Go dry yourself first." As far as she was concerned, anyone who violated the Clean-and-Dry-Feet Rule was stigmatized for life, and if we dared to go so far as to trespass on or dirty her flowered carpet, we were reminded of our wayward deed for many years to come. Lalla Mani appreciated being respected, that is to say, being left alone to sit elegantly dressed in her bejeweled head-dress, and look silently out into the courtyard. She liked being surrounded by heavy silence. Silence was the luxurious privilege of the happy few who could afford to keep the children away.

Finally, on the right side of the courtyard was the largest and most elegant salon of all—the men's dining room, where they ate, listened to the news, settled business deals, and played cards. The men were the only ones in the house supposed to have access to a huge cabinet radio which they kept in the right corner of their salon, with the cabinet doors locked when the radio was not in use. (Loudspeakers were installed outside, how-ever, to allow everyone to listen to it.) Father was sure that he and Uncle had the only two keys to the radio. However, curiously enough, the women managed to listen to Radio Cairo regularly, when the men were out. Chama and Mother often would be dancing away to its tunes, singing along with the Lebanese princess Asmahan *"Ahwa"* (I am in love), with no men in sight. And I remember quite clearly the first time the grownups used the word *khain* (traitors) to describe Samir and myself: when we told Father, who had asked us what we had done while he was away, that we had listened to Radio Cairo. Our answer indicated that there was an unlawful key going around. More specifically, it indicated that the women had stolen the key and made a copy of it. "If they made a copy of the radio key, soon they'll make one to open the gate," growled Father. A huge dispute ensued, with the women being interviewed in the men's salon one at a time. But after two days of inquiry, it turned out that the radio key must have fallen from the sky. No one knew where it had come from.

Even so, following the inquiry, the women took their revenge on us children. They said that we were traitors, and ought to be excluded from their games. That was a hor-rifying prospect, and so we defended ourselves by explaining that all we had done was tell the truth. Mother retorted by saying that some things were true, indeed, but you still could not say them: you had to keep them secret. And then she added that what you say and what you keep secret has nothing to do with truth and lies. We begged her to explain to us how to tell the difference, but she did not come up with a helpful answer. "You have to judge by yourselves the impact of your words," she said. "If what you say could hurt someone, then you keep quiet." Well, that advice did not help us at all. Poor Samir hated being called a traitor. He rebelled and shouted that he was free to say whatever he wanted. I, as usual, admired his audacity, but kept silent. I decided that if, on top of trying to distinguish truth from lies (which was already giving me a lot of trouble), I also had to distinguish this new category of "secret," I was headed for a lot of confusion, and I would just have to accept the fact that I often would be insulted and called a traitor.

One of my weekly pleasures was to admire Samir as he staged his mutinies against the grownups, and I felt that if I only kept following him, nothing bad could happen to me. Samir and I were born the same day, in a long Ramadan afternoon, with hardly one hour's difference.[1] He came first, born on the second floor, the seventh child of his mother. I was born one hour later in our salon downstairs, my parents' firstborn, and although Mother was exhausted, she insisted that my aunts and relatives hold the same celebration rituals for me as for Samir. She had always rejected male superiority as nonsense and totally anti-Muslim—"Allah made us all equal," she would say. The house, she later recalled, vibrated for a second time that afternoon, with the traditional *you-you-you-you* and festive chants, and the neighbors got confused and thought that two baby boys had been born.[2] Father was thrilled: I was very plump with a round face "like a moon," and he immediately decided that I was going to be a great beauty. To tease him a little, Lalla Mani told him that I was a bit too pale, and my eyes were too slanted, and my cheekbones too high, while Samir, she said, had "a beautiful golden tan and the largest black velvet eyes you ever saw." Mother told me later that she kept quiet, but as soon as she could stand on her feet, she rushed to see if Samir really had velvet eyes, and he did. He still does, but all the velvety softness disappears when he is in his seditious moods, and I have always wondered whether his inclination to jump up and down when rebelling against the grownups was not merely due to his wiry build.

In contrast, I was so plump then that it never occurred to me to leap when someone annoyed me; I just cried and ran to hide in my mother's caftan. But Mother kept saying that I could not rely on Samir to do all the rebelling for me: "You have to learn to scream and protest, just the way you learned to walk and talk. Crying when you are insulted is like asking for more." She was so worried that I would grow up to be an obsequious woman that she consulted Grandmother Yasmina, known to be incomparable at staging confrontations, when visiting her on summer vacations. Grandmother advised her to stop comparing me with Samir, and to push me instead to develop a protective attitude toward the younger children. "There are many ways to create a strong personality," she said. "One of them is to develop the capacity to feel responsible for others. Simply being aggressive, and jumping at your neighbor's throat whenever he or she makes a blunder is one way, and surely not the most elegant one. Pushing a child to feel responsible for the younger ones in the courtyard gives her room to build strength. Hanging on to Samir for protection could be okay, but if she figures out how to protect others, she can use that skill for herself."

But it was the radio incident that taught me an important lesson. It was then that Mother told me about the need to chew my words before letting them out. "Turn each word around your tongue seven times, with your lips tightly shut, before uttering a sentence," she said. "Because once your words are out, you might lose a lot." Then I remembered how, in one of the tales from *A Thousand and One Nights*, a single misspoken word could bring disaster to the unfortunate one who had pronounced it and displeased the caliph, or king. Sometimes, the *siaf*, or executioner, would even be called in.

---

1. Ramadan, the sacred ninth month of the Muslim calendar, is observed by daily fasting from sunrise to sunset.

2. *You-you-you-you* is a joyous song women chant to celebrate happy events from birth and marriage to simple ones such as finishing an embroidery piece, or organizing a party for an old aunt.

However, words could save the person who knew how to string them artfully together. That is what happened to Scheherazade, the author of the thousand and one tales. The king was about to chop off her head, but she was able to stop him at the last minute, just by using words. I was eager to find out how she had done it.

22. *Henna, Clay, and Men's Stares*   Father hated the smell of henna, and the stink of the argan and olive oil treatments that Mother used to fortify her hair. He always looked ill-at-ease on Thursday mornings when Mother put on her horrible, previously green but now dirty gray *qamis* (an ancient gift from Lalla Mani's pilgrimage to Mecca, which had taken place before my birth), and started running around with henna on her hair and a chick-pea-and-melon mask smeared on her face from one ear to the other. Her hip-long hair, moistened with henna paste and then braided and pinned to the top of her head, looked like an impressive helmet. Mother was wholeheartedly of the school that the uglier you made yourself before *hammam* [bathouse], the more beautiful you came out afterwards, and she invested an incredible amount of energy in transforming herself, so much so that my little sister would fail to recognize her through her masks and shriek whenever she approached.

Already on late Wednesday afternoons, Father would start looking gloomy, "Douja, I love you as natural as God made you," he would say. "You needn't go through all this trouble to please me. I am happy with you as you are, in spite of your quick temper. I swear, with God as my witness, that I am a happy man. So, please, why don't you forget about the henna tomorrow." But Mother's answer was always the same. "Sidi (my lord), the woman you love is not natural at all! I have been using henna since I was three. And I need to go through this process for psychological reasons too—it makes me feel reborn. Besides, my skin and hair are silkier afterwards. You can't deny that, can you?"

So, on Thursdays, Father would sneak out of the house as early as he could. But if, by chance, he needed to come back, he would run away from Mother whenever she came near. It was a game that the courtyard loved. Occasions when men showed any terror in front of women were rare indeed. Mother would start chasing Father between the columns, and everyone would be screaming with laughter, until Lalla Mani, in her imposing headdress, appeared on her threshold. Then everything would come to a sudden stop. "You know, Madame Tazi," she would call out, using my mother's family name to remind her that she was a stranger in the family, "in this respected household, husbands are not to be terrorized. Maybe at your father's farm that's how things are. But here, in the middle of this very religious city, and only a few meters away from the Qaraouiyine Mosque—one of the centers of Islam worldwide—women behave by the book. They are obedient and respectful. Outrageous behavior of the type practiced by your mother Yasmina is only good for entertaining peasants." At that, Mother would look furiously at Father, and then disappear upstairs. She hated the harem's lack of privacy and the constant interference of his mother. "Her behavior is unbearable and vulgar too," Mother would say, "especially for someone who is always lecturing about manners and respect for others."

At the beginning of their marriage, Father had tried to keep Mother away from traditional beauty treatments by getting her to use the French beauty products which took much less time to prepare and had immediate results. Beauty products were the only area in which Father favored the modern over the traditional. After long consultations with Cousin Zin, who translated the beauty ads in the French newspaper and magazines for him, he made a long list. Then they went shopping in the Ville Nouvelle, coming back with a big bagful of beautiful packages, all wrapped in cellophane and tied with colorful silk ribbons. Father asked Zin to sit down in our salon while Mother opened the packages, in case she needed help understanding the French directions, and looked on with a great deal of interest as she carefully opened each item. It was evident that he had spent a fortune. Some packages were hair dyes, others shampoos, and then there were three kinds of creams for both the face and the hair, not to mention perfume in jewel-like bottles. Father especially disliked the musk fragrance that Mother insisted on putting on her hair, and so he eagerly helped her open the bottle of Chanel N° 5, swearing that "It has all the flowers in it that you like the best." Mother looked at everything with a lot of curiosity, made some inquiries about their composition, and asked Zin to translate the instructions. Finally she turned to Father and asked him a question he did not expect. "Who made these products?" He then made the fatal mistake of telling her that they had been made by scientific men in clinical laboratories. Upon hearing that, she picked up the perfume, and threw everything else away. "If men are now going to rob me of the only things I still control—my own cosmetics—then they will be the ones who have power over my beauty. I will never allow such thing to happen. I create my own magic, and I am not relinquishing my henna." That settled the matter once and for all, and Father had to resign himself, along with all the other men in the courtyard, to the inconveniences of the beauty treatments.

On the night before the *hammam,* when Mother put henna in her hair, Father deserted our salon and took refuge at his mother's. But he would always come back immediately when Mother returned home, wearing Chanel N° 5. She would stop by Lalla Mani's salon first to kiss her hand. That was a traditional ritual. A daughter-in-law was obliged to stop at her mother-in-law's to kiss her hand after the *hammam.* However, thanks to the nationalist revolution and all the talk about women's liberation, the ritual was dying out in most places, except for on important religious festival days. Still, since Lalla Radia continued to respect the ritual, Mother had to do so as well.

But Mother also used the hand-kissing ritual as an opportunity to joke a little. "Dear Mother-in-law," she would say, "do you think your son is ready to face his wife again, or does he want to stay with mom?" Mother would be smiling as she spoke, but Lalla Mani would respond with a frown, and raise her chin. She thought that humor in general was a form of disrespect, and that when it came from Mother, in particular, it was a kind of straightforward aggression. "You know dear," she would inevitably retort, "you are lucky to have married such an easygoing man as my son. Others would have cast out a wife who disobeyed them and insisted on putting henna in her hair when they begged her not to. Besides, don't forget that Allah has given men the right to have four wives. If my son ever uses his sacred right, he could go to his second wife's bed, when you drive him out with your henna stink." Mother would listen to Grandmother calmly and serenely, until she finished her sermon. Then, without any another word, she would kiss her hand and proceed towards her own salon, with Chanel N° 5 trailing close behind.

The *hammam* that we went to in order to bathe and wash off our beauty treatments was all white marble walls and floors, with a lot of glass in the ceilings to keep the light flowing in. That combination of ivory light, mist, and nude adults and children running all around made the *hammam* seem like a steamy-hot, exotic island that had somehow become adrift in the middle of the disciplined Medina. Indeed, the *hammam* would have been paradise, if it had not been for its third chamber.

The first chamber of the *hammam* was steamy, yes, but nothing exceptional, and we passed through it quickly, using it mainly as a way to get used to the misty heat. The second chamber was a delight, with just enough steam to blur the world around us into a sort of extraterrestrial place, but not enough to make breathing difficult. In that second chamber, women would get into a cleansing frenzy, sloughing off dead skin with *mhecca,* or round pieces of cork wrapped up in hand-crocheted woolen covers.

To wash out the henna and oils, the women used *ghassoul,* a miraculous clay shampoo and lotion which made your hair and skin feel incredibly smooth. "The *ghassoul* is what transforms your skin into silk," claimed Aunt Habiba. "That's what makes you feel like an ancient goddess when you step out of the *hammam.*" It took many seasons, and two to three days of hard work, to make *ghassoul,* which was actually fragrant brown chips of dried clay. Once they were made, all you needed to do with the chips was to sprinkle a handful of them into rosewater, and you had a magical solution.

The making of *ghassoul* started in the spring, and the whole courtyard would get involved. First, Sidi Allal would bring in heaps of rosebuds, myrtle, and other fragrant plants from the countryside, and the women would rush to take them upstairs and spread them out on clean sheets away from the sun. Once dried, the flowers would be put away until the big *ghassoul*-making day in mid-summer, when they would be combined with clay and dried again into a thin crust—this time by the hot summer sun. No child ever wanted to miss that day because then, not only did the grownups need our assistance, but we were also allowed to knead the clay and become as dirty as we liked, with no one complaining. The perfumed clay smelled good enough to eat, and once Samir and I did try some, only to come down with stomach aches which we kept carefully secret.

As with the other beauty treatments, the making of *ghassoul* took place around the fountain. Women would bring their stools and charcoal fires, and sit near the water, so as to be able to wash their hands and pots and pans easily. First, kilos of dried roses and myrtle would be placed in separate deep pots and left to simmer slowly for a while. Then, they would be taken off the fire, and allowed to cool down. Women who were fond of a special kind of flower—like Mother, who loved lavender—would put these flowers in smaller pots to simmer. Again, as with the other beauty treatments, some women believed that all the magical effect of their *ghassoul* formula would evaporate if it became common knowledge, and so these women would disappear into dark corners on the top floors, close doors, and mix their mysterious plants and flowers in secrecy. Some women, like Aunt Habiba, dried their roses in the moonlight. Others restricted themselves to flowers of specific colors, and still others recited magic incantations over their plants to enhance their enchanting powers.

Then the kneading process would start. Aunt Habiba would give the signal by putting a few handfuls of raw clay in a wide earthenware pan like those used to knead bread. She would then pour a bowlful of myrtle or rosewater over the clay, allow it to sink in, and start kneading it until it became a smooth paste. Next, she would spread the paste over a wooden board, and call on us children to take the board to the terrace to dry.

We children loved that part, and sometimes one of us would get so excited that he forgot that the clay was still soft, and started running faster and faster, until the whole contents of the board slipped off onto his head. That was horribly embarrassing, especially because then someone would have to lead him back down to the courtyard, his eyes sealed shut with clay. This kind of incident never happened to me, however, since I was so desperately slow in everything. But *ghassoul*-making day was one of the rare occasions when that quality was appreciated.

Once we children emerged on the terrace with the wooden boards on our heads, huffing and puffing away to show how important our contribution was, Mina would take charge. Her job was to watch over the boards and monitor the drying process. At night, she would instruct us to take the boards in, so that the humidity would not affect them, and around noon the next day, when the sun was hot, she would instruct us to bring them back out again. After five days, the clay would have dried into a thin crust, and split into small pieces. Then, Mina would dump it all out onto one big clean sheet and divide it up among all the adult women. Those who had children got proportionally more, because their needs were greater.

Ghassoul was used in the second chamber of the *hammam* as a shampoo, and in the third and hottest chamber, where the most compulsive cleansing took place, as a smoothing and cleansing cream. Samir and I hated that third room, and even called it the torture chamber, because it was there that the grownups insisted on "seriously" taking care of us children. In the first two chambers of the *hammam*, the mothers would forget about their offspring, so involved were they with their beauty treatments. But in the third chamber, just before undertaking their own purification rituals, the mothers felt guilty about neglecting us, and tried to make up for it by turning our last moments in the *hammam* into a nightmare. It was then and there that everything suddenly went wrong, and we started sliding from one misfortunate experience to the next.

First of all, the mothers filled buckets of cold and hot water directly from the fountains, and poured it over our heads before testing it properly first. And they never succeeded in getting the right temperature. The water was either scaldingly hot or ice cold, never anything in between. Officially, too, we were not even allowed to scream in the third chamber because all around us, the women were conducting their purification rituals. To purify oneself, that is, to prepare for the prayer that took place immediately after stepping out of the *hammam*, adults needed to use the purest of waters. The only way to insure that purity was to be as near to the source (in this case, the fountains) as possible. That meant that the third chamber was always crowded and you had to line up in order to fill your buckets. (Actually, the third chamber of the *hammam* was the only place where I ever saw Moroccans line up in an orderly way.) Every minute spent waiting for that fountain was simply unbearable, because of the heat.

As soon as the buckets were filled, the adults immediately started in on the purification ritual, right at the front of the line. The ritual washing was distinguished from routine washing by a silent concentration and a prescribed order in which the body parts were washed—hands, arms, face, head, and finally the feet. You were not supposed to run in front of a woman doing her ritual, which meant that you could barely move. So between that and the too-hot or too-cold water being poured over your head, you could always hear children shrieking and howling all over the place. Some would manage to escape from their mother's grip for a moment, but since the marble floor was slippery with water and clay, and the room so crowded, they never got away for very long. Some would try to avoid going into the third chamber in the first place, but in that case, which was often what happened to me, they would just be picked up off their feet and forced in, despite their shrill screams.

Those were the few terrible moments that practically erased the whole delightful effect of the *hammam* session, nearly wiping out in a single stroke the long string of wonderful hours spent concealing Aunt Habiba's precious Senegalese ivory comb, only to magically produce it again when she started frantically searching for it; stealing a few of Chama's oranges that she kept in a cold bucket of water; watching the fat women with huge breasts, the skinny ones with protruding behinds, or the tiny mothers with giant teen-age daughters; and, most of all, comforting the grownups when they fell down on the slippery clay- and henna-coated floors.

I discovered, at one point, a way to speed up the process in the torture chamber and force Mother to rush me to the door. I faked fainting, a talent at which I had already became rather skillful, to keep people from bothering me. Fainting when the other children imitated the *djinnis* as we rushed down the stairs late at night, would often result in the child who had frightened me dragging me down to the courtyard or at least alerting Mother. That, in turn, would result in Mother raising hell, and going to complain to the child's mother on my behalf. But performing my strategic fainting in the *hammam*, when I was dragged to the third chamber, was more rewarding because I had an audience. First, I would grip Mother's hand to make sure she was looking my way. Then I would close my eyes, hold my breath, and start sliding down towards the wet marble floor. Mother would beg for help. "For God's sake, help me get her out of here! This child is having heart failure again." I told my trick to Samir, and he tried it too, but he was caught smiling when his mother started howling for help. She reported this to Uncle 'Ali, and

Samir was publicly chided the next Friday, just before the prayer, for fooling his own mother, "the most sacred creature walking on two feet on God's vast planet." Samir then had to ask her pardon, kiss Lalla Mani's hand, and ask her to pray for him. To get to paradise, a Muslim had to pass under his mother's feet *(al-janatu tahta aqdami l-umma-hat)*, and Samir's prospects at that moment looked rather dim.

Then came the day that Samir was thrown out of the *hammam* because a woman noticed that he had "a man's stare." That event made me realize that we were both somehow drifting into a new era, maybe into adulthood, even though we still looked terribly small and helpless compared to the giant-sized grownups around us.

The incident occurred one day in the second chamber when a woman suddenly started shouting and pointing at Samir. "To whom does this boy belong?" she cried, "He is not a child anymore." Chama rushed up to her and told her that Samir was just nine, but the woman was adamant. "He might be four, but I am telling you, he looked at my breast just like my husband does." All the women who were sitting around, washing the henna out of their hair, stopped what they were doing to listen to the exchange, and they all started laughing when the woman went on to say that Samir "had a very erotic stare." Then Chama got nasty: "Maybe he looked at you like that because you have a strange breast. Or maybe, you're getting an erotic kick out of this child. If so, you're going to be in for some serious frustration." At that, everyone started laughing uproariously, and Samir, standing there in the middle of all those naked ladies, suddenly realized that he unquestionably had some kind of unusual power. He pounded his skinny chest and shouted out with aplomb his now-historic retort which became a sort of witticism in the Mernissi household: "You are not my type. I like tall women." This put Chama in an awkward position. She could no longer keep defending her surprisingly precocious brother, especially since she herself could not refrain from laughing along with the crowd. Their laughter reverberated around the room. But that comic incident signaled, without Samir and I realizing it, the end of childhood, when the difference between the sexes did not matter. After that, Samir was less and less tolerated in the woman's *hammam*, as his "erotic stare" began disturbing more and more women. Each time it happened, Samir would be taken back home as a triumphant male, and his manly behavior commented on and joked about in the courtyard for days. Finally, though, news of the incidents reached Uncle 'Ali, who decided that his son should stop going to the women's *hammam* and join the men's.

I was very sad to go to the *hammam* without Samir, especially since we could no longer play the games we had usually played during the three hours we spent there. Samir made equally sad reports on his experiences in the men's *hammam*. "The men don't eat there, you know," he said. "No almonds, no drinks, and they don't talk or laugh either. They just clean themselves." I told him that if he could just avoid looking at the women the way he did, maybe he could still convince his mother to let him join us again. But to my great amazement, he said that that was no longer possible and that we needed to think about the future. "You know," he said, "I am a man, although it does not show yet, and men and women have to hide their bodies from each other. They need to separate." That sounded profound, and I was very impressed, although not convinced. Samir then remarked that in the men's *hammam* they did not use henna and face masks. "Men don't need beauty preparations," he said.

That remark brought me back to the old discussion we had had on the terrace, and I felt that it was an attack on me. I had been the first to jeopardize our friendship, by insisting on my need to get involved in the beauty treatments, so I started to defend my position. "Aunt Habiba says that skin is important," I began, but Samir interrupted me. "I think that men have a different skin," he said. I just stared at him. There was nothing I could say because I realized that for the first time in our children's games, all that Samir had said was right, and that whatever I said did not matter that much. Suddenly, it all seemed so strange and complicated, and beyond my grasp. I could feel that I was crossing a frontier, stepping over a threshold, but I could not figure out what kind of new space I was stepping into.

Suddenly I felt sad for no reason, and I went up to Mina on the terrace and sat by her side. She stroked my hair. "Why are we so quiet today?" she asked. I told her about my conversation with Samir, and also about what had happened in the *hammam*. She listened with her back to the western wall, her yellow headdress as elegant as ever, and when I had finished, she told me that life was going to be tougher from now on for both me and Samir. "Childhood is when the difference does not matter," she said. "From now on, you won't be able to escape it. You'll be ruled by the difference. The world is going to turn ruthless."

"But why?" I asked her, "and why can't we escape the rule of the difference? Why can't men and women keep on playing together even when they are older? Why the separation?" Mina replied not by answering my questions but by saying that both men and women live miserable lives because of the separation. Separation creates an enormous gap in understanding. "Men do not understand women," she said, "and women do not understand men, and it all starts when little girls are separated from little boys in the *hammam*. Then a cosmic frontier splits the planet in two halves. The frontier indicates the line of power because wherever there is a frontier, there are two kinds of creatures walking on Allah's earth, the powerful on one side, and the powerless on the other."

I asked Mina how would I know on which side I stood. Her answer was quick, short, and very clear: "If you can't get out, you are on the powerless side."

PART 5

BEYOND "THE DECADE OF THE WOMAN"

1975 to the Present

21

MOTHERS, GUERRILLAS, AND REVOLUTIONARIES

Women's Mobilization and Activism in Latin America

M. Cristina Alcalde

How have women sought to transform their societies into more just spaces? Does participation in groups and movements for social justice qualify a woman as feminist? Can a woman be feminist even if she does not identify with that label? Women's experiences in motherist, guerrilla, and revolutionary movements from the 1970s to the early 1990s in Latin America reveal multiple paths to and various labels under which women have organized for social justice and change. This essay presents women's struggles against racial and class inequality as well as political repression. It invites us to consider how struggles for social change that do not have gender equity as their primary goal may also empower women and address feminist goals related to social justice. It also invites us to consider what role, if any, violence may play in women's struggles for social justice.

BACKGROUND TO WOMEN'S ACTIVISM IN LATIN AMERICA

Activism and feminism are not new to Latin America, nor are they replicas of activism and feminism in other parts of the world. Gender inequality is one of several forms of oppression in the region. The region's history of colonialism has greatly influenced social justice struggles that are equally, and sometimes more, concerned with racism and economic inequality as they are with sexism. Even today, the power associated with whiteness and the persistent discrimination against indigenous peoples can be traced to the colonial experience, and is felt by nonwhite women individually and as parts of broader communities. In 1992, the indigenous Guatemalan activist Rigoberta Menchú won the Nobel Peace Prize for her activism against sexism, racism, and human rights abuses.

Feminism has deep roots in the region. The first International Feminist Congress took place in Buenos Aires in 1910. Since 1981, Latin American and Caribbean feminist *encuentros* (encounters) have taken place every three years. These meetings were originally organized in response to the United Nations' declaration of the International Decade of the Woman (1975–85), and have become vital spaces for transnational networks of feminist activism and discussion in the region. Topics addressed in these meetings have included the relationships between feminist and nonfeminist activist women; the historically close relationship between feminist and leftist movements in the region; national, regional, and international feminism; feminists in government posts and autonomous feminists; globalization; social and economic justice; motherhood and reproductive rights; and the inclusiveness of feminism (especially in connection to race and sexual orientation).

In spite of the history of feminist organizing in Latin America, feminist mobilization was particularly challenging under military, dictatorial regimes and during internal wars that took over parts of the region from roughly the 1960s to the 1980s. On the one hand, authoritarian conservative governments considered feminism subversive and therefore sufficient justification for persecution. Decreased tolerance for feminist movements and increased oppression resulted in a decrease in visible feminist mobilization. On the other hand, increasingly violent and unjust living conditions led women to organize themselves as mothers, grandmothers, sisters, and wives to protect their loved ones and themselves from human rights abuses and to ensure survival in ways that have not typically been associated with feminism in Latin America or the United States.

MOTHERING AND ACTIVISM: ARGENTINA AND BEYOND

Within the 1960s and 1970s feminist movements in North America, motherhood came to be generally identified with women's oppression within the patriarchal family. It was rarely analyzed as a space of empowerment and social transformation. In contrast, in Latin America mothering has a long trajectory of being studied and publicly performed as a site of collective resistance and social change, particularly during times of political repression. Women purposefully used their maternal role to assert authority within contexts in which governments viewed the family as central to the state's well-being and women who stepped out of traditional gender roles within the family as potentially subversive and dangerous to the state. Those who were identified as subversive, a category that could include anyone suspected of not agreeing with the ideologies of the regime in power, risked abduction, torture in secret detention centers, and death at the hands of secret government agents. Bodies were rarely found, and the state refused to accept responsibility for the abduction, detainment, torture, and death of thousands.

In Argentina, thirty thousand people were disappeared between 1976 and 1983. Approximately 30 percent of the disappeared were women. This period is known as the "Dirty War," a time when suspected opponents of the professedly Christian military regime were rounded up and disappeared. Typically, individuals working for the regime but dressed in civilian clothes would break into a home in the middle of the night and abduct those the government viewed as a threat—students, teachers, labor union activists, human rights activists, and many other individuals who were viewed as having or potentially having leftist leanings or otherwise challenging the status quo. The mothers and fathers who witnessed their loved ones being taken could do little to protect them, and began to search for alternative ways to demand justice from a government that denied the abductions of their children had even taken place.

The Mothers of the Plaza de Mayo are women who, most of them housewives, had until the abduction of their children rarely became involved in political debates. After their children were abducted, however, they drew on their grief and maternal role to publicly protest a powerful and corrupt professedly Catholic regime that promoted the Christian imagery of self-sacrificing motherhood. Because in the late 1970s the law prohibited groups of three or more people from congregating on the street, the women decided to walk together in circles outside the Pink House (the equivalent of the U.S. White House, and the traditional place for protests), covering their hair with white kerchiefs and carrying the images and names of their disappeared children, to protest the state's violent repression. Some of the group's early leaders and members were disappeared, tortured, and killed as a result of their participation. In spite of this, more and more women participated.

To this day, the mothers and their allies meet every Thursday at 3:30 P.M. in the Plaza de Mayo opposite the Pink House in Buenos Aires, Argentina's capital. They know their children were killed during the Dirty War, yet most still do not know exactly how they were killed or where to find their remains. The women continue to meet to remember their children and to hold the state accountable for its actions. Through their roles as mothers, women transgressed the public/private distinction by making their "private" pain public and demanding accountability in an increasingly dangerous political landscape, and at great personal costs.

The experiences of the Mothers of the Plaza de Mayo have inspired a multitude of books, articles, films, documentaries, and even songs around the globe (for example, U2's 1987 "Mothers of the Disappeared" and Sting's 1988 "They Dance Alone"). They have also led some of the mothers in the group to publish their own texts, which provide us with glimpses of the thoughts, pain, and actions that give women strength to continue to struggle for social change and justice, even decades after their loved ones have been taken from them.

In Carmen Robles de Zurita's testimony, one of several compiled in Mellibovsky's (1997) collection, we learn that in 1975 her twenty-five-year-old son Nestor was violently taken from his home at two in the morning and that her twenty-one-year-old daughter

María Rosa was abducted ninety days later from her workplace. Both Nestor and María Rosa were disappeared, never to be heard from again. Like other women who searched for their children, Carmen sought the support of the Catholic Church, relatives, friends, and anyone who might be able to help, yet she faced indifference and more violence—even the lawyer who helped her was murdered. It was only in joining with other women in similar situations through the Mothers of the Plaza de Mayo that she found the support and space to organize collective protests during a tremendously dangerous political period. It was also in joining with other women that she found the strength and resources to find ways to make ends meet and create a new home.

The Mothers of the Plaza de Mayo may be the best known motherist activist group in the region, but it is far from the only one. Groups of mothers of the disappeared spread throughout Latin America during and after the military dictatorships of the 1960s through the 1980s. In El Salvador in the late 1970s mothers organized themselves into a group called the Co-Madres to locate children and other family members who were disappeared before and during the civil war there (1979–92). In the process of protesting human rights abuses and discussing their individual and collective experiences, women also questioned the constrictive gender roles they were expected to perform (Stephen). Today, the association between mothering and public protest continues. In Juarez, Mexico, for example, the ongoing murders and disappearances of hundreds of young women since 1993 and the authorities' failure to find those responsible for the murders have led mothers of disappeared young women to organize themselves in order to demand justice from local and national authorities on both sides of the U.S.-Mexico border.

VIOLENCE AND NONVIOLENCE: PERU'S SHINING PATH AND MARÍA ELENA MOYANO

Whereas some women respond to state and institutional violence through nonviolent, collective protest, other women embrace collective violence as necessary in the struggle for social transformation. In the 1960s, after the Cuban Revolution, guerrilla movements were common throughout the region, and women took on various roles within these movements. However, even within revolutionary movements the roles assigned to women tended to center on the family and support for others, and women rarely received the same privileges from participation in these movements as did men. In the 1970s, revolutionary movements throughout Central America grew and women went from playing supporting roles to having central roles fighting as soldiers and leading troops.

In Peru, political violence wreaked havoc in the 1980s and early 1990s. The Peruvian Truth and Reconciliation Committee report (2003) documents 69,280 deaths during the 1980–2000 period. Most of the dead were poor and indigenous. The entities responsible for these deaths were the Peruvian state, predominantly through the military, and the radical Maoist-Leninist-Marxist group Shining Path. Women fought on both sides of the conflict. What is particularly noteworthy for the purposes of this essay is that approximately 40 percent of Shining Path militants were women, and they employed violence as a way to achieve their group's goals. Both the women in Shining Path and women community activists struggled to survive and create social change, yet the means they used to achieve change could not have been more different.

Shining Path originated in the late 1960s in Ayacucho, one of the most impoverished and indigenous areas in Peru, under the rallying cry of class struggle and anti-imperialism. It advocated armed struggle as the only way to create a new, more just society from the ruins of the old, unjust order in which the majority was poor and exploited. Although armed revolutionary movements have not been uncommon in Latin America, Shining Path stands out because of its particularly violent and bloody form of revolution, which has more often been compared to Pol Pot's Khmer Rouge than to other Latin American revolutionary movements. Unlike other Latin American revolutionary movements, it rejected human rights as a legitimate concept.

Recruitment into Shining Path was both voluntary and coercive, and focused mostly on rural areas that had been largely abandoned by the state. The group was particularly appealing to young women and men who felt stuck between their parents' indigenous and rural roots and the more modern but racist city, which rejected them. Given the few opportunities poor indigenous and mestiza women have for upward mobility in a largely racist society, participation in Shining Path provided a rare opportunity for women to achieve political power. Women's participation also made women's violence especially visible because it occurred in a traditionally masculine domain: armed struggle.

Shining Path targeted for assassination community and union leaders, elected officials, development workers, police, church personnel, feminist nongovernmental organizations, and women community leaders because it believed they were maintaining the status quo and thus preventing the creation of a new society. Traditionally, women from the working and poor sectors in Latin America have organized at the neighborhood level and beyond to fight for basic services the state refuses to provide. Women have ensured their children's survival through such collective grassroots enterprises as communal kitchens and communal day care. For Shining Path, the only way to change society was to completely destroy it first. Women grassroots leaders were viewed as enemies because their work was not directly tied to Shining Path's armed struggle.

In 1992, María Elena Moyano, a thirty-two-year-old Afro-Peruvian feminist organizer and the deputy mayor of the Villa El Salvador, a large and impoverished district in Peru's capital, defied Shining Path's orders to stop her community work. She also publicly condemned the group's violent methods and promised to continue her work to provide the people in her community with basic necessities. In February of that year, Shining Path militants, including women, gunned down Moyano and dynamited her body in front of her two young sons and dozens of other people at a public event in Villa El Salvador.

In Moyano's autobiography, we get a glimpse of Moyano's life and her daily struggles. Growing up poor and experiencing inequality on a personal level made the political personal in her life from very early on and informed her activism. Moyano became an activist to challenge the injustice all around her, and the necessity of action to change these injustices were never far from her mind. She writes that even as she entered the church on her wedding day, "I thought only of the young people in the strike and remembered the struggle."

In the poem she includes in her autobiography, Moyano writes that attending the funeral of a murdered political activist in her community and seeing his grieving family made her think of her own family, and in particular of her two young sons and the pain they would feel if she too were killed because of her leadership in the community. She then tells us that "in spite of the deep sorrow I might cause / I had lived the best years of my life." Moyano understood the danger she faced, yet she continued working to help people in her community because of her deep commitment to social justice. Her struggles, although difficult, also constituted that which she highly valued. A few days after writing in that same poem that she thanked "God for continuing to give me life," she was murdered. Thousands of people attended Moyano's funeral to celebrate her life. Hundreds of individuals also continued to participate in Shining Path, searching for a way to create a better society, even if that meant destroying the current one first.

MOBILIZATION, ACTIVISM, FEMINISM

Historically as well as in the contemporary world women across borders have taken great risks and placed themselves in dangerous situations to secure basic rights and for the sake of social change—for themselves, for their children, for their communities, and for society as a whole. In this anthology, for example, in their coauthored essay section in chapter 6, Rosenman, Abney, and Kern examine how women's struggles for suffrage from the mid-1800s to the early 1900s in England and India sometimes included militant tactics and could result in "outright brutality from men"; Hopson in chapter 14 introduces readers to Mary Ann Weathers, an African American "feminist revolutionary willing to take up arms to effect a necessary and fundamental change in society" in the 1960s and 1970s; and Al-Ali in chapter 28 discusses women's activism against oppressive regimes in the decades before as well as during the Arab Spring.

In Latin America in the 1970s and 1980s, women concerned with the social injustice that surrounded them fought to change situations that did not necessarily center on gender inequality but rather on other social issues, such as racism, economic inequality, and political ideologies. For the Mothers of the Plaza de Mayo, the mothering role became a vehicle through which to transgress gendered spaces and seek justice in private and public realms. In the case of women in Shining Path and in the case of María Elena Moyano—as well as other community activists—they understood the country to be highly unequal, unjust, and in need of change. Their views about violence, however, marked their fundamentally different paths to social change. These are just some of the experiences of women in Latin America that underscore that there is no one way of being an activist, a woman, or a feminist.

WORKS CITED

Mellibovsky, Matilde. *Circle of Love over Death: Testimonies of the Mothers of the Plaza de Mayo.* Seattle: Curbstone Books, 1997.

Miloslavich Tupac, Diana, and María Elena Moyano. *The Autobiography of María Elena Moyano: The Life and Death of a Peruvian Activist.* Gainesville: University Press of Florida, 2000.

Stephen, Lynn. *Women and Social Movements in Latin America: Power from Below.* Austin: University of Texas Press, 1997.

Truth and Reconciliation Committee. *Informe final.* Lima: Comisión de la Verdad y Reconciliación, 2003.

DISCUSSION QUESTIONS

1. In what ways have Latin American women transgressed and conformed to norms of femininity in their struggles for social justice?

2. Can a woman be feminist if she does not identify as feminist? Consider the cases of the Mothers of the Plaza de Mayo and María Elena Moyano.

3. In your opinion, is the use of violence ever justified in the name of social justice? In the name of feminism? When? Why or why not?

CARMEN ROBLES DE ZURITA, FROM MATILDE MELLIBOVSKY, *CIRCLE OF LOVE OVER DEATH: TESTIMONIES OF THE MOTHERS OF THE PLAZA DE MAYO*

Testimony of Carmen Robles de Zurita, the mother of Nestor Juan Agustín Zurita, abducted at the age of 25, August 1, 1975, and of María Rosa Zurita, abducted at the age of 21, November 1, 1975

What Weapons Are You Talking About?

I am going to start by telling you about the abduction. It was on August 1, 1975, at two o'clock in the morning. They came in by smashing down the large front gate and proceeded to smash down all the other doors standing in their way. My son was in his bedroom of course—in his underwear. By the time I got up to answer and open the door, the

SOURCE: Matilde Mellibovsky, *Circle of Love over Death: Testimonies of the Mothers of the Plaza de Mayo*, trans. Maria and Matthew Proser (Willimantic, CT: Curbstone Press, 1997), 64–70.

men were already inside because by then they had knocked the door down. All of them were armed, all of them were wearing masks, and they ordered me to give them the weapons and asked me for Juan Zurita.

These men confronted me and asked me for the weapons, so I told them: "Me? Weapons? What weapons are you talking about? I have two bicycles here—the ones the kids use to collect the newspapers and then take them to the vending places, those are the weapons I have, I don't have any other weapons."

Then they locked us up in the room where I slept with my girl and they went into action in my son's bedroom. When I realized that they had taken him away, I saw at the same time that they had torn all the mattresses. All of them were perforated. I came out and asked this guy where my kid was and where they had taken him because I wanted to give him his shoes and his clothes so he could get dressed. Then the guy tells me that it wasn't necessary, that he'd be back immediately. And eleven years have gone by and soon it's going to be twelve. I have gone through all the procedures, as we all have done. Because we have searched high and low in this country, we have gone abroad, we have complained to the Church, which is the party that's given us fewer answers than anybody else: they have never contacted us about anything, nobody has concerned himself about these cases, not in Tucumán City, nor anywhere else.

In Tucumán City very little, and even less in the small towns; at least here in the capital there is somebody who's been moved . . . at least surreptitiously . . . by so much suffering . . . who told us something, although he too was risking his head. And it should be very clear that those men of the Church who put themselves out for all those in pain also had their heads chopped off, like Monsignor Angelelli and a few others.

My son was an ordinary kid, like any other kid, but he would come and talk about the needs of others.

That was his politics: other people's needs. He hurt for those who didn't have enough, for anyone who needed to buy medicine. He would put himself in his place and say: "Well, I'm going to do it, I'm going to look for it and I am going to take it to that poor guy. . . ." He would fight even with me . . . now I understand what he was telling me. I would ask him: "And so, are you going?" "Yes, I'm going," he'd say, and well, when we calmed down, he'd start talking: "And so, what do you want? They're so ignorant that— you know what they do? They go and buy wine and some salami and they get drunk, and that's because of ignorance, Mom," he'd tell me. "And how are you going to cure it?" "It's difficult, because those men on top—they don't want to cure this, because the greater the need is, the more servants there are . . . and you go and you talk to those poor guys, it's as if you threw stones at them, because they're so ignorant that they can't understand, so you figure it out: they live five in a one-room hut and they have ten children. . . ."

Sometimes I would ask him: "Juancito, what did you do with the shirt I bought you fifteen days ago?" He'd answer: "Look, I gave it to someone who didn't have any." My son was one of those people who'd go without eating bread so I could give it to you, so that you'd give it to somebody else's son who didn't have any, that sort of a kid. And since such people should not be walking around loose, their heads have to be cut off, because other people—what they want least is that there should be people like this.

My son was a skinny kid, one of those kids who . . . how can I say it? . . . like the king of the birds . . . everybody liked him: and where is that skinny kid now? What's become of that skinny kid? Where is he? Because everybody loved him. He was a kid without any vices, a hard-working kid who helped me with my work because I had to work so they could study, because I had nothing. Look, I had to work in my kiosk, selling newspapers, magazines. That was my work and their work. He would finish with that and would leave because he worked at an electric plant—he wasn't one of those boys who'd spend nights out, passing the time. He was a hard-working kid like any other.

I'll go on telling you about the abduction. On that same day I went out ready to fight for him. I went out immediately to question one person after another. We got connected with Pisarello, a defender of political prisoners and he told us: "Well, look dear, you have to leave, because there's no other alternative, dear, because they're going to take you too." And me, with this idea that you didn't believe in anything because you couldn't believe in anything . . . the only thing you believed was that, yes, you were going to find your son. Then Pisarello was abducted, they took him away too, dear; it didn't look like an abduction, he was taken from his house in a gentle way, his wife told me afterwards. They allowed him to put on his shoes, they allowed him to get dressed and they took him away. After fifteen days he reappeared—those who saw him told me—in a bag, cut up with a saw, his eyes jabbed out. . . . Well, when that happened, I told myself I'd better run because if they did that to him, why wouldn't they do something worse to me? Then I came to Buenos Aires without knowing anything about anything. I didn't know anybody, they had already taken my girl too, they took her after my son, ninety days later. When they took her, I went immediately to talk to Pisarello, and he told me: "Look, do you know why they've done this to you? The girl doesn't have anything to do with this, the girl is innocent, but they have taken her because you stirred up things for them every hour of the day and night—what they've done to you is their revenge. There are those who could be witnesses for the girl, but who'd offer to be a witness? Nobody, because nobody wants to talk, they're all blind, they're all dumb."

My son was taken with another kid whose name is Roberto, who is also one of the disappeared; there are lots of disappeared during that period, 1975.

Look, I didn't mention the children's names: Nestor Juan Agustín Zurita, my son, who was abducted at dawn on August 1st, 1975 . . . because my son didn't "disappear," my son was taken . . . and my daughter, María Rosa Zurita, they took her ninety days later. And up until today they are still disappeared. All these cases happened in the city of Tucumán, in that same capital city of the province.

Yes, I did get the habeas corpus, like everybody else. When they answered you, if they answered you, they said they didn't know. In Tucumán, everything was no.

The Church didn't answer. I wrote outside the country, I wrote to the Pope, who never answered, though he knew better than anybody else, and maybe was satisfied with this genocide being carried out. Because everything was looked upon favorably by them, because if they had not looked on things favorably, those bums in the military wouldn't have done anything and things wouldn't have gone so far.

They've gotten to the point they have with the complicity of the Head of the Church.

I came here since I could no longer do anything and they had murdered my lawyer, who was more or less in charge of my papers and who had already warned me about what could happen to me when that really terrible thing happened to him. I got myself a job as a sleep-in maid. I didn't do anything but go around in circles. Well, those times went by until I was able to establish myself a bit and get connected with the Mothers, but dear, it was tough going. During that time I didn't have a thing, because I didn't know anybody. The Mothers helped me a bit and found a place for me to work; they gave me a hand.

I did any kind of work to eat until—I don't know why—somebody said to me, why don't you buy yourself a bit of land and I got myself this plot with some pesos that I had left, dear, for which today I thank God, who gave me the courage and the will power to build this roof, and now I'm living in my own place. And I have to give thanks every day while I am alive to those who have backed me, to those who have given me loans, to those who have trusted me. And I built my little house, and that's where I'm living now.

To Me Your Daughter Is My Daughter

But without forgetting what has already happened, I keep on looking for my children and everybody else's children, because to me your daughter is my daughter, she's a little bit mine. My children are a little bit yours, because I hope yours will appear so that she can tell me, so I can find some consolation, know, know what happened to some of them . . . because the children belong to everyone, to every person in those circles we walk in. . . . Ten years have gone by already since we started these circles. Sometimes I don't know why we keep marching in them, because nobody listens to us. The policies of Alfonsín's government promised so many things. . . . And now three years have gone by and nobody tells us anything.

When the civilian government came to power, didn't you have hopes? But how could we not be hopeful? It wasn't me alone who was hopeful, all of us were hopeful. It's time for the constitutional government to make use of its weapons because they have promised us so many things . . . they've promised the country so many things, and it has not fulfilled even one of them. I want somebody to tell me which of their promises they have fulfilled.

But it was everybody's illusion. Not just my hope, it was the country's hope: that the disappeared would reappear, that Alfonsín was going to give an answer, that he was going to tell the Mothers about the children, that there was going to be justice. But what answer did he give us? NONE.

In spite of everything, I am going to keep on asking for justice, I am going to keep on marching, because I want to know who is the guy who gave the order, who pulled the trigger, and where . . . and where they threw the bones, of each and every one of the disappeared. Of each and every one of the disappeared! Because I am not interested in what some people say: that my son was a guerrilla. Because it's a lie, because they yanked my child out of my house, they stole him from my own house, so nobody can say that my son was in the mountains. And they came and dragged my daughter out of her workplace because I stirred things up every single day, and they didn't like that and they had to do something or other to shut me up.

I now feel calm because I have my own place to live in, a house that's mine, and a job. I can escape sometimes to Tucumán to see my sons, the two of them who stayed there, and my two daughters as well.

All of them are all right, thank God. I have a daughter who's a doctor, but she doesn't work because what they pay her is hardly anything. I go there, my grandchildren are all happy, the older one is now nine years old and didn't know anything about things, but now he knows because his parents told him what happened to his aunt, what happened to his uncle; so he asks me things like: "Why did they do it? Who did it? Why did they do that to my uncle? Why did they do that to my aunt?" Because they had a big photo made and they told the children: "This was your uncle, some bad men came and took him from his house." Then he says to me: "Grandma, if I knew who took him away, who did that to him, I don't know what I'd do to that guy." He's a child barely ten years old, but he already has the notion—in his very veins—that he isn't sure what he'd do to that insolent scum who took it upon himself to barge into other people's homes, to knock down other people's doors, to steal people.

Translated by Maria and Matthew Proser

MARÍA ELENA MOYANO, FROM *THE AUTOBIOGRAPHY OF MARÍA ELENA MOYANO: THE LIFE AND DEATH OF A PERUVIAN ACTIVIST*

I Spent the Best Days of My Life in Villa El Salvador

My name is María Elena Moyano Delgado. I was born on November 29, 1958, in the Barranco District of Lima. My parents were Eugenia Delgado Cabrera and Hermógenes Moyano Lescano. I have six brothers and sisters: Rodolfo, Raúl, Carlos, Narda, Eduardo, and Martha. I am married and have two children. I am busy with my family and my organization. I live in Sector 3, Group 18, Lot 15. I studied two years of sociology at the university level.

I have happy memories of my father and family, at least until I reached the age of five. We lived in Surco, in a house near the park and my school. The best part of my childhood

SOURCE: María Elena Moyano, *The Autobiography of María Elena Moyano: The Life and Death of a Peruvian Activist*, ed. Diana Miloslavich Tupac, trans. Patricia S. Taylor Edmisten (Gainesville: University Press of Florida, 2000), 75–90.

was having my parents together and my time in school. I could read and write at an early age. I attended the little school on the park. I remember that my teacher's name was René. Later I attended a state-run primary school. My teacher was named Asunción; she was very good. I never did receive a diploma. Well, I was very active, unlike my brothers, who were glued to the books. But I never repeated a school year. I was one of a group of children that was always making mischief.

I felt useless when I lived in Barranco and Surco, although I admit it was also frustrating moving to a desert. [Villa El Salvador lies on a barren coastal strip.] I remember that first day when we were dropped off with our things. There was my mother and my brothers and sisters. My siblings were a little older than I, and they fought to see who would go to buy the straw mats and poles. My sister [Narda] and I were very afraid.

By evening, we finished making a basic shack. Four mats made a square room, with one on top for the roof. I remember there was a lot of wind, and that the roof almost blew off at night. Everything was dark, and all you could hear was the whistle of the wind. We didn't even have a candle. My sister and I couldn't sleep all night. I joined my brothers and sisters in telling my mother that the situation was horrible. We said, "And now what do we do?" But my mother thought that here, at least, nobody would throw us out of this shack, and that here, one day, we would build our home. She told us where the bathroom would be, the living room, the bedroom. She said that each of us would have our own bedroom, and if the lot wasn't large enough, we would make a spiral staircase and have more bedrooms on the second floor.

I remember when they threw us out of our house and seized our furniture. That experience gave us even more desire to endure and more dreams for our own pretty house with a little living room, kitchen, bath, and bedrooms. I wouldn't need a patio. We would have a huge one; it would be the central park in which, one day, there would also be a place for us to gather and play volleyball.

Those first months we all worked hard to finish our house of straw mats and poles. We eventually added several rooms.

Later I got involved in the church. We formed a youth group and prepared a theatrical production for Holy Week about the passion and death of our Lord, Jesus Christ. Once, I played the role of Mary Magdalene. These events took place on Sundays. On weekdays, I traveled to a school in Surco called Jorge Chávez. I left with my brother at five in the morning to get in line to take bus number 55, which dropped us at the stop near Higuereta. From there, we walked about a half hour. We were on the school's volleyball team, and so we had to return to school in the afternoons to train.

I also remember that we were hungry a lot. My brothers and sisters didn't work, and my mother couldn't find clothes to wash. Nevertheless, we always returned home for lunch. To my mother, everything that had to do with school came first. At times we lied, saying that we had classes in the afternoon, knowing she would give us bus money so we could go to volleyball practice. During the summers, I would play volleyball in the Villa championships.

I Spent My Days at the Secondary School or at Church

At age fifteen I finished secondary school at Jorge Chávez in Surco. My brothers wanted Narda and me to apply to the university. A school friend and I wanted to enroll in a secretarial program instead. There was an extension course offered by the University of Lima. When the time came, I asked my brothers if it could be my sister who applied to the university because, otherwise, there would not be enough money for the two of us. I reminded them that I preferred a practical career. My sister applied to the University of San Marcos; I did not. She was not admitted.

Later, the entrance exams for the Garcilaso de la Vega University came up. My brother Carlos asked us to apply, but we didn't want to. He promised to work for us and said that he would pay our fees. We agreed and applied together. I added the condition that I be allowed to choose my own career. My mother opposed this arrangement. She wanted me to study law. I lied to her, saying that, yes, I would, but instead I applied to the sociology program. Anyway, I thought that I'd never be accepted. Unlike my sister, I had never been educated in an academy; I only wanted to read books about different societies. Unfortunately, I was admitted.

When the exam results were released, I was already in love with Gustavo, who is now my husband. I didn't want to go to the university, but he insisted. I went with my fiancé, and my sister went with hers. The first thing I did was look at the acceptance list for the accounting program, the career track that my sister had chosen, but her name was not on the list. "Well," I told Gustavo, "this university is off limits for the poor," and I angrily commented that we should not have wasted time or money in applying, least of all at a private university. This was my brothers' madness. And we had even lied, saying we lived in Barranco, and had also put on the personal data sheet that we had a very wealthy father, who was a businessman, and a number of other things, and still we were not admitted. I thought I was right to think one had to have a lot of money to get into that university.

My sweetheart then insisted that we look at the sociology list. I was very surprised to see my name on it. I couldn't believe it. I was sad because I couldn't understand why they had not admitted my sister, who was more studious and better prepared than I, and who now would not have the same chances in life. I didn't say anything at home for one week. I was so sad, but I finally had to tell my brother.

I Became Director of a Musical Theater Group Shortly after Entering the University

There were fifty young people from different neighborhoods who, independently of the Church, gathered in the local hall. It was a beautiful group. I remember each one of them, the activities we had, and how we reflected on the Bible, the problems of the young, drugs, and the lack of communication with our parents.

We were just young people, with Christian convictions, who were loyal to our community. There was no adult to guide or influence us. We were youths with a desire to do something for our community. We helped the directors and sang and performed before large meetings, where neighbors would debate the issues. We developed our own themes. I must say that we did not see the people from the Popular Communication Center. We thought they would try to manipulate us politically. We were always careful around them, and we competed with them when we learned they would be performing in one of the neighborhoods; we polished our acts and rehearsed to leave a good impression of our group.

I can't forget the time there was a youth conference, and we were invited. I remember Yoni, who told me that the Bible wasn't sufficient to end the problems of young people. I argued with him, trying to convince him and the others that what was important was love of our neighbor; that if we could just be good and united, it would be enough.

I studied historical and dialectical materialism at the university—class struggle, et cetera. Then I began to question myself. I didn't understand why so many of the poor had to struggle so hard to study or to get work. They couldn't succeed. What was our problem? Incapacity? What? I asked myself many questions, and finally I began to question the existence of God, and, if He existed, why did He allow so many children to die from hunger, and why were there so many frustrated young people?

About the same time, some university students approached our youth group. They promised to help us with the theater, to write the scripts, to train our voices, et cetera. At first, they tried to teach us something, but they were very boring. We had our own way of thinking, our own music, and our own way of dancing. Later, we turned off the music, and we shared our problems or accounts of something that had mortified us, and we helped each other; we would reflect on a problem together. They [on the other hand] wanted to teach us the thesis of Mao, who spoke of the obligations of the individual, but the lessons were boring, and they turned off the students. Very few of us remained with them.

They [the university students] began a class to teach us about Marxism and about the Chinese revolution. We talked about class struggle. I, who had only a minimal amount of university instruction, and they, who were much older, spoke about the same things. They said that the Church was the opiate of the people. A point came when I no longer believed in God. Only a few remained from our original group, and all of us were leaders. Now, I very much regret not having been able to help some of the other students, younger than we, who are now marginalized. They still respect us, however, and have never harmed us. On the contrary, they have always been supportive.

The directors decided there was a need for a school for the young children of the members of our circle. The school had to belong to the people and not to the state. They asked all of the young women who had finished their secondary educations, and who wanted to care for children aged three to five years, to come forward at the next meeting because they would select someone to be in charge. I was chosen, and they asked me to prepare myself for the task. It was exciting for me to become a teacher that easily.

I began to work with a group of children in the mornings. I remember that we had very little. The children sat on stones or bricks. One day my fiancé, Gustavo, brought some wood and made a table for us. He shaped it into a circle, and the children had a place to draw and paint. I dreamed about an ideal, early childhood education facility, about the kind the directors talked about doing with the help of UNICEF. I dreamed about having a bathroom and a real classroom for the children. I worked for four years in the local community center while the module was being constructed. I never had the chance to teach there, but my youngest son attended that facility.

I Worked Alone at the First PRONOEI [Nonformal, Experimental] Early Childhood Program in Villa El Salvador

The following year, more educational programs began in Villa El Salvador. I was chosen to be the specialist in charge of educational evaluation. The teachers got together so that the instructional coordinator could train us, but we were unsuccessful when we tried to apply the information. We had neither the materials nor the kind of children they had in Miraflores [a much wealthier Lima neighborhood]. So we formed the Study Circle for Nonformal Teachers (CEA). We taught ourselves the instructional methodology and the curriculum used by the Ministry of Education.

We never thought of a salary until more coordinators arrived. We learned that some of them were not specialists, did not have experience but were, nevertheless, earning salaries. Then, through our study circle, we asked the Community Education Nucleus (NEC) to keep our own promoters in mind—those who had experience and some train-ing—when they contracted for future coordinators.

The year that the Education Workers of Peru (SUTEP) struck, the union leaders came to our circle and asked us for our support, telling us that we, too, had grievances, and that the state should be responsible for the education of the children by paying teachers. They told us that we were teachers, uncredentialed, but teachers. The educational leaders of the Urban Self-Management Committee also supported the strike. All of the parents did, too. So we decided to form a committee of strikers from Villa El Salvador. We asked for a minimum salary and the right to be coordinators. The community decided to form the Central Strike Committee, composed of a member from the Urban Self-Management Committee, one from the Education Workers of Peru group, a parent, and a representa-tive from the education promoters. I was elected as the representative from Villa El Sal-vador. As a show of strength, the committee agreed to occupy the schools, demonstrate, and throw paint on the yellows [scabs].

They Assign Me to a School

The Central Strike Committee delegated responsibility for the occupation of the schools. I was assigned to a school. I had no experience, but I still participated with great conviction and a sense of mythical proportion. I was convinced that only societal change could end the injustice against the people. I remember when the Pachacútec school was occupied—the school that turned out to be the model. It was considered the strongest school because the educational nucleus was there. I remember the woman who became famous as Comandante Zero. She was a mother with children in the school. I spent my first night away from home in that school. My mother was desperate, thinking that something had happened to me. Well, tanks did come. I don't remember how they entered because there was so much sand.

That stage in my life really changed me. I did not live at home; I lived at the "Pacha" school. I left my family; I had a different family during the entire strike. My mother was Comandante Zero, and the teachers, students, and promoters were my brothers and sisters. It was our home. I remember how we rotated tasks, in such a disciplined way, and with a feeling we were involved in a spiritual revolution. The occupation was disciplined, especially during the night watches. I didn't sleep one moment the first night. Every time I saw a car pass, I blew a whistle that made everyone jump out of their beds and leave through the windows. I didn't let anyone sleep. They never assigned me to that watch again.

It was such an emotional time! I remember how we would go out early in the morning to gather food at the markets and the solidarity of the people. It was so beautiful! What unity! I remember how we walked from school to school as though it were nothing. Everyday the people would prepare communal kettles. I'll never forget the famous soups, so delicious: sweet potato, cauliflower, yucca, *olluco*, and all of the vegetables that would be donated, prepared with great gusto by Comandante Zero and "Fat Alfred."

I also remember when the *apros* [members of APRA, the American Popular Revolutionary Alliance] removed the parents from "school occupation number five," Public School 6065. All of the Central Strike Committee prepared to retake "five." All of the families gathered and planned, minute by minute, how we would recapture the school and throw out the *apros*. It was said that they had guns and knives. We got clubs. I was responsible for getting the self-defense weapons. Although I was very afraid, I accepted this duty. I can't forget a *compañero* who was bleeding profusely from a head injury. We were even told that one of us could die; that we should take care of each other. That day I gathered stones for the *compañeros* who had to oust the yellows. I remember the mobilizations, the tear gas, and the clubs.

I Believed We Were Engaging in Revolution

I must say that even though I had a revolutionary consciousness, I knew nothing about political parties. I knew only that APRA was opposed to our cause.

It was my experience that the education promoters who did not actively participate in the strike, were not invited to the meetings. I believed that it was our cause, and that we had to fight for it together. I understood that not everyone was in favor of the strike. Some of the nonformal teachers even replaced the regular teachers during the long strike, although we really wouldn't let anyone work. Ms. Vilcachagua had a list of the yellows who were "working."

To Pay My University Fees, I Substituted for Teachers on Maternity Leave

I forgot to mention that, to earn money to pay my university fees, I substituted for teachers who were on maternity leave. During the strike, I taught at Public School 6063 in the mornings and at one PRONOEI school in the afternoons. I also remember that although Ms. Vilcachagua knew I was coordinator of the preschool, nonformal teachers, she offered me a contract and even guaranteed me a position in a school. She tried to convince me that those who initiated the strike were politicians. I rejected the offer. Of course, I couldn't return to any school once the strike ended. But I had the satisfaction of knowing that Vilcachagua promised there would be no retaliation against the directors and nonformal teachers once the strike ended, on the condition that I not return to teach at any PRONOEI school. I remember how all the *compañeras* turned their backs on Vilcachagua and unanimously agreed to continue with the strike if she did not allow me to return. She had no other recourse, and I was able to finish the year at my PRONOEI school.

Later, I didn't have any work, and my mother was pressuring me because I wasn't helping out at home. I couldn't substitute-teach anymore because of my strike involvement, and so I couldn't pay for the academic term. I also learned that the political parties took advantage of each school occupation. Some teachers were even inviting me to insider meetings. So, with all the pressure from my family, with hundreds of teachers replaced, with some *compañeros* in prison, I felt frustrated, as if I had accomplished nothing. My only consolation was my ever-patient fiancé. We had been together for five years, and my mother adored him—the ideal son-in-law.

I decided to surrender to him and to have a baby. I had wanted to have one. I didn't understand it, but I wanted to raise, educate, and give my child everything that I could not have: a family with an exemplary father. I got pregnant. I didn't want to get married and didn't even want Gustavo to be responsible for supporting the baby. Gustavo had his own economic problems. He was the oldest of seven orphaned brothers and sisters, and his father was in prison. He also had a pregnant sister to take care of. An entire family for which he was responsible. I would have been too much.

I looked for work but couldn't find any, and, to top it off, the pregnancy caused me to become very anemic—a product of the communal kettles and my bad kidneys. I couldn't sleep at night. My brothers learned that I was pregnant. My pregnancy created total chaos in the family. My mother cried and shamed me. She scolded me, saying that if she couldn't get married in white, her daughter should. My brothers wanted to kill me. While I was ill and at home, my youngest brother psychologically abused me. No one forgave me for losing my job and leaving the university for some strike that produced no visible gains. They threw it in my face that I had been used by the politicians. While I was in bed, they would ask me, "Where are your friends now that you are going to have a child?"

My Mother Speaks to Gustavo and Asks Him to Marry Me

Gustavo was, of course, delighted. He had already told me that in spite of all the economic difficulties, we would get married. I believed that marriage was not the solution to any problem, least of all the problem of having a baby. But I remembered how I had suffered when I was a little girl, when my parents separated, without a father at my side, and the oft-repeated words of my mother, "Since I didn't have luck in marriage, and did not have the good fortune to get married in white, you, my daughters, will certainly leave this house in white."

My mother arranged all the details of the civil and religious ceremonies. She paid the expenses. My oldest brother rented the bridal dress; my youngest brother, Eduardo, gave us the cake and the appetizers; my sister-in-law, Beatriz, and my other brothers and sisters provided the food and beer. My mother did the invitations, and I got married just as my mother had dreamed of getting married herself: in the Barranco church, where I had also been baptized, with a white gown and a train, three bridesmaids, two nephews carrying my train, and one niece bearing the rings. As I entered the church, I thought only of the young people in the strike and remembered the struggle. I could see my *compañeros* Miguel and Josefina. I felt sad. Was I beginning a new life only to leave my people's revolutionary struggle? On the other hand, I dreamed of the ideal family and awaited the birth of my child.

I Begin a New Life

I had problems in creating the ideal family—my new goal. I lived in a room made of straw mats that belonged to my mother. My brothers were not working. I was sick because of the pregnancy. My husband had another family to support. We lived on the little that my *compañero* earned, and he also helped to feed my brothers. I remember that my brother Carlos, who had children, was also jobless. My sister Narda was the only one working. I remember the fights, the absolute subordination to my husband. I cooked for him, but he did not like the taste of the food I prepared, and so I cried. I did not eat so I could save the best for him. I didn't want him to ever reproach me by saying that he supported my family.

I remember the birth of my child in those poor circumstances. I used the little money that Gustavo gave me for diapers and maternity fees for food.

The day my pains began, my mother looked for Felícita, the health worker. She checked me and said I was not yet ready. My mother and husband decided to wait a little longer so the maternity hospital would not send me back home. At 7:00 P.M. on August 2, 1980, my son was born in my mother's bed. I was attended by my husband and Señora Felícita. My husband held his son at birth. It was a marvelous experience. My child, so longed for.

I lived with my mother. Gustavo also had to support his own family. His sister had a child, but her *compañero* did not assume responsibility. My family had its own problems. Then an opportunity arose for Gustavo and me to live on our own. There was a custodial job in Miraflores. In exchange for keeping the building clean, we got an apartment on the roof. I lived in that apartment for eight months, acting like the ideal mother and wife, but I could not stand people's indifference. Everybody lived their own lives; no one spoke to anyone else. I just took care of my child and waited for my husband's return. I remember feeling that, on the one hand, I was happy with my family, but, on the other, totally frustrated as a person. I missed Villa El Salvador, its gatherings, the neighbors, and the life of my people.

I Return to Villa El Salvador

One day a neighbor's clothes were stolen from the roof, and a lady shouted at me, suggesting it was my family who had stolen them during one of their visits. I became furious at the very idea. I shouted at her, expressing all of my frustration and all of my feelings about class discrimination. I couldn't take it any longer. We said our good-byes and returned to Villa El Salvador.

In 1983 I returned to my community. I again lived with my mother; there wasn't an alternative. I did it with the hope of helping out my husband, so we could get a house. I got a job in a private school and did some substitute-teaching work in Public School 6070. Later, David, our second and unexpected child, came. My husband gave me the strength to have the baby, and my mother and youngest sister helped to care for both of our children. I taught literacy classes in the evenings. We founded a mothers' club, Micaela Bastidas, hoping to prevent any manipulation of the mothers by institutions such as OFASA [Adventist Philanthropic Office for Social Action] and others. It was a good experience. I worked morning, afternoon, and night.

I Was Director of a Mothers' Club for Three Years

Being director of a mothers' club helped me to understand women's problems. I became conscious of women's roles and of their marginalization. Even though they worked outside the home, because they were women, their household duties didn't diminish. I understood, too, just how macho my own husband was. There were constant fights because I wanted him to assume some of the household chores.

At the end of 1983, a group of women from the mothers' club wanted to clean the streets, as other women's groups had been doing. I agreed and helped them with some cleaning tasks. Previously, a group of them had come to my house to propose the formation of a women's federation within our own group so that some could donate food [to the communal kitchen] instead of participating in cleaning duties. They asked my advice. I said that I didn't understand the role of a women's federation if its only purpose was to acquire food. They said that Señora Erlinda asked them to form the women's club with the women who do the sweeping. I told them I didn't understand why a women's club was needed if we already had a mothers' club because only women could be mothers. I didn't perceive any difference, and it also seemed like a duplication of effort. If it was a question of getting food, we could change the name from mothers' club to women's club.

It Was Time for a Women's Conference in Villa El Salvador

The señoras asked me, along with two other delegates, to represent them at the convention where the Women's Federation was formed. I attended with my son David. When we got to the movie theater Madrid, we met many women from other organizations, including those from mothers' clubs. They were all trying to be part of the conference. Erlinda decided who would enter. I knew her because she had participated in the occupation of Public School 6066. When she recognized me, she refused to allow me to participate as a delegate. The women from the cleaning group told her that I was their representative, and that she should let me enter. Juana Bendezú, who also had participated in the school occupations, convinced Erlinda that I should be allowed to enter. I thought about the role of various factions at that convention, even though I did not understand them very well. Queta headed up the minority faction and Erlinda, the majority. They asked me to serve as secretary. I did not understand this federation business because it seemed that the only women who were attending were those from the cleaning groups; the majority of the women in the other organizations did not participate.

I had a small child, and I did not have time to dedicate to any federation. I thought of the manipulation that probably had occurred during the time of the school occupations. I began to think that maybe I should take the job, so I could better work for the women from my mothers' club. I was elected as undersecretary of the organization, and a new stage began in my personal life and in terms of my growth as a director. I was named president during the second Women's Federation convention of 1986, and I was reelected in May 1988.

From María Elena's Notebook, January–February 1992

> Ayer tuve a la muerte cerca.
> Al ver a la familia de Andrés Sosa,[1]
> a sus hijos que se desgarraban de dolor,
> de impotencia,
> sentí la muerte cerca.
> Más cerca que antes.
> Comprendí que difícil es el sacrificio.
> Pensé en mis hijos, mi vida y mi historia,

---

1. *Miembro del Bloque Populario Revolucionario (BPR), agrupación conformada por disidentes del prosoviético Partido Comunista Peruano. Fue asesinado en Villa El Salvador el 24 de enero de 1992 presuntamente por miembros del Movimiento Revolucionario Tupac Amaru (MRTA). María Elena asistió a su funeral.*

pero cerca a la muerte sentí el amor,
este amor que ahora siento por ti,
mis hijos y mi pueblo,
y volví a sentir la vida cerca de mí.
Pensé que pese al dolor profundo que pudiera dejar,
siento que ya viví lo mejor de mi vida.
De mi niñez recuerdo a mi madre trabajando,
a mis hermanos enérgicos en nuestra educaciòn,
la tristeza de no tener a mi padre cerca.
Pero también cuando pisé por primera vez el desierto
empecé a vivir los mejores años de mi vida.
Aunque con mis hermanos nos íbamos al colegio sín comer,
estábamos felices.
Recuerdo cuando iba a la iglesia y me hice catequista.
Recuerdo a "Los Hijos del Pueblo,"
al grupo "Renovación,"
a los niños de los grupos 12 y 18
sentados en los ladrillos y en los tablones que ponía Gustavo
para que pintaran.
Recuerdo las luchas para organizarnos y estudiar,
las faenas comunales y las escuelas populares.
A Ana, a los profesores del SUTEP,
las ollas comunales.
Las marchas interminables e incontables
y a las mujeres organizadas.
Nuestras alegrías, penas y logros alcanzados.
A mis niños del colegio Miguel Grau, el 6070.
Entonces sigo recordando
y siento que he vivido lo más hermoso de mi vida.
A mis hijos,
la ternura de David y la timidez de Gustavito.
Este amor tan infinito,
a mis hijos,
a mi pueblo que sufre y se corroe el alma.
Su alegría de las polladas y festivales deportivos.
Cómo vivo, Dios mío.
Gracias por darme ¡todo!

El amor,
el dar todo lo que pude
de mí misma.
Todo.
Gracias Dios mío por seguirme dando la vida.
—Febrero de 1992

Yesterday death came near to me
when I saw the family of Andrés Sosa,[2]
his children rent by grief,
and impotence.
I felt death near,
nearer than before.
I understood how difficult sacrifice is.
I thought about my children, my life and my history.
But close to death, I felt love, too,
that love I now feel for you,
my children and my people,
and I felt life rise within me again.
In spite of the deep sorrow I might cause,
I had lived the best years of my life.
I remembered my mother, working when I was a child,
my lively brothers at school, the sadness of
not having my father near.
Yet, when I first stepped onto the desert,
the best years of my life began.
Even though we went to school hungry,
we were happy.
I remember when I went to church
and studied catechism.
I remember the "Children of the People,"
and the youth from Renovación,
the children from groups 12 and 18
seated on the bricks and boards that Gustavo brought
so they could paint.
I remember the struggle to organize and the struggle to study,
the communal tasks and the people's schools,

2. Member of the Popular Revolutionary Block, formed by dissidents of the pro-Soviet Peruvian Communist Party. Sosa was assassinated in Villa El Salvador on January 24, 1992, presumably by members of the Túpac Amaru Revolutionary Movement (MRTA). María Elena attended his funeral.

and Ana, and the professors from SUTEP,
the communal kettles.
I recall the interminable and innumerable marches
and the women—organized.
Our happiness, pain and accomplishments,
and my students in the Miguel Grau School, number 6070.
Then I continue to remember
and know I've already lived the most beautiful years of my life.
My children,
the tenderness of David and the shyness of Gustavito.
This infinite love
for my children,
for my people whose souls are consumed,
yet they are happy at the barbecues and sport celebrations.
My God, how I've lived.
Thank you for giving me so much!
Love,
the opportunity to give my all—
Everything.
Thank you my God for continuing to give me life.
—February 1992

Translated by Patricia S. Taylor Edmisten

22

FEMINIST ORGANIZING AROUND VIOLENCE AGAINST WOMEN IN MALI, PERU, AND INDIA

M. Cristina Alcalde, Srimati Basu, and Emily Burrill

The home is one of the most dangerous spaces for women. In the United States, for example, domestic violence is the leading cause of injury for women between the ages of fifteen and forty-four. Available country studies from around the world indicate that between 10 percent and 50 percent of women are abused by an intimate partner and that the perpetrators are almost exclusively men (WHO 2001). International feminist mobilization around issues of violence against women acquired momentum in the 1980s, spurred by the activities of the UN Decade for Women (1975–1985). The UN Declaration of the Elimination of Violence against Women came in 1993. The UNIFEM Report contends that "the violence against women movement is perhaps the greatest success story of international mobilization around a specific human rights issue, leading to the articulation of international norms and the formulation of international programs and policies" (Coomaraswamy 2).

Although internationally feminists agree on the need to eradicate violence against women, the definition of domestic violence and the practices, ideologies, laws, and resources available within specific national settings have led to divergent approaches, successes, and obstacles . This essay provides an overview of feminist organizing in three countries, each on a different continent, in the post-UN Conference era. In examining feminist organizing around violence against women from the 1970s to the 1990s (and in the case of Mali, until the present), the essay invites readers to appreciate similarities, differences, and points of contention across borders and how local conditions shape this global issue.

MALI

The Republic of Mali is a signatory to major international organization treaties of the rights of women, including the International Covenant on Civil and Political Rights (ICCPR), the International Covenant on Economic, Social and Cultural Rights (ICESCR), the African Charter on Human and People's Rights (Banjul Charter), the International Convention on the Elimination of All Forms of Discrimination Against Women (CEDAW), and the Convention on the Rights of the Child (CRC). However, being a state signatory to international conventions and bills does not automatically lead to changes in the state constitution, legal codes, or especially, social and cultural norms and expectations when it comes to domestic violence. There are no laws on the books in the Republic of Mali that outlaw domestic violence or gender-based violence, though the penal code in Mali does prohibit rape. Still, the penal code itself does not outline the definition of domestic abuse, and there are no state-funded shelters or programs to assist survivors of domestic abuse.

On one level, an important question to ask is this: what are developing states such as Mali to do—Mali is one of the poorest countries in the world, according to every major metric—when they are expected to maintain standards and protocols that require a certain level of infrastructure and funding, and when they operate in a neocolonial context of tremendous debt and dependence upon international aid? Mali's political history since colonial independence from France in 1960 is defined by five decades of social and political struggle and renewal in the face of overwhelming economic challenges in the postcolonial decade of the 1960s, a single-party political system and dictatorship from 1968 to 1991, a successful coup followed by free elections and democratic renewal in the early 1990s, and continued entrenchment in the development-aid-poverty cycle which defines the relationship between many former colonies and former colonial powers. All of these aspects of post-independence Mali impact the struggle to define and combat domestic violence in Mali.

One way to approach the issue of domestic violence is to compare what governmental and nongovernmental Malian organizations are doing in the face of the global structural and institutional challenges of poverty and development, how they are defining the problem of gender-based violence in the household, how they cope with challenges, and what strategies they are employing to combat such violence. Such a comparison allows us to see what constraints and opportunities are tied to working within the framework of a state government, as well as those that are tied to the nongovernmental sector.

In 1991, when President Moussa Traore was overthrown in a coup, Mali began to make forward movement as a state in the arena of social programs and reform. The UN Decade for Women occurred during a politically repressed time for Mali; while Mali renegotiated structural adjustment programs with the International Monetary Fund (IMF) during the 1980s, there was little government programming for social welfare during the repressive Traore years, and political organizing of any sort was outlawed. Malians did not begin to see the effects of the UN Decade for Women until well into the 1990s, under Alpha Konare's presidency and through the presidency of Amadou Toumani Toure, who was democratically elected in 2002 and who was overthrown in a military coup in March 2012.

The activities and initiatives of two distinct organizations help us to understand how some have recently attempted to combat domestic violence in Mali, despite various hurdles. One is a state ministry, le Ministère de la promotion de la femme, de l'enfant et de la famille (the Ministry for the Promotion of the Family, Women, and Children, hereafter MPFEF) and one is a nongovernmental organization, l'Association pour le progrès et la defense des droits des femmes (the Association for the Progress and Defense of Women's Rights, hereafter APDF). Both organizations were formed after the UN Decade for Women, during the Konare presidency, and both have worked very hard and to varying degrees of success to promote the rights of women in Mali.

Founded in 1997, the MPFEF established its goals as threefold: to elaborate and implement measures to ensure the well-being of women, children, and the family; to work towards a better economic, social, and cultural status for women and children; and to ensure that the realm of the family becomes a realm of equality in social relationships. Specific targets include economic empowerment, improvement of health conditions, literacy programs, educating women about their legal rights, and improving sanitation (access to clean water, for example). Many of these strategies—particularly increasing economic access, literacy programs, and legal rights education—can mitigate domestic violence, but none of the programs or initiatives directly name violence in the home as a threat to the well-being of women, children, or the family. However, in 2002 and in 2009, MPFEF conducted targeted studies of violence against women. The 2002 study outlined eight different forms of violence: sexual, physical, psychological, institutional, economic, psychosocial, neglect and discrimination, and woman-on-woman violence. This provided a useful set of standards that adhered to UN and World Health Organization (WHO) protocols, and could be applied to determine whether or not the state of Mali was implementing successful programming to combat gendered violence.

In their follow-up 2009 study, the United Nations Population Fund (UNFPA) and the MPFEF appraised the international human rights conventions to which Mali is a signatory and concluded with a discussion of genital cutting (FGM) and the necessity of eradicating it in Mali. Despite the 2002 report's detailed description of domestic violence and the conclusion that it is a dire problem, the UNFPA and the MPFEF were primarily focused on FGM. We learn from the reports that state-based organizations are under a tremendous amount of pressure to participate in international conversations about the universal rights of women, but they are ill-equipped to combat domestic violence because of the various infrastructural and institutional requirements. When certain practices and agendas have international backing and funding—such as the campaign against FGM—these initiatives tend to take precedence over domestic violence.

The APDF is the largest organization devoted to women's rights in Mali and one of the most visible NGOs for women's affairs. The APDF was created in 1991, and since 1994 it has run a legal counseling and resource center for women who are victims and survivors of violence. From its first years, the APDF has been on the front lines of combating violence against women. Formed by Madame Fatoumata Sire Diakite, the APDF has successfully won a seat at the table for many state-level conversations about marriage and the rights of women. Its members have consistently argued for women's rights in a way that adheres to international protocols centered on the rights of the individual, definitions of violence and abuse of the person in mind and body, and in definitions of adulthood and one's capacity to provide consent.

One of the reasons why the APDF is successful is that while it works in conjunction with lawyers, most of the legal aid that it provides is from laypeople, typically older women, who are concerned with two factors: facilitating successful reconciliation and productive conversation between men and women on the subject of violence in the home and alternative solutions to violence; and maintaining follow-up relationships with clients beyond the office visit. This is a sort of peri-legal form of assistance whose power lies in the sociocultural embeddedness of the counselor. In this way, the APDF achieves "vernacularization" of international protocols (Merry). However, the APDF faces regular obstacles. It is underfunded and many Malian women are unaware of its existence because of infrastructural and funding challenges.

In the end, it seems that if nongovernmental and governmental organizations can work in tandem—organizations such as the APDF on the ground with women and men in Mali, and ministries such as MPFEF in the drafting of reports and protocols to be read and integrated in international communities of human rights reform—successful outcomes may be achieved.

PERU

In Peru, trial transcripts dating back to the colonial period provide evidence of the long history of women's suffering from and resistance to men's violence against them (see Chambers, Christiansen, and van Deusen). More recently, studies on the lives of women living in Peru and neighboring countries provide evidence of men's brutal acts of violence against their wives and partners in the twentieth and twenty-first centuries (see Femenias, Weismantel). In Peru's capital, Lima, 51 percent of women have experienced physical or sexual violence by a partner (Güezmes, Palomino, and Ramos).

As is also mentioned in Mogrovejo's essay in chapter 17, in Latin America from the 1960s to the early 1980s several countries were either under military authoritarian regimes or in the midst of internal armed conflicts, and this left little space for national attention to the violence many women experienced in their homes. As countries transitioned to democracy and were no longer mired in internal armed conflicts, and with the momentum provided in part by the UN Decade for Women, women's human rights and feminist organizations found more opportunities to organize in order to demand a more just and equitable society in which men's violence against women would not be tolerated. It was thus largely in the 1980s that women's human rights and feminist organizations in Latin America brought the global issue of violence against women out of the private sphere of secrecy and into the public sphere of attention. By the 1990s almost all Latin American countries had established national women's offices to focus on eradicating violence against women. Unlike the Mali case, by 2000 the majority of the countries in the region had passed domestic violence legislation.

Political and economic crises and an internal armed conflict between the state and the insurgent group Shining Path throughout the 1980s and into the early 1990s made organizing around violence against women dangerous in Peru, yet both middle-class and working-class women struggled (sometimes together, sometimes separately) to bring attention to and end men's violence against women. Many successes, including shelters for battered women, all-women's police stations, a family violence law, and Peru's signing of international treaties condemning violence against women as a human rights violation have resulted. These successes, however, must be understood against a backdrop of a developing country with high rates of poverty, rampant racism, and the absence of funding to fully implement existing international and national laws pertaining to violence against women.

Shelters

It was not until the late twentieth century, in 1982, and in the midst of the armed conflict between the state and Shining Path, that the first shelter designed specifically for battered women opened in Peru, in Lima. Rosa Dueñas, an indigenous woman and respected leader on women's and human rights issues, opened the modest house she had inherited from her mother to women and children seeking to leave violent homes. By 2001 there were six shelters in the country. Shelters are not state-funded; they are small, independent spaces founded by women community leaders who open their homes to women in the community or who are able to secure a house or lot in which to build a shelter for women in the community. It is common for shelter personnel, including the director, to experience poverty on a personal level as they struggle to assist other women and children on a day-to-day basis.

Women's Police Stations

Women's police stations were specifically created to respond to women's complaints of violence against them and have opened in various parts of the world since they were first created in India. In Peru, the first and main women's police station opened in downtown

Lima in 1988, largely as a result of the efforts of local women's organizations to push for more and better resources for women trapped in violent relationships. In many cases, women would visit regular police stations to denounce an abusive partner only to be turned away by a police officer. The opening of the first women's police station in Peru came only three years after the creation of the first women's police station in Latin America in São Paulo, Brazil. By 2002, six women's police stations (staffed exclusively by women police officers) had opened in Lima and seven more in other parts of the country. Police officers in these stations were to be sensitized and trained to respond to women's experiences of domestic violence, so that women would no longer be turned away or further victimized by the state institution charged with protecting citizens' rights.

At the main women's police station, lawyers from the prominent feminist organizations Center for Peruvian Women Flora Tristán, the Manuela Ramos Movement, and Research for the Defense of Women's Rights (DEMUS) take turns counseling women in domestic violence situations. Flora Tristán began to offer legal assistance at the main women's police station just a year after the station opened. In addition to staffing the main women's police station with lawyers, these organizations offer free legal counsel at their main offices and work on multiple projects related to women's rights. Manuela Ramos has offered free legal counsel since the mid-1980s and counseled over fifteen thousand women between the mid-1980s and 2001 at its main office.

The creation of women's police stations marked an important milestone in the struggle against violence against women, yet some women continued to experience indifference, hostility, and discrimination when they attempted to denounce abusive partners at these police stations. The practices in women's police stations thus also make clear that staffing police stations with women has its merits but cannot guarantee women the right to be heard or protected from their partner's violence (Hautzinger, Nelson). In Peru, as in other settings, individual police officers interpret existing laws through the filter of cultural values and norms, as well as individual prejudices about race, class, sexuality, and gender.

National Law and International Treaties

In 1993 pressure from women's and feminist organizations on the government resulted in the passing of the first National Family Violence Law, which includes physical, psychological, and sexual violence as forms of domestic violence, regardless of class, race, or gender. The law applies to violence between spouses, ex-spouses, current and former common-law spouses, and between those who have had children together, even if the individuals never lived together. As is the case with many domestic violence laws in Latin America, however, the law excludes same-sex partners.

Additionally, although Peruvian feminist organizations have consistently rejected conciliation as a solution in domestic violence cases because conciliation presumes two equal partners and situations of domestic violence are characterized by unequal power relations between partners, the law included mandatory conciliation procedures between 1997 and 2001. Although today it is no longer mandatory for women to undergo a conciliation proceeding, some women continue to be pressured to reconcile with their abusive partners due to the high value placed on family unity within Peru's predominantly Catholic society.

In the 1980s and 1990s the Peruvian government took several additional steps to condemn gender violence publicly, largely as a result of pressure from women's and feminist organizations. At the regional level, Peru ratified the Inter-American Convention on the Prevention, Punishment, and Eradication of Violence against Women, known as the Convention of Belém do Pará, in 1996. It establishes that women have the right to live free of violence and that violence against women violates women's human rights and fundamental freedoms.

Looking Ahead

Without accompanying structural changes, however, passing laws and signing treaties cannot end violence. Because of this, over the last four decades, feminist organizations working to end violence against women through research, education, and legislation have also focused their efforts on other aspects of society, such as health (especially reproductive health), political participation and political violence, employment, and rural development. Although the successes of feminist organizing are evident in the laws, institutions, and ongoing campaigns to educate the public about violence against women, the struggle for a more equitable and just society is far from over in Peru.

INDIA

The 1980s were a vibrant decade of feminist mobilization in India. In the 1950s though the 1970s, following the activism of the anticolonial Independence struggle, there were a number of land and labor struggles that incorporated issues of gender, as well as anti-alcohol and consumer movements led by women. Starting in the mid-1970s, urban groups arose that consciously represented themselves as "feminist" and sought to theorize gendered discrimination (Kumar). But the rallies and campaigns of the late 1970s and 1980s made the women's movement a formidable public entity, and these dealt centrally with questions of violence against women, particularly rape ("custodial rape," by police or other agents of the state, being a critical focus) and domestic violence (especially "death by fire" episodes, which were often linked to dowry demands).

While domestic violence was front and center as a concern, the activities of the Indian women's movement are primarily remembered as being dominated by protests against "dowry deaths." Here, the practice of marriage-related gifts or "dowry," which increasingly took the form of extravagant and unreasonable demands, was linked with the murders and abetted suicides of young brides, who are victims of multiple kinds of domestic violence beyond marriage gifts, though gifting became the focus of protest. As Uma Narayan perceptively points out in *Dislocating Cultures,* in these deaths by fire the figure of a burning bride ("cooking accidents" of kerosene stoves being a popular mode of murder at the time) and extravagant payments from brides' families coalesced neatly with Orientalist images of burning Indian women in need of rescue. A number of women's movement groups too made the link between the violence and marriage payments: they challenged "suicide" verdicts often attributed to deaths by fire, held extended families (rather than just husbands) accountable for domestic violence, and pointed out that ongoing demands for goods or cash often continued long after weddings. The feminist social movement around dowry worked on several fronts: legal interventions such as filing public interest lawsuits and mobilizing to lobby politicians and publicly shame dowry murderers were undertaken alongside sustained campaigns to interrogate norms of gender, as Radha Kumar describes at length in *The History of Doing* (117). The Progressive Organization of Women, Stri Sangharsh, Mahila Dakshata Samiti, and Nari Raksha Samiti all organized demonstrations which gave a great deal of national visibility to the issue of domestic violence and murder connected to dowry, as well as marches which protested the commercialization of weddings (Kumar). Sometimes, demonstrations exerted pressure by taking place in the victim's workplace and home, as well as the victim's and husband's workplaces. Street plays such as *Om Swaha* in Delhi and *Meye Dilam Shajiye* in Calcutta became an important and popular means of interrogating the culpability of families in providing dowry, reveling in displays of status, staying silent on domestic violence, and making married dependence the ideal of women's lives.

Such deaths provided spectacular and effective moments for mobilization, and became the basis for a number of legal provisions which continue to carry force. However, "dowry deaths" are too narrow an analysis of the phenomenon: much evidence exists that demands for dowry were typically only one of the grounds of harassment of married women. It is much more useful to name this phenomenon as a form of family violence, parallel to that experienced in other parts of the world. The Indian women's movement did consistently acknowledge this broader basis for identifying and redressing violence against women: most feminist organizations involved in the antidowry movement pointed to the ways in which monetization and conspicuous consumption contributed to the problem, but located the problem fundamentally in the political economy of patriarchy. The 1982 memorandum of the Dahej Virodhi Chetana Manch (the antidowry consciousness forum) insisted that dowry not be viewed as an isolated phenomenon: "Its increasing incidence is symptomatic of the continuing erosion of women's status and devaluation of female life in independent fashion. It is equally related to the worsening socioeconomic crisis within which structural inequalities have accentuated and black money power grown to fuel greater human oppression" (Palriwala 943).

The 1975 *Towards Equality* report prepared by the Committee on the Status of Women in India (CSWI) for the UN Decade for Women, arguably the most significant feminist policy document of the decade, highlighted broader social and economic issues, identifying the problem of women's oppression as "against the goal of a socialistic society," and rooted in women's economic dependence (76), as well as kinship and property: "It is not the fact of patriliny by itself but its association with joint property, and joint household and certain rules and patterns of marriage which lead to greater constraints over women and affect their position in an adverse way" (CSWI 58). To this end, they advocated, "social consciousness needs to be aroused particularly amongst women, to enable them to understand that by encouraging dowry they are perpetuating the inequality of the sexes. Reforms in marriage custom to simplify the ceremony, increasing opportunities for employment, condemnation of the ideal of a parasitic existence for women, a reassessment of the value of household work and homemaking as socially and economically productive, and the enforcement of the Anti-Dowry Act are some of the measures necessary" (76).

The influence of the women's movement in pressuring a nation-state that saw itself as both progressive and equitable is demonstrated in the number of legal provisions that were instituted as a result. The amended Dowry Prohibition Act (1984) makes the giving and taking of dowry "as a condition of marriage" punishable by law while excluding "voluntary gifts." Suicides and murders attributed to dowry have a special apparatus of evidence and arrest: Section 304B of the Indian Penal Code and Sections 113A and 113B of the Evidence Act relate to presumption of dowry deaths for unnatural deaths within seven years of marriage and carry a term of seven years to life, Section 174 of the Criminal Procedure Code relates to compulsory postmortems for women dying within seven years of marriage, and Section 32(1) of the Evidence Act relates to the weight given to dying declarations in assessing the guilt of the accused. Section 498A of the Indian Penal Code pertains to "cruelty" which may drive a woman to suicide or "harassment" related to "unlawful demands for property," but is also much more broadly treated as a "domestic torture" provision including physical, verbal, sexual, and emotional violence.

That feminist struggles over law and culture involve ongoing negotiation, rather than resting with institutionalized reform, is well illustrated in the legacies of these legal provisions. Death-by-fire cases have vanished as a popular mode of murder (perhaps along with the popularity of kerosene stoves), and the Indian women's movement has largely moved on from focusing on questions of dowry per se to economic entitlements of marriage and the dailiness of violence (Basu). However, "dowry" continues to be a powerful legal strategy with spectacular gendered appeal, such that adding dowry harassment to either domestic torture cases or divorce cases alleging cruelty, or seeking return of dowry goods in divorce settlements carries overwhelming force (whether or not dowry happened to be a major point of discord or harassment). Meanwhile S498A cases, used to prosecute domestic violence, are now arguably the frontier of strategy and controversy.

The criminal threat of S498A is often used by women to negotiate better settlements in divorce or towards reconciliation; that is, it is less a tool for curbing widespread domestic violence, and more a way of blocking the economic devastation of marital dissolution. Despite the unwillingness of police and courts to prosecute under this clause, and incredibly low conviction rates, S498A has become the locus of emergent vociferous men's movements (and some women's groups who claim to be kin to these persecuted men, such as the newly formed Forgotten Women's Association in Hyderabad) who allege that it is used as a tool of revenge and lacks sufficient curbs on capricious imprisonment. Feminist organizations find themselves ambivalent towards S498A in very different ways: they recognize its power (and limitations) as a legal strategy, but they also acknowledge that it can easily be disproportionately deployed by elite women to harass, while in fact there is no substantive legal redress, through that provision or others, for the routine family violence most women face. Economic settlements thus function as the leverage of domestic violence prosecution, while the violence itself is normalized and rendered invisible.

FROM THE NATIONAL TO THE GLOBAL

Domestic violence, it seems from these comparisons, has been at the forefront of feminist organizing at least since the 1970s in a number of countries. International feminist discourses and parameters developed during the UN Decade for Women play a strong role in the political leverage that can be asserted in each national context. Vibrant local movements provide the force behind political negotiations and shape the specific forms of intervention, continuing to develop innovative strategies in the face of recurring oppositions within diverse cultural, social, and economic landscapes.

In the trajectories that we have traced since the 1970s, we also notice the ways in which domestic violence begins to be understood on multiple intersectional fronts. Paralleling international development policy initiatives, which change from having separate "women in development" projects to "gender mainstreaming," and from a focus on addressing violence by state intervention through law to a focus on individual empowerment, domestic violence reform begins to include economic arenas, health care, and politics. The imprint of growing international discourses of mediation and alternate dispute resolution since the 1970s are also evident in the reform strategies.

Despite the energetic national movements, we cannot help but notice that change is particularly difficult to ensure in subjects relating to family and marriage, to domestic authority and the distribution of resources, and to questions of violence, shame, and privacy.

WORKS CITED

Basu, Srimati. "Transformations of Dowry in Contemporary India: Marriage Practices and Feminist Discourses." In *Dowry: Bridging the Gap between Theory and Practice*, 177–96. Edited by Tamsin Bradley, Emma Tomalin, and Mangala Subramanian. London: Zed Books, 2010.

Burrill, Emily, Richard Roberts, and Elizabeth Thornberry. *Domestic Violence and the Law in Colonial and Postcolonial Africa*. Athens, OH: Ohio University Press, 2010.

Chambers, Sarah. *From Subjects to Citizens: Honor, Gender, and Politics in Arequipa, Peru, 1780–1854*. University Park: Penn State University Press, 1999.

Christiansen, Tanja. *Disobedience, Slander, Seduction, and Assault: Women and Men in Cajamarca, Peru, 1862–1900*. Austin: University of Texas Press, 2004.

Committee on the Status of Women in India. *Towards Equality: Report of the Committee on the Status of Women in India*. New Delhi: Government of India Ministry of Education and Social Welfare, 1975.

Coomaraswamy, Radhika. "The Varied Contours of Violence against Women in South Asia." Report prepared for the Fifth South Asia Regional Ministerial Conference Celebrating Beijing Plus Ten, jointly organized by Government of Pakistan and UNIFEM South Asia Regional Office. May 3–5, 2005.

Femenias, Blenda. *Gender and the Boundaries of Dress in Contemporary Peru*. Austin: University of Texas Press, 2005.

Güezmes, Ana, Nancy Palomino, and Miguel Ramos. *Violencia sexual y física contra las mujeres en el Perú*. Lima: Flora Tristan, 2002.

Kumar, Radha. *The History of Doing: An Illustrated Account of Movements for Women's Rights and Feminism in India, 1800–1990*. London: Verso, 1993.

Merry, Sally Engle, and Peggy Levitt. "Vernacularization in Action: Using Global Women's Human Rights Locally." *Global Networks* 9, no. 4 (2009): 441–61.

Narayan, Uma. *Dislocating Cultures: Identities, Traditions and Third-World Feminism*. New York: Routledge, 1997.

Palriwala, R. "Reaffirming the Anti-Dowry Struggle." *Economic and Political Weekly* (April 1989): 942–44.

van Deusen, Nancy. "Determining the Boundaries of Virtue: The Discourse of *Recogimiento* among Women in Seventeenth-Century Lima." *Journal of Family History* 22, no. 4 (1997): 373–90.

Weismantel, Mary. *Cholas and Pishtacos: Stories of Race and Sex in the Andes*. Chicago: University of Chicago Press, 2001.

DISCUSSION QUESTIONS

1. How do women's experiences of domestic violence in the United States differ from or overlap with the experiences of violence for women in Peru? Mali? India? Why do these experiences differ or overlap?

2. Trace the difference in forms of feminist thought and feminist organizing in Mali, Peru, and India in the context of their different histories. How do international feminisms influence national feminisms, and vice versa?

3. India and Peru both have domestic violence laws, while Mali does not. In what ways, if any, do you think legislation affects the experience of domestic violence?

4. Notice the ways in which reconciliation appears as a solution in all three situations. What makes this problematic? On the other hand, why does this appear an attractive solution?

FROM *AFRICAN (BANJUL) CHARTER ON HUMAN AND PEOPLES' RIGHTS*

Adopted 27 June 1981, OAU Doc. CAB/LEG/67/3 rev. 5, 21 I.L.M. 58 (1982), entered into force 21 October 1986

Preamble

The African States members of the Organization of African Unity, parties to the present convention entitled "African Charter on Human and Peoples' Rights,"

Recalling Decision 115 (XVI) of the Assembly of Heads of State and Government at its Sixteenth Ordinary Session held in Monrovia, Liberia, from 17 to 20 July 1979 on the preparation of a "preliminary draft on an African Charter on Human and Peoples' Rights providing inter alia for the establishment of bodies to promote and protect human and peoples' rights";

Considering the Charter of the Organization of African Unity, which stipulates that "freedom, equality, justice and dignity are essential objectives for the achievement of the legitimate aspirations of the African peoples";

Reaffirming the pledge they solemnly made in Article 2 of the said Charter to eradicate all forms of colonialism from Africa, to coordinate and intensify their cooperation and efforts to achieve a better life for the peoples of Africa and to promote international cooperation having due regard to the Charter of the United Nations, and the Universal Declaration of Human Rights;

Taking into consideration the virtues of their historical tradition and the values of African civilization which should inspire and characterize their reflection on the concept of human and peoples' rights;

Recognizing on the one hand, that fundamental human rights stem from the attributes of human beings which justify their national and international protection and on the other hand that the reality and respect of peoples' rights should necessarily guarantee human rights;

Considering that the enjoyment of rights and freedoms also implies the performance of duties on the part of everyone;

Convinced that it is henceforth essential to pay a particular attention to the right to development and that civil and political rights cannot be dissociated from economic, social and cultural rights in their conception as well as universality and that the satisfaction of economic, social and cultural rights is a guarantee for the enjoyment of civil and political rights;

Conscious of their duty to achieve the total liberation of Africa, the peoples of which are still struggling for their dignity and genuine independence, and undertaking to eliminate colonialism, neo-colonialism, apartheid, Zionism and to dismantle aggressive foreign military bases and all forms of discrimination, particularly those based on race, ethnic group, color, sex, language, religion or political opinions;

Reaffirming their adherence to the principles of human and peoples' rights and freedoms contained in the declarations, conventions and other instruments adopted by the Organization of African Unity, the Movement of Non-Aligned Countries and the United Nations;

Firmly convinced of their duty to promote and protect human and peoples' rights and freedoms taking into account the importance traditionally attached to these rights and freedoms in Africa;

Have agreed as follows:

Part I: Rights and Duties

Chapter I: Human and People's Rights [. . . .]

Article 2

Every individual shall be entitled to the enjoyment of the rights and freedoms recognized and guaranteed in the present Charter without distinction of any kind such as race, ethnic group, color, sex, language, religious, political or any other opinion, national and social origin, fortune, birth or other status.

Article 3

1. Every individual shall be equal before the law.

2. Every individual shall be entitled to equal protection of the law.

Article 4

Human beings are inviolable. Every human being shall be entitled to respect for his life and the integrity of his person. No one may be arbitrarily deprived of this right.

Article 5

Every individual shall have the right to the respect of the dignity inherent in a human being and to the recognition of his legal status. All forms of exploitation and degradation of man particularly slavery, slave trade, torture, cruel, inhuman or degrading punishment and treatment shall be prohibited. [. . .]

Article 18

1. The family shall be the natural unit and basis of society. It shall be protected by the State which shall take care of its physical health and moral.

2. The State shall have the duty to assist the family which is the custodian of morals and traditional values recognized by the community.

3. The State shall ensure the elimination of every discrimination against women and also ensure the protection of the rights of the woman and the child as stipulated in international declarations and conventions.

4. The aged and the disabled shall also have the right to special measures of protection in keeping with their physical or moral needs.

Article 19

All peoples shall be equal; they shall enjoy the same respect and shall have the same rights. Nothing shall justify the domination of a people by another.

INTER-AMERICAN CONVENTION ON THE PREVENTION, PUNISHMENT, AND ERADICATION OF VIOLENCE AGAINST WOMEN (CONVENTION OF BELÉM DO PARÁ, 1994)

Preamble

THE STATES PARTIES TO THIS CONVENTION,

RECOGNIZING that full respect for human rights has been enshrined in the American Declaration of the Rights and Duties of Man and the Universal Declaration of Human Rights, and reaffirmed in other international and regional instruments;

AFFIRMING that violence against women constitutes a violation of their human rights and fundamental freedoms, and impairs or nullifies the observance, enjoyment and exercise of such rights and freedoms;

CONCERNED that violence against women is an offense against human dignity and a manifestation of the historically unequal power relations between women and men;

RECALLING the Declaration on the Elimination of Violence against Women, adopted by the Twenty-fifth Assembly of Delegates of the Inter-American Commission of Women, and affirming that violence against women pervades every sector of society regardless of class, race or ethnic group, income, culture, level of education, age or religion and strikes at its very foundations;

CONVINCED that the elimination of violence against women is essential for their individual and social development and their full and equal participation in all walks of life; and

CONVINCED that the adoption of a convention on the prevention, punishment and eradication of all forms of violence against women within the framework of the Organization of American States is a positive contribution to protecting the rights of women and eliminating violence against them,

HAVE AGREED to the following:

Chapter I: Definition and Scope of Application

Article 1

For the purposes of this Convention, violence against women shall be understood as any act or conduct, based on gender, which causes death or physical, sexual or psychological harm or suffering to women, whether in the public or the private sphere.

Article 2

Violence against women shall be understood to include physical, sexual and psychological violence:

a. that occurs within the family or domestic unit or within any other interpersonal relationship, whether or not the perpetrator shares or has shared the same residence with the woman, including, among others, rape, battery and sexual abuse;

b. that occurs in the community and is perpetrated by any person, including, among others, rape, sexual abuse, torture, trafficking in persons, forced prostitution, kidnapping and sexual harassment in the workplace, as well as in educational institutions, health facilities or any other place; and

c. that is perpetrated or condoned by the state or its agents regardless of where it occurs.

Chapter II: Rights Protected

Article 3

Every woman has the right to be free from violence in both the public and private spheres.

Article 4

Every woman has the right to the recognition, enjoyment, exercise and protection of all human rights and freedoms embodied in regional and international human rights instruments. These rights include, among others:

a. The right to have her life respected;

b. The right to have her physical, mental and moral integrity respected;

c. The right to personal liberty and security;

d. The right not to be subjected to torture;

e. The right to have the inherent dignity of her person respected and her family protected;

f. The right to equal protection before the law and of the law;

g. The right to simple and prompt recourse to a competent court for protection against acts that violate her rights;

h. The right to associate freely;

i. The right of freedom to profess her religion and beliefs within the law; and

j. The right to have equal access to the public service of her country and to take part in the conduct of public affairs, including decision-making.

Article 5

Every woman is entitled to the free and full exercise of her civil, political, economic, social and cultural rights, and may rely on the full protection of those rights as embodied in regional and international instruments on human rights. The States Parties recognize that violence against women prevents and nullifies the exercise of these rights.

Article 6

The right of every woman to be free from violence includes, among others:

a. The right of women to be free from all forms of discrimination; and

b. The right of women to be valued and educated free of stereotyped patterns of behavior and social and cultural practices based on concepts of inferiority or subordination.

Chapter III: Duties of the States

Article 7

The States Parties condemn all forms of violence against women and agree to pursue, by all appropriate means and without delay, policies to prevent, punish and eradicate such violence and undertake to:

a. refrain from engaging in any act or practice of violence against women and to ensure that their authorities, officials, personnel, agents, and institutions act in conformity with this obligation;

b. apply due diligence to prevent, investigate and impose penalties for violence against women;

c. include in their domestic legislation penal, civil, administrative and any other type of provisions that may be needed to prevent, punish and eradicate violence against women and to adopt appropriate administrative measures where necessary;

d. adopt legal measures to require the perpetrator to refrain from harassing, intimidating or threatening the woman or using any method that harms or endangers her life or integrity, or damages her property;

e. take all appropriate measures, including legislative measures, to amend or repeal existing laws and regulations or to modify legal or customary practices which sustain the persistence and tolerance of violence against women;

f. establish fair and effective legal procedures for women who have been subjected to violence which include, among others, protective measures, a timely hearing and effective access to such procedures;

g. establish the necessary legal and administrative mechanisms to ensure that women subjected to violence have effective access to restitution, reparations or other just and effective remedies; and

h. adopt such legislative or other measures as may be necessary to give effect to this Convention.

Article 8

The States Parties agree to undertake progressively specific measures, including programs:

a. to promote awareness and observance of the right of women to be free from violence, and the right of women to have their human rights respected and protected;

b. to modify social and cultural patterns of conduct of men and women, including the development of formal and informal educational programs appropriate to every level of the educational process, to counteract prejudices, customs and all other practices which are based on the idea of the inferiority or superiority of either of the sexes or on the stereotyped roles for men and women which legitimize or exacerbate violence against women;

c. to promote the education and training of all those involved in the administration of justice, police and other law enforcement officers as well as other personnel responsible for implementing policies for the prevention, punishment and eradication of violence against women;

d. to provide appropriate specialized services for women who have been subjected to violence, through public and private sector agencies, including shelters, counseling services for all family members where appropriate, and care and custody of the affected children;

e. to promote and support governmental and private sector education designed to raise the awareness of the public with respect to the problems of and remedies for violence against women;

f. to provide women who are subjected to violence access to effective readjustment and training programs to enable them to fully participate in public, private and social life;

g. to encourage the communications media to develop appropriate media guidelines in order to contribute to the eradication of violence against women in all its forms, and to enhance respect for the dignity of women;

h. to ensure research and the gathering of statistics and other relevant information relating to the causes, consequences and frequency of violence against women, in order to assess the effectiveness of measures to prevent, punish and eradicate violence against women and to formulate and implement the necessary changes; and

i. to foster international cooperation for the exchange of ideas and experiences and the execution of programs aimed at protecting women who are subjected to violence.

Article 9

With respect to the adoption of the measures in this Chapter, the States Parties shall take special account of the vulnerability of women to violence by reason of among others, their race or ethnic background or their status as migrants, refugees or displaced persons. Similar consideration shall be given to women subjected to violence while pregnant or who are disabled, of minor age, elderly, socio-economically disadvantaged, affected by armed conflict or deprived of their freedom.

Chapter IV: Inter-American Mechanisms of Protection

Article 10

In order to protect the right of every woman to be free from violence, the States Parties shall include in their national reports to the Inter-American Commission of Women information on measures adopted to prevent and prohibit violence against women, and to assist women affected by violence, as well as on any difficulties they observe in applying those measures, and the factors that contribute to violence against women.

Article 11

The States Parties to this Convention and the Inter-American Commission of Women may request of the Inter-American Court of Human Rights advisory opinions on the interpretation of this Convention.

Article 12

Any person or group of persons, or any nongovernmental entity legally recognized in one or more member states of the Organization, may lodge petitions with the Inter-American Commission on Human Rights containing denunciations or complaints of violations of Article 7 of this Convention by a State Party, and the Commission shall consider such claims in accordance with the norms and procedures established by the American Convention on Human Rights and the Statutes and Regulations of the Inter-American Commission on Human Rights for lodging and considering petitions.

Chapter V: General Provisions

Article 13

No part of this Convention shall be understood to restrict or limit the domestic law of any State Party that affords equal or greater protection and guarantees of the rights of women and appropriate safeguards to prevent and eradicate violence against women.

Article 14

No part of this Convention shall be understood to restrict or limit the American Convention on Human Rights or any other international convention on the subject that provides for equal or greater protection in this area.

Article 15

This Convention is open to signature by all the member States of the Organization of American States.

Article 16

This Convention is subject to ratification. The instruments of ratification shall be deposited with the General Secretariat of the Organization of American States.

Article 17

This Convention is open to accession by any other state. Instruments of accession shall be deposited with the General Secretariat of the Organization of American States.

Article 18

Any State may, at the time of approval, signature, ratification, or accession, make reservations to this Convention provided that such reservations are:

a. not incompatible with the object and purpose of the Convention, and

b. not of a general nature and relate to one or more specific provisions.

Article 19

Any State Party may submit to the General Assembly, through the Inter-American Commission of Women, proposals for the amendment of this Convention. Amendments shall enter into force for the states ratifying them on the date when two-thirds of the States Parties to this Convention have deposited their respective instruments of ratification. With respect to the other States Parties, the amendments shall enter into force on the dates on which they deposit their respective instruments of ratification.

Article 20

If a State Party has two or more territorial units in which the matters dealt with in this Convention are governed by different systems of law, it may, at the time of signature, ratification or accession, declare that this Convention shall extend to all its territorial units or to only one or more of them. Such a declaration may be amended at any time by subsequent declarations, which shall expressly specify the territorial unit or units to which this Convention applies. Such subsequent declarations shall be transmitted to the General Secretariat of the Organization of American States, and shall enter into force thirty days after the date of their receipt.

Article 21

This Convention shall enter into force on the thirtieth day after the date of deposit of the second instrument of ratification. For each State that ratifies or accedes to the Convention after the second instrument of ratification is deposited, it shall enter into force thirty days after the date on which that State deposited its instrument of ratification or accession.

Article 22

The Secretary General shall inform all member states of the Organization of American States of the entry into force of this Convention.

Article 23

The Secretary General of the Organization of American States shall present an annual report to the member states of the Organization on the status of this Convention, including the signatures, deposits of instruments of ratification and accession, and declarations, and any reservations that may have been presented by the States Parties, accompanied by a report thereon if needed.

Article 24

This Convention shall remain in force indefinitely, but any of the States Parties may denounce it by depositing an instrument to that effect with the General Secretariat of the Organization of American States. One year after the date of deposit of the instrument of denunciation, this Convention shall cease to be in effect for the denouncing State but shall remain in force for the remaining States Parties.

Article 25

The original instrument of this Convention, the English, French, Portuguese and Spanish texts of which are equally authentic, shall be deposited with the General

Secretariat of the Organization of American States, which shall send a certified copy to the Secretariat of the United Nations for registration and publication in accordance with the provisions of Article 102 of the United Nations Charter.

IN WITNESS WHEREOF the undersigned Plenipotentiaries, being duly authorized thereto by their respective governments, have signed this Convention, which shall be called the Inter-American Convention on the Prevention, Punishment and Eradication of Violence against Women—Convention of Belém do Pará.

DONE IN THE CITY OF BELÉM DO PARÁ, BRAZIL, the ninth of June in the year one thousand nine hundred ninety-four.

MALINI BHATTACHARYA, *TO GIVE A DAUGHTER AWAY*, SCENE 3

Dramatis Personae

Bride/Devi (girl masquerading as Devi Chaudhurani)[1]

Groom

Bride's father

Groom's father

Rangaraj, Devi Chaudhurani's lieutenant

Choruses

Devi Chaudhurani is seated in the court. On one side of her stand the groom and his father, tarred as a mark of shame and with fools' caps on their heads; the bride's father and Rangaraj stand on the other side.

GROOM:	Call this justice—our names are trash!
BRIDE'S FATHER:	I thank thee God, for thou art kind.
GROOM'S FATHER:	Well, it's not fair and we do mind.
FIRST CHORUS:	But you must admit they haven't taken cash.
DEVI:	That's sheer luck—for otherwise
	They'd be in jail. And the one who buys
	The mirrors, the safes, the bed, and the bedding
	Empties his purse for a daughter's wedding,
	That's money too, wouldn't you agree?

SOURCE: Malini Bhattacharya, "To Give a Daughter Away," in *Women Writing in India, 600 B.C. to the Present*, vol. 2, ed. Susie Tharu and K. Lalita, trans. Chandreyee Neogy and Piyali Sengupta (New York: Feminist Press, 1993), 478–86.

1. Devi Chaudhurani, the eponymous character in a nineteenth-century novel by Bankim Chandra Chatterji, becomes a bandit queen after being oppressed by her husband and father-in-law. The play often references and quotes the novel.—Ed.

SECOND CHORUS: Quite true—call a rose by any name—you see!

THIRD CHORUS: And what about the gold the bride must bring?

The armlet, the bracelet, the necklace, the ring?

No money might have been taken this time,

But that doesn't at all excuse your crime.

GROOM'S FATHER: Honestly, ma'am, this is grossly unfair!

I am a poor man and wouldn't dare

To cross you or to go against your will.

But what about those who are richer still

Than scores of me—why are they free?

Why let them go and punish me?

FOURTH CHORUS: Sadhu Khan the businessman

Who has his ways with the government,

His granddaughter wed a big shot's son

And do you know what a fortune he spent?

FIFTH CHORUS: Three hundred grams of gold, and oh!

There was money double that amount.

And the marriage over, they did go

For a honeymoon that could account

For thousands more, and there was talk

That they'd honeymooned in Bangkok.

You pick on us because we're poor—

And they range in safety sure.

DEVI: You're really beneath all contempt,

For you're the ones—who attempt

To cow the weak. Before the strong

You bow your heads and go along

With all they say and all they do—

And in their turn when they kick you

Or suck your blood you lose your cool

And take that out on your bride—you fool!

SIXTH CHORUS: Today's new brides in time will grow

Into mothers-in-law who proceed to show

What misery means to other young brides.

Generations go, yet each strides

By this cruel law which rules her life.

Mother, daughter, sister, wife!

SECOND CHORUS: If the bride and groom agree to marry

It's simple enough! Why tarry?

All this fuss for a dressing table?

A wardrobe with a Godrej label?

Oh come now, sir, she wed your son.

And as for him, why what's he done

That's great enough to deserve a wife,

A girl he's promised to keep for life?

THIRD CHORUS: I say, everybody, did you know

In wealthy homes it happens so—

Pretty brides are burned to death

When dowries prove inadequate?

A stove bursts and goes up in flame;

A death a day statistics claim.

It's high time now you stopped those games

Of seeking rich prospects with rich names.

The times have changed and you must, too

Or else these times won't forgive you.

GROOM'S FATHER: Do you have a son, sir? No? I thought so.

Marry a son and then you'll know

How much one spends on the food at the wedding,

And apart from that there's the bread and the bedding

Of a girl who'll stay with you all her life,

And besides, who's to pay when children arrive?

FOURTH CHORUS: Will surprises never cease?

When you get a horse on a lifetime lease

Do you calculate the fodder cost in years?

This is a woman that you will buy,

Put her to work till she should die,

So she'll pay you back in sweat and tears.

GROOM'S FATHER: Come now, friends, let's start anew

And forget this ruckus and ballyhoo.

I'm good at heart, don't you see?

I'll take her home should my son agree.

GROOM: Though I've always dreamed of a fair-skinned wife

I suppose I must keep this one for life.

Some powder can mend her unfair face.

It's Father who's got me into this mess.

DEVI: That's enough now. Where's the bride's father?

You can't decide without him.

BRIDE'S FATHER: O ma'am, you've saved my face.

DEVI: I? Your face? And what about your daughter?

Doesn't she have face too?

BRIDE'S FATHER: She's saved too, ma'am.

She'll bless you with all her soul.

Now she'll have her home and husband.

All the money I've spent has been worth it.

DEVI: But you haven't been tried yet!

BRIDE'S FATHER: Good God! Why should I be tried?

FIFTH CHORUS: But he's the plaintiff.

Why should he have a trial?

DEVI: Because he's brought his daughter up

To believe that her only place is at home—

That her husband is her destiny,

That she mustn't leave the four walls of her jail

Unless fate and circumstance play a cruel trick on her.

FIFTH CHORUS: Is that true?

BRIDE'S FATHER: No, no—I've paid for her education.

She has a bachelor's degree too—

I've never stopped her from going out.

DEVI: And why, pray? Because you knew

That a B.A. would help you make a match—

A degree would help you catch a catch.

Today, if she cannot envisage a life

Apart from the parasite's life she leads—

Then you're to blame entirely for it.

SIXTH CHORUS: No, it's the women's fault.

It's the girls who insist on money and jewelry.

Their father is their golden goose.

Behold their tears, should he fail

To lay the golden egg.

DEVI: What father, then, for his daughter buys

Poison, since she, wayward, cries?

In spite of her, shouldn't he strive

To save her, to keep her alive?

RANGARAJ: To pay in cash can't staunch her blood,

With none forthcoming, her life's at stake!

If marriage kills so many, early or late,

It's foolish to sign and say, "All is fate!"

DEVI: Give her a million, she's still a doll,

Sometimes petted, sometimes mauled!

BRIDE'S FATHER: *[Kneeling]* Yes, I see it now.

It's for me that my daughter suffered.

Madam, you are a goddess.

Won't you tell us how we can make amends?

CHORUS: *[Kneeling]* Yes, tell us how we can make amends.

RANGARAJ: Man has no divinity

Whatever be his woes,

And no god brings you felicity

Or shows the way to freedom.

[Drops cane and moves aside]

DEVI: I am not of today.

I am that which has existed forever.

I am the desire in your heart of hearts.

So many times have I been here and yet

You have forgotten me. So I have come again.

I am not a goddess, nor am I a queen.

I am that I am.

[Removes her mask]

BRIDE'S FATHER: It's my daughter!

GROOM: Prafulla—thou art a bandit!

Fie on you!

GROOM'S FATHER: What! Not Devi Chaudhurani,

But our first daughter-in-law?

Where was she until this day?

Who has she been living with?

BRIDE'S FATHER: She's insane. Her grief—

Her sorrows have made her insane! She wouldn't

Have done something of this sort otherwise.

You stupid girl, aren't you ashamed of yourself?

Go home at once—or I'll

Beat your bones to pulp.

[Rises to hit]

BRIDE: No! *[Stays his hand]*

CHORUS: No, you cannot hit her.

GROOM'S FATHER: Do you see now?

That's not an easy girl to handle.

Look how she's humiliated us,

Her husband, and her in-laws!

GROOM: She's a real spitfire!

If she were a good girl,

She'd have sat at home and shed tears.

She wouldn't have come out

And raised such a hue and cry.

Look here, this must stop.

I shall not take you in otherwise.

BRIDE: Take me in? How many times have I

Been beaten up and starved, just to be taken in!

What haven't I done for that?

Now it's all up to you. You won't

Find me crying to be taken in.

GROOM'S FATHER: What? Don't forget you're a woman,

My girl. How do you plan to live?

What are you going to eat?

Your father's not going to feed you.

That seems to be his major problem anyway.

BRIDE: Who says he needs to feed me?

[Pointing to Rangaraj]

These people run a primary school in the village

And he's given me a job there.

That's what I shall live on.

BRIDE'S FATHER: Look what you've done now.

They're not going to take you in anymore.

BRIDE: That's no longer our care, Father.

It's their problem now.

CHORUS: Yes, it's their problem. It's their problem now.

FIRST CHORUS: Riddle me the riddle of this vanity fair—

You can buy the moon with good cheer,

With gold and money and a tear

And you're pleased as punch when you've given it all away.

SECOND CHORUS: And the seller gets it all back anew.

THIRD CHORUS: Two hands to work and serve him too,

And children? That's the least she'll do.

And she'd never have it done in any other way.

FOURTH CHORUS: Oh yes, she's ready with a smile

To give herself up all the while.

FIFTH CHORUS: To work to death, to neither rant nor rile.

SIXTH CHORUS: And burst with pride in her home each day.

A woman? A wife? A human being?

A parasite, I'd rather say.

DEVI: A woman—a mere human—must turn every stone

To be able to call her work her own,

Or else, she's a ware for exchange

And none can solve this riddle strange!

RANGARAJ: Come, let's go now.

[About to go out with the Devi]

FIRST CHORUS: Wait a minute! It sounds like a fairy tale.

You can't get jobs that easily these days.

Forget about women, even men can't—

SECOND CHORUS: Take my younger sister now. She's finished school.

Now she can't get into a college. She's plain.

The prospective groom and his parents take one look

At her and ask for so much money it makes me giddy.

Even if I can't get her married off I'd like to see

Her settled with a job. But where would she get one?

BRIDE: Yes, you're quite right. It's a fairy tale

You have just witnessed.

Do you want to know what really happened?

Listen to this—

RANGARAJ: The bride's father throws her out—

That is the truth without a doubt.

She comes back to her husband's home

And with thrashings for her sin atones.

BRIDE'S FATHER: That's what happened. Yes sir,

That's what happens even today. A girl of our breed

Can't be like Devi Chaudhurani.

They'll leave her alone only when

They've thrashed her wits out of her.

She's looking for trouble if she wants it otherwise.

GROOM: *[To the bride]* You aren't looking for trouble, I hope.

Come, come, let's not talk big now—we're going home.

BRIDE: Have I been talking big?

Do I have to go home, after all? Tell me, all of you—

Isn't there any other way out?

CHORUS: Isn't there any other way out?

THIRD CHORUS: Look at the girl next door. Her brothers spent

Thousands on her marriage—but she was treated so

Badly she hanged herself after six months.

There's nothing for it but to endure.

BRIDE: Should I hang myself?

CHORUS: No!

FIRST CHORUS: I got my daughter married to a rich man's son

When she was only fourteen. I gave

Them a lot of jewelry and bundles of money.

But my daughter didn't survive.

Year after year they'd pester her for more.

One day she talked back—

And they hit her on the head and killed her.

A million rupees couldn't save her.

BRIDE: May I not be saved? Will I also be killed?

CHORUS: No!

BRIDE: Well then what SHOULD I do?

It's a fairy tale I've told you—of Devi Chaudurani.

If you can't make it come true, there's no end to this life.

For years we've been pushed back

To a hated life.

For our families, we've been told,

For our children, for love.

Is marriage the only place for me if I want to live?

Would you marry me to a lifetime of shame?

Speak! Speak! Oh, you must speak!

CHORUS: My daughter is the light of my life.

She will not be a scoundrel's wife.

I'm not going to give her away.

I gave her a ring and a golden chain,

They took it all and sent her back again.

Oh, that was a terrible day—

She was all laughter, she became all tears,

Lived day and night with unknown fears,

I didn't know what to say.

Now she's going to school, she'll forget her fears,

If I can help it, I won't have those tears.

I won't have her crying away.

I'll have her wed whomever she wants,

There must be real stuff 'neath whatever he flaunts.

No dowry this time, no way—

I'm not going to give her away.

Translated by Chandreyee Neogy and Piyali Sengupta

23

FREEDOM FROM SEXISM VERSUS SEXUAL FREEDOM

A Short History of the Feminist Sex Wars

Bernadette Barton

In 2012, when I am writing this, U.S. citizens contend with an enormous number of contradictory messages about sexuality. On the one hand, sexually explicit imagery is literally everywhere. Open any magazine, turn on the television, glance at a billboard on the freeway, and you will encounter provocative representations of youth and desire. At the same time, although we are assaulted with images of jiggling booties in every media form we encounter, Americans are prudish when it comes to speaking about sex. Sexual education in many of our public schools typically consists of urging abstinence, frightening adolescents with the threat of STDs, and only grudgingly mentioning condoms. Discussions of sexual desire, sexual behavior, sexual orientation, sexual pleasure, and sexual difference are notably absent from this curriculum. We lack both the language and confidence to have meaningful conversations about sexuality even while sexually graphic images permeate our media landscape. Who can help us make sense of this disconnect? Radical and sex radical feminists can, and do. Although these two schools of feminist thought have a contentious history, they work best in concert, offering the curious and committed intellectual tools to dissect a flood of sexist imagery in the media, and develop a personal sexual subjectivity.

FREEDOM FROM SEXISM

The Second Wave of the Women's Movement (1960s—1970s) took on institutional sexism with wit and passion. Key publications such as Betty Friedan's *The Feminine Mystique*, and

Germaine Greer's *The Female Eunuch,* were part of a dawning national realization that 1950s-style gender roles were suffocating, that discrimination against women was rampant, and that women could fight for social change. No longer would women docilely accept a second-class status in the courts, streets, and their bedrooms. Inspired and fueled by social justice movements for civil rights and peace, women came together in consciousness-raising groups and began to question the taken-for-granted inequality they daily experienced (sexual harassment, wage gap, double shift, rape myths, unfair laws), so commonplace it was part of the air they breathed. Thus emerged the Second Wave feminist demand for economic, political, and sexual freedom. Of these three, radical feminists such as Andrea Dworkin, Susan Brownmiller, and Robin Morgan focused their attention on violence against women, especially visible in the extremely profitable pornography industry.

Through closely examining pornographic images, collecting the stories of sex-abuse survivors, and giving tours of the red light district in Times Square in New York City, radical feminists examined the subordination of women's sexuality in patriarchal social systems. *Radical* comes from the Latin for "root." Radical feminists believe social change must happen at the foundation of society, not within existing political systems. Andrea Dworkin, for example, featured in this anthology, critiqued the politics of both the left and right for promoting their political agendas on the bodies of women. She argued that the men of the right attempt to control women's sexuality through access to birth control, abortion, and the institution of marriage. Those on the left, she explained, use arguments of free speech to justify the exploitation of women in the sex industry. Throughout her career, which ended too soon at the age of fifty-eight, Dworkin repeatedly emphasized the dialectical relationship between pornography and male supremacy. In the essay included in this anthology Dworkin explains:

> Pornography functions to perpetuate male supremacy and crimes of violence against women because it conditions, trains, educates and inspires men to despise women, to use women, to hurt women. Pornography exists because men despise women, and men despise women in part because pornography exists. (439)

Radical feminists argued, and continue to argue, that pornographic images eroticize hierarchy, domination, violence, and inequality. Representations of women, both those in the mainstream media as well as in pornography, are typically overtly sexual. Open any magazine, watch almost any music video and you will immediately see the sexualization and objectification of women's bodies. When violence is sexualized, as it often is in representations of women within patriarchal social systems, viewers do not see the violence, they see the sexualization. Fusing women's sexuality with violence and objectification in people's minds maintains male dominance. As Dworkin eloquently explained,

> The slicing of our skins and the rattling of our bones are the energizing sources of male-defined art and science, as they are the essential content of pornography. The visceral ex-

perience of a hatred of women that literally knows no bounds has put me beyond anger and beyond tears; I can only speak to you from grief. (437)

Dworkin, like Brownmiller and Morgan, used evocative language and provocative images to arouse the emotions of a generation of women in the fight against pornography. The radical feminists took, and continue to take, an uncompromising moral stand that made, and continues to make, many people uncomfortable.

SEXUAL FREEDOM

Among those influenced by radical feminist theory were the literal and figurative daughters of the Second Wave—women, young and older, who benefited from the Second Wave Women's Liberation Movement, and were thus in a position to complicate the arguments of radical feminism. Where radical feminist theory focuses on the institutional effects of patriarchy—the society-wide consequences of women's sexual subordination—sex radical feminism begins with an exploration of how one's individual experience does or does not align with a radical feminist critique of social phenomenon, especially sexual behavior. As individual women, themselves burgeoning feminists, listened to radical feminist arguments about sexuality, many began to whisper, at first to themselves, and then with others, that the radical feminists sounded a little too monolithic and puritanical. Everyday lived sexual experiences were lost in the institutional analysis of the radical feminists. As Dorothy Allison explored in her essay in this anthology,

> In fact, it is difficult to frame questions about sex without getting caught up in endless considerations of the *meaning* of the acts, sometimes quite astonishing philosophical, political, and spiritual treatments of meaning that I cannot quite bring back down to the level of my everyday life. In all questions about sex, it is the everyday life that interests me the most. All the impassioned rhetoric serves no purpose but greater obscurity, if it does not originate and flow from an examination of the specific—how we all actually live out our sexuality. (445)

In this climate, tireless radical feminist opposition to pornography began to be read as antisex by many new feminists, though that was not its intent. Amber Hollibaugh, a sex radical contemporary of Dorothy Allison, wondered if the seemingly inexhaustible anger expressed by radical feminists did not hint at some fear of sex. Hollibaugh suggested that perhaps "our horror at pornography is often horror at sex itself" (402). Feminists worried that there was a right, feminist way to have sex in contrast to wrong, bad, patriarchal sex. What exactly "feminist sex" was and how one achieved it was a matter of much speculation and confusion. But, one thing radical feminists were clear on was that feminist sex must not reproduce the violence, objectification, and domination so visible in pornography. Hence, a new generation of women questioned, "What does it mean if I get turned on by power play, or pornography—am I a bad feminist? How do I clean my mind of politically incorrect fantasies?"

Dorothy Allison perceived such sexual self-censure, a censure that was partly fueled by radical feminist theories of sexuality, as problematic, destructive, dangerous, and, ultimately antifeminist. Indeed, many sex radical feminists, like Allison and Hollibaugh, noted that part of women's sexual history within patriarchy had been sexual repression, sexual incoherence, and the erasure of female sexual pleasure and sexual subjectivity. Allison asked:

> How might our lives be different, I began to ask, if we were not being constantly subjected to this fear of ourselves and each other? What kind of women might we be if we did not have to worry about being too sexual, or not sexual enough, or the wrong kind of sexual for the company we keep? More and more I have grown impatient with the limitations placed on bringing this kind of discussion out of the closed group and into the public debate that continues among feminists. Not addressing these issues reinforces the rage and fear we all hide, while supporting the status quo of oppression. (449)

Thus, some sex radical feminists, like Allison, interpreted radical feminist arguments against pornography as closing down an important conversation about women's sexual subjectivity, narrowing women's range of sexual choices, and limiting women's overall sexual agency.

Further, sex radical feminism dovetailed with new developments in feminist theory that emerged in the 1980s and early 1990s: intersectional theory and Third Wave feminism. By the early 1980s, working-class feminists and feminists of color had already begun to critique radical feminist theory for homogenizing and totalizing women's experiences from a white, middle-class perspective. The publication of *This Bridge Called My Back* in 1981 signaled an emerging feminist perspective—intersectional theory—which critiques radical feminism for not adequately attending to how women's experiences of inequality differ based on multiple axes of inequality, such as race, class, and sexual orientation. For example, pornography may not be the most important issue facing a poor woman of color, and gender not her only, or even her most significant, site of oppression and exploitation.

Third Wave feminism explores individual differences, choices, and resistance—at the "level of one's everyday life"—in an increasingly complex and fragmented social world. Theorists of the Third Wave typically find suspect any kind of global claim about gendered experience, such as Andrea Dworkin's assertion that "the most terrible thing about pornography is that it tells male truth" (289). In response, the sex radical feminist might ask, "Which male? What truth?" Using the tools of intersectional theory to examine gender relations at the individual as well as the institutional level, some sex radical feminists theorized sexual behavior, sexual identity, and sexual difference as a contested landscape within which women's participation in the sexist social order, including the sex industry, has the potential not only to reinforce patriarchy, but also, at times, destabilize it.

A KEY MOMENT IN FEMINIST THEORIZING: THE BARNARD CONFERENCE

What is commonly referred to as the "Barnard Conference" gave voice to feminists struggling to articulate a new discourse of women's sexuality—one focusing on women's sexual pleasure—and heralded the beginning of the "feminist sex wars." In 1982, Barnard College hosted a feminist conference titled "Towards a Politics of Sexuality" with the intent "to explore the ambiguous and complex relationship between sexual pleasure and danger in women's lives and feminist theory" (Vance 3). The Barnard Conference emerged from a collective desire to address complicated issues of "pleasure, danger and feminism" in a safe space. It was ironic then, and damaging and hurtful, when those organizing and attending the conference found that safe space threatened by an unexpected adversary: antipornography feminists.

Among the range of topics on the Barnard Conference program were butch-femme identities among lesbians, women's use of pornography, women's participation in the sex industry, and the ways that BDSM (bondage, domination, sado-masochism) figured in women's fantasies and sexual lives. Upon learning that these themes would be explored in some conference papers, some antipornography feminists organized to protest the event on the grounds that discussion of such subjects promoted patriarchal values. The antipornography feminists succeeded in suppressing the distribution of the conference's major text, the *Diary of a Conference on Sexuality*.

Questions and concerns about what constituted "feminist sex" or "politically incorrect sex" among those at the Barnard Conference transmuted into anger at the perceived line drawn in the sand by some radical feminists. Between the increasingly heated exchanges of words, the protest, and the picketing, radical and sex radical feminist ideological positions solidified, and an ugly divisiveness emerged among feminists theorizing about sexuality and the sex industry. Camps developed, publications advocating one or the other side were fired off, and the "sex wars" commenced.

FINDING COMMON GROUND

It is possible to straddle this once antagonistic feminist divide. A body of scholars, including myself, has adopted a blended theoretical position that draws on the strongest elements of each. For example, in my research on exotic dancers, I found evidence to support both sex radical and radical feminist theories of women's participation in the sex industry. Many of the dancers I interviewed enjoyed parts of their work, and felt powerful at times, in strip bars. They were also stereotyped, abused, insulted, and stigmatized. Theoretically, I found that both radical and sex radical feminist arguments were valid depending upon the focus. On an individual level, having control over one's body means having the freedom to take off one's shirt as well as leave it on. It all depends on the political and cultural context. At the same time, on an institutional level, women's overall participation in the sex industry reinforces a sexist social order that negatively impacts all women. As sociologist Lynn Chancer noted, the radical feminist goal of freedom from sexism *is* compatible with the sex radical goal of sexual freedom. These need not be in tension. Indeed, a feminist reenvisioning of the social world *requires* that we attend to both these goals simultaneously, for one without the other leads to uneasy and problematic alliances: the radical feminists with conservative Christians, and the sex radical feminists with pornographers. Finally, one glance at our hyperbolic, over-sexualized "raunch culture" (Levy), of stripper poles and "bad girls" relentlessly instructing young people, especially young women, that their most important resource is how "hot" they are, warns us that we need all our feminist tools close at hand.

WORKS CITED

Allison, Dorothy. "Public Silence, Private Terror." In *Pleasure and Danger: Exploring Female Sexuality*, 103–14. Edited by Carole S. Vance. London: Pandora Press, 1989.

Chancer, Lynn. *Reconcilable Differences: Confronting Beauty, Pornography and the Future of Feminism*. Berkeley: University of California Press, 1998.

Dworkin, Andrea. "Pornography and Grief." In *Take Back the Night: Women on Pornography*, 286–91. Edited by Laura Lederer. New York: Bantam Books, 1980.

Hollibaugh, Amber. "Desire for the Future: Radical Hope in Passion and Pleasure." In *Pleasure and Danger: Exploring Female Sexuality*, 401–10. Edited by Carole S. Vance. London: Pandora Press, 1989.

Levy, Ariel. *Female Chauvinist Pigs: Women and the Rise of Raunch Culture*. New York: Free Press, 2005.

Moraga, Cherríe, and Gloria Anzaldúa, *This Bridge Called My Back: Writings by Radical Women of Color*. New York: Kitchen Table Women of Color Press, 1981.

Vance, Carole S., ed. *Pleasure and Danger: Exploring Female Sexuality*. London: Pandora Press, 1989.

DISCUSSION QUESTIONS

1. What are the "feminist sex wars"? Do you identify more with the arguments made by sex radical feminists or radical feminists? Why?

2. What kinds of messages do young people receive from current media representations of sexuality? In what ways have contemporary feminists shaped, influenced, and/or interpreted these messages?

3. Barton writes that the 1982 Barnard Conference was a "key moment in feminist theorizing." What other key moments, events, elections, and/or phenomena have you observed that have served to galvanize people around issues of women's liberation and gender equality?

ANDREA DWORKIN, *PORNOGRAPHY AND GRIEF*

This paper was originally a speech presented in 1978 at the "Feminist Perspectives on Pornography" conference in San Francisco. Embodying a sweeping vision of the problem, it was delivered directly before a Take Back the Night March. The march was held as a way of demonstrating our commitment to stopping the tide of violence against women, whether by rapists or batterers or imagemakers in the mass media.

As night fell, three thousand marchers gathered to hear Andrea Dworkin's "Exhortation to March." Then we wound our way toward Broadway, which was crowded with tourists, neon signs advertising live sex shows, adult bookstores, and pornographic theaters. Chanting slogans such as "No More Profit off Women's Bodies," we filled the street entirely, blocking off traffic and completely occupying the Broadway strip for three blocks. For an hour, and for the first time ever, Broadway belonged not to the barkers, pimps, or pornographers, but instead to the songs, voices, rage, and vision of thousands of women.

I searched for something to say here today quite different from what I am going to say. I wanted to come here militant and proud and angry as hell. But more and more, I find that anger is a pale shadow next to the grief I feel. If a woman has any sense of her own intrinsic worth, seeing pornography in small bits and pieces can bring her to a useful rage. Studying pornography in quantity and depth, as I have been doing for more months than I care to remember, will turn that same woman into a mourner.

The pornography itself is vile. To characterize it any other way would be to lie. No plague of male intellectualisms and sophistries can change or hide that simple fact. Georges Bataille, a philosopher of pornography (which he calls "eroticism"), puts it clearly: "In essence, the domain of eroticism is the domain of violence, of violation."[1] Mr. Bataille, unlike so many of his peers, is good enough to make explicit that the whole idea is to violate the female. Using the language of grand euphemism so popular with male intellectuals who write on the subject of pornography, Bataille informs us that "[t]he passive, female side is essentially the one that is dissolved as a separate entity."[2] To be "dissolved"—by any means necessary—is the role of women in pornography. The great

---

SOURCE: Andrea Dworkin, "Pornography and Grief," in *Take Back the Night: Women on Pornography*, ed. Laura Lederer (New York: Bantam Books, 1980), 286–91.

1. Georges Bataille, *Death and Sensuality* (New York: Ballantine Books, 1969), 10.
2. Bataille, *Death and Sensuality*, 11.

male scientists and philosophers of sexuality, including Kinsey, Havelock Ellis, Wilhelm Reich, and Freud, uphold this view of our purpose and destiny. The great male writers use language more or less beautifully to create us in self-serving fragments, half-"dissolved" as it were, and then proceed to "dissolve" us all the way, by any means necessary. The biographers of the great male artists celebrate the real-life atrocities those men have committed against us, as if those atrocities are central to the making of art. And in history, as men have lived it, they have "dissolved" us—by any means necessary. The slicing of our skins and the rattling of our bones are the energizing sources of male-defined art and science, as they are the essential content of pornography. The visceral experience of a hatred of women that literally knows no bounds has put me beyond anger and beyond tears; I can only speak to you from grief.

We all expected the world to be different than it is, didn't we? No matter what material or emotional deprivation we have experienced as children or as adults, no matter what we understood from history or from the testimonies of living persons about how people suffer and why, we all believed, however privately, in human possibility. Some of us believed in art, or literature, or music, or religion, or revolution, or in children, or in the redeeming potential of eroticism or affection. No matter what we knew of cruelty, we all believed in kindness; and no matter what we knew of hatred, we all believed in friendship or love. Not one of us could have imagined or would have believed the simple facts of life as we have come to know them: the rapacity of male greed for dominance; the malignancy of male supremacy; the virulent contempt for women that is the very foundation of the culture in which we live. The Women's Movement has forced us all to face the facts, but no matter how brave and clear-sighted we are, no matter how far we are willing to go or are forced to go in viewing reality without romance or illusion, we are simply overwhelmed by the male hatred of our kind, its morbidity, its compulsiveness, its obsessiveness, its celebration of itself in every detail of life and culture. We think that we have grasped this hatred once and for all, seen it in its spectacular cruelty, learned its every secret, got used to it or risen above it or organized against it so as to be protected from its worst excesses. We think that we know all there is to know about what men do to women, even if we cannot imagine why they do what they do, when something happens that simply drives us mad, out of our minds, so that we are again imprisoned like caged animals in the numbing reality of male control, male revenge against no one knows what, male hatred of our very being.

One can know everything and still not imagine snuff films. One can know everything and still be shocked and terrified when a man who attempted to make snuff films is released, despite the testimony of the women undercover agents whom he wanted to torture, murder, and, of course, film. One can know everything and still be stunned and paralyzed when one meets a child who is being continually raped by her father or some close male relative. One can know everything and still be reduced to sputtering like an idiot when a woman is prosecuted for attempting to abort herself with knitting needles or when a woman is imprisoned for killing a man who has raped or tortured her or is raping or torturing her. One can know everything and still want to kill and be dead simultaneously when one sees a celebratory picture of a woman being ground up in a meat grinder on the cover of a national magazine, no matter how putrid the magazine. One can know everything and still somewhere inside refuse to believe that the personal, social, culturally sanctioned violence against women is unlimited, unpredictable, pervasive, constant, ruthless, and happily and unselfconsciously sadistic. One can know everything and still be unable to accept the fact that sex and murder are fused in the male consciousness, so that the one without the imminent possibility of the other is unthinkable and impossible. One can know everything and still, at bottom, refuse to accept that the annihilation of women is the source of meaning and identity for men. One can know everything and still want desperately to know nothing because to face what we know is to question whether life is worth anything at all.

The pornographers, modern and ancient, visual and literary, vulgar and aristocratic, put forth one consistent proposition: erotic pleasure for men is derived from and predicated on the savage destruction of women. As the world's most honored pornographer, the Marquis de Sade (called by male scholars "The Divine Marquis"), wrote in one of his more restrained and civil moments: "There's not a woman on earth who'd ever have had cause to complain of my services if I'd been sure of being able to kill her afterward."[3] The eroticization of murder is the essence of pornography, as it is the essence of life. The torturer may be a policeman tearing the fingernails off a victim in a prison cell or a so-called normal man engaged in the project of attempting to fuck a woman to death. The fact is that the process of killing—and both rape and battery are steps in that process—is the prime sexual act for men in reality and/or in imagination. Women as a class must remain in bondage, subject to the sexual will of men, because the knowledge of an imperial right to kill, whether exercised to the fullest extent or just partway, is necessary to fuel sexual appetite and behavior. Without women as potential or actual victims, men are, in the current sanitized jargon, "sexually dysfunctional." This same motif also operates among male homosexuals, where force and/or convention designate some males as female or feminized. The plethora of leather and chains among male homosexuals, and the newly fashionable defenses of organized rings of boy prostitution by supposedly radical gay men, [is] testimony to the fixedness of the male compulsion to dominate and destroy that is the source of sexual pleasure for men.

The most terrible thing about pornography is that it tells male truth. The most insidious thing about pornography is that it tells male truth as if it were universal truth. Those depictions of women in chains being tortured are supposed to represent our deepest erotic aspirations. And some of us believe it, don't we? The most important thing about pornography is that the values in it are the common values of men. This is the crucial fact that both the male Right and the male Left, in their differing but mutually

3. Marquis de Sade, *Juliette*, trans. Austryn Wainhouse (New York: Grove Press, 1976), 404.

reinforcing ways, want to keep hidden from women. The male Right wants to hide the pornography, and the male Left wants to hide its meaning. Both want access to pornography so that men can be encouraged and energized by it. The Right wants secret access; the Left wants public access. But whether we see the pornography or not, the values expressed in it are the values expressed in the acts of rape and wife-beating, in the legal system, in religion, in art and in literature, in systematic economic discrimination against women, in the moribund academies, and by the good and wise and kind and enlightened in all of these fields and areas. Pornography is not a genre of expression separate and different from the rest of life; it is a genre of expression fully in harmony with any culture in which it flourishes. This is so whether it is legal or illegal. And, in either case, pornography functions to perpetuate male supremacy and crimes of violence against women because it conditions, trains, educates, and inspires men to despise women, to use women, to hurt women. Pornography exists because men despise women, and men despise women in part because pornography exists.

For myself, pornography has defeated me in a way that, at least so far, life has not. Whatever struggles and difficulties I have had in my life, I have always wanted to find a way to go on even if I did not know how, to live through one more day, to learn one more thing, to take one more walk, to read one more book, to write one more paragraph, to see one more friend, to love one more time. When I read or see pornography, I want everything to stop. Why, I ask, why are they so damned cruel and so damned proud of it? Sometimes, a detail drives me mad. There is a series of photographs: a woman slicing her breasts with a knife, smearing her own blood on her own body, sticking a sword up her vagina. *And she is smiling.* And it is the smile that drives me mad. There is a record album plastered all over a huge display window. The picture on the album is a profile view of a woman's thighs. Her crotch is suggested because we know it is there; it is not shown. The title of the album is *Plug Me to Death*. And it is the use of the first person that drives me mad. "Plug Me to Death." The arrogance. The cold-blooded arrogance. And how can it go on like this, senseless, entirely brutal, inane, day after day and year after year, these images and ideas and values pouring out, packaged, bought and sold, promoted, enduring on and on, and no one stops it, and our darling boy intellectuals defend it, and elegant radical lawyers argue for it, and men of every sort cannot and will not live without it. And life, which means everything to me, becomes meaningless, because these celebrations of cruelty destroy my very capacity to feel and to care and to hope. I hate the pornographers most of all for depriving me of hope.

The psychic violence in pornography is unbearable in and of itself. It acts on one like a bludgeon until one's sensibility is pummeled flat and one's heart goes dead. One becomes numb. Everything stops, and one looks at the pages or pictures and knows: this is what men want, and this is what men have had, and this is what men will not give up. As lesbian-feminist Karla Jay pointed out in an article called "Pot, Porn, and the Politics of Pleasure," men will give up grapes and lettuce and orange juice and Portuguese wine and tuna fish, but men will not give up pornography. And yes, one wants to take it from them, to burn it, to rip it up, bomb it, raze their theaters and publishing houses to the ground. One can be part of a revolutionary movement or one can mourn. Perhaps I have found the real source of my grief: we have not yet become a revolutionary movement.

Tonight we are going to walk together, all of us, to take back the night, as women have in cities all over the world, because in every sense none of us can walk alone. Every woman walking alone is a target. Every woman walking alone is hunted, harassed, time after time harmed by psychic or physical violence. Only by walking together can we walk at all with any sense of safety, dignity, or freedom. Tonight, walking together, we will proclaim to the rapists and pornographers and woman-batterers that their days are numbered and our time has come. And tomorrow, what will we do tomorrow? Because, sisters, the truth is that we have to take back the night every night, or the night will never be ours. And once we have conquered the dark, we have to reach for the light, to take the day and make it ours. This is our choice, and this is our necessity. It is a revolutionary choice, and it is a revolutionary necessity. For us, the two are indivisible, as we must be indivisible in our fight for freedom. Many of us have walked many miles already—brave, hard miles—but we have not gone far enough. Tonight, with every breath and every step, we must commit ourselves to going the distance: to transforming this earth on which we walk from prison and tomb into our rightful and joyous home. This we must do and this we will do, for our own sakes and for the sake of every woman who has ever lived.

DOROTHY ALLISON, *PUBLIC SILENCE, PRIVATE TERROR*

I urge each one of us to reach down into that deep place of knowledge inside herself and touch that terror and loathing of any difference that lives there.

> AUDRE LORDE, "THE MASTER'S TOOLS WILL NEVER
> DISMANTLE THE MASTER'S HOUSE"

What drew me to politics was my love of women, that agony I felt in observing the straight-jackets of poverty and repression I saw people in my family in. But the deepest political tragedy I have experienced is how with such grace, such blind faith, this commitment to women in the feminist movement grew to be exclusive and reactionary.

CHERRÍE MORAGA, "PREFACE," *THIS BRIDGE CALLED MY BACK*

Her voice on the phone was a surprise, not only because the call had come so late in the evening or even that she was so hesitant to identify herself. She had never been a friend—

SOURCE: Dorothy Allison, "Public Silence, Private Terror," in *Pleasure and Danger: Exploring Female Sexuality*, ed. Carole S. Vance (London: Pandora Press, 1989), 103–14. The following notes are from that publication.
Epigraphs: Audre Lorde, "The Master's Tools Will Never Dismantle the Master's House," in *This Bridge Called My Back*, ed. Cherríe Moraga and Gloria Anzaldúa (New York, Kitchen Table Women of Color Press, 1981/1983), 105; Cherríe Moraga, "Preface," in Moraga and Anzaldúa, *This Bridge Called My Back*, xiv.

only an acquaintance, another lesbian whose writing I had admired but whom I'd spoken to less than half a dozen times in all the years we'd been aware of each other's existence. There was also the too present memory of the last time I'd seen her, the way her eyes had registered, stared and then avoided mine. I'd seen in her face the same look I'd been seeing in other women's faces for all the months since the Barnard sex scandal—a look of fascination, contempt, and extreme discomfort. She'd gotten away as quickly as possible, and at the time I had reminded myself again that it really wasn't any different from the way straight women used to avoid me back in 1971.

"I didn't wake you, did I?" Her voice almost trembled with anxiety and automatically I told her, "No, I don't go to bed this early." I started to make a joke, to try to put her a little more at ease, but I stopped myself. After all she was the one who had called me; she had to know what she wanted.

But it didn't seem that way. She rambled, made small talk, her voice so soft and hesitant that I couldn't bring myself to grab hold of the conversation, to say "Just why was it you called anyway?" I don't remember now just how we steered through it, her fear so palpable that gradually I figured out that whatever else she wanted, some part of it had to be about sex. When she finally said, "Well I thought I could talk to *you* anyway," I was so relieved that she was going to get around to the point that it almost overcame my sudden, tired anger at her for being one more person to put it that way.

"Yeah, you should be able to say anything to me," I thought but did not say, and she finally got around to it. Sex, and her terror, her disgust with herself. I listened to her voice and felt my anger melt to grief. It was that same old tone I'd heard before, choked with shame and desperation. She had been doing these things—no, she couldn't say what exactly—but there was no one she could talk to about it. She had tried to stop herself, stop the fantasies, masturbation, stray thoughts. But it didn't go away, either her fear or her desire, and finally she had tried to talk to another woman she thought she was close to, someone she had thought would understand. That woman had stared at her, hesitated and then told her she was sick.

"Sick," she said in a very small voice.

I put my head down onto my arm and cradled the phone close to my shoulder. I didn't know her well enough to be having this conversation. I didn't know what to say. I didn't even know exactly what she'd been doing, or imagining doing. I remembered an old lover whose terror had been so great, who liked to imagine herself held down, unable to reach the mouth that hovered over hers until she had to beg for it—that mouth, that release. I started to tell the voice on the phone that story, of how I noticed that when we made love, my lover's mouth worked and worked but never made a sound, of how gradually I'd teased her and comforted her and reassured her until finally she let go and shouted and roared her passion.

"She was so afraid," I said, "so certain that she was a terrible, sick person but when it all came out, there was so little to it, nothing to match all those years of knotted up silent grief. It's usually like that, you know. We're very rarely as terrible as we believe ourselves to be."

Silence answered me and stretched out. I pushed my hair back, waiting, wondering if I was saying the absolutely wrong thing. Maybe she really was terrible, maybe she was even a little bit sick? What did I know? Maybe her desire was to slice little pieces of herself off and feed them to her cat. What good was it for me to tell her about someone she didn't know, who after all had a desire that was relatively easy to accomplish, that didn't really demand much of anyone else or herself except the strength to put it out. What lover would refuse to pin her down and tease her? What friend would call her sick for that?

"I'm not an expert," I finally said, "not a sex therapist. Sometimes I think the only thing I understand is myself, and that not very well—just a few of the ways I've fucked myself over, let myself be fucked over, invited it or cooperated with it." Talk to me, I wanted to say, I can't say anything if you don't give a little.

"I've been putting stuff inside me," she whispered. I just about dropped the phone in relief. OK, what was she putting inside her, and inside her where? But she wouldn't give me that. Quickly, it became clear that she would never be able to stand having said that little bit, and I knew that after this phone call she would never speak to me again. She would always feel vulnerable to me, imagine I knew more than I did—all her secret thoughts, what she did alone in her bed in the dark—and she would always feel that I had betrayed her or would when the chance came.

I grabbed onto that phone like a lifeline. Did she know there was a group—a lesbian group she could go talk to? No, but as I repeated the address I knew she wasn't writing it down. I could hear her urge to run and hide, knew certainly that whatever she did, she wasn't ready to talk to people—not about this tender stuff. Well, did she have any books about sex? "I'm sure you've seen *Sapphistry*," I said, "but I could loan you some others, or you could buy them if you wanted." Probably she wouldn't want to see me, but if she had the titles she could get them herself in some store where no one knew her. But there was so little to recommend. How few feminists write about sex, I thought for perhaps the hundredth time.

"Seen what? *Sapphistry?*"

I made myself talk quietly, slowly, though all I really wanted was to start yelling, not really at her but at anything, kicking furniture, and screaming in frustration.

"That's Pat Califia's book from Naiad Press.[1] It's good, very good with lots of practical information, especially about what's dangerous and what's not."

"Oh." I could hear it in her voice. She'd heard that name before, read some review that had growled indignation about all that s/m stuff and probably reinforced all her own sexual terrors. It didn't matter that, if she really was pushing something into her cunt or ass, *Sapphistry* would be one of the few books that would tell her what was involved in

---

1. Pat Califia, *Sapphistry* (Tallahassee, FL: Naiad, 1981).

plain and simple terms, that wouldn't play into all the guilt and self-hatred she was carrying. Odds were, the same *friend* who had told her she was sick told her all about Pat Califia.

Suddenly she had to get off the phone. Her cat was getting into the garbage. She thought she heard someone at the door. It was an excuse, and we both knew it, and the phone went silent. I sat holding the receiver until the hum broke into a howl. Then I put it down and went to wrap myself around my lover, so angry I couldn't even speak, couldn't even say, "It was just another one of those terrible phone calls."

On the wall over my desk, I hang pictures, clippings and notes to myself. It is crowded with fantasy images, lists, and ideas, even love letters several years old. The picture of the young woman in a black lace dress and feathered hat has been up there almost as long as the samurai woman sweeping her long sword into the sunlight. Each inspires me, though in very different ways. Some days I want to become one or the other. Some days I want to write the story of how they became lovers. Other days I can't stand to look at them at all and turn instead to notecards pinned up between the pictures, reading the words over and over to myself, knowing I have not yet exhausted all I need to learn from them.

The quote from Adrienne Rich's introduction to the reprint of her *Compulsory Heterosexuality and Lesbian Existence* is pinned next to the paragraphs I copied from Barbara Smith's short story, "Home," so that the words follow each other and echo an idea that has been worrying me for months.

> There has recently been an intensified debate on Female sexuality among feminists and lesbians, with lines often furiously drawn, with sado-masochism and pornography as key words which are variously defined according to who is talking. The depth of women's rage and fear regarding sexuality and its relation to power and pain is real, even when the dialogue sounds simplistic, self-righteous, or like parallel monologues.
>
> Adrienne Rich[2]
>
> I knew when I first met her that it would be all right to love her, that whatever happened we would emerge from this not broken. It would not be about betrayal. Loving doesn't terrify me. Loss does. The women I need literally disappearing from the face of the earth. It has already happened.
>
> Barbara Smith[3]

I keep wanting to take down the card that holds Adrienne Rich's words and file them away, not to have to think any more about the fact that it is certainly fear that has dominated the debate on female sexuality, that it is fear that has provoked the shouting, name-calling, and rejection. I am tired of trying to understand why people fall into self-righteous hatred, but I keep the card up for just that reason, to remember the human

2. Adrienne Rich, *Compulsory Heterosexuality and Lesbian Existence* (San Francisco: Antelope, 1983).
3. Barbara Smith, "Home," *Conditions*, no. 8 (Fall 1982): 105.

dimensions of the debate. The quote from "Home" serves the same purpose, but it also reaches my own fear and goes deeper still to a level of desire I have known since I first realized just what it would mean to my life to be queer. *Home* is what I want, what I have always wanted—the trust that my life, my love does not betray those I need most, that they will not betray me.

You confuse the two, a friend once told me. When we talk about love, we are not necessarily speaking of sex. When we talk about sex, love is not at issue. Is that true? I ask myself and read the cards over again.

Underneath those two, held by the same pin that positions a picture of my younger sister with her two children, is a line I have written for myself, the beginning to an article I know I must someday finish: "The terrors of sex are real," it reads, "the awful vulnerability of the individual exposed physically and emotionally—and we are too often betrayed by our own desires or the failures of our lovers." Betrayal again, I notice, and this time failure. It does not appear that I am so very much different from the woman who called me that night. We are both stumbling over our private fears, worrying at desire from the downhill side, not speaking to the trust and joy I know we both are seeking.

When we speak of sex, grief should not be where we have to start. But the idea of a life in which rage, physical fear or emotional terror prevents even the impetus of desire—that is the image that haunts the discussion for me now. The thought that we could all be forced to live isolated in our own bodies, never safe enough to risk ourselves in naked intimacy with others rides me now like an old nightmare from my childhood: a dream of silence, cold hands, and suspicious eyes. It was a nightmare I used to believe was common to all lesbians but one I thought had grown less powerful in our everyday lives. It was the fear behind our politics, a unifying and radicalizing perception that we did not need to voice since we all knew it so well. The experience of having the meaning of our love and desire for women twisted, misused, or denied totally seemed to me central and basic to feminism in the same way that our politics itself was supposed to rest in the actual lived experience of women who must name for themselves their needs, hopes, and desires. But I never wanted fear to be the only impulse behind political action. As deeply as I wanted safety or freedom, I wanted desire, hope, and joy. What after all was the worth of one without the other?

All those notes hang on my wall and stare back at me as piteously as the pictures of my lovers, sisters, and fantasy figures. I can neither answer them, tear them down nor ignore them because, in trying to write about sex, I am always faced with the fear that any conclusion I make will betray someone. If I outline, even if only for myself, a new understanding of how our desire for sex is used against us, some face always stares back at me unsatisfied. If I demand my right as a lesbian to examine and explore my relationships with other women, both as sources of passion and grief, I am flat up against it again. I imagine not only faceless heterosexual feminists who cannot understand any human relationship not rooted in the dynamics of male-female interaction; but also the lesbians who will tell me I am betraying them by putting such information out for the perusal and possible use of "boys" or non-feminists; or even the lesbians who will dismiss me, because my life is nothing like theirs, the sources of my passions strange or frightening to them.

In fact, it is difficult to frame questions about sex without getting caught up in endless considerations of the meaning of the acts, sometimes quite astonishing philosophical, political, and spiritual treatments of meaning that I cannot quite bring back down to the level of my everyday life. In all questions about sex, it is the everyday life that interests me most. All the impassioned rhetoric serves no purpose but greater obscurity, if it does not originate and flow from an examination of the specific—how we all actually live out our sexuality. Without that detail, I have concluded that there are no valid generalizations to be made about sex and women's lives except for the central fact that we are all hungry for the power of desire and we are all terribly deeply afraid.

The hardest lesson I have learned in the last few years is how powerful is my own desire to hang on to a shared sense of feminist community where it is safe to talk about dangerous subjects like sex, and also—how hopeless is that desire. Even within what I have thought of as my own community, and, worse, even within the community of my friends and lovers, I have never felt safe. I have never been safe and that is only partly because everyone else is just as fearful as I am. None of us is safe, because we have never made each other safe. We have never even recognized the fearfulness of the territory. We have addressed violence and exploitation and heterosexual assumption without establishing first the understanding that for each of us desire is unique and necessary and simply terrifying. Without that understanding, and the compassion and empathy that must be part of it, I do not know how to avoid those acts of betrayal. But it is one thing for me to confront my own fear of those different from me—whether they are women of color, middle-class women or heterosexuals—and another entirely to demand of feminists that we begin again with this understanding. Yet that is exactly what I want to do. I want to begin again by saying that as women we don't know enough about each other, our fears, our desires or the many ways that this society has acted upon us. Nor do I want to give ground and allow sex to be exempted from the discussion.

As feminists we have committed our whole lives to struggling to change what most people in this society don't even question, and sometimes the intensity of our struggle has persuaded us that the only way to accomplish change is to make hard bargains, to give up some points and compromise on others; in the end what that has always meant is trading some people for some others.

I don't want to do that.

I don't want to require any other woman to do that.

I don't want to claim a safe or comfortable life for myself that is purchased at the cost of some other woman's needs or desires. But over and over again I see us being pushed to do just that. I know for myself how easily I used to dismiss heterosexual desire. I was kind about it, and even gently patient, but I used to look at heterosexual feminists with a kind of superior disdain, wondering how long it would take them to realize the hopelessness of their position. Crawling head first through the eye of a needle didn't seem to me half as difficult as dragging a man through your life. I took as whole cloth the notion that, yes, feminism is the theory while lesbianism is the practice, and only a childhood of forced politeness kept me from preaching that conviction to the less enlightened. I made no connection then between such expectations and the kind of pressure to "reform" myself that had hurt me so badly for so many years.

I can't pinpoint the act that changed all that for me, that made me see the absurdity of such a theory. I know that a piece of it was my relationship with my sisters. I could imagine some theoretical stranger deciding that rational lesbianism was the solution. I could not face my baby sister with her children, her half-tamed boyfriend and her hard won self-respect and try to tell her that she'd be better off in a lesbian collective. I know that once when we had stayed up talking almost all night, and she'd told me how her husband was sleeping around, and I'd admitted that yes, that woman I'd told her about had hurt me almost more than I could stand, she had put her hand on mine, squeezed and said, "I know. I know that pain." I knew she was right, that she understood, and I knew too that all the things wrong in her life wouldn't be solved by her trying to be something she was not.

My understanding of what feminism meant changed even more from reading and listening to the many women who contributed to *This Bridge Called My Back*.[4] It was not then only a matter of looking at the personal racism that blights all our lives but also examining the institutional racism that shapes our convictions of who is or can be "right," and what it is that we really know as feminists. In a very real sense, *Bridge* gave me a new way to look at my life because it was so full of the lives of women who, while they were very different from me, voiced the same hopes, the same desperate desire to change what any of us is allowed. Throughout, while addressing the very real ways racism tears at all of us, the writers spoke again and again of joy, of love, of power, of lives shared and things accomplished. Most of all it offered a vision that struggle between white women and women of color did not have to be framed in terms of betrayal, that just as Barbara Smith had put it we might "emerge from this not broken."[5] If we could hope for this across the barriers of color and class, why not across sexuality and gender?

Bridge raised also the question of the difference between politics and personal style— a complicated, critical, and painful issue that no one has addressed sufficiently. Part of the power of the writers' voices lay in how different they were from what I had come to think of as the same old, slightly distant and carefully respectable aura of feminist theory. Here were all kinds of voices speaking of their real lives, not abstract generalities, not shielding or obscuring anger or impatience. I thought of all the meetings I had attended and papers I had read where the dominant tone was academic, polite, and distant, while

4. Moraga and Anzaldúa, *This Bridge Called My Back*.
5. Smith, "Home," 100.

the undercurrent was personal and vicious: the desire I had always had to say, "Can we stop a minute and talk about what is *really* going on here?"

When Cherríe Moraga spoke of how "with such grace, such blind faith, this commitment to women in the feminist movement grew to be exclusive and reactionary," she was speaking specifically about racism, and the tendency to ignore or misinterpret the lives of women of color.[6] But her words not only made me look at my own fears, avoidance, and racism but they made me also see that I had the same criticisms of the movement around the issues of class and sex. Moreover, just as I was terrified of addressing my own racism, so too other women were afraid of stepping into the deep and messy waters of class and sexual desire. If we get into this, what might we lose? If we expose this, what might our enemies do with it? And what might it mean? Will we have to throw out all that theory we have built with such pain and struggle? Will we have to start over? How are we going to make each other safe, while we work through all it means?

My first response to these questions was that it was all too hard, too deep, too terrible. It was only when I took my second breath and let go a little that I began to think in terms of going ahead anyway. We learn prejudice and hatred at the same time as we learn who we are and what the world is about, at the same time as we learn all our convictions about sex. The choice of our lives is whether we will simply swallow all we are handed, or whether we will risk our whole lives shaking down and changing just those bottle-fed convictions.

Essential political decisions are made not once but again and again in all kinds of situations, always against that pressure to compromise, to bargain. I have found that in my own slow reassessment of my own politics, the most telling factor has been the gap between the rhetoric of lesbian feminism and the reality of my own life. It didn't matter how many times I was told that I was oppressed as a woman, I found that that fact did not answer all the contradictions of my life. Simple answers do not satisfy, and I rarely find that only one dynamic is going on in any given situation—a fact that makes me sharply suspicious of reductionist politics. Such politics are the most prone to compromise, to say we're addressing the essential contradiction and all that other stuff can slide. It is people who slide.

All my life I have been subject to the fact that somebody is always trying to set the boundaries of who and what I will be allowed to be—if queer, an acceptable queer, not too forward about the details of one's sexual practice; if working-class, an intellectual, upwardly mobile type who knows her place or at least the virtues of gratitude; if a writer, a humble, consciously female one who understands her relationship to "real" writers and who is willing to listen to her editor. What is common to all these boundary lines is that their true power lies in what I can be persuaded to do to myself—the walls of fear, shame, and guilt I am encouraged to build in my own mind. I have learned, in fact, that all systems of oppression feed on public silence and private terror, but few do so more forcefully than the system of sexual oppression.

6. Moraga, "Preface," in *This Bridge Called My Back*, xiv.

Within the feminist movement we have developed a major analysis around the issue of silence—the impact on all our lives of all the things that must not be said. Nor has this been an analysis contained only within lesbian feminism. When I have spoken as a lesbian about my own struggles to understand and publicly acknowledge the full meaning of my love for women, I have watched straight women nod back at me, heard them speak of their own terrible secrets, their own impossible desires. For all women it is the public expression of desire that is impossible, any vestige of deviation from what we are supposed to want and how we are supposed to behave. The myth prevails that "good girls"—even modern, enlightened, liberal or radical varieties—don't really have such desires.

For ten years now I have been sharing with other women the rage with which I began my work as a feminist organizer—outrage at anybody telling us what we will be allowed to do with our lives, and what we will not. And always for me this struggle has been about sex and class; shattering the silence that has been imposed on us not only around our terrifying sexual desires, but also around the powerful details of all the different ways we approach the world. When in 1981, I helped to organize the Lesbian Sex Mafia [LSM], I felt very much in that tradition. It was to be a CR [consciousness-raising] support group whose whole concern would be the subject of sex. To be sure that we would begin focused on our outrageousness, we chose our deliberately provocative name and concentrated on attracting members whose primary sexual orientation was s/m, butch/femme, fetishes, or otherwise "politically incorrect." We drew more women from the bars than the movement, but we brought back the principles of CR in our organization and insisted that within the group we would make no assumptions, no judgments, and no conclusions. We began by asking each other: what would it be like to organize for our sexual desire as strongly as we have tried to organize for our sexual defense?

The failings of LSM were largely the failings of early CR groups. With the concentration on sharing stories, it was hard to move on to taking any action as a group or to any kind of public, political identity. Some members felt frustrated with this, while others wanted the group to concentrate only on meeting the needs of members. In fact, there were limits on how the latter could be achieved. Integrating new people was extremely difficult and in fact the membership has always been concentrated on individuals who had already come to some state of self-acceptance. The kind of hesitant, fearful young woman who called me might never have come back after an initial orientation, and women who came expecting that LSM was going to provide them with an instant source of sex and adventure could get bored with all the talk and business. But the worst failure of the organization was that none of us really expected the kind of attacks that took place at the time of the Barnard conference and the organization's only public event—a speak-out on politically incorrect sex. Concentrating on supporting each other, we had put no work into confronting critics who were horrified at our behavior as lesbians, never mind "queer" queers. Nonetheless, the group—both before and after April 24, 1982—fulfilled its function as a forum to talk about our pleasure, rage, and fear about sex.

Even for those of us with backgrounds as political activists who had thought we had some handle on sex and its variations in this society, the revelation of shame, fear, and guilt that we produced was overwhelming. Women talked about years of celibacy, self-hatred, rejection, and abandonment by lovers, helplessness after rape or incest, social censure and street violence, family ostracism and constantly—the fear of what our desires might mean. Even though we had set up the group to avoid judgments we would still depressingly ask: "Do you think I'm sick?" The great strength of the group was the emphasis placed on how to turn those fears and experiences to a source of insight rather than confusion. That we could feel safe while being so vulnerable to each other was a constant source of energy and power. Every forbidden thought that was spoken enriched us. Every terrible desire that we shared suddenly assumed human dimensions, and our meetings were full of warmth and laughter.

How might our lives be different, I began to ask, if we were not being constantly subjected to this fear of ourselves and each other? What kind of women might we be if we did not have to worry about being too sexual, or not sexual enough, or the wrong kind of sexual for the company we kept? More and more I have grown impatient with the limitations placed on bringing this kind of discussion out of the closed group and into the public debate that continues among feminists. Not addressing these issues reinforces the rage and fear we all hide, while supporting the status quo of sexual oppression.

Instead of speaking out in favor of sex, most feminists seem to avoid this discussion in any way possible. It is too dangerous, too painful, too hopeless—like racism, class, anti-Semitism, and all the important issues that require so much of us. Everyone is afraid of what might be revealed about our personal fears and desires. It is easier to dismiss any discussion of sexuality as irrelevant or divisive than to have to look at all the different ways we have denied and dismissed each other.

But we have no choice about this issue. We cannot continue to be circumspect in how we challenge this system of sexual oppression. We cannot continue to be willing to allow each other to deny ourselves, to be so quick to make those bad bargains that look so good at the time. I think for example of all those times we have pandered to this sex-hating society: as lesbians by pretending that we're really no different from heterosexuals and by placing such a strong emphasis on monogamy; as feminists by speaking for "reproductive freedom" rather than abortion, talking about our right to control our bodies but never going on to demand all that might mean; and by talking of morality as if that word didn't stick in our mouths with the memory of every lesbian ever attacked for the "immoral" acts we all commit. Our enemies are not confused about this issue. The preachers, psychologists, and politicians who want us to be silent, frightened women they can control—they are not avoiding the issue of sex. Sex is their favorite subject for attack, because they know how vulnerable we are to it.

I know from my own life that none of us wants to go on with this fear, this sense of loss, betrayal, risk. I know that I want most what Barbara Smith described in her short story—the ability to love without fear of betrayal, the confidence that we can expose ourselves and not have the women we love literally disappear from our lives. I know too that we will not get that safe ground easily. If we are not to sacrifice some part of ourselves or our community, we will have to go through all the grief of exposure and struggle, with only a thin line of trust that we will emerge whole and unbroken. The only way I know to begin this is to start by saying, "I will give up nothing. I will give up no one."

For my lovers, my sisters, the women who are now afraid to speak to or be seen with me, I have only one promise to make. I promise someday to provide a gathering place where in the center of the room will stand a huge, open book, a book where women will write out their fearful secrets and sign them or not as they choose. The only requirement will be that they should not feel they have to lie.

24

TWO GENERATIONS OF
FEMINIST ACTIVISM

Snapshots from the Middle East and North Africa since 1970

Diane E. King

Ethnographic research first brought me to the Middle East and North Africa (MENA) region in 1995, when I began work in Kurdistan, in the northwest corner of Iraq. I taught at American University of Beirut between 2000 and 2006, and I continue to make research trips to Kurdistan. In both Kurdistan and Lebanon, as well as in nearby countries that I have visited, I have observed and experienced a great deal of gendered oppression. Men tend to have many advantages over women in daily life, and can, if they wish, behave abusively toward the girls and women in their lives with few consequences. I once met a group of female secondary teachers in Kurdistan who asked what had brought me to the area, and I reported that I was writing about their society. They immediately brought up the subject of gender relations and proceeded to list the ways in which they felt restricted by men. In the end, one summed up their points by urging, "We speak for all women here. . . . Just write that life for women here is hell!" On many other occasions, women have been quicker to tell me about the positive aspects of their lives than to litanize about any gendered oppression they may have experienced. MENA women's "empowerment" and "disempowerment" are more complex than it might initially appear (Abu Odeh). In this chapter I draw primarily on ethnographic research and two novels written by women from the MENA region to highlight some of the challenges faced by many MENA women and how some women have responded through activism.

The MENA region is home to girls and women who live diverse lives, and women's life experiences are certainly not limited to subjugation by males. Many women have not been victims and are anything but passive, anything but desirous of outsiders' condescension or, in many cases, help. Many urban career women, such as those in bustling Beirut, have a day-to-day experience that closely resembles that of their counterparts in the West; probably the greatest difference is that the Beiruti career woman is much more likely to have a full-time domestic employee (usually a woman from Sri Lanka or the Philippines). Most rural women, in contrast, spend their days engaging in the labor of agriculture, food preparation, childcare, cleaning, and entertaining guests.

In spite of this diversity, research on MENA women indicates that the oppression of women is a significant problem across many ethnic, class, religious, regional, and national divisions. They are not alone: globally, at least one in three women has been "beaten, coerced into sex, or otherwise abused in her lifetime." Until recently, systematic research on female subjugation and abuse in the MENA region was extremely rare, and while it remains scarce, some recent studies have revealed alarming statistics. Kocacıka, Kutlarb, and Erselcanb cite a number of studies in Turkey that reveal high levels of domestic violence toward women, ranging from around 20 percent to much higher; in a survey of 1,259 women in Turkey, 68 percent of wives reported being hit by their husbands (Purple Roof Foundation 34–35, cited in Kocacıka, Kutlarb, and Erselcanb 700). In research with wives regarding husband-perpetrated violence in a Palestinian refugee camp in Jordan, Khawaja and Barazi found that the reported prevalence of lifetime beating was 44.7 percent. The Arab Human Development Report, while having a broad mandate to report on many aspects of development, had a special focus on women in 2005 (UNDP) and perhaps represented the broadest analysis of gender inequality in Arab countries undertaken to that point. The report highlighted recent successes, such as impressive gains in female education rates, but was mainly scathing, pointing out deficiencies such as the statistic that over half of Arab women were still nonliterate.

The question of female status in the MENA region is, in many instances and settings, tied to religion and the ways in which people and governments may use it to justify social policies both informal and formal. Most people in the region are Muslim, so Islam plays a more important role than other faiths, and indeed, particular understandings of Islam are sometimes used to justify female exclusion from public life and subjugation by males. Minority religions such as Christianity and that of the Druze are also influential where their adherents are found. In fact, I have heard religious justifications from non-Muslims for some of the region's most restrictive treatment of women, as well as a sexual double standard. For example, an Iraqi Christian leader told me that in his branch of Christianity, a woman could not ask her husband to remain sexually faithful to her and that she would be required to stay with him if she knew him to be unfaithful, but that the reverse was not true and a man had the right to divorce an unfaithful wife. In general, the MENA region is led today by Muslim men, and in many instances these male leaders interpret the Quran in a conservative fashion in those areas of policy that pertain to women and "the family," even if few regimes in the region can be labeled "Islamist."

MENA PERSONAL STATUS CODES

In the modern state, patriliny and its associated practices and conventions have been made "legible" (Scott)—written and made official in state records and databases and identification cards. Thus a very old form of understanding the family and descent has been adapted to the modern setting. Most of the modern states of the MENA region have a special set of legal codes that govern family life, referred to as personal status codes (PSCs). These laws were developed during the twentieth century in a period of European colonial control that gave way to autocratic independent states. Their roots lie in tradition, religion, European law, and "modern" ideals. While their authors may have seen the codes' treatment of women as "protecting" and "honoring" them, compared to the laws of other contemporary societies, the PSCs of the MENA region uphold some of the most rigid gender segregation and female denigration practices in the world.

Recently a number of efforts have been mounted to change PSCs for the benefit of women. Some have been successful. In Morocco, the young king Mohammed IV has responded positively to calls for reform. In 2004, sweeping changes to the Moroccan personal status code, the Moudawana, went into effect. The table in this chapter shows some of these changes to the Moudawana.

Despite the great deal of attention paid to religion however, the low status of many girls and women in the MENA region may also be more tied to kinship conventions upheld by the modern state than to religion or any other factor. Despite the diverse life experiences found in the MENA region, many girls and women there have one important feature in common that I argue may contribute to their subjugation: almost all live in societies and under governments that follow a patrilineal way of ordering society. (Israel is largely an exception, since Israeli citizenship can be passed on by both mothers and fathers, and many Jews regard *mothers* to be the main source of Jewishness, as opposed to fathers, even though fathers also pass on categories such as membership in priestly lines.) The adjective *patrilineal* and its noun *patriliny* (or the older form *patrilineality*) come from anthropological kinship studies, which address how family is defined, how identity and goods are passed on to the next generation, marriage conventions, and the like. Patrilines are male lines of descent through which identity categories such as tribe, ethnicity, and religion are passed on. For example, in the MENA region, a child of an ethnic Turkish mother and ethnic Arab father is seen as Arab, and not of "mixed" ethnicity. The social degree of emphasis on male lines of descent varies greatly in the MENA region. Some people belong to prestigious patrilines and others do not. Despite the variation, patriliny is very widespread and upheld by numerous policies and laws. The need to be certain about which men fathered which children, and to uphold other patrilineal ideals, may be a major reason why large numbers of women in the MENA region tend to be cloistered, their bodies covered to a greater degree than in many other parts of the world, and their daily freedom and movements restricted.

Legal Status of Moroccan Women

	Moudawana of 1957–1958	Moudawana of 2004
Marital Age and Consent	Marriage is legal at 18 years of age for males, 15 for females; judges can authorize marriage of girls younger than 15 years of age. *Wali* (marital tutor) is mandated.	Marriage is legal at age 18 for both males and females; judges are now required to provide a written justification if authorizing underage marriage. *Wali* is optional.
Polygamy	Men may have up to four spouses. Permission of the first wife is not required to take an additional wife; it is recommended but not legally required that the new wife be informed of her husband's first wife at the time of marriage. Theoretically, it is possible for a wife to ask her husband to commit to monogamy in the marriage contract, but there is no legal mechanism for enforcing the agreement.	Judicial authorization is required to take a second wife; husband must have an exceptional reason for seeking an additional wife and prove his ability to financially support both wives and offspring equally. The first wife must be present when the husband appears before the judge to seek authorization. A wife can stipulate a monogamy clause in the marriage contract.
Responsibilities and Rights	Husband is the legal head of household and the wife is legally required to obey the husband. Husband is legally required to financially support the wife.	Husband and wife are joint heads of household; the legal requirement of obedience is abolished. The husband is still legally required to financially support the wife.
Divorce and Repudiation	Repudiation is executed through verbal pronouncement ("I repudiate thee"), and does not require cause or judicial control, though it must be notarized by an *adoul;* only the husband may repudiate and the wife's presence not required. Two types of divorce are available to women: (1) divorce "for cause" (harm, financial non-maintenance, abandonment, long-term imprisonment, or abstinence), or (2) a "negotiated repudiation" (*khul'* divorce), in which the wife pays the husband to repudiate her.	Repudiation is placed under judicial oversight and wife must be present so she knows she is being repudiated; it remains an option available only to males. All previously specified forms of divorce are retained, and two new forms of divorce are added: (1) mutual consent (initiated by both spouses), and (2) irreconcilable differences (can be initiated by either spouse).

	Moudawana of 1957–1958	Moudawana of 2004
Filiation and Nationality	Filiation is legally conceived of as a child's integration into his or her father's patrilineage. Children can only acquire Moroccan nationality through their father.	The child of a non-Moroccan father and Moroccan mother can acquire his or her nationality through the mother. Judges can order paternity testing to establish paternal filiation.*
Custody and Guardianship	Sons are to remain with their mother until puberty, when the father assumes custody. Daughters remain with their mothers until marriage, at which time they become the legal responsibility of their husbands. The father is always the legal tutor (guardian), even if the mother is the physical custodian. A mother can lose custody of her children upon remarriage or if she moves to a location too distant for the father to exercise his rights as the legal tutor. The father is "third in line" in the legally dictated sequence for custody, after the mother and maternal female relatives. (The 1993 revision made the father "second in line," ahead of maternal female relatives.)	Upon reaching fifteen years of age, children can choose either their mother or father as custodian. Distinction between physical custody and legal tutorship remains. A mother no longer automatically loses custody for remarrying or moving; in such cases the father must petition the court within a specified period of time to gain custody.
Marital Property	The husband and wife have completely separate estates in terms of both property/wealth brought into the marriage and property/wealth acquired during the marriage.	Spouses can opt to enter into a prenuptial agreement specifying alternative arrangements.

SOURCE: Compiled by Beth Malchiodi, "Assessing the Impact of the 2004 Moudawana on Women's Rights in Morocco: A Curriculum Unit" (2008). Data for 1958–1959 are derived from Charrad, *States and Women's Rights*, 31–45, 158–68; data for 2004 are based upon Bordat, "Women's Rights and the Family Code In Morocco" and the HREA unofficial English translation of the Moudawana.

* From Gomez-Rivas, "Morocco's Imperfect Remedy for Gender Inequality"; paternity tests reportedly cost over six hundred USD and can only be performed at one location in Rabat.

The period from 1970 to the present, the focus of this chapter, follows several decades during which the states of the MENA region emerged as independent from European colonial rule, only to solidify their own brands of authoritarianism. Conflict wracked the region—in Palestine, Algeria, Lebanon, Iraq, and elsewhere. Conflict, nationalism, modern aspirations, and state-supported religion were major influences in women's lives.

During the past two generations, while modernizing, "secular" authoritarianism and other previously prominent features of MENA life have not dissipated, and war and occupation continue, a new order in the form of Islamism has been on the rise. Movements labeling themselves as Islamic have had only limited success in assuming governing power (Iran and Gaza are two exceptions), but they are very influential. Some, such as the Islamic State in the Levant (ISIL), may hold swaths of territory and exercise heavy-handed control over the local population without necessarily controlling the central government. ISIL has abused, displaced, and killed thousands of people and, as of this writing in 2014, is growing in strength in Iraq, Syria, and Lebanon. In most MENA countries governments that might otherwise have been gravitating away from Islamic-influenced policy have instead placed renewed emphasis on it in order to appease their increasingly Islamicized citizens and remain in power.

The Islamist trend has had an important bearing on women's lives and is often a factor in preventing improvements in women's condition. It has also prompted some feminists to use parts of the Quran and Hadith to justify arguments for better treatment of women, where earlier generations might have used more secular arguments. Lara Deeb, in *An Enchanted Modern*, has shown how Shi'i women in Lebanon deftly combine a vision of the modern and the Islamic in a lifestyle that appears anything but disempowered. Muslim feminists in the MENA region now generally fall into two camps: those who advocate a move away from the Quran as a guide for gender relations, and those who insist that the Quran has been misinterpreted by conservatives and that it can be used to elevate women's status. Quran 4:34, for example, appears to allow a man to beat his wife. Interpretations on this verse vary tremendously, however. Some commentators argue that when taken in context, the verse does not justify violence, while others argue that it does.

Despite discouraging social and political conditions, throughout the MENA region a new generation of activists is working to foster change in the gender system. Its members are building on the successes of earlier feminists such as Fatima Mernissi of Morocco and Nawal al-Saadawi of Egypt (see chapter 20 for selections by Mernissi). They include Saudi Wajeha al Huwaider, who successfully sparked debate in 2008 by placing a video of herself driving a car on YouTube; Saudi Arabia prohibits driving by females (except in some rural areas and behind walled compounds). Rola Dashti of Kuwait is the first woman member of the Kuwaiti parliament and an outspoken advocate for women's rights. Iranian lawyer and former judge Shirin Ebadi was awarded the Nobel Peace Prize in 2003 for her work on behalf of children's and women's rights in the face of intense pressure from the government; she moved to Canada in 2009 because the pressure on her in Iran became too much to bear. In 2008, twenty-seven-year-old Noha Ostadh became the first Egyptian woman to win a court case against a man who had sexually harassed her and in the process became well-known to the Egyptian public ("Egyptian Sexual Harasser Jailed"). In the Arab Spring that began in early 2011, young women played a major role in largely peaceful revolutions that brought down two authoritarian leaders, in Tunisia and Egypt, and other revolts with significant female participation are under way. Millions of young women are studying in or are on track to enter the MENA region's universities, and many more have recently graduated. For many, pursuing higher education itself constitutes activism. However, high unemployment rates among young women mean that graduates must continue to exercise persistence and creativity in order to be able to apply their training.

My friend Nesreen Barwari became Iraq's minister of public works in 2003, making her one of the two highest-ranking women in the history of modern Iraq. I watched many of the difficult steps that preceded that role, some of which seemed to me at the time to require even more courage than becoming a minister. As far as either of us knows, she was the first local woman to drive a car in the town of Dohuk, Iraq. Once in the late 1990s, a local woman and I were walking on the street in Dohuk when we saw Barwari driving a sport utility vehicle with male passengers, in her capacity as head of a local United Nations office. She stopped briefly to say hello. After they drove off, the friend with me on the street said, "Did you see the man in the back seat? I could see on his face that he was embarrassed for me to see him in the back of a car being driven by a local woman!" In her estimation, to be driven by a woman was a terribly humiliating role for a local man, one made even worse by being in the back rather than in the passenger seat and having been seen by a local person who might gossip about him. Small acts of resisting such social pressure, repeated by increasing numbers of women until the status quo has changed, are the stuff of widespread gender system change. Such change is happening, albeit in many cases slowly, in diverse corners of the MENA region.

Finally, the Internet and other technologies such as satellite television have been major factors in women's activism, especially during the past twenty years. In 1990, few MENA homes had satellite dishes, but now they can be seen on nearly every urban rooftop and on most rural ones (except where they are banned, as in Iran). The Internet has had a much smaller impact to date, but tremendous growth is surely ahead. Social networking has been used by some Arab Spring protesters. Bloggers are having an impact, such as the woman in her twenties who wrote under the pseudonym Riverbend. From 2003 to 2007 she chronicled the Iraq war and subsequent occupation with candor, for the whole world to read, and in the process allowed the complexities of young female life in a war zone to receive unprecedented exposure.

Riding a new wave of media, travel, networks, external funding, and awareness of trends in the broader world, many women's NGOs have arisen during the past two decades. Some are very local and small-scale, and others are transnational networks that also serve as information clearinghouses, such as Women Living under Muslim Laws.

REPRESENTING MENA WOMEN: NEW FEMALE LITERARY VOICES

Too often, the status of women in the MENA region is linked in Western popular culture and media to broader issues of economics and geopolitical contests, sometimes in ways that border on the absurd. For example, a 2009 Time.com article on improvements for women in the Saudi workplace had hyperlinks to other articles inserted at the end of some of its paragraphs (Butters, "Saudi Arabia's Small Steps"). One read, "See pictures of Osama Bin Laden." Would it have made sense for *Time* to have included a link to a story on Timothy McVey, the American who detonated a truck bomb that killed and injured hundreds of people in Oklahoma City in 1995, in a piece on advances by women in the United States? This seems highly unlikely, but the presence of the link, whether auto-generated or intentionally inserted by editors, implies that a connection may be made between a famous terrorist originally from Saudi Arabia and the struggle for Saudi women's rights.

Fortunately, women in the MENA region have plenty of means of representing themselves, and they use those means in rich and creative ways. For example, during the past several decades, they have been publishing books in numbers far greater than previously. These works belong to every imaginable fiction and nonfiction genre. This chapter highlights two excerpts, one from the autobiography *An Iranian Odyssey* by Gohar Kordi (1991), and the other from the novel *B as in Beirut* by Iman Humaydan Younes (2006). The portions of these two works are very different from each other, deliberately chosen to highlight the varied nature of women's experience in MENA life.

Gohar Kordi's book is a methodical protest against multiple injustices, starting with her birth and persisting into adulthood. Born to an ethnically Turkish father and a Kurdish mother in an Iranian village, Kordi overcomes gendered discrimination, her family's poverty, a variety of difficult circumstances including abuse at a boarding school run by Westerners, and the loss of her sight at the age of four, to earn a degree in psychology at Tehran University in 1970. Her young adulthood took place during a paradoxical time in Iran. The shah's government was brutal to some people, torturing and killing at will. Others, however, were seemingly unaffected and lived well. Kordi relates that the conditions in her dormitory were much better than in her parents' home. But discontent was increasingly widespread. The angst that fueled the 1979 Iranian revolution is evident even though she covers a prior period.

Kordi's account is packaged as a story of personal triumph against the odds, but it is much more. Her challenges represent some of the most prominent aspects of female subjugation and abuse and the social structures that may facilitate them, found across the MENA region, as in other patrilineal societies globally. Those mentioned in the excerpt include son preference, daughter neglect, forced marriage, early marriage, and patrilocal residence. "You neglected me, didn't you, because I was a girl. You neglected my sister as well, and she died," Kordi writes to her mother (9).

At the same time, Kordi's account is fraught with a nostalgia that seems guilt-ridden and laden with dilemmas. She ends the book with a description of an encounter on an intercity bus with strangers who offered to help her reach her final destination in a taxi. She recounts that she wanted very deeply to trust them but ultimately chose not to. With this unvarnished vignette, she ends the book. In Kordi's story, issues of abuse and longing are rendered in context and in one human life. Solutions are not offered; that is a job for the reader.

Iman Humaydan Younes's novel profiles the experiences of four diverse women during the Lebanese civil war (1975–90). In the excerpt included here, a woman named Camilia reminisces about her earlier life in a Lebanese town during the war. Raised in a household without any men, a highly unusual arrangement, she remembers a youth at once socially carefree and fraught with wartime fear and danger. In the excerpt, we learn that her parents had emigrated to Argentina to work, and that her father had subsequently died there and her mother remarried. She is bitter at her mother for leaving her behind as a suckling infant and rebellious toward her aunt and the uncle who periodically visit. In the excerpt we witness gender segregation in the *majlis* (Druze prayer room), which Camilia flouts before being driven off by an appropriately clad woman inside, and her growing knowledge about relations between women and men despite her sheltered upbringing.

Camilia later realizes her dream of moving abroad and lives in London for several years before returning with a filmmaker to document wartime Lebanon. She has jobs and affairs; she philosophizes. She remains rootless, a woman caught between generations, places, relationships, and dreams as her homeland is partially destroyed. A traditionalist might find Camilia's life shocking, and a cosmopolitan might take much of it for granted. In any case, Humaydan Younes adroitly shows, through her portrayal of the circumstances and choices of Camilia and the other women, how empowerment and disempowerment are not mutually exclusive categories but always entwined in individual lives and cultures.

The contrasts represented by Kordi's and Humaydan Younes's works can be taken as emblematic of the variety of life experiences, choices, meanings, conundrums, and causes facing MENA girls and women at present. There is much conversation in the West and elsewhere about MENA women's lives, but nowhere is the conversation more lively than among MENA women themselves. May these brief samples of literature serve to encourage further reading of MENA women authors.

WORKS CITED

Bordat, Stephanie Willman. "Women's Rights and the Family Code In Morocco." Presentation delivered at the Moroccan American Commission for Educational and Cultural Exchange (MACECE), Rabat, July 2, 2008.

Butters, Andrew Lee. "Saudi Arabia's Small Steps for Women." October 19, 2009. *Time*. www.time.com/time/magazine/article/0,9171,1929152,00.html. Accessed November 2, 2009.

Charrad, Mounira M. *States and Women's Rights: The Making of Postcolonial Tunisia, Algeria, and Morocco*. Berkeley: University of California Press, 2001.

Deeb, Lara. *An Enchanted Modern: Gender and Public Piety in Shi'i Lebanon*. Princeton: Princeton University Press, 2006.

"Egyptian Sexual Harasser Jailed." October 21, 2008. *BBC News*. http://news.bbc.co.uk/2/hi/africa/7682951.stm. Accessed July 14, 2010.

Gomez-Rivas, Camilo. "Morocco's Imperfect Remedy for Gender Inequality." *Middle East Report Online 24/7*. www.merip.org/mer/mer247/gomez-rivas.html. Accessed November 1, 2008.

Khawaja, Marwan and Rana Barazi. "Prevalence of Wife Beating in Jordanian Refugee Camps: Reports by Men and Women." *Journal of Epidemiology and Community Health* 59, no. 10 (2005): 840–41.

Kocacıka, Faruk, Aziz Kutlarb, and Feray Erselcanb. "Domestic Violence against Women: A Field Study in Turkey." *Social Science Journal* 44, no. 4 (2007): 698–720.

Kordi, Gohar. *An Iranian Odyssey*. London: Serpent's Tail, 1991.

Malchiodi, Beth. "Assessing the Impact of the 2004 Moudawana on Women's Rights in Morocco: A Curriculum Unit." 2008. *Outreach World*. www.outreachworld.org/Files/u_texas/Women_and_family_law_Morocco_curriculum.pdf. Accessed June 15, 2012. .

Odeh, Lama Abu. "Post-colonial Feminism and the Veil: Thinking the Difference." *Feminist Review* 43 (1993): 26–37.

Purple Roof Foundation. *My Future in My Hands (Geleceğim Elimde)*. Istanbul: Mor Çatı Kadın Sığınağı Vakfı, 1997.

Scott, James C. *Seeing Like a State: How Certain Schemes to Improve the Human Condition Have Failed*. New Haven: Yale University Press, 1999.

UNDP. "The Arab Human Development Report 2005: Towards the Rise of Women in the Arab World." 2005. *United Nations Development Programme*. http://hdr.undp.org/en/reports/regionalreports/arabstates/RBAS_ahdr2005_EN.pdf. Accessed July 5, 2010.

UNIFEM. "2010 Facts & Figures on VAW." 2010. *UN Women*. www.unifem.org/gender_issues/violence_against_women/facts_figures.php. Accessed July 14, 2010.

Younes, Iman Humaydan. *B as in Beirut*. Translated by Max Weiss. Northhampton, MA: Interlink Books, 2007.

DISCUSSION QUESTIONS

1. What kinds of gendered oppression are experienced by some women in the MENA region? How do the readings represent them?

2. How do Kordi and Camilia attempt to resist these forms of oppression? How successful are they, and why? What are the costs of their resistance?

3. What is patriliny and how does it influence culture and law in the MENA region? Do you see its effects in the readings?

GOHAR KORDI, FROM *AN IRANIAN ODYSSEY*
Chapter One

I must have been about four years old and I was playing outside in the street, when an older boy who would have been about seven, said to me. "You can't see. You're blind."

"No. I'm not," I said confident, resolute.

"Yes, you are."

"No, I'm not," I repeated.

"If you're not," he said, "then drop that coin you have in your hand and pick it up."

I dropped the coin and picked it up again straightaway. The boy walked off without a word.

I stood there with the coin in my hand, proud, triumphant. I had proved . . .

I wonder how long I went on with this illusion?

Maybe I still do not know that I am blind.

What happened during that period of my life?

It was as though the world came to a standstill. I was shut out. Doomed. Forgotten. I vegetated and yet lived. I was shut out from light, love, and wrapped in a curtain of darkness which lay all around me, touching me, squeezing me, hurting me, suffocating me.

Fear fills my heart, cripples me. I lose any attempt, any effort to struggle, protest.

I feel the bandages on my eyes, on my body, on my soul.

I dare not struggle, scream, protest—too dangerous. I have lost my voice. If I make the slightest protest the bandages will be pulled tighter and that will be the end of me.

Not a sound. "She slept the whole time," mother said.

If I were to meet my mother now, what would I say to her? I have a lot to say to you, mother, a lot! I want to show you some of my achievements. This is my son, meet him. Isn't he beautiful? And this is my husband. Isn't he handsome? And he loves me, I love him. Unlike you and your husband, you hated each other, didn't you?

And this is my house. Isn't it beautiful? Look, we've done it all by ourselves, my husband and I. It was a derelict house when we moved in. And look what we've made of it.

My son's room:—look we've just finished it. Decorated it, no, renovated it. I sanded it and scraped it with my own hands. Isn't it beautifully painted? The colour scheme, everyone says how beautiful it is. I can't see it.

But I want you to see it, mother. You tell me how nice it is.

People say this room is a child's paradise. Look at all these hand-made wooden toys. Aren't they beautiful to touch? I can't see them.

SOURCE: Gohar Kordi, *An Iranian Odyssey* (London: Serpent's Tail, 1991), 7–19.

And his globe. He finds Iran, where I was born, on it. I can't see it.

Look at the carpets. Aren't they beautiful? Everyone admires them. Oriental, they think. They didn't cost much money and we did extremely well in finding them.

Everything is just so beautiful. Everyone says so. And I feel it, although I can't appreciate it to the full. I can't see it.

Look mother. I want you to see everything. See how well I have done? I have given birth to this beautiful child, and he is so wonderful. Such a perfect little boy. Sometimes people are taken by surprise. "Is he your child?" people ask in dismay, just as people used to comment about me when I was a little girl. "Is this your daughter? But she is beautiful!" You dressed me like a dolly, you said. Now I understand how proud you must have felt. This was, of course, before I lost my sight. With it I lost my beauty in your eyes. In spite of that, I have done well, mother. I am a good mother, mother. A good mother, unlike you. And I am a good wife and a good friend, too. Friends say so. After all, I haven't let you down, mother.

I said I lost my sight. No, I did not lose it. It was lost for me. Did you do it, mother? You neglected me, didn't you, because I was a girl. You neglected my sister as well, and she died. I survived. Miracles happen, mother. How come nothing happened to your sons? They were taken good care of, because they were male. Isn't that right, mother? Admit it. And, in doing so, free yourself from the terrible guilt and free me from my anger.

I feel angry with you, mother. A terrible anger has been locked inside me all these years and it has been eating me away. It is time now to be released. I know, I know you had a hard time. But I wasn't responsible for it. You negated my existence because I was female. You put a death-wish on me when I became blind, you said so many times, "I wish she was dead and had not recovered from her illness!" And now look what I have done with my life. Who were you to prejudge my future? "What has life got in store for her?" you used to say. I have not failed you, mother.

Have a good look round my house. Oh, no, not in the drawers, not yet, they are untidy, I have to sort them out. I want to show you good things about me for once. Look at my kitchen. I am a good cook, everyone says so, even my mother-in-law. They had a meal with us this Christmas for the first time. My mother-in-law, father-in-law, sister-in-law, brother-in-law, the lot, and I cooked them a good meal, they were most impressed. They enjoyed the visit. They didn't criticize anything as we feared they would. I proved myself. But look, I want to know what *you* think, mother, what would *you* say, have I done well?

Look at my curtains. Would you like to know how I got them? We didn't have money to get new ones. I rang the local library and asked them to read out jumble sales advertised in the local newspaper. Then I rang them to see if they had curtains and went round. Eventually I found a huge piece of curtain material. I found someone to make it to measure. They are all right, aren't they? People thought we had spent hundreds of pounds on them.

You see how I manage, do things, achieve? I can't see, but I have a mind and I use it, that is how I have survived despite what you put me through, mother.

I haven't told this to anyone before and I am telling you now: you've hurt me deeply, you've scarred me for life, you've crushed me but, look, I have survived.

I have no recollection of events early in my life such as my illness and before that of my sight. No visual memory except faint memories of colour, blues in particular, sky, maybe. I have blocked everything off, hidden the memories deep down, lost them, cannot find them even though I search.

What went through my mind during those three months of illness and then recovery? How did I feel? When did I discover that I could see no longer? At what moment was that? How did I feel?

Chapter Two

I was born on New Year's Day in Iran, *Norooz,* the twenty-first of March, the first day of spring. In Iran *Norooz* is a major celebration. People prepare months in advance. They spring-clean, buy new clothes, decorate and prepare delicacies. Having survived the harsh winter they celebrate, everything is cleaned and freshened, people wear their new clothes, especially the children. Children must have new clothes. If adults can't afford them somehow they manage for the children. They have to. Everyone tries to wear something new. People start visiting to wish each other Happy New Year, the senior members of the family first, grandparents, great uncles and aunts, senior members, who give presents to the young ones. Children receive coins from aunts and uncles, and coloured eggs and sweets from friends. Young married women receive a trayful of goodies from their parents and brothers—sweets, cakes, coloured eggs, a scarf, bits of jewelery maybe, and a piece of material for a dress, usually, or a chador, and this is called *pi,* a share, signifying that the women still play a part in their lives, that they have not been forgotten. Women who live far away receive their presents a few days before.

I was born early in the morning at about five o'clock. The news of my birth was taken to my father who stayed in a nearby house as was the custom in the village. Congratulations, it's a girl, the messenger shouted.

"Congratulations for a girl?" my father asked. The woman expected this response. She wasn't dismayed. The news had to be taken. She'd done her duty. "It would have been better if a child had brought the news," she thought, but it was too late. Had it been a boy it would have been totally different. The women would have argued over who was to take the news and she would have arrived breathless with running. "You have a boy." "Wonderful," he would laugh. "Here." And he would place a coin in her hand. He would go out and treat everyone in the neighbourhood to fruit or sweets. Everyone in the village would know that he had a boy. He would hold his head high, proud. In some cases, fathers of daughters would not return home for a while, or not speak to their wives for a time. What does a wife expect, giving birth to a girl? It wasn't too bad in my case, since luckily my father already had a son.

He was called Ali. I was called Monir. And then my second brother, Akbar, was born. Their last child was my sister, Khanomtaj.

Ali, the eldest, the first male, was always given special treatment. He was given the best of the soup, the best of everything. He was the family's hope, because he was male, the first son, the eldest. The first son was always regarded as the family's future security. He would carry the family burden, look after his parents in their old age. He was the life line of the generations. Daughters left home when married but sons stayed, even after they had married. The eldest son always stayed with the parents, and eventually took over the running of the household. There was great prestige in giving birth to a male child first. It was even more wonderful if the second and third were also male, just in case something happened to the first son. The parents would register the birth of a son late, thus their age was given as a few years younger on the birth certificate and the parents could benefit from having their son stay with them longer before he had to leave to do national service. On the other hand daughters were registered as a few years older than they actually were so they could be married off early. The legal age for marriage was fifteen so, a girl would often, in fact, be married at twelve. National service age for boys was at eighteen but they often went at twenty-one or twenty-two.

I do not know much about the first couple of years of my life except that my mother used to say, "She was a beautiful girl before she lost her sight. She was so pretty, clever, full of life. I used to dress her like a doll. She could attract attention straightaway. 'Whose daughter is this?' strangers would ask. 'She's mine,' I would say proudly. 'Yours? What a beautiful daughter you have.'"

"You know," my mother would go on, "that admiration did for her in the end. Yes, one of those people gave her the evil eye. That's why she lost her sight. Look at her, what is she now?"

The words "look at her"—and she said them often enough—made me feel diminished, worthless. And yet I said to myself, there is nothing wrong with me. I am here after all.

"She is not the girl she was," mother would go on, "she's totally changed, she's not the daughter I had." The only time I received recognition, admiration, acceptance was when I still had my sight. Maybe that gave me the strength to fight for my survival later on.

At around the age of three I fell ill with smallpox. "A disaster struck," as my mother would often say, "she was ill for three months. She did not open her eyes." They bandaged them. "She didn't cry, she just slept." I just slept for three months. I must have been petrified. It was too dangerous for me to be awake, to make demands or protest. I felt the danger right to the bone. I demanded just enough to keep me alive, no more, no less. Female, I wasn't wanted in the first place and now how dare I ask for attention?

"After three months when we opened her eyes," my mother would go on, "she'd lost her sight in both. I wish she'd died really. Now look at her." Those three words "look at her" would always come up when she talked about me. I used to wonder if the other person was watching me then. I used to feel like hiding, going to sleep maybe, just as I slept those three months. I can imagine her, hear her voice when she opened my eyes and saw how damaged I was. I can feel the horror on her face, and hear her voice saying, "As if having a girl wasn't bad enough, but a blind girl." She repeated it often. "What a misfortune. What have I done to be punished like this? What a burden on the family for life. An extra mouth to feed." I often heard that—an extra mouth to feed—because being blind meant I'd also lost the chance of being married off.

Mother had one other story about my birth which she often talked about. "She's *bab-ghadam*," she said of me. She believed that my arrival brought bad luck to the family. "Anything we touched turned to stone after her birth, everything went wrong for us." I never knew for sure what did go wrong although I understood that I had evil power and ought to be avoided, put away, to sleep forever maybe. This feeling that I had evil power was to have an enormous effect on my life. When I was about four or five, mother was talking to a woman about me and said, as usual, that I had brought bad luck. The other woman said, "Don't say that in front of her." "Oh, she doesn't understand," mother replied.

Chapter Three

My mother's name was Mahi. She was born in a small Kurdish village named Khorben-deh. There were five children in the family, three boys and two girls, and she was the fourth child. She had been happy as a little girl in the village among her own people, until she had been married off against her wishes at the age of twelve, as was customary, to another Kurd from the next village. The marriage had not worked—that is to say, she had not allowed it to be consummated. She was eventually divorced and after a while was married off to my father, a Turk from a distant Turkish village, Kahleh, also against her wishes. Father's name was Reza. He was a good and gentle man, but mother did not love him; in fact, she hated him because she had already fallen in love long before, with a young Kurd from her own village.

It was the month of July, the height of the summer heat. People slept on the roof in the night for the coolness. Sometimes they ate their supper on the roof as well. One night after supper during which Mahi and Reza, her husband, had not spoken one word, she started to lay out the bedding. Bedding was normally kept on the roof in summer, folded into a pile and covered with a large cloth. She put two small mattresses down next to each other, just long enough and wide enough for the three of them. The little boy would go in the middle, Mahi would sleep on one side and her husband on the other. Then she put down the pillows, one small cushion in the middle for the boy and two pillows long and round, like sausages, on each side which she had brought with her as part of her dowry. Her mother had made them as mothers did for their daughters long before their marriage and stuffed them with all sorts of things, bits of raw wool, bits of left-over fabrics, some hair including her own, and bits of feather. Sometimes Mahi would stick her finger into the pillow to see what interesting things she could find in there. The mattresses were filled with old clothes, rags, bits of cottonwool, and wool sewn together. Then she put down a couple of folded quilts in case it became cool later in the night. The quilts were made of cotton wool. They also came with her dowry and had been made by her mother. She'd brought all the bedding with her when she married. Then she put the little boy in the middle and covered him with her old chador to protect him from the mosquitoes. She did this with care. She raised the chador over his face so that he could breathe easily. She stopped for a moment and looked at her son. She was clever to produce this first child, a boy. She would share her old chador with her son but she would not share anything with her husband, she would rather he slept at the other end of the roof, or even downstairs. If only she could leave his bed downstairs, as far away as possible from her. That would be ideal. But such hopes were fantastic and never went beyond wishful thinking. She handled the child with great care. Each time she touched him *Besmella he rob-manehnabim* she said, "in the name of God." He was a gift from God and should be handled with great care and respect. Every child was God given but this one was special to her, a boy, her first child. The family's hopes focused on him. He had to be well looked after and well cared for. Her second pregnancy had failed and she'd miscarried the year before. She didn't mind. She already had a boy. Many second pregnancies ended badly. She was very young, there was still time. Her first was three now so it was time for another child. People kept asking whether she was pregnant. Her mother, her sister. "It's God's will. The time will come." She took a last look at the child as he slept, deeply, peacefully.

There was still a lot to do before going to bed. She collected everything she had to take downstairs, the pot, bowls, spoons, the *sofreh,* the cloth the bread was wrapped in; she put them all on a tray, lifted it on to her head and started to climb down the ladder. That's how she carried things around. On her head. Holding the tray with one hand and holding the ladder with the other. The steps squeaked as she climbed down. She had to wash the dishes, make the dough for the next morning's bread, attend to the milk, make the cheese, and then mend her husband's trousers. She hated doing that. It wasn't the sewing she hated. She enjoyed sewing but she hated doing anything for him. She'd been putting it off for days while he grumbled and told friends she wasn't doing anything for him, not even mending his trousers. "I feel I haven't got a wife," he'd joke. "Look at my trousers, they're still not mended." She worked away gently, quietly. At times she sang to herself as she worked in the cool, fresh air of the evening. She enjoyed the peace and quiet of the evening, being on her own and taking things gently, quietly. She loved doing things in the garden in the moonlight. It didn't seem very long to her before everything was done.

Before going up to bed she had to say her prayers. She prayed three times a day, once in the morning before sunrise, once in the afternoon, and once in the evening after sunset—if she was menstruating or if she'd had intercourse, she had to go through the cleansing ritual before prayer. This was in three stages and was called *ghusl baze.* First she would place her head under running water, then she would stretch her right arm under the running water, then her left arm. She would accompany these gestures with the words: "In *gbusl baze* I cleanse myself so that I may get close to the Lord." Otherwise, she would take a jug, an *afta-beb,* of water into the toilet and wash between her legs, then squat in the garden and splash water on her face and on her arms three times. Then with two fingers of her right hand she marked her head and her feet repeating verses from the Koran. After this she was cleansed and ready to say her prayers. If she passed wind during prayer she would have to repeat the cleansing process. After cleansing, she put on her chador and fetched the prayer mat. She chose a spot in the middle of the room and stood facing north towards Mecca. There was one large mat and one medium and one smaller. She unrolled all three. Inside them she kept a *mobr,* a little rectangular block of clay from Mecca onto which she placed her forehead, a Koran prayer book, a *tasbeb,* with lots of beads also from Mecca, as well as a few other special items. She'd brought the prayer mats as part of her dowry. They were beautifully embroidered. The fabrics were from Mecca. She set them all out and started to pray. She had to bend down seven times, each time resting her forehead on the *mobr.* Sometimes she should say extra prayers for the days she had missed (for having a period), but this evening she didn't feel like saying more than seven, the necessary number. She wanted to get out up on to the roof as soon as she could, and look at the stars and the moon and enjoy the cool fresh air of the evening. When she had finished praying, she folded all the mats and put them away.

Before leaving the room she stood for a moment and wondered whether to take the trousers up with her. No, she didn't feel like it, she didn't feel up to it, she'd do it tomorrow, in the morning, in the daylight. She just wanted to get up there and let her mind drift and enjoy the coolness of the evening and look at the stars. She loved looking at the stars and just dreaming, letting her mind wander far away. She looked forward to that each evening. She longed for it. As usual, she felt lighter after saying her prayers, revived, happy, content and at peace with herself. She felt she'd been listened to, accepted and gained strength. No, she would leave the trousers, she would do them tomorrow, in the daylight. She promised herself she'd do them. She didn't even feel so angry with her husband now, after having said her prayers. What's more she felt a little ashamed for not having mended his trousers. She was his wife after all. It was the least she could do for him. It was a wife's duty to serve her husband. She took a last look around. She'd better take some drinking water upstairs. She closed the window and then locked the door. She picked up a copper bowl from a large basket where she'd left the dishes to dry, filled it with fresh water and climbed the ladder.

The steps squeaked as she went up. She put the bowl of water down next to her husband, and the key next to that. He would be going down later to say his prayers. He would know where the key was kept. They needn't talk to each other at all. During the day the little boy would carry messages between them, at times with disastrous results. "Go and tell your father we're going to dinner at auntie's tonight," or "Go and tell mother we are having two visitors for dinner tonight."

"Mother, father said to tell you we have two visitors for dinner tonight." "Your father be damned," mother replied and the little boy ran down the street in excitement, and said in a loud and clear voice, "Mother said father be damned," in front of the visitors. This meant trouble for her afterwards.

She watched over the boy. He was fine, he slept peacefully. She felt proud of him. She went to bed, adjusted her pillow and lay down covering herself and the boy with the chador.

She lay there on her back, looking at the stars, counting them. How many could she see? She'd seen the moon earlier in the evening. Whenever she saw the moon for the first time she always tried to look straight after at water or in a mirror for luck; and to avoid looking at the face of a person who was not a friend, which might mean bad luck. She always made sure not to look at her husband's face. She hated him. She looked far off into the distance, at the stars. Could she see? She tried to penetrate to the most distant, tiniest stars, taking her mind further and further away from her body. It was like flying. She felt so weightless. The sky was beautiful, full of stars. Occasionally a light breeze stroked her cheeks and brought her the fresh, pure smells of the country, of flowers and herbs. It was magical. Everything felt so beautiful, so perfect, so unique, complete. She let her mind float. She felt herself lifted, going further away from the earth, excited, liberated, enriched. She felt part of it all, and yet in control. She went over and above everything, everything she'd known, everything she'd experienced. She felt the joy, the happiness, deep down inside her, which nourished her, cherished her, fulfilled her. This was ultimate beauty, perfection, and she saw herself as part of it all. She was young, beautiful, healthy, full of energy. She was creative, clever, capable. She saw herself as powerful. Nothing could limit her, restrict her, cut her down, not even her husband or the landlord, or her mother. No one could tell her what to do or how to be. She would decide what to do, how to be, what to be. She was in charge, in control of herself. Just like the nature she saw around her, part of nature and yet apart, powerful. She felt wonderful. Her dreams carried her away into the night. She was happy sleeping on the roof in the open. Here she was safe. All the neighbours slept on their roofs. He dare not touch her. She would protest. They would hear. He knew this, so never touched her. People slept all around her. She slept with them in mind. Their presence gave her a sense of security, safety, peace. With her family she slept together and yet apart—with the neighbours she slept apart and yet together. She was pleased to get to bed, she sighed with relief, the day was over and now she could be herself. She could dream, sleep, escape. In a moment all her tensions, all her exhaustion, her anxiety, would be over.

IMAN HUMAYDAN YOUNES, FROM *B AS IN BEIRUT*

Not a single man lived in our house. I was born and raised and grew up, and not a single man lived in our house. "It's hard for a household to carry on without a man around," my grandmother used to say, and still stay as bright as my aunt's sheets on the laundry

SOURCE: Iman Humaydan Younes, *B as in Beirut*, trans. Max Weiss (Northhampton, MA: Interlink Books, 2007), 116–21.

line. "If your father were here, I wouldn't have this burden of raising a girl all by myself," my aunt added. His absence didn't bother me; I felt an extreme, boundless freedom, a freedom that was apparent in my eyes and my behavior. Whenever I talked to my girl-friends about it, I could read in their eyes how much they longed for the sudden death of their own fathers. I secretly enjoyed it, but also concealed jealousy that gnawed at me from inside whenever I saw mothers coming to school in the afternoon with lunch for their daughters.

"I'm sending you to your father's. To hell with you," my aunt said in the night, grab-bing me by the hand and shoving me inside the house. After my father died in a car accident in Argentina, my aunt stopped saying such things. After his death, my mother married their partner in the spinning factory and then had another child. She rushed to have another child. She gave birth to a girl who she named Camilia—that is, she gave her my name. She said that she missed me. Is that why she gave my name to her other daughter? Did she miss me that much? I would ask, as the anger grew inside me like a tumor. I really was furious: at my father, at my mother, at all the women around me, at the war that my mother used as a pretense not to come back. Why didn't the two of them take me with them? I asked the same question over and over. My mother kept on writing that she was going to come back at the beginning of the summer. Every letter ended with a sentence that I had memorized. "I'll see you this summer *inshallah*." But she kept on delaying her return from one summer to the next. Meanwhile I grew up and my mother got closer to old age. When my aunt got upset with me, she would remind me how she had begged my mother to take me with her and how my father had refused, claiming that she was going to be working, just like him, and that the two of them didn't know anyone there to entrust with a breastfeeding child. They were moving away to make some money. My grandmother cried and said that our land can't hold onto its children, while my aunt started to beat her breast, claiming that I was the reason she still wasn't married.

My uncle was the only man who ever visited us and stayed over at our house. One day, through my classroom window, I saw him get out of a taxi in the town square and head down the road that slopes to our house carrying thin, dark paper bags. I slipped out dur-ing the last hour of class, while the teacher had his face to the blackboard explaining the Arabic lesson in a muted voice. Our teacher, Daoud, immersed himself in his explana-tions like someone talking to himself while we sat still, staring at him, monitoring the lethargic movements of his body in front of the blackboard, chalk dust flying all around him. We made paper airplanes out of the handouts he gave us and threw them at one another. They flew high into the air, as light as moths, not making a sound. The day before my uncle arrived, some girls from my class dared me to come to school barefoot. When the next day I did, winning the bet, they sat in a circle around me and squawked in amazement. My uncle looked down at my small, blackened feet and asked me angrily if I showed up to school like that every day, if I had any shoes at all. I tried explaining to him about the class dare, but he just handed me the bags of candy and motioned to tell me that there was no use in trying to explain, urging me ahead of him toward home. I walked slowly because I wanted to see the look on his face. I thought, I want to see how men look when they get angry. Do they get angry like my aunt and beat their chests, scream and wail? I didn't want to turn around so I started bringing my steps closer together, shortening them and slowing my pace, staring at the ground so he would think I was just making sure I didn't step on pebbles and thorns in my bare feet. When we arrived at home, there was nobody there. My aunt was out in the field. I quickly put some shoes on and went to escort my grandmother home from the *majlis*. My uncle had letters from my mother; she had also sent pictures and money.

The entrance to the *majlis* was lit dimly. Lights flickered in lanterns spread out on the ground all around those praying. Inside was a large salon with a wooden ceiling, divided into two areas by a white curtain. The curtain was held up on one side by nails hammered into the wall and was left hanging open slightly so people could pass through to the other side. The salon looked onto the outer room, which was for men, but the inner room behind the curtain was reserved for women. If a woman wanted to go outside before the men were finished, she had to be sure that her head and face were completely covered except for one eye. She would have to cover her hands and the upper part of her body with a long white muslin *mandeel*, which she also wrapped around her head. I stood there confused, forgetting why I had come in the first place. I stood there staring at the bearded old men sitting in a circle. In front of some of them there were religious books on low tables, opened to pages with words scrawled on them in longhand. They were reading. I stood there listening to the slow rhythm of their voices. Their voices were deep, as though they were coming from some distant place. Their voices sounded as though they had just finished a high, long cry: pure and crystal clear. When one of them noticed me, he stopped reading. He averted his gaze and twice asked for almighty God's forgiveness. May God disgrace the devil, said another. A terrifying silence prevailed in the room, followed by a similar silence in the women's room. A woman peeked her covered head through the curtain and scolded me, telling me I had to leave because my clothes were inappropriate in that place. I took off running scared toward home.

Translated by Max Weiss

25

MEN AND WOMEN'S STUDIES
Promise, Pitfalls, and Possibility

Michael Kimmel

What is the position of men in women's studies? How do men engage with women's studies? I want to take the position that women's studies is *also* about men. Or, rather that it makes *masculinity* potentially visible as a specific construction, and not simply the unexamined norm.

Before women's studies, men—as men—were invisible—especially to themselves. By making women visible, women's studies also made men visible both to women and to men themselves. If men are now taking up the issue of gender, it is probably less accurate to say, "Thank goodness they've arrived," the way one might when the cavalry appears in a western film, than to say, "It's about time."

Of course, making men visible has not been the primary task of women's studies. But it has been one of its signal successes. The major achievement of women's studies, acting independently and as a force within traditional disciplines, has been making women visible through the rediscovery of long-neglected, undervalued, and understudied women who were accomplished leaders, artists, composers, and writers and placing them in the pantheons of significance where they rightly belong. In addition, women's studies has rediscovered the voices of ordinary women—the laundresses and the salesgirls, the union maids and the union organizers, the workers and the wives—who have struggled to scratch out lives of meaning and dignity. For all these voices—whether they know it or not, whether they acknowledge it or not—women all over the world owe a debt.

But in making women visible, feminism has been at the epicenter of a seismic shift in the university as we know it. Women's studies has made *gender* visible. Women's studies has demonstrated that gender is one of the axes around which social life is orga-nized, one of the most crucial building blocks of our identities. Before women's studies, we didn't know that gender mattered. Twenty-five years ago, there were no women's stud-ies courses in colleges or universities, no women's studies lists at university presses across the country. By making women visible, women's studies decentered men as the unexamined, disembodied authorial voice of the academic canon and showed that men, as well as women, are utterly embodied, their identities as socially constructed as those of women. When the voice of the canon speaks, we can no longer assume that the voice is going to sound masculine or that the speaker is going to look like a man.

The problem is that many men do not yet know this. Though ubiquitous in positions of power, many men remain invisible to themselves as gendered beings. Courses on gender in the universities are populated largely by women, as if the term applied only to them. "Woman alone seems to have 'gender' since the category itself is defined as that aspect of social relations based on difference between the sexes in which the standard has always been man," writes historian Thomas Lacquer. Or, as the Chinese proverb has it, the fish are the last to discover the ocean.

I know this from my own experience: women's studies made gender visible to me. In the early 1980s I participated in a graduate-level women's studies seminar in which I was the only man among about a dozen participants. During one meeting, a white woman and a black woman were discussing whether all women were, by definition, "sisters" because they all had essentially the same experiences and because all women faced a common oppression by all men. The white woman asserted that the fact that they were both women bonded them, in spite of racial differences. The black woman disagreed.

"When you wake up in the morning and look in the mirror, what do you see?" she asked.

"I see a woman," replied the white woman.

"That's precisely the problem," responded the black woman. "I see a black woman. To me, race is visible every day, because race is how I am not privileged in our culture. Race is invisible to you, because it's how you are privileged. It's why there will always be dif-ferences in our experience."

As I witnessed this exchange, I was startled, and groaned, more audibly, perhaps, than I had intended. Someone asked what my response meant. "Well," I said, "when I look in the mirror, I see a human being. I'm universally generalizable. As a middle-class white man, I have no class, no race, no gender. I'm the generic person!"

Sometimes, I like to think it was on that day that I became a middle-class white man. Sure, I had been those things before, but they had not meant much to me. Since then, I have begun to understand that race, class, and gender do not refer only to other people, who are marginalized by race, class, or gender privilege. Those terms also describe me. I enjoy the privilege of invisibility. The very processes that confer privilege to one group and not another group are often invisible to those upon whom that privilege is conferred. American men have come to think of ourselves as genderless, in part because gender privilege affords us the luxury of ignoring the centrality of gender. But women's studies offers the possibility of making gender visible to men as well and, in so doing, creating the possibilities of alliances between women and men to collaboratively investigate what gender means, how it works, and what its consequences are.

Though this story took place over twenty years ago, I was reminded of it recently when I went to give a guest lecture for a female colleague at my university. As I walked into the auditorium, one student looked up at me and said, "Oh, finally, an objective opinion!" All that semester, whenever my female colleague opened her mouth, what this student saw was "a woman." Biased. But when I walked in, I was, in this student's eyes, *unbiased,* an objective opinion. Disembodied Western rationality—standing right in front of the class! This notion that middle-class white men are "objective" and everyone else is "biased" is the way that inequalities are reproduced.

To speak personally, the perspectives of women's studies have transformed both my research and my teaching. Women's studies made it possible for me to do the work I do. And for that I am grateful. Inspired by the way women's studies made gender visible, I offered a course called Sociology of the Male Experience in 1983 at Rutgers University, where I was then a young assistant professor. This was the first such course on men and masculinity in the state of New Jersey. Today, I teach that course as well as a course enti-tled Sex and Society at Stony Brook to over 350 students each semester. Now, as then, the course is cross-listed with women's studies. But I also teach our department's classical sociological theory course, the course on the historical development of social and political theory. In that course, students traditionally read works by Hobbes, Locke, Rousseau, Smith, Marx, Durkheim, Tocqueville, Weber, and Freud. This is probably the most intractably canonical "dead white European men" course we offer in the social sciences. But it has become impossible for me to teach the works of those "great men" without reference to gender—without noting, for example, the gendered creation myths that characterize the move from the state of nature to civil society in the thought of Locke or Hobbes, or the chronic anxiety and loss of control attendant upon modern society docu-mented by Tocqueville, Marx, Weber, or Freud. Moreover, I find that I cannot teach about the rise of nineteenth-century liberal individualism without including Frederick Doug-lass or Mary Wollstonecraft; nor can I teach about the late-nineteenth-century critiques of individualism without reference to W. E. B. Du Bois or to Charlotte Perkins Gilman.

If women's studies has made gender, and hence men, visible, then it has also raised a question about men: where have they been in women's struggles for equality? Taking my cues from women's history, I began to research men's responses to feminism. *Against the Tide* tries to provide part of the answer, a missing chapter from women's history: the chapter about the men who supported women's equality.

I'm sure you are saying to yourself: "A book about men who supported feminism? Now that will surely be the world's shortest book!" It turns out that in every arena in which women have struggled for equal rights—education (the right to go to college or professional school), economic life (the right to work, join unions, receive equal wages), social life (the right to own property, have access to birth control, get a divorce), or political life (the right to vote, to hold elective office, to serve on juries)—there have been men, some prominent, many unheralded, who have supported them.

Men have been supporting women's equality at every step. And if men have been there, it means that men can be there and that they will be there. This legacy of men who supported women's equality allows contemporary men to join what I like to think of as the Gentlemen's Auxiliary of the Women's Movement. Neither passive bystanders nor the frontline forces—and especially not the leaders of those troops—men still have a pivotal role to play. Men can join this epochal struggle and provide support both individually and collectively. This strikes me as an utterly honorable relationship to feminism, quite different from an impulse I've encountered among newly enlightened men that I liken to the cavalry rescuing feminist-damsels in distress. It goes something like, "Thanks for bringing all this to my attention, ladies. We'll take it from here." (This is an example of what I call premature self-congratulation.) The Gentleman's Auxiliary position also serves as an important corrective to many men's fears, which often boil down to "How can I support feminism without feeling like—or being seen as—a wimp?" To be a member of the Auxiliary is to know that the central actors in the struggle for gender equality will be, as they always have been, women.

But women's studies has done more than make the study of gender possible; it has made it necessary. The issues raised by women in the university and outside it have not "gone away" or subsided now that women have been offered a few resources and an academic room of their own. Women's studies has not been content with one room while the rest of the university goes about its androcentric business, any more than the Women's Movement has been convinced of its political victory because 100 percent of the U.S. senators from California in 2010 were women.

Gender as a power relation is the "it" that men "just don't get" in the current discussion. Women's studies scholars have demonstrated that masculinity and femininity are identities that are socially constructed in a field of power. Gender, like race and class, is not simply a mode of classification by which biological creatures are sorted into their respective and appropriate niches. Gender is about power. Just because both masculinity and femininity are socially constructed does not mean that they are equivalent, that there are no dynamics of power and privilege in operation. The problem with bringing men into this discussion about gender and power is that these issues are invisible to men.

Men are often confused about the question of power because some feminist insights do not resonate for men as they do for women. In its simplest formulation, feminism offered women a symmetry between their analysis of the world and their individual experiences. First, feminists argued, at the social level women were not "in power." This was an empirical observation, easily apprehended by anyone who cared to look. Every board of trustees of every university, every board of directors of every law firm and corporation, every legislature at every level in every state in the country—all were illustrations that women, as a group, did not have the power. Second, this aggregate analysis provided a social analogue for women's individual experience: women were not in power and women did not feel powerful.

To apply this symmetry to men's lives, however, missed something crucial in men's experiences. Certainly, at the political and institutional levels men are in power. But when that syllogism is presented to men—that individually, then, men must feel powerful—most men respond as if you came from outer space. "What are you talking about?" they say. "I have no power at all! My wife bosses me around. My kids boss me around! My boss bosses me around! I'm completely powerless!" This is a critical blind spot. All the economic, social, and political power in the world has not left individual men feeling powerful. The argument that men are powerful does not address the felt experience of most American men. Antifeminists and men's rights advocates do address that felt experience: "You're right, men have no power," they say. "Women have the power, in custody battles, in alimony, in the draft. Men are the real victims of reverse discrimination." And mythopoetic male bonders respond to that experience as well. "You're right," they say. "We have no power. Let's go off to the woods and get some. Here's the power ritual, the power drumming, the power chant."

But power is not a quality one can acquire by trooping off to a mythic summer camp for a weekend with the boys. At the individual level, power is experienced as a person's ability to do the kinds of things in his or her life that he or she wants to do. At the social level, power is an expression of the distribution of rewards and resources in a society; as such it is the property of groups, not of individuals. A gendered analysis must bridge these two levels, addressing both men's aggregate power and men's individual feelings of powerlessness. Much of the thinking about men has focused on opposite sides of the issue: antifeminists have seen individual men as powerless; many feminists have defined socially constructed masculinity as the drive for power, domination, and control.

I began the historical research for my book *Manhood in America* guided by this perspective. Surely masculinity was nothing if not the drive for domination. Men were possessed with a craving for power and control. But the historical record has revealed a different picture: American men do not experience manhood as a drive for domination. Manhood is actually more about the fear of others dominating us, having power or control over us. We have constructed a vision of masculinity that sees others, especially other men, as frightening potential aggressors. We are afraid that others will see us as less than manly, weak, timid, and frightened. We are afraid of not measuring up to some vaguely defined notions of what it means to be a man; we are afraid of failure. Acting masculine becomes a way to ward off the fears that we will not be seen as manly by other men, or by ourselves. What we call masculinity is more a defensive hedge against revealing those fears than it is the offensive and intentional initiation of aggression.

John Steinbeck wrote in *Of Mice and Men:* "Funny thing [Curly's wife] said. 'If I catch any one man, and he's alone, I get along fine with him. But just let two of the guys get together an' you won't talk. Jus' nothin' but mad.' She dropped her fingers and put her hands on her hips. 'You're all scared of each other, that's what. Ever'one of you's scared the rest is goin' to get something on you.'"

My reading of American history documents this theme. American masculinity has been propelled not by a drive for domination, but by fears of failure and fears that other men will "get something on you." In this sense, homophobia is the animating condition of American manhood. I do not mean homophobia in its current limited sense as the irrational fear of homosexuals or the fear of homosexual impulses in ourselves. It is those fears as well, of course, but it is also something deeper: homophobia is the fear of other men. It is this fear that propels many men to engage in the drive to dominate and to control. Homophobia keeps us isolated from one another, and eager to use what few resources we do have—racism, sexism, heterosexism, nativism—to dominate others lest they dominate us first. Such domination serves only as a hedge, keeping fears only temporarily at bay. If those other "isms"—racism, sexism, and the like—are compensatory mechanisms by which men can shield themselves from their fears of other men, then those who advocate equality for women, for people of color, for gays and lesbians, must also address men's deeper-seated homophobic fears. Since admitting fear is itself emasculating, these fears lie deeply buried in the hearts of men. We cannot even admit their presence, let alone work collectively to challenge the mechanisms that have placed those fears there.

Homophobia is part of our earliest experiences; it is inscribed into our psyches and becomes as familiar as our skin. Imagine, for example, a playground where a dozen five-year-old boys are happily playing. By asking one question, I would wager that I could immediately start a fight among these boys. The question? "Who's a sissy around here?" One of two things will likely happen. Two of the boys may square off, each pointing his finger at the other and shouting, in turn, "He is!" "No! He is!" before they come to blows. Or all the boys may gang up on the smallest, youngest, weakest boy and point at him in unison, shouting, "He is! He is!" Faced with a challenge that will haunt him for the rest of his life, he can either fight it out against overwhelming odds or take the more rational route and run away. Since this will forever brand him a coward, the manly response would probably be the less rational one.

Does anyone recall the 1992 Academy Awards presentations? As veteran actor Jack Palance came to the podium to accept the award for Best Supporting Actor, for his role in *City Slickers,* he observed that many Hollywood producers believed that at the age of seventy-one he was washed up as an actor, that he was past his prime. Then he dropped to the stage and commenced a set of one-armed push-ups. When he stood up and returned to the microphone, he clutched his Oscar tightly and notified a couple of hundred million viewers that he could "still get it up." "When does it end?" I groaned, wincing a bit at the pathos of a man old enough to be my grandfather who still had something to prove.

When does it end? And why does it start so young? Why does it seem that men always have to prove their manhood? Why is masculinity such a relentless test, never assured,

always in doubt? How is it that a man can spend a lifetime collecting the props that signify successful manhood—wealth, power, status, women—and have it all unravel in a
flash because of a trivial innuendo? Why do men spend their lifetimes in pursuit of signs
of strength, power, resolve, and courage, when our inner sense of manhood is ultimately
so fragile? These are the questions that my participation in women's studies has led me
to ask. And these are questions that are, at once, both scholarly and political.

Like studies of race and class, women's studies has made gender visible as a power
relation, as an expression of the unequal distribution of rewards and resources in society.
Women's studies connected that analysis to the social movement—feminism—that was
about reallocating those rewards and resources more equitably so that women might
make choices, widen their sphere of action, and claim their voices, their agency, and their
lives. In the process, women's studies came to understand that those voices, agencies,
and lives are very different among different women. Women, differently situated in society by race, class, age, sexuality, or region of the country, experience their lives in different
ways. We have come to acknowledge that a singular construction of women's experience
is inadequate.

The same is true for men. Women's studies has made gender visible to men, but it is
not a monolithic, singular construction. There are many masculinities, many different
definitions of masculinity, many different voices. These constructions of masculinity
have taken shape on a contradictory terrain—a terrain of privilege conferred by gender,
yet equally a terrain of inequality and powerlessness organized by race, or class, or sexuality, or ethnicity, or religion. Masculinity is about power, but it is the power of men as a
group over women as a group, and additionally it is about the power of some men over
other men. It is about the construction of masculinities within that field of power—
the ways in which racism or homophobia, for example, construct the identities of both
white men and men of color, of both heterosexual and homosexual men. Thus we
speak of masculinities to denote this variety of men's experiences, and also of a hegemonic masculinity, a normative standard against which every other masculinity may be
measured.

Many men resist the insights of women's studies because they do not understand how
it relates to their experiences of not feeling powerful. They are told they are in power and
must be aware of holding that power; yet they do not feel powerful. One of the most
crucial tasks facing women's studies and the men who support it is to bring men into the
discussion, to develop pedagogical techniques that will analyze men's power as a social
group and simultaneously acknowledge men's individualized feelings of powerlessness,
for it is only by acknowledging these feelings that we will be able to bring more men into
the discussion. The ensuing conversation will further strengthen women's studies. Any
metallurgist can tell you that the way to strengthen a metal, to make it stronger, more
resilient, and more reliable, is not to add more of the same metal to it but to add different
metals to it—to make an alloy. I would argue that diversity in women's studies, like diversity in the university, is certainly such a source of strength.

Men can learn so much from women's studies. And whether men acknowledge it or not, we need women's studies—desperately. All across the country, men are saying that they want to live more emotionally responsive lives, that they want their interior lives to play an increasingly important role, that they want to be more responsive lovers and better friends both with women and with other men. Virtually all men say they want to be better fathers than their own fathers were. In every arena—the university, the workplace, the home—it has been women who have advocated precisely those changes that will allow us to live the kinds of lives we say we want to live. At home, women demand that we share housework and childcare. In the workplace women campaign for family-friendly workplace policies, such as flex time, parental leave, on-site child care. These are not women's issues—these are *parents'* issues. And to the extent that men seek to be better fathers and better partners, men, too, have to make them our issues.

On campus and in the workplace women campaign for an end to sexual harassment and an end to date and acquaintance rape. Surely, as long as women fear us, they cannot claim the sexual and emotional and intellectual agency that they take as their right. If heterosexual men want the kinds of relationships they say they want—relationships with women who are passionate, strong, sexy, women who are in every way our equals in desire—then the only way to accomplish this is to join with feminist women in their struggles against these abuses of power.

When women's studies makes gender visible to women, it not only reveals the ways in which women's lives have been obscured by traditional scholarship, but also provides to women a model of how engaged research, passionate pedagogy, and critical thought can be brought to bear in order to enlarge the range of opportunities open to them. And when women's studies fulfills its promise of making gender visible to men—or, even more acutely, makes it possible for men to make gender visible to other men—it also opens up possibilities for men to live healthier, more emotionally responsive, more nurturing and compassionate lives, lives animated by a passion for equality and justice.

In 1917 a New York City writer named Floyd Dell wrote an essay in the popular magazine *The Masses* entitled "Feminism for Men." In it, Dell outlined how gender inequality also impoverished men's lives:

> When you have got a woman in a box, and you pay rent on the box, relationship to you insensibly changes character. It loses the live excitement of democracy. It ceases to be companionship, for companionship is only possible in a democracy. It is no longer a sharing of life together—it is a breaking of life apart. Half a life—cooking, clothes, and children; half a life—business, politics, and baseball. It doesn't make much difference which is the poorer half. Any half, when it comes to life, is very near to none at all.

In the first line of this essay, Dell underscores the promise of feminism. "Feminism is going to make it possible for the first time for men to be free," he writes. Women's studies has provided the opportunity for men to glimpse that possibility. And for that, we men are both inspired and grateful.

DISCUSSION QUESTIONS

1. What does Kimmel mean when he writes that "gender is invisible to men"? In what ways is privilege invisible?

2. What does Kimmel mean when he argues that much of American masculinity is "homophobic"?

3. How does women's studies contribute to understanding men's lives?

JOHN STOLTENBERG, *HOW MEN HAVE (A) SEX: AN ADDRESS TO COLLEGE STUDENTS*

In the human species, how many sexes are there?
Answer A: There are two sexes.
Answer B: There are three sexes.
Answer C: There are four sexes.
Answer D: There are seven sexes.
Answer E: There are as many sexes as there are people.

I'd like to take you, in an imaginary way, to look at a different world, somewhere else in the universe, a place inhabited by a life form that very much resembles us. But these creatures grow up with a peculiar knowledge. They know that they have been born in an infinite variety. They know, for instance, that in their genetic material they are born with hundreds of different chromosome formations at the point in each cell that we would say determines their "sex." These creatures don't just come in XX or XY; they also come in XXY and XYY and XXX plus a long list of "mosaic" variations in which some cells in a creature's body have one combination and other cells have another. Some of these creatures are born with chromosomes that aren't even quite X or Y because a little bit of one chromosome goes and gets joined to another. There are hundreds of different combinations, and though all are not fertile, quite a number of them are. The creatures in this world enjoy their individuality; they delight in the fact that they are not divisible into distinct categories. So when another newborn arrives with an esoterically rare chromosomal formation, there is a little celebration: "Aha," they say, "another sign that we are each unique."

These creatures also live with the knowledge that they are born with a vast range of genital formations. Between their legs are tissue structures that vary along a continuum,

SOURCE: John Stoltenberg, "How Men Have (a) Sex," in *Refusing to Be a Man: Essays on Sex and Justice* (Portland: Breitenbush Books, 1989), 18–31.

from clitorises with a vulva through all possible combinations and gradations to penises with a scrotal sac. These creatures live with an understanding that their genitals all developed prenatally from exactly the same little nub of embryonic tissue called a genital tubercle, which grew and developed under the influence of varying amounts of the hormone androgen. These creatures honor and respect everyone's natural-born genitalia—including what we would describe as a microphallus or a clitoris several inches long. What these creatures find amazing and precious is that because everyone's genitals stem from the same embryonic tissue, the nerves inside all their genitals got wired very much alike, so these nerves of touch just go crazy upon contact in a way that resonates completely between them "My gosh," they think, "you must feel something in your genital tubercle that intensely resembles what I'm feeling in my genital tubercle." Well, they don't exactly *think* that in so many words; they're actually quite heavy into their feelings at that point; but they do feel very connected—throughout all their wondrous variety.

I could go on. I could tell you about the variety of hormones that course through their bodies in countless different patterns and proportions, both before birth and throughout their lives—the hormones that we call "sex hormones" but that they call "individuality inducers." I could tell you how these creatures think about reproduction: For part of their lives, some of them are quite capable of gestation, delivery, and lactation; and for part of their lives, some of them are quite capable of insemination; and for part or all their lives, some of them are not capable of any of those things—so these creatures conclude that it would be silly to lock anyone into a lifelong category based on a capability variable that may or may not be utilized and that in any case changes over each lifetime in a fairly uncertain and idiosyncratic way. These creatures are not oblivious to reproduction; but nor do they spend their lives constructing a self-definition around their variable reproductive capacities. They don't have to, because what is truly unique about these creatures is that they are capable of having a sense of personal identity without struggling to fit into a group identity based on how they were born. These creatures are quite happy, actually. They don't worry about sorting *other* creatures into categories, so they don't have to worry about whether they are measuring up to some category they themselves are supposed to belong to.

These creatures, of course, have sex. Rolling and rollicking and robust sex, and sweaty and slippery and sticky sex, and trembling and quaking and tumultuous sex, and tender and tingling and transcendent sex. They have sex fingers to fingers. They have sex belly to belly. They have sex genital tubercle to genital tubercle. They *have* sex. They do not have *a* sex. In their erotic lives, they are not required to act out their status in a category system—because there *is* no category system. There are no sexes to belong to, so sex between creatures is free to be between genuine individuals—not representatives of a category. They have sex. They do not have a sex. Imagine life like that.

Perhaps you have guessed the point of this science fiction: Anatomically, each creature in the imaginary world I have been describing could be an identical twin of every human being on earth. These creatures, in fact, *are us*—in every way except socially and politically. The way they are born is the way we are born. And we are not born belonging to one or the other of two sexes. We are born into a physiological continuum on which there is no discrete and definite point that you can call "male" and no discrete and definite point that you can call "female." If you look at all the variables in nature that are said to determine human "sex," you can't possibly find one that will unequivocally split the species into two. Each of the so-called criteria of sexedness is itself a continuum—including chromosomal variables, genital and gonadal variations, reproductive capacities, endocrinological proportions, and any other criterion you could think of. Any or all of these different variables may line up in any number of ways, and all of the variables may vary independently of one another.[1]

What does all this mean? It means, first of all, a logical dilemma: Either human "male" and human "female" actually exist in nature as fixed and discrete entities and you can credibly base an entire social and political system on those absolute natural categories, or else the variety of human sexedness is infinite. As Andrea Dworkin wrote in 1974:

> The discovery is, of course, that "man" and "woman" are fictions, caricatures, cultural constructs. As models they are reductive, totalitarian, inappropriate to human becoming. As roles they are static, demeaning to the female, dead-ended for male and female both.[2]

The conclusion is inescapable:

> *We are, clearly, a multisexed species which has its sexuality spread along a vast continuum where the elements called male and female are not discrete.*[3]

"We are . . . a multisexed species." I first read those words a little over ten years ago—and that liberating recognition saved my life.

All the time I was growing up, I knew that there was something really problematical in my relationship to manhood. Inside, deep inside, I never believed I was fully male—I never believed I was growing up enough of a man. I believed that someplace out there, in other men, there was something that was genuine authentic all-American manhood—the real stuff—but I didn't have it: not enough of it to convince *me* anyway, even if I managed to be fairly convincing to those around me. I felt like an impostor, like a fake. I agonized a lot about not feeling male enough, and I had no idea then how much I was not alone.

Then I read those words—those words that suggested to me for the first time that the notion of manhood is a cultural delusion, a baseless belief, a false front, a house of cards.

---

1. My source for the foregoing information about so-called sex determinants in the human species is a series of interviews I conducted with the sexologist Dr. John Money in Baltimore, Maryland, in 1979 for an article I wrote called "The Multisex Theorem," which was published in a shortened version as "Future Genders" in *Omni* magazine (May 1980): 67–73 ff.

2. Andrea Dworkin, *Woman Hating* (New York: Dutton, 1974), 174.

3. Dworkin, *Woman Hating*, 183 (italics in original).

It's not true. The category I was trying so desperately to belong to, to be a member of in good standing—it doesn't exist. Poof. Now you see it, now you don't. Now you're terrified you're not really part of it; now you're free, you don't have to worry anymore. However removed you feel inside from "authentic manhood," it doesn't matter. What matters is the center inside yourself—and how you live, and how you treat people, and what you can contribute as you pass through life on this earth, and how honestly you love, and how carefully you make choices. Those are the things that really matter. Not whether you're a real man. There's no such thing.

The idea of the male sex is like the idea of an Aryan race. The Nazis believed in the idea of an Aryan race—they believed that the Aryan race really existed, physically, in nature—and they put a great deal of effort into making it real. The Nazis believed that from the blond hair and blue eyes occurring naturally in the human species, they could construe the existence of a separate *race*—a distinct category of human beings that was unambiguously rooted in the natural order of things. But traits do not a race make; traits only make traits. For the idea to be real that these physical traits comprised a race, the race had to be socially constructed. The Nazis inferiorized and exterminated those they defined as "non-Aryan." With that, the notion of an Aryan race began to seem to come true. That's how there could be a political entity known as an Aryan race, and that's how there could be for some people a personal, subjective sense that they belonged to it. This happened through hate and force, through violence and victimization, through treating millions of people as things, then exterminating them. The belief system shared by people who believed they were all Aryan could not exist apart from that force and violence. The force and violence created a racial class system, *and* it created those people's membership in the race considered "superior." The force and violence served their class interests in large part because it created and maintained the class itself. But the idea of an Aryan race could never become metaphysically true, despite all the violence unleashed to create it, because there simply *is* no Aryan race. There is only the idea of it—and the consequences of trying to make it seem real. The male sex is very like that.

Penises and ejaculate and prostate glands occur in nature, but the notion that these anatomical traits comprise a sex—a discrete class, separate and distinct, metaphysically divisible from some other sex, *the* "other sex"—is simply that: a notion, an idea. The penises exist; the male sex does not. The male sex is socially constructed. It is a political entity that flourishes only through acts of force and sexual terrorism. Apart from the global inferiorization and subordination of those who are defined as "nonmale," the idea of personal membership in the male sex class would have no recognizable meaning. It would make no sense. No one could be a member of it and no one would think they *should* be a member of it. There would be no male sex to belong to. That doesn't mean there wouldn't still be penises and ejaculate and prostate glands and such. It simply means that the center of our selfhood would not be required to reside inside an utterly fictitious category—a category that only seems real to the extent that those outside it are put down.

We live in a world divided absolutely into two sexes, even though nothing about human nature warrants that division. We are sorted into one category or another at birth based solely on a visual inspection of our groins, and the only question that's asked is whether there's enough elongated tissue around your urethra so you can pee standing up. The presence or absence of a long-enough penis is the primary criterion for separating who's to grow up male from who's to grow up female. And among all the ironies in that utterly whimsical and arbitrary selection process is the fact that *anyone* can pee both sitting down and standing up.

Male sexual identity is the conviction or belief, held by most people born with penises, that they are male and not female, that they belong to the male sex. In a society predicated on the notion that there are two "opposite" and "complementary" sexes, this idea not only makes sense, it *becomes* sense; the very idea of a male sexual identity produces sensation, produces the meaning of sensation, becomes the meaning of how one's body feels. The sense and the sensing of a male sexual identity [are] at once mental and physical, at once public and personal. Most people born with a penis between their legs grow up aspiring to feel and act unambiguously male, longing to belong to the sex that is male and daring not to belong to the sex that is not, and feeling this urgency for a visceral and constant verification of their male sexual identity—for a fleshy connection to manhood—as the driving force of their life. The drive does not originate in the anatomy. The sensations derive from the idea. The idea gives the feelings social meaning; the idea determines which sensations shall be sought.

People born with penises must strive to make the idea of male sexual identity personally real by doing certain deeds, actions that are valued and chosen because they produce the desired feeling of belonging to a sex that is male and not female. Male sexual identity is experienced only in sensation and action, in feeling and doing, in eroticism and ethics. The feeling of belonging to a male sex encompasses both sensations that are explicitly "sexual" and those that are not ordinarily regarded as such. And there is a tacit social value system according to which certain acts are chosen because they make an individual's sexedness feel real and certain other acts are eschewed because they numb it. That value system is the ethics of male sexual identity—and it may well be the social origin of all injustice.

Each person experiences the idea of sexual identity as more or less real, more or less certain, more or less true, depending on two very personal phenomena: one's feelings and one's acts. For many people, for instance, the act of fucking makes their sexual identity feel more real than it does at other times, and they can predict from experience that this feeling of greater certainty will last for at least a while after each time they fuck. Fucking is not the only such act, and not only so-called sex acts can result in feelings of certainty about sexual identity; but the act of fucking happens to be a very good example of the correlation between *doing* a specific act in a specific way and *sensing* the specificity of the sexual identity to which one aspires. A person can decide to do certain acts and not others just because some acts will have the payoff of a feeling of greater certainty about sexual identity and others will give the feedback of a feeling of less. The transient reality of one's sexual identity, a person can know, is always a function of what one does and how one's acts make one feel. The feeling and the act must conjoin for the idea of the sexual identity to come true. We all keep longing for surety of our sexedness that we can feel; we all keep striving through our actions to make the idea real.

In human nature, eroticism is not differentiated between "male" and "female" in any clear-cut way. There is too much of a continuum, too great a resemblance. From all that we know, the penis and the clitoris are identically "wired" to receive and retransmit sensations from throughout the body, and the congestion of blood within the lower torso during sexual excitation makes all bodies sensate in a remarkably similar manner. Simply put, we all share all the nerve and blood-vessel layouts that are associated with sexual arousal. Who can say, for instance, that the penis would not experience sensations the way that a clitoris does if this were not a world in which the penis is supposed to be hell-bent on penetration? By the time most men make it through puberty, they believe that erotic sensation is supposed to *begin* in their penis; that if engorgement has not begun there, then nothing else in their body will heat up either. There is a massive interior dissociation from sensations that do not explicitly remind a man that his penis is still there. And not only there as sensate, but as *functional and operational.*

So much of most men's sexuality is tied up with gender-actualizing—with feeling like a real man—that they can scarcely recall an erotic sensation that had no gender-specific cultural meaning. As most men age, they learn to cancel out and deny erotic sensations that are not specifically linked to what they think a real man is supposed to feel. An erotic sensation unintentionally experienced in a receptive, communing mode—instead of in an aggressive and controlling and violative mode, for instance—can shut down sensory systems in an instant. An erotic sensation unintentionally linked to the "wrong" sex of another person can similarly mean sudden numbness. Acculturated male sexuality has a built-in fail-safe: Either its political context reifies manhood or the experience cannot be felt as sensual. Either the act creates his sexedness or it does not compute as a sex act. So he tenses up, pumps up, steels himself against the dread that he be found not male enough. And his dread is not stupid; for he sees what happens to people when they are treated as nonmales.

My point is that sexuality does not *have* a gender; it *creates* a gender. It creates for those who adapt to it in narrow and specified ways the confirmation for the individual of belonging to the idea of one sex or the other. So-called male sexuality is a learned connection between specific physical sensations and the idea of a male sexual identity. To achieve this male sexual identity requires that an individual *identify with* the class of males—that is, accept as one's own the values and interests of the class. A fully realized male sexual identity also requires *nonidentification with* that which is perceived to be nonmale, or female. A male must not identify with females; he must not associate with females in feeling, interest, or action. His identity as a member of the sex class "men" absolutely depends on the extent to which he repudiates the values and interests of the sex class "women."

I think somewhere inside us all, we have always known something about the relativity of gender. Somewhere inside us all, we know that our bodies harbor deep resemblances, that we are wired inside to respond in a profound harmony to the resonance of eroticism inside the body of someone near us. Physiologically, we are far more alike than different. The tissue structures that have become labial and clitoral or scrotal and penile have not forgotten their common ancestry. Their sensations are of the same source. The nerve networks and interlock of capillaries throughout our pelvises electrify and engorge as if plugged in together and pumping as one. That's what we feel when we feel one another's feelings. That's what can happen during sex that is mutual, equal, reciprocal, profoundly communing.

So why is it that some of us with penises think it's sexy to pressure someone into having sex against their will? Some of us actually get harder the harder the person resists. Some of us with penises actually believe that some of us without penises want to be raped. And why is it that some of us with penises think it's sexy to treat other people as objects, as things to be bought and sold, impersonal bodies to be possessed and consumed for our sexual pleasure? Why is it that the some of us with penises are aroused by sex tinged with rape, and sex commoditized by pornography? Why do so many of us with penises want such antisexual sex?

There's a reason, of course. We have to make a lie seem real. It's a very big lie. We each have to do our part. Otherwise the lie will look like the lie that it is. Imagine the enormity of what we each must do to keep the lie alive in each of us. Imagine the awesome challenge we face to make the lie a social fact. It's a lifetime mission for each of us born with a penis: to have sex such a way that the male sex seems real—and so that we'll feel like a real part of it.

We all grow up knowing exactly what kind of sex that is. It's the kind of sex you can have when you pressure or bully someone else into it. So it's a kind of sex that makes your will more important than theirs. That kind of sex helps the lie a lot. That kind of sex makes you feel like someone important and it turns the other person into someone unimportant. That kind of sex makes you feel real, not like a fake. It's a kind of sex men have in order to feel like real men.

There's also the kind of sex you can have when you force someone and hurt someone and cause someone suffering and humiliation. Violence and hostility in sex help the lie a lot too. Real men are aggressive in sex. Real men get cruel in sex. Real men use their penises like weapons in sex. Real men leave bruises. Real men think it's a turn-on to threaten harm. A brutish push can make an erection feel really hard. That kind of sex helps the lie a lot. That kind of sex makes you feel like someone who is powerful and it turns the other person into someone powerless. That kind of sex makes you feel dangerous and in control—like you're fighting a war with an enemy and if you're mean enough you'll win but if you let up you'll lose your manhood. It's a kind of sex men have *in order to have* a manhood.

There's also the kind of sex you can have when you pay your money into a profit system that grows rich displaying and exploiting the bodies and body parts of people without penises for the sexual entertainment of people with. Pay your money and watch. Pay your money and imagine. Pay your money and get real turned on. Pay your money and jerk off. That kind of sex helps the lie a lot. It helps support an industry committed to making people with penises believe that people without are sluts who just want to be ravished and reviled—an industry dedicated to maintaining a sex-class system in which men believe themselves sex machines and men believe women are mindless fuck tubes. That kind of sex helps the lie a lot. It's like buying Krugerrands as a vote of confidence for white supremacy in South Africa.

And there's one more thing: That kind of sex makes the lie indelible—burns it onto your retinas right adjacent to your brain—makes you remember it and makes your body respond to it and so it makes you believe that the lie is in fact true: You really are a real man. That slavish and submissive creature there spreading her legs is really not. You and that creature have nothing in common. That creature is an alien inanimate thing, but your penis is completely real and alive. Now you can come. Thank god almighty—you have a sex at last.

Now, I believe there are many who are sick at heart over what I have been describing. There are many who were born with penises who want to stop collaborating in the sex-class system that needs us to need these kinds of sex. I believe some of you want to stop living out the big lie, and you want to know how. Some of you long to touch truthfully. Some of you want sexual relationships in your life that are about intimacy and joy, ecstasy and equality—not antagonism and alienation. So what I have to say next I have to say to you.

When you use sex to have a sex, the sex you have is likely to make you feel crummy about yourself. But when you have sex in which you are not struggling with your partner in order to act out "real manhood," the sex you have is more likely to bring you close.

This means several specific things:

1. *Consent is absolutely essential.* If both you and your partner have not freely given your informed consent to the sex you are about to have, you can be quite certain that the sex you go ahead and have will make you strangers to each other. How do you know if there's consent? You ask. You ask again if you're sensing any doubt. Consent to do one thing isn't consent to do another. So you keep communicating, in clear words. And you don't take anything for granted.

2. *Mutuality is absolutely essential.* Sex is not something you do to someone. Sex is not a one-way transitive verb, with a subject, you, and an object, the body you're with. Sex that is mutual is not about doing and being done to; it's about being-with and feeling-with. You have to really be there to experience what is happening between and within the two of you—between every part of you and within both your whole bodies. It's a matter of paying attention—as if you are paying attention to someone who matters.

3. *Respect is absolutely essential.* In the sex that you have, treat your partner like a real person who, like you, has real feelings—feelings that matter as much as

your own. You may or may not love—but you must always respect. You must respect the integrity of your partner's body. It is not yours for the taking. It belongs to someone real. And you do not get ownership of your partner's body just because you are having sex—or just because you have had sex.

For those who are closer to the beginning of your sex lives than to the middle or the end, many things are still changing for you about how you have sex, with whom, why or why not, what you like or dislike, what kind of sex you want to have more of. In the next few years, you are going to discover and decide a lot. I say "discover" because no one can tell you what you're going to find out about yourself in relation to sex—and I say "decide" because virtually without knowing it you are going to be laying down habits and patterns that will probably stay with you for the rest of your life. You're at a point in your sexual history that you will never be at again. You don't know what you don't know yet. And yet you are making choices whose consequences for your particular sexuality will be sealed years from now.

I speak to you as someone who is closer to the middle of my sexual history. As I look back, I see that I made many choices that I didn't know I was making. And as I look at men who are near my age, I see that what has happened to many of them is that their sex lives are stuck in deep ruts that began as tiny fissures when they were young. So I want to conclude by identifying what I believe are three of the most important decisions about your sexuality that you can make when you are at the beginning of your sexual history. However difficult these choices may seem to you now, I promise you they will only get more difficult as you grow older. I realize that what I'm about to give is some quite unsolicited nuts-and-bolts advice. But perhaps it will spare you, later on in your lives, some of the obsessions and emptiness that have claimed the sexual histories of many men just a generation before you. Perhaps it will not help, I don't know; but I hope very much that it will.

First, you can start choosing now not to let your sexuality be manipulated by the pornography industry. I've heard many unhappy men talk about how they are so hooked on pornography and obsessed with it that they are virtually incapable of a human erotic contact. And I have heard even more men talk about how, when they do have sex with someone, the pornography gets in the way, like a mental obstacle, like a barrier preventing a full experience of what's really happening between them and their partner. The sexuality that the pornography industry needs you to have is not about communicating and caring; it's about "pornographizing" people—objectifying and conquering them, not being with them as a person. You do not have to buy into it.

Second, you can start choosing now not to let drugs and alcohol numb you through your sex life. Too many men, as they age, become incapable of having sex with a clear head. But you need your head clear—to make clear choices, to send clear messages, to read clearly what's coming in on a clear channel between you and your partner. Sex is no time for your awareness to sign off. And another thing: Beware of relying on drugs or alcohol to give you "permission" to have sex, or to trick your body into feeling something that it's not, or so you won't have to take responsibility for what you're feeling or for the sex that you're about to have. If you can't take sober responsibility for your part in a sexual encounter, you probably shouldn't be having it—and you certainly shouldn't be zonked out of your mind *in order* to have it.

Third, you can start choosing now not to fixate on fucking—especially if you'd really rather have sex in other, noncoital ways. Sometimes men have coital sex—penetration and thrusting then ejaculating inside someone—not because they particularly feel like it but because they feel they *should* feel like it: It's expected that if you're the man, you fuck. And if you don't fuck, you're not a man. The corollary of this cultural imperative is that if two people don't have intercourse, they have not had real sex. That's baloney, of course, but the message comes down hard, especially inside men's heads: Fucking is *the* sex act, the act in which you act out what sex is supposed to be—and what sex you're supposed to be.

Like others born with a penis, I was born into a sex-class system that requires my collaboration every day, even in how I have sex. Nobody told me, when I was younger, that I could have noncoital sex and that it would be fine. Actually, much better than fine. Nobody told me about an incredible range of other erotic possibilities for mutual lovemaking—including rubbing body to body, then coming body to body; including multiple, nonejaculatory orgasms; including the feeling you get when even the tiniest place where you and your partner touch becomes like a window through which great tidal storms of passion ebb and flow, back and forth. Nobody told me about the sex you can have when you stop working at having a sex. My body told me, finally. And I began to trust what my body was telling me more than the lie I was supposed to make real.

I invite you too to resist the lie. I invite you too to become an erotic traitor to male supremacy.

R. W. CONNELL, *MASCULINITIES AND GLOBALIZATION*
The Ethnographic Moment in Studies of Masculinity

The current wave of research and debate on masculinity stems from the impact of the women's liberation movement on men, but it has taken time for this impact to produce a new intellectual agenda. Most discussions of men's gender in the 1970s and early 1980s centered on an established concept, the male sex role, and an established problem: how men and boys were socialized into this role. There was not much new empirical research. What there was tended to use the more abstracted methods of social psychology (e.g., paper-and-pencil masculinity/femininity scales) to measure generalized attitudes and

SOURCE: This article is revised from an address, "Men in the World: Masculinities and Globalization," given at the Colloquium on Masculinities in Southern Africa, University of Natal–Durban, July 1997. It appeared in *Men and Masculinities* 1, no. 1 (Thousand Oaks, CA: Sage, 1998), 3–23.

expectations in ill-defined populations. The largest body of empirical research was the continuing stream of quantitative studies of sex differences—which continued to be disappointingly slight (Carrigan, Connell, and Lee 1985).

The concept of a unitary male sex role, however, came under increasing criticism for its multiple oversimplifications and its incapacity to handle issues about power (Kimmel 1987; Connell 1987). New conceptual frameworks were proposed that linked feminism, work on institutionalized patriarchy, gay theoretical work on homophobia, and psycho-analytic ideas about the person (Carrigan, Connell, and Lee 1985; Hearn 1987). Increasing attention was given to certain studies that located issues about masculinity in a fully described local context, whether a British printing shop (Cockburn 1983) or a Pauan mountain community (Herdt 1981). By the late 1980s, a genre of empirical research based on these ideas was developing, most clearly in sociology but also in anthropology, history, organization studies, and cultural studies. This has borne fruit in the 1990s in what is now widely recognized as a new generation of social research on masculinity and men in gender relations (Connell 1995; *Widersprueche* 1995; Segal 1997).

Although the recent research has been diverse in subject matter and social location, its characteristic focus is the construction of masculinity in a particular milieu or moment—a clergyman's family (Tosh 1991), a professional sports career (Messner 1992), a small group of gay men (Connell 1992), a bodybuilding gym (Klein 1993), a group of colonial schools (Morrell 1994), an urban police force (McElhinny 1994), drinking groups in bars (Tomsen 1997), a corporate office on the verge of a decision (Messer-schmidt 1997). Accordingly, we might think of this as the "ethnographic moment" in masculinity research, in which the specific and the local are in focus. (This is not to deny that this work *deploys* broader structural concepts, simply to note the characteristic focus of the empirical work and its analysis.)

The ethnographic moment brought a much-needed gust of realism to debates on men and masculinity, a corrective to the simplifications of role theory. It also provided a corrective to the trend in popular culture where vague discussions of men's sex roles were giving way to the mystical generalities of the mythopoetic movement and the extreme simplifications of religious revivalism.

Although the rich detail of the historical and field studies defies easy summary, certain conclusions emerge from this body of research as a whole. In short form, they are the following.

Plural Masculinities.   A theme of theoretical work in the late 1980s, the multiplicity of masculinities has now been very fully documented by descriptive research. Different cultures and different periods of history construct gender differently. Striking differences exist, for instance, in the relationship of homosexual practice to dominant forms of masculinity (Herdt 1984). In multicultural societies, there are varying definitions and enactments of masculinity, for instance, between Anglo and Latino communities in the United States (Hondagneu-Sotelo and Messner 1994). Equally important, more than one kind of masculinity can be found within a given cultural setting or institution. This is particularly well documented in school studies (Foley 1990) but can also be observed in workplaces (Messerschmidt 1997) and the military (Barrett 1996).

Hierarchy and Hegemony. These plural masculinities exist in definite social relations, often relations of hierarchy and exclusion. This was recognized early, in gay theorists' discussions of homophobia; it has become clear that the implications are far-reaching. There is generally a hegemonic form of masculinity, the most honored or desired in a particular context. For Western popular culture, this is extensively documented in research on media representations of masculinity (McKay and Huber 1992). The hegemonic form need not be the most common form of masculinity. Many men live in a state of some tension with, or distance from, hegemonic masculinity; others (such as sporting heroes) are taken as exemplars of hegemonic masculinity and are required to live up to it strenuously (Connell 1990a). The dominance of hegemonic masculinity over other forms may be quiet and implicit, but it may also be vehement and violent, as in the important case of homophobic violence.

Collective Masculinities. Masculinities, as patterns of gender practice, are sustained and enacted not only by individuals but also by groups and institutions. This fact was visible in Cockburn's (1983) pioneering research on informal workplace culture, and it has been confirmed over and over: in workplaces (Donaldson 1991), in organized sport (Whitson 1990; Messner 1992), in schools (Connell 1996), and so on. This point must be taken with the previous two: institutions may construct multiple masculinities and define relationships between them. Barrett's (1996) illuminating study of hegemonic masculinity in the U.S. Navy shows how this takes different forms in the different subbranches of the one military organization.

Bodies as Arenas. Men's bodies do not determine the patterns of masculinity, but they are still of great importance in masculinity. Men's bodies are addressed, defined and disciplined (as in sport; see Theberge 1991), and given outlets and pleasures by the gender order of society. But men's bodies are not blank slates. The enactment of masculinity reaches certain limits, for instance, in the destruction of the industrial worker's body (Donaldson 1991). Masculine conduct with a female body is felt to be anomalous or transgressive, like feminine conduct with a male body; research on gender crossing (Bolin 1988) shows the work that must be done to sustain an anomalous gender.

Active Construction. Masculinities do not exist prior to social interaction, but come into existence as people act. They are actively produced, using the resources and strategies available in a given milieu. Thus the exemplary masculinities of sports professionals are not a product of passive disciplining, but as Messner (1992) shows, results from a sustained, active engagement with the demands of the institutional setting, even to the point of serious bodily damage from "playing hurt" and accumulated stress.

With boys learning masculinities, much of what was previously taken as socialization appears, in close-focus studies of schools (Walker 1988; Thorne 1993), as the outcome of intricate and intense maneuvering in peer groups, classes, and adult-child relationships.

Contradiction. Masculinities are not homogeneous, simple states of being. Close-focus research on masculinities commonly identifies contradictory desires and conduct; for instance, in Klein's (1993) study of bodybuilders, the contradiction between the heterosexual definition of hegemonic masculinity and the homosexual practice by which some of the bodybuilders finance the making of an exemplary body. Psychoanalysis provides the classic evidence of conflicts within personality, and recent psychoanalytic writing (Chodorow 1994; Lewes 1988) has laid some emphasis on the conflicts and emotional compromises within both hegemonic and subordinated forms of masculinity. Life-history research influenced by existential psychoanalysis (Connell 1995) has similarly traced contradictory projects and commitments within particular forms of masculinity.

Dynamics. Masculinities created in specific historical circumstances are liable to reconstruction and any pattern of hegemony is subject to contestation, in which a dominant masculinity may be displaced. Heward (1988) shows the changing gender regime of a boys' school responding to the changed strategies of the families in its clientele. Roper (1991) shows the displacement of a production-oriented masculinity among engineering managers by new financially oriented generic managers. Since the 1970s, the reconstruction of masculinities has been pursued as a conscious politics. Schwalbe's (1996) close examination of one mythopoetic group shows the complexity of the practice and the limits of the reconstruction.

If we compare this picture of masculinity with earlier understandings of the male sex role, it is clear that the ethnographic moment in research has already had important intellectual fruits.

Nevertheless, it has always been recognized that some issues go beyond the local. For instance, mythopoetic movements such as the highly visible Promise Keepers are part of a spectrum of masculinity politics; Messner (1997) shows for the United States that this spectrum involves at least eight conflicting agendas for the remaking of masculinity. Historical studies such as Phillips (1987) on New Zealand and Kimmel (1996) on the United States have traced the changing public constructions of masculinity for whole countries over long periods; ultimately, such historical reconstructions are essential for understanding the meaning of ethnographic details.

I consider that this logic must now be taken a step further, and in taking this step, we will move toward a new agenda for the whole field. What happens in localities is affected by the history of whole countries, but what happens in countries is affected by the history of the world. Locally situated lives are now (indeed, have long been) powerfully influenced by geopolitical struggles, global markets, multinational corporations, labor migration, transnational media. It is time for this fundamental fact to be built into our analysis of men and masculinities.

To understand local masculinities, we must think in global terms. But how? That is the problem pursued in this article. I will offer a framework for thinking about masculinities as a feature of world society and for thinking about men's gender practices in terms of the global structure and dynamics of gender. This is by no means to reject the ethnographic moment in masculinity research. It is, rather, to think how we can use its findings more adequately. [. . .]

Globalizing Masculinities

In this section, I will offer a sketch of major forms of globalizing masculinity in the three historical phases identified above in the discussion of globalization.

Masculinities of Conquest and Settlement The creation of the imperial social order involved peculiar conditions for the gender practices of men. Colonial conquest itself was mainly carried out by segregated groups of men—soldiers, sailors, traders, administrators, and a good many who were all these by turn (such as the Rum Corps in early New South Wales, Australia). They were drawn from the more segregated occupations and milieu in the metropole, and it is likely that the men drawn into colonization tended to be more rootless. Certainly the process of conquest could produce frontier masculinities that combined the occupational culture of these groups with an unusual level of violence and egocentric individualism. The vehement contemporary debate about the genocidal violence of the Spanish conquistadors—who in fifty years completely exterminated the population of Hispaniola—points to this pattern (Bitterli 1989).

The political history of empire is full of evidence of the tenuous control over the frontier exercised by the state—the Spanish monarchs unable to rein in the conquistadors, the governors in Sydney unable to hold back the squatters and in Capetown unable to hold back the Boers, gold rushes breaking boundaries everywhere, even, an independent republic set up by escaped slaves in Brazil. The point probably applies to other forms of social control too, such as customary controls on men's sexuality. Extensive sexual exploitation of indigenous women was a common feature of conquest. In certain circumstances, frontier masculinities might be reproduced as a local cultural tradition long after the frontier had passed, such as the gauchos of southern [South] America, the cowboys of the western United States.

In other circumstances, however, the frontier of conquest and exploitation was replaced by a frontier of settlement. Sex ratios in the colonizing population changed, as women arrived and locally born generations succeeded. A shift back toward the family patterns of the metropole was likely. As Cain and Hopkins (1993) have shown for the British empire, the ruling group in the colonial world as a whole was an extension of the dominant class in the metropole, the landed gentry, and tended to reproduce its social customs and ideology. The creation of a settler masculinity might be the goal of state policy, as it seems to have been in late-nineteenth-century New Zealand, as part of a general process of pacification and the creation of an agricultural social order (Phillips 1987). Or it might be undertaken through institutions created by settler groups, such as the elite schools in Natal studies by Morrell (1994).

The impact of colonialism on the construction of masculinity among the colonized is much less documented, but there is every reason to think it was severe. Conquest and settlement disrupted all the structures of indigenous society, whether or not this was intended by the colonizing powers (Bitterli 1989). Indigenous gender orders were no exception. Their disruption could result from the pulverization of indigenous communities (as in the seizure of land in eastern North America and southeastern Australia), through gendered labor migration (as in gold mining with Black labor in South Africa; see Moodie 1994), to ideological attacks on local gender arrangements (as in the missionary assault on the *berdache* tradition in North America; see Williams 1986). The varied course of resistance to colonization is also likely to have affected the making of masculinities. This is clear in the region of Natal in South Africa, where sustained resistance to colonization by the Zulu kingdom was a key to the mobilization of ethnic-national masculine identities in the twentieth century (Morrell 1996).

Masculinities of Empire   The imperial social order created a hierarchy of masculinities, as it created a hierarchy of communities and races. The colonizers distinguished "more manly" from "less manly" groups among their subjects. In British India, for instance, Bengali men were supposed effeminate while Pathans and Sikhs were regarded as strong and warlike. Similar distinctions were made in South Africa between Hottentots and Zulus, in North America between Iroquois, Sioux, and Cheyenne on one side, and southern and southwestern tribes on the other.

At the same time, the emerging imagery of gender difference in European culture provided general symbols of superiority and inferiority. Within the imperial "poetics of war" (MacDonald 1994), the conqueror was virile, while the colonized were dirty, sexualized, and effeminate or childlike. In many colonial situations, indigenous men were called "boys" by the colonizers (e.g., in Zimbabwe; see Shire 1994). Sinha's (1995) interesting study of the language of political controversy in India in the 1880s and 1890s shows how the images of "manly Englishman" and "effeminate Bengali" were deployed to uphold colonial privilege and contain movements for change. In the late nineteenth century, racial barriers in colonial societies were hardening rather than weakening, and gender ideology tended to fuse with racism in forms that the twentieth century has never untangled.

The power relations of empire meant that indigenous gender orders were generally under pressure from the colonizers, rather than the other way around. But the colonizers too might change. The barriers of late colonial racism were not only to prevent pollution from below but also to forestall "going native," a well-recognized possibility—the starting point, for instance, of Kipling's famous novel *Kim* ([1901] 1987). The pressures, opportunities, and profits of empire might also work changes in gender arrangements among the colonizers, for instance, the division of labor in households with a large supply of indigenous workers as domestic servants (Bulbeck 1992). Empire might also affect the gender order of the metropole itself by changing gender ideologies, divisions of labor, and the nature of the metropolitan state. For instance, empire figured prominently as a source of masculine imagery in Britain, in the Boy Scouts, and in the cult of Lawrence of Arabia (Dawson 1991). Here we see examples of an important principle: the interplay of gender dynamics between different parts of the world order.

The world of empire created two very different settings for the modernization of masculinities. In the periphery, the forcible restructuring of economies and workforces tended to individualize, on one hand, and rationalize, on the other. A widespread result was masculinities in which the rational calculation of self-interest was the key to action, emphasizing the European gender contrast of rational man / irrational woman. The specific form might be local—for instance, the Japanese "salaryman," a type first recognized in the 1910s, was specific to the Japanese context of large, stable industrial conglomerates (Kinmonth 1981). But the result generally was masculinities defined around economic action, with both workers and entrepreneurs increasingly adapted to emerging market economies.

In the metropole, the accumulation of wealth made possible a specialization of leadership in the dominant classes, and struggles for hegemony in which masculinities organized around domination or violence were split from masculinities organized around expertise. The class compromises that allowed the development of the welfare state in Europe and North America were paralleled by gender compromises—gender reform movements (most notably the women's suffrage movement) contesting the legal privileges of men and forcing concessions from the state. In this context, agendas of reform in masculinity emerged: the temperance movement, companionate marriage, homosexual rights movements, leading eventually to the pursuit of androgyny in "men's liberation" in the 1970s (Kimmel and Mosmiller 1992). Not all reconstructions of masculinity, however, emphasized tolerance or moved toward androgyny. The vehement masculinity politics of fascism, for instance, emphasized dominance and difference and glorified violence, a pattern still found in contemporary racist movements (Tillner 1997).

Masculinities of Postcolonization and Neoliberalism   The process of decolonization disrupted the gender hierarchies of the colonial order and, where armed struggle was involved, might have involved a deliberate cultivation of masculine hardness and violence (as in South Africa; see Xaba 1997). Some activists and theorists of liberation struggles celebrated this, as a necessary response to colonial violence and emasculation; women in liberation struggles were perhaps less impressed. However one evaluates the process, one of the consequences of decolonization was another round of disruptions of community-based gender orders and another step in the reorientation of masculinities toward national and international contexts.

Nearly half a century after the main wave of decolonization, the old hierarchies persist in new shapes. With the collapse of Soviet communism, the decline of postcolonial socialism, and the ascendancy of the new right in Europe and North America, world politics is more and more organized around the needs of transnational capital and the creation of global markets.

The neoliberal agenda has little to say, explicitly, about gender: it speaks a gender-neutral language of "markets," "individuals," and "choice." But the world in which neo-liberalism is ascendant is still a gendered world, and neoliberalism has an implicit gender politics. The "individual" of neoliberal theory has in general the attributes and interests of a male entrepreneur, the attack on the welfare state generally weakens the position of women, while the increasingly unregulated power of transnational corporations places strategic power in the hands of particular groups of men. It is not surprising, then, that the installation of capitalism in Eastern Europe and the former Soviet Union has been accompanied by a reassertion of dominating masculinities and, in some situations, a sharp worsening in the social position of women.

We might propose, then, that the hegemonic form of masculinity in the current world gender order is the masculinity associated with those who control its dominant institutions: the business executives who operate in global markets, and the political executives who interact (and in many contexts, merge) with them. I will call this *transnational business masculinity*. This is not readily available for ethnographic study, but we can get some clues to its character from its reflections in management literature, business journalism, and corporate self-promotion, and from studies of local business elites (e.g., Donaldson 1997).

As a first approximation, I would suggest this is a masculinity marked by increasing egocentrism, very conditional loyalties (even to the corporation), and a declining sense of responsibility for others (except for purposes of image making). Gee, Hull, and Lank-shear (1996), studying recent management textbooks, note the peculiar construction of the executive in "fast capitalism" as a person with no permanent commitments, except (in effect) to the idea of accumulation itself. Transnational business masculinity is char-acterized by a limited technical rationality (management theory), which is increasingly separate from science.

Transnational business masculinity differs from traditional bourgeois masculinity by its increasingly libertarian sexuality, with a growing tendency to commodify relations with women. Hotels catering to businessmen in most parts of the world now routinely offer pornographic videos, and in some parts of the world, there is a well-developed prostitution industry catering for international businessmen. Transnational business masculinity does not require bodily force, since the patriarchal dividend on which it rests is accumulated by impersonal, institutional means. But corporations increasingly use the exemplary bodies of elite sportsmen as a marketing tool (note the phenomenal growth of corporate "sponsorship" of sport in the last generation) and indirectly as a means of legitimation for the whole gender order.

Recognizing global society as an arena of masculinity formation allows us to pose new questions about masculinity politics. What social dynamics in the global arena give rise to masculinity politics, and what shape does global masculinity politics take?

The gradual creation of a world gender order has meant many local instabilities of gender. Gender instability is a familiar theme of poststructuralist theory, but this school of thought takes as a universal condition a situation that is historically specific. Instabilities range from the disruption of men's local cultural dominance as women move into the public realm and higher education, through the disruption of sexual identities that produced "queer" politics in the metropole, to the shifts in the urban intelligentsia that produced "the new sensitive man" and other images of gender change.

One response to such instabilities, on the part of groups whose power is challenged but still dominant, is to reaffirm *local* gender orthodoxies and hierarchies. A masculine fundamentalism is, accordingly, a common response in gender politics at present. A soft version, searching for an essential masculinity among myths and symbols, is offered by the mythopoetic men's movement in the United States and by the religious revivalists of the Promise Keepers (Messner 1997). A much harder version is found, in that country, in the right-wing militia movement brought to world attention by the Oklahoma City bombing (Gibson 1994), and in contemporary Afghanistan, if we can trust Western media reports, in the militant misogyny of the Talibaan. It is no coincidence that in the two latter cases, hardline masculine fundamentalism goes together with a marked anti-internationalism. The world system—rightly enough—is seen as the source of pollution and disruption.

Not that the emerging global order is a hotbed of gender progressivism. Indeed, the neoliberal agenda for the reform of national and international economies involves closing down historic possibilities for gender reform. I have noted how it subverts the gender compromise represented by the metropolitan welfare state. It has also undermined the progressive-liberal agendas of sex role reform represented by affirmative action programs, antidiscrimination provisions, childcare services, and the like. Right-wing parties and governments have been persistently cutting such programs, in the name of either individual liberties or global competitiveness. Through these means, the patriarchal dividend to men is defended or restored, without an *explicit* masculinity politics in the form of a mobilization of men.

Within the arenas of international relations, the international state, multinational corporations, and global markets, there is nevertheless a deployment of masculinities and a reasonably clear hegemony. The transnational business masculinity described above has had only one major competitor for hegemony in recent decades, the rigid, control-oriented masculinity of the military, and the military-style bureaucratic dictatorships of Stalinism. With the collapse of Stalinism and the end of the cold war, Big Brother (Orwell's famous parody of this form of masculinity) is a fading threat, and the more flexible, calculative, egocentric masculinity of the fast capitalist entrepreneur holds the world stage.

We must, however, recall two important conclusions of the ethnographic moment in masculinity research: that different forms of masculinity exist together and the hegemony is constantly subject to challenge. These are possibilities in the global arena too. Transnational business masculinity is not completely homogenous; variations of it are embedded in different parts of the world system, which may not be completely compatible. We may distinguish a Confucian variant, based in East Asia, with a stronger commitment to hierarchy and social consensus, from a secularized Christian variant, based in North America, with more hedonism and individualism and greater tolerance for social conflict. In certain arenas, there is already conflict between the business and political leaderships embodying these forms of masculinity: initially over human rights versus Asian values, and more recently over the extent of trade and investment liberalization.

If there are contenders for hegemony, there is also the possibility of opposition to hegemony. The global circulation of "gay" identity (Altman 1996) is an important indication that nonhegemonic masculinities may operate in global arenas, and may even find a certain political articulation, in this case around human rights and AIDS prevention.

Critiques of dominant forms of masculinity have been circulating for some time among heterosexual men, or among groups that are predominantly heterosexual. English-language readers will be most familiar with three Anglophone examples: the antisexist or profeminist men's groups in the United States, with their umbrella group NOMAS (National Organization for Men Against Sexism), which has been running since the early 1980s (Cohen 1991); the British new left men's groups, which produced the remarkable magazine *Achilles Heel* (Seidler 1991); and the Canadian White Ribbon campaign, the most successful mass mobilization of men opposing men's violence against women (Kaufman 1997).

There are parallel developments in other language communities. In Germany, for instance, feminists launched a discussion of the gender of men in the 1980s (Metz-Goeckel and Mueller 1986; Hagemann-White and Rerrich 1988), which has been followed by an educational (Kindler 1993), a popular-psychology (Hollstein 1992), and a critical (*Widersprueche* 1995; BauSteineMaenner 1996) debate among men about masculinities and how to change them. In Scandinavia, gender reform and debates about men (Oftung 1994) have led to the "father's quota" of paternal leave in Norway (Gender Equality Ombudsman 1997) and to a particularly active network of masculinity researchers. In Japan, a media debate about men's liberation and some pioneering books about changing masculinities (Ito 1993; Nakamura 1994) have been followed by the foundation of a men's center and diversifying debates on change.

These developments at national or regional levels have very recently begun to link internationally. An International Association for Studies of Men has begun to link men involved in critical studies of masculinity. Certain international agencies, including the United Nations Educational, Scientific and Cultural Organization (UNESCO) (1997), have sponsored conferences to discuss the policy implications of new perspectives on masculinity.

Compared with the concentration of institutional power in multinational businesses, these initiatives remain small scale and dispersed. They are, nevertheless, important in potential. I have argued that the global gender order contains, necessarily, greater plurality of gender forms than any local gender order. This must reinforce the consciousness that masculinity is not one fixed form. The plurality of masculinities at least symbolically prefigures the unconstrained creativity of a demographic gender order.

WORKS CITED

Altman, Dennis. 1996. "Rupture or Continuity? The Internationalization of Gay Identities." *Social Text* 48 (3): 77–94.

Barrett, Frank J. 1996. "The Organizational Construction of Hegemonic Masculinity: The Case of the U.S. Navy." *Gender, Work and Organization* 3 (3): 129–42.

BauSteineMaenner, ed. 1996. *Kritische Maenerforschung* (Critical Research on Men). Berlin: Argument.

Bitterli, Urs. 1989. *Cultures in Conflict: Encounters between European and Non-European Cultures, 1492–1800*. Stanford, CA: Stanford University Press.

Bolin, Anne. 1988. *In Search of Eve: Transsexual Rites of Passage*. Westport, CT: Bergin & Garvey.

Bulbeck, Chilla. 1992. *Australian Women in Papua New Guinea: Colonial Passages 1920–1960*. Cambridge, UK: Cambridge University Press.

Cain, P. J., and A. G. Hopkins. 1993. *British Imperialism: Innovation and Expansion, 1688–1914*. New York: Longman.

Carrigan, Tim, Bob Connell, and John Lee. 1985. "Toward a New Sociology of Masculinity." *Theory and Society* 14 (5): 551–604.

Chodorow, Nancy. 1994. *Femininities, Masculinities, Sexualities: Freud and Beyond*. Lexington: University Press of Kentucky.

Cockburn, Cynthia. 1983. *Brothers: Male Dominance and Technological Change*. London: Pluto.

Cohen, Jon. 1991. NOMAS: Challenging Male Supremacy. *Changing Men* (Winter/Spring): 45–46.

Connell, R. W. 1987. *Gender and Power*. Cambridge, MA: Polity.

———. 1990a. "An Iron Man: The Body and Some Contradictions of Hegemonic Masculinity." In *Sport, Men and the Gender Order: Critical Feminist Perspectives*, edited by Michael A. Messner and Donald F. Sabo, 83–95. Champaign, IL: Human Kinetics Books.

———. 1990b. "The State, Gender and Sexual Politics: Theory and Appraisal." *Theory and Society* 19:507–44.

———. 1992. "A Very Straight Gay: Masculinity, Homosexual Experience, and the Dynamics of Gender." *American Sociological Review* 57 (6): 735–51.

Dawson, Graham. 1991. "The Blond Bedouin: Lawrence of Arabia, Imperial Adventure and the Imagining of English-British Masculinity." In *Manful Assertions: Masculinities in Britain since 1800*, edited by Michael Roper and John Tosh, 113–44. London: Routledge.

Donaldson, Mike. 1991. *Time of Our Lives: Labour and Love in the Working Class*. Sydney: Allen & Unwin.

———. 1997. "Growing up Very Rich: The Masculinity of the Hegemonic." Paper presented at the conference Masculinities: Renegotiating Genders, June, University of Wollongong, Australia.

Foley, Douglas E. 1990. *Learning Capitalist Culture: Deep in the Heart of Tejas*. Philadelphia: University of Pennsylvania Press.

Gee, James Paul, Glynda Hull, and Colin Lankshear. 1996. *The New Work Order: Behind the Language of New Capitalism*. Sydney: Allen & Unwin.

Gender Equality Ombudsman. 1997. *The Father's Quota*. Information sheet on paternal leave entitlements, Oslo.

Gibson, J. William. 1994. *Warrior Dreams: Paramilitary Culture in Post-Vietnam America*. New York: Hill and Wang.

Hagemann-White, Carol, and Maria S. Rerrich, eds. 1988. *FrauenMaennerBilder* (Women, Imaging, Men). Bielefeld: AJZ-Verlag.

Hearn, Jeff. 1987. *The Gender of Oppression: Men, Masculinity and the Critique of Marxism*. Brighton, U.K.: Wheatsheaf.

Herdt, Gilbert H. 1981. *Guardians of the Flutes: Idioms of Masculinity*. New York: McGraw-Hill.

———, ed. 1984. *Ritualized Homosexuality in Melanesia*. Berkeley: University of California Press.

Heward, Christine. 1988. *Making a Man of Him: Parents and Their Sons' Education at an English Public School 1929–1950*. London: Routledge.

Hollstein, Walter. 1992. *Machen Sie Platz, mein Herr! Teilen statt Herrschen* [Sharing instead of dominating]. Hamburg: Rowohlt.

Hondagneu-Sotelo, Pierrette, and Michael A. Messner. 1994. "Gender Displays and Men's Power: The 'New Man' and the Mexican Immigrant Man." In *Theorizing Masculinities*, edited by Harry Brod and Michael Kaufman, 200–218. Thousand Oaks, CA: Sage.

Ito Kimio. 1993. *Otokorashisa-no-yukue* [Directions for masculinities]. Tokyo: Shinyo-sha.

Kaufman, Michael. 1997. "Working with Men and Boys to Challenge Sexism and End Men's Violence." Paper presented at UNESCO expert group meeting on Male Roles and Masculinities in the Perspective of a Culture of Peace, September, Oslo.

Kimmel, Michael S. 1987. "Rethinking "Masculinity": New Directions in Research." In *Changing Men: New Directions in Research on Men and Masculinity*, edited by Michael S. Kimmel, 9–24. Newbury Park, CA: Sage.

———. 1996. *Manhood in America: A Cultural History*. New York: Free Press.

Kimmel, Michael S., and Thomas E. Mosmiller, eds. 1992. *Against the Tide: Pro-Feminist Men in the United States, 1776–1990, a Documentary History*. Boston: Beacon.

Kinmonth, Earl H. 1981. *The Self-Made Man in Meiji Japanese Thought: From Samurai to Salary Man*. Berkeley: University of California Press.

Klein, Alan M. 1993. *Little Big Men: Bodybuilding Sub-Culture and Gender Construction*. Albany: State University of New York Press.

Lewes, Kenneth. 1988. *The Psychoanalytic Theory of Male Homosexuality*. New York: Simon & Schuster.

McElhinny, Bonnie. 1994. "An Economy of Affect: Objectivity, Masculinity and the Gendering of Police work." In *Dislocating Masculinity: Comparative Ethnographies*, edited by Andrea Cornwall and Nancy Lindisfarne, 159–71. London: Routledge.

McKay, Jim, and Debbie Huber. 1992. "Anchoring Media Images of Technology and Sport." *Women's Studies International Forum* 15 (2): 205–18.

Messerschmidt, James W. 1997. *Crime as Structured Action: Gender, Race, Class, and Crime in the Making*. Thousand Oaks, CA: Sage.

Messner, Michael A. 1992. *Power at Play: Sports and the Problem of Masculinity*. Boston. Beacon.

———. 1997. *The Politics of Masculinities: Men in Movements*. Thousand Oaks, CA: Sage.

Metz-Goeckel, Sigrid, and Ursula Mueller. 1986. *Der Mann: Die Brigitte-Studie* [The male]. Beltz. Weinheim & Basel.

Moodie, T. Dunbar. 1994. *Going for Gold: Men, Mines, and Migration.* Johannesburg: Witwatersrand University Press.

Morrell, Robert. 1994. "Boys, Gangs, and the Making of Masculinity in the White Secondary Schools of Natal, 1880–1930." *Masculinities* 2 (2): 56–82.

Nakamura Akira. 1994. *Watashi-no Danseigaku* [My men's studies]. Tokyo: Kindaibugei-sha.

Oftung, Knut, ed. 1994. *Menns bilder og bilder av menn* [Images of men]. Oslo: Likestillingsradet.

Phillips, Jock. 1987. *A Man's Country? The Image of the Pakeha Male, a History.* Auckland: Penguin.

Roper, Michael. 1991. "Yesterday's Model: Product Fetishism and the British Company Man, 1945–85." In *Manful Assertions: Masculinities in Britain since 1800,* edited by Michael Roper and John Tosh, 190–211. London: Routledge.

Schwalbe, Michael. 1996. *Unlocking the Iron Cage: The Men's Movement, Gender Politics, and the American Culture.* New York: Oxford University Press.

Segal, Lynne. 1997. *Slow Motion: Changing Masculinities, Changing Men.* 2d ed. London: Virago.

Seidler, Victor J. 1991. *Achilles Heel Reader: Men, Sexual Politics and Socialism.* London: Routledge.

Shire, Chenjerai. 1994. "Men Don't Go to the Moon: Language, Space and Masculinities in Zimbabwe." In *Dislocating Masculinity: Comparative Ethnographies,* edited by Andrea Cornwall and Nancy Lindisfarne, 147–58. London: Routledge.

Sinha, Mrinalini. 1995. *Colonial Masculinity: The Manly Englishman and the Effeminate Bengali in the Late Nineteenth Century.* Manchester: U.K.: Manchester University Press.

Theberge, Nancy, 1991. "Reflections on the Body in the Sociology of Sport." *Quest* 43:123–34.

Thorne, Barrie. 1993. *Gender Play: Girls and Boys in School.* New Brunswick, NJ: Rutgers University Press.

Tillner, Georg. 1997. "Masculinity and Xenophobia." Paper presented at UNESCO meeting on Male Roles and Masculinities in the Perspective of a Culture of Peace, September, Oslo.

Tomsen, Stephen. 1997. "A Top Night: Social Protest, Masculinity and the Culture of Drinking Violence." *British Journal of Criminology* 37 (1): 90–103.

Tosh, John. 1991. "Domesticity and Manliness in the Victorian Middle Class: The Family of Edward White Benson." In *Manful Assertions: Masculinities in Britain since 1800,* edited by Michael Roper and John Tosh, 44–73. London: Routledge.

Walker, James C. 1988. *Louts and Legends: Male Youth Culture in an Inner-City School.* Sydney: Allen & Unwin.

Whitson, David. 1990. "Sport in the Social Construction of Masculinity." In *Sport, Men, and the Gender Order: Critical Feminist Perspectives,* edited by Michael A. Messner and Donald F. Sabo, 19–29. Champaign, IL: Human Kinetics Books.

Widersprueche. 1995. Special issue: Maennlichkeiten. Vol. 56/57.

Williams, Walter L. 1986. *The Spirit and the Flesh: Sexual Diversity in American Indian Culture.* Boston: Beacon.

Xaba, Thokozani. 1997. "Masculinity in a Transitional Society: The Rise and Fall of the 'Young Lions.'" Paper presented at the conference Masculinities in Southern Africa, June, University of Natal-Durban, Durban.

26

IDENTITY, ACTIVISM, AND THIRD WAVE FEMINISM IN THE UNITED STATES

Ashley Bourgeois

In 1992, inflamed by the Supreme Court confirmation of Clarence Thomas and the general disregard and disrespect shown Anita Hill throughout the infamous Senate hearings, Rebecca Walker penned a letter to *Ms.* magazine that made public both her irrepressible anger and her impassioned intent to fight what she deemed the blacklash of female oppression in the United States. "Becoming the Third Wave" was nothing short of a manifesto that chronicled (among other things) the increasing limitations placed upon women's credibility and power. In summation, Walker declared her feminist position: "I am not a postfeminism feminist. I am the Third Wave." Today, Third Wave feminism remains a meaningful political category for many young feminist thinkers and activists—both within and beyond the academy—who have no first-hand experience of the Women's Liberation or Second Wave movement that swept the United States in the late 1960s and early 1970s. Others struggle to pinpoint the Third Wave's political objectives and in some cases even challenge its veracity as a feminist movement. A child of the late eighties, I grew up alongside Third Wave feminism. Now a feminist scholar, I often question the categorization of feminist movements, but as its near twenty-year run would indicate, the Third Wave has both earned and solidified its spot in feminist history.

As the daughter of renowned "womanist" and political activist, Alice Walker, Rebecca Walker sought in the early nineties to define a new brand of feminism when she declared herself the Third Wave. Whether Rebecca Walker attempted to downplay or to emphasize a generational divide between movements in her letter, she was very clear in her dismissal of postfeminism, a brand of antifeminism that flourished during the 1980s and reflected the social conservatism of a decade branded the "Reagan Era." Although the term has since acquired a slew of fuzzy definitions, this postfeminist position held that Second Wave feminism had served its purpose and run its course. Deeming the battle for equality over and won, postfeminists found the need for feminist activism nonexistent and the feminist label disagreeable. Although for Walker the postfeminist mentality was distinct from, and oppositional to, the position of Third Wave feminism, more recent accounts often find the two positions conflated, or at least to some degree, overlapping. In their introduction to *Third Wave Agenda* (1997), Leslie Heywood and Jennifer Drake report that popular media often mislabel Third Wave feminism as post-feminism, and both strongly oppose the slippage as their conception of Third Wave does not signify a break with, but rather builds upon older traditions of the feminist movement.

In fact, feminism was not entirely absent or even dormant throughout the eighties, though it did to some extent get comfortable behind the walls of the academy. In *Around 1981* (1992), Jane Gallop situates the rise of academic feminism and the proliferation of formal feminist criticism at a time when the social movement encountered major set-backs. Across college campuses and across disciplines, scholars welcomed feminist theories as valid points of inquiry and useful tools for analysis.

Perhaps the most exciting and influential work being done by feminists to change the face of feminist theory itself was done by women of color who raised questions regarding the white elitism of the Second Wave movement. In 1981, Cherríe Moraga and Gloria Anzaldua coedited *This Bridge Called My Back: Writings by Radical Women of Color,* a seminal work that gave voice to "third-world" feminists living in the United States and commanded the attention of white feminists who made claims for sisterhood without critical consideration of the ways in which oppression affects women of color. That same year, bell hooks published *Ain't I A Woman: Black Women and Feminism,* in which she too addressed racist priorities and terms of exclusion that characterized aspects of the Women's Liberation Movement. In "Intersectionality and Feminist Politics," Niral Yuval-Davis describes hooks's work as a "political move to deconstruct the categories of both 'women' and 'Blacks' and to develop an analysis of the intersectionality of various social divisions, most often—but not exclusively—focusing on gender, race and class." In short, these feminist thinkers emphasized a need to acknowledge and appreciate the differ-ences among women. This emphasis upon intersectionality—coordinating points of identity including class, race, and sexual orientation in addition to gender, is one that both informs and permeates the Third Wave movement.

Although an educated woman, Walker in 1992 had not joined the ranks of academic feminism. Her letter to *Ms.* was a more generalized call to arms that increased visibility for a new wave of feminism reaching beyond the academy and propelling younger women to feminist activism. While she is most often credited for popularizing the term "Third Wave feminism," Walker was not alone in promoting the movement. Naomi Wolf and Katie Roiphe dominated early popular media accounts of Third Wave feminism with their highly publicized critiques of what came to be known as "victim feminism." These self-identified Third Wavers argued that dominant discourses of the Second Wave overstressed the position of women as victims, and in turn, undermined female agency. In *Fire with Fire: A New Female Power and How to Use It*, Wolf describes an "elaborate vocabulary in which to describe sexual harm done by men, but almost no vocabulary in which a woman can celebrate sex with men." Many criticized Wolf for attempting to fit all women of the Second Wave into the same mold. While she supported her case by calling upon positions espoused by antiporn feminists Catherine MacKinnon and Andrea Dworkin, Wolf conveniently overlooked feminists like Germaine Greer and Audre Lorde who made arguments for the creative potential of sex and encouraged women to make pleasure a priority of sex, as opposed to procreation.

To correct the "problem" of victim feminism, Wolf proposed "power feminism" as a subset of the Third Wave. Power feminism, as such, has its detractors both within and beyond the Third Wave community. Some claim that power feminists oversimplify the work of women activists who sought both to "recognize and inspire women's agency" while at the same time calling attention to the victimization women do experience (Stringer 24). Heywood and Drake associate power feminism with a conservative agenda for the ways in which it depends upon materialism and popular beauty ideals to express an empowered sexuality, without engaging a critique of capitalism, desire, and power.

Publishing alongside Walker and Wolf in the early nineties was Kathleen Hanna (included here), author of "Riot Grrrl Manifesto," and front-woman for the female punk band Bikini Kill. Riot grrrls were musicians and members of the female punk rock community of the Pacific Northwest. These feminist rockers are often associated with the girl power movement, another subset of the Third Wave that addressed issues of rape, domestic abuse, sexuality, queer identity, and female empowerment. If Wolf's approach to female power was conservative, Hanna's might be characterized as anything but. In her manifesto she demonstrates contempt for the "capitalist way of doing things" and urges girls who constitute a "revolutionary soul force" to "take over the means of production." Hanna also envisions unconventional definitions of power that promote creativity and are nonhierarchical in structure.

As a quick survey of these early Third Wavers indicates, the movement is marked by difference. Third Wavers embrace contradiction on the grounds that their Second Wave predecessors were too restrictive in defining proper womanhood; in other words, Third Wavers reject any arguments about the right and wrong ways to be a feminist. (What they tend to overlook are ways in which diversity characterized the Women's Liberation Movement.) So in order to correct what they term exclusionary tactics of the Second Wave, Third Wavers promote inclusion. Inclusion can be a beautiful thing, an inspiring thing, a powerful thing. However, when inclusion comes at the cost of a united political front, it's time to reevaluate and regroup. While thinkers such as hooks, Spivak, and Patricia Hill-Collins (among others) advanced early theories of difference, they did not depart from political principles of equality, humanity, and self-ownership. In other words, arguments for inclusion can be taken too far. A troubling example might be found in 2008 Republican vice-presidential candidate Sarah Palin, who embraced an "emerging, conservative, feminist identity" in a speech for the Susan B. Anthony List, a political action committee (PAC) for antiabortion female congressional candidates.

The selections included here represent a range of Third Wave voices, and while they have several points of overlap, I've chosen to highlight the ways in which they address two fundamental concerns of Third Wave feminism: identity politics and activism. These authors settle on difference in different ways, in some cases by highlighting their own claims to difference, and in other cases, by embracing constructive concepts of difference that work toward feminist collaborations. Activist strategies of Third Wave feminism serve to illuminate ways in which feminist issues have evolved since the first organized feminist protest of the Miss America Pageant in 1968. The world is a different place, in some respects. In the period that followed the decline of Second Wave involvement, changes to the cultural landscape include events and phenomena as varied as the rise of AIDS culture, the Internet boom, technological advances in medicine and cosmetic procedures, and globalization efforts.

Third Wavers face different societal pressures. Whereas Second Wave women fought for job opportunities and felt forced to choose between staying home as wives and mothers and working, women now feel pressured to dominate both domestic and professional spheres. Problems plaguing the workplace include fewer job opportunities, overqualification, and increasing costs of education (Heywood and Drake). Media images that peddle society's idea of the perfect woman are inescapable and the expectations they foster, for the most part, unattainable. As a result, more women and young girls suffer from eating disorders and low self-esteem. Of course some of today's most pressing issues aren't new at all; just look at the most recent political attacks on women that question the validity of rape and challenge a woman's right to choose. Looking at Third Wave feminist agendas, I hope to uncover what makes Third Wavers angry and what they propose to do about it.

In "Do the Ladies Run This . . . ? Some Thoughts on Hip-Hop Feminism," Gwendolyn Pough struggles to reconcile her love of hip-hop culture with her feminist values. For her, hip-hop is an extension of the African American community she belongs to. Her identification with hip-hop culture is something she takes pride in, and yet she is discouraged by what she sees as its increasing preoccupation with "scantily clad bitches, hos, stunts, skeezers, and hoochies." Assessing the cultural landscape of hip-hop, she encounters an onslaught of lyrics and images that devalue black women; still she argues that hip-hop and feminism can work for each other.

Pough uses identity politics to validate her claim. One of the ways in which Pough emphasizes her racial and cultural identity is by contextualizing the hip-hop movement within a larger history of African American culture in the twentieth century. In hip-hop she seeks out the "continued legacy of black feminism," and also identifies hip-hop development as a youth movement that "grew out of the rubble of a dying Black Power

Movement." Along with Black Power, she nods to Black Panthers, the Student Non-Violent Coordinating Committee (SNCC), and the Black Liberation Army. By acknowledging the proactive campaigns of both black feminism and the more patriarchal institutions of Black Power and the Panther Party, Pough unites historic traditions that were at times at odds politically. These contradictions inform her unique position as a Third Wave hip-hop feminist. As she aligns herself with other hip-hop feminists, she also demonstrates her cultural commitment to, and admiration for, hip-hop icons Queen Latifah and Erykah Badu. Pough seems unaffected by the fact that Queen Latifah wouldn't label herself a hip-hop feminist; she insists that Latifah remains a "strong black presence in hip-hop culture that inspired [. . .] black feminist consciousness" and applauds Latifah's pro-woman perspective, which speaks to contemporary concerns of black women.

Pough's brand of feminism sounds made to order:

> Hip-hop feminists need to create a feminism that fits their lives. Although black feminism offers useful analytical tools, I contend that these too have had to change. Black feminism has had to take on a hip-hop slant in order to reach the generation that needs to utilize it.

Plain ol' feminism just won't do. Pough's feminism isn't only Third Wave feminism; it's not only black feminism either. For Pough, the specific terms of a hip-hop feminist identity are essential to her feminist agenda.

Similarly, Alana Suskin stresses identity politics in "Hearing the Daughter Voice: The *Bat Kol* as Rrrabi Grrrl," through which she contemplates her position as a Jewish feminist. Suskin begins by recalling herself as a young girl who did "not think much" about God or religion; by the end of the article, she is a practicing rabbi. She credits her involvement in women's studies as a graduate student for her change of heart: "Although many faculty members in the department were Jewish by birth, I found that many were often subtly hostile to Judaism, particularly traditional Judaism, while being open to diversity among other groups." And so, though at one time nonreligious, Suskin found herself suddenly defending Jewish religious traditions:

> I once found myself arguing that departmental meetings shouldn't be scheduled on Friday nights, the night when our Sabbath begins. I found myself defending even the possibility of being both a ritually observant Jew and a feminist. I did not even know why I felt the need to defend a religion in which I participated very little.

But she did, and like Pough, she set out to define a feminism that would work for her. Her determination to repair the troubled relationship between Judaism and feminism was fueled in part by lasting feminist prejudices "against those who are nonwhite and non-middle class." After immersing herself within Jewish studies, an undertaking that ultimately put her on the rabbinic track, Suskin claims that the voice of the feminist,

Third Wave daughter is one that the Jews need to hear because both feminism and Judaism are marked by resistance to "degrading paradigms of the dominant culture."

These essays by Pough and Suskin both appeared in the 2003 anthology *Catching a Wave: Reclaiming Feminism for the 21st Century,* and what underlies both arguments is the initial fear, and ultimate rejection, of restrictive terms of feminism. Both women underscore, if indirectly, the assumption that proponents of a more traditional feminism might force them to deny their cultural traditions altogether. Pough seems convinced that the larger feminist community has no use for the sexist contributions of hip-hop, and Suskin recalls a feminist article claiming that any observance of Judaism would be capitulation to "patriarchal values and rules." As Third Wave feminists, both seek to reclaim and repurpose their cultural identities for feminist use.

While Pough and Suskin defend their own claims to difference, Hanna, in "The Riot Grrrl Manifesto" outlines priorities of the feminist "grrrl" community while simultaneously making room for difference. Published in the band's small distribution zine, Hanna's manifesto would presumably find its way into the hands of like-minded "grrrls," and yet Hanna's scope for change is more far-reaching. Within the riot grrrl movement she identifies an "angry grrrl rock revolution which seeks to save the psychic and cultural lives of girls and women *everywhere, according to their own terms,*" not on the terms prescribed by the riot grrrls themselves (my emphasis). She also identifies a "sense of community" as essential to the fight against oppression.

The "Third Wave Manifesta: A Thirteen Point Agenda," by Jennifer Baumgardner and Amy Richards, is similar in form to "Riot Grrrl Manifesto" in that it comprises a list of social and political imperatives as opposed to the more personal accounts by Pough and Suskin. Baumgardner and Richards are ambitious, defining their intended audience as all participants in the Third Wave movement as opposed to a specific subset of it. Their thirteen points make repeated references to difference. In points two and three, they acknowledge difference as it relates to women's roles. While they advocate for all women (and men) who choose to have children, regardless of sexual orientation and social class, they similarly support "the choice to be childless." In point five they celebrate a diverse feminist legacy and women's history, nodding to radical feminists, womanists, and mujeristas. They address difference in terms of sexual orientation in point number six, their commitment to

> Support and increase the visibility and power of lesbians and bisexual women in the feminist movement, in high schools, colleges, and the workplace. To recognize that queer women have always been at the forefront of the feminist movement and that there is nothing to be gained—and much to be lost—by downplaying their history . . .

Finally, like Hanna, they acknowledge that feminists have "disparate values [but] share the same goal of equality and of supporting one another in efforts to gain the power to make our own choices."

Feminist activism is the outward expression of political and social motivations that define a feminist community. It is Walker's call to activism in 1992 that sets her apart from the "postfeminism feminists," and today, Walker's letter to *Ms.* remains a useful measure for attempts to define a Third Wave agenda. Walker's first step toward activism is anger. In her letter she recounts a personal encounter with sexism and her estimation of its effects upon all those who are poisoned by it. She writes:

> I am so angry that thoughts of murder, [. . .] of separatism, engulf me. I am almost out of body, just shy of being pure force. I am sick of the way women are negated, violated, devalued, ignored. I am livid, unrelenting in my anger at those who invade my space, who wish to take away my rights, who refuse to hear my voice. [. . .] My involvement must reach beyond my own voice in discussion, beyond voting, beyond reading feminist theory. My anger and awareness must translate into tangible action.

For Walker, there was a natural progression from anger to action. Following publication of her letter, Walker answered her own call to activism by initiating a voter registration campaign targeting apathetic youth and helped to create (along with Amy Richards, included here) the Third Wave Foundation, an organization to support women in politics.

More than any other Third Wave writer featured here, Kathleen Hanna of Bikini Kill communicates impassioned anger, and she directs her anger at a society that tells her: "Girl = Dumb, Girl = Bad, Girl = Weak." Hanna identifies an enemy in capitalism, and exudes pure contempt for the "bullshit christian capitalist way of doing things." Her activist agenda includes (among other things) the support of female artists, rebellion against sexist authorities, and the rejection of capitalist consumer culture and any efforts to maintain the status quo. At times, her proposals invoke the same desire for separatism that Walker describes. Measured up against activist efforts of the Second Wave, "The Riot Grrrl Manifesto" might best be characterized as a "radical" Third Wave agenda that supports the eradication of existing social institutions in favor of something completely new.

The "Third Wave Manifesta" reconsiders pressing issues addressed by activists of the Women's Liberation Movement. It urges feminists to vote, to fight for reproductive rights, and to pass the Equal Rights Amendment. Other echoes of an earlier wave include demands for partners to share equally the burden of family planning and efforts to raise awareness of women's history and feminist legacy. One might argue that the "Third Wave Manifesta" represents a more liberal approach to feminist activism—one that operates within the existing social structure, but seeks to afford women the same rights under law as are afforded to men.

Particularly interesting are the very different ways in which Pough and Suskin define a Third Wave feminist agenda. Pough urges women of the hip-hop community to embrace self-love and challenges MCs to move their crowds toward change. While Pough calls out to many different members of the hip-hop community, Suskin's call to activism is perhaps more limited. Unlike Hanna, who makes an argument for "non-hierarchial ways of being," Suskin finds value in a hierarchical approach, soliciting activism from female Jewish rabbis who have the power to identify new directions and new positions for women within the Jewish religion. The agendas of Pough and Suskin are not easily aligned with popular models of Second Wave feminist activism. Rather, their activism seeks to increase visibility of specific feminist communities before they reach beyond them. If the feminist movement continues to grow, activist strategies will be rethought and reinvented. I hear rumors of a fourth wave.

WORKS CITED

Stringer, Rebecca. "Rethinking the Critique of Victim Feminism." In *Victim No More: Women's Resistance to Law, Culture and Power*, 19–27. Edited by Ellen Faulkner and Gayle MacDonald. Halifax. Ferwood Publishing. 2009.

Wolf, Naomi. *Fire with Fire: A New Female Power and How to Use it*. New York: Random House, 1993.

DISCUSSION QUESTIONS

1. The *Third Wave Manifesta* was published in 2000. If you were advising Baumgardner and Richards on ways to revise for reprint, what changes would you suggest? What new issues face young women today? What, if any, issues seem obsolete?

2. Identify ways in which the activist priorities of the *Third Wave Manifesta* align with priorities identified by the Second Wave. Which items can you identify as "new" and distinctly Third Wave?

3. After reading the selections, go back and read the brief definition of power feminism offered by Bourgeois. How would you guess that Gwendolyn Pough might respond to the concept of power feminism? The others? What are your own thoughts regarding power feminism?

KATHLEEN HANNA, *RIOT GRRRL MANIFESTO*

In the 1990s, despite American media descriptions of a "postfeminist" culture that took for granted the gains of earlier social movements, a new generation of activists confronted persistent obstacles to women's equality. The problems of girls, ranging from low self-esteem to eating disorders to sexual abuse, stimulated a range of "girl power" campaigns to counteract societal pressures. Within the punk rock musical subculture, young women who felt marginalized by men reclaimed the term "girl,"

SOURCE: Kathleen Hanna, "Riot Grrrl Manifesto," *Bikini Kill* zine 2 (1991).

proclaiming their strength in a variety of "riot grrrl" fanzines. With graphic language and hard-driving music, female punk bands such as Bikini Kill screamed with rage against male abuse, celebrated an independent female sexuality, and called for a grrrl-style revolution. The following declaration, written by Kathleen Hanna of Bikini Kill, illustrates the political spirit of this movement, which questioned male dominance in music and throughout society. Her critique of capitalism and rejection of internalized sexism echoes the anarchist feminism of Emma Goldman, while the band's music added a queer sexual sensibility that embraced lesbian as well as heterosexual pleasure.

BECAUSE us girls crave records and books and fanzines that speak to US that WE feel included in and can understand in our own ways.

BECAUSE we wanna make it easier for girls to see/hear each other's work so that we can share strategies and criticize-applaud each other.

BECAUSE we must take over the means of production in order to create our own meanings.

BECAUSE viewing our work as being connected to our girlfriends-politics-real-lives is essential if we are gonna figure out how we are doing impacts, reflects, perpetuates, or DISRUPTS the status quo.

BECAUSE we recognize fantasies of Instant Macho Gun Revolution as impractical lies meant to keep us simply dreaming instead of becoming our dreams AND THUS seek to create revolution in our own lives every single day by envisioning and creating alternatives to the bullshit christian capitalist way of doing things.

BECAUSE we want and need to encourage and be encouraged in the face of all our own insecurities, in the face of beergutboyrock that tells us we can't play our instruments, in the face of "authorities" who say our bands/zines/etc are the worst in the U.S. and

BECAUSE we don't wanna assimilate to someone else's (boy) standards of what is or isn't cool.

BECAUSE we are unwilling to falter under claims that we are reactionary "reverse sexists" AND NOT THE TRUEPUNKROCK-SOULCRUSADERS THAT WE KNOW we really are.

BECAUSE we know that life is much more than physical survival and are patently aware that the punk rock "you can do anything" idea is crucial to the coming angry grrrl rock revolution which seeks to save the psychic and cultural lives of girls and women everywhere, according to their own terms, not ours.

BECAUSE we are interested in creating non-hierarchical ways of being AND making music, friends, and scenes based on communication + understanding, instead of competition + good/bad categorizations.

BECAUSE doing/reading/seeing/hearing cool things that validate and challenge us can help us gain the strength and sense of community that we need in order to figure out how bullshit like racism, able-bodieism, ageism, speciesism, classism, thinism, sexism, anti-semitism and hererosexism figures in our own lives.

BECAUSE we see fostering and supporting girl scenes and girl artists of all kinds as integral to this process.

BECAUSE we hate capitalism in all its forms and see our main goal as sharing information and staying alive, instead of making profits or being cool according to traditional standards.

BECAUSE we are angry at a society that tells us Girl = Dumb, Girl = Bad, Girl = Weak.

BECAUSE we are unwilling to let our real and valid anger be diffused and/or turned against us via the internalization of sexism as witnessed in girl/girl jealousy and self defeating girltype behaviors.

BECAUSE I believe with my wholeheartmindbody that girls constitute a revolutionary soul force that can, and will change the world for real.

GWENDOLYN D. POUGH, *DO THE LADIES RUN THIS . . . ? SOME THOUGHTS ON HIP-HOP FEMINISM*

I was nine years old when the first rap record hit the airwaves. "Rapper's Delight" came out in 1979, and I memorized every line. I wanted to be an MC even then. I started making up my own rhymes: "I'm the K-I-Double-TT-Y. I'm the fresh female that ya can't deny!" I used to write rhymes and listen to rap music every day, I dragged around a miniature boom box long before LL could not live without his radio. I guess you could say rap music and hip-hop culture were my first loves. I still love the music and the culture, but I have to admit that my relationship to them has become somewhat troubled. The music that I grew up on has changed, and so have I. The music and the culture used to validate me in real and significant ways. I had no problem being a certified B-girl, with my Kangol hat, pink Lee jeans, and pastel pink Nikes (or pink construction boots, depending on the weather). I had LL Cool J crooning that he needed an "Around the Way Girl" and the Boogie Boys calling me a "Fly Girl." Hip-hop culture had me feeling like we were going to be tight forever. And then Apache started rapping about needing a "Gangsta Bitch," and rap lyrics began to be laced with more bitches, hos, stunts, skeezers, and hoochies than I could count. I did not want to go from B-girl to scantily clad video ho, so I chilled. But I still loved hip-hop; I just needed to find a way to make the culture mesh with the feminist politics I had started to develop when I took my first women's studies class as an undergraduate. Luckily, I'm not alone. There are several young black women writing about their need to combine hip-hop with feminism. They have begun to create a tremendous body of work and begun to think about what it means to be a hip-hop feminist.

SOURCE: Gwendolyn Pough, "Do the Ladies Run This . . . ? Some Thoughts on Hip-Hop Feminism," in *Catching a Wave: Reclaiming Feminism for the 21st Century*, ed. Rory Dicker and Alison Piepmeier (Lebanon, NH: University Press of New England), 232–43.

There is indeed a large contingent of young black feminists who are grappling with the tenuous relationship between black women, hip-hop culture, rap music, and feminism. At the May 1999 Power Moves Hip Hop Conference at U.C.L.A., during the pre-conference in which graduate students presented their works-in-progress on hip-hop, several young black women—including myself—spoke passionately about issues of gender and hip-hop culture. We bespoke the need for a feminist critique and tried to continue the lineage of black feminist/womanist dialogue in the black community. Hip-hop feminists are trying to find ways both to be true to themselves and to listen to the music and participate in the culture that stimulates the very depth of their souls. And they are trying to be true to themselves while building on the legacies and the promises left by the black women who went before them. These black women grew up knowing freedom in ways that just a generation before were not possible. In spite of the disbelief, discrediting, dismissals, and straight-up disses these women encounter, they have begun to write about their lives in relation to hip-hop culture and the feminist movement in real and honest ways.

I will attempt to theorize and document hip-hop feminism by examining the work of black women involved in hip-hop culture for common themes and a continued legacy of black feminism. I take the stance that hip-hop is a cultural phenomenon that extends beyond rap music. Hip-hop has been defined by many as a way of life that encompasses everything from dress to speech. Hip-hop as a culture originally included graffiti writing, dee-jaying, break dancing, and rap music. It has recently expanded to include genres such as film, spoken word, autobiography, literature, journalism, and activism. I examine several of these genres in order to document a potentially activist agenda for hip-hop that is tied to feminism. I explore the hip-hop feminism that has come from the music of both women rappers and hip-hop soul artists, the essays and poetry of third wave hip-hop feminists, and music video images and representations. The images and representations are sending harmful messages about materialism and can be linked to the growing black female incarceration rate. Feminism can give young women and men of today the critical interpretive tools they need to understand the world they live in—the tools of black feminism with a hip-hop slant. Some of these tools can be found in the work of third wave black feminist writers, such as Eisa Davis, Eisa Nefertari Ulen, dream hampton, Joan Morgan, Tara Roberts, and Angela Ards, who are expanding black feminist theory and black women's intellectual traditions in fascinating ways. What started out as a few young black feminist women who loved hip-hop and who tried to mesh that love with their feminist/womanist consciousness is now a rich body of articles, essays, poetry, and creative nonfiction.

Hip-hop as a youth movement grew out of the rubble of a dying Black Power movement. Just as the Black Power movement was taking its last breath in the mid-1970s in America's inner cities, hip-hop was being created by black and Latino youth in the South Bronx. It's important to note hip-hop's proximity to the Black Power movement, because out of nationalist movements by people of color against oppression came not only hip-hop but also what we currently call woman-of-color feminisms. For example, many of the women who pioneered black feminist thought, activism, and art as we now know them started out in the Black Power movement and Black Arts movement of the 1970s. Many of them, while working to end oppression for all black people by forming alliances in groups such as the Black Panther Party, Student Nonviolent Coordinating Committee (SNCC), and the Black Liberation Army, found that the movement they thought would free them all was centered on freeing black masculinity and establishing a black patriarchy. These women began to address issues of gender and found that the women's movement going on at that time was too focused on the issues of white, middle-class women. Thus, the title of Gloria T. Hull, Patricia Bell Scott, and Barbara Smith's anthology, *All the Women Are White, All the Blacks Are Men, but Some of Us Are Brave* (1981), becomes a fitting description of the ways in which black women were marginalized in both race-based movements and gender-based movements. So they began to shape and build a feminism to fight for their needs. And the feminism they created is the feminism that hip-hop feminism grows out of. The hip-hop generation sees a link between itself and the Black Power movement. Young black feminists of today also see themselves in relation to their black feminist foremothers.

The one thing that most third wave feminists grappling with their love for hip-hop have in common is that they were all born in the early to mid-1970s and they all came of age in a post–Black Power era. This is not to say that they came of age without the outlet for black consciousness that the Black Power movement encouraged. Although they did not have the Black Panther Party and Huey P. Newton to listen to, they did have the political rap stylings of groups such as Public Enemy, X-Clan, KRS-One, Paris, and Conscious Daughters. These rappers produced rap songs with political themes of unity, racial uplift, self-definition, self-determination, and black diasporic connections. There were also mass movements to end "black on black" crime and violence with projects such as "Stop the Violence: Self Destruction" and "We're All in the Same Gang." These kinds of projects used rap as a vehicle to stop black youth from killing one another and worked to bring various rappers together for a similar cause. Thus, the connections to the ideals of Black Power remained in some form. These connections are also evident in the third wave black feminists' openly stated appreciation for the Black Power movement and the second wave black feminists who went before them.

The most striking visual representation of this connection can be seen in Queen Latifah's video for "Ladies First." At the start of the video, we see image after image of black women leaders, from Sojourner Truth to Angela Davis. Later in the video, we view a scene in which Queen Latifah is dressed as a high-ranking military commander poised over a map of the world with little white men all over it. She knocks the little white men off the map and replaces them with little Black Power fists. Queen Latifah's video visually represents the connection between this generation's black women and the black female leaders of the past. Also, by replacing the white men with Black Power fists, she is showing the connection between this generation and the Black Power movement. The two scenes from the video highlight the indebtedness that hip-hop feminists feel both to the Black Power movement and to the black feminist leaders of the past.

Although Queen Latifah probably would not label herself a hip-hop feminist—or a womanist, for that matter—she has been claimed by several hip-hop feminists as the strong black female presence in hip-hop culture that inspired their own black feminist consciousness. Through her presence and her lyrics, Queen Latifah becomes not only a model for showing the legacy of Black Power in the hip-hop generation but also a model for contemporary black womanhood that hip-hop feminists aspire to be. And songs such as "Ladies First" and "U.N.I.T.Y."—because of their pro-woman messages—give voice to the issues that contemporary black women find most pressing. For example, in "U.N.I.T.Y.," she addresses the word "bitch," domestic violence, and gang violence. In "Ladies First," she addresses the need for women to be respected in society. By document-ing or demonstrating this connection, Queen Latifah enacts hip-hop feminism.

Another example of hip-hop feminism—and a visual representation of the connection between third wave hip-hop feminism and black feminism—is Erykah Badu's remix of Ntozake Shange's *For Colored Girls Who Have Considered Suicide/When the Rainbow Is Enuf* (1975). In her video for her hit single "Bag Lady," Badu and six other women dress as the ladies in brown, yellow, purple, red, green, blue, and orange. Shange's 1970s response to the sexism of the Black Arts movement encouraged black women to find God in themselves and love "her fiercely" in an attempt to circumvent the negative responses that most black women internalize when faced with the multiple oppressions they encounter. Similarly, Badu's "Bag Lady" encourages twenty-first-century black women to let go of the baggage that weighs them down.[1] Badu's lyrics serve as a twenty-first-cen-tury remix of Shange's choreo-poem. She tells women to hold on to themselves and hold on to love. Implicit in Badu's lyrics is the message that self-love will make life better. In addition, the messages of self-redemption, self-love, and fighting against the oppressive systems and circumstances that inhibit self-love are present in Badu's work, as they are in Shange's.

The hip-hop feminist writer Eisa Davis offers another example of third wave hip-hop feminism's indebtedness to the black women who grappled with these issues before them. Her poem "if we've gotta live underground and everybody's got cancer / will poetry be enuf?: A Letter to Ntozake Shange" essentially questions how useful the tools that the women of Shange's generation fought with are for this generation. The poem lists the ways in which the problems that this generation faces are quite different. She notes that there is now "high definition tragedy." And she asks the questions, "if we've gone and burnt up everything in the sky / if there's nothing else to eat but landfill stroganoff / if we've gotta live underground and everybody's got cancer / will poetry be enuf?"[2] The

---

1. Erykah Badu, "Bag Lady," *Mama's Gun* (UNI/Motown, 2000).

2. Eisa Davis, "If we've gotta live underground and everybody's got cancer/ will poetry be enuf?: A Letter to Ntozake Shange," in *Step into a World: A Global Anthology of the New Black Literature*, ed. Kevin Powell, 380–84 (New York: John Wiley & Sons, 2000), 383.

poem ends on the hopeful note that "poetry just might be enuf." Clearly, it is a different kind of poetry: it is poetry made to question and fight today's problems. Some of the issues are the same. But most have been amplified, and still others are totally new.

Hip-hop feminists need to create a feminism that fits their lives. Shange's generation did not have to contend with the reality of AIDS. Although the heroin epidemic was horrific, it in no way matched the trauma inflicted by crack in African American communities. Add to those differences the impact of an urban environmental poisoning that amounts to genocide and a global capitalist structure that leads to fewer and fewer jobs just as welfare is being reformed, and we can see how the issues in the poetry would need to change. And although black feminism offers useful analytical tools, I contend that these, too, have had to change. Black feminism has had to take on a hip-hop slant in order to reach the generation that needs to utilize it.

The need for a different kind of poetry leads to rap music and hip-hop culture. Countless academics have traced rap's connection to African American oral and musical traditions. Rap is the most recent addition to a culture that is steeped in history and talent. Rap has been categorized in a variety of genres, from music to storytelling to poetry. Rap is the contemporary art form that gives voice to a part of the population that would not have a voice otherwise. It is my belief that rap is the poetry that just might be "enuf." I think that rap has political potential—potential that should be honed by the feminist movement in general and by third wave hip-hop feminists in particular.

This might sound crazy, given rap music's track record of sexism and misogyny. Bitches, hos, and scantily clad women hardly make for a strong feminist agenda. Or do they? The fact is that rap music and hip-hop culture have brought issues concerning women into the public space. Rap videos that subjugate women have become fodder for much feminist activism and academic discussion and debate. We use them now to talk about what is wrong in the entertainment industry and the world. What would happen if we pushed these kinds of discussions and debates further? What would happen if we took the advice of cultural critics such as bell hooks and Cheo Coker and expanded our critique of rap music? Both hooks and Coker note that rap music does not occur in a vacuum and that sexism and misogyny are as American as apple pie. The only difference between rappers and the "suits" in the boardroom is race and socioeconomic status. While rap does give us some startling and, indeed, ugly representations of female objectification, rap is not responsible for other travesties, such as the feminization of poverty, welfare reform, and the glass ceiling, to name only a few.

I believe we can use rap music as teaching moments. Rap can help us to enact a public pedagogy that can be used not only to bring women's issues into the public sphere but also to mobilize action. One of the main things an MC does is to move the crowd. What would happen if we combined hip-hop and feminism to work toward that political end? What would happen if we had feminist MCs moving millions toward a critique of gender that motivated them toward change? We have not had any female MCs with this kind of feminist agenda. Although rappers like Queen Latifah, Salt-N-Pepa, and Yo-Yo have come close, they will not openly claim a feminist agenda or even call themselves feminists. What would happen if we could harness the power that rap music has to make people dance and make them work toward change in women's lives? The current power of hip-hop works on a variety of levels. Not only does it intersect borders of race, class, and gender in terms of its listening audience, but the messages that the music brings to its multiple listeners can influence them. Also, the power of hip-hop is worldwide; it is causing young men and women all over the world to learn English—more specifically the black English vernacular—just so that they can follow rap lyrics. When one adds to this equation the fact that an enormous number of white youths in America are buying the music and identifying with the culture, the power of rap music and hip-hop culture becomes clear.

Finding a way to combine feminism and hip-hop in politically meaningful ways is one of the premier goals of hip-hop feminism. [. . .] Joan Morgan notes, "I needed a feminism that would allow us to continue loving ourselves and the brothers who hurt us without letting race loyalty buy us early tombstones."[3] I would add that we also need a feminism that would encourage a self-love that would prohibit the internalization of negative self-images—the kinds of self-images that are fed by rampant materialism and usually end in prison jumpsuits. We are losing a whole generation of young women of color; feminism has to at least attempt to address that problem. I see the salvation of young women of color as one of the crucial goals for hip-hop feminism. Giving them the tools they need to critique, and indeed to survive, the negative images is the only way that the ladies can truly run this—*this* being our very lives. Otherwise, the messages will run and ruin us.

3. Joan Morgan, *When Chickenheads Come Home to Roost: My Life as a Hip-Hop Feminist* (New York: Simon & Schuster, 1999), 36.

ALANA SUSKIN, *HEARING THE DAUGHTER VOICE: THE "BAT KOL" AS RRRABBI GRRRL*

I.

I doubt that as I was growing up, I would have considered myself religious. My family went to synagogue for holidays and on Friday nights, but I certainly did not think much about God. At the same time, I always knew that I was Jewish. I have always been proud to be Jewish, even among people who informed me that it was a shame that I was going to hell because, other than being a Jew, I seemed like an all right person. [. . .]

II.

Oddly enough, it was my work in women's studies that made me rethink Judaism. While completing my master's degree, I had decided that I would work toward the graduate

SOURCE: Alana Suskin, "Hearing the Daughter Voice: The *Bat Kol* as Rrrabbi Grrrl," in *Catching a Wave: Reclaiming Feminism for the 21st Century*, ed. Rory Dicker and Alison Piepmeier (Lebanon, NH: University Press of New England), 263, 265–67, 268–71, 277–78.

certificate offered by the women's studies department. Although many faculty members in the department were Jewish by birth, I found that many were often subtly hostile to Judaism, particularly traditional Judaism, while being open to diversity among other groups. Sometimes the hostility existed even while these same faculty members were fighting anti-Semitism on the left and within women's movements. I once found myself arguing that departmental meetings shouldn't be scheduled on Friday nights, the night when our Sabbath begins. I once noted the number of conferences and meetings that were scheduled on Saturday—our Sabbath—or on Jewish holidays. I found myself defending even the possibility of being both a ritually observant Jew and a feminist. In one class, we read an article that argued that Judaism was so patriarchal that any observance of it beyond the most nominal level amounted to submitting to patriarchal values and rules. It was very frustrating to read article after article that only criticized Judaism. Some of these articles' authors were Jewish women who seemed to know very little about what they were criticizing. Others were Christian authors who used Judaism as a foil for Christianity's own misogyny, attempting to show that early Christianity was a feminist alternative to that shameful patriarchal Judaism, despite the fact that this perspective has little historical validity. I felt extremely peculiar: I couldn't defend a religion that I really knew very little about.

I did not even know why I felt the need to defend a religion in which I participated very little. As I grew older, I had certainly come to see that Judaism, or at least practicing Jews, were not perfect. Yet, reading feminist essays that said that Jewish women should throw out Judaism as it was and start over left a sour taste in my mouth. If that was the only solution, why bother calling it Judaism at all? If Judaism was unsalvageable, why do so many of us who are feminist and Jewish want to keep something called Judaism around? I found myself defending Judaism, trying to show a truly feminist side to Judaism that was and always had been a part of the Jewish religious tradition.

This is how I became involved in Jewish women's studies. Every time a secular Jewish woman stated that we needed to reject men's traditions and start our own totally unrelated religion—but still call it Judaism—I thought to myself, what do we know about these traditions? Why do we assume that they are all men's traditions? And how could we simply invent new laws and just throw out the old ones? How could that be Jewish? Where is God in that? So I did what Jews have always done: I studied.

In studying Judaism, I became disappointed and pleased. Within my tradition was a strain of liberation theology, but in many places another strain that rejected modernity had turned a radical tradition into one that was so afraid of its own destruction by assimilation that it had rejected all that was radical within it.

Women's studies gave me the tools to evaluate the strengths and weaknesses of Judaism. I was not alone in this pursuit: since the mid-1980s, a growing number of Jewish feminists have begun to evaluate our traditions. Feminism has grown to a point where it is able to examine itself and its own prejudices. This has made room for more women and more feminisms.

Jewish women's studies, like womanism (African American feminism) and Xican-isma (Chicana feminism), has become a movement in itself. However, because many second wave feminists equate Jews with "white and middle-class," they have not attempted to differentiate Jewish feminism from the broader category of feminism in general. This is a mistake, for within Judaism there are many ethnic groups: Jews of color from Africa and the Middle East, as well as other Jews of color, all of whom have their own critiques of secular culture as well as the Ashkenazi-centric Jewish world. Moreover, even the Ashkenazi—Eastern European Jews—are ethnically differentiated from the "white" culture around us.

It is true that Judaism is not only a religion but also a culture, and not just one, but many; at the same time, all Jews are a single people. These intertwined matrices of iden-tity make it difficult to tease out which feminist critiques of Judaism—even by Jewish women—fairly question women's treatment in Jewish religious life and which of these critiques are something else. Academic feminists, Jewish or not, still struggle with a society that makes women hate their bodies and people of color hate their skin and hair. Jewish women have been disproportionately represented in feminism in every wave, just as Jews are disproportionately represented in all social justice movements. However, despite our numbers, it is only recently that, like other ethnic feminists, Jewish women have begun to see that feminists have not yet weeded out all of their own prejudices against those who are nonwhite and non-middle-class.

Feminist prejudices against religious Jews are part of that struggle. One of the best classes that I ever took examined colonialism and race; the course also introduced me to the work of Karen Brodkin, who talks about the shifting racial identities of Jews (whether we are considered white or not depends upon a variety of factors).[1] Her work points toward other Jewish women's analyses of the rejection of Jewish identity. Evelyn Torton Beck, for instance, analyzes both the misogyny and racism or anti-Semitism of the JAP-bashing that was common in the 1990s (JAP refers to "Jewish American Princess").[2] Inherent in the rejection of our identities as Jewish women are the poisonous attitudes that Jewish women have come to accept about ourselves. When we reject Judaism, we are also rejecting a nonwhite immigrant identity in which we are seen and see ourselves as "too Jewish." Caricatures of Jewish women—as people with hair that is too curly, noses too big, bodies too round, voices too loud (both literally and figuratively), breasts too big, and sometimes skin, hair, and eyes too dark—are also part of these "critiques" of Juda-ism. Such "critiques" are unfair; they are not really critiques, but rather prejudice beneath the surface. The struggle to be secular is not necessarily different from any other kind of hair straightening or nose bobbing. [. . .]

1. Karen Brodkin, *How Jews Became White Folks and What That Shows about Race in America* (New Bruns-wick, NJ: Rutgers University Press, 1998). I was introduced to Brodkin's work through her article "How Jews Became White Folks," in *Race*, ed. Steven Gregory and Roger Sanjek (New Brunswick, NJ: Rutgers University Press, 1994), which became the first chapter of her book.

2. Evelyn Torton Beck, ed., *Nice Jewish Girls: A Lesbian Anthology*, rev. ed. (Boston: Beacon Press, 1989).

When I began to learn about my tradition, I found it a daily struggle. It became very difficult to read that historically only men determined the law in those texts, with little or no input from women, thus ignoring the realities of women's daily lives. Sometimes the rabbis would make pronouncements about women's biology that were patently ridiculous; a simple question put to a woman might have provided them with a more accurate answer. However, these men were sitting in male spaces that were "uncontaminated" by women. Their study spaces were sacred and exclusive, a boys' club. Apparently, to ask a woman a question about her body would have been too unseemly. Yet, here and there, one does encounter the individual rabbi who says he must discuss with his wife before taking a position, or a rabbi who rules that a certain law is harmful to women or who takes it upon himself to ask a woman about something on which she is the expert.

Today these texts are records of the divine voice: religious Jews must take them into account. However, as a woman who will be a rabbi, I have the opportunity to take dissenting voices and make them my own, to take minority opinions and show why they are the correct interpretation of law, to make my voice, a woman's voice, a part of that recorded struggle to hear God's voice.

But this is not enough. Our tradition asks us if it is better to study or to do. The answer is that to study is better, when it leads to action. The Jewish world has in many places become alienated from its tradition of textual study. Even in those places where text study (generally conducted primarily among men) is still central to the community, action has somehow slipped away. American life is safe, open, and full of opportunities that have been denied to Jews historically, and in many places still are. In this atmosphere, many observant Jews have forgotten that the point of all those laws is to repair the flaws of the world, to teach us what justice is, to remind us that, in everything we do, our hands should be God's hands. Somehow, the measure of observance has become limited to certain kinds of ritual behavior such as keeping kosher or not driving on the Sabbath. It does not occur to many Jews that preventing women from participating in the public forms of religious life might violate the laws we keep. It is ordained that one must give to the poor, and so we do, because that is justice (indeed, the Hebrew word for giving to the poor means "justice"). I have heard many men say that it disturbs them that women are not counted in all public prayer quorums, but they continue to take honors and go up to lead prayer in places where this is true, rather than try to change the status quo there.

The role of the rabbi in the world needs to become more activist. The rabbi who ensured that our tradition would continue after the Temple in Jerusalem was destroyed knew that the world had been turned upon its head and things would have to change. He made sure that they did, without destroying the tradition itself; we as rabbis have to do this again. The world has changed and is still changing. No longer do constant pregnancies and births prevent women from participating in the public arena. Although being excused from public prayer may have initially relieved women of a responsibility they did not have time for, this exclusion now has become an excuse to bar us from the community. No longer should women alone bear the burdens and joys of childrearing and care. In legislating participation by both sexes in both roles, we ensure a world that is truer to God's vision of justice.

Jews need feminism because without feminism, Judaism ceases to be true to itself. Judaism has always been a religion that resisted the degrading paradigms of the dominant culture. When Palestine was ruled by Rome, the Romans valued the male body as the epitome of all that was sacred. Like today's American culture, the Roman culture was a gymnasium culture, one that viewed human perfection as the perfection of the body, and a very narrow perfection at that. The rabbis rebelled then and said that male sexuality must be reined in and set to God's service. The Romans saw the rebellion of the Jews, our insistence on circumcision for male children and the study of Torah, as defying their belief that Roman culture was the only true civilization. The way of those rabbis was to resist the dominant ideology of power. Today, Judaism is true to its rabbinic roots when we—Jewish women as well as men—are a countercultural force.

Feminism is today the basis of resistance to the dominant paradigm. Feminism is now the method by which we are able to analyze that dominant culture and reject what are accepted universally as truths simply because these truths have been indoctrinated into us since we were born. Judaism has those methods of resistance still embedded in its laws, its hermeneutics, and its traditions, but we need feminism to reawaken us to them. Feminism is what will remind Jews of the traditional flexibility of our method of interpretation of Jewish law and of the radical nature of our resistance to the status quo.

Today, the world needs rabbis who have adopted feminist methods, an ideology of activism that hears the reality of injustice and addresses it, without depending upon "it's always been that way" as satisfactory and sufficient. Feminism made me someone who went out and interacted with actual people, someone who worked in the community to change the world, and not just someone who thought about what was wrong with it without even attempting to conceive of a solution. Truth is important, but it's only a beginning. Feminism taught me that to do God's will means to listen to people's pain, but then to take action to change society so that people do not have to adjust to injustice. To do God's will means to work to see justice ring out across the land. [. . .]

My goal as a rabbi is to make the community hear the voice of the disenfranchised. This is what makes me a feminist: the knowledge that God is present in every voice, and so every voice must have the chance to speak. I am not the first female rabbi; hundreds have gone before me. Similarly, I'm part of the third wave—not the first or second—of American feminists; there has been much feminist movement long before I came along. The struggle still continues. The Haggada, the text Jews read at Passover, says, "In every generation it is obligatory for each person to see themselves as if they themselves had been redeemed from slavery in Egypt." As a feminist, I can add that in each and every generation of feminism, we are all obligated to see ourselves as undertaking the redemption of humanity from inequality. Women, the stranger, the minority, and the poor—

none has reached equality. The powerful of humanity still greedily grab all the resources they can and make war, literal or metaphoric, to keep "what is theirs."

There is no doubt that traditional Judaism is now well on its way to including women; what has yet to be discussed at any length are the repercussions for the community as a whole and the fact that men's visions of faith must also be transformed by feminism. What Judaism looks like to outsiders is often the result of the struggle within our community both to change and to resist change. The struggle within Judaism is one mirrored by the wider world, whether within other religious traditions, or politics, or even feminism itself. In the Talmud, there is occasionally a voice that speaks from the heavens, to make known God's will, and it is called the *bat kol*—that is, "the daughter voice." It is time that Her voice is heard.

JENNIFER BAUMGARDNER AND AMY RICHARDS, *THIRD WAVE MANIFESTA: A THIRTEEN-POINT AGENDA*

1. To out unacknowledged feminists, specifically those who are younger, so that Generation X can become a visible movement and, further, a voting block of eighteen- to forty-year-olds.

2. To safeguard a woman's right to bear or not to bear a child, regardless of circumstances, including women who are younger than eighteen or impoverished. To preserve this right throughout her life and support the choice to be childless.

3. To make explicit that the fight for reproductive rights must include birth control; the right for poor women and lesbians to have children; partner adoption for gay couples; subsidized fertility treatments for all women who choose them; and freedom from sterilization abuse. Furthermore, to support the idea that sex can be—and usually is—for pleasure, not procreation.

4. To bring down the double standard in sex and sexual health, and foster male responsibility and assertiveness in the following areas: achieving freedom from STDs; more fairly dividing the burden of family planning as well as responsibilities such as child care; and eliminating violence against women.

5. To tap into and raise awareness of our revolutionary history, and the fact that almost all movements began as youth movements. To have access to our intellectual feminist legacy and women's history; for the classics of radical feminism, womanism, *mujeristas*, women's liberation, and all our roots to remain in print; and to have women's history taught to men as well as women as a part of all curricula.

6. To support and increase the visibility and power of lesbians and bisexual women in the feminist movement, in high schools, colleges, and the workplace. To recognize

SOURCE: Jennifer Baumgardner and Amy Richards, "Third Wave Manifesta: A Thirteen-Point Agenda" in *Manifesta: Young Women, Feminism, and the Future*, ed. Jennifer Baumgardner and Amy Richards (New York: Farrar, Straus and Giroux, 2000), 278–80.

that queer women have always been at the forefront of the feminist movement, and that there is nothing to be gained—and much to be lost—by downplaying their history, whether inadvertently or actively.

7. To practice "autokeonony" ("self in community"): to see activism not as a choice between self and community but as a link between them that creates balance.

8. To have equal access to health care, regardless of income, which includes coverage equivalent to men's and keeping in mind that women use the system more often than men do because of our reproductive capacity.

9. For women who so desire to participate in all reaches of the military, including combat, and to enjoy all the benefits (loans, health care, pensions) offered to its members for as long as we continue to have an active military. The largest expenditure of our national budget goes toward maintaining this welfare system, and feminists have a duty to make sure women have access to every echelon.

10. To liberate adolescents from slut-bashing, listless educators, sexual harassment, and bullying at school, as well as violence in all walks of life, and the silence that hangs over adolescents' heads, often keeping them isolated, lonely, and indifferent to the world.

11. To make the workplace responsive to an individual's wants, needs, and talents. This includes valuing (monetarily) stay-at-home parents, aiding employees who want to spend more time with family and continue to work, equalizing pay for jobs of comparable worth, enacting a minimum wage that would bring a full-time worker with two children over the poverty line, and providing employee benefits for freelance and part-time workers.

12. To acknowledge that, although feminists may have disparate values, we share the same goal of equality, and of supporting one another in our efforts to gain the power to make our own choices.

13. To pass the Equal Rights Amendment so that we can have a constitutional foundation of righteousness and equality upon which future women's rights conventions will stand.

27

CAPTURED IN TRANSLATION
Africa and Feminisms in the Age of Globalization

Obioma Nnaemeka

"Women are the Blacks of the human race." Can they tell us then what or who are
Black Women? The Blacks of the Blacks of the human race?"

AWA THIAM

Colonialism, development, and even current so-called globalization—all processes of
unequal power relations—focus more on the material and less on the human. Colonialism's focus on natural resources, institutions, and frameworks is matched by development's focus on economics, institutions, and processes. The same goes for "the world in
motion" of this age of globalization, in which resources, capital, and skills are more "in
motion" than certain categories of humans—mostly poor, unskilled, people of color from
the so-called third world, whose movements are, by design, regulated and managed by
the immigration policies of many Western nations. The humanity that is at best mini-
mized and at worst ignored in the discourse and practice of globalization in general takes
center stage in discourses and practices that I see evolving in Africa.

Globalization discourses' tendency to totalize and dwell on abstractions—flows, time-
space compression, the world in motion, et cetera—creates the picture of this monolith
called the world moving. But we are not told what specifically this world consists of. What
is moving? Who is moving? When is the movement? By what means is the movement
enacted? What is the cost of the movement? The disaggregation of the actors and stake-
holders in this motion or flows will produce a more useful and accurate reading of the
phenomenon we call globalization. It will be instructive to know why the human movement from Cape Verde and Edo State in Nigeria to Italy is feminized or why the Filipino
migration to some Gulf States is almost exclusively female. It is not sufficient to talk
about abstractions, such as flows and time-space compression in these instances; it is
necessary to account for the feminization of the flows. In short, we cannot account fully

for the phenomenon we have come to know as globalization by navigating in and out of abstractions and homogeneity. We can come to terms with globalization's complexity, impact, and implications only when we put a human face on the phenomenon. It is only in this context that we can adequately interrogate and account for the myriad of issues this phenomenon brings in its wake—human rights, health, poverty, migration, environment, et cetera.

Alison Jaggar poses an important question: "Is Globalization Good for Women?" and answers by claiming that it is not good for most women. She argues that

> neoliberal globalization, despite its glowing promises . . . [has created a world that] is characterized by a rapidly widening gulf between rich and poor, both within and among nations. To the extent that global neoliberalism undermines women's special interests in peace, prosperity, democracy, environmental health, and the abolition of racism and ethnocentrism, it is a system hostile or antagonistic to women. Although neoliberal globalization is making the lives of many women better, it is making the lives of even more women worse. (Jaggar 301)

What is certain is that globalization has exacerbated old global inequalities and created new ones.

Globalization brings in its wake all sorts of anxieties inside and outside the academy. The academy is faced with disciplinary anxieties. "By providing a complex picture of the relationship between globalization from above (as defined by corporations, major multilateral agencies, policy experts, and national governments) and below (grassroots, civil society), collaborative research on globalization could contribute to new forms of pedagogy that could level the theoretical playing field for grassroots activists in international fora" (Appadurai 17). My work with nongovernmental organizations (NGOs) and civil society, particularly in the so-called third world and my collaboration worldwide with transnational advocacy networks (TANs) has informed and radically transformed my scholarship and made it possible for me to see globalization from a different angle— from below. It is from this angle, this different location, that one can delineate sub-Saharan African women's engagement with feminism and take the next step to pose a probing question: Is feminism translatable? Transnational feminist work unfolds at borders; transnational feminist workers are border-crossers par excellence. What one gains at the border is transformative understanding.

Mapping the trajectory of feminist engagement, in theory and practice, in the past half century is a study in contrasts, relatedness, and shifting boundaries—autonomy and connectedness, exclusion and the demand for inclusion, conflict and collaboration, border-crossing and intersectionality, and, more important, the expansion of horizons. In seeking to remake the world by demanding an end to all forms of gender-based discrimination, feminism, as ideology and struggle, has taken location-specific and culturally defined forms across time and space. As both a movement and an intellectual tradition, Western feminism has in the last five decades contended with challenges from within (disagreements among Western feminists based on difference) and without (challenges by non-Western women) and along the way engaged in the self-interrogation and redefinition that has given it its current breath, depth, relevance, and salience. Many have suggested that to account fully for the many faces of feminism—theories, methodologies, and practices—the plural form of the word, feminisms, is more appropriate and encompassing.

The location of African women (as knowledge producers and as subjects of / objects for knowledge production) in feminist epistemological quarrels is both specific and complex. African women's critique of feminist theories goes beyond the issues of relevance, adequacy, and appropriateness to include crucial questions about representation and task-allocation/sharing. The challenges from minority voices in feminist theorizing and practice—from the insurgency of women of color in the 1970s and the opposition from third world women in the 1980s to the intervention of African women in the 1990s—have compelled feminism to expand its horizons. Through their writings and practices, feminists of African descent have intervened to redefine feminism and extend its boundaries. Similar to Black feminism, the "womanist idea strikes at the heart of some of the basic issues in feminism. . . . The question of encountering the Other underlines womanist intervention in feminist politics" (Allan 119–21). In many ways, African feminisms respond to Zillah Eisenstein's probing questions: "What are the other-than-western cores of feminism? Is there a polyversal core—a universal idea with local expressions—to feminisms across the globe?" (Eisenstein).

Arguing against the notion that the West owns feminism, Zillah Eisenstein affirms that "feminism belongs to anyone who has fought for or died in the struggle to improve the lot of women. As such, no one simply owns its meaning" (Eisenstein). Throughout African history, women have played leadership roles in society and participated in liberation struggles and movements for social change. Most women who have mobilized against women's oppression in Africa—from Algeria, Egypt, and Nigeria to Kenya, Zimbabwe, and South Africa—did not claim the feminist label and they did not have to; the majority of them did not speak English and could not have pinned an English word on their struggle. The feminist spirit pervades Africa and is folded into all sorts of struggles, from liberation movements to gender-specific insurgencies. Not surprisingly, some African women who came to the United States to study in the 1970s and 1980s were attracted to the feminist agenda that was consolidating at that time, particularly the new path that had been opened by the theorizing and practice of women of color and third world women. Facing marginalization in the Women's Movement and backlash from their own patriarchal societies for disloyalty and selling-out, African feminists searched for appropriate responses. They combined challenges to the imperialism and maternalism of Western feminists (white and of color) with a critique of the gender-based discrimination that runs deep in their own societies.

In the 1990s, debates about female circumcision galvanized African feminists against the ethnocentrism and imperial arrogance of Western feminists. As I noted elsewhere, "the polemic at the heart of the debates about female circumcision revolved around the questions of rights, culture, and civilization—individual versus communal rights, cultural relativism versus universalism, and barbarism versus civilization" (Nnaemeka, *Colonial Discourses* 28). Unfortunately, in these debates, the "West is arguing with itself for/against women used as tools to affirm and perpetuate a long history of political, imperialist, and racist positions anchored in moralizing (but morally bankrupt) feelings of superiority" (Nnaemeka, *Challenges* 8). African feminists neither supported female circumcision nor objected to women from other parts of the world participating in their struggles. African feminists have, through their scholarly writing and publishing, fieldwork, and collaboration with nongovernmental organizations, registered their opposition to the practice and worked vigorously to end it.

Seeking culturally defined tools for the analysis of African women's experiences, African feminists have proposed various frameworks that are rooted in local realities. I have proposed "negofeminism" as a definitional tool and analytical framework for understanding African women's experiences. But what is negofeminism? Negofeminism, which stands both for feminism of negotiation and for "no ego" feminism, is grounded in African cultural reality. The diversity of the African continent notwithstanding, there are shared values that can be used as organizing principles in formulating a feminist framework that is location-specific and relevant. In the foundation of shared values in many African cultures are the principles of negotiation, give and take, compromise, and balance. Here, negotiation has double meanings: it means both to give and take or exchange, and to cope with successfully or go around.

African feminism (or feminism as I have seen it practiced in Africa) challenges through negotiations and compromise. It knows when, where, and how to confront patriarchal challenges; it also knows when, where, and how to go around patriarchal obstacles. In other words, it knows when, where, and how to negotiate with or negotiate around patriarchy in different contexts. Furthermore, negofeminism is structured by cultural imperatives and modulated by ever shifting local and global exigencies. For example, the theology of nearness in the Igbo worldview (*ife kwulu, ife akwudebie,* or "when something stands, something else stands beside it") is grounded in the indigenous and shapes feminism in Africa as a performance and an altruistic act.

The negotiations that are made at the level of gender and language are rooted in the indigenous as well: "African patterns of feminism can be seen as having developed within a context that views human life from a total, rather than a dichotomous and exclusive, perspective. For women, the male is not 'the other' but part of the human same. Each gender constitutes the critical half that makes the human whole. Neither sex is totally complete in itself. Each has and needs a complement, despite the possession of unique features of its own" (Steady 8).

African women's willingness and readiness to negotiate with and around men and patriarchal structures even in difficult circumstances is quite pervasive. As the Cameroonian writer Calixthe Beyala puts it at the beginning of her 1995 book *Lettre d'une Africaine à ses soeurs occidentales, "Soyons clairs: tous les hommes ne sont pas des salauds"* (Let's face it, all men are not bastards) (7). Another example is also by a Francophone African woman writer, Mariama Bâ of Senegal, who dedicated her fine novel, *Une si longue lettre* (1980), to many constituencies including *"aux hommes de bonne volonté"* (men of goodwill). By not casting a pall over men as a monolith, African women are more inclined to reach out and work with men in achieving set goals. Sexual politics were huge in Western feminism about two decades ago, but it would be inaccurate to suggest that those politics no longer exist. In my view, Western feminism has turned down the volume on sexual politics, but the residues are still a driving force. The resistance in institutions across the United States against changing women's studies programs to gender studies programs is rooted principally in the argument that women's issues will be relegated to the back burner in a gender studies program. I don't see a similar argument flourishing in Africa.

Like bell hooks, African women believe that sisterhood amongst women from different races and backgrounds is possible but must be interrogated not assumed. The flowering of true sisterhood rooted in mutual respect requires a great deal of sustained hard work. Culturally, for African women, group identification is based less on gender and more on their location in the patriarchal structure—mothers, daughters, wives—that is, categories that are linked to males. In effect, feminism without men is a challenge at least and an impossibility in the extreme in such an environment. Women's communities and alliances coalesce around female statuses and social and cultural locations but women's allegiances go beyond these alliances; they cross gender boundaries.

Convinced that feminism is translatable, and cognizant of the specificity of their own cultural and social locations, African feminist scholars in the West and on the continent burst on the feminist theorizing scene in the 1990s. Rejecting the notion of a monolithic feminism, African feminists insist on engaging and fully accounting for the plurality of feminisms unfolding on the continent. They argue that it is not sufficient to denounce the construction of African women in Western feminist discourses; it is imperative to develop culturally specific and relevant analytical tools and frameworks for examining the experiences of African women. As I have argued elsewhere, the feminist spirit pervades the African continent although it distinguishes itself from Western feminism by marking specific areas of disagreement and resistance—"radical feminism, motherhood, language, sexuality, priorities, (gender) separatism, and universalism" (Nnaemeka, *Sisterhood* 6). Unlike radical feminism, African feminism does not subscribe to the argument that social transformation can only occur when the existing social structure is uprooted and replaced with a new one. Closer to liberal feminism in its argument, African feminism affirms that the social structure can be salvaged through modifications. In its insurgency, African feminism speaks the language of negotiation and compromise. Additionally, African feminism challenges Western feminism's universalization of Western notions and values.

Susan Arndt's insightful work examines how ethnic, cultural, social, economic, political, and religious diversity on the African continent produces diverse feminisms (Arndt 2002). Many African feminists have proposed different concepts for grasping the complexities of African feminisms. Chikwenye Okonjo Ogunyemi developed her concept of *womanism* independently of Alice Walker and prior to Walker's 1983 publication (see Hopson's essay in chapter 14) although Ogunyemi's article in which the concept was elaborated did not appear until 1985. Ogunyemi argues that womanism differs from feminism because it views patriarchy differently and has its own specific concerns: a womanist "will recognize that, along with her consciousness of sexual issues, she must incorporate racial, cultural, national, economic, and political considerations into her philosophy" (Ogunyemi, "Womanism" 64). In her book published a decade later, Ogunyemi distinguishes her brand of womanism (African womanism) not only from white Western feminism but also from African American womanism: "since feminism and African American womanism overlook African peculiarities, there is a need to define African womanism . . . . It is necessary to reiterate that the womanist praxis in Africa has never totally identified with all the original Walkerian concepts" (Ogunyemi, *Africa Wo/Man* 114, 133). Mary Kolawale, another African feminist scholar drawn to the womanist concept, argues that "any African woman who has the consciousness to situate the struggle within the African cultural realities by working for a total and robust self-retrieval of the African woman is an African or Africana womanist" (Kolawale 34). Like Ogunyemi, Kolawale grounds her concept of womanism in local realities but unlike Ogunyemi, she claims affinity with African American womanism.

Molara Ogundipe-Leslie proposes another concept, *stiwanism*, from STIWA (Social Transformation Including Women in Africa), that insists on the prominent role of gender issues in social engineering: "This new term 'STIWA' allows me to discuss the needs of African women today in the tradition of the spaces and strategies provided in our indigenous cultures for the social being of women . . . 'STIWA' is about the inclusion of African women in the contemporary social and political transformation of Africa" (Ogundipe-Leslie 229–30). Catherine Acholonu's *motherism* centers motherhood and maternal politics. By linking motherhood, nurture, and nature, Acholonu's concept reveals its ecofeminist concerns: "[Motherism] is concerned about the menace of wars around the globe, racism, malnutrition, political and economic exploitation, hunger and starvation . . . the degradation of the environment and the depletion of the ozone layer through pollution" (Acholonu 111).

As indicated earlier, I propose *negofeminism* as a definitional tool and analytical framework for understanding African women's experiences (Nnsemeka, *Sisterhood; Nego-feminism*). Negofeminism in Africa is living those legacies in theory, practice, and policy matters. African women's engagement still nurtures the compromise and hopefulness needed to build a harmonious society. As far as theory goes, Barbara Christian, in "The Race for Theory," rightly noted that people of color theorize differently. But can feminist theory create the space for the unfolding of "different" theorizing not as an isolated engagement outside feminist theory but as a force that can have a defamiliarizing power on feminist theory? In other words, seeing feminist theorizing through the eyes of the "other," from the "other" place, through the "other" worldview has the capacity to defamiliarize feminist theory as we know it and assist it not only in interrogating, understanding, and explaining the unfamiliar but also in refamiliarizing the familiar in more productive and enriching ways. Thus, the focus will not be on what feminist theory can do in terms of explicating other lives and other places but on how feminist theory is and could be constructed. In this instance, Westerners are led across borders so that they can cross back enriched and defamiliarized and ready to see the familiar anew. How do we deal with the theorizing emanating from other epistemological centers in the so-called third world? How do we come to terms with the multiplicity of centers bound by coherence and decipherment and not disrupted perpetually by endless differences?

Although African feminist scholars name their analytical frameworks differently and have different takes on what constitutes African feminism, they all agree that the tools for theorizing and analyzing African feminism must be grounded in local realities. Through their contributions, African feminists urge Western feminist scholarship to rethink its exclusionary practices and expand its horizon by making room for feminisms from elsewhere. It is by accommodating "other" feminisms that feminism can survive and grow in a truly polyversal form: "Feminism has suffered from this overdrawn divide palpably. It has been wrongly homogenized as a unity, and then defined as of the west. This negates multiple forms of feminisms in the west AND the multiple forms of feminisms outside the west. As such feminisms lose their plurality of meanings which also express the similarities among women. A polyversal feminism—multiple and connected—expresses women's potential humanity which does not recognize irreconcilable divides" (Eisenstein).

WORKS CITED

Acholonu, Catherine O. *Motherism: The Afrocentric Alternative to Feminism.* Owerri: Afa Publications, 1995.

Allan, Tuzyline Jita. *Womanist and Feminist Aesthetics: A Comparative Review.* Athens: Ohio University Press, 1995.

Appadurai, Arjun. "Grassroots Globalization and the Research Imagination." *Public Culture* 12, no. 1 (2000): 1–19.

Arndt, Susan. *The Dynamics of African Feminism: Defining and Classifying African Feminist Literatures.* Trenton: African World Press, 2002.

Bâ, Mariama. *Une si longue lettre.* Dakar: Les Nouvelles Editions Africaines, 1979.

Beyala, Calixthe. *Lettre d'une Africaine à ses soeurs occidentales.* Paris: Spengler, 1995.

Christian, Barbara. "The Race for Theory." *Cultural Critique* 6 (1987): 51–63.

Eisenstein, Zillah. *Against Empire: Feminisms, Racism, and the West.* London: Zed Books, 2004.

hooks, bell. "Sisterhood: Political Solidarity between Women." In *Feminism and Community,* 293–316. Edited by Penny A. Wise and Marilyn Friedman. Philadelphia: Temple University Press, 1995.

Jaggar, Alison M. "Is Globalization Good for Women?" *Comparative Literature* 53, no. 4 (2001): 298–314.

Kolawale, Mary Modupe. *Womanism and African Consciousness*. Trenton: Africa World Press, 1997.

Morgan, Robin, ed. *Sisterhood Is Global: The International Women's Movement Anthology*. Garden City: Anchor Press/Doubleday, 1984.

———, ed. *Sisterhood Is Powerful: An Anthology of Writings from the Women's Liberation Movement*. New York: Random House, 1970.

Nnaemeka, Obioma. "African Women, Colonial Discourses, and Imperialist Interventions: Female Circumcision as Impetus." In *Female Circumcision and the Politics of Knowledge*, 27–45. Edited by Obioma Nnaemeka. Westport: Praeger, 2005.

———. "The Challenges of Border-Crossing: African Women and Transnational Feminisms." In *Female Circumcision and the Politics of Knowledge: African Women in Imperialist Discourses*, 3–18. Edited by Obioma Nnaemeka. Westport: Praeger, 2005.

———. "Mapping African Feminisms." In *Readings in Gender in Africa*, 31–41.. Edited by Andrea Cornwall. Bloomington: Indiana University Press, 2005.

———. "Nego-feminism: Theorizing, Practicing, and Pruning Africa's Way." *Signs: Journal of Women in Culture and Society* 29, no. 2 (2004): 357–86.

———, ed. *Sisterhood, Feminisms, and Power: From Africa to the Diaspora*. Trenton: Africa World Press, 1998.

Ogundipe-Leslie, Molara. *Re-Creating Ourselves: African Women and Critical Transformations*. Trenton: Africa World Press, 1994.

Ogunyemi, Chikwenye Okonjo. "Womanism: The Dynamics of the Contemporary Black Female Novel in English." *Signs* 11 (1985/86): 63–80.

———. *Africa Wo/Man: The Nigerian Novel by Women*. Chicago: University of Chicago Press, 1996.

Steady, F. C. "African Feminism: A Worldwide Perspective." In *Women in Africa and the African Diaspora*, 3–24. Edited by Rosalyn Terborg-Penn, Sharon Harley, and Andrea Benton. Washington, D.C.: Howard University Press, 1987.

Thiam, Awa. *Black Sisters Speak Out: Feminism and Oppression in Black Africa*. London: Pluto Press, 1986.

DISCUSSION QUESTIONS

1. What are some of the criticisms African women have had of Western feminist theories?

2. In what ways is the concept of "negofeminism" grounded in African realities? How is it different from Western feminism?

3. Nnaemeka suggests that because there are several different ways of being feminist, it is more appropriate to speak of "feminisms." Do you agree or disagree? Why?

28

GENDERING THE ARAB SPRING

Nadje Al-Ali

It has almost been impossible over the last few months to keep up with political developments in the Middle East: small-scale demonstrations, and mass protests; revolutionary
processes that not only involve the political sphere but that have also touched the social
fabric; the ousting of several dictators; the brutal crackdown and killing of peaceful protesters; armed struggles, NATO involvement and wider debates about international
intervention; not to mention various forms of counterrevolutionary backlash and the
struggles of old regimes to hold on to power.

In the initial phase of these rapid changes and developments, I was frequently asked:
"Where are the women?" The first images we saw of protests in Tunisia and Egypt were
largely of men. Later on the images and the coverage of the protests changed and it
became clear that women were involved at all levels. Individual women were given particular media attention: in Egypt, Asma Mahfouz became known by many as the "leader
of the revolution" after posting an online video calling young people to demonstrate en
masse, helping to spark the protests that forced President Hosni Mubarak's resignation.
In Bahrain, political activist Munira Fakhro played a leading role as an organizer and
spokesperson for the Pearl Square demonstrations, demanding government reform and
building a movement that was "not Sunni, not Shia, but Bahraini." In Yemen, human

SOURCE: This contribution is based on and developed from Nadje Al-Ali's inaugural lecture entitled "On Not
Travelling Lightly: Transnational Feminist Journeys to and from the Middle East," May 18, 2011, School of Oriental and African Studies, University of London. A version of it was published in *Middle East Journal of Culture
and Communication* 5, no. 1 (2012): 26–31.

rights activist and journalist Tawakul Karman has protested nonviolently outside Sanaa University every Tuesday since May 2007, demanding that President Ali Abdullah Saleh step down from power.

Yet it was not just individual women—women participated side by side with men in the protests across the region. In light of western media representations and widespread perceptions among the public in western countries that women in the region did not just appear on the scene in 2011, we should clarify: for decades they had been active members in trade unions, political opposition parties, and more informal networks and organizations that were all instrumental in the recent political developments. Women have been very much involved in the virtual communities of bloggers and Facebook users. And during the height of the actual protests to oust Ben Ali and Mubarak, women of all generations and social classes were on the streets in large numbers. Notably in places like Tahrir Square in Cairo, where men and women mingled for weeks in extremely crowded and volatile situations, many Egyptian women reported that they had never felt as safe and been treated as respectfully as during the time of these protests.

Without doubt, it has been easier for women to participate in politics in Egypt, where the protest movement had initially taken an explicitly nonviolent character—*silmiya*—and where there exists a long history of large-scale women's political participation. Indeed, in Egypt and also in Iran, which to my mind should not be left out in current discussions about people's power and resistance, women activists have been spearheading civic rights, democracy, and human rights movements in the context of their women's rights struggles. My own work on the Egyptian women's movement in the mid-1990s revealed that women's rights activists were engaged in contestations with the state about the shaping of gender policies as well as wider issues of citizenship and social justice. To varying degrees, Egyptian women have engaged for a long time in grassroots activism and have aspired to find nonhierarchical ways of organizing, thereby engaging in the process of democratization.

Yet, even in the more socially conservative countries like Yemen, Libya, Bahrain, and Syria—and they are all very different from each other—we find that women have increasingly pushed the boundaries of what is socially acceptable when joining the protests and making their own gender-specific demands, in addition to joining in the wider calls for reforms, democratization, an end to corruption, political transparency, and human rights.

It is not surprising that revolutionary processes should open up social and political spaces for women. History is full of comparable examples around the world. If we speak of the Middle East, the most commonly cited examples are the Egyptian anticolonial and independence movement at the turn of the twentieth century, which gave rise to the Egyptian women's movement, the Algerian war of independence in the time of French colonialism, and the Palestinian struggle against Israeli occupation.

Yet, history also teaches us that during political transitions, women are regularly marginalized and tend to lose many of the gains they might have acquired, or have been promised at the height of a revolutionary struggle. We see this development most clearly in the Egyptian context, where the institutionalization of the various aspects of the protest movement and political representation has not only been male-dominated but has also been controlled by the military. Here the issue is not only the lack or very limited representation of women in crucial transitional bodies, such as the constitutional review committee, but perhaps more significantly, we see women's rights being actively violated and women's and gender-based issues sidelined, occasionally even ridiculed, sometimes by women themselves.

Unfortunately all cross-cultural and historical evidence suggests that unless women explicitly insist on their gender-specific needs, rights, and problems, these will be sidelined, ignored, and swept under the carpet. I suggest that the failure to stress women's specific demands within the respective wider struggles is a strategic mistake and will lead to history repeating itself.

Ironically, but again not surprisingly, we can see that women and gender issues are taking center stage in the old regimes' attempts to hold on to power and privilege, and in the violent backlash and counterrevolutionary processes we have been witnessing recently. Egyptian women who participated in demonstrations during International Women's Day on 8 March 2011 were harassed and accused of taking away attention from the main issues. Some men who attacked the female protesters claimed that they were seeking to destroy Egypt and undermine family values and the sanctity of the family, by telling women to desert their husbands. In this instance it was obvious that the men surrounding them were divided into those who are threatened by a women's bloc making their own demands and thereby challenging the prevailing gender order, and those who stood in solidarity with them, recognizing that the women's demands were at the core of their own visions and ideas of a new Egypt.

The treatment of female protesters has taken very different forms from that of their male counterparts. Harassment and brutalization by the police, the *mukhabarat,* or secret police, and the army often have sexual connotations for women. Egyptian female protesters have been strip-searched; pictures have been taken while they were without clothes; they have been accused of prostitution and in some cases forced to undergo virginity testing. Yemeni president Ali Abdullah Saleh suggested in April 2011 that antigovernment protesters in the capital Sanaa were in violation of Islamic law because women were not allowed to mix with men. He engaged in smear campaigns on national TV implying that women in pro-change demonstrations were "loose."

The heart-wrenching case of Iman al-Obeidy, a Libyan woman from Benghazi who was raped by a group of military men loyal to Qaddafi, is a cruel reminder of the way rape is a commonly used weapon in warfare. Here rape is not only meant to violate and harm an individual woman, but is a way to humiliate and violate entire communities. What made this case so different from the many others that go unreported is that Iman al-Obeidy did not allow herself to be silenced by prevailing notions of shame and codes of honor. She went public, enabling the international media to widely circulate images of her anguish and terror. For me personally, most shocking in the scenes we saw broadcasted around the world were the Libyan women working in the hotel who tried to silence her, calling her a traitor and at some point throwing a coat over her face. Those images made crystal clear what we have known for many years but is still painful to watch and experience in practice: sisterhood is not global. It might not even be local. Women do not necessarily act in solidarity with each other, just because they are women.

In those places in which the protests or revolutionary developments have taken a largely militarized form, the gendered outcomes are from the outset problematic. The images of armed men fighting other armed men in Libya are a huge cause for concern. Documented cases of female African migrant workers being raped in Tripoli and elsewhere by anti-Qaddafi forces might be individual instances of gender-based violence and human rights violation; however, given the frequently close relationship between the glorification of militarized masculinities and the increase in gender-based violence, I am personally not very optimistic where gender relations in Libya are concerned.

The backlash against women in some current contexts also reminds us that women's reliance on the state to champion and support gender equality and social justice is problematic. It has already become obvious—and I have seen it most clearly in the context of postinvasion developments in Iraq—that politicians and governments in the region have been prone to compromise women's rights in order to shore up support among socially conservative constituencies. In Iraq, for example, the central as well as the Kurdish regional government have been sidelining gender-related issues in the context of negotiating political disputes, such as federalism, regulation of oil, and the status of Kirkuk.

Historically, regional women's rights activists have been challenged to not be co-opted by the largely secular authoritarian state's modernizing gender policies and forms of state feminism. When dealing with a dictatorship and a one-party system it is very difficult for women's rights activists to operate independently outside given state structures. Yet, in the past authoritarian regimes have implemented measures to increase gender equality and social justice, as long as these were perceived to be harmless to the regime and the status quo. We have seen this most conspicuously in Tunisia and Iraq, but also to a lesser extent in Egypt, where many women's rights activists collaborated with Suzanne Mubarak's National Union for Women. An exaggerated belief in the ability of the state and the main political party to promote women's rights might seriously diminish women activists' credibility and might limit their strategies and possible achievements in the long run.

Another cause of concern are Islamist constituencies whose gender politics are viewed with great anxiety by secular women and men across the region. At the height of the euphoria in the early phase of the Arab Spring, I often argued with Iranian friends whose own revolutionary experiences made them rather skeptical and worried about recent developments in the region. A few months later, there is no doubt that Islamist groups are not only the best organized in terms of political parties but also that they appear to be well placed to convince many people that they would provide a viable alternative to the previous secular authoritarian regimes. It is too early to assess their impact on the evolving situation, but it is already evident that we have to recognize the variations and range of Islamist groups and their differing gender ideologies and visions. Analytically, it is important to consider the specific historical and current contexts of individual Islamist parties and groups. Al-Nahda in Tunisia, for example, has, so far, gone out of its way to stress its commitment to women's rights, which marks it as very different from the Muslim Brotherhood in Egypt. But even the Brotherhood appears moderate and favorable in comparison to the Salafis, who increasingly claim their space on the political map in Egypt and elsewhere in the region.

Theoretically and politically, several issues emerge from these recent events: the centrality of women and gender when it comes to constructing and controlling communities, be they ethnic, religious, or political; the significance of the state in reproducing, maintaining, and challenging prevailing gender regimes, ideologies, discourses, and relations; the instrumentalization of women's bodies and sexualities in regulating and controlling citizens and members of communities; the prevalence of gender-based violence; the historically and cross-culturally predominant construction of women as second-class citizens; the relationship between militarization and a militarized masculinity that privileges authoritarianism and social hierarchies and tries to marginalize and control not only women but also men who by virtue of their class, ethnicity, religion, sexuality, or politics do not fit into the image of the normative "ideal man."

The various theoretical and political issues emerging in relation to recent processes and events in the Middle East illustrate what many of us have been narrating, documenting, and analyzing over the past decades but what often remains misunderstood: a gendered lens is not just about women, even though in some contexts that continues to be an important and necessary focus of inquiry, as women are still systematically absent from official accounts, analyses, and projected future scenarios. Yet zooming in on what happens to and is going on with femininities, masculinities, and sexualities; to gender norms, ideologies, and discourses as well as gender roles and relations and the various processes of gendering within all aspects of social, cultural, political, and economic lives tells us a great deal about the nature of and dynamics within the state, citizenship, civil society, the military, the economy, et cetera. When Cynthia Enloe famously and provocatively asked a few years ago whether gender might be the bigger picture, she was alluding to the way we can learn from a gendered lens about power, both the more oppressive top-down variety, but also the more subtle micro-politics of power; and the way we can learn about hierarchies and inequalities. A gendered lens also allows us to explore the various ways subjects are materially and discursively constituted and circumscribed, at both local and global levels.

DISCUSSION QUESTIONS

1. Although we may not see this reflected in Western media coverage, Arab women have engaged in multiple forms of activism for decades. According to

Al-Ali, what are some of the forms of activism in which Arab women have been involved? How are these forms similar to or different from the forms of activism that U.S. women have engaged in?

2. Al-Ali emphasizes the importance of insisting on gender-specific needs and rights during times of political transition. What gender-specific needs and rights do you think women in Egypt viewed as most important at the beginning of the Arab Spring?

3. Al-Ali discusses how both women and men, and women from different backgrounds, can come together to mobilize for change. She also provides examples to illustrate that sisterhood should not be assumed simply because of gender. What are some of the examples she provides? What are some examples from your own community of how women don't necessarily act in solidarity or support each other?

CONTRIBUTORS

JILL ABNEY is a doctoral candidate in history at the University of Kentucky. Winner of the John Snell Prize from the European History Section of the Southern Historical Association in 2010, she is working on a dissertation titled "Negotiating an Electorate: Class, Gender and the British Reform Acts."

NADJE AL-ALI is Professor in Gender Studies and Chair of the Centre for Gender Studies, at the School of Oriental and African Studies, University of London. Her main research interests revolve around gender theory; feminist activism; women and gender in the Middle East; transnational migration and diaspora mobilization; war, conflict, and reconstruction. Her publications include *What Kind of Liberation? Women and the Occupation of Iraq* (2009), *Iraqi Women: Untold Stories from 1948 to the Present* (2007), and *Secularism, Gender and the State in the Middle East* (2000) as well as numerous book chapters and journal articles.

M. CRISTINA ALCALDE is Associate Professor of Gender and Women's Studies at the University of Kentucky. Her research areas include Latin America, migration, gender, race, violence, and Latinos/as in the United States. Her publications include *The Woman in the Violence: Gender, Poverty, and Resistance in Peru* (2010) and the coedited *Visiones del Perú de académicos peruanos en Estados Unidos* (Visions of Peru of Peruvian Academics in the United States) (2008), as well as several book chapters and journal articles.

PAULA GUNN ALLEN was one of the foremost scholars of Native American literature. She was also a poet and novelist. She held positions at San Francisco State University, the University of New Mexico, Fort Lewis College in Durango, Colorado, the University of

California at Berkeley, and the University of California at Los Angeles. Her publications include *Studies in American Indian Literature: Critical Essays and Course Designs* (1983) and *The Sacred Hoop: Recovering the Feminine in American Indian Traditions* (1986). She passed away in 2008.

BERNADETTE BARTON is Professor of Sociology and Women's Studies at Morehead State University. She is the author of *Stripped: Inside the Lives of Exotic Dancers* (2006) and *Pray the Gay Away: The Extraordinary Lives of Bible Belt Gays* (2012). Barton writes and lectures on contemporary issues of gender, sexuality, religion, and the sex industry.

SRIMATI BASU is Associate Professor of Gender and Women's Studies and Anthropology at the University of Kentucky. Her teaching, research, and community work interests include legal anthropology, women in development, feminist jurisprudence, South Asia, feminist theory and methodology, work, property, and violence against women. Dr. Basu's research on Indian women and inheritance laws has been published in *She Comes to Take Her Rights: Indian Women, Property and Propriety* (1999) as well as numerous journal articles, and she is also the editor of the *Dowry and Inheritance* volume in the Kali for Women series *Issues in Indian Feminism*.

TAMARA BEAUBOEUF-LAFONTANT is Professor of Women's, Gender, and Sexuality Studies at DePauw University. She offers courses in women and education, girls' and women's lifespan development, and feminist inquiry. Her published work has examined teachers' negotiations of race and gender in their identities and pedagogy, and the racialized embodiment of standards of feminine goodness. The latter is most recently investigated in her book *Behind the Mask of the Strong Black Woman: Voice and the Embodiment of a Costly Performance* (2009).

MAYLEI BLACKWELL is Associate Professor of Chicana/o Studies and Women's Studies at University of California at Los Angeles. She is an interdisciplinary scholar, activist, oral historian, and author of *¡Chicana Power! Contested Histories of Feminism in the Chicano Movement*. Her research has two distinct, but interrelated trajectories that broadly analyze how women's social movements in the United States and Mexico are shaped by questions of difference and factors such as race, indigeneity, class, sexuality, or citizenship status and how these differences impact the possibilities and challenges of transnational organizing. Her most recent research with farmworker women and indigenous migrants seeks to better understand new forms of grassroots transnationalism.

SUSAN BORDO is the Otis A. Singletary Chair in the Humanities at the University of Kentucky. Her first book, *The Flight to Objectivity*, has become a classic of feminist philosophy. In 1993, increasingly aware of our culture's preoccupation with weight and body image, she published *Unbearable Weight: Feminism, Western Culture, and the Body*, a book that is still widely read and assigned in classes today. Other notable books include *The Male Body: A New Look at Men in Public and in Private* (1999) and *The Creation of Anne Boleyn: A New Look at England's Most Notorious Queen* (2013).

ASHLEY BOURGEOIS is a Ph.D. student in American literature at the University of Kentucky, where she also completed a graduate certificate in Gender and Women's Studies. She is currently at work on her dissertation project, entitled "Remnants of the New Left: Scenes of Liberation in Fiction and Film."

EMILY BURRILL is Associate Professor of Women's and Gender Studies at the University of North Carolina at Chapel Hill. Her research centers on twentieth-century francophone West Africa and histories of gender and power within colonial and postcolonial contexts. She is currently completing a book entitled *States of Marriage: Gender, Justice, and Rights in Colonial Mali*. Burrill is also engaged in a long-term collaborative and interdisciplinary study on the marital form in global context.

ANN M. CIASULLO is Associate Professor of English and Women's and Gender Studies at Gonzaga University. She has presented and published on a wide range of topics, including feminist pedagogy, representations of women's sexuality in popular culture, and the television series *Mad Men*. She is passionate about the history and influence of Second Wave feminism and is particularly interested in how the writings of the U.S. Women's Liberation Movement grappled with the complex relationship between sexuality, desire, and power. Most of all, she appreciates how the Second Wave embraced rather than denied the role of anger as an essential and productive force in feminist consciousness. She believes we should continue to heed the words of black lesbian feminist Audre Lorde: "Every woman has a well-stocked arsenal of anger potentially useful against those oppressions, personal and institutional, which brought that anger into being. Focused with precision it can become a powerful source of energy serving progress and change."

JACQUELINE COUTI is Assistant Professor of French at the University of Kentucky. She specializes in francophone Caribbean, African, and New World literatures and cultures, examining how the notion of local knowledge in the colonial and postcolonial eras has shaped literatures and awarenesses of self in former colonies through what she terms a "sexual edge"—a sharp, violent representation of sexuality as a societal construction. She has published articles on women writers, diasporic identities, memory, and exile as well as on issues of nationhood, sexuality, gender, and violence.

MÓNICA DÍAZ is Associate Professor of Spanish at the University of Kentucky. She specializes in the history and literature of colonial Latin America and the early modern Atlantic. Her research focuses on indigenous cultures and discursive production. Her other area of specialization is women's cultural history and literature. Díaz's book *Indigenous Writings from the Convent: Negotiating Ethnic Autonomy in Colonial Mexico* (2010) examines the existence of the only three convents opened exclusively for indigenous women in colonial Mexico.

CHERYL R. HOPSON is Assistant Professor of African American literature at Georgia Regents University in Augusta. She specializes in twentieth-century African American and American literature and culture and has secondary interests in Black feminist thought and generational feminisms. Her most recent publication, "Zora Neale Hurston as Womanist," is included in the edited collection *Critical Insights: Zora Neale Hurston* (2013). She is currently revising her book manuscript on Alice and Rebecca Walker. Dr. Hopson's poetry chapbook *Black Notes* was published by Finishing Line Press in 2013.

KATHI KERN is Associate Professor of History at the University of Kentucky. Her research centers on the women's rights movement in nineteenth-century America and focuses particularly on the ways in which politics, gender, and religion have mixed to create new ideological positions and social change in the United States. In 2008, Kern was the cowinner (with Linda Levstik and Kathy Swan) of the National Technology Leadership Initiative Award in Social Studies for their research project on digital storytelling and history instruction. Her publications include *Mrs. Stanton's Bible* (2001).

MICHAEL KIMMEL is Distinguished Professor of Sociology at Stony Brook University. He is among the leading researchers and writers on men and masculinity. He is the author or editor of more than twenty volumes, including *Changing Men: New Directions in Research on Men and Masculinity* (1987), *Men Confront Pornography* (1990), *The Politics of Manhood* (1996), *The Gender of Desire* (2005), and *The History of Men* (2005). He is also coeditor of *The Encyclopedia on Men and Masculinities* (2 volumes, 2004) and *The Handbook of Studies on Men and Masculinities* (2004).

DIANE E. KING is Associate Professor of Anthropology at the University of Kentucky. She works on kinship and descent, gender, collective identity, and the modern state in the Middle East. Her main field site is the Kurdistan region of Iraq. She has published a variety of articles and an edited volume called *Middle Eastern Belongings* (2010), as well as "Kurdistan on the Global Stage: Kinship, Land, and Community in Iraq" (2014). Between 2000 and 2006, she was on the faculty at American University of Beirut. She has held fellowships sponsored by the University of Kentucky, the William and Flora Hewlett Foundation, and the George A. and Eliza Gardner Howard Foundation.

LIANG LUO is Associate Professor of Chinese Literature and Culture at the University of Kentucky. She is interested in the intersection of gender, class, youth, and radicalism in East Asia through studies of literature, performing arts, and film. Her first book, *The Avant-garde and the Popular in Modern China: Tian Han and the Intersection of Performance and Politics*, was published in 2014 by the University of Michigan Press.

FATIMA MERNISSI is a Moroccan feminist writer and sociologist. In 2003, she was awarded the Prince of Asturias Award along with Susan Sontag. Mernissi was a lecturer at the Mohammed V University of Rabat and a research scholar at the University Institute for Scientific Research in Rabat. She retired from the university in 2005 in order to focus on writing. Her publications include *Dreams of Trespass: Tales of a Harem Girlhood, Beyond the Veil, The Veil and the Male Elite: A Feminist Interpretation of Islam*, and *Islam and Democracy: Fear of the Modern World*.

NORMA MOGROVEJO is on the faculty at Universidad de la Ciudad de México. Her research interests and publications focus on Latin American and Caribbean lesbian feminist movements. Her publications include *Teoria Lesbica: Participacion Politica Y Literatura* (Lesbian Theory: Political Participation and Literature) and *Un amor que se atrevio a decir su nombre: La lucha de las lesbianas* (A Love That Dared to Speak Its Name: The Lesbian Struggle).

OBIOMA NNAEMEKA is Chancellor's Distinguished Professor of French, Women's/Gender Studies, and Africana Studies at Indiana University, Indianapolis. She is originally from

Agulu in southeastern Nigeria. Professor Nnaemeka—a former Rockefeller Humanist-in-Residence (University of Minnesota), Edith Kreeger-Wolf Distinguished Visiting Professor (Northwestern University), and Verne Wagner Distinguished Visiting Professor (University of Kansas)—is the president of the Association of African Women Scholars, the president/CEO of the Jessie Obidiegwu Education Fund, and board member of numerous national and international NGOs and academic journals. She has published extensively in the following areas: development, postcolonial literature, women/gender studies, human rights, and African/African diaspora studies. She is the author of over sixty scholarly articles and book chapters, editor of the ten-volume WAAD collection, and author/editor of eleven books, including *The Politics of (M)Othering; Sisterhood, Feminisms and Power; Agrippa d'Aubigné and the Poetics of Change;* and *Female Circumcision and the Politics of Knowledge.*

RUTH PERRY is the Ann Friedlaender Professor in the School of Humanities at MIT. She was the founding director of the MIT Women's Studies program; in 2000 she was elected president of the American Society for Eighteenth-Century Studies. The author of numerous books and articles, many reprinted in anthologies, she has written on such canonical figures as Pope, Sterne, Richardson, and Austen as well as on contemporary women writers such as Grace Paley and Mary Gordon. Her books include *Women, Letters, and the Novel* (1980); *Mothering the Mind: Twelve Studies of Writers and Their Silent Partners* (1985); an edition of *George Ballard's 1752 Several Ladies of Great Britain* (1984); *The Celebrated Mary Astell* (1986); *Novel Relations: The Transformation of Kinship in English Culture and Literature, 1748–1818* (2004); and a scholarly edition of Charlotte Lennox's *1758 Henrietta* (2008).

AMY RICHLIN is Professor of Classics at University of California at Los Angeles. She has published widely on the history of sexuality, on Latin literature, and on Roman women's history; her books include *The Garden of Priapus* (1983, rev. ed. 1992), *Rome and the Mysterious Orient: Three Plays by Plautus* (2005), and *Marcus Aurelius in Love* (2006); she edited *Pornography and Representation in Greece and Rome* (1992) and coedited *Feminist Theory and the Classics* (1993). She is now revising a book on epistolarity, the end of the ancient sex/gender system, and the circulation of knowledge about that system in the nineteenth and early twentieth centuries, with the working title *How Fronto's Letters Got Lost: Reading Roman Pederasty in Modern Europe.* A book of her collected essays on Roman women's history is forthcoming from the University of Michigan Press. Other current interests include Roman comedy as slave theater and the teaching of classical literature to Native Americans in the seventeenth and eighteenth centuries.

ELLEN ROSENMAN is the Provost's Distinguished Service Professor of English at the University of Kentucky. She is the author of *The Invisible Presence: Virginia Woolf and the Mother-Daughter Relationship* (1986), *A Room of One's Own: Women Writers and the Politics of Creativity* (1995), and *Unauthorized Pleasures: Accounts of Victorian Erotic Experience* (2003) and the coeditor, with Claudia Klaver, of *Other Mothers: Beyond the Maternal Ideal* (2008).

KAREN W. TICE is Chair of the Department of Gender and Women's Studies and Associate Professor of Educational Policy Studies at the University of Kentucky. Her teaching and research interests include gender and education, media and popular culture, social movements, class, the body, economies of beauty and makeover, and feminist theory. Her publications include *Tales of Wayward Girls and Immoral Women: Case Records and the Professionalization of Social Work* (1998) and *Queens of Academe: Beauty, Bodies and Campus Life, 1920-Present* (2012).

PRAMILA VENKATESWARAN, author of *Thirtha* (Yuganta Press, 2002), *Behind Dark Waters* (Plain View Press, 2008), *Draw Me Inmost* (Stockport Flats, 2009), and *Trace* (Finishing Line Press, 2011), is an award-winning poet who teaches English and Women's Studies at Nassau Community College, New York. Her essays on gender and literature have appeared in *The Women's Studies Quarterly, Journal of Postcolonial Studies, The Writer's Chronicle, Language Crossings,* and anthologies of literary criticism. She was the 2011 Walt Whitman Birthplace Association Long Island Poet of the Year.

CREDITS

CHAPTER 1: FEMINIST THOUGHT BEFORE THE RENAISSANCE

Translations of Sappho, Sulpicia the elegist, Sulpicia the satirist, Hrotsvit, and Plautus are by Amy Richlin and were commissioned for this volume.

Nossis. "Poem 11." In *Sappho's Lyre: Archaic Lyric and Women Poets of Ancient Greece,* translated by Diane Rayor, 133. Berkeley: University of California Press, 1991.

Euripides. "Medea." In *Women on the Edge: Four Plays by Euripides,* translated by Ruby Blondell, 177. New York: Routledge, 1999. Reproduced with permission of Taylor & Francis Group LLC—Books via Copyright Clearance Center.

"The Roman Socrates", translated by Cora E. Lutz, 41, 43, 45, 47. Hartford: Yale University Press, 1947. ©1947. Reprinted by permission of Yale University Press.

CHAPTER 2: CHRISTINE DE PIZAN AND THE *QUERELLE DES FEMMES*

de Pizan, Christine. *The Book of the City of Ladies,* translated by Earl Jeffrey Richard, 3–5, 62–64, 142, 164–65, 256–57. New York: Persea, 1982. ©1982 by Persea Books, Inc. Reprinted by permission of Persea Books, Inc. All rights reserved.

CHAPTER 3: SOR JUANA INÉS DE LA CRUZ AND EARLY FEMINISM

de la Cruz, Sor Juana Inés. "The Poet's Answer to the Most Illustrious Sor Filotea de la Cruz." In *The Answer / La Respuesta,* edited and translated by Electa Arenal and Amanda Powell,

39, 41, 47, 49, 51, 53, 73, 75, 77, 79, 81, 85, 87. New York: Feminist Press, 1994. Reprinted with the permission of The Permissions Company, Inc., on behalf of The Feminist Press, www.feministpress.org. All rights reserved.

de la Cruz, Sor Juana Inés. "First Dream." In *A Sor Juana Anthology*, translated by Alan S. Trueblood, 171–73, 179, 180, 181, 194–95. Cambridge, MA: Harvard University Press, 1988. ©1988 by the President and Fellows of Harvard College. Reprinted by permission of the publisher.

CHAPTER 4: RADICAL DOUBT AND THE LIBERATION OF WOMEN

Perry, Ruth. "Radical Doubt and the Liberation of Women." *Eighteenth-Century-Studies* 18, no. 4 (Autumn 1985): 472–93. ©1985 by The American Society for Eighteenth-Century Studies. Reprinted with permission of the Johns Hopkins University Press.

Descartes, René. *Meditations on First Philosophy*, edited by David B. Manley and Charles S. Taylor, translated by John Veitch. www.wright.edu/~charles.taylor/descartes/.

Astell, Mary. "A Serious Proposal to the Ladies." In *The Essential Feminist Reader*, edited by Estelle Freedman, 20–23. New York: Modern Library, 2007.

CHAPTER 5: SEXUAL POLITICS IN ENGLAND AND INDIA

Butler, Josephine E. *Personal Reminiscences of a Great Crusade*, 4–12, 78–80. London: Horace Marshall and Son, 1911; rpt. Westport, CT: Hyperion Press, 1976.

Ramamirthammal, Muvalur. *Web of Deceit: Devadasi Reform in Colonial India*, edited by Kalpana Kannabiran and Vasanth Kannabiran, 48–59, 82–84. New Delhi: Kali for Women, 2003.

CHAPTER 6: WOMEN'S SUFFRAGE

Lytton, Lady Constance. "A Speech by Constance Lytton." In *Speeches and Trials of the Militant Suffragettes: The Women's Social and Political Union, 1903–1918*, edited by Cheryl R. Jorgensen-Earp, 107–13. Madison, NJ: Farleigh Dickinson Press, 1999.

Fawcett, Millicent Garrett. "Home and Politics." In *Before the Vote Was Won: Arguments for and against Women's Suffrage*, edited by Jane Lewis, 418–24. New York: Routledge and Kegan Paul, 1987.

Ali, Aruna Asaf. "Women's Suffrage in India." In *Our Cause: A Symposium by Indian Women*, edited by Shyam Tumari Neiru, 364–71. Allahabad, Kitabistan: n.p., n.d.

Catt, Carrie Chapman. Excerpt, untitled manuscript on the position of women in the "Orient," 1913. Box 7, folder 1, Carrie Chapman Catt Papers, New York Public Library.

Colby, Clara. "An Attack on the Tagore 'Craze.'" *The Literary Digest*, August 21, 1915 p. 352. Clipping, box 5, folder 11, Clara Bewick Colby Papers, State Historical Society of Wisconsin.

Colby, Clara. "Notes on the Writings of Rabindranath Tagore." Box 5, folder 11, Clara Bewick Colby Papers, State Historical Society of Wisconsin.

CHAPTER 7: THE MYTHOLOGY OF THE *DOUDOU*

Hearn, Lafcadio. *"La fille de couleur."* In *Two Years in the French West Indies.* New York: Harper and Brothers, 1890.

Hearn, Lafcadio. *Youma: The Story of a West-Indian Slave.* New York: Harper and Brothers, 1890.

CHAPTER 8: LOCATING THE FEMINIST SPIRIT IN INDIA

Shinde, Tarabai. "Stri Purush Tulana" (A Comparison of Men and Women). In *Women Writing in India, 600 BC to the Present,* edited by Susie Tharu and K. Lalita, translated by Maya Pandit, 223–35. Vol. 1. New York: Feminist Press, 1991.

Antherjanam, Lalithambika. "Praticaradevatha" (The Goddess of Revenge). In *Women Writing in India, 600 B.C. to the Present,* edited by Susie Tharu and K. Lalita, 490–500. Vol. 1. New York: Feminist Press, 1991.

CHAPTER 9: TRANSLATION AND TRANSNATIONAL FEMINISMS

Gu Ruopu. "Rebuttal of Ridicule." In *The Red Brush: Women Writing Imperial China,* edited and translated by Wilt Idema and Beata Grant, 418–20. Cambridge, MA: Harvard University Asia Center, 2004. ©2004 The President and Fellows of Harvard College. Reprinted by permission of the Harvard University Asia Center.

Li Ruzhen. "Flowers in the Mirror." In *The Essential Feminist Reader,* edited by Estelle Freedman, translated by Lin Tai-yi, 37–46. New York: Modern Library, 2007. Reprinted by permission of Peter Owen Ltd, London.

CHAPTER 10: *A ROOM OF ONE'S OWN* IN TRANSRACIAL PERSPECTIVE

Woolf, Virginia. *A Room of One's Own.* New York: Houghton Mifflin Harcourt, 1929. Reprinted by permission of Houghton Mifflin Harcourt Publishing Company. All rights reserved. The Society of Authors as the Literary Representative of the Estate of Virginia Woolf.

CHAPTER 11: BEAUVOIR: FEMINIST PHILOSOPHER AS OTHER

de Beauvoir, Simone. *The Second Sex,* translated by H. M. Parshley, xv–xxx. New York: Alfred A. Knopf, 1957. ©1952 and renewed 1980 by Alfred A. Knopf, a division of Random House, Inc. Used by permission of Alfred A. Knopf, a division of Random House, Inc. Any third-party use of this material, outside of this publication, is prohibited. Interested parties must apply directly to Random House, Inc. for permission.

de Beauvoir, Simone. "Interview with Alice Schwarzer and Simone de Beauvoir." In *New French Feminisms: An Anthology,* edited by Elaine Marks and Isabelle de Courtivron, translated by Elaine Marks, 151–53. Amherst: University of Massachusetts Press, 1980.

CHAPTER 12: THE "PERSONAL POLITICS" OF CLASS

Brown, Rita Mae. "The Last Straw." *Motive* 32, no. 1 (1972): 2–5. Reprinted by permission of Rita Mae Brown.

Berson, Ginny. "Class Revisited: One Step forward, Two Steps Back." *The Furies: Lesbian/ Feminist Monthly* 2, no. 3 (1973): 8–9.

CHAPTER 13: FEMINISTS REIMAGINE THE BODY

Greer, Germaine. "Sex." In *The Female Eunuch.* New York: Harper Collins, 1970. ©1970 by Germaine Greer. Reprinted by permission of Harper Collins Publishers.

Koedt, Anne. "The Myth of the Vaginal Orgasm." In *Radical Feminism,* edited by Anne Koedt, Ellen Levine, and Anita Rapone, 158–62. New York: Quadrangle Books, 1973. Reprinted with permission of Anne Koedt.

Irigaray, Luce. "This Sex Which Is Not One." In *New French Feminisms: An Anthology,* edited by Elaine Marks and Isabelle de Courtivron, translated by Claudia Reeder, 99–106. Amherst: University of Massachusetts Press, 1980. ©1980 by University of Massachusetts Press.

Lorde, Audre. *Uses of the Erotic: The Erotic as Power.* Pamphlet. Tucson, AZ: Kore Press, 1978. ©1984, 2007 by Audre Lorde. Reprinted by permission of the Charlotte Sheedy Literary Agency.

CHAPTER 14: WOMEN'S LIBERATION AND BLACK "SISTERHOOD"

Weathers, Mary Ann. "An Argument for Black Women's Liberation as a Revolutionary Force." In *Words of Fire: An Anthology of African-American Feminist Thought,* edited by Beverly Guy-Sheftall, 158–62. New York: The New Press, 1995.

Murray, Pauli. "The Liberation of Black Women." In *Words of Fire: An Anthology of African-American Feminist Thought,* edited by Beverly Guy-Sheftall, 186–98. New York: The New Press, 1995.

Wallace, Michele. "Anger in Isolation: A Black Feminist's Search for Sisterhood." In *Words of Fire: An Anthology of African-American Feminist Thought,* edited by Beverly Guy-Sheftall, 220–28. New York: The New Press, 1995.

Lorde, Audre. "Eye to Eye: Black Women, Anger, and Hatred." In *Sister Outsider: Essays and Speeches by Audre Lorde,* 174–75. Berkeley: The Crossing Press, 1984. ©1984, 2007 by Audre Lorde. Reprinted by permission of the Charlotte Sheedy Literary Agency.

CHAPTER 15: *TRIPLE JEOPARDY*

Triple Jeopardy, September–October 1971.

CHAPTER 16: STRAINED SISTERHOOD

Radicalesbians. "The Woman-Identified Woman." In *Out of the Closets: Voices of Gay Liberation,* edited by Karla Jay and Allen Young. New York: NYU Press, 1972, 1978, 1992. Used by permission of the editors.

Hollibaugh, Amber, and Cherríe Moraga. "What We're Rollin around in Bed With: Sexual Silences in Feminism." In *Powers of Desire: The Politics of Sexuality*, edited by Ann Snitow, Christine Stansell, and Sharon Thompson, 395–98, 401–5. New York: Monthly Review Press, 1983. Reprinted by permission of Monthly Review Press.

CHAPTER 17: THE LATIN AMERICAN LESBIAN MOVEMENT

The text of *Declaration of Lesbians from Mexico* is by Norma Mogrovejo and was commissioned for this volume.

CHAPTER 18: WHO IS YOUR MOTHER?

Allen, Paula Gunn. "Who Is Your Mother? Red Roots of White Feminism." In *The Sacred Hoop*. Boston: Beacon Press, 1992. Reprinted by permission of Beacon Press.
Nancy Ward/Nanye'hi. "Speeches to the U.S. Treaty Commissioners," and Cherokee Women, "Speech to General Greene's Commission" and "Letter to Governor Benjamin Franklin." In *Transatlantic Feminism in the Age of Revolutions*, edited by Lisa L. Moore, Joanne Brooks, and Catherine Wigginton, 178–82. New York: Oxford University Press, 2011.

CHAPTER 19: SUFFERING LIKE AN AFRICAN GIRL

Dangarembga, Tsitsi. *Nervous Conditions*. Banbury, UK: Ayebia Clarke, 1988. Permission granted by Ayebia Clarke Publishing Limited, copyright and world rights holding publisher.

CHAPTER 20: THE MEANING OF SPATIAL BOUNDARIES

Mernissi, Fatima. "The Meaning of Spatial Boundaries." In *Beyond the Veil: Male-Female Dynamics in Muslim Society*. London: Al Saqi Books, 1975. Reprinted with permission of Indiana University Press
Mernissi, Fatima. *Dreams of Trespass: Tales of a Harem Girlhood*. Jackson, TN: Perseus, 1994. Reprinted by permission of Basic Books, a member of the Perseus Books Group.

CHAPTER 21: MOTHERS, GUERRILLAS, AND REVOLUTIONARIES

Mellibovsky, Matilde. *Circle of Love over Death: Testimonies of the Mothers of the Plaza de Mayo*, translated by Maria and Matthew Proser, 64–70. Willimantic: Curbstone Press, 1997.
Miloslavich Tupac, Diana, and María Elena Moyano. *The Autobiography of María Elena Moyano: The Life and Death of a Peruvian Activist*, translated by Patricia S. Taylor Edmisten. Gainesville: University Press of Florida, 2000. Reprinted with permission of the University Press of Florida.

CHAPTER 22: FEMINIST ORGANIZING AROUND VIOLENCE

Bhattacharya, Malini. "To Give a Daughter Away." In *Women Writing in India, 600 B.C. to the Present*, edited by Susie Tharu and K. Lalita, translated by Chandreyee Neogy and Piyali Sengupta, 478–86. Vol. 2. New York: Feminist Press, 1993.

CHAPTER 23: FREEDOM FROM SEXISM VERSUS SEXUAL FREEDOM

Dworkin, Andrea. "Pornography and Grief." In *Take Back the Night: Women on Pornography,* edited by Laura Lederer, 286–91. New York: Bantam Books, 1980.

Allison, Dorothy. "Public Silence, Private Terror." In *Pleasure and Danger: Exploring Female Sexuality,* edited by Carole S. Vance, 103–14. London: Pandora Press, 1989.

CHAPTER 24: TWO GENERATIONS OF FEMINIST ACTIVISM

Kordi, Gohar. *An Iranian Odyssey.* London: Serpent's Tail, 1991. Permission granted by Profile Books Limited.

Younes, Iman Humaydan. *B as in Beirut.* Translated by Max Weiss. Northhampton, MA: Interlink Books, 2007.

CHAPTER 25: MEN AND WOMEN'S STUDIES

Stoltenberg, John. "How Men Have (a) Sex." In *Refusing to Be a Man: Essays on Sex and Justice.* Portland: Breitenbush Books, 1989. Reprinted with permission.

Connell, R. W. "Masculinities and Globalization." *Men and Masculinities* 1, no. 1 (1998): 3–23. ©1998 by SAGE publications. Reprinted by permission of SAGE Publications.

CHAPTER 26: IDENTITY, ACTIVISM, AND THE THIRD WAVE

Hanna, Kathleen. "Riot Grrrl Manifesto." *Bikini Kill* zine 2 (1991).

Pough, Gwendolyn. "Do the Ladies Run This . . . ? Some Thoughts on Hip-Hop Feminism." In *Catching a Wave: Reclaiming Feminism for the 21st Century,* edited by Rory Dicker and Alison Piepmeier, 232–43. Lebanon, NH: University Press of New England, 2003. Reprinted with permission.

Suskin, Alana. "Hearing the Daughter Voice: The *Bat Kol* as Rrrabbi Grrrl." In *Catching a Wave: Reclaiming Feminism for the 21st Century,* edited by Rory Dicker and Alison Piepmeier, 263, 265–67, 268–71, 277–78. Lebanon, NH: University Press of New England, 2003. Reprinted with permission.

Baumgardner, Jennifer, and Amy Richards. "Third Wave Manifesta: A Thirteen-Point Agenda." In *Manifesta: Young Women, Feminism, and the Future,* edited by Jennifer Baumgardner and Amy Richards, 278–80. New York: Farrar, Straus and Giroux, 2000. Reprinted by permission of Farrar, Straus and Giroux, LLC.

CHAPTER 28: GENDERING THE ARAB SPRING

Al-Ali, Nadje. "Gendering the Arab Spring." *Middle East Journal of Culture and Communication* 5, no. 1 (2012): 26–31. Reproduced with permission of Brill via Copyright Clearance Center.

AUTHOR AND TITLE INDEX

For ease of access, this index contains the authors and titles of the primary readings only.

African (Banjul) Charter on Human and People's Rights, 413–15

Ali, Aruna Asaf, 119–24

Allison, Dorothy, 440–50

"Anger in Isolation" (Wallace), 275–78

Antherjanam, Lalithambika, 160–68

"Argument for Black Women's Liberation as a Revolutionary Force, An" (Weathers), 270–73

Astell, Mary, 69–74

"Attack on the Tagore 'Craze'" (Colby), 125–26

Autobiography of María Elena Moyano (Moyano), 389–98

B as in Beirut (Humaydan Younes), 468–70

Baumgardner, Jennifer, 520–21

Beauvoir, Simone de, 199–210

Berson, Ginny, 226–30

Bhattacharya, Malini, 421–29

Book of the City of Ladies, The (Christine de Pizan), 23–27

Brown, Rita Mae, 221–26

Butler, Josephine, 83–88

Catt, Carrie Chapman, 124–25

Christine de Pizan, 23–27

Circle of Love over Death (Mellibovsky), 385–89

"Class Revisited" (Brown), 226–30

Colby, Clara, 125–27

"Comparison of Men and Women, A" (Shinde), 150–60

Connell, R. W., 488–98

Convention of Belém do Pará (1994), 415–21

Dangarembga, Tsitsi, 340–49

Declaration of Lesbians from Mexico, 319–20

Descartes, René, 68–69

"Do the Ladies Run This . . . ?" (Pough), 510–15

Dreams of Trespass (Mernissi), 363–75

Dworkin, Andrea, 436–40

Euripides, 14]

"Eye to Eye" (Lorde), 278–79

Fawcett, Millicent Garrett, 114–19

Female Eunuch, The (Greer), 236–42

"Fille de Couleur, La" (Hearn), 139–42
"First Dream" (Sor Juana), 44–61
"Flowers in the Mirror" (Li), 176–82
Fragment (Sulpicia the Satirist), 11
Fragment 16 (Sappho), 10–11

"Goddess of Revenge, The" (Antarjanam), 160–68
Greer, Germaine, 236–42
Gu Ruopu, 175–76

Hanna, Kathleen, 508–10
"Hearing the Daughter Voice" (Suskin), 515–20
Hearn, Lafcadio, 139–43
Hollibaugh, Amber, 305–11
"Home and Politics" (Fawcett), 114–19
"How Men Have (a) Sex" (Stoltenberg), 479–88
Hrotsvit, 12–14
Humaydan Younes, Iman, 468–70

Inter-American Convention on the Prevention, Punishment, and Eradication of Violence against Women (1994), 415–21
Iranian Odyssey, An (Kordi), 461–68
Irigaray, Luce, 248–54

Katteuha, 333–34, 334n6. See also Nanye'hi (Nancy Ward)
Koedt, Anne, 242–48
Kordi, Gohar, 461–68

"Last Straw, The" (Brown), 221–26
Letter to Certain Wise Men, Supporters of This Book (Hrotsvit), 13–14
"Liberation of Black Women, The" (Murray), 273–75
Li Ruzhen, 176–82
Lorde, Audre, 254–59, 278–79
Lytton, Constance, 109–14

Marie-Claire, Beauvoir interview in, 199
"Masculinities and Globalization" (Connell), 488–98
Medea (Euripides), 14
Meditations on First Philosophy (Descartes), 68–69
Mellibovsky, Matilde, 385–89
Mercator (Plautus), 15

Mernissi, Fatima, 363–75
Moraga, Cherríe, 305–11
Mothers of the Plaza de Mayo, 385–89
Moyano, María Elena, 389–401
Murray, Pauli, 273–75
Musonius Rufus, 15–18
"Myth of the Vaginal Orgasm, The" (Koedt), 242–48

Nanye'hi (Nancy Ward), 331–34, 334n6
Nervous Conditions (Dangarembga), 340–49
Nossis, 11
Notebook (Moyano), 398–401
"Notes on the Writings of Rabindranath Tagore" (Colby), 127

Personal Reminiscences of a Great Crusade (Butler), 83–88
Plautus, 15
Poem 1 (Sulpicia the Elegist), 11
Poem 11 (Nossis), 11
"Poet's Answer to the Most Illustrious Sor Filotea de la Cruz, The" (Sor Juana), 36–44
"Pornography and Grief" (Dworkin), 436–40
Pough, Gwendolyn D., 510–15
"Praticaradevatha" (Antherjanam), 160–68
Preface to Her Plays (Hrotsvit), 12
"Public Silence, Private Terror" (Allison), 440–50

Radicalesbians, 301–5
Ramamirthammal, Muvalur, 88–97
"Rebuttal of Ridicule" (Gu), 175–76
Richards, Amy, 518–19
"Riot Grrrl Manifesto" (Hanna), 508–10
Robles de Zurita, Carmen, 385–89
Room of One's Own, A (Woolf), 187–92

Sappho, 10–11
Schwarzer, Alice, 208–10
Second Sex, The (Beauvoir), 199–207
"Serious Proposal to the Ladies, A" (Astell), 69–74
"Sex," from The Female Eunuch (Greer), 236–42
Shinde, Tarabai, 150–60
"Should Daughters Receive the Same Education as Sons?" (Musonius Rufus), 17–18
Sor Juana (Juana Inés de la Cruz), 36–61

"Speech Delivered at the Queen's Hall, January
31, 1910" (Lytton), 109–14
Speeches and Letters (Nanye'hi and Cherokee
women), 331–34
Stoltenberg, John, 479–88
"Stri Purush Tulana" (Shinde), 150–60
Sulpicia the Elegist, 11
Sulpicia the Satirist, 11
Suskin, Alana, 515–20

"That Women Too Should Study Philosophy"
(Musonius Rufus), 15–17
"Third Wave Manifesta" (Baumgardner and
Richards), 520–21
Third World Women's Alliance (TWWA),
288–91
"This Sex Which Is Not One" (Irigaray), 248–54
Tibullus Book 3, Poem 13 (Sulpicia the Elegist), 11
"To Give a Daughter Away" (Bhattacharya),
421–29

Triple Jeopardy (TWWA newspaper), 288–91
Two Years in the French West Indies (Hearn),
139–42

Untitled Manuscript on the Position of Women
in the "Orient" (Catt), 124–25
"Uses of the Erotic, The" (Lorde), 254–59

Wallace, Michele, 275–78
Ward, Nancy (Nanye'hi), 331–34, 334n6
Weathers, Mary Ann, 270–73
Web of Deceit (Ramamirthammal), 88–97
"What We're Rollin' around in Bed With"
(Hollibaugh and Moraga), 305–11
"Woman-Identified Woman, The" (Radicalesbi-
ans), 301–5
"Women's Suffrage in India" (Ali), 119–25
Woolf, Virginia, 187–92

Youma (Hearn), 142–43

SUBJECT INDEX

Page references in **bold print** indicate primary readings or their authors. For easier access, please consult the author and title index beginning on page 549.

Abderahman al-Majoub, Sidi, 358–59

ableism, 510

Abney, Jill, 384

abortion, 197, 274, 283, 504

academic feminism, 502

Academy Awards (1992), 476

acculturation, 338

Achilles Heel (magazine), 497

Acholonu, Catherine, 525

acquaintance rape, 478

activism. *See* Arab Spring; Latin American
    women's activism; prostitution reform;
    Second Wave feminism; Third Wave
    feminism; United States, Women's
    Liberation Movement; *specific organization;
    person*

"Adieu foulard, adieu madras" (song), 132–33

Adult Suffragists, 185

affirmative action, 283, 496

Africa: British colonial education in, 335–36;
    diverse cultures of, 525; feminist spirit in,
    522; women's oppression in, 522

African Americans: community culture of, 261;
    equal but separate status of (Beauvoir on),
    204; Native American intermarriage with,
    326–27; tokenism and, 222. *See also* Black
    feminists

African American women: anger of, 275–78;
    liberation of, **270–75**; self-love needed for,
    278–79; as writers, 186

African Charter on Human and People's Rights
    (1986), 403, **413–15**

African feminisms: female circumcision
    activism, 523; frameworks proposed for,
    523–25; men and, 524; sisterhood as viewed
    in, 524; theorizing of, 525–26; use of term,
    522, 525

ageism, 510; in women's movement, 229

Agrippa von Nettesheim, Heinrich Cornelius,
    22

Aguiar y Seijas, Francisco, 31

AIDS, 497, 504, 514

Ain't I a Woman (hooks), 502

Ain't I a Woman (magazine), 227

Aisha Kandisha (female demon), 358

Alberti, Leon Battista, 21

alcohol, 117, 487–88

Algerian revolution, 271, 355, 456, 529

Algren, Nelson, 195

Ali, Aruna Asaf, 103, **119–25**

Al-Ali, Nadje, 384

Allan, Tuzyline Jita, 522

All India Women's Deputation, 119–20

Allison, Dorothy, 432, 433, **440–50**

Altman, Dennis, 497

America, 125

American Popular Revolutionary Alliance
    (APRA), 394–95

Anatomy of Human Bodies Epitomised, The
    (Collins), 238

Ancien Régime, 133

Anderson, Benedict, 285

androgyny, 494

"Anger in Isolation" (Wallace), 263–64, 266–67,
    275–78

Annie John (Kincaid), 336

anorexia, 337–39, **345–49**

Antherjanam, Lalithambika, 144, 145, 146–49,
    160–68

Anthony, Susan B., 105, 106, 324

antiabortion movement, 504

antidiscrimination legislation, 496

Anti-Dowry Act (India), 410

antifeminism, 204–5, 475, 501–2

anti-Semitism, 510, 516

antislavery movements, 99, 101

Antoine, Régis, 132–33

anxiety, 196

Anzaldúa, Gloria, 502

Apology (Plato), 9

Appadurai, Arjun, 523

appearance. *See* beauty standards/treatments;
    clothing/jewelry

Arab Americans, 287

Arab Human Development Report, 452

Arab-Israeli conflict, 284, 355–56, 529

Arab Spring: Islamist gender politics and,
    531–32; protest movement institutionaliza-
    tion, 530; women as activists in, 457,
    528–29; women marginalized in, 529–30;
    women protesters brutalized during, 530–31

Arce, Juan, 33, 42

Ards, Angela, 511

Arenal, Electa, 31, 34

Arendt, Hannah, 173

Argentina: Dirty War in, 381; homosexual
    groups in, 313; lesbian feminist groups in,
    315; women as activists in, 380–82, **385–89**

"Argument for Black Women's Liberation as a
    Revolutionary Force, An" (Weathers),
    262–63, 265, **270–73**

Aristophanes, 7

Aristotle, 7, 8, 30, 34n4, 200

Arnaud, Antoine, 67

Arndt, Susan, 525

Around 1981 (Gallop), 502

aryana (unveiled woman), 355

Aryan race, 482

Asia, Westernization of, 124–25

Association pour le progrès et la defense des
    droits des femmes, l' (APDF), 404, 405

Astell, Mary, 22; Cartesian rationalism and
    feminism of, 65–66, 67, **71–74**; publica-
    tions of, 66–67, **69–74**

Athenian comedy, 7

Atkinson, Ti-Grace, 246

"Attack on the Tagore 'Craze,'" An (Colby),
    125–26

Attakullakulla (Cherokee chief), 332

Augustine, Saint, 204

Augustus (Roman emperor), 5

Australia, 492

Autobiography of María Elena Moyano (Moyano),
    389–98

autoeroticism, 138, 249–50, 254

autokeonomy, 521

"Awakening of Race Consciousness" (P. Nardal),
    137

Ayacucho (Peru), 383

Ayuquelén (Chilean lesbian feminist group),
    315, 318n2

Bâ, Mariama, 524

Bacon, Francis, 62–63

bad faith, 196

Bad Girl's Club (TV show), 220

Badu, Erykah, 505, 513

Bahrain, 528, 529

Bair, Deidre, 193, 194, 198

Baker, Josephine, 137

Balibar, Etienne, 131

ballads, vagina in, 237

Banana Garden Poetry Club (*jiaoyuan shishe*), 169

Banjul Charter (1986), 403, **413–15**

Ban Zhao, 171, 173

Barnard Conference (1982), 294, 434

Barnett, Ida B. Wells. *See* Ida B. Wells

Barranco (Peru), 390

Barre, Poullain de la, 63, 203

Barrett, Frank J., 490

Barrett, William, 194

Barthes, Roland, 231

Barwari, Nesreen, 457

B as in Beirut (Humaydan Younes), 458, 459, **468–70**

Basu, Srimati, 410

Bataille, Georges, 436–37

bat kol (daughter voice), 520

battered women's shelters, 208, 406

Baumgardner, Jennifer, 506, 507, **520–21**

BauSteineMaenner, 497

BDSM, 434

Beal, Frances, 281–82

beauty standards/treatments: body as social construction and, 232; foot-binding, 171, **176–77**, **179–82**, 232; Moroccan, **369–75**; of Native Americans, 322; power feminism and, 503; role-reversal satire on (Li), 171, **176–82**; Second Wave protests against, 213, 292, 504

Beauvoir, Simone de, 231; death of, 198; interview (1976), **208–10**; popular media portrayals of, 193; privileged life of, 195; as reproductive rights advocate, 197. *See also Second Sex, The* (Beauvoir)

Beck, Evelyn Torton, 517

being, 196

Being and Nothingness (Sartre), 196–98

Beirut (Lebanon), 452

Belghiti, Malika, 353–54

belle affranchie (free mulatto woman), 133, 134, **140**

Bénassy-Berling, Marie-Cecile, 34

Benda, Julien, 200

Bengali men, 493

Benjamin, Walter, 169, 170

berdache tradition, 493

Berkeley, Elizabeth, 65

Berson, Ginny: class background of, 217; on class consciousness, 213, 215, 217, **229–30**; on classism in women's movement, 214, **226–30**; as Furies member, 216; as Olivia Records founder, 216

Besant, Annie, 103, 119

Beyala, Calixthe, 523–24

Bhattacharya, Malini, **421–29**

Biggest Loser, The (TV show), 219–20

Bikini Kill (punk band), 503, 509

birth control, 197, 520; mandatory, 283

birtherism, 195

bisexuality, 248

bisexual women, 506, 520–21

Bitterli, Urs, 491, 492

Black Arts movement, 512, 513

black English vernacular, 515

Black feminists: anger of (Wallace), 275–78; legacy of, 504–5, 511; as revolutionaries (Weathers), 270–73; self-love needed for (Lorde), 278–79; sisterhood as viewed by, 262–64, 472; as sisters, 261–62, 268–69; Third-Wave, 511; in U.S. Women's Liberation Movement, 260–61, 276–78

Black Liberation, 265–66

Black Liberation Army, 505, 512

black masculinity, 512

black matriarchy, myth of, 271–72, 281

black men, liberation of, 270–71

Black Movement, 261, 262, 263

Black Nationalism, 263

Black Panthers, 505, 512

black patriarchy, 336, 512

Black Power movement, 232, 504–5, 511–13

Black Women's Alliance, 216, 281–82

Black Women's Liberation Committee, 281

bladder weakness, 238–39

Bluest Eye, The (Morrison), 336

body: adornment of, in Morocco, 353; as "constructed", 232; as discursive product (Greer on), 233; male poststructuralist view of, 231–32; mind vs., 19, **68–69**; slavery and, 3; social consciousness of, 232; soul vs., 30–31. *See also* female body

Boletina, La (Costa Rican lesbian feminist publication), 318n4

Bolin, Anne, 490

Bonaparte, Marie, 244

bondage and discipline, 241, 434

Book of the City of Ladies, The (Christine de Pizan), 20–21, 22, **23–27**, 31–32

Borde, Constance, 198n1

Bordo, Susan, 232, 235, 338

bourgeoisie, 202

Boyarin, Daniel, 10

Boy Scouts, 493

"bra burners," feminists as, 213

Brandauer, Frederick P., 173

Brandon, William, 326

Brazil: lesbian feminist groups in, 313, 315; women's movement in, 284; women's police stations in, 407

Bread & Roses (Boston, MA), 215–16

British Empire, 102–3, 104, 145, 335–36, 492–93

British Parliament, 77, 99, 114

Brodkin, Karen, 517

Brown, Rita Mae: on class consciousness, 217–18; on classism in women's movement, **221–26**; on education and class, 219; as Furies member, 216; on U.S. class mythologies, 216–17

Brownmiller, Susan, 431, 432

Buddhism, 125

Buenos Aires (Argentina), 380, 381

Bulbeck, Chilla, 494

bulimia, 338

Bunch, Charlotte, 215, 216, 218, 293, 297

bureaucratization, 356

Burnet, Elizabeth Berkeley, 65

Burton, Antoinette, 80

Burton, Richard D. E., 132

Butler, Josephine, 78–79, 80, 82, **83–88**, 101

Butler, Judith, 232

Cain, P. J., 491–92

Calcutta (India), 409

Califia, Pat, 442–43

Cambridge University (England), 183, 187

Camus, Albert, 194

Canada, 497

Cape Verde, 522

capitalism, 62; as elastic, 217, 222; "fast", 495; pornography and, 361n8; sexuality and, 233; Third Wave opposition to, 503, 507, 509, 514; tokenism and, 222; U.S. mythologies involving, 217. *See also* neoliberalism

Caprio, Frank S., 243–44

Cárdenas, Nancy, 313

car-driving, by women, 456, 457

Carmelites, 29, 32

Carney, Virginia, 332

Carrigan, Tim, 489

Cartesian assumptions, 62

Cartesian method, 62

Casablanca (Morocco), 362n18

Castro, Yan Maria, 314

Catching a Wave (ed. Rory Dicker and Alison Piepmeier), 505–6

Catholic Church: Argentine Dirty War and, 381, 382, 386, 387–88; Beauvoir *Second Sex* banned by, 194; humanist questioning of, 20; New World religious environment, 28–29; Spanish colonialism and, 28; women canonized in, 33; women censored by, 34; women writers in, 33

Catt, Carrie Chapman, 105, 106, 107, **124–25**

Catullus, 5

censorship, 33–34

Center for Peruvian Women Flora Tristán, 407

Center for Women's Global Leadership (Rutgers University), 216

Central Intelligence Agency, 284

Central Strike Committee (Peru), 393–94

Césaire, Aimé, 136

Chambers, Sarah, 405

Chamoiseau, Patrick, 136, 138

Champion of Women, The (Le Franc), 21

Chana com chana (bulletin), 313

Chancer, Lynn, 435

Chang, Kang-I Sun, 169–70, 172

chaperoning, 354

chastity belts, 297

Cherokee General Council, 332

Cherokee Indians, 329

Cherokee women, **331–34**

Cheyenne Indians, 323, 493

Chicago Women's Liberation Union, 216

Chicana feminism, 517

Chicanos, 222

child care, 274, 282, 283, 478, 496

child custody rights, 77, 78, 455

child marriages, 81, 145, 297, 459

childrearing, 327

children: decision to have, and Third Wave
  feminism, 506; international treaties
  regarding rights of, 403; Mali organizations supporting, 404; parental rights over,
  197; right to have, for lesbians/poor
  women, 520
child sexual abuse, 241
Chile, lesbian feminist groups in, 315, 318n2
China, 271
Chinese National People's Congress, 284
Chodorow, Nancy, 491
choice, 196
Christian, Barbara, 525–26
Christianity: early, as feminist alternative, 516;
  early gnostic, 8; in MENA region, 452;
  misogyny and, 7–8, 516; prostitution
  reform movement and, 80; radical
  feminism and, 435; Roman antiquity and,
  9–10; Sappho's work destroyed by, 4–5;
  sexuality as viewed in, 359; Third Wave
  opposition to, 503, 507, 509; women's
  education and, 8–9; women's rights in,
  3–4. *See also* Catholic Church
Christiansen, Tanja, 405
Christine (Queen of Sweden), 63
Christine de Pizan, 20–21, 22, **23–27**, 31–32
Cicero, 8, 33, 35n7
Circle of Love over Death (Mellibovsky), **385–89**
Cistellaria (Plautus), 6
Civil Rights Act (1964), 269n3
Cixous, Helene, 231
Claire-Solange (Lacascade), 137
class consciousness: Berson on, 213, 215, 217,
  229–30; Brown on, 217–18; socialist
  feminism and, 219. *See also* social class
classism: eating disorders as result of, 338;
  higher education and, 218–19, **223–24**;
  Latin American lesbian movement and,
  317; Third Wave feminism and, 510; in
  women's movement, 214, 215, 217–20,
  221–26. *See also* social class
"Class Revisited" (Berson), 213, **226–30**
Cleaver, Eldridge, 276
Cliff, Michelle, 6
clitoral orgasm, 233–34, 243–44, 245–46
clitoridectomies, 247, 248, 404–5
clitoris: anatomy of (Koedt), **244–45**; female
  sexual gratification through, 239, 240, **242**,

244–45; as "little penis" (Irigaray), 234;
  male gynecological descriptions of, 237, 238
clothing/jewelry: coverture doctrine and, 77; *da*
  and, 139; feminist protests involving
  (1968), 213, 292, 504; hip-hop, 510; in
  India, 96–97; male transvestite use of, 232;
  Moroccan use of, 353; role-reversal satire on
  (Li), 171, **176–82**
Cobbe, Francis Power, 78, 102
Cockburn, Cynthia, 489
Codo a Codo (Argentine lesbian feminist
  publication), 318n3
Coker, Cheo, 514
Colby, Clara, 106–8, **125–27**
Collins, Jackie, 241–42
Collins, Samuel, 237–38
Colombia, lesbian feminist groups in, 315
colonial desire: *doudou* and, 133–35; enduring
  legacy of, 136; proto-feminist reaction to,
  136–38; use of term, 132
colonialism: bureaucratization as result of, 356;
  colonial desire and, 132; female body and,
  232; feminism and, in India, 144–49;
  gynarchies destroyed by, 325; hooks on
  history of, 335; Latin American lesbian
  movement and, 316–17; Latin American
  women's activism and, 379; legacy of, in
  MENA region, 453; masculinity and,
  492–94; Native American traditions and,
  322; neocolonialism, 317; Otherness and,
  195; postcolonialism, 494–95; power focus
  of, 522; women's education under, 335–36;
  women's suffrage movement and, 98
colonial subject, 335–36
Columbus, Christopher, 325, 328
Combahee River Collective, 215–16
Comité de Lucha Feminista, 313
Committee on the Status of Women in India
  (CSWI), 409–10
communism, 329–30
community activism, 383–84
"Comparison of Men and Women, A" (Shinde),
  145–46, **150–60**
"Compulsory Heterosexuality and Lesbian
  Existence" (Rich), 294–95, 296–98,
  300n16, 443–44
Conference for International Women's Year
  (1975), **287n7**, 313, 319–20

Confiant, Raphael, 136, 138

Confucianism, 169, 170–71, 172–73

Congress on Public Morality (Geneva, Switzerland; 1877), 79

Congress to Unite Women (1970), 292, 294

Connell, R. W., **488–98**

Conscious Daughters (rap group), 512

consciousness raising (CR), 277, 448

conservatism: postfeminism and, 501–502; power feminism and, 503; WLM and, 299

"Conspiracy of Silence", 85

Constitution of Deganawidah, 324

consumerism, 225

Contagious Disease Acts (England; 1864/1866/1869), 78–79, 80, 99

contraception, 197

Convention of Belém do Pará (1996), 408

Convention on the Rights of the Child (CRC), 403

Convent of Saint Paula (Mexico City), 29

Convocatoria Lesbiana (Argentine lesbian feminist group), 315, 318n3

Coomaraswamy, Radhika, 402

Corinthians, Book of, 33

corseting, 232

cosmetics, 504; male transvestite use of, 232; Moroccan use of, 353

Costa Rica, lesbian feminist groups in, 315, 318n2, 318n4

Counter-Reformation, 28–29

court salons, 20, 22n1

Cousins, Margaret, 103

coverture, doctrine of, 77, 100

cowboys, 492

crack (drug), 514

Craig, Maxine Leeds, 262

Creoles, 28–29

Crick Crack, Monkey (Hodge), 336

Crimean War, 77

criminal sex, 241

cross-dressing, 232

Cuadernos de Existencia Lesbiana (Argentine lesbian feminist publication), 318n3

Cuarto Creciente (Mexican lesbian feminist group), 315, 318n2

Cuba, 271, 284, 312, 382

cultural criticism, 231–32

cultural nationalism, 285

Curiel, Ochy, 317

Cynics, 8

da (French Caribbean maternal figure), 132, 133, 134–35, **139–40**, **142**

Dahej Virodhi Chetana Manch, 409

Dangarembga, Tsitsi, 335, 338–39, **340–49**. *See also Nervous Conditions* (Dangarembga)

Dashti, Rola, 456–57

Dasigal Mosavalei (*Web of Deceit;* Ramamirthammal), 82, **88–97**

date rape, 478

daughters: African women and, 524; Confucian education of, 171, 173, **175–76**; education of, 8, **17–18**, 25–26, 43; Indian marriage customs and, 153–54, **421–29**; in MENA region, 455, 464; *mujeristas* and, 388–89; in Native American matriarchies, 329; neglect of, 459; of Second Wave feminists, 432; voice of (*bat kol*), 505–6, **515–20**; womanist sisterhood and, 264, 267–68

Davis, Angela, 283

Davis, Eisa, 511, 513–14

Davison, Emily, 100

Dawson, Graham, 493

day care, 282, 283

Declaration of Lesbians from Mexico, 319–20

Declaration of Sentiments (U.S.; 1848), 105–6

decolonization, 494–95

Deeb, Lara, 456

Defence of Good Women (Vives), 21–22

deities, female, 323

Delgado Cabrera, Eugenia, 389

Delhi (India), 409

Dell, Floyd, 478–79

De Partitione Oratoria (Cicero), 35n7

Dépêche africaine, La (journal), 137

Derrida, Jacques, 231

Descartes, René: cross-sex intellectual friendships of, 63–64; philosophy of, as liberating influence, 62–63, 64, 65–66, 67, **68–69**; social disconnection of, 64–65

devadasis (Hindu temple dancers), 81, 82, **88–97**

development, 522

Dewey, John, 171

Diakite, Fatoumata Sire, 405

Diary of a Conference on Sexuality, 434

Diderot, Denis, 204

difference, 198

Dirty War (Argentina; 1976–1983), 381

disability, 195

disability studies, 197

Discipline and Punish (Foucault), 195, 232

Discourse on Method (Descartes), 64

Dislocating Cultures (Narayan), 409

diversity: in Greco-Roman antiquity, 4; in India, 102

divorce law, 77, 78; in MENA region, 452, 454; Roman vs. Christian, 3–4

Dohuk (Iraq), 457

domesticity/the home: Black feminists and, 272, 282; feminist revaluation of, 186; freedom from, 183; male control of, in India, 81; Muslim sphere of, 351–54; nationalism and, 145, 149; public sphere vs. (Naidu on), 104; "white middle-class female" model of, 282; women's intellect and (Astell), 66; women's suffrage vs. (Ali on), **121–22**; women's suffrage vs. (Fawcett on), **114–19**

domestic violence: Beauvoir on, 208; Indian reforms, 408–11; international feminist organizing against, 402; international treaties regarding, 403, 408, **413–21**; Mali reforms, 403–5; in MENA region, 452; Peruvian reforms, 405–8; rates of, 402; Third Wave feminism and, 503, 513

domestic workers, 286, 452, 494

Dominican Republic, lesbian feminist groups in, 315

Donaldson, Mike, 490, 495"Do the Ladies Run This . . . ?" (Pough), 504–5, **510–15**

double shift, 431

doudou (Caribbean mulatto woman): *da* and, 133; exotic/racialized discourse portraying, **139–42**; polysemic facets of, 131–33

Doudou et la da, La (Burton), 132

doudouisme (French exoticism), 136–37

Douglass, Frederick, 473

dowries, 408–11, **421–29**

dowry deaths, 408–9

Drake, Jennifer, 502, 503, 504

Dream of the Red Chamber, The, 172

Dreams of Trespass (Mernissi), **363–75**

drug abuse, 487–88

drunkenness, 117

Druze people, 452

duBois, Page, 5

Du Bois, W. E. B., 473

Dueñas, Rosa, 406

Durkheim, Émile, 473

Dworkin, Andrea: on body as social construction, 232; on gender as social construction, 481; on pornography and male supremacy, 433; on pornography as violence, 431–32, **436–40**; as radical feminist, 431, 503; Wolf and, 503

Dye, Eva Emery, 326

"dyke," use of term, 302, 303

earning power, 228–29

eating disorders, 337–39, **345–49**, 504, 508

Ebadi, Shirin, 457

Ebony (magazine), 276

ecofeminism, 525

economic exploitation, 282–83

economic inequality, 379, 523

education. *See* women's education

education, higher: classism and, 218–19, **223–24**; cost of, and Third Wave feminism, 502; as political opportunity, 219

Education of a Christian Woman, The (Vives), 21

Education Workers of Peru (SUTEP), 393

Edwards, Brent Hayes, 131

Edwards, Louise, 98

Egypt, 124, 456, 457, 528, 529, 530

Ehrenreich, Barbara, 214–15

Eiljersen, Mette, 239

Eiljersen, Mette, 246

Eisenstein, Zillah, 522, 526

elite women: as activists, 78; class prejudice of, 102; in Victorian-era England, 77–78; women's suffrage movement and, 99–100, 102

Elizabeth (Princess of Bohemia), 63–64

Elizabeth I (Queen of England), 22

Ellis, Albert, 248

Ellis, Havelock, 193, 437

Ellman, Mary, 243

El Salvador, women as activists in, 382

Elyot, Thomas, 21–22

empire, masculinities of, 493–94

empiricism, 62–63

employee benefits, 521

employment, 283

Enchanted Modern, An (Deeb), 456

Encore (magazine), 276

Encuentros Feministas Latinoamericanos y del
    Caribe, 315, 316, 318n2, 380

Encuentros Lésbicos Feministas de América
    Latina y el Caribe (ELFLAC), 315–17, 318n2

Engels, Friedrich, 325, 330

England: antislavery movement in, 99, 101;
    class distinctions in, 78, 98; common law
    system of, 328; Contagious Disease Acts in,
    78–79, 80, 99; prostitution in, 82n1;
    prostitution reform in, 79, **83–88**, 101;
    seventeenth-century, women's liberation
    during, 62; vagrancy laws in, 82n1;
    Victorian-era elite, 77–78; voting rights in,
    102; women's political activity in, 114–15;
    women's suffrage granted in, 183; women's
    suffrage movement in, 98, 99–102, **109–19**

Enigmas ofrecidos a la Casa del Placer (Sor
    Juana), 34

Enlightenment, 20, 103

Enloe, Cynthia, 532

environment, 322, 523, 525

epic, as male tradition, 5

Epicureans, 8

Epiphanes, 8

Equal Rights Amendment (ERA), 507, 521

Erasmus, 20

erotic, the: Lorde on, 235, **254–59**; redefining
    (Rich on), 295, 298

eroticism: autoeroticism, 138, 249–50, 254;
    clitoral orgasm and, 233; the gaze and, 250;
    Latin American lesbian movement and,
    318n2; Lorde on, 235; male sexual identity
    and, 483–85 (Stoltenberg); pornography as,
    256, 436; redeeming potential of (Dwor-
    kin), 437

Erselcanb (Turkey), 452

essentialism, 101, 105–6, 185, 195–96, 198

ethnocentrism, 102–3, 198, 274–75

Euripides, 7, **14**

Eurocentrism, 316

"Éveil de la conscience noir, L'" (P. Nardal), 137

exhibitionism, 355

"Exhortation to March" (Dworkin), 436

existentialism, 193–94, 196. *See also Second Sex,*
    The (Beauvoir)

exotic dancers, 434–35

extramarital affairs, 148, 248

Extreme Makeover (TV show), 219–20

"Eye to Eye" (Lorde), 264, 267, **278–79**

"faggot," use of term, 302

Faithfull, Theodore, 238

Fakhro, Munira, 528

family: arranged marriages and (India), 81;
    Beauvoir on, 204; black, 262, 274; Black
    feminists and, 271, 281–83; capitalism and,
    62; colonialism and, 337; communal
    structures for, 282; dowries and (India),
    409–11; -friendly workplace policies, 214,
    478, 521; Latin American lesbian move-
    ment and, 312, 314; male dominance in,
    338, 352; Mali organizations supporting,
    404; in MENA region, 452, 453; in Muslim
    societies, 351–52; nationalism and, 145;
    Native American women and, 327, 328, 331;
    nuclear, 305; ostracism by, 449; patriarchal,
    women's oppression in, 380; racialized
    romances portraying, 135, 143; revolution-
    ary women and, 382; social class and, 215,
    220; Third Wave feminism and, 507, 520;
    WLM and, 295, 303–4; women's suffrage
    movement and, 101. *See also* children;
    daughters; husbands; motherhood; sons

family planning, 283, 507, 520

family violence, 406, 407. *See also* domestic
    violence

fascism, 494

Fawcett, Millicent Garrett, 99, 101–2, 104,
    114–19

Federalists, 328

female body: black, male exoticization/
    racialization of, 131; colonization of, 232;
    degradation of, and homosociality, 361n8;
    eating disorders as rebellion, 337–39;
    gender and, 490; pornography and
    objectification of, 431–32

female chastity, 171

female circumcision, 524–25

female empowerment, 503

Female Eunuch, The (Greer), 233, **236–42**, 431

female inferiority theories: antifeminist sources
    for, 204–5; Beauvoir on, 195, 203–6,
    209–10; Christine de Pizan on, 22;

female inferiority theories *(continued)*
  colonialism and, 144; Dangarembga on,
  344; educational opportunity and, 417–18;
  Enlightenment philosophy and, 204–5;
  Freudian view of, 243–44; in Greco-Roman
  philosophy, 8; humanism and, 20, 22;
  international treaties involving, 417–18;
  Koedt on, 247; Lorde on, 255; in Protestant
  thought, 22; sexuality and, 247, 255; Shinde
  on, 145; Woolf and, 185. *See also* sexism
female orgasm, **236**, **242**, 245–46. *See also*
  clitoral orgasm; vaginal orgasm
female punk bands, 509
Female Sexuality (Bonaparte), 244
feminine, eternal, 205, 210
Feminine Mystique, The (Friedan), 430–31
femininity: fear of, in Muslim societies, 358–59;
  French Caribbean, external exoticization/
  racialization of, 133–35; as myth (Beauvoir
  on), 207; as social construction, 185,
  209, 474–75, 481; women's education
  and, 117; women's political activity and,
  117–19
feminism: academic, 502; African feminisms
  and, 522; Cartesian rationalism and, 65–66,
  67, **71–74**; conservatism and, 299; epithets
  for, 213; first New World feminist, 31; first
  theorist of, 20; hegemonic, 316; during
  Indian colonial period, 144–49; institutionalization processes in, 316; internal
  tensions in, 100–101; Judaism and, 505–6;
  male supporters of, 473–74, 478–79, 497;
  in MENA region, 456–58; as monolithic,
  524; movement categorization in, 501; as
  multifaceted, 522; postfeminism and, 502;
  power, 503; pre-Renaissance existence of, 3;
  radical, 430–32; as "sex-positive", 5–6, 294,
  298–99; socialist, 214–16; translatability of,
  523; use of term, 31, 172; victim, 503;
  Western ownership of, 522; white, as racist,
  235; womanism vs., 525
"Feminism for Men" (Dell), 478–79
feminist organizations: social class and, 214;
  socialist feminist, 215–16
Feminist Perspectives on Pornography
  Conference (San Francisco; 1978), 436
feminist rebellion, first in U.S., 324
"feminist sex", 432, 434

feminist "sex wars", 294; Barnard Conference
  (1982) and, 434; radical feminist/
  anti-pornography position, 430–32,
  436–40; resolution of, 434–35; sex
  radical/"sex-positive" position, 432–34,
  440–50
feminists of color, 433
feminization, 171, **176–82**, 247
Femmes savantes, Les (Molière), 65
Fernández de Santa Cruz, Manuel, 31, 32, 33
Ferrat, Jean, 209
fetishes, 242
Fifteenth Amendment, U.S. Constitution, 105
filiation, 455
filles de couleur, 134, 135, **139–42**
Filotea de la Cruz, 31, 32
Fire with Fire (Wolf), 503
First Blast of the Trumpet Against the Monstrous
  Regiment of Women, The (Knox), 22
Fish, Stanley, 231
fitna (chaos), 357–58
Flavor of Love: Charm School (TV show), 219–20
Flowers in the Mirror (*Jing hua yuan*; Li), 171–74,
  176–82
Foley, Douglas, 489–90
foot-binding, 171, **176–77**, **179–82**, 232
Forbes, Geraldine, 81
force feeding, during hunger strikes, 104,
  109–14
For Colored Girls Who Have Considered Suicide
  (Shange), 513
"foremothers", 184
Forgotten Women's Association (Hyderabad,
  India), 411
Foucault, Michel, 195, 231, 232
Fourth French Republic, 197
Fourth Wave feminism, rumors of, 508
France: Ancien Régime, 133; colonial exhibi-
  tions in, 136, 137; intellectual women in,
  65; negrophilia/primitivism craze in, 131,
  136; post-WWII, women's rights in, 197;
  prostitution reform in, 79; proto-feminism
  of color in, 136–38; women's liberation
  movement in, 208n1
Franklin, Benjamin, 332, 333–34
"Freedom Trash Can", 213
freelance workers, benefits for, 521
French Caribbean Studies, 132

French Caribbean women. *See belle affranchie* (free mulatto woman); *da* (French Caribbean maternal figure); *doudou* (Caribbean mulatto woman)

French Empire, 136, 403, 529

French feminism, 185, 198, 234

French Resistance, 197

French Revolution, 329

Frente de Liberación Homosexual (FLH), 313

Frente Homosexual de Acción Revolucionaria (FHAR), 314

Frente Sáfico (FRESA), 315

Freud, Sigmund, 473; female sexuality theories of, 234, 243–44, 356, 359; Marcuse vs., 233; as sexist, 243–44, 437

Friedan, Betty, 292, 293, 430–31

frigidity, 208, 243–44

frontier masculinities, 492–93

Fronto, 8

Furies, The (lesbian feminist collective), 216–19

Furies, The (magazine), 216, 227, 229

Fuskova, Ilse, 315

Gaca, Kathy, 8

GALF. *See* Grupo de Acción Lésbico Feminista (GALF)

Galla Placidia (Roman empress), 5

Gallop, Jane, 502

Gandersheim, abbey of (Germany), 9

Garcia, Inéz, 283

Gassendi, Pierre, 63

gauchos, 492

gay identity, 497

gay power movement, 313

gay rights movement, 494

gay theory, 490

Gaza, 456

gaze, the, 196–98

Gee, James Paul, 495

gender: African vs. Western feminist views of, 524; Black feminist sisterhood and, 262; colonialism and, 493–94; constructionist principles of, 185, 316, 481; intersectional theory and, 433–34, 502; materialist cultural analysis of (Woolf), 183–84; neoliberalism and, 495; as performative, 232, 238, **240–42**; as power relation, 474–77, 532; racialized, 335; rap music and,

515; sexuality and, 484–85; women-of-color feminists and, 284; women's studies and visibility of, 471–74, 477

gender-based violence, 403

gender crossing, 490

gender-egalitarianism: during Greco-Roman antiquity, 8; during Renaissance, 20

Gender Equal Ombudsman, 497

gender reform movements, 494, 496

gender separatism, 524

Genesis, Book of, 200

genital cutting (FGM), 404–5

genocide, 514

geopolitics, 491–92

George V (King of England), 100

Germany, 497

ghassoul (shampoo/lotion), 371–72

Al-Ghazali, Abu-Hamid, 353, 359, 360

Gibson, J. William, 496

Gilbert, Sandra, 231

Gilman, Charlotte Perkins, 216, 473

girdles, 213

girl power movement, 503, 508–9

girls' studies, 336–37

Girton and Newnham (Cambridge women's colleges), 183, 185, 186–87

glass ceiling, 514

globalization: inequalities as result of, 522–23; Latin American lesbian movement and, 316; masculinity and, 491–92, 496–98; power focus of, 522; Third Wave feminism and, 504. *See also* neoliberalism

gnosticism, 8

goddesses, 145, 323

"Goddess of Revenge, The" (Antarjanam), 146–49, **160–68**

Goldman, Emma, 216, 509

Grandmothers' Society, 325

Grant, Beata, 169–70

Great Britain: as imperialist country, 102–3, 104; masculine imagery in, 493; new left men's groups in, 497

Great Law of the Iroquois, 323–24

Greco-Roman antiquity, **15–18**; Christianity and, 9–10; diversity in, 4; male writers as ventriloquists for women during, 6–7, **14–15**; misogyny during, 5; philosophy and feminism during, 7–9, **15–18**; U.S. colonial

Greco-Roman antiquity *(continued)*
government based in, 328; women's rights
in, 3–4; women writers during, 4–6, 9, **10–14**
Greene, Nathanael, 331, 332–33
Greer, Germaine: the erotic as viewed by, 235;
on female sexuality, **236–42**; Koedt and,
234; male poststructuralist view of, 194,
231; Second Wave feminism and, 431; as
sex radical feminist, 233, 503
group sex, 241
Grupo Autogestivo de Lesbianas (GAL), 315
Grupo de Acción Lésbico Feminista (GALF),
313, 315, 318n2
Grupo de Reflexión de Lesbianas (GRL), 315
Guadeloupe, 131, 136
Gubar, Susan, 231
guerrilla movements, 382–84
Guevara, Che, 285, 312
Güezmes, Ana, 405
Guinea-Bissau, 284
Gulf States, Filipino migration to, 522
Gu Ruopu, 169–71, 173, 174n2, **175–76**
Guy-Sheftall, Beverly, 266, 269n3
gynarchy, 323, 325, 328
gynecology, 237–40

Hadith, 456
Hagemann-White, Carol, 497
Haggada, 519
hagiographies, 32
Hall, Edward, 355, 360–61n1
Hall, Stuart, 231
Hamer, Fannie Lou, 268
hammam (public baths), 354, **369–75**
hampton, dream, 511
Han Dynasty, 173
Hangzhou (China), 169
Hanna, Kathleen, 503, 506, **508–9**
harems, 354, **363–69**
Harper's Weekly, 133
Harvey, Tamara, 30–31
Hautzinger, Sarah, 407
health care, access to, 521, 523
"Hearing the Daughter Voice" (Suskin), 505–6,
515–20
Hearn, Jeff, 489
Hearn, Lafcadio: career overview, 138n2; *doudou*
exoticized/racialized by, 131, 132, 133–35,

139–42; U.S. audience of, 136; writings of,
133, 136, **139–43**
hegemonic feminism, 316
hegemonic masculinity, 490, 494, 495
Heidegger, Martin, 202n2
henna, 369, 370–71
Henry VIII (King of England), 21
Herdt, Gilbert H., 489
heterocentric hermeticism, 314
heterocentrism, 316
heterosexism, 195, 476, 510
heterosexuality: of Black male/female relationships, 260; compulsory, 232, 317; as
ideological, 296; as institution, 294, 296;
sexism and, 296; sex radical/"sex-positive"
feminism and, 444–46; Third Wave
feminism and, 503; women's movement
and, 228, 444–46
Heward, Christine, 491
Heywood, Leslie, 502, 503, 504
Hidden Dimension, The (Hall), 355, 360–61n1
high heels, 213
Hill, Anita, 501
Hill-Collins, Patricia, 503–4
Hinduism: prescriptions for women in, 125,
144, 145; temple dancers (*devadasis*), 81, 82,
88–97
Hindu-Muslim Reform (India), 119–20
hip-hop feminism, 504–5, **510–15**
history, feminism as, 172
History of Doing, The (Kumar), 409
Hobbes, Thomas, 473
Hodge, Merle, 336
Hollibaugh, Amber: as sex radical feminist, 295,
432, 433; on sexuality and feminism, 292,
298–99, **305–11**
Hollstein, Walter, 497
"Home" (Smith), 443–44, 449–50
"Home and Politics" (Fawcett), **114–19**
Home Rule movement (India), 119
homophobia, 338, 476, 477, 490
homosexual groups, Latin American, 313
homosexuality, 241; male vs. female, 302–3;
masculinity and, 489. *See also* lesbian
entries
homosexual rights movement, 494
homosociality, 352–53, 361n8
Hondagneu-Sotelo, Pierrette, 489

hooks, bell, 335, 502, 503–4, 514, 526

Hopewell, Treaty of (1785), 332

Hopi Indians, 493

Hopkins, A. G., 491–92

Hopson, Cheryl R., 260, 384

Horace, 5

Hottentots, 493

housework, 282, 478

"How Men Have (a) Sex" (Stoltenberg), **479–88**

Hrotsvit, 9; *Letters to Certain Wise Men*, **13–14**; Preface to plays of, **12**

Huber, Debbie, 490

hudud (sacred frontier), 363, 364

Hull, Glynda, 495

Hull, Gloria T., 512

humanism, 20–22, 22n1, 194

human rights, 100–101, 103, 105–6, 380, 497, 523

Humaydan Younes, Iman, 458, 459, **468–70**

Hunger So Wide and So Deep, A (Thompson), 338

hunger strikes, 104, **109–14**

Hurtado, Aida, 337

husbands: Beauvoir on, 202, 208; Confucianism and, 170–71, 173, 175; coverture doctrine and, 77, 100; domestic violence committed by, 208, 409, 452; extramarital affairs of, 148, 248; in 15th/16th-century "gender wars", 21, 26; in Greco-Roman philosophy, 8, 14–15; in MENA region, 454–55; Muslim sexuality and, 353, 354, 358, 361–62n16; in Native American cultures, 329; in post-WWII France, 197; sexuality and, 243; Shinde on, 152, 153–55; wife as property of, in Latin America, 248; women's suffrage movement and, 116, 121

Hu Shi, 171, 173

al-Huwaider, Wajeha, 456

Huygens, Constantijn, 63

I Accuse! (Eiljersen), 239, 246

Idema, Wilt, 169–70

identity politics, 504–6

if we've gotta live underground and everybody's got cancer (poem; Davis), 513–14

Igbo people, 523

imagination: Astell on, 73; Black feminist sisterhood and, 269; Descartes on, 69; in everyday life (Walker on), 186; female sexuality and, 233, 234, 246; male, 146, 438; pornography and, 438; Sartre on, 196; Woolf and, 187

imagined communities, 285–86

imitatio Christi, 32

immanence, 196, 207

imperialism. *See* colonialism

incest, 449

Index of Forbidden Books, 194

India: colonialism and feminist spirit in, 144–49; colonialism and masculinity in, 493–94; as diverse country, 102; domestic violence reforms in, 408–11; dowry deaths in, 408–9; feminist writings in, **150–68**; independence movement in, 102, 103–4, 107–8, 119, 144–49; marriage customs in, 80–81, **421–29**; as "Orient", 124–25; prostitution reform in, 79–82, **88–97**; as spiritually superior society, 98, 106–8; street plays in, 409; women as nationalistic symbols in, 144–45; women's police stations in, 406; women's suffrage movement in, 102–5, **119–25**

Indian Constitution, 121

Indian drama, dowries as portrayed in, **421–29**

Indianization, 327–28, 330

Indian National Conference (1917), 103

Indian National Congress, 103–4, 120

Indian Penal Code, 410–11

In Search of Our Mothers' Gardens (Walker), 186, 264, 267–68

Inter-American Convention on the Prevention, Punishment, and Eradication of Violence against Women (1994), **415–21**

Inter-American Convention on the Prevention, Punishment, and Eradication of Violence against Women (1996), 408

intermarriage, 326–27

International Association for Studies of Men, 497

International Convention on the Elimination of all Forms of Discrimination Against Women (CEDAW), 403

International Covenant on Civil and Political Rights (ICCPR), 403

International Covenant on Economic, Social, and Cultural Rights (ICESCR), 403

International Decade of the Woman (1975–
 1985), 380, 402, 403–4, 406, 411
International Feminist Congress (Buenos Aires;
 1910), 380
internationalism, 102, 281
International Lesbian Information Service
 (ILIS), 315
International Monetary Fund (IMF), 403
International Women's Day (2011), 530
International Women's Suffrage Alliance, 99,
 102
International Women's Year (1975), 284. *See also*
 Conference for International Women's
 Year (1975)
Internet, 457–58, 504, 531
"Intersectionality and Feminist Politics"
 (Yuval-Davis), 502
intersectional theory, 433–34, 502, 523
Iran, 456, 457, 458–59
Iranian Odyssey, An (Kordi), 458–59, **461–68**
Iranian Revolution (1979), 458
Iraq, 451, 456, 457, 531
Iraq War, 457
Irigaray, Luce, 185, 234–35, **248–54**
Iroquois Confederation of Nations, 324
Iroquois Constitution, 323–24
Iroquois Indians, 323–24, 328–30, 493
Irrational Man (Barrett), 194
"Is Globalization Good for Women?" (Jaggar),
 523
Islam: body ornamentation discouraged in, 353;
 in MENA region, 452–53; sexual segrega-
 tion in, 125; spatial rules in, 350–51; women
 debased in, 359. *See also* Muslim sexuality
Islamic State in the Levant (ISIL), 456
Islamism, 452, 456, 531–32
"Is Marriage a Handicap for the Pursuit of
 Philosophy?" (Musonius Rufus), 8
Israel, 453
Israel-Arab conflict, 284, 355–56, 529
Ito, Kimio, 497

Jackson, Andrew, 329
Jaggar, Allison, 523
Jameson, Frederic, 231
Jamie Oliver's Food Revolution (TV show), 220
Jane Crow, 273
Jansen, Sharon, 22

Japan, 494, 497
Jay, Karla, 439
Jerome, Saint, 33, 34n1
Jet (magazine), 276
jewelry. *See* clothing/jewelry
"Jewish American Princess" (JAP), 517
Jewish feminism, 505–6, **515–20**
Jewishness, mothers as source of, 453
Jewish women's studies, 517
Jews of color, 517
jiaoyuan shishe (Banana Garden Poetry Club),
 169
Jim Crow laws, 204, 273
Jing hua yuan (*Flowers in the Mirror;* Li), 172,
 176–82
job opportunities, 504, 514
Johnson, Virginia E., 239, 240, 244
Johnston, Jill, 292, 296, 297
Jordan, Constance, 22, 34n4
Juana Inés de la Cruz. *See* Sor Juana
Juarez (Mexico), 382
Judaism, 505–6, 515–20
Judge Judy (TV show), 220
Julia (daughter of Augustus), 5
Justice, Daniel Heath, 332

Karman, Tawakul, 529
Kaufman, Michael, 497
Kegel, A. H., 238–39
Kelly, G. Lombard, 244, 245
Kelly, Joan, 20
Kennedy, Florence, 266
Kennedy, John F., 269n3
Keres Indians, 321–22
Kern, Kathi, 103
Khmer Rouge, 383
Kilmer, Joyce, 125–26
Kim (Kipling), 492
Kimmel, Michael, 475, 489, 491, 494
Kincaid, Jamaica, 336
Kindler, Heinz, 497
King, Margaret, 22
King, Martin Luther, Jr., 273
Kinmonth, Earl H., 494
Kinsey, Alfred, 199, 199n1, 244, 245, 437
Kipling, Rudyard, 492
Klein, Uta, 489, 491
Knopf, Alfred, 193

Knox, John, 22

Kocacƒıka (Turkey), 452

Koedt, Anne, 233–34, **242–48**

Kolawale, Mary, 525

Konare, Alpha, 404

Kordi, Gohar, 458–59, **461–68**

KRS-One (rap group), 512

Kuhn, Thomas, 231

Kumar, Radha, 408, 409

Kurdistan, 451, 531

Kutlarb (Turkey), 452

Kuwait, 456–57

labia minora, 245

labor migration, 491–92

labor unrest, 393–95

Lacascade, Suzanne, 131, 136–37

La Comuna de Morelos, 314

Lacquer, Thomas, 472

"Ladies First" (music video; Queen Latifah), 512–13

ladies-in-waiting, 29

Ladies National Association (LNA), 78–79, 80

Laguna Pueblo, 321

Lamda de Liberación Homosexual, 313, 314

Lamentations (Mathéolus), 21, 23–24

Lankshear, Colin, 495

Las Entendidas (Costa Rican lesbian feminist group), 315, 318n2, 318n4

Las Lunas y las Otras, 315

Latifah, Queen, 505, 512–13, 514–15

Latin America: civil wars in, 380, 382, 405–6; homosexual groups in, 313; military dictatorships in, 380, 382, 405–6; revolutionary struggles in, 283–84, 312; women as property in, 248; women's police stations in, 407

Latin American lesbian movement: autonomous organization experiences of, 313–15, 318nn1–4; *Declaration of Lesbians from Mexico*, **319–20**; ELFLACs and, 315–17, 318n2; emergence of, 312–13, 380

Latin American women's activism: community activism, 383–84; historical background, 379–80; militant groups, 382–83; mothering and, 380–82; violence and, 382–85

Lauretis, De, 317

Lavendar Menace, 292–93, 294

Lawrence of Arabia, 493

Laws (Plato), 8

Lebanese Civil War (1975–1990), 459

Lebanon, 355–56, 451–52, 456, 459

Lebron, Lolita, 283

Lecoeur, M., 79, 87

Lee, John, 489

Le Franc, Martin, 21

lesbian continuum, 294–95, 297–98, 300n16

lesbian feminism: downward mobility and, **224–26**; forum on (1975), 319–20; social class and (Berson on), **226–30**; social class and (Brown on), **221–26**; Third Wave feminism and, 520–21; U.S. WLM and, 277, 292–93. *See also* Latin American lesbian movement

lesbian media, 226

Lesbian Nation (Johnston), 292, 297

lesbians: Barnard discussions about, 434; bisexuality and, 248; butch-femme relations among, 434; cultural marginalization of, 297; defined (Radicalesbians), 301–2; eating disorders of, 338; male homosexuals vs., 302–3; as parents, 520; stigmatization as, 314; woman-identified, 293–96, **301–5**

lesbian separatism, 227, 313, 317

Lesbian Sex Mafia, 448

lesbian sexuality: men as sexually irrelevant, 247–48; as political choice, 294

"Lesbians in Revolt" (Bunch), 293, 297

lesbians of color, 283

lesbian subject, 317

Lésbico Feminista (Brazilian lesbian feminist group), 313

lesbophobia, 316

Lesbos, 4, 5

Lesbos (Mexican lesbian feminist group), 313–14

Lettre d'une Africaine à ses soeurs occidentales (Beyala), 523–24

Levy, Ariel, 435

Lewes, Kenneth, 491

Lewis and Clark expedition, 326

"Liberation of Black Women, The" (Murray), 263, 265–66, **273–75**

Libya, 529, 530–31

Ligue du droit des femmes, 208

Lima (Peru), 383–84, **389–90**, 406–7
Lin Yutang, 171, 173
Li Ruzhen, 171–74, **176–82**
literacy qualifications, 120–21
literacy rates, 452
Literary Digest, 125–26
literary translations, 169–70
literature: ballad, 237; Caribbean, 132; castrating
  female in, 358; feminine style in (Woolf),
  185; French, women as treated in, 204;
  French colonial, 137; Greco-Roman, male
  ventriloquism in, 6–7; hip-hop, 511; Indian,
  146, 147; lesbians marginalized in, 297,
  306; male imagination in, 146; public
  recognition for, 186; sexism in, 295; "the
  look" in, 198; women and "Tagore craze",
  125–26. *See also individual author; women
  writers*
Little, Joanne, 283
location, politics of, 285
Locke, John, 65, 473
Logé, Marc, 136
look, the, 196–98
Lorde, Audre: on Black female distrust, 264; on
  Black female self-love, 267, **278–79**; on
  difference, fear of, 440; the erotic as viewed
  by, 235, **254–59**, 298; as sex radical
  feminist, 503; sisterhood hopes of, 262,
  265; Weathers and, 265
Lothian Committee (India), 120–22
Ludmer, Josefina, 33
Lumsden, Ian, 312
"lyric" poetry, 4–5
Lysistratas, 324
Lytton, Constance, 104, **109–14**

MacDonald, Robert H., 493
MacDonald, Dwight, 194
MacKinnon, Catherine, 503
Macrobius, 5
Mahfouz, Asma, 528
makeover shows, 219–20
Makin, Bathsua, 63
male body, 490
male chauvinism, 247
male orgasm, **242–43**, 246–47
male poststructuralists, 231–32
male privilege, 472–73

male responsibility, 520
male sexuality: alcohol/drugs and, 487–88;
  feminist critiques of, 107; pornography
  and, 487; Stoltenberg on, **479–88**;
  transnational businessman masculinity
  and, 495; vagina and, 234, **239–42**;
  women's sexuality defined in terms of,
  242–43
male supremacy: ahistorical feminist explana-
  tions for, 214; Beauvoir on, 201; black men
  and, 270–71; Freudian view of, 243–44;
  lesbians as threat to, 222, **226**; pornography and, 431, 437–40, 485–86; social class
  and, **227**
male transvestism, 232
Mali, domestic violence reforms in, 403–5
Mali Ministère de la promotion de la femme, de
  l'enfant, et de la famille (MPFEF), 404
Manhood in America (Kimmel), 475
Manuela Ramos Movement, 407
Marcuse, Herbert, 233, 235
Marguerite de Navarre, 22n1
marital property, 455
marriage: arranged, 81, 360; child marriages,
  81, 145; companionate, 62, 494; convent
  entrance vs., 29; dowries for, 408–11,
  421–29; forced, in MENA region, 459;
  fulfillment in, and social class, 228; during
  Greco-Roman antiquity, 8; heterosexual,
  idealization of, 297; in India, and domestic
  violence reform, 408–11; in India, and
  nationalism, 145; in India, and prostitution
  reform, 80–81; intermarriage with Native
  Americans, 326–27; legal age, in MENA
  region, 454; power relations within,
  17th-century attacks on, 67; as voting
  qualification, 120–21; as woman's destiny
  (Beauvoir on), 207; women's education
  and, 8, 66
Martinique, 131, 133–35, 136
Martyr, Peter, 325, 328
Marx, Karl, 218, 221, 329–30, 473
Marxism, 214, 392
Mary (Queen of England), 21
"Masculinities and Globalization" (Connell),
  488–98
masculinity/masculinities: Beauvoir on, 200;
  black, 512; Connell on, **488–98**; ethnogra-

phy of, 488–92, 497; globalization of, 492–95, 496–98; homophobia and, 476, 477; penis as epitome of, 247; politics of, 494, 495–98; revolutionary, 285; sex and, 486–88; as social construction, 185, 474–77, 481–84, 490–91; Stoltenberg on, **479–88**; women's studies and visibility of, 471

masochism, 356

Masters, William H., 239, 240, 244

Masters and Johnson reports, 239, 240, 244

"Master's Tools Will Never Dismantle the Master's House, The" (Lorde), 440

masturbation, 244, 441

materialism: downward mobility and, 225–26; power feminism and, 503; women's movement and, 228–29

maternity. *See* motherhood

maternity leave, 274, 283

Mathéolus, 21, 23–24

matriarchies, 323–24, 328–30

matriliny, 321

Matrons, Council of (Iroquois executive council), 323–24, 328–29

McElhinny, Bonnie, 489

McKay, Jim, 490

Mead, Margaret, 222

Medea (Euripides), 7, **14**

Meditations on First Philosophy (Descartes), **68–69**

Mellibovsky, Matilde, 381–82, **385–89**

men: African feminist engagement with, 524; Beauvoir on, 199–200; black, liberation of, 270–71; clitoral orgasm, and sexual irrelevance of, 247–48; "dead white European", 473; as feminist supporters, 473–74, 478–79, 497; feminization of, 171, **176–82**; as genderless, 472–73; "lesbian" as term used by, 302–3; monolithic view of, 524; sex as performance for, 238; sexual identity of, 483–84; U.S. WLM lesbianism opposition and, 295–96; women compared to (Shinde on), **150–60**; women's studies and, 471–73, 477–79. *See also* husbands; male *entries;* masculinity/masculinities; patriarchy; sons

MENA region. *See* Middle East and North Africa (MENA) region

Menchú, Rigoberta, 380

men's liberation movement, 494

men's rights, 475

men's studies, 497–98

Mercator (Plautus), 6–7

meritocracy, 217

Mernissi, Fatima, **363–75**, 456

Merrim, Stephanie, 32, 34

Merry, Sally Engle, 405

Mersenne, Marin, 63

Messerschmidt, James W., 489, 489–90

Messner, Michael A., 489, 490, 491

Metz-Goeckel, Sigrid, 497

Meun, Jean de, 21

Meung, Jean de, 204

Mexico: lesbian feminist groups in, 313–14, 315–16, 318n2; Spanish colonization of, 28–29; women as activists in, 382

Meye Dilam Shajiye (Indian street play), 409

Micaela Bastidas (mothers' club), 397–98

Michelet, Jules, 200

Middle East: clitoridectomies in, 247, 248; Jews of color from, 517; spatial rules in, 355. *See also* Morocco; *specific country*

Middle East and North Africa (MENA) region: conflicts in, 456; female literary voices in, 458–59, **461–70**; feminist activism in, 456–58; Jews of color from, 517; patriliny in, 453, 459; religion in, 452–53, 456; women as activists in, 529; women's diverse lives in, 451–52, 459; women's legal status in (PSCs), 453, 454–55; women's oppression in, 452. *See also* Morocco; *specific country*

migrations, 522–23

military, women in, 521

Mill, John Stuart, 78, 99, 204

Millett, Kate, 295

mind/body dualism, 19, **68–69**

minimum wage, 521

miscegenation, 134

misogyny: Christianity and, 7–8, 516; during Greco-Roman antiquity, 5; masculinity politics and, 496; philosophy and, 7–8; *querelle des femmes* and, 19–20; during Renaissance, 19–20, 30

Miss America pageant, feminist protests against (1968), 213, 292, 504

Mitchell, Julie, 216

Mitilene (Dominican lesbian feminist group), 315

Mitsein, 202, 202n2

modernization, 354

Mogrovejo, Norma, 312, 313, 314, 315, 405

Mohammed IV (King of Morocco), 453

Moi, Toril, 197, 198, 198n1

Molière, 65

Mommy Wars, 186

Money, John, 481n1

mons veneris, 237

Montagu, E. S., 119

Montaigne, Michel de, 204, 329

Moodie, T. Dunbar, 492

Moraga, Cherríe: on feminist movement reactionary views, 440, 447; as sex radical feminist, 295; on sexuality and feminism, 292, 298–99, **305–11**; "Third World women" as term used by, 286; as *This Bridge Called My Back* co-editor, 286, 440, 502

Moran, Paul, 137

More, Thomas, 20

Morgan, Joan, 511, 515

Morgan, Lewis Henry, 329–30

Morgan, Robin, 431, 432

Moroccan folk culture, 358–59, 36n4

Morocco: female sexuality as threat in, 357–60; *hammam* beauty treatments in, **369–75**; harems in, **363–69**; PSC in, 453, 454–55; sexual segregation in, 352–54; women's trespasses in, 354–57

Morrell, Robert, 489, 492

Morrison, Toni, 336

Mosmiller, Thomas E., 494

mosques, sexual segregation at, 361–62n16

motherhood, 115–17; African American women and, 272; African vs. Western feminist views of, 524; *da* (French Caribbean maternal figure), 132, 133, 134–35, **139–40**, **142**; "foremothers", 184; Jewishness and, 453; Latin American women's activism and, 380–82; in MENA region, 453; Mommy Wars, 186; in Muslim societies, 360; in Native American cultures, 321, 323–24, 328–30; negofeminism and, 525; revolutionary, 286; Second Wave feminism and, 504; womanist sisterhood and, 267–68

motherism, 380–82, 525

mothers' clubs, 397–98

Mothers of the Plaza de Mayo, 381–82, 384, **388–89**

Moudawana (Moroccan personal status code), 453, 454–55

Movement de libération de femmes (MLF), 208, 208n1, 209

Movimiento Revolucionario Tupac Amaru (MRTA), 318n2

Moyano, María Elena: as community activist, 383–84, **393–98**; education of, **391**; family background of, **389–90**; marriage of, **396–97**; as mother, **395–96**, 398; as musical theater group director, **391–93**; notebook poetry by, **398–401**

Moyano Lescano, Hermógenes, 389

Ms. magazine, 276, 501, 502, 507

Mubarak, Hosni, 528

Mubarak, Suzanne, 531

Mueller, Ursula, 497

mujeristas, 506

MULA (Mexican lesbian feminist group), 315, 318n2

mulatto women. *See belle affranchie* (free mulatto woman); *da* (French Caribbean maternal figure); *doudou* (Caribbean mulatto woman)

multinational corporations, 491–92, 496–97

"Multisex Theorem, The" (Stoltenberg), 481n1

Municipal Boards (England), 114

Murray, Pauli, 262, 263, 265–66, 269n3, **273–75**

Muskogee Indians, 329

Muslim, Imam, 358

Muslim Brotherhood, 532

Muslims, 287

Muslim sexuality: female sexuality as threat in, 357–60, 361n4; homosociality in, 352–53, 361n8; modernization and, 354; public sphere (*umma*) vs. domestic sphere in, 351–54, **363–75**; territorial nature of, 350–51, 360–61n11; women's tresspasses in, 354–57

Musonius Rufus, 8–9, **15–18**

Myron, Nancy, 219, 222

"Myth of the Vaginal Orgasm" (Koedt), 233–34, **242–48**

mythopoetic men's movements, 491, 496

Al-Nahda (Islamist group), 532
Naidu, Sarajini, 103, 104
Nakamura, Akira, 497
Nanye'hi (Nancy Ward), 331–32, **333–34**
Narayan, Uma, 409
Nardal, Jane, 131, 136–38
Nardal, Paulette, 131, 136–38
Natal region (South Africa), 493
National American Woman's Suffrage
    Association, 330
National Black Feminist Organization, 277
National Black Theatre, 263
National Congress of Vietnamese Women
    (Hanoi; 1975), 285
National Family Violence Law (Peru), 407–8
nationalism: cultural, 285; patriarchal, BWA
    critique of, 282; women as symbols of,
    144–45, 286; women's rights and, 103–4
National Organization for Men Against Sexism
    (NOMAS), 497
National Organization for Women (NOW), 215,
    269n3, 293
National Union for Women (Egypt), 531
National Union of Women's Suffrage Societies
    (NUWSS; England), 99, 100, 101–2, 104
"native," going, 493
Native Americans: berdache tradition, 493;
    masculinities of empire and, 493;
    matriarchal culture of, 323–24, 328–29;
    matriliny among, 321; traditions as honored
    by, 321–22; U.S. culture influenced by,
    326–28; U.S. feminism influenced by,
    324–26; U.S. history and, 328–30
Native American women: as decision-makers,
    323–24; forced sterilization of, 285; popular
    media portrayals of, 325
Native Caribbeans, 325
nativism, 476
naturalism, critiques of, 316
Nazi Germany, 482
Nefertari Ulen, Eisa, 511
negofeminism, 523, 525
negotiation, 523–24
negrophilia, 131, 136
Nelson, Sara, 407
neocolonialism, 317
neoliberalism, 316, 317, 495, 496. *See also*
    globalization

Neoplatonism, 30
Nervous Conditions (Dangarembga), **340–49**;
    anorexia as rebellion in, 337–39, **345–49**;
    colonial subject portrayed in, 335–36;
    girlhood/adolescence portrayed in, 336–37;
    other's other in, 337
New Left, 224, 233, 285, 497
New Spain, 28–29, 492
New Women, 78
New York Yoruban Temple, 276
New Zealand, 493
Nickel and Dimed (Ehrenreich), 214
Nietzsche, Friedrich, 235
Nigeria, 522
Nightingale, Florence, 77
Nineteenth Amendment, U.S. Constitution, 105
Nnaemeka, Obioma, 523, 525
Nobel Peace Prize, 380, 457
No Exit (Sartre), 196
No More Miss America protest (1968), 213, 292,
    504
non-consumerism, 225
Norris, John, 66
Norton, Caroline, 77
Norton, Eleanor Holmes, 266
Norway, 497
Nossis, 5; Poem 11, 11
"Notes on the Writings of Rabindranath Tagore"
    (Colby), **127**
Nuestro Mundo (Argentine homosexual group),
    313
Núñez de Miranda, Antonio, 29, 31
nurse training, 77

Oakely, Judith, 198
Oasis (Mexican lesbian feminist group), 315,
    318n2
Obama, Barack, 195
al-Obeidy, Iman, 530–31
objectification, 196–98
objects, 196
Odeh, Lama Abu, 451
Of Mice and Men (Steinbeck), 475–76
Of the Nobilitie and Excellencye of Womankynde
    (Agrippa von Nettesheim), 22
Oftung, Knut, 497
Ogundipe-Leslie, Molara, 525
Ogunyemi, Chikwenye Okonjo, 525

O'Higgins, Laurie, 6
Oklahoma City bombing (1995), 496
old gay/new gay duality, 229
oligarchy, 328
Olivia Records, 216
Ollin Iskan Katuntat Bebeth Thot (OIKABETH),
    314
Omni magazine, 481n1
Om Swaha (Indian street play), 409
"One Child of One's Own" (Walker), 264, 268
On the Family (Alberti), 21
Oppian Law, 3
Organization of African Unity, 413–15
orgasm: clitoral, 233–34; female, **236**, **242**, 245–46
    (*see also* clitoral orgasm; vaginal orgasm);
    male, **242–43**, 246–47; politics of, 232
Orientalism, 106, 107–8
Ostadh, Noha, 457
Other/Otherness: Beauvoir on, 195–98,
    199–207; as multifaceted, 195; womanism
    and, 522
other's other, 335, 337
overeating, compulsive, 338
overqualification, 504
Ovid, 5
Oxford University (England), 187

pacifism, 102, 322, 323
Palance, Jack, 476
Palestine, 456, 529
Palin, Sarah, 504
Palomino, Nancy, 405
Pankhurst, Christabel, 99, 103
Pankhurst, Emmeline, 99, 103
Pankhurst, Sylvia, 99, 103
"Pantins exotiques" (J. Nardal), 137
Paraguay, women's movement in, 284
Paris (rap group), 512
Parshley, H. M., 193, 198n1
part-time workers, benefits for, 521
Pascon-Bentahar survey, 354
Passionate Politics (Bunch), 216
paternal leave, 497
Pathans, 493
patriarchy: African feminisms and, 524;
    ahistorical feminist explanations for, 214;
    black, 336, 512; in Black Movement/
    culture, 262; colonial desire and, 132;

heterosexuality as compulsory in, 296–97;
    Indian nationalism and, 104, 144; Jewish,
    516; Latin American lesbian movement
    and, 317; motherhood and, 380; socialist
    feminism and, 214–15; Sor Juana and, 28;
    in Tang-dynasty China, 173; U.S. WLM
    and, 295; white feminism and, 235;
    womanist vs. feminist views of, 525;
    women's suffrage movement and, 103, 104
patriliny, 453, 459
patrilocal residence, 459
Paul, Saint, 8, 33
Paz, Octavio, 30
Pearson, Gail, 104
penis: male orgasm and, 242–43, 246–47;
    masculinity and, 247, 482–83; vagina as
    "home" for (Irigaray), 234
Perelmuter Pérez, Rosa, 33, 34
performative ethic, **240–42**
perfume, 370
Perpetua, 3
Persia, 124
personal as political, the, 228, 264, 294,
    298–99, 305
Personal Reminiscences of a Great Crusade
    (Butler), 82, **83–88**
personal status codes (PSCs), 453
Peru: domestic violence reforms in, 405–8;
    feminist organizations in, 407–8; lesbian
    feminist groups in, 315, 318n2; terrorist
    groups in, 318n2, 382–84, 406; women as
    activists in, 382–84
Peruvian Truth and Reconciliation Committee,
    382
phallocentrism, 234
Philippines, 452, 522
Phillips, Jock, 491, 492
philosophy: classical education and, 63;
    cross-sex learned discussions of, 63–65;
    existentialist, 193–94, 196; "new"
    (17th-century), liberating influence of,
    62–63; women as conundrum in, 19–22,
    23–27
plantation system, 134–35
Plato, 7, 8, 9, 30, 34n5
Plautus, 6–7, **15**
Playboy magazine, 213
Plessix Gray, Francine du, 198n1

Pliny, 8
police repression, 282–83, 530–31
police stations, women's, 406–7
political prisoners, 282–83
Politics (Aristotle), 8, 34n4
politics of location, 285
pollution, 514
polygamy, 360, 454
polysemy, 131–33
Poor Law (England), 114
poor women, 272, 338, 520
popular culture, social class and, 219–20
pornography, 232, 294; Barnard discussions
    about, 434; Dworkin on, **436–40**;
    homosociality and, 361n8; male sexuality
    and, 487; radical feminist opposition to,
    431–32, 436–40, 503; sex radical/"sex-posi-
    tive" feminism and, 432–33, 435; as site of
    male power, 297, 431, 437–40, 485–86;
    transnational businessman masculinity
    and, 495; U.S. WLM and, 298
"Pornography and Grief" (Dworkin), **436–40**
postcolonialism, masculinities of, 494–95
postfeminism, 316, 501–2, 508
poststructuralism, 194, 231–32
"Pot, Porn, and the Politics of Pleasure" (Jay), 439
Pough, Gwendolyn D., 504–5, 506, 507–8,
    510–15
poverty, 274, 338, 514, 523
Powell, Amanda, 31
power feminism, 503
Power Moves Hip Hop Conference (UCLA;
    1999), 511
Praise of Folly, The (Erasmus), 20
"Praticaradevatha" (Antherjanam), 146–49,
    160–68
précieuses, les, 65
priamel, 5
Primero sueño ("First Dream"; Sor Juana), 29–31,
    44–61
primitivism, 131, 136
proletariat, 201–2
Promise Keepers, 491, 496
property ownership, as voting qualification,
    120–21
property rights: in India, and prostitution
    reform, 81; Roman vs. Christian law, 3–4;
    in Victorian-era England, 77, 99–100

prostitution, 495
prostitution reform: in India, 79–82, **88–97**; as
    transnational movement, 80–82; in
    Victorian-era England, 78–79, **83–88**, 101;
    women's suffragists active in, 101
Protestant convents, seventeenth-century
    proposals for, 66–67
Protestant Reformation, 20, 22, 328
protests/demonstrations: at Barnard Confer-
    ence (1982), 434; eating disorders as,
    337–39; No More Miss America protest
    (1968), 213, 292, 504; Take Back the Night
    March (San Francisco; 1978), 436, 440
proto-feminism: Aristophanes and, 7; of color,
    in France, 136–38
Proust, Marcel, 197–98
proxemics, 360–61n1
Psychology of Women (Freud), 243
Public Enemy (rap group), 512
"Public Silence, Private Terror" (Allison),
    440–50
pubococcygeal muscles, 238–39
Pueblo Indians, 493
Puerto Rican independence movement, 216,
    284
Purple Roof Foundation, 452
Pythagoreans, 8

queer identity, 503
queer people, 286
queer women, 506, 520–21
querelle des femmes ("woman question"), 19–22,
    23–27, 31–32, 33, 77
Quran, 353, 452, 456

Rabat (Morocco), 362n18
rabbis, women as, 518–20
race: Black feminist sisterhood and, 262, 472;
    intersectional theory and, 433, 502;
    Otherness and, 195; rap music and, 515;
    Third Wave feminism and, 515; women-of-
    color feminists and, 284; in women's
    movement, 219, 226, 228, 229
"Race for Theory, The" (Christian), 525–26
race studies, 197
racial essentialism, 137
racism, 104; eating disorders as result of, 338;
    Latin American lesbian movement and,

racism *(continued)*
317; Latin American women's activism and, 379–80; male domination through, 476, 477; masculinities of empire and, 493–94; origins of, in U.S., 273–74; sexism and, 131, 136–38; Third Wave feminism and, 510; of white feminism, 235; women-of-color feminists and, 282–83; women's suffrage movement and, 98, 105

racist movements, 494

Radi, Abelwanad, 361n4

Radicalesbians, 294, 295–96, **301–5**

radical feminism, 430–32, **436–40**, 503, 506, 526

Ramamirthammal, Muvalur, 82, **88–97**

Ramírez y Asbaje, Juana. *See* Sor Juana (Juana Inés de la Cruz)

Ramos, Miguel, 405

Randle, Gloria Thomas, 261

rape, 449, 478, 485, 503, 504, 532–33

rape myths, 431

rap music, 511, 514–15. *See also* hip-hop feminism

Rapport d'Uriel (Benda), 200

rationalism, 62–63, 65–66, 67, **71–74**

"Reagan Era," 501–2

"Rebuttal of Ridicule" (Gu), 170–71

Rebuttal of Ridicule (Yang Xiong), 174n1

Reddy, Muthulakshmi, 80–81, 103

Reform Acts (England; 1866/1867), 102

Reich, Wilhelm, 437

Reid, Coletta, 215, 218–19, 229

religion. *See* Catholic Church; Christianity; Hinduism; Islam; Judaism; *specific religion*

Remembrance of Things Past (Proust), 197–98

Renaissance: *querelle des femmes* during, 19–22, **23–27**, 31–32, 33; rhetorical conventions of, 33

reproductive justice movements, 197, 283–84, 520

Republic (Plato), 8, 34n5

repudiation, 360, 454

Rerrich, Maria S., 497

Research for the Defense of Women's Rights (DEMUS), 407

Respuesta, La (Sor Juana), 29, 31–33, **36–44**

revolutionary iconography, 285–86

Revue du monde noir (journal), 137

Rhodesia, 335–36, 337

Rich, Adrienne: on compulsory heterosexuality, 296–97; on feminist "sex wars", 443; lesbian continuum theory of, 294–95, 297–98, 300n16; on politics of location, 285

Richards, Amy, 506, 507, **520–21**

Richelieu, Cardinal, 63

Richlin, Amy, 19–20

right-wing militias, 496

Ringgold, Faith, 263, 266

"Riot Grrrl Manifesto" (Hanna), 503, 506, **508–9**

riot grrrl movement, 502, 506, 507, **508–9**

Roberts, Tara, 511

Robles de Zurita, Carmen, 381–82, **385–89**

Roces, Mina, 98

Rodriguez del Padron, Juan, 21

Rogers, Annie, 336–37

Roiphe, Katie, 502–3

Romance of the Rose, The, 21, 32

Roman comedy, 6–7

Roman law, 3–4, 204

Room of One's Own, A (Woolf), **187–92**; feminist influence of, 185; gender-specific originality of, 184; literary influence of, 186; naming of, 183; narration in, 186–87; women's economic self-sufficiency promoted in, 183–84; Woolf as "insider-outsider" in, 185–86

Roper, Michael, 491

Rosenman, Ellen, 384

Ross, Diana, 222

Rousseau, Jean-Jacques, 473

Roussi-Césaire, Suzanne, 136–37

Roy, Anupuma, 104

Rum Corps, 492

Rutgers University, 216, 473

al-Saadawi, Nawal, 456

Sabat de Rivers, Georgina, 30, 34

Sacagawea (Native American guide/translator), 326, 330

Sade, Marquis de, 438

Said, Edward, 106, 194, 231

Salafis (Islamist group), 532

salaries, 228–29

"salaryman," Japanese, 494

Saleh, Ali Abdullah, 529

Salt-N-Pepa (rapper), 514–15

Sanaa University (Yemen), 529

Sandoval, Chela, 281

São Paulo (Brazil), 407

Sapphistry (Califia), 442–43

Sappho: LP 1, 5; LP 16, 4–5, **10–11**

Sartre, Jean-Paul, 196–98

sati, 145

Saudi Arabia, 456

Saussy, Haun, 169–70

School Boards (England), 114

Schwalbe, Michael, 491

Schwarzer, Alice, 198, **208–10**

scientific revolution, 20

Scott, James C., 453

Scott, Patricia Bell, 512

Second Sex, The (Beauvoir): critical reviews of, 194; existentialist concepts contained in, 196; feminist critiques of, 198; Parshley English translation of, 193–94, 198n1; popular media portrayals of, 193; publication environment of, 197; translations of, 198, 198n1; women as Others in, 195–98, **199–207**

Second Wave feminism: Black feminists and, 262; decline of, 504; exclusionary tactics of, 503; institutional sexism opposed by, 430–32; Latin American lesbian movement and, 313; lesbian feminism and, 292–94, 313; postfeminism and, 502; sisterhood as viewed in, 262; Third Wave critiques of, 503, 512; as white elitist, 502; Woolf and, 185; writing style of, 234. *See also* feminist "sex wars"

secularism, 517

seduction, in Muslim societies, 352–53

Segal, Lynn, 489

Seidler, Victor J., 497

self-censorship, 184

self-esteem, 504

self-help advice, 220

self-improvement, 220

Sen, Samita, 145

Sendero Luminoso. *See* Shining Path (Peruvian terrorist group)

Seneca Falls Convention (Seneca Falls, NY; 1848), 105–6, 324

Serious Proposal to the Ladies, A (Astell), 66–67, **69–74**

settler masculinity, 493

sex: double standards in, 520; female superior position during, 239; "feminist sex", 432; as male skill, 238, **240–42**; sex radical/"sex-positive" feminism and, 432–34, **440–50**. *See also* feminist "sex wars"

"Sex," from *The Female Eunuch* (Greer), 233, **236–42**

sex industry, 434–35. *See also* pornography

sexism: in Black Arts movement, 513; eating disorders as result of, 338; heterosexuality and, 296; in higher education, 224; during Indian colonial period, 144–49; institutional, radical feminist opposition to, 430–32, 435; Latin American women's activism and, 379–80; lesbianism and, 302–3; male domination through, 476; racism and, 131, 136–38; Third Wave feminism and, 510, 513; women-of-color feminists and, 282–83. *See also* female inferiority theories

sex radical/"sex-positive" feminism, 432–34, **440–50**, 503

sexual abuse, 338

sexual education, 430

sexual exploitation, 274

sexual fantasies, 242, 295; Allison on, 441; Barnard discussions about, 434; sex radical/"sex-positive" feminism and, 432–33

Sexual Feeling in Married Men and Women (Kelly), 245

sexual harassment: during Arab Spring, 530–31; in Muslim societies, 354–57, 362n18; radical feminist opposition to, 431; at workplace, 478

sexual health, 520

sexuality: African vs. Western feminist views of, 524; capitalism and, 233; consensual, 486–88; feminism and, 5–6, 298–99; Freudian view of, 233; gender and, 484–85; "the look" and, 196–98; male philosophers of, 437; permissive society and, 241; as political choice, 294; Third Wave feminism and, 503, 509, 520; U.S. contradictory views of, 430; violence and, 485–86; women-of-color feminists and, 283;

sexuality (continued)
    women's oppression and (Beauvoir on),
        208–9. See also male sexuality; Muslim
        sexuality; women's sexuality
Sexually Adequate Female, The (Caprio), 243–44
sexually transmitted diseases (STDs), 520
sexual orientation, intersectional theory and,
        433, 502
sexual politics, 78, 101, 524
Sexual Politics (Millett), 295
sexual segregation, 351–54, 361–62n16, 363–75,
        459
Shange, Ntozake, 513
Sharpley-Whiting, T. Denean, 136, 137
Shaw, Anna Howard, 330
shelters, 208, 406
Shi'i women, 456
Shinde, Tarabai, 144, 145–46, 148–49, 150–60
Shining Path (Peruvian terrorist group), 318n2,
        382–84, 406
Shire, Chenjerai, 493
Shona people, 336
"Should Daughters Receive the Same Education
        as Sons?" (Musonius Rufus), 8, 17–18
Showalter, Elaine, 231
Sikhs, 493
silence: Arab Spring police brutality and, 531;
        about class differences, 217–20; "Conspir-
        acy of Silence", 85; about extramarital
        affairs, in India, 148; prostitution reform
        and, 82, 84; sexual (Allison on), 440–50;
        sexual (Moraga and Hollibaugh on), 295,
        298, 299, 305–11; slave women and, 6; Sor
        Juana on, 42, 44, 45, 46, 48, 50, 57
Si longue lettre, Une (Bâ), 524
Simon Commission (India), 121
Simons, Margaret, 194
Sinha, Mrinalini, 493
Sioux Indians, 493
sisterhood: African feminist view of, 524; Black
        feminist, 268–69; as global, 285; lesbians
        and, 292; Lorde on, 267; as process,
        268–69; race and, 472; U.S. "Second
        Wave" Black feminist perspectives on,
        262–64; Wallace on, 266–67; Weathers
        on, 265; womanist (Walker on), 267–68
Sister Outsider (Lorde), 269n2
skin-color testing, 232

slavery: abolition of, in Martinique (1848), 135;
        mammy stereotype, 134; nostalgia for,
        134–35; as theater performers, 6; U.S.
        retention of, 328; women and, 3
slave women, 186
Smith, Barbara, 443–44, 449–50, 512
Smitherman, Geneva, 261
snuff films, 437–38
social class: alliance-shattering potential of, 226;
        Berson on, 226–30; Black feminist
        sisterhood and, 262; Brown on, 221–26;
        components of, 220, 222; downward
        mobility and, 224–26; hegemonic
        masculinity and, 494; intersectional theory
        and, 433, 502; personal nuances of ("nooks
        and crannies" of), 217–20; politics of, 213,
        227–28; rap music and, 515; socialist
        feminism and, 214–19; in Victorian-era
        England, 78, 98; women-of-color feminists
        and, 284; in women's studies programs,
        213–14; women's suffrage movement and,
        98. See also social mobility
social conservatism, 502
socialism, 102
socialist feminism, 214–16, 219
social mobility: downward, 224–26; upward,
        218–20, 224; U.S. mythologies involving,
        216–17, 219–20, 222
social purity, 78–79, 80–81, 106, 115–17
Socrates, 9
Somos (Brazilian lesbian feminist group), 313
sons: education of, 8, 17–18, 25; in MENA
        region, 459; preference for, 459
Sor Juana (Juana Inés de la Cruz): birth of, 28;
        censorship of, 34; death of, 34; as feminist,
        31, 33, 34; as nun, 28–29; as poet, 29, 31;
        Primero sueño, 29–31, 44–61; La Respuesta,
        29, 31–33, 36–44
Sor Juana Inés de la Cruz (Paz), 30
soul, as genderless, 30–31
Soul on Ice (Cleaver), 276
South Africa, 493, 494
Southeast Asian immigrants, 287
Southern Rhodesia, 335–36, 337
South Vietnam Liberation Women's Union, 285
Soviet Union, collapse of, 495
Spain, Counter-Reformation in, 28–29
Spanish Empire, 492

speciesism, 510

"Speech Delivered at the Queen's Hall, January 31, 1910" (Lytton), **109–14**

Speeches and Letters (Nanye'hi/Nancy Ward/ Cherokee women), **331–34**

Spivak, Gayatri, 194, 231, 503–4

sports, corporate "sponsorship" of, 495

spousal abuse, 78

Sri Lanka, 452

Stalinism, collapse of, 496

Stanton, Elizabeth Cady, 105

stay-at-home-parents, 521

Steady, F. C., 523

Steinbeck, John, 475–76

sterilization, forced, 232, 283, 284

Sting (singer), 381

STIWA (Social Transformation Including Women in Africa), 525

stiwanism, 525

St. Lazare Prison/Hospital (Paris, France), 79, 86–87

Stoics, 8

Stoltenberg, John, **479–88**

Stone, Lawrence, 62

Stonewall riots (1969), 312–13

street plays, 409

"Stri Purush Tulana" (Shinde), 145–46, **150–60**

Student Nonviolent Coordinating Committee (SNCC), 281–82, 505, 512

subjects, 196, 200

subordination, 337

Sulpicia the elegist, 5; Poem 1, 11

Sulpicia the satirist, 5–6; fragment, 11

Surco (Peru), 390, 391

Susan B. Anthony List, 504

Suskin, Alana, 505–6, 507–8, **515–20**

Sweeney, Carole, 137

Syria, 456, 531

Tagore, Rabindranath, 107, **125–27**

Take Back the Night March (San Francisco; 1978), 436, 440

Taliban, 496

Talking Back (hooks), 335

Talmud, 520

Tang Dynasty, 172, 173

Tatian, 8

Taylor, Harriet, 78

television: makeover shows, 219–20; satellite, and MENA women's activism, 457

temperance movement, 494

Tepoztlán (Mexico), 318n2

Terence (Roman comic playwright), 9

Teresa of Avila, Saint, 32

territoriality, 350, 360–61n1

Tertullian, 8

"That Women Too Should Study Philosophy" (Musonius Rufus), 8, **15–17**

Theberge, Nancy, 490

theory, feminism as, 172

thinism, 510

Thinking About Women (Ellman), 243

Third Wave Agenda (Heywood and Drake), 502

Third Wave feminism, 293; activist strategies of, 504, 506–7; agenda of, 507–8, **520–21**; Black feminists, 511; difference as characteristic of, 503–4; hip-hop feminism, 504–5, **510–15**; identity politics of, 504; intersectional theory and, 502; Jewish feminism, 504–5, **515–20**; origins of, 501–2; popular media accounts of, 502–3; riot grrrl feminism, 506, 507, **508–9**; Second Wave as viewed in, 503; sex radical/"sex-positive" feminism and, 433

Third Wave Foundation, 507

"Third Wave Manifesta" (Baumgardner and Richards), 506, 507, **520–21**

Third World, bureaucratization in, 356

Third World women: in revolutionary iconography, 285–86; theorizing of, 522; use of term, 286

Third World Women's Alliance (TWWA): legacy of, 286–87; origins of, 281–82; publications of, 280 (*see also Triple Jeopardy* (newspaper)); as socialist feminist organization, 215–16; transnational roots of, 280–81

This Bridge Called My Back (ed. Moraga and Anzaldúa), 286, 433, 440, 446–47, 502

"This Sex That Is Not One" (Irigaray), 234, **248–54**

Thomas, Clarence, 501

Thomas Aquinas, Saint, 8, 200

Thompson, Becky, 337

Thorne, Barrie, 491

Thousand and One Nights, 368–69

Tillion, Germaine, 361n14

Tillner, Georg, 494

Time magazine, 194

Title VII (Civil Rights Act; 1964), 269n3

Tocqueville, Alexis de, 473

"To Give a Daughter Away" (Bhattacharya), **421–29**

tokenism, 216, 217, 222

Tomsen, Stephen, 489

torture, 104, **109–14**

Tosh, John, 489

Toure, Amadou Toumani, 404

Towards Equality (CSWI), 409–10

tradition: Native American view of, 321–22; U.S. rejection of, 322, 323

transcendence, 196

transgender people, 286

transnational advocacy networks (TANs), 523

transnational businessman masculinity, 495, 496–97

transnational women's alliances: African feminists and, 523–24; limitations of, 80; in MENA region, 458; prostitution reform, 80–82; TWWA as, 280; women-of-color feminists and, 280–81; women's suffrage movement, 98–99, 103, 106–8

Traore, Moussa, 403–4

treaties: on domestic violence, 403, **413–21**; with Native Americans, 332; on women's rights, 403

Triple Jeopardy (newspaper): coalitional politics covered in, 283; International Women's Year issue (1975), 284; issues covered by, 283–85; multiple women-of-color feminist insurgencies revealed through, 280–81; revolutionary female subjectivity as portrayed in, 283–86, **289–91**; as socialist feminist publication, 216

Triumph of Women, The (Rodriguez del Padron), 21

Truculentus (Plautus), 6

Truth, Sojourner, 264, 268

Tsu-la (Cherokee man), 331

Tubman, Harriet, 264, 268

Tucumán (Argentina), 386, 387

Tunisia, 457, 531

Turkey, 124, 452

Two Years in the French West Indies (Hearn), 132, 133, 134, 135, 136, **139–42**

umma (public sphere), 351–54

Um Outro Olhar (Latin American lesbian feminist group), 313

UN Decade for Women. *See* International Decade of the Woman (1975–1985)

underemployment, 504

unemployment, 283

UNIFEM Report, 402

United Nations, 205

United Nations Declaration of the Elimination of Violence against Women (1993), 402

United Nations Educational, Scientific, and Cultural Organization (UNESCO), 497

United Nations Population Fund (UNFPA), 404

United States: domestic violence in, 402; frontier masculinities in, 492, 493; gay power movement in, 313; masculinity politics in, 496; Native American-focused history of, 328–30; Native American influence in, 326–28; post-911 backlash in, 286; profeminist men's groups in, 497; racial prejudice in, 98, 105; sexuality as viewed in, 430; social mobility mythology in, 216–17, 219–20, 222; Tagore craze in, **125–26**; third-world women in, 280–82, 286, 502; tradition rejected in, 322, 323; women's suffrage movement in, 98, 105–8, **125–26**

United States, Women's Liberation Movement: anti-pornography vs. "sex-positive" conflict, 294, 298; anti-Semitism in, 516; Black feminists participating in, 260–61, 276–78; diversity as characteristic of, 503; empirical strain of, 233; as heterosexist, 292–93; as imperialist/maternalist, 522; lesbian feminism and, 277, 292–93, 295–96; media coverage of, 293; Native American roots of, 324–26; as political force, 292; sisterhood concept within, 261–62; Third Wave repositioning of, 507; as transracial social/political movement, 261. *See also* Second Wave feminism; Third Wave feminism

United States Constitution: Equal Rights Amendment proposal, 507, 521; Fifteenth

Amendment, 105; Native American influence on, 323; Nineteenth Amendment, 105
United States Supreme Court, 501
United States Treaty Commissioners, Cherokee women's speeches to, **332–33**
"U.N.I.T.Y" (song; Queen Latifah), 513
universalism, 524
universities, 20
urban environmental degradation, 514
Uruguay, women's movement in, 284
"Uses of the Erotic, The" (Lorde), **254–59**
U2 (rock band), 381

vagina: anatomy of (Koedt), **244–45**; in ballad literature, 237; cultural imagination and (Greer), 233; male gynecological descriptions of, 237–40; modesty about, 237; penis as "home" for (Irigaray), 234; scientific/mechanistic view of (Koedt), 233–34
vaginal orgasm, 234; Greer on, **239–42**; Koedt on, **242–48**
vagrancy laws, 82n1
Van Deusen, Nancy, 405
Van Schurman, Anna, 63
"Variations on Negation and the Heresy of Black Feminist Creativity" (Wallace), 335
Vatican, 194
veiling, 352, 353, 355, 361n14
venereal disease, 78
Venkateswaran, Pramila, 104
ventriloquism, 6–7, **14–15**
Vichy France, 197
victim feminism, 503
Victoria (Queen of England), 118
Vietnam War, 271, 284
Vieyra, Antonio de, 31
Vindication of the Rights of Women, A (Wollstonecraft), 77
violence: gender-based, 403, 408; homophobic, 490; Latin American women's activism and, 382–84; masculinity politics and, 494, 496; pornography and, 437–40, 485–86; sexualization of, 431–32; Third Wave feminism and, 521. *See also* domestic violence
Vives, Juan Luis, 21–22

Voet, Gisbert, 63
voting rights, 99, 105
Voting Rights Act (U.S.; 1965), 105

wage gap, 431
wages, 228–29, 521
Walker, Alice: as Black feminist, 266; sisterhood hopes of, 262, 265; Weathers and, 265; womanist schema of, 264, 267–68; Woolf's influence on, 186
Walker, James C., 491
Walker, Rebecca, 268, 501–503, 507
Walkowitz, Judith, 82n2
Wallace, Michele: on Black female distrust, 263–64, 266–67, **275–78**; on other's other, 335, 336; sisterhood hopes of, 262, 265, 266; Weathers and, 265
Ward, Bryant, 332
Ward, Nancy (Nanye'hi), 331–32
Ware, Caroline F., 275
Weathers, Mary Ann, 262–63, 265, 270–73, 384
Weber, Max, 356, 473
Web of Deceit (Dasigal Mosavalei; Ramamirthammal), 82, **88–97**
welfare, 284
welfare reform, 514
Wells, Ida B. (Ida B. Wells Barnett), 264, 268
Western feminism: as imperialist/maternalist, 522–23, 526; internal divisions in, 523–24; sexual politics of, 524
"What We're Rollin around in Bed With" (Hollibaugh and Moraga), 292, 295, 298–99, **305–11**
Wheatley, Phillis, 186
White, Hayden, 231
White Ribbon campaign (Canada), 497
White Roots of Peace, 323–24
Whitson, David, 490
Widersprueche, 489, 497
widow remarriage, 145
wifehood qualification, 121
wigs, 361n9
Williams, Walter L., 492
Williams, Raymond, 231
Wolf, Naomi, 502–3
Wollstonecraft, Mary, 77, 473
woman-identified woman, 293–96, 297, **301–5**

"Woman-Identified Woman, The" (Radicalesbians), 294, **301–5**

womanism: African American, 264, 267–68; African feminisms and, 522, 525; feminism vs., 525; Jewish feminism and, 517; Third Wave feminism and, 506, 511, 520

"woman question" (*querelle des femmes*), 19–22, **23–27**, 31–32, 33, 77

"Woman's Suffrage in India" (Ali), **119–25**

Woman's Tribune, The, 106

women: being vs. becoming (Beauvoir), 195–96; canonization of, 33; as community activists, 383–84; as domestic workers, 452; eating disorders among, 338; economic self-sufficiency of (Woolf on), 183–84; frigidity in, 243–44; human equality vs. female essentialism views of, 100–101, 105–6; male writers as ventriloquists for, 6–7, **14–15**; men compared to (Shinde on), **150–60**; as militants, 382–83; as mothers, 115–17; nationalistic portrayals of, 144–45; as Others, 195–98, **199–207**; as philosophical conundrum (*querelle des femmes*), 19–22, **23–27**; as property, 248; seclusion of, in Muslim societies, 352–54, 361n4, 361–62n16; slavery and, 3; tokenism and, 222; as victims, 503. *See also* daughters; female *entries*; motherhood

Women at the Thesmophoria (Aristophanes), 7

Women Living under Muslim Laws, 458

women of color, 338, 522

women-of-color feminism: coalitional politics of, 282–84; origins of, 502, 511–12; political identities of, 286; political platforms supported by, 283; transnational roots of, 280–81; transnational solidarity of, 286–287

women philosophers, 6

women's colleges, seventeenth-century proposals for, 66–67

Women's Co-operative Guild, 185

women's education: British colonial, 335–36; Christianity and, 8–9; classism and, 218–19; in Confucian societies, 169, 171, 172–73; economic self-sufficiency through (Woolf on), 183–84; femininity and, 117; during Greco-Roman antiquity, 8, **15–18**; Gu on, **175–76**; during Indian colonial

period, 145; as marriage alternative, 66; in MENA region, 452; in Muslim societies, 354; *querelle des femmes* and, 21–22, 33; seventeenth-century proposals for, 66–67, **69–71**; in Victorian-era England, 78

Women's Federation (Peru), 398

women's history, 284

Women's Indian Association, 103

women's movement: classism within, 214, 215, 217–20; classism within (Berson on), **226–30**; classism within (Brown on), **221–26**; downward mobility and, **224–26**; heterosexual feminists in, 444–46; Latin American, 284; money-pooling in, **228–29**; social consciousness of the body awakened by, 232

women's oppression: in Africa, 522; Beauvoir on, 208–9; in MENA region, 452; sexual, 208–9, 447

women's police stations, 406–7

Women's Protest (England; 1870), 84–85

women's rights: international treaties regarding, 403; male writers supporting, 33; nationalism and, 103–4; in post-WWII France, 197; Roman vs. Christian law, 3–4

women's sexuality: Barnard discussions about, 434; fear of, in Muslim societies, 357–60, 361n4; Greer on, **236–42**; Irigaray on, **248–54**; Koedt on, **242–48**; lesbian, 247–48; Lorde on, **254–59**; as political issue, 78–79, 101; redefining, **243**; subordination of, 431–32; Third Wave feminism and, 509. *See also* clitoral orgasm; vaginal orgasm

women's studies programs: changed to "gender studies", 524; gender made visible through, 471–74, 477; Jewish, 517; Judaism and, 505–6, 515–208; men and, 471–73, 477–79; social class as taught in, 213–14

women's suffrage movement: difficulties facing, 100; divisions within, 98–99, 100–102, 105–6; in England, 99–102, 104, **109–19**; gender compromises made as result of, 494; imprisonment/torture during, **109–14**; in India, 102–5, **119–25**; nationalism and, 103–4; Native Americans and, 324, 326, 330; opposition to, 116–17; transnational nature of, 98–99, 103,

106–8, **125–27**; in U.S., 98, 105–8, **125–26**, 324

Women's Suffrage Political Union (WSPU; England), 99, 100, 101, 103, 104

women writers: African American, 186; Catholic, 33; economic self-sufficiency needed for (Woolf), 183–84, **187–92**; during Greco-Roman antiquity, 4–6, 9, **10–14**; male artistic standards and, 184; in MENA region, 458–59, **461–70**; during Renaissance, 20–21, 33. *See also individual author*

Woolf, Virginia, 183–87. *See also Room of One's Own, A* (Woolf)

Woolworth's bra action (1971), 213

working women: industrial revolution and, 204; in MENA region, 451–52; in Muslim societies, 354, 356–57

workplace: family-friendly policies at, 478, 521; masculinity at, 490; as site of male power, 297; Third Wave feminism and problems of, 504

World Health Organization (WHO), 402, 404

World War I, 102, 106

Wright, Doris, 277

Wright, Richard, 195

Wu Zetian (Empress of China), 172–73

Xaba, Thokozani, 494

X-Clan (rap group), 512

Xicanisma (Chicana feminism), 517

Yang Xiong, 170, 174n1

Yeats, William Butler, 125–26

Yemen, 284, 528–29

yin/yang duality, 170

Youma (Hearn), 133–35, 136, **142–43**

Young, Iris, 232

Young, Robert, 132

Young, Whitney, 222

YouTube, 456

Yo-Yo (rapper), 514–15

Yuval-Davis, Niral, 502

Zimbabwe, 335–36, 337, 493

Zulus, 493

Zurita, María Rosa, 381–82, 385, 387

Zurita, Nestor Juan Agustín, 381–82, 385–88

TEXT: 9.5/14 Scala Pro
DISPLAY: Scala Sans Pro
COMPOSITOR: IDS Infotech Ltd
INDEXER: Kevin Millham
PRINTER AND BINDER: Maple Press